Vol. 11 *The Doctrine of the Saints' Perseverance Explained and Confirmed.*

Vol. 12 *Vindiciae Evangelicae: or, the Mystery of the Gospel Vindicated.*
Of the Death of Christ, and of Justification.
A Review of the Annotations of Grotius.

Vol. 13 *The Duty of Pastors and People Distinguished.*
Eshcol: a Cluster of the Fruit of Canaan.
Of Schism; in Three Books.
Nonconformity Vindicated.
Tracts on the Power of the Magistrate, Indulgence, Toleration, etc.

Vol. 14 *Animadversions on 'Fiat Lux'.*
Vindication of Animadversions.
The Church of Rome no safe Guide.
On Union among Protestants.
The State and Fate of Protestantism.

Vol. 15 *Discourse concerning Liturgies.*
Discourse concerning Evangelical Love, Church Peace, and Unity.
Inquiry concerning Evangelical Churches.
Answer to Dr Stillingfleet on the unreasonableness of Separation.
Instruction in the Worship of God.

Vol. 16 *The Nature of a Gospel Church.*
Tracts on Excommunication, Church Censures, Baptism, etc.
On the Divine Original of the Scriptures.
Posthumous Sermons.
Indices.

DIVISION 4 : EXPOSITORY

Vol. 17 *Concerning the Epistle to the Hebrews.*
Concerning the Messiah.
Concerning the Jewish Church.

Vol. 18 *The Sacerdotal Office of Christ.*
A Day of Sacred Rest.
Summary of Observations on Hebrews.

Vol. 19 *Exposition of Hebrews, 1–3:6.*

Vol. 20 *Exposition of Hebrews, 3:7–5:14.*

Vol. 21 *Exposition of Hebrews, 6:1–7:28.*

Vol. 22 *Exposition of Hebrews, 8:1–10:39.*

Vol. 23 *Exposition of Hebrews, 11:1–13:25.*

The Works of John Owen

VOLUME XIV

The Works of JOHN OWEN

EDITED BY

William H. Goold

VOLUME XIV

The Banner of Truth Trust

This Edition of
THE WORKS OF JOHN OWEN
first published by Johnstone & Hunter, 1850-53

Reprinted by
THE BANNER OF TRUTH TRUST
3 Murrayfield Road, Edinburgh EH12 6EL, UK
P.O. Box 621, Carlisle, PA 17013, USA

VOLUME XIV

1965

Second printing 1976
Third printing 1983
Fourth printing 1991
Fifth printing 1999
Sixth printing 2009
Seventh printing 2019

THIS VOLUME ISBN: 978 0 85151 062 0
16-VOLUME SET ISBN: 978 0 85151 392 8

*

Printed in the USA by
Versa Press, Inc.,
East Peoria, IL

CONTENTS OF VOL. XIV.

ANIMADVERSIONS ON A TREATISE ENTITLED "FIAT LUX."

A VINDICATION OF THE ANIMADVERSIONS ON "FIAT LUX."

PAGE

THE CHURCH OF ROME NO SAFE GUIDE.

SOME CONSIDERATIONS ABOUT UNION AMONG PROTESTANTS.

A BRIEF AND IMPARTIAL ACCOUNT OF THE NATURE OF THE PROTESTANT RELIGION.

ANIMADVERSIONS

ON

A TREATISE ENTITLED "FIAT LUX;"

OR,

"A GUIDE IN DIFFERENCES OF RELIGION BETWEEN PAPIST AND PROTESTANT, PRESBYTERIAN AND INDEPENDENT."

PREFATORY NOTE.

The Restoration revived the hopes of the Roman Catholics that their Church would ere long recover its ancient influence in Britain. The re-action by which the dynasty of the Stuarts recovered possession of the British crown extended in some measure to the doctrines held by the great body of Protestant Nonconformists, who had raised Cromwell to the Protectorate. The members of the English Church, who were really attached to Protestantism, and at the same time zealous for the Restoration, were too apt, under the bias of their political views, to regard Nonconformity as synonymous with rebellion. It was but a step farther to insinuate that Nonconformity was only Protestantism under another name and with slight modifications; that Protestantism was really the fountain of bitterness which had recently overflowed in rebellion and anarchy; and that unless the doctrines of the Church of Rome were embraced and generally diffused throughout the nation, the ark of the State would never alight on any Ararat of settled peace and permanent safety.

The Church of Rome has always emissaries at command to seize such an opening as now presented itself. It is certainly remarkable, however, that it produced at this time, and down to the Revolution, no British controversialist, in whom the Barrows and Owens of the Protestant cause could recognise "a foeman worthy of their steel." The Jesuits were busy in their own style of secret and successful intrigue, but on the Popish side of the controversy no work appeared exceeding in importance and plausibility the "Fiat Lux" of John Vincent Cane. It was published in 1661, and a good conception of its leading design may be gathered from its title if given at length; "Fiat Lux; or, a general conduct to a right understanding in the great combustions and broils about religion here in England, betwixt Papist and Protestant, Presbyterian and Independent, to the end that moderation and quietness may at length happily ensue after so various tumults in the kingdom. By Mr J. V. C., a friend to men of all religions, 1661." Cane was a Franciscan friar, and had previously been the author of a work entitled "The Reclaimed Papist." When he was eighteen years of age, he had gone to the University of Cambridge, and, having studied there for two years, left it for London, whence he entered for some time on a course of foreign travel. He professes to have become attached to the Romish Church from the solemnity of its ritual abroad, though he admits hereditary prepossessions in its favour, as his grandfather was a Papist, and had been "so far impeached about the rising of the Earls in the north, that he lost estate and life." "Fiat Lux" consists of five chapters, in which, under a subdivision of thirty-one "paragraphs," it is shown,—1. That there is no occasion for fiery zeal about religion; 2. That all things are so obscure that no man should presume to guide his neighbour in matters of religion; 3. That no religion is superior to Popery; 4. That the Roman religion is truly innocent and unblamable,—quite as much so as other religions opposed to it are to one another; and lastly, follow "moral topics for charity and peace."

The character of the times gave importance to such a publication. Though not remarkable either for learning or argument, it is crafty and plausible, contains some dexterous hits at the differences among Protestants, and, when the weak points of Romanism are to be covered, is written with a misty vagueness, in which sentimentalism is made to do the work of logic. It assumes as its text a passage in a speech by the Lord Chancellor, which seems to have brought it speedily into notice with the higher circles of society. Before Owen had finished his "Animadversions" in reply to it, it was in a second edition. It is believed that Clarendon, the Lord Chancellor, is "the person of honour," who, according to Asty, sent the work to Owen, requesting him to prepare an answer to it.

Our author had the book in his possession for "a few days only." The "Animadversions," published in 1662, were the result of the attention he bestowed on it. He answers Cane most successfully. The readers of Owen will not much wonder that the Franciscan should be quite overwhelmed by the superior learning of the Puritan, but they will hardly be prepared for the resources of wit, humour, and irony, by which these "Animadversions" retain all their freshness and pungency to the present day, and Cane found his own favourite weapons of ridicule and sarcasm turned upon himself with irresistible effect. Cane, it may be added, found another antagonist in Mr Samuel Mather, who wrote, in reply to "Fiat Lux," "A Defence of the Protestant Religion." It was published in Dublin, 1671, 4to.—Ed.

TO THE READER.

READER,

THE treatise entitled "Fiat Lux," which thou wilt find examined in the ensuing discourse, was lent unto me, not long since, by an honourable person, with a request to return an answer unto it. It had not been many hours in my hand before the same desire was seconded by others. Having made no engagement unto the person of whom I received it, the book, after some few days, was remanded; yet, as it fell out, not before I had finished my Animadversions upon it. But before I could send my papers to the press, I heard of a second edition of that treatise; which also occasionally coming to my hands, I perceived it had been printed some good while before I saw or heard of the first. Finding the bulk of the discourse increased, I thought it needful to go through it once more, to see if any thing of moment were added to that edition which I had considered, or any alterations made by the author's second thoughts. This somewhat discouraged me, that, my first book being gone, I could not compare the editions, but must trust to my memory,—none of the best,—as to what was, or was not, in that I had perused. But not designing any use in a mere comparing of the editions, but only to consider whether in either of them any thing material was remaining, either not heeded by me, in my hasty passage through the first, or added in the second undiscussed, I thought it of no great concernment to inquire again after the first book. What of that nature offered itself unto me, I cast my thoughts upon into the margin of what was before written, inserting it into the same continued discourse. I therefore desire the reader, that he may not suspect himself deceived, to take notice, that whatever quotations out of that treatise he meets withal, the number of pages throughout answers the first edition of it.

Of the author of that discourse, and his design therein, I have but little to premise. He seems at first view to be a Naphtali, a hind let loose, and to give goodly words. But though the voice we hear from him sometimes be the voice of Jacob, yet the hands that put forth themselves, in his progress, are the hands of Esau. Moderation is pretended; but his counsels for peace centre in an advice for the extermination of the Ishmael (as he esteems it) of Protestancy. We know full well that the words he begins to flourish withal are not "Vox ultima Papæ." A discovery of the inconsistency of his real and pretended design is one part of our business. Indeed, an attentive reader cannot but quickly discern, that persuasions unto moderation in different professions of Christian religion, with a relinquishment of all others to an embracement of Popery, be they never so finely smoothed, must needs interfere. But yet, with words at such real variance among themselves doth our author hope to impose his sentiments in religion on the minds of noble and ingenuous persons, not yet accustomed to those severer thoughts and studies which are needful to form an exact judgment in things of this nature. That he should upon any obtain both his ends,—moderation and Popery,—is impossible. No two things are more inconsistent. Let him cease the pursuit of the latter, and we will follow after the former with him or without him. And if any man be so unhappily simple as to think to come to moderation in religion-feuds by turning Romanist, I shall leave him for his conviction to the mistress of such wise men. My present business is, as I find, to separate between his pleas for the moderation pretended, and those for Popery really aimed at. What force there may be in his reasons for that which he would not have, I shall not examine; but shall manifest that there is none in them he uses for what he would. And, reader, if this hasty attempt for the prevention of the application of them find acceptance with thee I shall, it may be ere long, give thee a full account of the new ways and principles which our author, and the men of the same persuasion, have of late years resolved on for the promotion of their cause and interest.

FAREWELL.

PREFACE.

Considering the condition of affairs in these nations, in reference to the late miscarriages and present distempers of men about religion, it was no hard conjecture that some would improve the advantage, seeming so fairly to present itself unto them, unto ends of their own: men of prudence, ability, and leisure, engaged by all bonds imaginable in the pursuit of any special interest, need little minding of the common ways of wisdom for its promotion. They know that he that would fashion iron into the image and likeness which he hath fancied *must strike whilst it is hot*,—when the adventitious efficacy of the fire it hath admitted makes it pliable to that whereunto, in its own nature, it is most opposite. Such seems to be, in these days, the temper of men in religion, from those flames wherewith some have been scorched, others heated, all provoked, and made fit to receive new impressions, if wisely hammered. Neither was it a difficult prognostication for any one, to foretell what arguments and mediums would be made use of to animate and enliven the persuasions of men, who had either right or confidence enough to plead or pretend a disinterest in our miscarriages for an embracement of their profession. Commonly, with men that indulge to passion and distempers, as the most of men are apt to do, the last provocation blots out the remembrance of preceding crimes no less heinous. And, whatever to the contrary is pretended, men usually have not that indignation against principles which have produced evils they have only heard or read of, that they have against practices under which they have personally suffered. Hence it might easily be expected that the Romanists, supposing, at least, by the help of those paroxysms they discern amongst us, that the miscarriages of some of their adversaries would prove a garment large enough to cover and hide their own, would, with much confidence, improve them to their special advantage. Nor is it otherwise come to pass. This persuasion, and suitable practice thereon, runs through all the veins of the discourse we have proposed to consideration; making that seem quick and sprightly which otherwise would have been but a heap or a carcase.

That then this sort of men would not only be *angling* in the lesser brooks of our troubled waters, endeavouring to inveigle wandering, loose, and discontented individuals (which hath been their constant employment), but also come with their nets into our open streams, was the thoughts of all men who count themselves concerned to think of such things as these. There is scarce a forward emissary amongst them who cries not, in such a season, "An ego occasionem mihi ostentatam, tantam, tam bonam, tam optatam, tam insperatam, amitterem?" What baits and tacklings they would principally make use of was also foreknown. But the way and manner which they would fix on for the management of their design, now displayed in this discourse, lay not, I confess, under an ordinary prospect. For, as to what course the wisdom of men will steer them, in various alterations, *μάντις ἄριστος ὅστις εἰκάζει καλῶς*, [Eurip. Frag. inc. cxxviii.]—"he is no mean prophet that can but indifferently guess." But yet there wanted not some beams of light to guide men in the exercise of their stochastic[1] faculty, even as to this also. That accommodation of religion and all its concernments unto the humours, fancies, and conversations of men, wherewith some of late have pleased themselves, and laid snares for the ruin of others, did shrewdly portend what, in this attempt of the same party, we were to expect. Of this nature is that poetical strain of devotion so much applauded and prevailing in our neighbour kingdom; whereby men, ignorant of the heavenly power of the gospel, not only to resist but to subdue the strongest lusts and most towering imaginations of the sons of men, do labour, in soft and delicate rhymes, to attemperate religion unto the loose and airy fancies of persons wholly indulging their minds to vanity and pleasure;—a fond attempt of men not knowing how to manage the sublime, spiritual, severe truths of the gospel, to the ingenerating of faith and devotion in the souls of sinners; but yet that which they suppose is the only way left them to prevent the keeping of religion and the most of their party at a perpetual distance! So Mohammed saw it necessary to go to the mountain, when the mountain, for all his calling, would not come to him. And of the same sort is the greatest part of the casuistical divinity of the Jesuits. A mere accommodation of the principles of religion to the filthy lusts and wicked lives of men, who on no other terms would resign the conduct of their souls unto them, seems to be their main design in it. On these defects of others, he that would have pondered what a wise and observing person of the same interest with them might apprehend of the present tempers, distempers, humours, interests, provocations, fancies, lives of them with whom he intends to deal, could not have failed of some advantage in his conjectures at the way and manner wherein he would proceed in treating of them. It is of the *many* of whom we speak,—on whose countenances, and in whose lives, he that runs may read provocations from former miscarriages; supine negligence of spiritual and eternal concernments; ignorance of things past, beyond what they can remember in their own days; sloth in the disquisition of the truth; willingness to be accommodated with a religion pretended secure and unconcerned in present disputes, that may save them and their sins together without farther trouble; delight in quaint language and poetical strains of eloquence, whereunto they are accustomed at the stage; with sundry other inward accoutrements of mind not unlike to these. To this frame and temper of spirit, this composition of humours, it was not improbable but that those who should first enter into the lists in this design would accommodate their style and manner of procedure,—"Nec spem fefellit expectatio." The treatise under consideration hath fully answered whatever was of conjecture in this kind. Frequent repetitions of late provocations, with the crimes of the provokers; confident and undue assertions of things past in the days of old; large promises of security, temporal and eternal, to nations and all individuals in them,—of facility in coming to perfection in religion without more pains of teaching, learning, or fear of opposition; all interwoven with tart sarcasms, pleasant diversions, pretty stories of himself and others, flourished over with a smooth and handsome strain of rhetoric, do apparently make up the bulk of our author's discourse. Nor is the *romance* of his conversion, much influenced by the *tinkling of bells* and *sweeping of churches*, suited unto any other principles: a matter, I confess, so much the more admirable, because, as I suppose it, in the way mentioned, to have been his singular lot and good hap, so it was utterly impossible that for five hundred, I may say a thousand years after Christ, any man should on these motives be turned to any religion, most of them being not in those days "in rerum natura." A way of handling religion he hath fixed on which, as I suppose, he will himself acknowledge that the first planters of it were ignorant of; so I will promise him, that if he can, for a thousand years after they began their work, instance in any one book of an approved Catholic

[1] Conjectural, skilful in framing conjectures.—Ed.

author, written with the same design that this is, he shall have one proselyte to his profession; which is more, I suppose, than otherwise he will obtain by his learned labour. That this is no other but to persuade men that they can find no certainty or establishment for their faith in Scripture, but must for it devolve themselves solely on the authority of the pope, will afterward be made to appear; nor will himself deny it. But, it may be, it is unreasonable that when men are eagerly engaged in the pursuit of their interest, we should think, from former precedents, or general rules of sobriety, with that reverence which is due to the things of the great and holy God, to impose upon them the way and manner of their progress. The event and end aimed at is that which we are to respect; the management of their business in reference to this world and that which is to come is their own concernment. No man, I suppose, who hath any acquaintance with the things he treats about, can abstain from smiling, to observe how dexterously he turns and winds himself in his cloak (which is not every one's work to dance in); how he gilds over the more comely parts of his Amasia with brave suppositions, presumptions, and stories of things past and present, where he has been in his days; covering her deformities with a perpetual silence; ever and anon bespattering the first Reformation and reformers in his passage;—yea, their contentment must needs proceed to a high degree of complacence, in whom compassion for the woful state of them whom so able a man judgeth like to be inveigled by such flourishes and pretences doth not excite to other affections. The truth is, if ever there blew a wind of doctrine on unwary souls,—'Εν τῇ κυβείᾳ τῶν ἀνθρώπων, ἐν πανουργίᾳ πρὸς τὴν μεθοδείαν τῆς πλάνης, (Eph. iv. 14),—we have an instance of it in this discourse. Such a disposition of cogging sleights,[1] various crafts in enticing words, is rarely met with. Many, I think, are not able to take this course in handling the sacred things of God, and eternal concernments of men; and more, I hope, dare not. But our author is another man's servant; I shall not judge him; he "stands or falls to his own master." That which the importunity of some noble friends hath compelled me unto is, to offer somewhat to the judgment of impartial men that may serve to unmask him of his gilded pretences, and to lay open the emptiness of those prejudices and presumptions wherewith he makes such a tinkling noise in the ears of unlearned and unstable persons. Occasion of serious debate is very little administered by him; that which is the task assigned me I shall as fully discharge as the few hours allotted to its performance will allow.

In my dealing with him, I shall not make it my business to defend the several parties whereinto the men of his contest are distributed by our author as such; not all, not any of them. It is the common Protestant cause which, in and by all of them, he seeks to oppose. So far as they are interested and concerned therein, they fall all of them within the bounds of our present defensative. Wherein they differ one from another, or any or all of them do or may swerve from the principles of the Protestant religion, I have nothing to do with them in this business; and if any be so far addicted to their parties, wherein, it may be, they are in the wrong, as to choose rather not to be vindicated and pleaded for in that wherein with others I know they are in the right than to be joined in the same plea with them from whom in part they differ, I cannot help it. I pretend not their commission for what I do; and they may, when they please, disclaim my appearance for them. I suppose by this course I shall please very few, and I am sure I shall displease some, if not many. I aim at neither, but to profit all. I have sundry reasons for not owning or avowing particularly any party in this discourse, so as to judge the rest, wherewith I am not bound to acquaint the world. One of them I shall, and I hope it is such a one as may suffice ingenuous and impartial men; and thereunto some others may be added: The gentleman whose discourse I have

[1] Deceitful artifices.

undertaken the consideration of was pleased to front and close it with a part of a speech of my Lord Chancellor;[1] and his placing of it manifests how he uses it. He salutes it in his entrance, and takes his leave also of it, never regarding its intendment until coming to the close of his treatise; to his "salve" in the beginning he adds an "æternum vale." That the mention of such an excellent discourse (the best part in both our books) might not be lost, I have suited my plea and defensative of Protestantism to the spirit, and principles, and excellent ratiocinations of it. Behind that shield I lay the manner of my proceeding; where if it be not safe, I care not what becomes of it. Besides, it is not for what the men of his title-page are differenced amongst themselves that our author blames them; but for what he thinks they agree in too well in reference to the church of Rome: nor doth he insist on the evils of their contest to persuade them to peace amongst themselves, or to prevail over them to centre in any one persuasion about which they contend; but to lead them all over to the pope. And if any of them with whom our author deals and sports himself in his treatise are fallen off from the fundamental denominating principles of Protestant religion, as some of them seem to be, they come not within the compass of our plea, seeing as such they are not dealt with by our author. It is the Protestant religion in general, which he charges with all irregularities, uncertainties, and evils, that he expatiates about; and from the principles of it doth he endeavour to withdraw us. As to the case, then, under debate with him, it is enough if we manifest that that profession of religion is not liable or obnoxious to any of the crimes or inconveniences by him objected unto it; and that the remedy of our evils, whether real or imaginary, which he would impose upon us, is so far from being specifical towards their cure, that it is indeed far worse than the disease pretended,—to the full as undesirable as the cutting of the throat for the cure of a sore finger. There is no reason, therefore, in this business, wherefore I should avow any one persuasion, about which Protestants, that consent in general in the same confession of faith, may have, or actually have, difference amongst themselves; especially if I do also evince there is no cogency in them to cause any of them to renounce the truth wherein they all agree.

Much less shall I undertake to plead for, excuse, or palliate the miscarriages of any part or parties of men during our late unhappy troubles; nor shall I make much use of what offers itself in a way of recrimination. Certain it is, that, as to this gentleman's pretensions, sundry things might be insisted on that would serve to allay the fierceness of his spirit in his management of other men's crimes to his own ends and purposes. The sound of our late evils, as it is known to all the world, began in Ireland, amongst his good Roman Catholics, who were blessed from Rome into rebellion and murder, somewhat before any drop of blood was shed in England or Scotland,—

"—— Oculis male lippus inunctis,
Cur in amicorum vitiis tam cernis acutum,
Quam aut Aquila aut Serpens Epidaurius?"
[Hor. Sat. i. 3, 25.]

Let them that are innocent throw stones at others: Roman Catholics are unfit to be employed in that work. But it was never judged either a safe or honest way to judge of any religion by the practices of some that have professed it. Men by doctrines and principles, not doctrines by men, was the trial of old. And if this be a rule to guide our thoughts in reference to any religion,—namely, the principles which it avows and asserts,—I know none that can vie with the Romanists' in

[1] In the preface and in the conclusion to "Fiat Lux," the author quotes largely from a speech by the Earl of Clarendon, who, having been appointed Lord Chancellor by Charles II. during his exile, at the Restoration accompanied him in his return to London, and at once entered upon the office of Speaker in the House of Lords. The speech was delivered on the adjournment of Parliament in September 1660.—Ed.

laying foundations of, and making provision for, the disturbance of the civil peace of kingdoms and nations. For the present, unto the advantage taken by our author from our late unnatural wars and tumults to reflect on Protestancy, I shall only say, that if the religion of sinners be to be quitted and forsaken, I doubt that professed by the pope must be cashiered for company.

Least of all shall I oppose myself to that moderation in the pursuit of our religious interests which he pretends to plead for. He that will plead against mutual forbearance in religion can be no Christian, at least no good one. Much less shall I impeach what he declaims against,—that abominable principle of disturbing the peace of kingdoms and nations, under a pretence of defending, reforming, or propagating of our faith and opinions. But I know that neither the commendation of the former nor the decrying of the latter is the proper work of our author: for as the present principles and past practices of the men of that church and religion which he defends will not allow him to entertain such hard thoughts of the latter as he pretends unto; so as to the former, where he has made some progress in his work, and either warmed his zeal beyond his first intendment for its discovery, or has gotten some confidence that he hath obtained a better acceptance with his reader than, at the entrance of his discourse, he could lay claim unto, laying aside those counsels of moderation and forbearance which he had gilded over, he plainly declares that the only way of procuring peace amongst us is by the extermination of Protestancy! For, having compared the Roman Catholic to Isaac, the proper heir of the house, and Protestants to Ishmael vexing him in his own inheritance, the only way to obtain peace, he tells us, is, "Projice ancillam cum filio suo;"—"Cast out the handmaid with her son;" that is, in the gloss of their former practices, either burn them at home or send them to starve abroad. There is not the least reason, then, why I should trouble myself with his flourishes and stories, his characters of us and our neighbour nations, in reference unto moderation and forbearance in religion. That is not the thing by him intended, but is only used to give a false alarm to his unwary readers, whilst he marches away with a rhetorical persuasive unto Popery. In this it is wherein alone I shall attend his motions; and if, in our passage through his other discourses, we meet with any thing lying in a direct tendency unto his main end, though pretended to be used to another purpose, it shall not pass without some animadversion.

Also, I shall be far from contending with our author in those things wherein his discourse excelleth, and that upon the two general reasons of will and ability. Neither could I compare with him in them if I would, nor would if I could. His quaint rhetoric, biting sarcasms, fine stories, smooth expressions of his high contempt of them with whom he has to do, with many things of that sort, the repetition of whose names hath got the reputation of incivility, are things wherein, as I cannot keep pace with him (for "illud possumus quod jure possumus"), so I have no mind to follow him.

ANIMADVERSIONS

ON

A TREATISE ENTITLED "FIAT LUX."

CHAPTER I.

Our author's preface, and his method.

It is not any disputation or rational debate about differences in religion that our author intends; nor, until towards the close of his treatise, doth he at all fix directly on any thing in controversy between Romanists and Protestants. In the former parts of his discourse his design is sometimes covered, always carried on in the way of a rhetorical declamation; so that it is not possible, and is altogether needless, to trace all the particular passages and expressions, as they lie scattered up and down in his discourse, which he judgeth of advantage unto him in the management of the work he has undertaken. Some suppositions there are which lie at the bottom of his whole superstructure, quickening the oratory and rhetorical part of it (undoubtedly its best), which he chose rather to take for granted than to take upon himself the trouble to prove. These being drawn forth and removed, whatever he hath built upon them, with all that paint and flourish wherewith it is adorned, will of itself fall to the ground. I shall, then, first briefly discuss what he offers as to the method of his procedure, and then take this for my own,—namely, I shall draw out and examine the fundamental principles of his oration, upon whose trial the whole must stand or fall, and then pass through the severals of the whole treatise, with such animadversions as what remaineth of it may seem to require.

His method he speaks unto, p. 13. "My method," saith he, "I do purposely conceal, to keep therein a more handsome decorum; for he that goes about to part a fighting fray cannot observe a method, but must turn himself this way and that, as occasion offers, be it a corporeal or mental duel. So did good St Paul, in his Epistle to the

Romans; which, of all his other epistles, as it hath most of solidity, so it hath least of method in the context: the reason is," etc. These are handsome words of a man that seems to have good thoughts of himself and his skill in parting frays. But yet I see not how they hang well together as to any congruity of their sense and meaning. Surely, he that useth no method, nor can use any, cannot conceal his method,—no, though he purpose so to do. No man's purpose to hide will enable him to hide that which is not. If he hath concealed his method, he hath used one: if he hath used none, he hath not concealed it; for "that which is wanting cannot be numbered." Nor hath he by this or any other means kept any "handsome decorum," not having once spoken the sense, or according to the principles of him whom he undertakes to personate; which is such an observance of a decorum as a man shall not lightly meet with. Nor hath he discovered any mind so to part a fray as that the contenders might hereafter live quietly one by another; his business being avowedly to persuade as many as he can to a conjunction in one party for the destruction of all the rest. And whatever he saith of "not using a method," that method of his discourse, with the good words it is set off withal, is the whole of his interest in it. He pretends, indeed, to pass through "loca nullius ante Trita solo;" yet, setting aside his management of the advantages given him by the late miserable tumults in these nations, and the provision he has made for the entertainment of his reader is worts boiled a hundred times over; as he knows well enough. And for the method which he would have us believe not to be, and yet to be concealed, it is rather μεθοδεία than μέθοδος,—rather a crafty, various distribution of enticing words and plausible pretences, to inveigle and delude men unlearned and unstable, than any decent contexture of, or fair progress in, a rational discourse or regular disposition of nervous topics, to convince or persuade the minds of men who have their eyes in their heads. I shall, therefore, little trouble myself farther about it, but only discover it as occasion shall require; for the discovery of sophistry is its proper confutation.

However, the course he steers is the same that "good St Paul" used in his Epistle to the Romans; which hath, as he tells us, "most of solidity and least of method of all his epistles." I confess I knew not before that his church had determined which of St Paul's epistles had "most of solidity," which least; for I have such good thoughts of him, that I suppose he would not do it of his own head: nor do I know that he is appointed umpire to determine upon the writings that came all of them by inspiration from God, which is most solid. This, therefore, must needs be the sense of his church, which he may be acquainted with twenty ways that I know not of. And here his

Protestant visor, which by-and-by he will utterly cast off, fell off from him, I presume, at unawares. That he be no more so entrapped, I wish he would take notice, against the next time he hath occasion to personate a Protestant, that although, for method purely adventitious, and belonging to the external manner of writing, Protestants may affirm that one epistle is more methodical than another, according to those rules of method which ourselves, or other worms of the earth like to ourselves, have invented; yet, for their solidity, which concerns the matter of them, and efficacy for conviction, they affirm them all equal. Nor is he more happy in what he intimates of the immethodicalness of that epistle to the Romans; for, as it is acknowledged by all good expositors, that the apostle useth a most clear, distinct, and exact method in that epistle (whence most theological systems are composed by the rule of it), so our author himself assigneth such a design unto him, and the use of such ways and means in the prosecution of it, as argue a diligent observance of a method. I confess he is deceived in the occasion and intention of the epistle, by following some few late Roman expositors, neglecting the analysis given of it by the ancients. But we may pass that by; because I find his aim in mentioning a false scope and design was not to acquaint us with his mistake, but to take an advantage to fall upon our ministers, and I think a little too early for one so careful to keep a "handsome decorum," for "culling out of this epistle texts against the Christian doctrine of good works done in Christ, by his special grace, out of obedience to his command, with a promise of everlasting reward and intrinsic acceptability thence accruing." Thus we see still,—

"Inceptis gravibus plerumque et magna professis
Purpureus, late qui splendeat, unus et alter
Assuitur pannus;——
Sed nunc non erat his locus."—[Hor. ad Pis. 15.]

Use of disputing has cast him, at the very entrance of his discourse, upon, as he supposeth, a particular controversy between Protestants and Roman Catholics, quite besides his design and purpose; but, instead of obtaining any advantage by this transgression of his own rule, he is fallen upon a new misadventure, and that so much the greater, because it evidently discovers somewhat in him besides mistake. I am sure I have heard as many of our ministers preach as he, and read as many of their books as he, yet I can testify that I never heard or read them opposing "the Christian doctrine of good works." Often I have heard and found them pressing a universal obedience to the whole law of God; teaching men to abound in good works; pressing the indispensable necessity of them from the commands of law and gospel; encouraging men unto them by the blessed promises of acceptance and reward in Christ; declaring them to be the way of men's coming to the kingdom of heaven; affirming that all that believe are created in Christ Jesus unto good works, and for men to neglect, to despise them, is wilfully to neglect their own salvation. But "opposing the Christian doctrine of good works," and that with "sayings culled out of St Paul's Epistle to the Romans," I never heard, I never read, any Protestant minister. There is but one expression in that declaration of the doctrine of good works which, he saith, Protestants oppose, used by himself, that they do not own, and that is their "intrinsic acceptability;" which, I fear, he doth not very well understand. If he mean by it that there is in good works an intrinsical worth and value, from their exact answerableness to the law and proportion to the reward, so as on rules of justice to deserve and merit it, he speaks daggers, and doth not himself believe what he says, it being contradictious; for he lays their acceptability on the account of the promise. If he intend that, God having graciously promised to accept and receive them in Christ, they become thereupon acceptable and rewardable,—this, Protestant ministers teach daily. Against the former explication of their acceptability, in reference to the justice of God, on their own account, and the justification of their persons that perform them,—for them, I have often heard them speaking, but never with any authority or force of argument comparable to that used by St Paul, in his Epistle to the Romans, to the same purpose. But this tale of Protestants opposing the Christian doctrine of good works hath been so often told by the Romanists, that I am persuaded some of them begin to believe it, however it be not only false, but, from all circumstances, very incredible. And finding our author hugely addicted to approve any thing that passeth for current in his party, I will not charge him with a studied fraud; in the finding it so advantageous to his cause, he took hold of a very remote occasion to work an early prejudice in the minds of his readers against them and their doctrine whom he designeth to oppose. When he writes next, I hope he will mind the account we have all to make of what we do write and say, and be better advised than to give countenance to such groundless slanders.

CHAPTER II.

Heathen pleas—General Principles.

We have done with his method or manner of proceeding; our next view shall be of those general principles and suppositions which animate the parenetical part of his work, and whereon it is solely founded. And here I would entreat him not to be offended if, in the entrance of this discourse, I make bold to mind him that the most, if not all, of his pleas have been long since insisted on by a very learned man, in a case not much unlike this which we have in hand; and were also long since answered by one as learned as he, or as any the world saw in the age wherein he lived, or it may be since to this day, though he died now fourteen hundred years ago. The person I intend is Celsus[1] the philosopher, who objected the very same things, upon the same general grounds, and ordered his objections in the same manner against the Christians of old as our author doth against the Protestants. And the answer of Origen to his eight books will save any man the labour of answering this one, who knows how to make application of general rules and principles unto particular cases that may be regulated by them. Doth our author lay the cause of all the troubles, disorders, tumults, wars, wherewith the nations of Europe have been for some season, and are still, in some places, infested, on the Protestants?—so doth Celsus charge all the evils, commotions, plagues, and famines, wherewith mankind in those days was much wasted, upon the Christians. Doth our author charge the Protestants that, by their breaking off from Rome with schisms and seditions, they made way for others, on the same principles, to break off seditiously from themselves?—so did Celsus charge the Jews and Christians; telling the Jews that by their seditious departure from the common worship and religion of the world they made way for the Christians, a branch of themselves, to cast off them and their worship in like manner, and to set up for themselves; and, following on his objection, he applies it to the Christians, that they, departing from the Jews, had broached principles for others to improve into a departure from them: which is the sum of most that is pleaded, with any fair pretence, by our author against Protestants. Doth he insist upon the divisions of the Protestants, and, to make it evident that he speaks knowingly, boast that he is acquainted with their persons, and hath read the books of all sorts amongst them?—so doth Celsus deal with the Christians, reproaching them with their divisions, discords, mutual animosities, disputes about God and his worship, boasting that he had debated the matter with them, and read their books of all sorts. Hath he gathered a rhapsody of insignificant words, at least as by him put together, out of the books of the Quakers, to reproach Protestants with their divisions?—so did Celsus out of the books and writings of the Gnostics, Ebionites, and Valentinians. Doth he bring in Protestants pleading against the sects that are fallen from them, and these pleading against them, justifying the

[1] The earliest author who is known to have written against Christianity, and among the ablest of its opponents. He is called by Origen an Epicurean, though some of his views have a greater affinity with Platonism. He flourished during the latter half of the second century. His work against Christianity was entitled Λόγος Ἀληθής; his arguments assume the historical verity of revelation.—ED.

protestants against them, but at length equally rejecting them all?—so dealt Celsus with the Jews, Christians, and those that had fallen into singular opinions of their own. Doth he manage the arguments of the Jews against Christ, to intimate that we cannot well by Scripture prove him to be so?—the very same thing did Celsus, almost in the very words here used. Doth he declaim openly about the obscurity of divine things, the nature of God, the works of creation and providence, that we are not like to be delivered from it by books of poems, stories, plain letters?—so doth Celsus. Doth he insist on the uncertainty of our knowing the Scripture to be from God, the difficulty of understanding it, its insufficiency to end men's differences about religion and the worship of God?—the same doth Celsus at large, pleading the cause of Paganism against Christianity. Doth our author plead, that where and from whom men had their religion of old, there and with them they ought to abide, or to return unto them?—the same doth Celsus, and that with pretences far more specious than those of our author. Doth he plead the quietness of all things in the world, the peace, the plenty, love, union, that were in the days before Protestants began to trouble all, as he supposeth, about religion?—the same course steers Celsus, in his contending against Christians in general. Is there intimated by our author a decay of devotion and reverence to religious things, temples, etc.?—Celsus is large on this particular: the relinquishment of temples, discouragement of priests in their daily sacrifices and heavenly contemplations, with other votaries; contempt of holy altars, images, and statues of worthies deceased, all heaven-bred ceremonies and comely worship, by the means of Christians, he expatiates upon. Doth he profess love and compassion to his countrymen, to draw them off from their folly, to have been the cause of his writing?—so doth Celsus. Doth he deride and scoff at the first reformers, with no less witty and biting sarcasms than those wherewith Aristophanes jeered Socrates on the stage?—Celsus deals no otherwise with the first propagators of Christianity. Hath he taken pains to palliate and put new glosses and interpretations upon those opinions and practices in his religion which seem most obnoxious to exception?—the same work did Celsus undertake, in reference to his Pagan theology and worship. And in sundry other things may the parallel be traced; so that I may truly say, I cannot observe any thing of moment or importance, of the nature of a general head or principle, in this whole discourse made use of against Protestants, but that the same was used, as by others of old, so in particular by Celsus, against the whole profession of Christianity. I will not be so injurious to our author as once to surmise that he took either aim or assistance in his work from so bitter a professed enemy of Christ Jesus, and the religion by him revealed; yet he must give me leave to reckon this coincidence of argumentation between them amongst other instances that may be given where a similitude of cause hath produced a great likeness, if not identity, in the reasonings of ingenious men. I could not satisfy myself without remarking this parallel: and, perhaps, much more needs not to be added to satisfy an unprejudiced reader in or to our whole business; for if he be one that is unwilling to forego his Christianity, when he shall see that the arguments that are used to draw him from his Protestancy are the very same, in general, that wise men of old made use of to subvert that which he is resolved to cleave unto, he needs not much deliberation with himself what to do or say in this case, or be solicitous what he shall answer, when he is earnestly entreated to suffer himself to be deceived.

Of the pretences before mentioned, some, with their genuine inferences, are the main principles of this whole discourse. And seeing they bear the weight of all the pleas, reasonings, and persuasions that are drawn from them, which can have no farther real strength and efficacy than what is from them communicated unto them, I shall present them in one view to the reader, that he lose not himself in the maze of words wherewith our author endeavours to lead him up and down, still out of his way, and that he may make a clear and distinct judgment of what is tendered to prevail upon him to desert that profession of religion wherein he is engaged. For as I dare not attempt to deceive any man, though in matters incomparably of less moment than that treated about; so I hope no man can justly be offended, if in this I warn him to take heed to himself that he be not deceived. And they are these that follow:—

I. "That we, in these nations, first received the Christian religion from Rome, by the mission and authority of the pope."

II. "That whence and from whom we first received our religion, there and with them we ought to abide; to them we must repair for guidance in all our concernments in it; and speedily return to their rule and conduct, if we have departed from them."

III. "That the Roman profession of religion and practice in the worship of God is every way the same as it was when we first received our religion from thence; nor can ever otherwise be."

IV. "That all things, as to religion, were quiet and in peace, all men in union and at agreement amongst themselves in the worship of God, according to the mind of Christ, before the relinquishment of the Roman see by our forefathers."

V. "That the first reformers were the most of them sorry, contemptible persons, whose errors were propagated by indirect means, and entertained for sinister ends."

VI. "That our departure from Rome hath been the cause of all our evils, and particularly of all those divisions which are at this day found amongst the Protestants, and which have been ever since the Reformation."

VII. "That we have no remedy of our evils, no means of ending our differences, but by a return unto the rule of the Roman see."

VIII. "The Scripture, upon sundry accounts, is insufficient to settle us in the truth of religion, or to bring us to an agreement amongst ourselves; seeing it is,—1. Not to be known to be the word of God but by the testimony of the Roman church; 2. Cannot be well translated into our vulgar language; 3. Is in itself obscure; and, 4. We have none to determine of the sense of it."

IX. "That the pope is a good man, one that seeks nothing but our good, that never did us harm, and hath the care and inspection of us committed unto him by Christ."

X. "That the devotion of the Catholics far transcends that of Protestants, nor is their doctrine or worship liable to any just exception."

I suppose our author will not deny these to be the principal nerves and sinews of his oration; nor complain I have done him the least injury in this representation of them, or that any thing of importance unto his advantage, by himself insisted on, is here omitted. He that runs and reads, if he observe any thing that lies before him, besides handsome words and ingenious diversions, will consent that here lies the substance of what is offered unto him. I shall not need, then, to tire the reader and myself with transcriptions of those many words from the several parts of his discourse, wherein these principles are laid down and insinuated, or gilded over, as things on all hands granted. Besides, so far as they are interwoven with other reasonings, they will fall again under our consideration in the several places where they are used and improved. If all these principles, upon examination, be found good, true, firm, and stable, it is most meet and reasonable that our author should obtain his desire: and if, on the other side, they shall appear some of them false; some impertinent, and the deductions from them sophistical; some of them destructive to Christian religion in general; none of them singly, nor all of them together, able to bear the least part of that weight which is laid upon them,—I suppose he cannot take it ill if we resolve to be contented with our present condition, until some better way of deliverance from it be proposed unto us; which, to tell him the truth, for my part, I do not expect from his church or party. Let us, then, consider these principles apart, in the order wherein we have laid them down; which is the best I could think on upon the sudden, for the advantage of him who makes use of them:—

I. The first is a hinge, upon which many of those which follow do in a sort depend; yea, upon the matter, all of them. Our primitive receiving Christian religion from Rome is that which influences all persuasions for a return thither. Now, if this must be admitted to be true, that we in these nations first received the Christian religion from Rome, by the mission and authority of the pope, it either must be so because the proposition carries its own evidence in its very terms, or because our author, and those consenting with him, have had it by revelation, or it hath been testified to them by others who knew it so to be. That the first it doth not, is most certain: for it is very possible it might have been brought unto us from some other place, from whence it came to Rome; for, as I take it, it had not there its beginning. Nor do I suppose they will plead special revelation, made either to themselves or any others about this matter. I have read many of the revelations that are said to be made to sundry persons canonized by his church for saints, but never met with any thing concerning the place from whence England first received the gospel. Nor have I yet heard Revelation pleaded to this purpose by any of his copartners in design. It remains, then, that somebody hath told him so, or informed him of it, either by writing or by word of mouth. Usually, in such cases, the first inquiry is, whether they be credible persons who have made the report. Now, the pretended authors of this story may, I suppose, be justly questioned, if on no other, yet on this account, that he who designs an advantage by their testimony, doth not indeed believe what they say. For, notwithstanding what he would fain have us believe of Christianity coming into Britain from Rome, he knows well enough, and tells us elsewhere himself, that it came directly by sea from Palestine into France, and was thence brought into England by Joseph of Arimathea. And what was that faith and worship which he brought along with him we know full well, by that which was the faith and worship of his teachers and associates in the work of propagating the gospel, recorded in the Scripture. So that Christianity found a passage to Britain without so much as once visiting Rome by the way. "Yea, but one hundred and fifty years after, Fugatius and Damianus came from Rome, and propagated the gospel here; and four hundred years after them, Austin the monk." Of these stories we shall speak particularly afterward. But this quite spoils the whole market in hand This is not a *first* receiving of the gospel, but a *second* and *third* at the best; and if that be considerable, then so ought the proposition to be laid. These nations a second and third time, after the first from another place, received the gospel from Rome; but this will not discharge that bill of following items which is laid upon it. Whatever, then, there is considerable in the place or persons from whence or whom a nation or people receives the gospel, as far as it concerns us in these kingdoms, it relates to Jerusalem and Jews, not Rome and Italians. Indeed, it had been very possible that Christian religion might have been propagated at first from Rome into Britain, considering what in those days was the condition of the one place and the other: yet things were so ordered in the providence of the Lord, that it fell out otherwise; and the gospel was preached here in England probably before ever St Paul came to Rome, or St Peter either, if ever he came there. But yet, to prevent wrangling about Austin and the Saxons, let us suppose that Christian religion was first planted in these nations by persons coming from Rome,—if you will, men sent by the pope, before he was born, for that purpose; what then will follow? "Was it the pope's religion they taught and preached? Did the pope first find it out and declare it? Did they baptize men in the name of the pope? or declare that the pope was crucified for them?" You know whose arguings these are, to prove men should not lay weight upon, or contend about, the first ministerial revealers of the gospel, but rest all in him who is the author of it,—Christ Jesus. Did any come here and preach in the pope's name,—declare a religion of his revealing, or resting in him as the fountain and source of the whole business they had to do? If you say so, you say something which is near to your purpose, but certainly very wide from the truth. But because it is most certain that God had not promised originally to send the rod of Christ's strength out of Rome, I shall take leave to ask, Whence the gospel came thither? or, to use the words made use of once and again by our author, "Came the gospel from them, or came it to them only?" I suppose they will not say so, because they speak to men that have seen the Bible. If it came to them from others, what privilege had they at Rome, that they should not have the same respect for them from whom the gospel came to them, as they claim from those unto whom they plead that it came from themselves? "The case is clear: St Peter coming to Rome, brought his chair along with him; after which time that was made the head, spring, and fountain of all religion; and no such thing could befall those places where the planters of the gospel had no chairs to settle." I think I have read this story in a hundred writers; but they were all men of yesterday in comparison, who, whatever they pretend, know no more of this business than myself. St Peter speaks not one word of it in his writings, nor yet St Luke, nor St Paul, nor any one who by divine inspiration committed any thing to remembrance of the state of the church after the resurrection of Christ. And not only are they utterly silent of this matter, but also Clemens and Ignatius, and Justin Martyr and Tertullian, with the rest of knowing men in those days. I confess, in after ages, when some began to think it meet that the chiefest apostle should go to the then chiefest city in the world, divers began to speak of his going thither, and of his martyrdom there, though they agree not in their tales about it. But be it so; as for my part, I will not contend in a matter so dark, uncertain, of no moment in religion. This I know, that being the apostle of the circumcision, if he did go to Rome, it was to convert the Jews that were there, and not to found that Gentile church which in a short space got the start of the other. But yet neither do these writers talk of bringing his chair thither, much less is there in them one dust of that rope of sand which men of latter days have endeavoured to twist with inconsistent consequences and groundless presumptions, to draw out from thence the pope's prerogative. The case, then, is absolutely the same as to those, in respect of the Romans, who received the gospel from them, or by their means; and of the Romans themselves in respect of those from whom they received it. If they would win worship to themselves from others, by pretending that the gospel came forth from them unto them, let them teach them by the example of their devotion towards those from whom they received it. I suppose they will not plead that they are not now "in rerum natura," knowing what will ensue to their disadvantage on that plea. For if that church is utterly failed and gone from whence they first received the gospel, that which others received it from may possibly be not in a much better condition. But I find myself, before I was aware, fallen into the borders of the second principle or presumption mentioned. I shall therefore shut up my consideration of this first pretence with this only,—that neither is it true that these nations first received Christianity from Rome, much less by any mission of the pope; nor, if they had done so, in the exercise of a ministerial work and authority, would this make any thing to what is pretended from it; nor will it ever be of any use to the present Romanists, unless they can prove that the pope was the first author of Christian religion, which as yet they have not attempted to do: and thence it is evident what is to be thought of the second principle before mentioned, namely,—

II. "That whence and from whom we first received our religion, there and with them we must abide therein; to them we must repair for guidance; and return to their rule and conduct, if we have departed from them."

I have showed already that there is no privity of interests between us and the Romanists in this matter. But suppose we had been originally instructed in Christianity by men sent from Rome to that purpose (for unless we suppose this for the present, our talk is at an end), I see not, as yet, the verity of this proposition. With the truth, wherever it be, or with whomsoever, it is most certainly our duty to abide. And if those from whom we first received our Christianity, ministerially, abide in the truth, we must abide with them; not because they, or their predecessors, were the instruments of our conversion, but because they abide in the truth. Setting aside this consideration of truth, which is the bond of all union, and that which fixeth the centre, and limits the bounds of it, one people's or one church's abiding with another in any profession of religion, is a thing merely indifferent. When we have received the truth from any, the formal reason of our continuance with them in that union which our reception of the truth from them gives unto us, is their abiding in the truth, and no other. Suppose some persons, or some church or churches, do propagate Christianity to another, and, in progress of time, themselves fall off from some of those truths which they, or their predecessors, had formerly delivered unto those instructed by them (if our author shall deny that such a supposition can well be made, because it never did nor can fall out, I shall remove his exception by scores of instances out of antiquity, needless in so evident a matter to be here mentioned)—what in this case would be their duty who received the gospel from them? Must they abide with them, follow after them, and embrace the errors they are fallen into, because they first received the gospel from them? I trow not. It will be found their duty to abide in the truth, and not pin their faith upon the sleeves of them by whom ministerially it was at first communicated unto them. "But this case," you will say, "concerns not the Roman church and Protestants; for as these abide not in the truth, so they never did nor can depart from it." Well, then, that we may not displease them at present, let us put the case so as I presume they will own it. Suppose men, or a church, intrusted by Christ authoritatively to preach the gospel, do propagate the faith unto others according to their duties; these, being converted by their means, do afterward, through the craft and subtlety of seducers, fall in sundry things from the truths they were instructed in, and wherein their instructors do constantly abide ("Yea," say our adversaries, "this is the true case indeed")—I ask then, in this case, What is, and ought to be, the formal motive to prevail with these persons to return to their former condition, from whence they were fallen? Either this, That they are departed from the truth, which they cannot do without peril to their souls, and whereunto, if they return not, they must perish; or this, That it is their duty to return to them from whom they first received the doctrine of Christianity, because they so received it from them. St Paul, who surely had as much authority in these matters as either the pope or church of Rome can with any modesty lay claim unto, had to deal with very many in this case. Particularly, after he had preached the gospel to the Galatians, and converted them to the faith of Christ, there came in some false teachers and seducers amongst them, which drew them off from the truth wherein they had been instructed, in divers important and some fundamental points of it. What course doth the apostle proceed in towards them? Doth he plead with them about their falling away from him that first converted them? or falling away from the truth whereunto they were converted? If any one will take the pains to turn to any chapter in that epistle, he may be satisfied as to this inquiry: it is their falling away from the gospel, from the truth they had received, from the doctrine, in particular, of faith and justification by the blood of Christ, that alone he blamed them for; yea, and makes doctrines so far the measure and rule of judging and censuring of persons, whether they preach the word first or last, that he pronounceth a redoubled anathema against any creature in heaven or earth, upon a supposition of their teaching any thing contrary unto it, chap. i. 8. He pleads not, "*We* preached first unto you, by *us* you were converted; and therefore with *us* you must abide, from whom the faith came forth unto you:" but saith, "If we, or an angel from heaven, preach any other gospel, let him be accursed." This was the way he chose to insist on; and it may not be judged unreasonable if we esteem it better than that of theirs, who, by false pretending to have been our old, would very fain be our new masters. But the mentioned maxim lets us know that the persons and churches that have received the faith from the Roman church, or by means thereof, should abide under the rule and conduct of it, and, if departed from it, return speedily to due obedience. I think it will be easily granted, that if we ought to abide under its rule and conduct, whithersoever it shall please to guide us, we ought quickly to return to our duty and task, if we should make any elopement from it. It is not meet that those that are born mules to bondage should ever alter their condition. Only, we must profess we know not the springs of that unhappy fate which should render us such animals. Unto what is here pretended I only ask, Whether this right of presidency and rule in the Roman church, over all persons and churches pretended of old to be converted by her means, do belong unto her by virtue of any general right, that those who convert others should for ever have the conduct of those converted by them, or by virtue of some special privilege granted to the church of Rome above others? If the first or general title be insisted on, it is most certain that a very small pittance of jurisdiction will be left unto the Roman see, in comparison of that vast empire which now it hath or layeth claim unto, knowing no bounds but those of the universal nature of things here below. For all men know that the gospel was preached in very many places of the world before its sound reached unto Rome, and in most parts of the then known world before any such planting of a church at Rome as might be the foundation of any authoritative mission of any from thence for the conversion of others; and after that a church was planted in that city, for any thing that may be made to appear by story, it was, as to the first edition of Christianity in the Roman empire, as little serviceable in the propagation of the gospel as any other church of name in the world: so that, if such principles should be pleaded as of general equity, there could be nothing fixed on more destructive to the Romanists' pretences. If they have any special privilege to found this claim upon, they may do well to produce it. In the Scripture, though there be of many believers, yet there is no mention made of any church at Rome, but only of that little assembly that used to meet at Aquila's house, Rom. xvi. 5. Of any such privilege annexed unto that meeting we find nothing. The first general council, confirming power and rule over others in some churches, acknowledges, indeed, more to have been practised in the Roman church than I know how they could prove to be due unto it; but yet that very unwarrantable grant is utterly destructive to the present claim and condition of the pope and church of Rome. The wings now pretended to be like those of the sun, extending themselves at once to the ends of the earth, were then accounted no longer than to be able to cover the poor believers in the city and suburbs of it, and some few adjacent towns and villages. It would be a long story to tell the progress of this claim in after times: it is sufficiently done in some of those books of which our author says there are enough to fill the Tower of London; where, I presume, or into the fire, he could be contented they should be for ever disposed of: and therefore we may dismiss this principle also.

III. That which is the main pillar, bearing the weight of all this fine fabric, is the principle we mentioned in the third place,—namely, "That the Roman profession of religion and practice in the worship of God are every way the same as when we first received the gospel from the pope; nor can they ever otherwise be."

This is taken for granted by our author throughout his discourse. And the truth is, that if a man hath a mind to suppose and make use of things that are in question between him and his adversary, it were a folly not to presume on so much as should assuredly serve his turn. To what purpose is it to mince the matter, and give opportunity to new cavils and exceptions, by baby-mealy-mouthed petitions of some small things that there is a strife about, when a man may as honestly, all at once, suppose the whole truth of his side, and proceed without fear of disturbance? And so wisely deals our author in this business. That which ought to have been his whole work, he takes for granted to be already done! If this be granted him, he is safe; deny it, and all his fine oration dwindles into a little sapless sophistry. But he must get the great number of books that he seems to be troubled with out of the world, and the Scripture to boot, before he will persuade considerate and unprejudiced men that there is a word of truth in this supposition. That we in these nations received not the gospel originally from the pope (which, p. 354, our author tells us "is his, purely his," whereas we thought before it had been Christ's) hath been declared, and shall, if need be, be farther evinced. But let us suppose once again that we did so; yet we constantly deny the church of Rome to be the same, in doctrine, worship, and discipline, that she was when it is pretended that by her means we were instituted in the knowledge of truth. Our author knows full well what a facile work I have now lying in view,—what an easy thing it were to go over most of the opinions of the present church of Rome, and most if not all their practices in worship, and to manifest their vast distance from the doctrine, practice, and principles of that church of old. But though this were really a more serious work, and more useful, and much more accommodated to the nature of the whole difference between us, more easy and pleasant to myself, than the pursuit of this odd rambling chase that, by following of him, I am engaged in; yet, lest he should pretend that this would be a diversion into common-places, such as he hath purposely avoided (and that not unwisely, that he might have advantage all along to take for granted that which he knew to be principally in question between us), I shall dismiss that business, and only attend unto that great proof of this assertion which himself thought meet to shut up his book withal, as that which was fit to pin down the basket, and to keep close and safe all the long-billed birds that he hoped to lime-twig by his preceding rhetoric and sophistry. It is in pp. 362, 363. Though I hope I am not contentious, nor have any other hatred against Popery than what becomes an honest man to have against that which he is persuaded to be so ill as Popery must needs be, if it be ill at all; yet, upon his request, I have seriously pondered his queries (a captious way of disputing), and, falling now in my way, do return this answer unto them:—

The supposition on which all his ensuing queries are founded must be rightly stated, its terms freed from ambiguity, and the whole from equivocation;—which a word or two, unto, first, the subject; and then, secondly, the predicate of the proposition, or what is attributed unto the subject spoken of; and, thirdly, the proof of the whole, will suffice to do. The thesis laid down is this: "The church of Rome was once a most pure, excellent, flourishing, and mother church; this good St Paul amply testifies in his epistle to them, and is acknowledged by Protestants." The subject is, "The church of Rome;" and this may be taken either for the church that was founded in Rome in the apostles' days, consisting of believers, with those that had their rule and oversight in the Lord; or it may be taken for the church of Rome in the sense of latter ages, consisting of the pope its head, and cardinals, principal members, with all the jurisdiction dependent on them, and way of worship established by them and their authority; or that collection of men throughout the world that yield obedience to the pope in their several places and subordinations, according to the rules by him and his authority given unto them. That which is attributed to this church is, " That it was once a most pure, excellent, flourishing, and mother church;" all, it seems, in the superlative degree. I will not contend about the purity, excellence, or flourishing of that church. The boasting of the superlativeness of that purity and excellency seems to be borrowed from that of Rev. iii. 15–17. But we shall not exagitate that in that church which it would never have affirmed of itself, because it is fallen out to be the interest of some men in these latter days to talk at such a rate as primitive humility was an utter stranger unto. I somewhat guess at what he means by a mother church; for though the Scripture knows no such thing, but only appropriates that title to " Jerusalem that was above," which is said to be the " mother of us all," Gal. iv. 26,—which, I suppose, is not Rome (and I also think that no man can have two mothers), nor did purer antiquity ever dream of any such mother,—yet the vogue of latter days hath made this expression not only passable in the world, but sacred and unquestionable. I shall only say, that in the sense wherein it is by some understood, the old Roman church could lay no more claim unto it than most other churches in the world, and not so good as some others could.

The proof of this assertion lies first on the testimony of St Paul, and then on the acknowledgment of Protestants. First, " Good St Paul," he says, " amply testifies this in his Epistle to the Romans." This? What, I pray?—that the then Roman church was a mother church? Not a word in all the epistle of any such matter. Nay, as I observed before, though he greatly commends the faith and holiness of many believers, Jews and Gentiles, that were at Rome, yet he makes mention of no church there, but only of a little assembly that used to meet at Aquila's house; nor doth St Paul give any testimony at all to the Roman church in the latter sense of that expression. Is there any thing in his epistle of the pope, cardinals, patriarchs, etc.? any thing of their power and rule over other churches, or Christians not living at Rome? Is there any one word in that epistle about that which the Papists make the principal ingredient in their definition of the church,—namely, subjection to the pope? What, then, is the " this" that good St Paul so amply testifies unto in his Epistle to the Romans? Why this, and this only, that when he wrote this epistle to Rome, there were then living in that city sundry good and holy men, believing in Christ Jesus according to the gospel, and making profession of the faith that is in him; but that these men should live there to the end of the world, he says not, nor do we find that they do. The acknowledgment of Protestants is next, to as little purpose, insisted on. They acknowledge a pure and flourishing church to have been once at Rome, as they maintain there was at Jerusalem, Antioch, Ephesus, Smyrna, Laodicea, Alexandria, Babylon, etc. That in all these places such churches do still continue, they deny, and particularly at Rome. For that church which then was, they deny it to be the same that now is; at least, any more than Argo was the same ship as when first built, after there was not one plank or pin of its first structure remaining. That the church of Rome, in the latter sense, was ever a pure, flourishing church, never any Protestant acknowledged. The most of them deny it ever to have been, in that sense, any church at all; and those that grant it to retain the essential constituting principles of a church, yet aver that as it is, so it ever was, since it had a being, very far from a pure and flourishing church. For aught, then, that I can perceive, we are not at all concerned in the following queries; the supposition they are all built upon being partly sophistical and partly false. But yet, because he doth so earnestly request us to ponder them, we shall not give him cause to complain of us, in this particular at least (as he doth in general of all Protestants), that we deal uncivilly, and therefore shall pass through them; after which, if he pleaseth, he may deliver them to his friend of whom they were borrowed.

First, saith he, "This church could not cease to be such, but she must fall either by apostasy, heresy, or schism." But who told him so? Might she not cease to *be*, and so consequently to be such? Might not the persons of whom it consisted have been destroyed by an earthquake, as it happened to Laodicea? or by the sword, as it befell the church of the Jews? or twenty other ways? Besides, might she not fall by idolatry, or false worship, or by profaneness, or licentiousness of conversation, contrary to the whole rule of Christ? That, then, he may know what is to be removed by his queries, if he should speak any thing to the purpose, he may do well to take notice that this is the dogma of Protestants concerning the church of Rome: That the church planted there pure, did by degrees, in a long tract of time, fall, by apostasy, idolatry, heresy, schism, and profaneness of life, into that condition wherein now it is. But, says he,—

1. "Not by *apostasy;* for that is not only a renouncing of the faith of Christ, but the very name and title of Christianity; and no man will say that the church of Rome had ever such a fall, or fell thus." I tell you truly, sir, your church is very much beholden unto men, if they do not sometimes say very hard things of her fall. Had it been an ordinary slip or so, it might have been passed over; but this falling into the mire, and wallowing in it for so many ages, as

she has done, is in truth a very naughty business. For my part, I am resolved to deal as gently with her as possible; and therefore say, that there is a total apostasy from Christianity, which she fell not into or by; and there is a partial apostasy in Christianity from some of the principles of it, such as St Paul charged on the Galatians, and the old fathers on very many that yet retained the name and title of Christians; and this we say plainly that she fell by,—she fell by apostasy from many of the most material principles of the gospel, both as to faith, life, and worship. And there being no reply made upon this instance, were it not upon the ground of pure civility, we need not proceed any farther with his queries, the business of them being come to an end.

2. But, upon his entreaty, we will follow him a little farther. Supposing that he hath dispatched the business of apostasy, he comes to *heresy*, and tells us, "That it is an adhesion to some private or singular opinion or error in faith, contrary to the general approved doctrine of the church." That which ought to be subsumed is, that the church of Rome did never adhere to any singular opinion or error in faith, contrary to the general approved doctrine of the church; but our author, to cover his business, changes the terms in his proceeding into the Christian world. To clear this to us a little, I desire to know of him what church he means, when he speaks of the approved doctrine of the church? I am sure he will say, "The Roman Catholic church." And if I ask him, what age it is of that church which he intends? he will also say, "That age which is present when the opinions mentioned are asserted contrary to the approved doctrine." We have, then, obtained his meaning,—namely, *The Roman church did never at any time adhere to any opinion, but what the Roman church at that time adhered unto;* or taught or approved no other doctrine but what it taught and approved! Now, I verily believe this to be true, and he must be somewhat besides uncivil that shall deny it. But from hence to infer that the Roman church never fell from her first purity by heresy,—that is a thing I cannot yet discern how it may be made good. This conclusion ariseth out of that pitiful definition of heresy he gives us, coined merely to serve the Roman interest. The rule of judging heresy is made the "approved doctrine of the church." I would know of what church: of this or that particular church, or of the Catholic? Doubtless the Catholic must be pretended. I ask, Of this or that age, or of the first? "Of the first, certainly." I desire then to know how we may come to discern infallibly what was the approved doctrine of the Catholic church of old but only by the Scriptures, which we know it unanimously embraced, as given unto it by Christ for its rule of faith and worship. If we should then grant that the approved doctrine of the church were that, which a departure from, as such, gives formality

unto heresy, yet there is no way to know that doctrine but by the Scripture. But yet neither can or ought this to be granted. The formal reason of heresy, in the usual acceptation of the word, ariseth from its deviation from the Scripture as such; which is the rule of the church's doctrine, and of the opinions that are contrary unto it. Nor yet is every private or singular opinion, contrary to the Scripture or the doctrine of the church, presently a heresy. That is not the sense of the word, either in Scripture or antiquity; so that the foundation of the queries about heresy is not one jot better laid than that was about apostasy, which went before. This is that which I have heard Protestants say,—namely, "That the church of Rome doth adhere to very many opinions and errors in faith, contrary to the main principles of Christian religion delivered in the Scripture, and so, consequently, the doctrine approved by the catholic church;" and if this be to fall by heresy, I add, that she is thus fallen also from what she was. But then he asks,—(1.) "By what general council was she ever condemned?" (2.) "Which of the fathers ever wrote against her? By what authority was she otherwise reproved?" But this is all one as if a thief, arraigned for stealing before a judge, and the goods that he had stolen found upon him, should plead for himself, and say, "If ever I stole any thing, then by what lawful judge was I ever condemned? What officer of the peace did ever formally apprehend me? By what authority were writs issued out against me?" Were it not easy for the judge to reply, and tell him, "Friend, these allegations may prove that you were never before condemned, but they prove not at all that you never stole; which is a matter of fact that you are now upon your trial for." No more will it at all follow that the church of Rome did never offend, because she is not condemned. These things may be necessary that she may be said to be legally convicted, but not at all to prove that she is really guilty. Besides, the truth is, that many of her doctrines and practices are condemned by general councils, and most of them by the most learned fathers, and all of them by the authority of the Scripture. And whilst her doctrine and worship are so condemned, I see not well how she can escape; so that this second way also she is fallen.

3. To *apostasy* and *heresy* she hath also added the guilt of *schism* in a high degree. For schisms within herself, and her great schism from all the Christian world besides herself, are things well known to all that know her. Her intestine schisms were the shame of Christendom, her schisms in respect of others the ruin of it. And briefly to answer the triple query we are so earnestly invited to the consideration of, I shall need to instance only in that one particular of making subjection to the pope in all things the "tessera" and rule of all church communion, whereby she hath left the company of

all the churches of Christ in the world besides herself, is gone forth and departed from all apostolical churches, even that of old Rome itself; and the true church, which she hath forsaken, abides and is preserved in all the societies of Christians throughout the earth, who, attending to the Scripture for their only rule and guide, do believe what is therein revealed, and worship God accordingly. So that, notwithstanding any thing here offered to the contrary, it is very possible that the present church of Rome may be fallen from her primitive condition by apostasy, heresy, and schism,—which indeed she is; and worst of all, by *idolatry*, which our author thought meet to pass over in silence.

IV. It is frequently pleaded by our author (nor is there any thing which he more triumphs in), "That all things, as to religion, were quiet and in peace, all men in union and agreement amongst themselves in the worship of God, before the departure made by our forefathers from the Roman see." No man that hath once cast an eye upon the defensatives written by the ancient Christians, but knows how this very consideration was managed and improved against them by their Pagan impugners. That Christians, by their introduction of a new way of worshipping God, which their forefathers knew not, had disturbed the peace of human society, divided the world into seditious factions, broken all the ancient bonds of peace and amity, dissolved the whole harmony of mankind's agreement amongst themselves, was the subject of the declamations of their adversaries. This complaint, their books, their schools, the courts and judicatories were filled with; against all which clamours and violences that were stirred up against them by their means, those blessed souls armed themselves with patience, and the testimony of their consciences that they neither did nor practised any thing that in its own nature had a tendency to the least of those evils which they and their way of worshipping God were reproached with. As they had the opportunity, indeed, they let their adversaries know that that peace and union they boasted of in their religion, before the entrance of Christianity, was but a conspiracy against God, a consent in error and falsehood, and brought upon the world by the craft of Satan, maintained through the effectual influence of innumerable prejudices upon the innate blindness and darkness of their hearts. That upon the appearance of light, and publishing of the truth, divisions, animosities, troubles, and distractions did arise, they declared to have been no proper or necessary effect of the work, but a consequent, occasional and accidental, arising from the lusts of men, "who loved darkness more than light, because their works were evil;" which, that it would ensue, their blessed Master had long before foretold them, and forewarned them.

Though this be enough, yet it is not all that may be replied unto this old pretence and plea, as managed to the purpose of our adversaries. It is part of the motive which the great historian makes Galgacus, the valiant Briton, use to his countrymen to cast off the Roman yoke: "Ubi solitudinem faciunt, pacem adpellant." It was their way, when they had by force and cruelty laid all waste before them, to call the remaining solitude and desolation by the goodly name of peace; neither considered they whether the residue of men had either satisfaction in their minds or advantage by their rule. Nor was the peace of the Roman church any other before the Reformation. What waste they had, by sword and burnings, made in several parts of Europe, in almost all the chiefest nations of it, of mankind; what desolation they had brought by violence upon those who opposed their rule or questioned their doctrine, the blood of innumerable poor men, many of them learned, all pious and zealous,—whom they called Waldenses, Albigenses, Lollards, Wickliffites, Hussites, Calixtines, Subutraquians, Picards, or what else they pleased (being indeed the faithful witnesses of the Lord Christ and his truths),—will at the last day reveal. Besides, the event declared how remote the minds of millions were from an acquiescency in that conspiracy in the papal sovereignty, which was grown to be the bond of communion amongst those who called themselves the church, or an approbation of that doctrine and worship which they made profession of: for no sooner was a door of liberty and light opened unto them, but whole nations were at strife who should first enter in at it; which, undoubtedly, all the nations of Europe had long since done, had not the holy, wise God, in his good providence, suffered in some of them a sword of power and violence to interpose itself against their entrance. For, whatever may be pretended of peace and agreement to this day, take away force and violence, prisons and fagots, and in one day the whole compages of that stupendous fabric of the Papacy will be dissolved; and the life which will be maintained in it, springing only from secular advantages and inveterate prejudices, would, together with them, decay and disappear. Neither can any thing but a confidence of the ignorance of men in all things that are past, yea, in what was done almost by their own grandsires, give countenance to a man, in his own silent thoughts, for such insinuations of quietness in the world before the Reformation. The wars, seditions, rebellions, and tumults (to omit private practices), that were either raised, occasioned, or countenanced by the pope's absolving subjects from their allegiance, kings and states from their oaths, given mutually for the securing of peace between them, all in the pursuit of their own worldly interests, do fill up a good part of the stories of some ages before the Reformation. Whatever, then, is pretended, things were not so peaceable and quiet in those days as they are now represented to men that mind only things that are present; nor was their agreement their virtue, but their sin and misery, being centred in blindness and ignorance, and cemented with blood.

V. "That the first reformers were most of them sorry, contemptible persons, whose errors were propagated by indirect means, and entertained for sinister ends," is in several places of this book alleged, and consequences, pretended thence to ensue, urged and improved. But the truth is, the more contemptible the persons were that began the work, the greater glory and lustre is reflected on the work itself; which points out to a higher cause than any [which] appeared outwardly for the carrying of it on. It is no small part of the gospel's glory, that, being promulgated by persons whom the world looked on with the greatest contempt and scorn imaginable, as men utterly destitute of whatever was by them esteemed noble or honourable, it prevailed notwithstanding in the minds of men, to eradicate the inveterate prejudices received by tradition from their fathers, to overthrow the ancient and outward glorious worship of the nations, and to bring them into subjection unto Christ. Neither can any thing be written with more contempt and scorn, nor with greater undervaluation of the abilities or outward condition of the first reformers, than was spoken and written by the greatest, and wisest, and learnedst of men of old, concerning the preachers and planters of Christianity. Should I but repeat the biting sarcasms, contemptuous reproaches, and scorns wherewith, with plausible pretences, the apostles, and those that followed them in their work of preaching the gospel, were entertained by Celsus, Lucian, Porphyry, Julian, Hierocles, with many more, men learned and wise, I could easily manifest how short our new masters come of them in facetious wit, beguiling eloquence, and fair pretences, when they seek, by stories, jestings, calumnies, and false reports, to expose the first reformers to the contempt and scorn of men who know nothing of them but their names, and these as covered with all the dirt they can possibly cast upon them. But I intend not to tempt the atheistical wits of any to an approbation of their sin, by that compliance which the vain fancies of such men do usually afford them, in the contemplation of the wit and ingenuity, as they esteem it, of plausible calumnies. The Scripture may be heard: that abundantly testifies that the character given of the first reformers, as men poor, unlearned, seeking to advantage themselves, by the troubling of others better, greater, and wiser than they, in their religion, was received of the apostles, evangelists, and other Christians, in the first budding of Christianity. But the truth is, all these are but vain pretences; those knew of old, and these do now, that the persons whom they vilify and scorn were eminently fitted of God for the work that they were called unto.

The "receiving of their opinions for sinister ends," reflects principally on this kingdom of England; and must do so, whilst the surmises of a few interested friars shall be believed by Englishmen, before the solemn protestation of so renowned a king as he was who first cashiered the pope's authority in this nation: for what he, being alive, avowed on his royal word, and vowed, as in the sight of the Almighty God, was an effect of light and conscience in him, they will needs have to be a consequent of his lust and levity. And what honour it is to the royal government of this nation, to have those who swayed the sceptre of it but a few years ago publicly traduced and exposed to obloquy by the libellous pens of obscure and unknown persons, wise men may be easily able to judge. This I am sure, there is little probability that they should have any real regard or reverence for the present rulers, farther than they find or hope that they shall have their countenance and assistance for the furtherance of their private interest, who so revile their predecessors for acting contrary unto it,—and this loyalty the king's majesty may secure himself of from the most seditious fanatic in the nation,—so highly is he beholden to these men for their duty and obedience.

VI. "That our departure from Rome hath been the cause of all our evils, and particularly of all those divisions which are at this day found amongst Protestants, and which have been since the Reformation," is a supposition that not only insinuates itself into the hidden sophistry of our author's discourse, but is also everywhere spread over the face of it, with as little truth or advantage to his purpose as those that went before. So the Pagans judged the primitive Christians; so also did the Jews, and do to this day. Here is no new task lies before us. The answers given of old to them, and yet continued to be given, will suffice to these men also. The truth is, our divisions are not the effect of our *leaving* Rome, but of our *being* there. In the apostasy of that church came upon men all that darkness, and all those prejudices, which cause many needless divisions amongst them. And is it any wonder that men, partly led, partly driven, out of the right way, and turned a clean contrary course for sundry generations, should, upon liberty obtained to return to their old paths, somewhat vary in their choice of particular tracks, though they all agree to travel towards the same place, and, in general, steer their course accordingly? Besides, let men say what they please, the differences amongst the Protestants that are purely religious are no other but such as ever were, and, take away external force, ever will be, amongst the best of men, whilst they know but in part; however, they may not be managed with that prudence and moderation which it is our duty to use in and about them. Were not the consequences of our differences, which arise merely from our folly and sin, of more important consideration than our differences themselves, I should very little value the one or the other; knowing that none of them, in their own nature, are such as to impeach either our present tranquillity or future happiness. So that neither are the divisions that are among Protestants in themselves of any importance, nor were they occasioned by their departure from Rome. That all men are not made perfectly wise, nor do know all things perfectly, is partly a consequence of their condition in this world, partly a fruit of their own lusts and corruptions; neither to be imputed to the religion which they profess, nor to the rule that they pretend to follow. Had all those who could not continue in the profession of the errors and practice of the worship of the church of Rome, and were therefore driven out by violence and blood from amongst them, been as happy in attending to the rule that they chose for their guidance and direction as they were wise in choosing it, they had had no other differences among them than what necessarily follow their concreated different constitutions, complexions, and capacities. It is not the work of religion in this world *wholly* to dispel men's darkness, nor absolutely to eradicate their distempers: somewhat must be left for heaven; and that more is than ought to be is the fault of men, and not of the truth they profess. That religion which reveals a sufficient rule to guide men into peace, union, and all necessary truth, is not to be blamed if men in all things follow not its direction. Nor are the differences amongst the Protestants greater than those amongst the members of the Roman church. The imputation of the errors and miscarriages of the Socinians and Quakers unto Protestancy, is of no other nature than that of Pagans of old charging the follies and abominations of the Gnostics and Valentinians on Christianity; for those that are truly called Protestants, whose concurrence in the same confession of faith, as to all material points, is sufficient to cast them under one denomination, what evils, I wonder, are to be found amongst them, as to divisions, that are not conspicuous to all in the Papacy? The princes and nations of their profession are, or have all been, engaged in mortal feuds and wars, one against another, all the world over. Their divines write as stiffly one against another as men can do: mutual accusations of pernicious doctrines and practices abound amongst them. I am not able to guess what place will hold the books written about their intestine differences, as our author doth concerning those that are written by Protestants against the Papacy; but this I know, all public libraries and private studies of learned men abound with them: their invectives, apologies, accusations, charges, underminings of one another, are part of the weekly news of these days. Our author knows well enough what I mean. Nor are these the ways and practices of private men, but of whole societies and fraternities; which, if they are in truth such as they are by each other represented to be, it would be the interest of mankind to seek the suppression and extermination of some of them. I profess I wonder, whilst their own house is so visibly on fire, that they can find leisure to scold at others for not quenching theirs. Nor is the remaining agreement that they boast of one jot better than either their own dissensions or ours. It is not union or agreement amongst men absolutely that is to be valued. Simeon and Levi never did worse than when they agreed best, and "were brethren in evil." The grounds and reasons of men's agreement, with the nature of the things wherein they are agreed, are that which makes it either commendable or desirable. Should I lay forth what these are in the Papacy, our author, I fear, would count me unmannerly and uncivil; but yet, because the matter doth so require, I must needs tell him that many wise men do affirm that ignorance, inveterate prejudice, secular advantages, and external force, are the chief constitutive principles of that union and agreement which remains amongst them. But, whatever their evils be, it is pretended that they have a remedy at hand for them all. But,—

VII. "That we have no remedy of our evils, no means of ending our differences, but by a returnal to the Roman see." Whether there be any way to end differences among ourselves, as far and as soon as there is any need they should be ended, will be afterward inquired into. This I know, that a returnal unto Rome will not do it, unless, when we come thither, we can learn to behave ourselves better than those do who are there already; and there is indeed no party of men in the world but can give as good security of ending our differences as the Romanists. If we would all turn Quakers it would end our disputes; and that is all that is provided us if we will turn Papists. This is the language of every party,—and, for my part, I think they believe what they say,—"Come over to us, and we shall all agree." Only the Romanists are likely to obtain least credit as to this matter among wise men, because they cannot agree among themselves, and are as unfit to umpire the differences of other men as Philip of Macedon was to quiet Greece, whilst he, his wife, and children, were together by the ears at home.

"But why have not Protestants a remedy for their evils, a means of ending and making up their differences?" They have the word that is left them for that purpose, which the apostles commended unto them, and which the primitive church made use of, and no other. That this will not serve to prevent or remove any hurtful differences from amongst us, it is not its fault, but ours. And could we prevail with Roman Catholics to blame and reprove us, and not to blame the religion we profess, we should count ourselves beholden to them; and they would have the less to answer for another day. But as things are stated, it is fallen out very unhappily for them; that finding they cannot hurt us but that their weapons must pass through the Scripture, *that* is it which they are forced to direct their blows against "The Scripture is dark, obscure, insufficient, cannot be known to be the word of God, nor understood," is the main of their plea, when they intend to deal with Protestants. I am persuaded that they are troubled when they are put upon this work. It cannot be acceptable to the minds of men to be engaged in such undervaluations of the word of God. Sure they can have no other mind in this work than a man would have in pulling down his house to find out his enemy. He that shall read what the Scripture testifies of itself,—that is, what God doth of it,—and what the ancients speak concerning it, and shall himself have any acquaintance with the nature and excellency of it, must needs shrink extremely when he comes to see the Romanist's discourse about it,—indeed against it. For my part, I can truly profess, that no one thing doth so alienate my mind from the present Roman religion as this treatment of the word of God. I cannot but think that a sad profession of religion which enforceth men to decry the use and excellency of that which (let them pretend what they please) is the only infallible revelation of all that truth by obedience whereunto we become Christians. I do heartily pity learned and ingenious men, when I see them enforced, by a private corrupt interest, to engage in this woful work of undervaluing the word of God; and so much the more, as that I cannot but hope that it is a very ungrateful work to themselves. Did they delight in it, I should have other thoughts of them, and conclude that there are more atheists in the world than those whom our author informs us to be lately turned so in England. This, then, is the remedy that Protestants have for their evils,—this the means of making up all their differences; which they might do every day, so far as in this world it is possible that that work should be done amongst men, if it were not their own fault. That they do not so, blame them still, blame them soundly, lay on reproofs till I cry, Hold; but let not, I pray, the word of God be blamed any more. Methinks I could beg this of a Catholic, especially of my countrymen, that whatever they say to Protestants, or however they deal with them, they would let the Scripture alone, and not decry its worth and usefulness. It is not Protestants' book, it is God's, who hath only granted them a use of it, in common with the rest of men; and what is spoken in disparagement of it doth not reflect on them, but on him that made it and sent it to them. It is no policy, I confess, to discover our secrets to our adversaries, whereby they may prevent their own disadvantages for the future; but yet, because I look not on the Romanists as absolute enemies, I shall let them know for once, that when Protestants come to that head of their disputes or orations wherein they contend that the Scripture is so and so, obscure and insufficient, they generally take great contentment to find that their religion cannot be opposed without casting down the word of God from its excellency, and enthroning somewhat else in the room of it. Let them make what use of this they please, I could not but tell it them for their good; and I know it to be true. For the present it comes too late; for another main principle of our author's discourse is,—

VIII. "That the Scripture, on sundry accounts, is insufficient to settle us in the truth of religion, or to bring us to an agreement amongst ourselves; and that,—1. Because it is not to be known to be the word of God but by the testimony of the Roman church; and then,—2. Cannot be well translated into any vulgar language; and is also,—3. In itself obscure; and,—4. We have no way to determine of what is its proper sense." But, "Hic nigræ succus loliginis: hæc est Ærugo mera," [Hor. Sat. i. 4, 100.] I suppose they will not tell a Pagan or a Mohammedan this story; at least I heartily wish that men would not suffer themselves to be so far transported by their private interest as to forget the general concernments of Christianity. "We cannot," say they, "know the Scripture to be the word of God but by the authority of the church of Rome;" and all men may easily assure themselves that no man had ever known there was such a thing as a church, much less that it had any authority, but by the Scripture. And whither this tends, is easy to guess. But it will not enter into my head that we cannot know or believe the Scripture to be the word of God any otherwise than on the authority of the church of Rome. The greatest part of it was believed to be so before there was any church at Rome at all; and all of it is so by millions in the world who make no account of that church at all. Now some say there is such a church. I wish men would leave persuading us that we do not believe what we know we do believe, or that we cannot do that which we know we do, and see that millions besides ourselves do so too. There are not many nations in Europe wherein there are not thousands who are ready to lay down their lives to give testimony that the Scripture is the word of God, that care not a rush for the authority of the present church of Rome; and what farther evidence they can give that they believe so, I know not. And this they do upon that innate evidence that the word of God hath in itself and gives to itself, the testimony of Christ and his apostles, and the teaching of the church of God in all ages. I must needs say, there is not any thing for which Protestants are so much beholden to the Roman Catholics as this,—that they have with so much importunacy cast upon them the work of proving the Scripture to be of divine original, or to have been given by inspiration from God. It is as good a work as a man can well be employed in; and there is not any thing I should more gladly "ex professo" engage in, if the nature of my present business would bear such a diversion. Our author would quickly see what an easy task it were to remove those his reproaches of a private spirit, of an inward testimony of our own reason, which himself, knowing the advantage they afford him amongst vulgar unstudied men, trifles withal. Both Romanists and Protestants, as far as I can learn, do acknowledge that the grace of the Spirit is necessary to enable a man to believe savingly the Scripture to be the word of God, upon what testimony or authority soever that faith is founded or resolved into. Now, this with Protestants is no private whisper, no *enthusiasm,* no reason of their own, no particular testimony, but the most open, noble, known, that is or can be in the world,—even the voice of God himself speaking publicly to all, in and by the Scripture evidencing itself by its own divine innate light and excellency,—taught, confirmed, and testified unto, by the church in all ages, especially the first,—founded by Christ and his apostles. He that looks for better or other testimony, witness, or foundation to build his faith upon, may search till doomsday without success. He that renounceth this shakes the very root of Christianity, and opens a door to atheism and paganism. This was the anchor of Christians of old; from which neither the storms of persecution could drive them, nor the subtilty of disputations entice them. For men to come now, in the end of the world, and to tell us that we must rest in the authority of the present church of Rome in our receiving the Scripture to be the word of God, and then to tell us that that church hath all its authority by and from the Scripture,—and to know well enough all the while that no man can know there is any church authority but by the Scripture,—is to speak daggers and swords to us, upon a confidence that we will suffer ourselves to be befooled, that we may have the after pleasure of making others like ourselves.

2. Of the *translation of the Scripture into vulgar tongues* I shall expressly treat afterward; and therefore here pass it over.

3. Its *obscurity* is another thing insisted on, and highly exaggerated by our author. And this is another thing that I greatly wonder at. For as wise as these gentlemen would be thought to be, he that has but half an eye may discern that they consider not with whom they have to do in this matter. The Scripture, I suppose, they will grant to be given by inspiration from God; if they deny it, we are ready to prove it at any time. I suppose, also, that they will grant that the end why God gave it was that it might be a revelation of himself, so far as it was needful for us to know him, and his mind and will, so that we may serve him. If this were not the end for which

God gave his word unto us, I wish they would acquaint us with some other: I think it was not that it might be put into a cabinet, and locked up in a chest. If this were the end of it, then God *intended* in it to make a revelation of himself, so far as it was necessary we should know of him, and his mind and will, that we might serve him; for that which is any one end of any thing or matter, *that* he intends who is the author of it. Now, if God *intended* to make such a revelation of himself, his mind and will, in giving of the Scripture, as was said, he hath either done it plainly,—that is, without any such obscurity as should frustrate him of his end,—or he hath not; and that because either he would not, or he could not. I wish I knew which of these it was that the Roman Catholics do fix upon,—it would spare me the labour of speaking to the other; but seeing I do not, that they may have no evasion, I will consider them both. If they say it was because he could not make any such plain discovery and revelation of himself, then this is that they say: "That God, intending to reveal himself, his mind and will, plainly in the Scripture, to the sons of men, was not able to do it; and therefore failed in his design." This works but little to the glory of his omnipotency and omnisciency. But to let that pass, wherein men (so they may compass their own ends) seem not to be much concerned, I desire to know whether this plain, sufficient revelation of God be made any other way or no? If no otherwise, then, as I confess, we are all in the dark, so it is to no purpose to blame the Scripture of obscurity, seeing it is as lightsome as any thing else is or can be. If this revelation be made some other way, it must be by God himself, or somebody else. That any other should be supposed, in good earnest, to do that which God cannot (though I know how some Canonists have jested about the pope), I think will not be pleaded. If God, then, hath done this another way, I desire to know the true reason why he could not do it this way,—namely, by the Scripture,—and therefore desisted from his purpose? But it may be thought God could make a revelation of himself, his mind and will, in and by the Scripture, yet he would not do it plainly, but obscurely: let us then see what we mean by "plainly" in this business. We intend not that every text in Scripture is easy to be understood, nor that all the matter of it is easy to be apprehended; we know that there are things in it "hard to be understood," things to exercise the minds of the best and wisest of men unto diligence, and, when they have done their utmost, unto reverence. But this is that we mean by "plainly:"—The whole will and mind of God, with whatever is needful to be known of him, is revealed in the Scripture without such ambiguity or obscurity as should hinder the Scripture from being a revelation of him, his mind and will, to the end that we may know him, and live unto him. To say that God would not do this, would not make such a revelation (besides the reflection that it casts on his goodness and wisdom), is indeed to say that he would not do that which we say he would do. The truth is, all the harangues we meet withal about the obscurity of the Scripture, are direct arraignments of the wisdom and goodness of God. And if I were worthy to advise my Roman Catholic countrymen, I would persuade them to desist from this enterprise, if not in piety, at least in policy; for I can assure them, as I think I have done already, that all their endeavours for the extenuation of the worth, excellency, fulness, sufficiency of the Scripture, do exceedingly confirm Protestants in the truth of their present persuasion, which they see cannot be touched but by such horrible applications as they detest.

4. But yet they say, "Scripture is not so clear but that it needs interpretation, and Protestants have none to interpret it, so as to make it a means of ending differences." I confess, the interpretation of Scripture is a good and necessary work; and I know that He who "was dead, and is alive for ever," continues to give gifts unto men, according to his promise, to enable them to interpret the Scripture for the edification of his body, the church. If there were none of these interpreters among the Protestants, I wonder whence it is come to pass that his comments on and interpretations of Scripture, who is most hated by Romanists of all the Protestants that ever were in the world, are so borrowed and used (that I say not stolen) by so many of them; and that, indeed, what is praiseworthy in any of their church, in the way of exposition of Scripture, is either borrowed from Protestants or done in imitation of them. If I am called on for instances in this kind, I shall give them,—I am persuaded, to some men's amazement who are less conversant in these things; but we are beside the matter. "It is of an infallible interpreter, in whose expositions and determinations of Scripture sense all Christians are obliged to acquiesce; and such a one you have none." I confess we have not, if it be such a one as you intend, whose expositions and interpretations we must acquiesce in, not because they are true, but because they are his. We have infallible expositions of the Scripture in all necessary truths, as we are assured from the Scripture itself; but an infallible expositor, into whose authority our faith should be resolved, besides the Scripture itself, we have none. Nor do I think they have any at Rome, whatever they talk of to men that were never there: nor, I suppose, do they believe it themselves; for indeed if they do, I know not how they can be freed from being thought to be strangely distempered, if not stark mad. For, not to talk of the Tower of London, this I am sure of, that we have whole cart-loads of comments and expositions on the Scripture, written by

members of the church, men of all orders and degrees; and he that has cast an eye upon them knows that a great part of their large volumes are spent in confuting the expositions of one another, and those that went before them. Now, what a madness is this, or childishness, above that of very children, to lie swaggering and contending one with another, before all the world, with fallible mediums about the sense of Scripture, and giving expositions which no man is bound to acquiesce in any farther than he sees reason, whilst all this while they have one amongst them who can interpret all; and that with such an authority as all men are bound to rest in, and contend no farther! And the farther mischief of it is, that of all the rest this man is always silent as to exposition of Scripture, who alone is able to "part the fray." There be two things which I think, verily, if I were a Papist, I should never like in the pope, because methinks they argue a great deal of want of good nature. The one is (that we treat about), that he can see his children so fiercely wrangle about the sense of Scripture, and yet will not give out what is the infallible meaning of every place, at least that is controverted, and so stint the strife amongst them, seeing it seems he can if he would; and the other is, that he suffers so many souls to lie in purgatory when he may let them forth if he please, and, that I know of, hath received no order to the contrary. But the truth is, that neither the Romanists nor we have any infallible living judge, in whose determination of the sense of Scripture all men should be bound to acquiesce, upon the account of his authority. This is all the difference: we openly profess we have none such, and betake us to that which we have, which is better for us; they, pretending they have, yet acting constantly as if they had not, and as indeed they have not, maintain a perpetual inconsistency and contradiction between their pretensions and their practice. The Holy Ghost, speaking in and by the Scripture, using the ministry of men furnished by himself with gifts and abilities, and lawfully called to the work, for the oral declaration or other expositions of his mind, is that which the Protestants cleave unto for the interpreting of the Scripture, which itself discovers when infallible; and if Papists can tell me of a better way, I will quickly embrace it. I suppose I may, upon the considerations we have had of the reasons offered to prove the insufficiency of Scripture to settle us in the truth, and to end our differences, conclude their insufficiency to any such purpose. We know the Scripture was given us to settle us in the truth, and to end our differences; we know it is "profitable" to that end and purpose, and "able to make us wise to salvation." If we find not these effects wrought in ourselves, it is our own fault; and I desire that for hereafter we may bear our own blame, without such reflections on the holy word of the infinitely blessed God.

IX. We are come at length unto the pope, of whom we are told that "he is a good man, one that seeks nothing but our good, that never did us harm, but has the care and inspection of us committed unto him by Christ." For my part I am glad to hear such news of him, and should be more glad to find it to be true. Our forefathers and predecessors in the faith we profess, found it otherwise. All the harm that could be done unto them, by ruining their families, destroying their estates, imprisoning and torturing their persons, and, lastly, burning their bodies in fire, they received at his hands. If the alteration pretended be not from the shortening of his power, but the change of his mind and will, I shall be very glad to hear of it. For the present, I confess, I had rather take it for granted, whilst he is at this distance, than see him trusted with power for the trial of his will. I never heard of much of his repentance for the blood of those thousands that hath been shed by his authority, and in his cause; which makes me suspect he may be somewhat of the same mind still as he was. Time was when the very worst of popes exhausted more treasure out of this nation, to spend it abroad to their own ends, than some are willing to grant to the best of kings, to spend at home for their goods. It may be he is changed as to this design also, but I do not know it, nor is any proof offered of it by our author. Let us deal plainly one with another, and, without telling us that "the pope never did us harm," (which is not the way to make us believe that he will not, because it makes us suspect that all we have suffered from him is thought no harm,) let him tell us how he will assure us that if this good pope get us into his power again, he will not burn us, as he did our forefathers, unless we submit our consciences unto him in all things; that he will not find out ways to draw the treasure out of the nation, nor absolve subjects from their allegiance, nor excommunicate or attempt the deposition of our kings, or the giving away of their kingdoms, as he has done in former days. That these things he hath done we know; that he hath repented of them, and changed his mind thereupon, we know not. To have any thing to do with him, whilst he continues in such distempers, is not only against the principles of religion, but of common prudence also. For my part I cannot but fear, until I see security tendered of this change in the pope, that all the good words that are given us concerning him are but baits to inveigle us into his power; and, to tell you the truth, "terrent vestigia." How the pope employs himself in seeking our good, which our author paints out unto us, I know not; when I see the effects of it, I shall be thankful for it. In the meantime, being so great a stranger to Rome as I am, I must needs say, I know nothing that he does but seek to destroy us body and soul. Our author pleads, indeed, that "the care and inspection of our condition is committed to him by Christ:" but he attempts not to prove it, which I somewhat marvel at; for having professedly deserted the old way of pleading the Catholic cause and interest (which I presume he did upon conviction of its insufficiency),—whereas he is an ingenious person, he could not but know that "Pasce oves meas, tu es Petrus, tibi dabo claves," are as weak parts of the old plea as any made use of, belonging nothing at all to the thing whereunto they are applied,—it is somewhat strange that he would substitute no new proofs in their room. But it seems it is not every one's hap, with him of old, to want opinions sometimes, but no arguments. When he has got proofs to his purpose, we will again attend unto him: in the meantime, in this case shall only mind him, that the taking for granted, in disputations, that which should principally be proved, has got an ill name amongst learned men, being commonly called "begging."

X. The last principle which I have observed diffusing its influences throughout the whole discourse is, that "the devotion of Catholics far transcends that of Protestants; their preaching also" (which I forgot to mention before) "is far to be preferred above that of these; and for their religion and worship, it is liable to no just exception." I desire that our author would but a little call to mind that parable of our Saviour about the two men that went up into the temple to pray. To me this discourse smells rank of the Pharisee, and I wish that we might all rather strive to grow in faith, love, charity, self-denial, and universal conformity unto our Lord Jesus, than to bristle up and cry, "Stand farther off, for I am holier than thou." In the meantime, for the respect I bear him, I entreat our author to speak no more of this matter, lest some angry Protestant, or some fanatic, should take occasion to talk of old matters, and rip up old sores, or give an account of the present state of things in the church of Rome; all which were a great deal better covered. If he will not take my advice, he must thank himself for that which will assuredly follow. I must also say, by the way, that that devotion which consists so much, as our author makes it to do, in the sweeping of churches and tinkling of bells, in counting of beads and knocking of breasts, is of very little value with Protestants, who have obtained an experience of the excellency of spiritual communion with God in Christ Jesus. Now, whether these parts of the profession and practice of his church,—which he is pleased to undertake, not only the vindication, but the adorning of,—be liable to just exception or no, is the last part of our work to consider, and which shall in its proper place be done accordingly.

As I before observed, he that shall but cursorily run through this discourse will quickly find that these false suppositions, ungrounded presumptions, and unwarrantable pretensions, are things which are disposed of to be the foundations, nerves, and sinews of all the rhetoric that it is covered and wrought withal, and that the bare drawing of them out leaves all the remaining flourishes in a more scattered condition than the Sibyl's leaves, which no man can gather up and put together, to make up any significancy at all as to the design in hand. I might, then, well spare all farther labour, and here put a period to my progress; and indeed would do so, were I secure I had none to deal with but ingenuous and judicious readers, that have some tolerable acquaintance at least with the estate of religion of old and at present in Europe, and with the concernment of their own souls in these things. But that no pretence may be left unto any that we avoided any thing material in our author, having passed through his discourse unto the end of it, I shall once more return to the beginning, and pass through its severals, leaving behind, in the way, such animadversions as are any way needful to rescue such as have not a mind to be deceived, from the snares and cobwebs of his oratory.

CHAPTER III.

Motive, matter, and method of our author's book.

WHAT remains of our author's preface is spent in the pursuit of an easy task, in all the branches of it. To condemn the late miscarriages in these nations, to decry divisions in religion, with their pernicious consequences, to commend my Lord Chancellor's speech, are things that have little difficulty in them, to exercise the skill of a man pretending so highly as our author doth. He may secure himself that he will find no opposition about these things from any man in his right wits. No other man, certainly, can be so forsaken of religion and humanity as not to deplore the woful undertakings, and more woful issues, of sundry things whereunto the concernments of religion have been pleaded to give countenance. The rancour also of men, and wrath against one another on the same accounts, with the fruits which they bring forth all the world over, are doubtless a burden to the minds of all that love truth and peace. To prevent a returnal to the former, and remove or at least allay the latter, how excellently the speech of that great counsellor, and the things proposed in it, are suited, all sober and ingenuous men must needs acknowledge. Had this, then, been the whole design of this preface, I had given this book many an amen before I had come to the end.

But our author having wholly another mark in his eye, another business in hand, I should have thought it a little uncivil in him to make my Lord Chancellor's speech seemingly subservient to that which he never intended, never aimed at, which no word or expression in it leads unto, but that I find him afterward so dealing with the words of God himself. His real work in this compass of words is to set up a blind, or give a false alarm, to arrest and stay his unwary reader, whilst he prepares him for an entertainment which he thought not of. The pretence he flourisheth over, both in the preface and sundry other parts of his discourse, is the hatefulness of our animosities in and about religion, their dismal effects, with the necessity and excellency of moderation in things of that nature; the real work in hand is a persuasive unto Popery, and unto that end (not of moderation or forbearance) are all his arguments directed. Should a man go to him and say, "Sir, I have read your learned book, and find that heats and contests about differences in religion are things full of evil, and such as tend unto farther misery; I am therefore resolved quietly to persist in the way of Protestancy wherein I am, without ever attempting the least violence against others for their dissent from me, but only with meekness and quietness defend the truth which I profess;" —I presume he will not judge his design half accomplished towards such a man, if at all. Nay, I dare say, with some confidence, that in reference to such a one, he would say to himself, "Operam et oleum perdidi." And therefore doth he wisely tell us, p. 12, that his matter is perceived by the prefixed general contents of his chapters. His design, which he calls his method, he confesseth that he doth purposely conceal; but the truth is, it is easily discoverable, there being few pages in the book that do not display it.

The reader, then, must understand that the plain English of all his commendations of moderation, and all his exhortations to a relinquishment of those false lights and principles which have led men to a disturbance of the public peace, and ensuing calamities, is, that Popery is the only religion in the world, and that centring therein is the only means to put an end to our differences, heats, and troubles. Unless this be granted, it will be very hard to find one grain of sincerity in the whole discourse; and if it be, no less difficult to find so much of truth. So that, whatever may be esteemed suitable to the fancies of any of them whom our author courts in his address, those who know any thing of the holiness of God and the gospel, of that reverence which is due to Christ and his word, and wherewith all the concernments of religion ought to be managed, will scarcely judge that that blessed Fountain of light and truth will immix his pure beams and blessings with such crafty, worldly, sophistical devices, or such frothy ebullitions of wit and fancy, as this discourse is stuffed withal. These are things that may be fit to entangle unstable spirits, who, being regardless of eternity, and steering their course according to every blast of temptation that fills their lusts and carnal pleasures, are as ready to change their religion (if men can make any change in or of that which in reality they neither leave nor receive, but only sport themselves to and fro with the cloud and shadow of it) as they are their clothes and fashions. Those who have had experience of the power and efficacy of that religion which they have professed, as to all the ends for which religion is of God revealed, will be little moved with the stories, pretences, and diversions of this discourse.

Knowing, therefore, our author's design (and which we shall have occasion to deal with him about throughout his treatise), which is to take advantage, from the late miscarriages amongst us, and the differences that are in the world in religion, to persuade men, not indeed and ultimately to mutual moderation and forbearance, but to a general acquiescency in Roman Catholicism, I shall not here farther speak unto it. The five heads of his matter may be briefly run over as he proposeth them, p. 13; with whose consideration I shall take my leave of his preface.

1. The first is, "That there is not any colour of reason or just title to move us to quarrel and judge one another with so much heat about religion." Indeed there is not, nor can there be; no man was ever so mad as to suppose there could be any reason or just title for men to do evil: to quarrel and judge one another with heats about religion is of that nature. But if, placing himself to keep a decorum amongst Protestants, he would insinuate that we have no reason to contend about religion, as having lost all title unto it by our departure from Rome, I must take leave unto this general head to put in a general demurrer; which I shall afterward plead to and vindicate.

2. His second is, "That all things are so obscure, that no man in prudence can so far presume of his own knowledge as to set up himself a guide and leader in religion." I say so too; and suppose the words as they lie,. whatever be intended in them, are keenly set against the great papal pretension: whatever he may pretend, we know the pope sets up himself to be a guide to all men in religion; and if he do it not upon a presumption of his own knowledge, we know not on what better grounds he doth it. And though we wholly condemn men's setting up themselves to be guides and leaders to their neighbours, yet if he intend that all things are so obscure, that we have no means to come to the knowledge of the truth concerning God and his mind, so far as it is our duty to know it, and, therefore, that no man can teach or instruct another in that knowledge,—I say, as before, we are not yet of his mind: whether we shall be or no, the process of our discourse will show.

3. He adds, "That no sect hath any advantage at all over another, nor all of them together over Popery." Yes; they that have the truth, wherein they have it, have advantage against all others that have it not: and so Protestancy hath advantage over Popery. And here the pretext or visor of this Protestant begins to turn aside; in the next head it quite falls from him,—

That is, 4. "That all the several kinds of religion here in England are equally innocent to one another; and Popery, as it stands in opposition to them, is absolutely innocent and unblamable to them all." I am little concerned in the former part of these words, concerning the several kinds of religion in England, having undertaken the defence of one only,—namely, Protestancy. Those that are departed from Protestancy so far as to constitute another kind of religion, as to any thing from me, shall plead for themselves. However, I wish that all parties in England were all equally innocent to one another, or that they would not be willing to make themselves equally nocent. But the latter part of the words contains, I promise you, a very high undertaking: "Popery is innocent, absolutely innocent and unblamable to them all." I fear we shall scarce find it so when we come to the trial. I confess I do not like this pretence of absolute innocency and unblamableness. I suppose they are men that profess Popery, and I do know that Popery is a religion or profession of men's finding out. How it should come to be so absolutely innocent on a sudden, I cannot imagine; but we will leave this until we come to the proof of it, taking notice only, that here is a great promise made unto his noble and ingenuous readers, that cannot advantage his cause if he be not able to make it good. The close is,—

5. "That as there neither is nor can be any rational motive for disputes and animosities about matters of religion; so is there an indispensable moral cause obliging us to moderation," etc. But this, as I observed before, though, upon the first view of the sign hanging up at the door, a man would guess to be the whole work that was doing in the house, is indeed no part of his business; and is therefore thrust out at the postern in two short leaves, the least part of them in his own words, after the spending of three hundred and sixty-four pages in the pursuit of his proper design. But seeing we must look over these things again, in the chapters assigned to their adorning, we may take our leave of them at present and of his preface together.

CHAPTER IV.

Contests about religion and reformation, schoolmen, etc.

CHAP. I.[1] The title of this chapter was proposed; the pursuit of it now ensues. The first paragraph is a declamation about sundry things which have not much blameworthy in them. Their common weakness is, that they are common. They tend not to the furtherance of any one thing more than another, but are such as any party may flourish withal, and use to their several ends as they please. That "desire of honour and applause in the world" hath influenced the minds of men to great and strange undertakings, is certain; that it should do so is not certain nor true: so that when we treat of religion, if we renounce not the fundamental principle of it in self-denial, this consideration ought to have no place. What, then, was done by *emperors* and *philosophers* of old, or by the *later schoolmen* on this account, we are little concerned in. Nor have I either desire or design to vellicate any thing spoken by our author that may have an indifferent interpretation put upon it, and be separated from the end which he principally pursues. As there is but very little spoken in this paragraph directly tending to the whole end aimed at, so there are but three things that will any way serve to leaven the mind of his reader, that he may be prepared to be moulded into the form he hath fancied to cast him into; which is the work of all these previous harangues.

The first is his insinuation that the "reformation of religion is a thing pretended by emulous plebeians, not able to hope for that supervisorship in religion which they see intrusted with others." How unserviceable this is unto his design, as applied to the church of England, all men know: for, setting aside the consideration of the influence of sovereign royal authority, the first reformers amongst us were persons who, as they enjoyed the right of reputation for the excellencies of learning and wisdom, so also were they fixed in those places and conditions in the church which no reformation could possibly advance them above; and the attempt whereof cost them not only their dignities, but their lives also. Neither were Hezekiah, Josiah, nor Ezra of old, "emulous plebeians," whose lasting glory and renown arose from their reformation of religion. They who fancy men in all great undertakings to be steered by desire of applause and honour, are exceeding incompetent judges of those actions which zeal for the glory of God, love to the truth, sense of their duty to the Lord Jesus Christ, and compassion for the souls of others, do lead men unto, and

[1] This numeration refers to the chapter in "Fiat Lux," which Dr Owen is refuting.

guide them in; and such will the last day manifest the Reformation traduced to have been.

The second is a gallant commendation of the ingenuity, charity, candour, and sublime science of the schoolmen. I confess they have deserved good words at his hands. These are the men who, out of a mixture of philosophy, traditions, and Scripture, all corrupted and perverted, have hammered that faith which was afterward confirmed under so many anathemas at Trent. So that upon the matter he is beholden to them for his religion; which I find he loves, and hath therefore reason to be thankful to its contrivers. For my part, I am as far from envying them their commendation as I have reason to be; which, I am sure, is far enough. But yet before we admit this testimony, hand over head, I could wish he would take a course to stop the mouths of some of his own church, and those no small ones neither, who have declared them to the world to be a pack of egregious sophisters,—neither good philosophers nor any divines at all; men who seem not to have had the least reverence of God, nor much regard to the truth in any of their disputations, but were wholly influenced by a vain reputation of subtilty, desire of conquest, of leading and denominating parties, and that in a barbarous science, barbarously expressed, until they had driven all learning and divinity almost out of the world. But I will not contend about these fathers of contention: let every man esteem of them as he seems good.

There is the same respect in that bitter reflection which he makes on those who have managed differences in religion in this last age; the third thing observable. That they are the writers and writings that have been published against the Papacy which he intends, he doth more than intimate. Their disputes, he tells us, "are managed with so much unseemly behaviour, such unmannerly expressions, that discreet sobriety cannot but loathe and abhor to read them;" with very much more to this purpose. I shall not much labour to persuade men not to believe what he says in this matter; for I know full well that he believes it not himself. He hath seen too many Protestant books, I suppose, to think this censure will suit them all. This was meet to be spoken for the advantage of the Catholic cause: for what there hath been of real offence in this kind amongst us we may say, "Iliacos intra muros peccatur et extra;"—Romanists are sinners as well as others. And I suppose himself knows that the reviling and defamations used by some of his party are not to be paralleled in any writings of mankind at this day extant.

About the appellations he shall think meet to make use of in reference to the persons at variance, we will not contend with him; only I desire to let him know that the reproach of Galilean from the Pagans, which he appropriates to the Papists, was worn out of the world before that Popery which he pleads for came into it. As Roman Catholics never tasted of the sufferings wherewith that reproach was attended, so they have no special right to the honour that is in its remembrance. As to the sport he is pleased to make with his countrymen, in the close of this paragraph, about losing their wits in religious contests, with the evils thence ensuing, I shall no farther reflect upon [it], but once more to mind the reader, that the many words he is pleased to use in the exaggerating the evils of managing differences in religion with animosities and tumults, so, seemingly, to persuade men to moderation and peace, I shall wholly pass by, as having discovered that that is not his business, nor, consequently, at present mine.

It is well observed by him, in his second paragraph, that most of the great contests in the world about perishing things proceed from the unmortified lusts of men. The Scripture abounds in testimonies given hereunto: St James expressly, "From whence come wars and fightings among you? come they not hence, even of your lusts that war in your members? Ye lust, and have not: ye kill, and desire to have, and cannot obtain: ye fight and war, yet ye have not," chap. iv. 1, 2. Men's lusts put them on endless irregularities, in unbounded desires, and foolish, sinful enterprises, for their satisfaction. Neither is Satan, the old enemy of the welfare of mankind, wanting to excite, provoke, and stir up these lusts, by mixing himself with them in his temptations, thrusting them on, and entangling them in their pursuit. As to the contests about religion,—which, I know not with what mind or intention, he terms an "empty, airy business, a ghostly fight, a skirmish of shadows or horsemen in the clouds,"—he knows not what principle, cause, or source to ascribe them unto. That which he is most inclinable unto is, "That there is something invisible, above man, stronger and more politic than he, that doth this contumely to mankind, that casts in these apples of contention amongst us, that hisses us to war and battle, as waggish boys do dogs in the street." That which is intended in these words, and sundry others of the like quality that follow, is, that this ariseth from the enticements and impulsions of the devil. And none can doubt but that, in these works of darkness, the prince of darkness hath a great hand. The Scripture also assures us, that as the scorpions which vexed the world issued out of the bottomless pit, so also that these unclean spirits do stir up the powers of the earth to make opposition unto the truth of the gospel and religion of Jesus Christ. But yet neither doth this hinder but that even these religious feuds and miscarriages also proceed principally from the ignorance, darkness, and lusts of men. In them lies the true cause of all dissensions in and about the things of God. The best know but in part; and the most love darkness more than light, because their works are evil. A vain conversation received by tradition from men's fathers, with inveterate prejudices, love of the world, and the customs thereof, do all help on this sad work, wherein so many are employed. That some preach the gospel of God ἐν πολλῷ ἀγῶνι,—with all their strength, in much contention,—"and contend earnestly for the faith once delivered unto the saints," as it is their duty, so it is no cause, but only an accidental occasion, of differences amongst men. That the invisible substances our author talks of should be able to sport themselves with us as children do with dogs in the street, and that with the like impulse from them as dogs from these we should rush into our contentions, might pass for a pretty notion, but only that it overthrows all religion in the world, and the whole nature of man. There is evil enough in corrupted nature to produce all these evils, which are declaimed against to the end of this section, were there no demons to excite men unto them. The adventitious impressions from them, by temptations and suggestions, doubtless promote them, and make men precipitate above their natural tempers in their productions; but the principal cause of all our evils is still to be looked for at home,—

"Nec te quæsiveris extra."

Sect. iii. p. 34. In the next section of this chapter, whereunto he prefixes "Nullity of Title," he pursues the persuasive unto peace, moderation, charity, and quietness in our several persuasions, with so many reasonings and good words, that a man would almost think that he began to be in good earnest, and that those were the things which he intended for their own sakes to promote. I presume it cannot but at the first view seem strange to some, to find a man of the Roman party so ingeniously arguing against the imposition of our senses in religion magisterially, and with violence one upon the other: it being notoriously known to all the world that they are, if not the only, yet the greatest imposers on the minds and consciences of men that ever lived on the earth; and which work they cease not the prosecution of, where they have power, until they come to fire and fagot. I dare say there is not any strength in any of his queries, collections, and arguings, but an indifferent man would think it, at the first sight, to be pointed against the Roman interest and practice; for what have they been doing for some ages past, but, under a pretence of charity to the souls of men, endeavouring to persuade them to their opinions and worship, or to impose them on them whether they will or no? But let old things pass; it is well if now, at last, they begin to be otherwise minded. What, then, if we should take this gentleman at his word and cry, "A match! let us strive and contend no more. Keep you your religion at Rome to yourselves, and we will do as well as we can with ours in England: we will trouble you no more about yours; nor, pray, do not you meddle with us or ours. Let us pray for one another, wait on God for light and direction, it being told us, that 'if any one be otherwise minded' (than according to the truth), 'God shall reveal that unto him.' Let us all strive to promote godliness, obedience to the commands of Christ, good works, and peace in the world; but for this contending about opinions, or endeavouring to impose our several persuasions upon one another, let us give it quite over?" I fear he would scarcely close with us, and so wind up all our differences upon the bottom of his own proposals; especially if this law should extend itself to all other nations equally concerned with England. He would quickly tell us that this is our mistake; he intended not Roman Catholics, and the differences we have with them, in this discourse. It is Protestants—Presbyterians, Independents, Anabaptists, Quakers—that he deals withal, and them only; and that upon this ground, that none of them have any title or pretence of reason to impose on one another, and so ought to be quiet, and let one another alone in matters of religion: but for the Roman Catholics, they are not concerned at all in this harangue, having a sufficient title to impose upon them all. Now, truly, if this be all, I know not what we have to thank you for, "Tantumne est otii tibi abs re tua, aliena ut cures, eaque quæ ad te nihil attinent?" There are wise and learned men in England who are concerned in our differences, and do labour to compose them or suppress them. That this gentleman should come and justle them aside, and impose himself an umpire upon us, without our choice or desire, in matters that belong not unto him, how charitable it may seem to be I know not, but it is scarcely civil. Would he would be persuaded to go home and try his remedies upon the distempers of his own family, before he confidently vend them to us. I know he has no salves about him to heal diversities of opinions, that he can write "probatum est" upon, from his Roman church. If he have, he is the most uncharitable man in the world, to leave them at home brawling and together by the ears, to seek out practice where he is neither desired nor welcome, when he comes without invitation. I confess I was afraid, at the beginning of the section, that I should be forced to change the title before I came to the end, and write over it, "Desinit in piscem." The sum of this whole paragraph is, that all sorts of Protestants, and others here in England, do ridiculously contend about their several persuasions in religion, and put trouble on one another on that account, whereas it is the pope only that hath title and right to prescribe a religion unto us all; which is not, to me, unlike the fancy of the poor man in bedlam, who smiled with great contentment at their folly who imagined themselves either

Queen Elizabeth or King James, seeing he himself was King Henry the Eighth. But seeing that is the business in hand, let us see what is this title that the pope hath, which Protestants can lay no claim unto. It is founded on that of the apostle to the Corinthians, "Did the word of God come forth from you, or came it unto you only?" This is pretended the only rule to determine with whom the pre-eminence in religion doth remain. "Now the word came not out originally from Protestants or Puritans, nor came it to them alone; so that they have no reason to be imposing their conceptions on one another, or on others that differ from them." But our author seems here to have fallen upon a great misadventure; there is not, as I know of, any one single text of Scripture that doth more fatally cut the throat of papal pretensions than this that he hath stumbled on. It is known that the pope and his adherents claim a pre-eminence in religion, to be the sole judges of all its concernments, and the imposers of it on all the world. What men receive from them, that is truth; what they are any otherwise instructed in, it is all false and naught. On this pretence it is that this gentleman pleads nullity of title amongst us as to all our contests; though we know that truth carries its title with it, in whose hands soever it be found. Give me leave, then, to make so bold (at least at this distance) as to ask the pope and his adherents, "An a vobis verbum Dei processit, an ad vos solos pervenit?"—"Did the gospel first come from you, or only unto you," that you thus exalt yourselves above your brethren all the world over? Do we not know by whom it first came to you, and from whom? Did it not come to very many parts of the world before you? to the whole world as well as to you? Why do you then boast yourselves as though you had been the first revealers of the gospel, or that it had come unto you in a way or manner peculiar and distinct from that by which it came to other places? Would you make us believe that Christ preached at Rome, or suffered or rose from the dead there, or gave the Holy Ghost first to the apostles there, or first there founded his church, or gave order for the empaling it there when it was built? Would we never so fain, we cannot believe such prodigious fables. To what purpose, then, do you talk of title to impose your conceits in religion upon us? Did the gospel first come forth from you, or came it unto you only? Will not Rome, notwithstanding its seven hills, be laid in a level with the rest of the world, by virtue of this rule? The truth is, as to the oral dispensation of the gospel, it came forth from Jerusalem, by the personal ministry of the apostles; and came equally to all the world. That spring being long since dried up, it now comes forth to all from the written word; and unto them who receive it in its power and truth doth it come, and unto no other. What may farther be thought necessary to be discussed, as to the matter of fact, in reference to this rule, the reader may find handled under that consideration of the first supposition which our author builds his discourse upon.

Sect. iv. p. 48. "Heats and Resolution" is the title of this section; in which, if our author be found blameless, his charge on others will be the more significant: the impartial reader, that will not be imposed on by smooth words, will easily know what to guess of his temper. In the meantime, though we think it is good to be well resolved in the things that we are to believe and practise in the worship of God, yet all irregular and irrational heats, in the prosecution or maintenance of men's different conceptions and apprehensions in religion, we desire sincerely to avoid and explode. Nor is it amiss that, to further our moderation, we be minded of the temper of the Pagans, who, in their opinion-wars (we are told), used no other weapons but only of pen and speech; for our author seems to have forgotten, not only innumerable other instances to the contrary, but also the renowned battle between Ombi and Tentyra. But this forgetfulness was needful, to aggravate the charge on Christians that are not Romanists, for their heat, fury, and fightings, for the promotion of their opinions; as being in this so much the worse than Pagans, who in religion used another manner of moderation. And who, I pray, is it that manageth this charge? Whence comes this dove with an olive-branch, this orator of peace? If we may guess from whence he came by seeing whither he is going, we must say that it was from Rome. This is their plea, this the persuasion of men of the Roman interest, this their charge on Protestants: to this height the confidence of men's ignorance, inadvertency, and fulness of present things amounts. Could ever any one rationally expect that these gentlemen would be public decriers of fury, wars, and tumults for religion? May not Protestants say to them, "Quæ regio in terris nostri non plena cruoris?"—"Is there any nation under the heavens, whereunto your power extends, wherein our blood hath not given testimony to your wrath and fury?" After all your cursings and attempted depositions of kings and princes, translations of title to sovereignty and rule, invasions of nations, secret conspiracies, prisons, racks, swords, fire and fagot, do you now come and declaim about moderation? We see you not yet cease from killing of men, in the pursuit of your fancies and groundless opinions, anywhere but either where you have not power, or can find no more to kill; so that certainly, whatever reproach we deserve to have cast upon us in this matter, you are the unfittest men in the world to be managers of it. But I still find myself in a mistake in this thing: it is only Protestants, and others departed from the Roman church, that our author treats of: it is they who are more fierce and disingenuous than the Pagans, in their contests amongst themselves, and against the Romanists, as having the least share of reason of any upon the earth. His good church is not concerned; which, as it is not led by such fancies and motives as they are, so it hath right (where it hath power) to deal with its adversaries as seems good unto it. This then, sir, is that which you intend,—that we should agree amongst ourselves, and wait for your coming with power to destroy us all! It were well, indeed, if we could agree; it is our fault and misery if we do not, having so absolutely perfect a rule and means of agreement as we have. But yet, whether we agree or agree not, if there be another party distinct from us all, pretending a right to exterminate us from the earth, it behoves us to look after their proceedings. And this is the true state of all our author's pleas for moderation; which are built upon such principles as tend to the giving us up, unarmed and naked, to the power and will of his masters.

For the rest of this section, wherein he is pleased to sport himself in the miscarriages of men in their coining and propagating of their opinions, and to gild over the care and success of the church of Rome in stifling such births of pride and darkness, I shall not insist upon it. For as the first, as generally tossed up and down, concerns none in particular, though accompanied with the repetition of such words as ought not to be scoffed at; so the latter is nothing but what violence and ignorance may any where, and in any age, produce. There are societies of Christians not a few in the east, wherein mere darkness and ignorance of the truth hath kept men at peace in errors, without the least disturbance by contrary opinions amongst themselves, for above a thousand years; and yet they have wanted the help of outward force to secure their tranquillity. And is it any wonder, where both these powerful engines are set at work for the same end, if in some measure it be compassed and effected? And if there be such a thing among the Romanists (which I have reason to be difficult in admitting the belief of) as that they can stifle all opinions as fast as they are conceived, or destroy them as soon as they are brought forth, I know it must be some device or artifice unknown to the apostles and primitive churches, who, notwithstanding all their authority and care for the truth, could not with many compass that end.

Sect. v. p. 54. The last section of this chapter contains motives to moderation, three in number; and I suppose that no man doubts but that many more might be added, every one in weight outdoing all these three. The first is that alone which Protestants are concerned to look unto; not that Protestants oppose any motive unto moderation, but knowing that in this discourse moderation is only the pretence, Popery (if I may use the word without incivility) the design and aim, it concerns them to examine which of these pretended motives, that any way regards their real principle, doth tend unto. Now this motive is, "the great ignorance our state and condition is involved in concerning God, his works and providence;" a great motive to moderation. I wish all men would well consider it; for I must acknowledge that I cannot but suppose them ignorant of the state and condition of mortality, and so consequently their own, who are ready to destroy and exterminate their neighbours, of the same flesh and blood with them, and agreeing in the main principles of religion that may certainly be known, for lesser differences, and that by such rules as within a few years may possibly reach their nearest relations. Our author also lays so much weight on this motive, that he fears an anticipation by men saying, "That the Scripture reveals enough unto us;" which, therefore, he thinks necessary to remove. For my part, I scarce think he apprehended any real danger that this would be insisted on as an objection against his motive to moderation. For to prevent his tending on towards that which is indeed his proper end, this obstacle is not unseasonably laid, that, under a pretence of the ignorance unavoidably attending our state and condition, he might not prevail upon us to increase and aggravate it, by enticing us to give up ourselves by an implicit faith to the conduct of the Roman church. A man may easily perceive the end he intends, by the objections which he foresees. No man is so mad, I think, as to plead the sufficiency of Scripture revelation against moderation; when, in the revelation of the will of God contained in the Scripture, moderation is so much commended unto us, and pressed upon us. But against the pretended necessity of resigning ourselves to the Romanists, for a relief against the unavoidable ignorance of our state and condition, besides that we know full well such a resignation would yield us no relief at all, this plea of the sufficiency of Scripture revelation is full and unanswerable. This put our author on a work which I have formerly once or twice advised him to meddle no more; being well assured that it is neither for his reputation nor his advantage, much less for his soul's health. The pretences which he makes use of are the same that we have heard of many and many a time:—the abuse of it by some, and the want of an infallible interpreter of it as to us all. But the old tale is here anew gilded with an intermixture of other pretty stories, and application of all to the present humours of men; not forgetting to set forth the brave estate of our forefathers, that had not the use of the Scripture: which what it was we know well enough, and better than the prejudices of this gentleman will give him leave to tell us. But if the lawful and necessary use of any thing may be decried because of its abuse, we ought not only to labour [for] the abolishing of all Christian religion in general, and every principle of it in particular, out of the world, but the blotting out of the sun, and moon, and stars, out of the firmament of heaven, and the destruction of the greatest and most noble parts, at least, of the whole creation. But as the apostles continued in the work of preaching the gospel, though by some the grace they taught "was turned into lasciviousness;" so shall we abide to plead for the use of the Scripture, whatever abuse of them by the wicked lusts of men can be instanced in. Nor is there any reason in the world why food should be kept from all men, though some have surfeited, or may yet so do. To have a compendious narration of the story and morality of the Scripture in the room of the whole, which our author allows of, is so jejune, narrow, and empty a conception,—so unanswerable to all those divine testimonies given to the excellency of the word of God, with precepts to abide in the meditation and study of it, to grow in the knowledge of it and the mysteries contained in it, the commendations of them that did so in the Scripture itself,—so blasphemously derogatory to the goodness, love, and wisdom of God in granting us that inestimable benefit, —so contrary to the redoubled exhortations of all the ancient fathers, —that I wonder any one who dares pretend to have read it, or to be a Christian, can own and avow such a notion. All the fine stories, allusions, and speculations about madness, that he is pleased to flourish withal in this matter, are a covering too short and narrow to hide that wretched contempt of the holy word of the great God which in these notions discovers itself. Men who by corrupt principles have been scared from the study of the Scripture, or by their lusts kept from its serious perusal, or attendance unto it,—that value not the authority of God, of Christ, or his apostles, commanding and requiring the diligent study of it,—that disregard the glorious mysteries revealed in it, on set purpose that we might all come to an acquaintance with them,—and so, consequently, that have had no experience of the excellency or usefulness of it, nor lie under any conviction of their own duty to attend unto it,—may perhaps be glad to have their lusts and unbelief so far accommodated, as to suffer themselves to be persuaded that there is no need that they should any farther regard it than hitherto they have done; but "in vain is the net spread before the eye of any thing that hath a wing." For them who have tasted the sweetness of the good word of God, who have attained any acquaintance with its usefulness and excellency, who have heard the voice of God in it, making the knowledge of his will revealed therein of indispensable necessity to the salvation of their souls; believe me, sir, all your rhetoric and stories, your pretences and flourishes, will never prevail with them to cast away their Bibles, and resolve for the future to believe only in the pope. Of the interpretation of the Scripture I have spoken before, and showed sufficiently that neither are we at any such a loss therein as to bring us to any uncertainty about the principles of our religion; nor, if we were, have we the least reason to look for any relief from Rome. When I happen upon any of these discourses, I cannot but say to myself, What do these men intend? Do they know what they do, or with whom they have to deal? Have they ever read the Scriptures, or tasted any sweetness in it? If they instruct their disciples unto such mean thoughts of the holy word of God, they undo them for ever. And if I meet with these bold efforts against the wisdom of God twenty times, I cannot but still thus startle at them.

The two following motives, being taken up, as far as I can apprehend, to give our author an advantage to make sport for himself and others, in canvassing some expressions and discourses of our talkative times, and the vulgar, brutish management of our differences by some weak, unknowing persons, need not detain us. Did I judge it a business worthy of any prudent man's consideration, it were easy to return him for his requital a collection of the pretty prayers and devotions of his good Catholics, of their kind treatment one of another, or the doughty arguments they make use of amongst themselves and against us, abundantly enough to repay him his kindness, without being beholden to any of those legends which they formerly accommodated the people withal, in room both of Scripture and preaching, though of late they begin to be ashamed of them.

CHAPTER V.

Obscurity of God, etc.

CHAP. II. Unto the ensuing whole chapter, wherein our author expatiates with a most luxuriant oratory throughout, and ofttimes soars with poetical raptures in setting forth the obscurity and darkness of all things, our ignorance and disability to attain a right and perfect knowledge of them, canting by the way many of those pretty notions which the philosophical, discoursive men of our days do use to whet their wits upon over a glass of wine, I have not much to offer; nor should I once reflect upon that discourse, were it not designed to another end than that which it is ushered in by, as the thing aimed to be promoted by it. Forbearance of one another in our several persuasions, on a sense of our infirmity and weakness, and the obscurity of those things about which our minds and contemplations are conversant, is flourished at the entrance of this harangue:

after a small progress, the snake begins to hiss in the grass, and in the close openly to show itself in an enticement unto an embracing of the Roman religion; which, it seems, will disentangle our minds out of that maze about the things of God and man in which, without its guidance, we must of necessity wander for ever. As for his philosophical notions, I suppose they were only vented to show his skill in the learned talk of this age, and to tole on the gallants whom he hath most hope to inveigle, knowing them to be candidates for the most part unto that scepticism which is grown the entertainment of tables and taverns. How a man that is conversant in his thoughts about religion, and his choice of or settlement therein, should come to have any concernment in this discourse, I cannot imagine. That God, who is infinitely wise, holy, good, who perfectly knows all his own excellencies, hath revealed so much of himself, his mind and will, in reference to the knowledge which he requires of himself and obedience unto him, as is sufficient to guide us whilst we are here below, to steer our course in our subjection to him and dependence on him, in a manner acceptable unto him, and to bring us to our utmost end and blessedness in the enjoyment of him;—this Protestants think sufficient for them, who as they need not, so they desire not, to be wise above what is written, nor to know more of God than he hath so revealed of himself, that they may know it. Those barren, fruitless speculations which some curious serpentine wits, casting off all reverence of the sovereignty and majesty of God, have exercised themselves in and about, even in things too high and hard for them, darkening counsel and wisdom by words of pretended subtilty, but real folly, are fitter to be exploded out of the world than fomented and cherished in the minds of men.

Nor doth that discourse about God and his essence, which lies before us, seem to grow on any other roots than ignorance and curiosity: ignorance of what it is that God requireth us to know of him, and how; and curiosity in prying into and using words about what we do not understand, nor is it the mind of God that we should. Were poor sinners thoroughly sensible of their own condition, and what acquaintance with God their concernment doth lie in, they would little value such vain towering imaginations as some men's minds are exercised withal. Come, sir, let us leave these vain flourishes, and, in deepest abasement of soul, pray that we may know how "the Father, whom no man hath seen at any time, is revealed by the only-begotten Son, who is in his bosom;"—what he is in his law towards impenitent sinners, what in the covenant of his grace to them that fly for refuge to the hope that is set before them;—even "that the God of our Lord Jesus Christ, the Father of glory, would give unto us the spirit of wisdom and revelation in the knowledge of him; that the eyes of our understanding being enlightened, we may know what is the hope of his calling, and what the riches of the glory of his inheritance in the saints, and what is the exceeding greatness of his power towards them that believe, according to the working of the might of his power, which he wrought in Christ, when he raised him from the dead, and set him at his own right hand in heavenly places;"—"that our hearts may be comforted, being knit together in love, and unto all riches of the FULL ASSURANCE OF UNDERSTANDING, to the acknowledgment of the mystery of God, and of the Father, and of Christ; in whom are hid all the treasures of wisdom and knowledge," and by whom alone we may obtain any saving acquaintance with them; "who also is come, and hath given us an understanding that we may know him that is true."

This is the port-haven of Protestants, whatever real darkness may be about them, or whatever mists may be cast on them by the sleights of men that lie in wait to deceive,—that they need know no more of God, that they may love him, fear him, believe in him, and come to the enjoyment of him, than what he hath clearly and expressly in Christ revealed of himself by his word. Whether the storms of this gentleman's indignation be able to drive them, or the more pleasant gales of his eloquence to entice them from this harbour, time will show. In the meanwhile, that indeed they ought not so to do, nor will do so with any but such as are resolved to steer their course by some secret distempers of their own, a few strictures on the most material passages of this chapter will discover.

It is scarce worth while to remark his mistake, in the foundation of his discourse, of the "Obscurity of God," as he is pleased to state the matter, from that of the prophet, asserting that "God is a God who hideth himself," or, as he renders it, a "hidden God." His own prophet will tell him that it is not concerning the essence of God, but the dispensation of his love and favour towards his people, that these words were used by the prophet of old; and so are unwillingly pressed to serve in the design he hath in hand. Neither are we more concerned in the ensuing discourse of the "soul's cleaving to God by affection," upon the metaphysical representation of his excellencies and perfections unto it, it being purely Platonical, and no way suited to the revelation made of God in the gospel; which acquaints us not with any such amiableness in God as to endear the souls of sinners unto him, causing them to reach out the wings of their love after him, but only as he is in Christ Jesus reconciling the world to himself;—a consideration that hath no place, nor can obtain any, in this flourish of words; and the reason is, because they are sinners, and therefore, without the revelation of an atonement, can have no other apprehension of the infinitely holy and righteous God but as of a devouring fire, with whom no sinner can inhabit: nor yet in the aggravation of the obscurity of God from the restless endeavours of mankind in the disquisition of him; who, as he says, "show their love in seeking him, having at their birth an equal right to his favour, which they could nowise demerit before they were born,"—being directly contrary to the doctrine of his own church, in the head of original sin.

That which first draws up towards the design he is in pursuit of is his determination, "that the issuing of men's perplexities in the investigation of this hidden God must be by some prophet or teacher, sent from God unto men;" but the uncertainty of coming into any better condition thereby is so exaggerated by a contempt of those ways and means that such prophets have fixed on to evidence their coming forth from God, by miracles, visions, prophecies, a show of sanctity, with a concourse of threats and promises, as that means also is cashiered from yielding us any relief. Neither is there any thing intimated or offered to exempt the true prophets of God, nor the Lord Christ himself, from being shuffled into the same bag with false pretenders, in the close, that were brought forth to play their game in this pageant. Yea, the difficulty put upon this help, of the loss we are at in the knowledge of God by prophets and prophecies, seems especially to respect those of the Scripture, so to manifest the necessity of a farther evidence to be given unto them than any they carry about them or bring with them, that they may be useful to this end and purpose: and this intention is manifest a little after, where the Scripture is expressly reckoned among those things which all men boast of,—none can come to certainty or assurance by. Thus are poor unstable souls ventured to the borders of atheism, under a pretence of leading them to the church! Was this the method of Christ or his apostles, in drawing men to the faith of the gospel? this the way of the holy men of old that laboured in the conversion of souls from gentilism and heresy? Were ever such bold assaults against the immovable principles of Christianity made by any before religion came to be a matter of carnal interest? Is there no way to exalt the pope but by questioning the authority of Christ and truth of the Scripture? Truly, I am sorry that wise and considering men should observe such an irreverence of God and his word to prevail in the spirits of men, as to entertain thoughts of persuading them to desert their religion by such presumptuous insinuations of the uncertainty of all divine revelation. But all this may be made good on the consideration of the changes of men after their professions of this or that religion,—namely, that notwithstanding their former pretensions, yet indeed they know nothing at all, seeing that "from God and the truth no man doth willingly depart;" which, if it be universally true, I dare say there is not one word true in the Scripture. How often doth God complain in the Old Testament that his people "forsook him for that which was not God!" and how many do the apostles show us in the New to have "forsaken the truth!" It is true, that under the notion of God [as] the chiefest good, and of truth [as] the proper object and rest of the understanding, none can willingly and by choice depart; but that the minds of men might be so corrupted and perverted by their own lusts and temptations of Satan, as willingly and by choice to forsake the one or the other, to embrace that which in their stead presents itself unto them, is no less true than that twice two make four. And it is mere weakness, and ignorance of the condition of mankind since the entrance of sin, to conclude that because men may forsake the truth which they have professed, therefore there is no evidence in that truth which they so forsake; as though truth and its evidence were to be measured and judged by the carriage and deportment of corrupt and unstable men towards it. Though the sun continue to shine in the firmament, yet there be a thousand ways whereby men may become blind, and so rendered unable to see it; and there are no fewer ways whereby men either wilfully themselves darken the eyes of their understanding, or suffer them to be put out by others. Shall the truth be thence calumniated, as though it sent forth no beams whereby it may be clearly discerned? Are they not rather justly to be supposed blind themselves who can entertain such thoughts of it?

We dwell too much on these remote attempts towards the special end aimed at. The rhetoric of this discourse is wound up, pp. 76–79, in a persuasive unto Popery; the substance whereof is, that the Papacy being rejected, there is a necessity that all men must become atheists;—which requires a little farther consideration. He says, then, "That these dissensions of ours" (he means of Protestants, one of whom he most indecently personates) "about the faith, in its branches, so hot, so various, so extravagant, are apt to infer a suspicion in its very root. Are not a hundred in our own country become atheists already upon that very notion? and these men, supposing substantial change once made in religion, and deliberately admitted, are rather to be commended for their wit than blamed; for they do but that suddenly which all the land will come to by degrees." This in general; in which entrance into his farther application of what he had largely, and indeed loosely, before discoursed to his present purpose, I wish I could find any thing sound. If dissensions about the faith, however extravagantly managed, are apt to infer a suspicion in its very root, it is most certain that since the first preaching of it, or within a few years after its first revelation, causes of suspicion have been given, and will be given, and it is the mind of God should be given, who said, "There must be heresies, that the approved may be tried." And this very argument did Celsus press against Christianity almost fifteen hundred years ago: which is worthily answered by Origen; nor is there need of adding any thing to what that excellent man replied unto one of the first coiners of this objection. The truth is, our dissensions are evils,—our evils,—the evils of men that are engaged in them; and yet, it may be, not all out so evil in themselves as is pretended: they are far enough from meriting the title of, "Lo, here is Christ," and, "Lo, there is Christ." Protestants are all of them well enough agreed who is Christ, and where alone he is to be found. If they jump not wholly into the same conceptions about some few things of less importance in the way and manner of the worship of Christ, it is no more but what hath been the lot of the best of men, ever since Christ was preached on the earth, that were not infallibly inspired. Such contests ever were; and he that knows what men are, will have little cause given him to suspect the truth of the foundation of that about which they contend. Nor is any ground of such suspicion administered by these differences: men of corrupt minds may take occasion from them to vent the enmity which is in their hearts against the faith; ground of suspicion none is given unto them. Nay rather, it is a strong evidence of the certainty of the faith in general, that all those who contend about the branches of it do every one of them charge one another with the failure; and all agree that the faith itself about which they contend is certain, sure, and stable. And I hope the gentleman is mistaken in the calculation of the numbers that are become atheists in our country: or if he have brought them to the poll, I do not believe that he hath taken a particular account of the occasions and reasons that cast them on that commendable piece of "wit," as he styles it; and so knows not but that they may have been made witty by some of those ways whereby, if a learned friar may be believed, there were no less than sixty thousand become atheists, and that not of Protestants, but good Catholics, in one city in our neighbouring nation. But this falls out, saith he, by a "supposal of a substantial change made in religion, and deliberately admitted." This indeed were something; but who ever supposed so? The religion of Jesus Christ is the same "once delivered unto the saints." This is still one and the same, "yesterday, to-day, and for ever,"—unalterable as Christ himself. Men, indeed, who are liars, are changeable worms; and many, as to their profession in religion, alter, change, turn, apostatize, with or without deliberation; but he that shall thence conclude that his best course is speedily to be an atheist, will not deserve much commendation for his wit, less for his wisdom, and for his grace none at all. That the land will come to atheism by degrees is the prognostication of our author, calculated from the meridian of Rome. For my part, I fear not such kind of prophets. Protestant religion hath, by the blessing of God, retrieved the nation from the doors of atheism, and kept it safe almost these hundred years, notwithstanding the woful miscarriages of some that have professed it. Why they must now all by degrees turn atheists, I know no reason to fear, nor presume doth our author, but that he is prompted to like his conjecture by his love to his countrymen, desiring they may follow them who are so commended for their wit.

But we must proceed with the improvement of this consideration. Page 11,—" If the Papist, or Roman Catholic, who first brought the news of Christ and his Christianity into the land, as all men must needs know that have either heard or read of Christianity's ingress into England, or other countries and kingdoms (for we do no sooner hear news of Christianity than Popery, and its crucifixes, monasteries, relics, sacrifice, and the like); I say, if the Papist be now become so odious, as we see he is, and if the faith he brought and maintained a thousand years together be now rent all asunder by sects and factions, which bandy all to the ruin of that mother religion,—if all her practical truths, wherein chiefest piety consists, be already abandoned as erroneous,—doth not this justify the Pagan whom this Catholic Christian displaced to make way for his own law? And must not this be a certain way and means to introduce atheism, which naturally follows that faith once removed, even as a carcase succeeds a living body once deceased? For, one truth denied, is a fair way to question another which came by the same hand; and this, a third; till the very authority of the first revealer be at stake, which can no more defend himself than he can his law. For the same axe and instrument that cut down the branches can cut up the root too: and if his reverence, for which all the rest was believed, defend not their truth, it must needs at length utterly fail in his own; for all the authority they had was purely from him, and he fails in them before he fails in himself,—οὐδὲν ὑγιές." That the Papists, or Roman Catholics, first brought Christ and his Christianity into this land is most untrue; and I wonder how any one that hath read any story of the times that are past should so often aver what he cannot but know to be untrue. The gospel might have been brought into England by Romans, and yet not by Papists; for I cannot find, nor can this gentleman show, that the Romans St Paul wrote unto were any one of them, in any one point, Papists. But neither was it brought hither by Romans, but came immediately out of the east; from whence also, about the same time, it came to Rome. Nor is it any jot truer that " we no sooner heard news of Christianity than Popery, with its crucifixes, monasteries, relics, sacrifice" (that is, the mass), "and the like." "Apage nugas!" What! do we talk of t'other-day things, when we speak of the first news of Christianity? The first planting and watering of these things was in after ages, and their growing up to that consistency wherein they may justly be called Popery, a work of many centuries. And yet I shall grant that most of them got the start in the world of that papal sovereignty whence Popery is peculiarly denominated. But the first news we hear of Christianity is in the gospel, where there is not the least tidings of these trifles; nor was there in some ages that next succeeded the publication of it. If this gentleman give any farther occasion, the particulars shall be evinced to him. For my part, I know not how nor to whom a "Papist is become odious," which nextly he complains of. I can and do love their persons, pity them in their mistakes,—hate only their vices. But yet, certain it is a Papist may be odious; that is, men may not love those parts of his religion from whence he is so denominated, without the least impeachment of that faith that extirpated Gentilism in the world. It is for that faith which ruined Gentilism that we contend against Papists. Let us have that and no more, and there is an end of all our contests. The things we strive about sprang up since Gentilism was buried; the most of them out of its grave,—some from a deeper place, if there be a deeper place. For the "practical truths of the Papists," which he complains to be abolished, I was in good hope he would not have mentioned them. Their speculations are better than their practices, whether he intends their moral divinity or their "agenda" in worship. I would desire this gentleman to mention them no more, lest he hear that of them which I know he is not willing to do. As for the practical truths of the gospel, they are maintained and asserted in the church of England, and by all Protestants; and about others we are not solicitous. What tendency, then, the rejection of Popery, which had no hand in supplanting Gentilism, and which is no part of the religion of Christ, hath to the leading of men into atheism, is as hard to discover as the quadrature of a circle, or a subterranean passage into the Indies. But he gives his reasons: "If one truth be denied, a fair way is made to question another which came by the same hand; and this, a third; till the very authority of the first revealer be at stake, which can no more defend himself than he can his law." This first revealer I take to be the Lord Christ. He that grants a thing or doctrine to be taught and delivered by him, yet denies it to be true, doth indeed deny his authority; however, he will defend himself and his law, let men do what they please. But he that denies such a thing to be truth, because it is not revealed by him, nor consistent with what is revealed by him, doing this out of subjection of soul and conscience to his authority, is in no danger of questioning or opposing that authority. Nay, be it that it be indeed a truth which he denies,—being only denied by him because he is persuaded that it is not of Christ, the first revealer, and therefore not true,—there is no fear of the danger threatened. But the matter is, that all that is brought from Christ by the same hand must be equally received. It is true, if it be brought from Christ by the same hand, it must be so; not because by the same hand, but because from Christ. They that preached Christ, and withal that men must be circumcised, had put men into a sad condition if, in good sooth, they had been necessitated to embrace all that they taught,—the same men teaching Christ to be the Messiah, and circumcision to be necessary to life eternal. Amongst those that were converted to the gospel by the Jews that were zealous of the law, how easy had it been for their teachers to have utterly frustrated St Paul's doctrine of Christian liberty, by telling them that they could not forego circumcision but they must forego Christ also; for all those things they received by the same hand! If, indeed, a man comes and delivers a system of religion upon his own authority and reputation only, he that denies any one point of what he delivers is in a fair way of everting all that he asserts. But if he come as sent from another, and affirm that this other commanded him to declare that which he delivers for truth in his name, and produce for that end his commission, wherein all the truths that he is to deliver are written; [and] if he deliver what he hath not received in commission, that may honestly be rejected, without the least impeachment of any one truth that was really committed unto him by him that sent him. And this was the way, this the condition of them who planted the gospel in the name of Christ, not being themselves divinely inspired. So that if, in the second edition of Christianity in some parts of this nation, by Austin and his associates, any thing was taught or practised that was not according to the rule and commission given by Christ, it may be rejected without the least impeachment to the authority of the first revealer; nay, his authority, being once received, cannot be preserved entire without such rejection. I confess I do almost mistrust that by this revealer of Christianity, and his authority, which he discourses about, our author intends the pope; which, if so, what we have discoursed of Christ is, I confess, to little purpose: and it were easy to turn our reply that way; but because I have not clear evidence for it, I will not charge him with so horrid a presumptuous insinuation. When he declares his mind, he shall hear more of ours.

But he farther specifies his meaning in an enumeration of doctrines that were preached by the first planters of the gospel, in and unto the extirpation of Gentilism. "If," saith he, "the institution of monasteries, to the praise and service of God, day and night, be thought, as it hath been now these many years, a superstitious folly; if Christian priests and sacrifices be things of high idolatry; if the seven sacraments be deemed vain, most of them; if it suffice to salvation only to believe, whatever life we lead; if there be no value or merit in good works; if God's laws be impossible to be kept; if Christ be not our law-maker and director of doing well, as well as Redeemer from ill; if there be no sacramental tribunal for our reconciliation ordained for us by Christ on the earth; if the real body of our Lord be not bequeathed unto his spouse in his last will and testament; if there be not under Christ a general head of the church, who is chief priest and pastor of all Christians upon earth, under God, whose vicegerent he is in spiritual affairs,—all which things are now held forth by us, manifestly against the doctrine of the first preachers of Christianity in this land;—then, I say, Paganism was unjustly displaced by these doctrines, and atheism must needs succeed; for if Christ deceived us, upon whom shall we rely? and if they that brought us the first news of Christ, brought along with it so many grand lies, why may not the very story of Christ be thought a romance?"

I could wish there had been a little more clearness and ingenuity in this enumeration; the mixing of what he takes to be truths with some negatives that he condemns in the same series, breeds some confusion in the discourse: and I am also compelled to complain of want of candour and ingenuity in his representation of the Protestant doctrine, in every particular wherein he takes occasion to mention it. Let us, then, separate the things that have no place of their own in this argument, then what is ambiguously proposed; after which, what remains may be distinctly considered:—

1. What makes that inquiry in our way at this time, "If it suffice to salvation to believe, whatever life we lead?" Who ever said so, taught so, wrote so, in England? Is this the doctrine of the church of England? or of the Presbyterians or Independents? or whose is it? or what makes it in this place? If this be the way of gaining Catholics, let them that please make use of it. Protestants dislike the way as much as the end.

2. What is the meaning of that which follows, "If there be no value or merit in good works?" Who ever taught that there is no value in good works? that they are not commanded of God? that they are not accepted with him? that they are not our duty, to be careful in the performance of? that God is not honoured, the gospel adorned, the church and the world advantaged by them? Do all these things put "no value" on them? For their "merit," the expression being ambiguous, unscriptural, and, as commonly interpreted, derogatory to the glory of Christ and the grace of God, we shall let it pass as

proper to his purpose; and much good may it do him with all that he gains by it.

3. "If," saith he, "God's laws be impossible to be kept;"—but who said so? Protestants teach, indeed, that men in their own strength cannot keep the laws of God; that the grace received in this life extends not to an absolute sinless perfection in their observation, which is inconsistent with the covenant of grace, and men's walking with God therein: but, that the laws of God were in their own nature "impossible" to be observed by them to whom they were first given, or that they are yet impossible to be kept in that way of their sincere observation which is required in the gospel, Protestants teach not, that I know of. He proceeds:—

4. "If Christ be not our law-maker and director of doing well, as well as our Redeemer from ill." This is a little too open and plain. Doth he think any man will believe him, that Protestants or Presbyterians teach that "Christ is not our law-maker and director of doing well," etc.? I dare say he believes not one word of it himself, what confidence soever he hath taken upon him of imposing on the minds of weak and unstable men.

Other things mentioned by him are ambiguous; as, "If the seven sacraments be deemed vain, most of them," etc. Of the things themselves, which they term "sacraments," there is scarce any of them by Protestants esteemed vain; that one of Unction, which they judge now useless, they only say is an unwarrantable imitation of that which was useful. Of the rest which they reject, they reject not the things, but those things from being sacraments; and a practice in religion is not presently condemned as vain which is not esteemed a sacrament. There is no less ambiguity in that other supposition, "If the real body of our Lord be not bequeathed to his spouse in his last will and testament;" which no Protestant ever questioned, though there be great contests about the manner of the sacramental participation of that real body. The same may be said of some other of his supposals. But I need not go over them in particular; I shall only say in general, that take from amongst them what is acknowledged to be the doctrine of the Papists, and as such is opposed by the church of England or by Presbyterians (as papal supremacy, sacrifice of the mass, monasteries of votaries under special and peculiar vows and rules, necessity of auricular confession, transubstantiation, which are the things gilded over by our author), and prove that they were the doctrines, all or any of them, whereby and wherewith the first preachers of Christianity in this nation, or any where else in the old known world, displaced Paganism, and, for my part, I will immediately become his proselyte. What, then, can be bound with this rope of sand?—"The first preachers of Christianity preached the pope's supremacy, the mass, etc.; by these doctrines Paganism was displaced: if these doctrines now be decried as lies, why may not Christ himself be esteemed a romance?"—for neither did the first preachers of Christianity preach these doctrines, nor was Paganism displaced by them: nor is there any ground to question the authority and truth of Christ, in case those that do first preach him do therewithal preach somewhat that is not true, when they bring along with them an authentic conviction of their own mistakes, as was manifested before, and might be made good by innumerable other instances.

I shall not need to follow him in his declamation to the end of this paragraph; the whole foundation of his many flourishes and pretences being totally taken out of the way.

CHAPTER VI.

Scripture vindicated.

With his three following paragraphs, from p. 82 unto 108,—which have only a very remote and almost imperceptible tendency unto his purpose in hand, though they take up so long a portion of his discourse (seeming to be inserted either to manifest his skill and proficiency in philosophical scepticism, or to entertain his readers with such a delightful diversion, as that, having taken in it a taste of his ingenuity, they may have an edge given their appetite unto that which is more directly prepared for them),—I shall not trouble myself nor detain my reader about. If any one, a little skilled in the discourses of these days, have a mind to vie conjectures and notions with him, to vellicate commonly received maxims and vulgar opinions, to expatiate on the events of providence in all ages, he may quickly compose as many learned leaves: only, if he would be pleased to take my advice with him, I should wish him not to flourish and gild over things uncertain and unknown, to the disadvantage of things known and certain; nor to vent conjectures about other worlds and the nature of the heavenly bodies, derogatory to the love of God in sending his Son to be incarnate and to die for sinners that live on this earthly globe. Neither do I think it well done to mix St Paul and his writings in this scepticism, mentioning in one place his fancy, in another his conceit, which he seems to oppose,—such is the reverence these men bear to the Scripture and holy penmen thereof; so also that whole scorn, which he calls "man's dominion over the creatures," reflects principally on the beginning of Genesis and the eighth Psalm.

An unsearchable abyss in many of God's providential dispensations, wherein the infinite sovereignty, wisdom, and righteousness of him who giveth no account of his matters are to be adored, we readily acknowledge; and yet I dare freely say, that most of the things instanced in by our author are capable of a clear resolution, according to known rules and principles of truth revealed in the Scripture: such are, God's suffering the Gentiles to wander so long in the dark, not calling them to repentance; with the necessity of Christian religion, and yet the punishment of many of the professors of it by the power of idolaters and pagans, as the church of the Jews was handled of old by the Assyrians, Babylonians, and others. Of this sort, also, is his newly-inserted story of the Cirubrians; which, it may be, was added to give us a cast of his skill in the investigation of the original of nations, out of Camden; for if that which himself affirms of them were true, namely, "That they were devout, adoring the crucifix,"—which men usually are when they cease to worship aright him who was crucified (the sin mentioned, Rom. i. 25),—we need not much admire that God gave them up to be scourged by their pagan adversaries. But, not to mention that which is not only uncertain whether it be true, but is most probably false, it our author had ever read the stories of those times, and the lamentations made for the sins of them by Gildas, Salvianus, and others, he would have found enough to justify God in his proceedings and dealing with his Cirubrians, according to the known rules of his word. The like may be affirmed concerning the Irish, whose decay, like a true Englishman, he dates from the interest of our kings there, and makes the progress of it commensurate to the prevalency of their authority; when it is known to all the world that by that means alone they were reclaimed from barbarism, and brought into a most flourishing condition, until, by their rebellion and unparalleled cruelties, they precipitated themselves into confusion and ruin. As for that which is insinuated as the conclusion fit to be made out of all these premises, concerning the obscurity of God's nature and the works of providence,—namely, that we betake ourselves to the infallible determination of the Roman church, —I shall only say, that as I know not that as yet the pope hath undertaken pontifically to interpose his definite sentence in reference to these philosophical digladiations he glanceth on in the most part of his discourse, so I have but little reason, on the resignation required, to expect an illumination from that obscurity about the Deity which he insists on; finding the children, indeed the fathers of that church, of all men on the earth, most to abound in contradictory disputes and endless quarrels about the very nature and properties of God himself.

But his direct improvement of this long oration that he enters on, p. 122, may be farther considered. It is, in short, this: "That by the Scripture no man can come to the knowledge of, and settlement in, an assurance of the truth; nor is there any hope of relief for us in this sad condition but that living papal oracle, which, if we are wise, we will acquiesce in," pp. 125, 126. To this purpose men are furnished with many exceptions against the authority of the Scripture, from " the uncertainty of the rise and spring of it,—how it came to us,—how it was authorized, and by whom; the doubtfulness of its sense and meaning; the contemptible condition of the first penmen of it, seeming a company of men imposing their own fancies as oraculous visions upon us,—of whom how can we know that they were inspired, seeing they say no such thing of themselves, not those especially of the New Testament? besides the many appearing contradictions, with other human infirmities, seeming unto critics ever and anon to occur in them; and why may not illiterate men fail as well as," etc.?—with much more of the same nature and importance: unto all of which I shall need to say nothing but that of Job, " Vain man would be wise, but is like to the wild ass's colt." Never is the folly of men more eminently displayed, than when confidence of their wisdom makes them bold and daring. I doubt not but our author thought that he had so acquitted himself in this passage, as that his readers must need resolve to quit the Scripture and turn Papists; but there is an evident gulf between these reasonings and Popery, whereunto they will certainly carry any that shall give way to their force and efficacy. This is no other but downright atheism; this the supplying of men with cavils against the Scripture, its power and authority, does directly lead unto. Our author would have men to believe these suggestions, at least so far as not to seek for rest and satisfaction in the Scriptures, or he would not: if he would not, to what end doth he mention them, and sport himself in showing the luxuriancy of his wit and fancy in cavilling at the word of God? Is not this a ready way to make men atheists, if only by inducing them to an imitation of that which by his example he commends unto them? But it will be said, he only shows the uncertainties that are about Scripture, that men may not expect by or from them deliverance from the darkness and ignorance before spoken of? Suppose, then, they come to be persuaded of such an uncertainty, what course shall they take? "Apply themselves to the Roman church, and they are safe." But seeing the being of a church (much less the Roman church) hath no foundation in the light of nature, and men can never know any thing of it, especially of its prerogative, but by and from the Scripture, whose authority you have taught them to question, and made doubtful to them, what remains for rational men but to renounce both Scripture and church, and betake themselves to your commendable piece of witty atheism? This is the old lurry,—the

Scripture cannot be known, believed, understood, but by the church; the church cannot be proved to have being, constitution, or authority but by the Scripture: and then, if you doubt of the authority of that proof of the church, you must return to the church again; and so on, till all faith and reason vanish, or men make shipwreck of their faith, and become brutish in their understanding, pretending to believe they know neither what nor why. And this employment of raising surmises and stirring up jealousies about the word of God, its penmen and their authority, do men put themselves upon, I will not say to gratify the Roman court, but I will say in obedience to their prejudices, lusts, and darkness,—the saddest drudgery that any of the sons of men can be exercised withal. And, if he would be believed, he professeth himself an anti-scripturist, and in that profession, which he puts upon himself, an atheist. For my part, I am amazed to think how men are able to hold their pens in their hands,—that a horror of the work they have before them doth not make them shake them out, when they are thus traducing the holy word of Christ, and exciting evil surmises about it. Should they deal with a man of any power and authority, they might not expect to escape his indignation; even to publish to all the world that he is indeed an honourable person, but yet, if men will question his honour, truth, honesty, authority, and affirm him to be a cheat, thief, murderer, adulterer, they cannot see how they can be disproved,—at least, he would have a difficult task in hand that should endeavour to free him from objections of that nature. Yet thus men dare to deal with the Scripture, that word which God hath magnified above all his name. If this be the spirit that breathed in the apostles, the holy army of martyrs of old, and all the fathers of the primitive church, I am much mistaken; nay, I am greatly so, if with one consent they would not denounce an anathema against such a defence of any religion whatever. But you will say, the same person defends also the Scripture, just as he in the poet did Pelilius:—

> "Me Capitolinus convictore usus amicoque
> A puero est, causaque mea permulta rogatus
> Fecit; et incolumis lætor quod vivit in urbe;
> Sed tamen admiror quo pacto judicium illud
> Fugerit."—— [Hor. Sat. i. 4, 96.]

A defence worse and more bitter than a downright accusation. I am not now to observe what prejudice this excuse brings to the cause of our author with all intelligent persons, having noted it once and again before; nor what contentment Protestants take, to see that the truth they profess cannot be shaken without inducing men to question the fundamental principles of Christian religion, and if this course be persisted in, for aught that I can understand, the whole controversy between us and the Romanists must needs be at last reduced unto this head, Whether the Scripture of the Old and New Testament was given by divine inspiration? For the present, having, in the consideration of the general suppositions of this treatise, spoken before to this head, I shall not need to answer particular exceptions given in against its authority; nor do I think it incumbent on me so to do, unless our author own them for his sense: which if he be pleased to do, I promise him, if God give me life, to give him a distinct answer to every one of them, and all that is contained in them. Moreover, these things will again occur in his 15th section, where he expressly takes the Scripture to task, as to its pleas for judging of and settling men in the truth.

Proceed we to his next section, p. 126.

CHAPTER VII.

Use of Reason.

Sect. xi. THIS section is set apart for the cashiering of reason from having any hand in the business we deal about; and the truth is, if our author can persuade us first to throw away our Bibles, and then to lay aside the use of our reason, I suppose there is no doubt but we shall become Roman Catholics. This work, it seems, cannot be effected unless men are contented to part with Scripture and reason; all that whereby they are Christians and men. But unless our author have emptied Circe's box of ointment, whereby she transformed men into swine, he will confess it somewhat a difficult task that he hath undertaken. Methinks one of these demands might suffice at once. But he presumes he hath put his countrymen into a good humour, and, knowing them free and open-hearted, he plies them whilst they are warm.

We have indeed in this section as fair a flourish of words as in any other; but there can be but little reason in the words that men make use of to plead against reason itself. And yet I am persuaded most readers think as well of this section as any in the book. To whom the unreasonableness of this is evident, that of the others is so also; and those who willingly imbibe the other parts of his discourse, will little strain at this. Nothing is to be trusted unto prejudice; nor, if we will learn, are we to think strange of any thing. Let us, then, weigh impartially what is of reason in this discourse against the use of reason. Whatever he pretends, he knows full well that he hath no difference with any sort of Protestants about "finding out a religion by reason," and adhering only to its dictates in the worship of God.

All the world of Protestants profess that they receive their religion wholly by revelation from God, and no otherwise. Nor is it about ascribing a sovereignty to reason to judge of the particulars of religion so revealed, to accept or refuse them, according as that shall judge them suitable or not to its principles and liking. This is the sovereign dictate of reason,—that whatever God reveals to be believed is true, and as such must be embraced, though the bottom of it cannot be sounded by reason's line; and that because the reason of a man is not absolutely reason, but, being the reason of a man, is variously limited, bounded, and made defective in its ratiocinations. An objective truth our reason supposes: all that it hath to do is but to judge of what is proposed to it, according to the best principles that it hath; which is all that God in that kind requires of us, unless in that work wherein he intends to make us more than men, that is Christians, he would have us make ourselves less than men, even as brutes. That in our whole obedience to God we are to use our reason, Protestants say indeed, and, moreover, that what is not done reasonably is not obedience. The Scripture is the rule of all our obedience, grace the principle enabling us to perform it; but the manner of its performance must be rational, or it is not the supposition of rule or principle that will render any act of a man obedience. Religion, say Protestants, is revealed in the Scripture, proposed to the minds and wills of men for its entertainment by the ministry of the church; grace to believe and obey is supernaturally from God. But as to the proposals of religion from Scripture, they aver that men ought to admit and receive them as men; that is, judge of the sense and meaning of them, discover their truth, and, finding them revealed, acquiesce in the authority of him by whom they are first revealed. So far as men, in any things of their concernments that have a moral good or evil in them, do refuse, in the choice or refusal of them, to exercise that judging and discerning which is the proper work of reason, they unman themselves, and invert the order of nature; dethroning the τὸ ἡγεμονικὸν of the soul, and causing it to follow the faculties that have no light but what they receive by and from it. It is true, all our carnal reasonings against Scripture mysteries are to be captivated to the obedience of faith; and this is highly reasonable, making only the less, particular, defective collections of reason give place to the more noble, general, and universal principles of it. Nor is the denying of our reason anywhere required as to the sense and meaning of the words of the Scripture, but as to the things and matter signified by them. The former, reason must judge of, if we are men; the latter, if, in conjunction with unbelief and carnal lusts, it tumultuate against, it is to be subdued to the obedience of faith. All that Protestants, in the business of religion, ascribe unto men is but this, that in the business of religion they are, and ought to be, men; that is, judge of the sense and truth of what is spoken to them, according to that rule which they have received for the measure and guide of their understandings in these things. If this may not be allowed, you may make a herd of them, but a church never.

Let us now consider what is offered in this section about reason, wherein the concernment of any Protestants may lie. As the matter is stated about any "one's setting up himself to be a new and extraordinary director unto men in religion, upon the account of the irrefutable reason he brings along with him, which is the spring and source of that religion which he tenders unto them," I very much question whether any instance can be given of any such thing from the foundation of the world. Men have so set up, indeed, sometimes, as that good Catholic Vanini[1] did, not long since, in France, to draw men from all religions; but to give a new religion unto men, that this pretension was ever solely made use of, I much question. As true religion came by inspiration from God, so all authors of that which is false have pretended to revelation. Such were the pretensions of Minos, Lycurgus, and Numa of old, of Mohammed of late, and generally of the first founders of religious orders in the Roman church; all in imitation of real divine revelation, and in answer to indelible impressions on the minds of all men, that religion must come from God. To what purpose, then, the first part of his discourse, about the "coining of religion from reason," or the framing of religion by reason, is, I know not; unless it be to cast a blind before his unwary reader, whilst he steals away from him his treasure,—that is, his reason, as to its use in its proper place. Though, therefore, there be many things spoken unduly, and, because it must be said, untruly also, in this first part of his discourse, until toward the end of p. 131, which deserve to be animadverted on; yet, because they are such as no sort of Protestants hath any concernment in, I shall pass them over. That wherein he seems to reflect any thing upon our principles, is in a supposed reply to what he had before delivered; whereunto, indeed, it hath no respect or relation, being the assertion of a principle utterly distant from that imaginary one, which he had timely set up, and

[1] Owen most probably alludes to a weak enthusiast of the name of John Baptist Vanini. He was born at Taurosano, in the kingdom of Naples, in 1585. He published at Lyons, in 1615, a work entitled "Amphitheatrum æternæ Providentiæ," etc.; and in the following year another, entitled "De Admirandis Naturæ, Reginæ Deæque mortalium Arcanis." He was accused of atheism, and his book was burnt by a decree of the Sorbonne. To judge from the title of the last work, and the common accounts of his views, he seems to have deified the powers of nature. He was prosecuted on a charge of atheism at Toulouse, and burnt in 1619, under circumstances of gross brutality, though there is some dispute whether the charge of atheism was well founded. At his trial, he picked up a straw and declared it to be sufficient evidence to him that God existed. He was at one time in England, and held disputations in support of popish tenets; for which offence he suffered imprisonment for forty-nine days. After the publication of his second work, he offered his services to the papal nuncio at Paris, to write in defence of the Council of Trent. Hence the edge of Owen's sarcasm,—"That *good* Catholic."—Ed.

stoutly cast down before. It is this, "That we must take the words from Christ and his gospel; but the proper sense, which the words of themselves cannot carry with them, our own reason must make out." If it be the doctrine of Protestants which he intendeth in these words, it is most disadvantageously and uncandidly represented; which becomes not an ingenious and learned person. This is that which Protestants affirm:—religion is revealed in the Scripture; that revelation is delivered and contained in propositions of truth. Of the sense of those words that carry their sense with them, reason judgeth, and must do so, or we are brutes; and that every one's reason, so far as his concernment lies in what is proposed to him.

Neither doth this at all exclude the ministry or authority of the church, both which are intrusted with it by Christ, to propose the rules contained in his word unto rational creatures, that they may understand, believe, love, and obey them. To cast out this use of reason, with pretence of an *ancient sense* of the words, which yet we know they have not about them, is as vain as any thing in this section, and that is vain enough. If any such *ancient sense* can be made out or produced,—that is, a meaning of any text that was known to be so from their explication who gave that text,—it is by reason to be acquiesced in; neither is this to make a man a bishop, much less a chief bishop, to himself. I never heard that it was the office of a bishop to know, believe, or understand for any man but for himself. It is his office, indeed, to instruct and teach men; but they are to learn and understand for themselves, and so to use their reason in their learning. Nor doth the variableness of men's thoughts and reasonings infer any variableness in religion to follow; whose stability and sameness depends on its first revelation, not our manner of reception. Nor doth any thing asserted by Protestants, about the use of reason in the business of religion interfere with the rule of the apostle about "captivating our understandings to the obedience of faith," much less to his assertion that Christians "walk by faith, and not by sight," seeing that without it we can do neither the one nor the other: for I can neither submit to the truth of things to be believed, nor live upon them or according unto them, unless I understand the propositions wherein they are expressed; which is the work we assign to reason. For those who would resolve their faith into reason, we confess that they overthrow not only faith but reason itself; there being nothing more irrational than that belief should be the product of reason, being properly an assent resolved into authority; which, if not divine, is so also. I shall, then, desire no more of our author nor his readers as to this section but only this, that they would believe that no Protestant is at all concerned in it; and so I shall not farther interpose as to any contentment they may find in its review or perusal.

CHAPTER VIII.

Jews' objections.

THE title of this third chapter is, that "No religion, or sect, or way, hath any advantage over another, nor all of them over Popery." To this we excepted before, in general, that that way which hath the truth with it, hath, in that wherein it hath the truth, the advantage against all others. Truth turns the scales in this business, wherever and with whomsoever it be found; and if it lie in any way distant from Popery, it gives all the advantage against it that need be desired. And with this only inquiry, "With whom the truth abides?" is this disquisition, "What ways in religion have advantage against others?" to be resolved. But this course and procedure, for some reasons which he knows, and we may easily guess at, our author liked not; and it is now too late for us to walk in any path but what he has trodden before us, though it seem rather a maze than a way for travellers to walk in that would all pass on in their journey.

His first section is entitled, "Light and Spirit," the pretence whereof he treats after his manner, and cashiers from giving any such advantage as is inquired after. But neither yet are we arrived to any concernment of Protestants. That which they plead as their advantage is not the empty names of light and spirit, but the truth of Christ revealed in the Scripture. I know there are not a few who have impertinently used these good words and Scripture expressions, which yet ought no more to be scoffed at by others than abused by them; but that any have made the plea here pretended as to their settlement in religion, I know not. The truth is, if they have, it is no other upon the matter but what our author calls them unto. To a naked "Credo" he would reduce them; and that differs only from what seems to be the mind of them that plead light and spirit [in this], that he would have them resolve their faith irrationally into the authority of the church; they pretend to do it into the Scripture.

But what he aims to bring men unto, he justifies from the examples of Christians in ancient times, "who had to deal with Jews and Pagans, whose disputes were rational and weighty, and puzzled the wisest of the clergy to answer. So that after all their ratiocination ended, whether it sufficed or no, they still concluded with this one word, 'Credo;' which in logic and philosophy was a weak answer, but in religion the best and only one to be made." What could be spoken more untruly, more contumeliously, or more to the reproach of Christian religion, I cannot imagine. It is true, indeed, that as to the resolution, satisfaction, and settlement of their own souls, Christians always built their faith [on], and resolved it into, the authority of God in his word; but that they opposed their naked "Credo" to the disputes of Jews or Pagans, or rested in that for a solution of their objections, is heavenly-wide,—as far from truth ὡς οὐρανός ἐστ' ἀπὸ γαίης. I wonder any man who hath ever seen, or almost heard, of the disputes and discourses of Justin Martyr, Clemens Alexandrinus, Origen, Theophilus Antiochenus, Athenagoras, Tertullian, Lactantius, Chrysostom, Austin, Theodoret, and innumerable others, proving the faith of the Christian religion against the Jews from Scripture, and the reasonableness of it against the Pagans, with the folly and foppery of theirs, could on any account be induced to cast out such a reproach against them. But it seems "jacta est alea," and we must go on; and, therefore, to carry on the design of bringing us all to a naked "Credo," resolved into the authority of the present church,—a thing never heard of, spoken of, nor, that it appears, dreamed of, by any of the ancient Christians,—the objections of the Jews against the Christian religion are brought on the stage, and an inquiry made how they can be satisfactorily answered. His words are, p. 142, "In any age of the Christian church a Jew might say thus to the Christians then living, 'Your Lord and Master was born a Jew, and under the jurisdiction of the high priests; these he opposed, and taught a religion contrary to Moses (otherwise how comes there to be a faction?) But how could he justly do it? no human power is of force against God's, who spake (as you also grant) by Moses and the prophets; and divine power it could not be, for God is not contrary to himself. And although your Lord might say, as indeed he did, that Moses spake of him as of a prophet to come, greater than himself, yet who shall judge that such a thing was meant of his person? For since that prophet is neither specified by his name nor characteristical properties' (well said, Jew), 'who could say it was he more than any other to come? And if there were a greater to come than Moses were, surely born a Jew, he would, being come into the world, rather exalt that law to more ample glory than diminish it. And if you will farther contest that such a prophet was to abrogate the first law and bring in a new one, who shall judge in this case?—the whole church of the Hebrews, who never dreamed of any such thing? or one member thereof who was born a subject to their judgments?' This," saith he, "is the great œcumenical difficulty; and he that in any age of Christianity could either answer it, or find any bulwark to set against it, so that it should do no harm, would easily either salve or prevent all other difficulties," etc.

The difficulty, as is evident, lay in this, that the authority and judgment of the whole church of the Hebrews lay against Christ and the gospel. That church, when Christ conversed on earth, was a true church of God, the only church on earth, and had been so for two thousand years, without interruption in itself, without competition from any other. It had its high priest, confessedly instituted by

God himself, in an orderly succession to those days. The interpretation of Scripture, it pretended, was trusted with it alone; and traditions they had good store, whose original they pleaded from Moses himself, directing them in that interpretation. Christ and his apostles, whom they looked upon as poor, ignorant, contemptible persons, came and preached a doctrine which that church determined utterly contrary to the Scripture and their traditions. What shall now be answered to their authority, which was unquestionably all that ever was, or shall be, intrusted with any church on the earth? Our author tells us that this great "argument of the Jews could not be any way warded or put by, but by recourse unto the church's infallibility," p. 146; which, "sit verbo venia," is so ridiculous a pretence, as I wonder how any block in his way could cause him to stumble upon it. What church, I pray?—the church of Christians? When that argument was first used by the Jews against Christ himself, it was not yet founded; and if an absolute infallibility be supposed in the church, without respect to her adherence to the rule of infallibility, I dare boldly pronounce that argument indissoluble, and that all Christian religion must be thereon discarded. If the Jewish church,—which had at that day as great church power and prerogative as any church hath or can have,—were infallible in her judgment that she made of Christ and his doctrine, there remains nothing but that we renounce both him and it, and turn either Jews or Pagans, as we were of old. Here, then, by our author's confession, lies a plain judgment and definition of the only church of God in the world against Christ and his doctrine; and it is certainly incumbent on us to see how it may be waived. And this, I suppose, we cannot better be instructed in than by considering what was answered unto it by Christ himself, his apostles, and those that succeeded them in the profession of the faith of the gospel. 1. For Christ himself: it is certain he pleaded his miracles, the works which he wrought, and the doctrine that he revealed; but withal, as to the Jews, with whom he had to do, he pleads the Scriptures, Moses and the prophets, and offers himself and his doctrine to be tried, to stand or fall by their verdict, John v. 39, 46; Matt. xxii. 43; Luke xxiv. 27. I say, besides the testimony of his works and doctrine, to their authority of the church he opposeth that of the Scripture, which he knew the other ought to give place unto. And it is most vainly pretended by our author, in the behalf of the Jews, that the Messiah, or great prophet to come, was not in the Scripture specified by such characteristical properties as made it evident that Jesus was the Messiah; all the descriptions given of the one, and they innumerable, undeniably centring in the other. 2. The same course steered the apostle Peter, Acts ii. iii., and expressly in his second epistle, chap. i. 17–19; and Paul, Acts xiii. 16, 17, etc. And of Apollos, who openly disputed with the Jews upon this argument, it is said that he "mightily convinced the Jews, publicly, showing by the Scriptures that Jesus is the Christ," Acts xviii. 28. And Paul persuaded the Jews concerning Jesus at Rome, "both out of the law of Moses, and out of the prophets, from morning till evening," Acts xxviii. 23; concerning which labour and disputation the censure of our author, p. 149, is very remarkable. "There can be no hope," saith he, "of satisfying a querent, or convincing an opponent, in any point of Christianity, unless he will submit to the splendour of Christ's authority in his own person, and the church descended from him; which I take to be the reason why some of the Jews in Rome, when St Paul laboured so much to persuade Christ out of Moses and the prophets, believed in him, and some did not." Both the coherence of the words and design of the preface, and his whole scope, manifest his meaning to be, "That no more believed on him, or that some disbelieved," notwithstanding all the pains he took with them.

And what was the reason of this failure? Why, St Paul fixed on an unsuitable means of persuading them,—namely, Moses and the prophets,—when he should have made use of the authority of the church. Vain and bold man, that dares oppose his prejudices to the Spirit and wisdom of Christ in that great and holy apostle, and that in a way and work wherein he had the express pattern and example of his Master! If this be the spirit that rules in the Roman synagogue, that so puffs up men in their fleshly minds as to make them think themselves wiser than Christ and his apostles, I doubt not but men will every day find cause to rejoice that it is cast out of them, and be watchful that it returns to possess them no more. But this is that which galls the man: the difficulty which he proposeth as insoluble by any ways but an acquiescing in the authority of the present church, he finds assoiled in Scripture on other principles. This makes him fall foul on St Paul, whom he finds most frequent in answering it from Scripture; not considering that at the same time he accuseth St Peter of the like folly, though he pretend for him a greater reverence. However, this may be said in defence of St Paul, that by his arguments about Christ and the gospel from Moses and the prophets, many thousands of Jews, all the world over, were converted to the faith; when it is hard to meet with an instance of one in an age that will any way take notice of the authority of the Roman church. But to return. This was the constant way used by the apostles of answering that great difficulty pleaded by our author from the authority of the Hebrew church: They called the Jews to the Scripture, the plain texts and contexts of Moses and the prophets, opposing them to all their church's real or pretended authority, and all her interpretations pretended to be received by tradition from of old: so fixing this for a perpetual standing rule to all generations,—That the doctrine of the church is to be examined by the Scripture;

and where it is found contradictory of it, her authority is of no value at all, it being annexed unto her attendance on that rule. But it may be replied, that "the church in the days of the apostles was not yet settled, nor made firm enough to bear the weight that now may be laid upon it, as our author affirms, p. 149; so that now the great resolve of all doubts must be immediately upon the authority of the present church: after that was once well cleared, the fathers of old pleaded that only in this case, and removed the objections of the Jews by that alone." I am persuaded, though our author be a great admirer of the present church, he is not such a stranger to antiquity as to believe any such thing. Is the authority of the church pleaded by Justin Martyr, in that famous dispute with Trypho the Jew, wherein these very objections instanced by our author are thoroughly canvassed? Doth he not throughout his whole disputation prove out of the Scriptures, and them alone, that Jesus was the Christ, and his doctrine agreeable unto them? Is any such thing pleaded by Origen, Tertullian, Chrysostom, or any one that had to deal with the Jews? Do they not wholly persist in the way traced for them by Paul, Peter, and Apollos, mightily convincing the Jews out of Scripture? Let him consult their answers; he will not find them such poor, empty, jejune discourses as that he supposes they might make use of, p. 148; and to the proofs whereof, by texts of Scripture, he says the rabbis could answer by another interpretation of them. He will find another spirit breathing in their writings, another efficacy in their arguments, and other evidence in their testimonies, than it seems he is acquainted with, and such as all the rabbis in the world are not able to withstand. And I know full well that these insinuations, that Christians are not able justifiably to convince, confute, and stop the mouths of Jews from the Scripture, would have been abhorred as the highest piece of blasphemy by the whole ancient church of Christ; and it is meet it should be so still by all Christians.

Is there no way left to deny pretences of light and spirit but by proclaiming, to the great scandal of Christianity, that we cannot answer the exceptions of Jews unto the person and doctrine of our Saviour out of the Scriptures? And hath Rome need of these bold sallies against the vitals of religion? Is she no other way capable of a defence? Better she perished ten thousand times than that any such reproach should be justly cast on the Lord Jesus Christ and his gospel. But whatever our author thinks of himself, I have very good ground to conjecture that he hath very little acquaintance with Judaical antiquity, learning, or arguments, nor very much with the Scripture; and may possibly deserve on that account some excuse, if he thought those exceptions insoluble which more learned men than himself know how to answer and remove without any considerable trouble.

This difficulty was fixed on by our author, that upon it there might be stated a certain retreat and assured way of establishment against all of the like nature. This he assigns to be the authority of the present church; Protestants, the Scripture,—wherein, as to the instance chosen out as most pressing, we have the concurrent suffrage of Christ, his apostles, and all the ancient Christians: so that we need not any farther to consider the pretended pleas of light and spirit which he hath made use of, as the orator desired his dialogist would have insisted on the stories of Cerberus and Cocytus, that he might have showed his skill and activity in their confutation. For what he begs in the way, as to the constitution of St Peter and his successors in the rule of the church, as he produceth no other proof for it but that doughty one, that it must needs be so; so, if it were granted him, he may easily perceive, by the instance of the Judaical church, that himself thought good to insist upon, that it will not avail him in his plea against the final resolution of our faith into the Scripture, as its senses are proposed by the ministry of the church, and rationally conceived or understood.

CHAPTER IX.

Protestant Pleas.

HIS sect. xiii., p. 155, entitled, "Independent and Presbyterians' Pleas," is a merry one. The whole design of it seems to be, to make himself and others sport with the miscarriages of men in and about religion. Whether it be a good work or no, that day that is coming will discover. The Independents he divides into two parts,—Quakers and Anabaptists. Quakers he begins withal, and longer insists upon; being, as he saith, well read in their books, and acquainted with their persons. Some commendation he gives them, so far as it may serve to the disparagement of others, and then falls into a fit of quaking, so expressly imitating them in their discourses, that I fear he will confirm some in their surmises, that such as he both set them on work and afterward assisted them in it. For my part, having undertaken only the defence of Protestancy and Protestants, I am altogether unconcerned in the entertainment he hath provided for his readers in this personating of a Quaker; which he hath better done, and kept a better decorum in, than in his personating of a Protestant,—a thing, in the beginning of his discourse, he pretended unto. The Anabaptists, as far as I can perceive, he had not meddled with, unless it had been to get an advantage of venting his petty answer to an argument against infant baptism; but the truth is, if the Anabaptists had no other objections against infant baptism, nor Protestants no better answers to their objections, than what are mentioned here by our author, it were no great matter what become of the controversy; but it is merriment, not disputation, that he is designing, and I shall leave him to the solace of his own fancies.

No otherwise, in the next place, doth he deal with the Presbyterians, in personating of whom he pours out a long senseless rhapsody of words, many insignificant expressions, vehement exclamations, and uncouth terms, such as, to do them right, I never heard uttered by them in preaching, though I have heard many of them; nor read written by them, though, I suppose, I have perused at least as many of their books as our author hath done of the Quakers'. Any one with half an eye may see what it is that galls the man and his party, —which, whether he hath done wisely to discover, his *δεύτεραι φροντίδες* will inform him,—that is, the preaching of all sorts of Protestants, that he declares himself to be most perplexed with; and therefore most labours to expose it to reproach and obloquy. And herein he deals with us as in many of their stories their demoniacs do with their exorcists,—discover which relic, or which saint's name, or other engine in that bustle, most afflicts them, that so they may be paid more to the purpose. Somewhat we may learn from hence: "Fas est et ab hoste doceri." But he will make the Presbyterians amends for all the scorn he endeavours to expose them to, by affirming, when he hath assigned a senseless harangue of words unto them, that the Protestants are not able to answer their objections. Certainly, if the Presbyterians are such pitiful souls as not to be able any better to defend their cause than they are represented by him here to do, those Protestants are beneath all consideration who are not able to deal and grapple with them. And this is as it should be. Roman Catholics are wise, learned, holy, angelical, seraphical persons; all others, ignorant dolts, that can scarce say bo to a goose. These things, considered in themselves, are unserious trifles, but "seria ducunt." We shall see presently whither all this lurry tends; for the sting of this whole discourse is fixed in the Scripture.

Of the same importance is the next section, p. 170, entitled "Protestants' Pro and Con," wherein the differences that are amongst many in these nations are notably exagitated. I presume, in the intension of his mind upon his present design, he forgot that, by a new change of name, the same things may be uttered, the same words used, of and concerning Christians in general, ever since almost that name was known in the world. Was there any thing more frequent among the Pagans of old, than to object to Christians their differences and endless disputes? I wish our author would but consider that which remains of the discourse of Celsus on this subject; particularly his charge on them, that at their beginnings, and whilst they were few, they agreed well enough; but after they increased, and were dispersed into several nations, they were everywhere at variance among themselves, whereas all sorts of men were at peace before their pretended reformation of the worship of God: and he will find in it the sum of this and the four following sections, to the end of this chapter. And if he will but add so much to his pains as to peruse the excellent answers of Origen in his third book, he will, if not be persuaded to desist from urging the objections of Celsus, yet discern what is expected from him to reply unto if he persist in his way. But if we may suppose that he hath not that respect for the honour of the first Christians, methinks the intestine irreconcilable brawls of his own mother's children should somewhat allay his heat and confidence in charging endless differences upon Protestants, of whom only I speak. Yea, but you will say, "They have a certain means of ending their controversies; Protestants have none." And have they so?—the more shame for them to trouble themselves and others, from one generation unto another, with disputes and controversies, that have such a ready way to end them when they please: and Protestants are the more to be pitied, who perhaps are ready, some of them at least, as far as they are able, to live at peace. But why have not Protestants a sure and safe way to issue all their differences? "Why! because every one is judge himself, and they have no umpire in whose decision they are bound to acquiesce." I pray, who told you so? Is it not the fundamental principle of Protestantism, that the Scripture determines all things necessary unto faith and obedience, and that in that determination ought all men to acquiesce? I know few Roman Catholics have the prudence or the patience to understand what Protestancy is; and certain it is, that those who take up their knowledge of it from the discourses and writings of such gentlemen as our author, know very little of it, if any thing at all: and those who do at any time get leave to read the books of Protestants, seem to be so filled with prejudices against them, and to be so biassed by corrupt affections, that they seldom come to a true apprehension of their meanings; for who so blind as he that will not see? Protestants tell them that the Scripture contains all things necessary to be believed and practised in the worship of God, and those proposed with that perspicuity and clearness which became the wisdom of its author, who intended to instruct men by it in the knowledge of them; and in this word and rule, say they, are all men to rest and acquiesce. But says our author, "Why then do they not so? why are they at such feuds and differences amongst themselves?" Is this, in truth, his business? Is it Protestants he blames, and not Protestancy? men's miscarriages, and not their rule's imperfection? If it be so, I crave his pardon for having troubled him thus far. To defend Protestants for not answering the principles of their profession is a task too hard for me to undertake, nor do I at all like the business; let him lay on blame still, until I say, Hold. It may be we shall grow wiser by his reviling, as Monica was cured of her intemperance by the reproach of a servant. But I would fain prevail with these gentlemen, for their own sakes, not to cast that blame which is due to us upon the holy and perfect word of God. We do not say, nor ever did, that whoever acknowledgeth the Scripture to be a perfect rule must upon necessity understand perfectly all that is contained in it; that he is presently freed from all darkness, prejudices, corrupt affections, and enabled to judge perfectly and infallibly of every truth contained in it, or deduced from it. These causes of our differences belong to individual persons, not to our common rule; and if, because no men are absolutely perfect, and some are very perverse and froward, we should throw away our rule, the blessed word of God, and run to the pope for rule and guidance, it is all one as if at noonday, because some are blind and miss their way, and some are drunk and stagger out of it, and others are variously enticed to leave it, we should all conspire to wish the sun out of the firmament, that we might follow a Will-with-a-wisp.

I know not what in general needs to be added farther to this section; the mistake of it is palpable. Some particular passages may be remarked in it before we proceed: Page 173, he pronounceth a heavy doom on the prelate Protestants, making them prevaricators, impostors, reprobates;—a hard sentence, but that it is hoped it will prove like the flying bird, and curse causeless! But what is the matter? "Why, in dealing with the Presbyterians, they are forced to make use of those popish principles which themselves at first rejected, and so, building them up again, by the apostle's rule deserve no better terms." But what, I pray, are they? "Why, the difference betwixt clergy and laity, the efficacy of episcopal ordination, and the authority of a visible church, which all men are to obey." But there are two things our author needs to prove to make good his charge,—first, That these are popish principles; secondly, That as such they were at any time cast down and destroyed by prelate Protestants. I fear his mind was gone a little astray, or that he had been lately among the Quakers, when he hammered this charge against prelate Protestants; for as these have been their constant principles ever since the beginning of the Reformation, so they have as constantly maintained that, in their true and proper sense, they are not popish. Nor is the difference about these things, between any Protestants whatever, any more than verbal. For those terms of *clergy* and *laity*, because they had been abused in the Papacy, though anciently used, some have objected against them; but for the things signified by them,—namely, that in the church there are some teachers, some to be taught, bishops and flocks, pastors and people,—no Protestant ever questioned. Our author, then, doth but cut out work for himself, without order from any Protestant, when he sets up an excuse for this change in them by a relinquishment of their first principles, and re-assuming popish ones for their defence against the Presbyterians. He that set him a-work may pay him his wages. Protestants only tell him that what was never done needs never be excused.

Nor will they give him any more thanks for the plea he interposes in the behalf of episcopacy against Presbyterians and Independents, being interwoven with a plea for the Papacy, and managed by such arguments as end in the exaltation of the Roman see; and that partly because they know that their adversaries will be easily able to disprove the feigned monarchical government of the church under one pope, and to prove that that fancy really everts the true and only monarchical state of the church in reference to Christ, knowing that monarchy doth not signify two heads, but one; and partly because they have better arguments of their own to plead for episcopacy than those that he suggests here unto them, or than any man in the world can supply them with, who thinks there is no communication of authority from Christ to any on the earth but by the hands of the pope. So that upon the whole matter they desire him that he would attend his own business, and not immix their cause in the least with his, which tends so much to their weakening and disadvantage. If this may be granted, which is but reasonable, they will not much be troubled about his commendation of the pope, p. 178, as the substitute of Christ, our only visible pastor, the chief bishop of the Catholic church, presiding, ruling, and directing in the place of Christ, and the like eulogiums; being resolved, when he goes about to prove any thing that he says, that they will consider of it. But he must be better known to them than he is, before they will believe him on his bare word in things of such importance; and some suppose that the more he is known, the less he will be believed. But that he may not for the present think himself neglected, we will run over the heads of his plea, pretended for episcopacy, really to assert the papal sovereignty. First, he pleads, "That the Christian church was first monarchical, under one sovereign bishop, when Christ, who founded it, was upon the earth." True; and so it is still. There is one sheepfold, one shepherd and bishop of our souls; he that was then bodily present having promised that presence of himself with his church to the end of the world, wherein he continues its one sovereign bishop. And although the apostles after him had an equality of power in the church among themselves, as bishops after them have also, yet this doth not denominate the government of the church aristocratical, no more than the equality of the lords in parliament can denominate the government of this kingdom to be so. The denomination of any rule is from him or them in whom the sovereignty doth reside, not from any subordinate rulers. So is the rule of the church monarchical. The subversion of this episcopacy, we acknowledge, subverts the whole polity of the church, and so all her laws and rule; with the guilt whereof Protestants charge the Romanists. He adds, "It will not suffice to say that the church is still under its head, Christ, who, being in heaven, hath his spiritual influences over it." It will not indeed; but yet we suppose that his presence with it by his Spirit and laws will suffice? Why should it not? "Because the true church of Christ must have the very same head she had at first, or else she cannot be the same body." Very good, and so she hath; the very same Christ that was crucified for her, and not another. "But that head was man-God, personally present in both his natures here on earth." But is he not, I pray, the same man-God still? the same Christ, though the manner of his presence be altered? This is strange, that, being the same as he was, and being present still, one circumstance of the manner of his presence should hinder him from being the same head. I cannot understand the logic, reason, nor policy of this inference. Suppose we should on these trifling instances exclude Jesus Christ, "who is the same yesterday, to-day, and for ever," from being the same head of his church as he was, will the pope supply his room? Is he the same head that Christ was? Is he God-man bodily present? or what would you have us to conclude? "A visible head or bishop if the church hath not now over her, as at first she had, she is not the same she was; and, consequently, in the way to ruin." This, too, much alters the question: at first it was, that she must have the same head she had at first, or she is not the same; now, that she must have another head that is not the same, or she is not the same, for the pope is not Jesus Christ. These arguings hang together like a rope of sand; and what is built on this foundation (which, indeed, is so weak that I am ashamed farther to contend with it) will of its own accord fall to the ground.

CHAPTER X.

Scripture, and new principles.

The next paragraph, p. 182, is a naughty one. A business it is spent in and about that I have now often advised our author to meddle with no more. If he will not for the future take advice, I cannot help it; I have showed my good-will towards him. It is his debasing of the Scripture and its authority which I intend. This, with the intertexture of some other gentle suppositions, is the subject of this and the following section. And, because I will not tire myself and reader in tracing what seems of concernment in this discourse, backward and forward, up and down, as it is by him dispersed and disposed to his best advantage in dealing with unwary men, I shall draw out the principles of it; that he may know them wherever he meets them, though never so much masked and disguised, or never so lightly touched on; and also what judgment to pass upon them. Their foundation being so taken away, these sections, if I mistake not, will sink of themselves.

Some of these principles are coincident with those general ones insisted on in the entrance of our discourse; others of them are peculiar to the design of these paragraphs. The first I shall only point unto, the latter briefly discuss:—

1. It is supposed, in the whole discourse of these sections, that from the Roman church, so stated as now it is, or from the pope, we here in England first received the gospel, which is the Romanists' own religion, and theirs, by donation from them, whom they have here pleased to accommodate with it. This animates the whole, and is, besides, the special life of almost every sentence. A lifeless life! for that there is not a syllable of truth in it hath been declared before; nor, were it so that by the ministry of the Roman church of old the faith was first planted in these nations, would that one inch promote our author's pretensions, unless he could prove that they did not afterward lose, or corrupt at least, that which they communicated unto us; which he knows to be the thing in question, and not to be granted upon request, though made in never so handsome words. To say, then, "The gospel is the Romanists' own religion, from them you had it; you contend about that which is none of your own; hear them whose it is, from whom you had it, who have the precedency before you," is but to set up scarecrows to fright fools and children. Men who have any understanding of things past know that all this bluster and noise comes from emptiness of any solid matter or substance to be used in the case.

2. It is also doughtily supposed, "That whatever is spoken of the church in the Scripture belongs to the Roman church, and that alone:" the privileges, the authority, the glory of the church, are all theirs; as the madman at Athens thought all the ships to be his that came into the harbour. I suppose he will not contend but that, if you deny him this, all that he hath said besides is to little purpose. And I believe he cannot but take it ill that any of his readers should

call him to an account in that which he everywhere puts out of question. But this he knew well enough that all Protestants deny,—that they grant no one privilege of the catholic church, as such, to belong to the Roman. All that any of them will allow her, is but to be a putrid, corrupt member of it; some say cut off, dead and rotten. But yet that the catholic church and the Roman are the same must be believed, or you spoil all his market. "The church is before the gospel, gives testimony unto it; none could know it but by her authority, nothing can be accepted as such but what she sets her seals unto: so that to destroy the church is to destroy the gospel"! What then, I pray? Suppose all this, and all the rest of his assertions about the church, pp. 199, 200, etc., to be true, as some of them are most blasphemously false, yet what is all this to his purpose? "Why, this is the Roman church of which all these things are spoken." It may be the Roman church, indeed, of which much of it is spoken, even all that is sinfully derogatory to the glory of Christ and his apostles; upon whom and whose authority the church is built, and not their authority on it, Eph. ii. 19, 20. But what is truly spoken in the Scripture of the church doth no more belong to the Roman than to the least assembly of believers under heaven, wherein the essence of a true church is preserved, if it belongs unto it at all; and yet this rude pretence and palpable artifice is the main engine, in this section, applied to the removal of men from the basis of the Scripture. The church, the church! the Roman church, the Roman church! And these, forsooth, are supposed to be one and the same; and the pope to have monopolized all the privileges of the church, contrary to express statute-law of the gospel. Hence he pretends, that if to go out from the catholic be evil, then not to come into the Roman is evil; when, indeed, the most ready way to go out of the catholic is to go into the Roman.

3. Moreover, it is taken for granted, "That the Roman church is every way what it was when first planted." Indeed, if it were so, it would deserve as much particular respect as any church of any city in the world; and that would be all: as it is, the case is altered. But its *unalteredness* being added to the former supposition of its *oneliness* and *catholicism*, it is easy to see what sweet work a witty man, as our author is, may make with this church among good company. Many and many a time have the Romanists attempted to prove these things; but, failing in their attempt, they think it now reasonable to take them for granted. The religion they now profess must be that which first entered England. "And there," saith our author, "it continued in peace for a thousand years;" when the truth is, after the entrance of their religion,—that is, the corruption of Christianity by papal usurpations,—these nations never passed one age without tumults,

turmoils, contentions, disorders; nor many without wars, blood, and devastations;—and those arising from the principles of their religion.

4. To this is added, "That the Bible is the pope's own book, which none can lay claim to but by and from him." This will be found to be a doubtful assertion, and it will be difficult to conclude aright concerning it. He that shall consider what a worthy person the pope is represented to be by our author, especially in his just dealing and mercifulness, so that "he never did any man wrong," and shall take notice how many he hath caused to be burned to death for having and using the Bible without his consent, must need suppose that it is his book; for surely his heavenly mind would not have admitted of a provocation to such severity unless they had stolen his goods out of his possession. But, on the other side, he that shall weigh aright his vilifying and undervaluing of it, his preferring himself and church before and above it,—seeing we are all apt to set a high price upon that which is our own,—may be ready to question whether indeed he have such a property in it as is pretended. Having somewhat else to do, I shall not interpose myself in this difference, nor attempt to determine this difficulty, but leave it as I find it, free for every man to think as he seeth cause.

5. But that which is the chief ingredient of these sections is the plea, "That we know not the Scripture to be the word of God but by the church,—that is, the present church of Rome;" which he manageth by urging sundry objections against it, and difficulties which men meet withal in their inquiry whether it be so or no. Nor content with that plea alone, he interweaves in his discourse many expressions and comparisons, tending directly to the slighting and contempt both of its penmen and matter; which is said to be "laws, poems, sermons, histories, letters, visions, several fancies, in a diversity of composure; the whole a book whereby men may as well prove their negative in denying the immortality of the soul, heaven, or hell, or any other thing, which, by reason of many intricacies, are very difficult, if not impossible at all to be understood." See pp. 190–192, etc. Concerning all which I desire to know whether our author be in good earnest or no? or whether he thinks as he writes? or whether he would only have others to believe what he writes, that he may serve his turn upon their credulity? If he be in good earnest, indeed, he calls us to an easy, welcome employment,—namely, to defend the holy word of God, and the wisdom of God in it, from such slight and trivial exceptions as those he lays against them. This path is so trodden for us by the ancients, in their answers to the more weighty objections of his predecessors in this work, the Pagans, that we cannot well err or faint in it. If we are called to this task,—namely, to prove that we can know and believe the Scripture to be

the word of God without any respect to the authority or testimony of the present church of Rome; that no man can believe it to be so, with faith divine and supernatural, upon that testimony alone; that the whole counsel of God, in all things to be believed or done, in order to our last end, is clearly delivered in it, and that the composure of it is a work of infinite wisdom, suited to the end designed to be accomplished by it; that no difficulties in the interpretation of particular places hinder the whole from being a complete and perfect rule of faith and obedience,—we shall most willingly undertake it, as knowing it to be as honourable a service and employment as any of the sons of men can in this world be called unto. If, indeed, himself be otherwise minded, and believe not what he says, but only intend to entangle men by his sophistry, so as to render them pliable unto his farther intention, I must yet once more persuade him to desist from this course. It doth not become an ingenuous man, much less a Christian, and one that boasts of so much mortification as he doth, to juggle thus with the things of God. In the meantime, his reader may take notice, that so long as he is able to defend the authority, excellency, and usefulness of the Scripture, this man had nothing to say to him, as to the change of his religion from Protestancy to Popery; and when men will be persuaded to let that go, as a thing uncertain, dubious, useless, it matters not much where they go themselves. And for our author, methinks, if not for reverence to Christ, whose book we know the Scriptures to be, yet for the devotion he bears the pope, whose book he says it is, he might learn to treat it with a little more respect, or at least prevail with him to send out a book not liable to so many exceptions as this is pretended to be. However, this I know, that though his pretence be to make men Papists, the course he takes is the readiest in the world to make them atheists; and whether that will serve his turn or no as well as the other, I know not.

6. We have not yet done with the Scripture. "That the taking it for the only rule of faith, the only determiner of differences, is the only cause of all our differences, and which keeps us in a condition of having them endless," is also pretended and pleaded. But how shall we know this to be so? Christ and his apostles were absolutely of another mind; and so were Moses and the prophets before them. The ancient fathers of the primitive church walked in their steps, and umpired all differences in religion by the Scriptures,—opposing, confuting, and condemning errors and heresies by them; preserving through their guidance the unity of the Spirit in the bond of peace. In these latter days of the world, which surely are none of the best, we have a few unknown persons, come from Rome, would persuade us that the Scripture and the use of it is the cause of all our differ-

ences, and the means of making them endless. But why so, I pray? Doth it teach us to differ and contend? Doth it speak contradictions, and set us at variance? Is there any spirit of dissension breathing in it? Doth it not deliver what it commands us to understand so as it may be understood? Is there any thing needful for us to know in the things of God but what it reveals? Who can tell us what that is? "But do we not see, 'de facto,' what differences there are amongst you who pretend all of you to be guided by Scripture?" Yea, and we see also what surfeitings and drunkenness there are in the world, but yet do not think bread, meat, and drink to be the causes of them; and yet they are to the full as much so as the Scriptures are of our differences. Pray, sir, do not think that sober men will cast away their food and starve themselves, because you tell them that some continually abuse and surfeit on that very kind of food which they use. Nor will some men's abuse of it prevail with others to cast away the food of their souls, if they have any design to live eternally.

7. The great "safety and security that there is in committing ourselves, as to all the concernments of religion, unto the guidance, rule, and conduct of the pope," is another great principle of this discourse. And here our author falls into a deep admiration of the pope's "dexterity in keeping all his subjects in peace and unity and subjection to him, there being no danger to any one for forsaking him but only that of excommunication." The contest is between the Scripture and the pope. Protestants say, the safest way for men, in reference to their eternal condition, is to believe the Scripture and rest therein; the Romanists say the same of the pope. Which will prove the best course, methinks, should not be hard to determine. All Christians in the world ever did agree that the Scripture is the certain, infallible word of God, given by him on purpose to reveal his mind and will unto us. About the pope there were great contests ever since he was first taken notice of in the world. Nothing, I confess, little or low is spoken of him. Some say he is the head and spouse of the church, the vicar of Christ, the successor of Peter, the supreme moderator of Christians, the infallible judge of controversies, and the like; others, again, that he is antichrist, the man of sin, a cruel tyrant and persecutor, the evil servant characterized, Matt. xxiv. 48–51. But all, as far as I can gather, agree that he is a man: I mean, that almost all popes have been so; for about every individual there is not the like consent. Now, the question is, whether we shall rest in the authority and word of God, or in the authority and word of a man, as the pope is confessed to be? and whether is like to yield us more security in our affiance? This being such another difficult matter and case as that before mentioned, about the Bible being the pope's book, shall not be by me decided, but left to the judgment of wiser men. In

the meantime, for his feat of government, it is partly known what it is; as also what an influence into the effects of peace mentioned that gentle means of excommunication hath had. I know one that used, in the late times, to say of the excommunication in Scotland, "he would not care for their devil, were it not for his horn;" and I suppose had not papal excommunication been always attended with wars, blood, seditions, conspiracies, depositions and murders of kings, fire and fagot, according to the extent of their power, it would have been less effectual than our author pretends it to have been. Sir, do but give Christians the liberty that Christ hath purchased for them,—lay down your carnal weapons, your whips, racks, prisons, halters, swords, fagots, with your unchristian subtleties, slanders, and fleshly machinations,—and we and you shall quickly see what will become of your papal peace and power.

These are the goodly principles, the honest suppositions, of the discourse which our author ends his third book withal. It could not but have been a tedious thing to take them up by pieces, as they lay scattered up and down, like the limbs of Medeia's brother, cast in the way to retard her pursuers. The reader may now take a view of them together, and thence of all that is offered to persuade him to a relinquishment of his present profession and religion. For the stories, comparisons, jests, sarcasms, that are intermixed with them, I suppose he will know how to turn them to another use.

Some very few particulars need only to be remarked; as,—

1. "No man can say what ill Popery did in the world until Henry the Eighth's days." Strange! when it is not only openly accused, but proved guilty of almost all the evil that was in the Christian world in those days; particularly of corrupting the doctrine and worship of the gospel, and debauching the lives of Christians.

2. "With the Roman Catholics unity ever dwelt." Never! the very name of Roman Catholic, appropriating catholicism to Romanism, is destructive of all gospel unity.

3. "Some Protestants say they love the persons of the Romanists, but hate their religion; the reason is plain,—they know the one and not the other." No, they know them both; and the pretence that people are kept with, as from [not] knowing what the religion of the Romanists is, is vain, untrue; and as to what colour can possibly be given unto it, such an infant in comparison of that vast giant which of the same kind lives in the Romish territories, that it deserves not to be mentioned.

4. "Protestants are beholden to the Catholics" (that is, Romanists) "for their universities, benefices, books, pulpits, gospel." For some of them, not all; for the rest, as the Israelites were to the Egyptians for the tabernacle they built in the wilderness.

5. "The pope was anciently believed sole judge and general pastor over all." Prove it; ask the ancient fathers and councils whether they ever heard of any such thing? They will universally return their answer in the negative.

6. "The Scripture you received from the pope." Not at all, as hath been proved; but from Christ himself, by the ministry of the first planters of Christianity.

7. "You cannot believe the Scriptures to be the word of God but upon the authority of the church." We can and do upon the authority of God himself; and the influence of the church's ministry or authority into our believing concerns not the church of Rome.

8. "You account them that brought you the Scriptures as liars." No otherwise than as the Scripture affirms every man to be so; not in their ministry wherein they brought the word unto us.

9. "The gospel, separate from the church, can prove nothing." Yes, itself to be sent of God; and so doing is the foundation of the church.

Sundry other passages of the like nature might be remarked, if I could imagine any man would judge them worthy of consideration.

CHAPTER XI.

Story of religion.

THE fourth and last part of our author's discourse is spent in two stories,—one of religion, the other of himself. His first, of religion, is but a summary of what was diffused through the other parts of his treatise, being insinuated piecemeal, as he thought he could make any advantage of it to his purpose. Two things he aims to make his readers believe by it:—first, That we in these nations had our religion from Rome; and, secondly, That it was the same which is there now professed. Those whom he tells his tale unto are, as he professeth, such as are "ignorant of the coming in and progress of religion amongst us;" wherein he deals wisely and as became him, seeing he might easily assure himself that those who are acquainted before his information with the true state of these things, would give little credit to what he nakedly avers upon his own authority. For my part, I shall readily acknowledge, that for aught appears in this book, he is a better historian than a disputant; and hath more reason to trust to his faculty of telling a tale than managing of an argument. I confess, also, that a slight and superficial view of antiquity, especially as flourished over by some Roman legendaries, is the best advantage our adversaries have to work on, as a thorough, judicious search of it is fatal to their pretensions. He that, from the Scriptures and the writings extant of the first centuries, shall frame a true idea of the state and doctrine of the first churches, and then observe the adventitious accessions made to religion in the following ages, partly by men's own inventions, but chiefly by their borrowing from or imitation of the Jews and Pagans, will need very little light or help from artificial arguments to discover the defections of the Roman party, and the true means whereby that church arrived unto its present condition. To pursue this at large is not a work to be undertaken in this scambling chase. It hath been done by others; and those who are not unwilling to be at the cost and pains in the disquisition of the truth, which it is really worth, may easily know where to find it. Our present task is but to observe our author's motions, and to consider whether what he offers hath any efficacy towards that he aims at.

A triple conversion he assigns to this nation. The first by Joseph of Arimathea; about which, as to matter of fact, we have no contest[1]

[1] It was sufficient for our author's purpose to show that if, according to the statement in "Fiat Lux," Britain was indebted, in the first instance, to Joseph of Arimathea for a knowledge of the gospel, it is not Rome, but Palestine, that is entitled on such a ground to urge any claim to supremacy over the British churches. Subsequent inquiry has proved that no such degree of certainty attaches to the tradition as Dr Owen seems willing to concede to his opponent. The tradition is, that when the church at Jerusalem was dispersed by the persecution in which Stephen suffered martyrdom, Lazarus, Mary Magdalene, Martha, with her servant Marcella, a disciple of the name of Maximin, and Joseph of Arimathea, were placed on board of a vessel without sails, and that it was miraculously impelled and directed till it reached the haven of Marseilles in France. From Gaul Joseph is said to have been despatched by Philip on a mission to Britain, A.D. 63. He succeeded in converting many of its inhabitants to Christianity, obtained by royal grant land to the extent which could be included within twelve hides at Glastonbury, in Somersetshire, and built a wattled church,—the first erected for Christian worship in Britain. His staff, when stuck into the earth, took root, it is alleged, and grew into a species of thorn, which blossoms in winter, and still exists in the neighbourhood —an enduring memorial of the first evangelist who brought the gospel into this island. A famous abbey was afterwards erected, and, in virtue of its reputed antiquity, was held to prove the early origin of the British church; and precedence was therefore accorded to the English clergy over those of some other churches in the Council of Basle, A.D. 1434. The details of the legend on which this claim to high antiquity is founded are given by William of Malmesbury, who wrote in the twelfth century. It is repudiated and exposed as a monkish fiction by Bishop Stillingfleet, in his "Origines Britannicæ." Mosheim attributes it to the eagerness with which different nations vie with each other in magnifying the antiquity of their respective churches: the Gauls confounding a bishop of the same name, who lived at Paris during the second century, with Dionysius the Areopagite; and the Germans affirming that Eucharius, Valerius, and Maternus, of the third and fourth centuries, were contemporaries and companions of the apostle Peter; while the Britons, because the name was identical, would fain insist that the first Christian missionary who reached this country was Joseph of Arimathea.

The honour of having been the first to introduce the Christian faith into our island has also been claimed for James the son of Zebedee, who was killed by Herod, Acts xii. 2; and for Aristobulus, to whom, with his household, a salutation is addressed by Paul, Rom. xvi. 10. On the ground of some statements which occur in the martyrological calendar of the Greek church, Bishop Taylor and Dr Cave are inclined to believe that Simon Zelotes must have been in Britain. "But at last," it is said, "having

with him. That the gospel was preached here in the apostles' days, either by him or some other evangelist, is certain, and taken for granted on all hands; nor can our author pretend that it came hither from Rome, but grants it to have come immediately from Palestine. Whether this doth not overthrow the main of his plea in his whole discourse, concerning our dependence upon Rome for our religion, I leave to prudent men to judge. Thus far, then, we are equal. As the gospel came to Rome, so it came to England; to both from the same place, and by the same authority, the same ministry. All the question is, Whether religion they brought with them? that now

come to Britain, and enlightened many by the word of the gospel, being crucified and put to death by the unbelievers, he lies buried there."—Menologia Græca ad diem 10 Maii. According to the Roman martyrology, however, he suffered martyrdom in Persia. No definite conclusion seems likely to emerge from the sifting of authorities so vague and contradictory, unless it be the utter uncertainty of all such traditions.

Simon Metaphrastes, a writer of the tenth century, would have us to believe that Peter visited Britain. Baronius, perhaps from the wish, so natural to a Romanist, that every tradition tending to enhance the reputation of Peter, and to prove his connection with the western church, should be found true, extends credit to the story of Metaphrastes. It is accompanied, however, with details grossly inconsistent with authentic history, and is not supported by the testimony of any previous writer.

There is, however, some amount of historical evidence, which, if not conclusive, is at least entitled to respectful consideration, in favour of the notion that the Christian church was first planted in Britain by the apostle Paul. Four authorities are generally cited in order to justify this opinion,—Clemens Romanus, Eusebius, Jerome, and Theodoret. CLEMENS ("Epist. ad Corinth.," epist. i. cap. 5) speaks of Paul as "having preached the gospel in the east and the west, having come to the bounds of the west, —ἐπὶ τὸ τέρμα τῆς δύσεως,—and having testified before the rulers;" and immediately adds, "Thus he departed out of the world," etc. The question as to the precise import of this statement very much hinges on the interpretation to be affixed to the Greek words which we have just quoted. Dr Davidson (see his "Introduction to the New Testament," vol. ii. p. 98) sifts them very carefully, and doubts if they can be held to imply more than that Paul had reached Rome; while Neander founds upon them in proof that he must have visited Spain. In relation to the Corinthians, Rome might be the west intended by Clement; and had a region more to the west than Rome been intended by him, it is probable he would have spoken of Paul as having *gone*, not having *come*, to the "bounds of the west." Moreover, the statement of the apostolic father, in its scope and continuity, appears to identify the place where Paul bore his testimony before the rulers, and departed from this world, with "the boundary of the west," to which, by the preceding clause, he is represented as having come. These reasonings are of great weight in favour of the view which Dr Davidson adopts; but the strength of the phrase, τὸ τέρμα τῆς δύσεως, is hardly exhausted if we understand it to embrace a longitude not more distant from Corinth than Italy; and the intercourse of eastern nations with Spain was by no means so scanty and limited that the Corinthians, on perusing the letter of Clement, would naturally think of Rome as the extreme verge of the western world. The use of ἐλθὼν may be explained in relation to the point from which the apostle might have been viewed by Clement as commencing his journey. EUSEBIUS simply informs us, in his "Evangelical Demonstration" (lib. iii. cap. 7), that some of the apostolic body had crossed the seas ἐπὶ τὰς καλουμένας Βρεττανικὰς νήσους,—"to what are called the British islands." However valuable this testimony may be in proof of the early introduction of Christianity into Britain, it sheds no light on the question whether Paul was the founder of the British church. JEROME, too, commenting on Amos v., employs language far too indefinite to supply us with evidence on the point: "St Paul having been in Spain, went from one ocean to another." Then follows a comparison of Paul's labours to the Sun of Righteousness, "of whom it is said, that 'his going forth is from the end of the earth, and his circuit unto the ends of it.'" THEODORET gives the most distinct testimony which can be quoted from ancient writers on this subject: "St Paul,"

professed in England, or that of Rome? If this be determined, the business is at an issue. We are persuaded Joseph brought no other religion with him than what was taught by Peter and Paul, and the rest of the apostles and evangelists, in other parts of the world. What religion men taught "viva voce," in any age, is best known by their writings, if they left any behind them. No other way have the Romanists themselves, nor other do they use, in judging what was the doctrine of the fathers in the following ages. The writings of the apostles are still extant; by them alone can we judge of the doctrine that they preached. That doctrine, then, unquestionably taught

says he, after mentioning Spain, "preached salvation to the islands that lie in the ocean."—Vol. iv. Serm. 9. He makes a similar statement in his exposition of 2 Tim. iv. 17: "St Paul, after his release at Rome, went to Spain, and thence carried the light of the gospel to other nations."

If these testimonies do not prove that to the great apostle of the Gentiles in particular we are indebted for the first publication of the gospel in our island, they show that, coeval with the very origin of ecclesiastical history, a belief existed that within the first century, and even in the days of the apostles, Britain had been favoured, to some extent, with the light of divine revelation. If we discard, therefore, the tradition that the first evangelist in Britain was Joseph of Arimathea, to which Dr Owen seems willing to attach some importance, it is only to fall back upon an account of the introduction of the Christian religion into our country that has more of the weight and dignity of genuine history, and which supplies an answer more conclusive and satisfactory to the reasoning of his opponent in "Fiat Lux." The curious incident recorded by Tacitus ("Annal." xiii. cap. 32) has been regarded as proving that even in the reign of Claudius, A. D. 41–54, there might have been Christians in Britain. Pomponia Græcina, on the return of her husband from Britain, was accused of being tainted with a "foreign superstition;" and if this be the Christian religion, as is commonly supposed, her zeal as a primitive Christian, in diffusing the gospel, is not likely to have slumbered in Britain, where human degradation around her would serve so powerfully to evoke it into operation; and distance from Rome might lead her to avow her principles more freely than in a city where the martyrdom of Christians was no uncommon spectacle. Tertullian also affirms ("Adver. Jud.," cap. vii.) that by his time those parts of Britain inaccessible to the arms of Rome had been penetrated by the gospel. Mosheim ("De Rebus Christianis," p. 205) alludes to this testimony in disparaging terms: "Rhetoricatur paullulum vir bonus." If, however, there were no precise and definite facts to sustain his assertion, it is difficult to conceive how Tertullian could indulge in a statement so specific as that the gospel had entered countries which had checked the triumphant advance of the Roman legions, and so likely to offend the pride of the Roman, to provoke a denial and recoil upon its author if untrue. Gildas, writing in the sixth century, states that the sun of Christianity shone upon our island about the time when Boadicea revolted against the authority of Rome, A. D. 62; and seems to intimate that the Roman soldiers, of whom there were forty-eight thousand in Britain, and whom it was unlawful to accuse of Christianity, had been the means of diffusing a knowledge of the gospel. Mosheim, it may be added, in the work to which we have already referred, holds that the balance of probability is in favour of the view which ascribes the first publication of Christianity in our country to an apostle, or some companion of the apostles; and as the British churches were in the first century independent of the Roman see, had the same forms of worship, and observed Easter at the same time, with the churches of Gaul, which doubtless had an Asiatic origin, the evidence is very strong that the gospel reached us originally by a course exclusive of Rome. The "Origines" of Stillingfleet were published two years after the death of Owen; and the latter, accordingly, not having the advantage of the sifting discussion which the story about Joseph of Arimathea has since undergone, might the more readily commit himself to a profession of belief in its truth. His own language, however, "Either by him or some other evangelist," is sufficiently guarded. The facts we have stated enhance the strength of the general argument; and the knowledge of them will adapt it to the present state of the

Joseph in Britain; and that doctrine (blessed be God!) is still owned and professed amongst us. All, and only what is contained in their writings, is received with us as necessary to salvation. This conversion was wholly ours. "Quod antiquissimum id verissimum." Being the first, it was certainly the best. Our author, indeed, tells us of crosses, shrines, oratories, altars, monasteries, vigils, embers, honouring of saints (you must suppose all in the Roman mode), making oblations and orisons for the dead; and that this was the religion in those days planted amongst us. If this be so, I wonder what we do to keep the Bible, which speaks not one word of that religion which the apostles and apostolical men preached. Strange, that in all their writings they should not once mention the main parts and duties of the doctrines and worship which they taught and propagated! that Paul, in none of his epistles, should in the least give the churches any direction in or concerning the things and ways wherein their worship principally consisted, and their devotion was chiefly exercised! But how comes our author to know that these things, in the Roman mode, were brought into England at the first entrance of Christianity? Would he would give us a little information from what writings or monuments of those times he acquired his knowledge. I know it is unreasonable to put an historian to his oath; but yet, unless he can plead that he received his acquaintance with things that are so long past by inspiration, as Moses wrote the story of the creation and ages before the flood, being destitute of any other monuments or testimony that might give evidence to what he says, I hope he will not be offended if we suspend our belief. "Solus enim hoc Ithacus nullo sub teste canebat," [Juv., xv. 26]. This first conversion, then, as was said, is wholly ours; it neither came from Rome, nor knew any thing of that which is the present religion of Rome, wherein they differ from us.

That which is termed our second conversion, is the preaching of Damianus and Fugatius, sent hither by Eleutherius, bishop of Rome, in the days of king Lucius, in the year 190, as our author saith; Beda, 156; Nauclerus, Baronius, 178; Henricus de Erfordia, 169, in the days of Aurelius or Commodus. I have many reasons to question this whole story;[1] and sundry parts of it, as those about the epistles

controversy with Romanists, who are fond of urging the claims of the Roman see to supremacy, on the ground that Britain is indebted to it for its first acquaintance with Christianity. Besides the fact, that not till after the lapse of centuries did popes arise to usurp an impious lordship over the church of Christ, all the history which can be summoned in adjudication of the dispute shows that the Christian religion, in its pure and primitive form, reached our island by a different channel.—Ed.

[1] Several learned authors, such as Usher, Stillingfleet, Hooker, and others, concur in thinking that some British prince of the name of Lucius must have rendered eminent service in diffusing the Christian faith in some part of Britain. In the attempt to determine one point only,—the year of his admission into the Christian church,—Usher has occasion to quote upwards of fifty Latin authorities; and though it appears that one of the two coins on which he partly relied as evidence that such a royal personage once

of Lucius and Eleutherius, are palpably fictitious. But let us grant that about those days Fugatius and Damianus came hither from Rome, and furthered the preaching of the gospel, which had taken footing here so long before, and was no doubt preserved amongst many,—we know God in his providence used many various ways for the propagating of his gospel; sometimes he did it by merchants, sometimes by soldiers, sometimes by captives, as a poor maid gave occasion to the conversion of a whole province,—what will hence ensue to the advantage of the pretensions of the Romanists? The religion they planted here was doubtless that (and no other) which was then professed at Rome, and in most other places in the world, with some small differences in outward observances, wherein each church took liberty to follow traditions or prudential reasonings of its own. When our author, or any for him, can make it appear that any thing material in that which we call Popery was in those days taught, believed, preached, or known among the churches of Christ, they will do somewhat to the purpose; but the present flourish about the catholic faith planted here, which no man ever denied, is to none at all. It was the old catholic faith we at first received, and therefore not the present Romish.

After those days, wherein this propagation of Christianity by the ministry of Fugatius and Damianus in this province is supposed to have fallen out, a sad decay in faith and holiness of life befell professors, not only in this nation, but, for the most part, all the world over; which especially took place after God had graciously, in the

held sway in southern Britain is now pronounced false and counterfeit, this amount of historic testimony cannot be summarily discarded. There is extreme difficulty in discriminating the actual truth of history from the copious growth of fiction which loads the monkish narratives, from which all information respecting Lucius must be drawn. That there was such a native prince in Britain, while Antoninus and Commodus were emperors, amounts almost to a certainty; and his dominions seem to have comprised the modern counties of Surrey, Sussex, Oxfordshire, and Gloucestershire. Baronius states that from an early period of his life he had shown an inclination to espouse and befriend the Christian cause, having already obtained a partial knowledge of it from its adherents in Britain. Some account reaching him of the heroic constancy evinced by the martyrs at Vienne and Lyons amid their sufferings, and of conversions which had occurred among the nobility of Rome to the Christian faith, he could no longer refrain from a more careful inquiry into its principles and claims. He sent a deputation, consisting of two British Christians, to Eleutherius, at that time bishop of Rome, and deserving of respect for his personal integrity, although he had once given his sanction,—which indeed he afterwards revoked,—to the impious heresy of Montanus, who assumed to be the Paraclete promised by our Saviour, alleging that the term denoted not the Holy Ghost, but an inspired teacher authorized to prescribe a fuller rule of life than Christ himself had given. The result may be given in the words of Baronius, who cannot be suspected of any leanings to a version of the story unfavourable to the pretensions of the Romish church, and by whose account it appears, that whatever information Damianus and Fugatius (Duvianus and Faganus according to other authors) conveyed to the British prince, Christianity was already well known in the island before their arrival at his court:—"This pontiff sent into Britain Fugatius and Donatianus, otherwise named Damianus, that they might initiate in the sacred mysteries the king, and others who were imbued with the Christian religion,—a duty which they diligently fulfilled,—for long before (as Gildas the Wise testifies), the gospel of Christ had been carried thither."—Annal. Eccles. ii. A.D. 183.—Ed.

conversion of the emperors to the faith, intrusted them with outward peace and prosperity. I desire not to make naked their miscarriages whom I doubt not but in mercy God hath long since pardoned; but it cannot be denied that the stories of those days are full of nothing more than the oppressions, luxury, and sloth of rulers; the pride, ambition, and unseemly, scandalous contests for pre-eminence of sees and extent of jurisdiction, among bishops; the sensuality and ignorance of the most of men. In this season it was that the bishop of Rome, advantaged by the prerogative of the city, the ancient seat and spring of the empire, began gradually to attempt a superintendency over his brethren, according as any advantages for that end (which could not be wanting in the intestine tumults and seditions wherewith Christians were turmoiled) offered themselves unto him. Wherever an opportunity could be spied, he was still interposing his umpirage and authority amongst them, and that sometimes not without sinful artifices and downright forgeries; wherein he was always accepted or refused, according as the interest of them required with whom he had to do. What the lives of priests and people, what their knowledge and profession of the gospel, of the poor Britons especially, in those days were, our own countryman, Gildas, doth sufficiently testify and bewail. Salvianus doth the same for other parts of the world; and, generally, all the pious men of those ages. Whilst the priests strove for sovereignty and power, the people perished through ignorance and sensuality. Neither can we possibly have a more full conviction of what was the state of Christians and Christianity in those days in the world, than may be seen and read in the horrible judgments of God, wherewith he punished their wickedness and ingratitude. When he could no longer bear the provocations of his people, he stirred up those swarms of northern nations, Goths, Vandals, Huns, Franks, Longobards, Alans, Saxons, etc.,—some few of them Arians, the most Pagans,—and poured them out upon the western empire, to the utter ruin of it, and the division of the provinces amongst themselves. After a while, these fierce, cruel, and barbarous nations, having executed the judgments of God against the ungodliness of men,—seating themselves in the warmer climates of those whom they had in part subdued, in part extirpated, as is the manner of all persons in transmigration from one country to another, —began to unlearn their ancient barbarism, and to incline to the manners, fashions, and religion of the people to whom they were come, and with whom, after their heats were over and lusts satisfied, they began to incorporate and coalesce; together, I say, with their manners they took up, by various ways and means, the religion which they did profess. And the bishop of Rome having kept his outward station in that famous city during all those turmoils, becoming venerable unto them, unto him were many applications made; and his authority was first signally advanced by this new race of Christians. The religion they thus took up was not a little degenerated from its primitive apostolical purity and splendour. And they were among the first who felt the effects of their former barbarous inhumanity, in their sedulous endeavour to destroy all books and learning out of the world, which brought that darkness upon mankind wherewith they wrestled for many succeeding generations; for, having themselves made an intercision of the current and progress of studies and learning, they were forced to make use, in their entertainment of Christianity, of men meanly skilled in the knowledge of God or themselves, who, some of them, knew little more of the gospel than what they had learned in the outward observances and practices of the places where they had been educated. Towards the beginning of this hurry of the world, this shuffling of the nations, was the province of Britain,—not long before exhausted of its stores of men and arms and defeated by the Romans,—invaded by the Saxons, Picts, Angles, and others out of Germany, who, accomplishing the will of God, extirpated the greatest part of the British nation, and drove the remainders of them to shelter themselves in the western mountainous parts of this island. These new inhabitants, after they were somewhat civilised by the vicinity of the provincials, and had got a little breathing from their own intestine feuds, by fixing the limits of their leaders' dominions, which they called kingdoms, began to be in some preparedness to receive impressions of religion above that rude Paganism which they had before served Satan in. These were they to whom came Austin from Rome; —a man, as far as appears by the story,[1] little acquainted with the mystery of the gospel; yet one whom

[1] The Saxon invasion sufficiently accounts for the degree of barbarism and heathenism into which the most of Britain had relapsed before Augustine, with a commission from Gregory the Great, visited it to engage in the work of converting its inhabitants to the Christian faith. Galled by the repeated incursions of the Scots and Picts on the north, when the Roman soldiery had been recalled from the island to protect the sinking empire against the threatened descent of the Huns, the Britons invited the Saxons to assist them in repressing the encroachments of their warlike neighbours. The Saxons soon gained the ascendency; and the Britons, instead of being secured in the peaceable enjoyment of their territories, were driven to the west of the island, whilst their treacherous allies seized upon the largest portion of it. The arrival of the first Saxon army, at the invitation of Vortigern, was in the year 449. It was in the year 597 that the Roman abbot, Augustine, reached our island. In the interval, Christianity had been obliterated from Saxon England.

Augustine was soon able to report to Gregory considerable success in his mission, though the equivocal character of his proceedings may be understood from the fact, that, in his communications to Rome, he dwelt with especial pride and satisfaction on the baptism of ten thousand heathens in one Christmas-day. The vain-glory of the man did not altogether escape the notice of Gregory, if we may judge from the earnest admonition to be humble which he tenders in one of his earliest letters to the missionary. Along with such good advices, he sent a copy of the holy Scriptures to our island,—a rare and precious gift in those days.

The ancient Britons, however, still had their own Christian church. Neander states that " numerous clergy and monks" were connected with it. Augustine was anxious

it pleased God graciously to use to bring the Scripture amongst them,—that inexhaustible fountain of light and truth, and by which those to whom he preached might be infallibly freed from any mixture of mistakes that he might offer to them. That he brought with him a doctrine of observances not formerly known in Britain is notorious, from the famous story of those many professors of Christianity which he caused to be murdered by Pagans for not submitting to his power, and refusing to practise according to his traditions; whose unwillingness to be slain, if they could have otherwise chosen, is that which, I suppose, our author calls their "disturbing good St Austin in his pious work." But yet neither will this conversion of the Saxons, begun by Austin the monk, at all advantage our author as to his pretensions. The religion he taught here, as well as he could, was doubtless no other than that which at those days was professed at Rome: mixtures of human traditions, worldly policies, observances trenching upon the superstitions of the Gentiles, in many things it had then revived; but, however, it was far enough from the present Romanism, if the writers and chief bishops of those days knew what was their religion. Papal supremacy and infallibility, transubstantiation, religious veneration of images in churches, with innumerable other prime fundamentals of Popery, were as great strangers at Rome in the days of Gregory the Great as they are at this day to the church of England.

to secure their co-operation with him, and quite as anxious to obtain their recognition of his superiority as appointed by the see of Rome. The Britons, however, refused to own the supremacy of the pope. "We are all prepared," said Deynock, an abbot of Bangor, "to hearken to the church of God, to the pope of Rome, and to every pious Christian, in such a way as to manifest to all, according to their several stations, perfect charity, and to uphold them both by word and deed. We know not what other obedience we can owe to him whom you call pope, or father of fathers." A public conference between the representatives of the British and Romish churches had no effect in promoting the amalgamation at which Augustine aimed, and he died in 605 without effecting his object. The stand which the Britons made against the usurpation of the Roman see exerted a wide influence at the time. Neander ascribes to it the reaction which arose about this period, and continued for centuries afterwards, against the claims of the Romish hierarchy. The usages in which a difference existed between Rome and the earlier Christianity of the island, or the "Scotch church," to employ the designation of Neander,—so called in virtue of the fact that its ministers and missionaries were chiefly educated in the institutions founded by Columba and his successors,—relate to the time of Easter, the form of tonsure, and the administration of baptism. The Britons, moreover, sturdily resisted the supremacy which the Roman see arrogated over the western church. A century elapsed before the arts of Rome prevailed, with the help of Saxon ascendency, in enforcing its ritual on the Christians of this island, and supplanting the more ancient forms which they had learned, directly or indirectly, from the east.

It is said that, after a second conference had been without avail in securing the adhesion of the British Christians to the Roman see, Augustine threatened vengeance on them for thus refusing submission to a foreign prelate. Ethelfrid, king of Northumberland, at the head of an army, marched upon Bangor, and put nearly twelve hundred monks to the sword. To this carnage Owen alludes, though there is some difficulty in ascertaining what share in the atrocity belongs to Augustine, beyond the threatening which he had uttered of some impending calamity on the Britons. The massacre is dated seven years after his death.—Ed.

After these times, the world continuing still in troubles, religion began more and more to decline, and fall off from its pristine purity; at first, by degrees insensible and almost imperceptible, in the broaching of new opinions and inventing new practices in the worship of God; at length, by open, presumptuous transgressions of its whole rule and genius, in the usurpation of the pope of Rome, and impositions of his authority on the necks of emperors, kings, princes, and people of all sorts. By what means this work was carried on, what advantages were taken for, what instruments used in it, what opposition by kings and learned men was made unto it, what testimony was given against it by the blood of thousands of martyrs, others have at large declared; nor will my present design admit me to insist on particulars. What contests, debates, tumults, wars, were, by papal pretensions, raised in these nations, what shameful entreating of some of the greatest of our kings, what absolutions of subjects from their allegiance, with such like effluxes of an abundant apostolical piety, this nation, in particular, was exercised with from Rome, all our historians sufficiently testify. "Tantæ molis erat Romanam condere gentem!" The truth is, when once *Romanism* began to be enthroned, and had driven *Catholicism* out of the world, we had very few kings that passed their days in peace and quietness from contests with the pope, or such as acted for him, or were stirred up by him. The face, in the meantime, of Christianity was sad and deplorable. The body of the people being grown dark and profane, or else superstitious; the generality of the priests and votaries ignorant and vicious in their conversations; the oppressions of the Hildebrandine faction intolerable; religion dethroned, from a free, generous obedience, according to the rule of the gospel, and thrust into cells, orders, self-invented devotions and forms of worship superstitious and unknown to Scripture and antiquity,—the whole world groaned under the apostasy it was fallen into, when it was almost too late, the yoke was so fastened to their necks, and prejudices so fixed in the minds of the multitude. Kings began to repine, princes to remonstrate their grievances, whole nations to murmur, some learned men to write and preach against the superstitions and oppressions of the church of Rome; against all which complaints and attempts, what means the popes used for the safe-guarding their authority and opinions, subservient to their carnal, worldly interests,—deposing some, causing others to be murdered that were in supreme power, bandying princes and great men one against another, exterminating others with fire and sword,—is also known unto all who take any care to know such things, whatever our author pretends to the contrary. This was the state, this the peace, this the condition of most nations in Europe, and these in particular where we live; when occasion was administered, in the providence of God, unto that reformation which, in the next place, he gives us the story of. Little cause had he to mind us of this story; little to boast of the primitive catholic faith; little to pretend the Romish religion to have been that which was first planted in these nations. His concernments lie not in these things, but only in that tyrannical usurpation of the popes, and irregular devotions of some votaries, which latter ages produced.

CHAPTER XII.

Reformation.

THE story of the reformation of religion he distributes into three parts, and allots to each a particular paragraph. The first is of its occasion and rise in general; the second, of its entrance into England; the third, of its progress amongst us. Of the first he gives us this account:—"The pastor of Christianity, upon some solicitation of Christian princes for a general compliance to their design, sent forth in the year 1517 a plenary indulgence in favour of the cruciata[1] against the Turk. Albertus, the archbishop of Mentz, being delegated by the pope to see it executed, committed the promulgation of it to the Dominican friars; which the hermits of St Augustine in the same place took ill, especially Martin Luther, etc., who, vexed that he was neglected and undervalued, fell a writing and preaching first against indulgences, then against the pope," etc. He that had no other acquaintance with Christian religion but what the Scriptures and ancient fathers will afford him, could not but be amazed at the canting language of this story; it being impossible for him to understand any thing of it aright. He would admire who this "pastor of Christianity" should be, what this "plenary indulgence" should mean, what was the "preaching of plenary indulgence by Dominicans," and what all this would avail "against the Turk." I cannot but pity such a poor man, to think what a loss he would be at,—like one taken from home and carried blindfold into the midst of a wilderness, where, when he opens his eyes, every thing scares him, nothing gives him guidance or direction. Let him turn again to his Bible, and the Fathers of the first four or five hundred years, and I will undertake he shall come off from them as wise as to the true understanding of this story as he went unto them. The scene in religion is plainly changed, and this appearance of a "universal pastor, plenary indulgences, Dominicans, and cruciatas," all marching against the Turk, must needs affright

[1] The expression in full is "expeditio cruciata" and is now commonly rendered *crusade*.—ED.

a man accustomed only to the Scripture notions of religion, and those embraced by the primitive church. And I do know that if such a man could get together two or three of the wisest Romanists in the world,—which were the likeliest way for him to be resolved in the signification of these hard names,—they would never well agree to tell him what this "plenary indulgence" is. But for the present, as to our concernment, let us take these things according to the best understanding which their framers and founders have been pleased to give us of them. The story intended to be told was indeed neither so, nor so. There was no such solicitation of the pope by Christian princes at that time as is pretended; no cruciata[1] against the Turk undertaken; no attempt of that nature ensued; not a penny of indulgence money laid out to any such purpose. But the short of the matter is, that the church of Mentz, being not able to pay for the archiepiscopal pall of Albertus from Rome, having been much exhausted by the purchase of one or two for other bishops that died suddenly before, the pope grants to Albert a number of pardons, of, to say the truth, I know not what, to be sold in Germany, agreeing with him that one-half of the gain he would have in his own right, and the other for the pall. Now, the pope's merchants, that used to sell pardons for him in former days, were the preaching friars, who, upon holidays and festivals, were wont to let out their ware to the people, and, in plain terms, to cheat them of their money; and well had it been if that had been all. What share in the dividend came to the venders, well I know not: probably they had a proportion according to the commodity that they put off; which stirred up their zeal to be earnest and diligent in their work. Among the rest, one friar Tetzel was so warm in his employment, and so intent upon the main end that they had all in their eye, that, preaching in or about Wittenberg, it sufficed him not in general to make an offer of the pardon of all sins that any had committed, but, to take all scruples from their consciences, coming to particular instances, carried them

[1] The pretext for which a commission to sell indulgences was given to Tetzel was not a crusade against the Turks, but the completion of the church of St Peter at Rome. As for the allegation that Luther took offence at the commission being given to a member of the Dominican order, in preference to the Augustinian friars, to whom he belonged, it has been proved, that, with a single unimportant exception, no Augustinian friar was ever employed in the sale of indulgences from 1450 to 1517, when Luther made the assault on indulgences, and that they can hardly, therefore, be supposed to have taken umbrage from the motives imputed to them; that the business of prosecuting the sale had been offered to the Franciscans, and spurned by them; that the bitterest opponents of Luther,—Cajetan, Hochstrat, Emser, and even Tetzel,—never ascribe any such sinister motive to Luther; that Roman Catholic authors, such as De Prierio, Pallavicini, and Graveson, have confuted this charge against him; and that Cochlæus, who originally mooted it, never ventured on the fabrication till Luther was in his grave, and has never been esteemed of any authority by popish writers of respectable character. See an able and conclusive note appended to "Villers' Essay on the Spirit and Influence of the Reformation."—Ed.

up to a cursed, blasphemous supposition of ravishing the blessed Virgin; so cocksure he made of the forgiveness of any thing beneath it, provided the price were paid that was set upon the pardon. Sober men being much amazed and grieved at these horrible impieties, one Martin Luther, a professor of divinity at Wittenberg, an honest, warm, zealous soul, set himself to oppose the friar's blasphemies; wherein his zeal was commended by all, his discretion by few, it being the joint opinion of most that the pope would quickly have stopped his mouth by breaking his neck. But God, as it afterward appeared, had another work to bring about, and the time of entering upon it was now fully come. At the same time that Luther set himself to oppose the pardons in Germany, Zuinglius did the same in Switzerland. And both of them taking occasion, from the work they first engaged in, to search the Scriptures, so to find out the truth of religion, which they discovered to be horribly abused by the pope and his agents, proceeded farther in their discovery than at first they were aware of. Many nations, princes, and people, multitudes of learned and pious men, up and down the world, that had long groaned under the bondage of the papal yoke, and grieved for the horrible abuse of the worship of God which they were forced to see and endure, hearing that God had stirred up some learned men seriously to oppose those corruptions in religion which they saw and mourned under, speedily either countenanced them or joined themselves with them. It fell out, indeed, as it was morally impossible it should be otherwise, that multitudes of learned men, undertaking, without advising or consulting one with another, in several far distant nations, the discovery of the papal errors and the reformation of religion, some of them had different apprehensions and persuasions in and about some points of doctrine and parts of worship, of no great weight and importance. And he that shall seriously consider what was the state of things when they began their work, who they were, how educated, what prejudices they had to wrestle with, and remember withal that they were all men, will have ten thousand times more cause to admire at their agreement in all fundamentals than at their difference about some lesser things. However, whatever were their personal failings and infirmities, God was pleased to give testimony to the uprightness and integrity of their hearts; and to bless their endeavours with such success as answered, in some measure, the primitive work of planting and propagating the gospel. The small sallies of our author upon them, in some legends about what Luther should say or do, deserve not the least notice from men who will seriously contemplate the hand, power, and wisdom of God in the work accomplished by them.

The next thing undertaken by our author is the ingress of Protestancy into England, and its progress there. The old story of the love of King Henry the Eighth to Anne Bullen, with the divorce of Queen Katharine, told over and over long ago by men of the same principle and design with himself, is that which he chooseth to flourish withal. I shall say no more to the story, but that Englishmen were not wont to believe the whispers of an unknown friar or two, before the open redoubled protestation of one of the most famous kings that ever swayed the sceptre of this land, before the union of the crowns of England and Scotland. These men, whatever they pretend, show what reverence they have to our present sovereign, by their unworthy defamation of his royal predecessors. But let men suppose the worst they please of that great heroic person, what are his miscarriages unto Protestant religion? for neither was he the head, leader, or author of that religion, nor did he ever receive it, profess it, or embrace it; but caused men to be burned to death for its profession. Should I, by way of retaliation, return unto our author the lives and practices of some, of many, not of the great or leading men of his church, but of the popes themselves, the head, sum, and, in a manner, whole of their religion, at least so far that without him they will not acknowledge any, he knows well enough what double measure, "shaken together, pressed down, and running over," may be returned unto him. A work this would be, I confess, no way pleasing unto myself; for who can delight in raking into such a sink of filth as the lives of many of them have been? Yet, because he seems to talk with a confidence of willingness to revive the memory of such ulcers of Christianity, if he proceed in the course he hath begun, it will be necessary to mind him of not boxing up his eyes when he looks towards his own home. That poisonings, adulteries, incests, conjurations, perjuries, atheism, have been no strangers to that see, if he knows not, he shall be acquainted from stories that he hath no colour to except against. For the present, I shall only mind him and his friends of the comedian's advice:—

> "Dehinc ut quiescant, porro moneo, et desinant
> Maledicere, malefacta ne noscant sua."—[Ter. And. Prol., 22.]

The declaration made in the days of that king, that he was the head of the church of England, intended no more but that there was no other person in the world from whom any jurisdiction to be exercised in this church over his subjects might be derived, the supreme authority for all exterior government being vested in him alone. That this should be so, the word of God, the nature of the kingly office, and the ancient laws of this realm, do require. And I challenge our author to produce any one testimony of Scripture, or any one word out of any general council, or any one catholic father or writer, to give the least countenance to his assertion of two heads of the church in his sense: "a head of influence, which is Jesus himself; and a head of government, which is the pope, in whom all the sacred hierarchy ends." This taking of one half of Christ's rule and headship out of his hand, and giving it to the pope, will not be salved by that expression, thrust in by the way, "Under him:" for the headship of influence is distinctly ascribed unto Christ, and that of government to the pope; which evidently asserts that he is not, in the same manner, head unto his church in both these senses, but he in one, and the pope in another.

But whatever was the cause or occasion of the dissension between King Henry and the pope, it is certain Protestancy came into England by the same way and means that Christianity came into the world: the painful, pious professors and teachers of it sealed its truth with their blood; and what more honourable entrance it could make, I neither know, nor can it be declared. Nor did England receive this doctrine from others; in the days of King Henry it did but revive that light which sprung up amongst us long before, and, by the fury of the pope and his adherents, had been a while suppressed. And it was with the blood of Englishmen, dying patiently and gloriously in the flames, that the truth was sealed in the days of that king, who lived and died himself, as was said, in the profession of the Roman faith. The truth flourished yet more in the days of his pious and hopeful son. Some stop, our author tells us, was put to it in the days of Queen Mary. But what stop? of what kind? Of no other than that put to Christianity by Trajan, Diocletian, Julian: a stop by fire and sword, and all exquisite cruelties: which was broken through by the constant death and invincible patience and prayers of bishops, ministers, and people numberless; a stop that Rome hath cause to blush in the remembrance of, and all Protestants to rejoice, having their faith tried in the fire, and coming forth more precious than gold. Nor did Queen Elizabeth, as is falsely pretended, endeavour to continue that stop, but cordially, from the beginning of her reign, embraced that faith wherein she had before been instructed. And in the maintenance of it did God preserve her from all the plots, conspiracies, and rebellions of the Papists, curses and depositions of the popes, with invasion of her kingdoms by his instigation; as also her renowned successor, with his whole regal posterity, from their contrivance for their martyrdom and ruin. During the reign of those royal and magnificent princes, had the power and polity of the papal world been able to accomplish what the men of this innocent and quiet religion professedly designed, they had not had the advantage of the late miscarriages of some professing the Protestant religion, in reference to our late king, of glorious memory, to triumph in; though they had obtained that which would have been very desirable to them, and which we have but sorry evidence that they do not yet aim at and hope for. As for what he declares in the end of his 19th paragraph, about the Reformation here, that it followed wholly neither Luther nor Calvin,—which he intermixes with many unseemly taunts and reflections on our laws, government, and governors,—[it] is, as far as it is true, the glory of it. It was not Luther nor Calvin, but the word of God, and the practice of the primitive church, that England proposed for her rule and pattern in her reformation; and where any of the reformers forsook them, she counted it her duty, without reflections on them or their ways, to walk in that safe one she had chosen out for herself.

Nor shall I insist on his next paragraph, destined to the advancement of his interest, by a proclamation of the late tumults, seditions, and rebellions in these nations; which he ascribes to the Puritans. He hath got an advantage, and it is not equal we should persuade him to forego it; only I desire prudent men to consider what the importance of it is, as to this case in hand: for as to other considerations of the same things, they fall not within the compass of our present discourse. It is not of professions, but of persons, that he treats. The crimes that he insists on attend not any avowed principles, but the men that have professed them. And if a rule of choosing or leaving religion may from thence be gathered, I know not any in the world that any can embrace; much less can they rest in none at all. Professors of all religions have, in their seasons, sinfully miscarried themselves, and troubled the world with their lusts; and those who have possessed none, most of all. And of all that is called religion, that of the Romanists might by this rule be first cashiered. The abominable, bestial lives of very many of their chief guides in whom they believe; the tumults, seditions, rebellions, they have raised in the world; the treasons, murders, conspiracies, they have countenanced, encouraged, and commended, would take up, not a single paragraph of a little treatise, but innumerable volumes, should they be but briefly reported. They do so already; and,—which renders them abominable, whilst there is any in the world that see reason not to submit themselves unto the papal sovereignty,—their professed principles lead them to the same courses. And when men are brought to all the bestial subjection aimed at, yet pretences will not be wanting to set on foot such practices; they were not in former days, when they had obtained an uncontrollable omnipotency. If our author supposeth this a rational way for the handling of differences in religion, that, leaving the consideration of the doctrines and principles, we should insist on the vices and crimes, of those who have professed them, I can assure him he must expect the least advantage by it to his party of any in the world; nor need we choose any other scene than England to try out our contests by this rule. I hope, when he writes next, he will have better considered this matter, and not flatter himself that the crimes of any Protestants do enable him to conclude, as he doth, that the only way for peace is the extermination of Protestancy. And so his tale about religion is ended. He next brings himself on the stage.

CHAPTER XIII.

Popish contradictions.

THIS is our last task. Our author's own story of himself, and rare observations in the Roman religion, make up the close of his discourse, and merit, in his thoughts, the title of *discovery*. The design of the whole is to manifest his Catholic religion to be absolutely unblamable, by wiping off some spots and blemishes that are cast upon it; indeed by gilding over, with fair and plausible words, some parts of their profession and worship which he knew to be most liable to the exceptions of them with whom he intends to deal. His way of managing this design, that he may seem to do something new, is by telling a fair tale of himself and his observations, with the effects they had upon him; which is but the putting of a new tune to an old song, that hath been chanted at our doors these hundred years: and some, he hopes, are so simple as to like the new tune, though they were sick of the old song. His entrance is a blessing of the world with some knowledge of himself, his parentage, birth, and education, and proficiency in his studies; as not doubting but that great inquiry must needs be made after the meanest concernments of such a hero as, by his achievements and travels, he hath manifested himself to be. And, indeed, he hath so handsomely and delightfully given us the romance of himself and Popery, that it was pity he should so unhappily stumble at the threshold as he hath done, and fall upon a misadventure that to some men will render the design of his discourse suspected; for whereas he doth elsewhere most confidently aver that no trouble ever was raised amongst us by the Romanists, here, at unawares, he informs us that his own grandfather lost both his life and his estate, in a rebellion raised in the north, on the account of that religion!—just as before, attempting to prove that we received Christianity originally from Rome, he tells us that the first planters of it came directly from Palestina! It is in vain for him to persuade us that what hath been can never be again, unless he manifest the principles which formerly gave it life and being to be vanished out of the world; which, as to those of the Romanists, tending to the disturbance of these kingdoms, I fear he is not able to do.

There is not any thing else which Protestants are universally bound to observe in the course of his life before he went beyond the seas, but only the offence he took at men's preaching at London against Popery; not that he was then troubled, if we may believe him, that Popery was ill reported of, but the miscarriage of the preachers in bringing in the papal church hand over head in their sermons, speaking all evil and no good of it, and charging it with contradictions, was that which gave him distaste. He knows himself best what it was that troubled him, nor shall I set up conjectures against his assertions. The triple evil mentioned, so far as it is evil, I hope he finds now remedied. For my part, I never liked of men's importune diversions from their texts to deal with or confute Papists; which is the first part of the evil complained of. I know a far more effectual way to preserve men from Popery,—namely, a solid instruction of them in the principles of truth, with an endeavour to plant in their hearts the power of those principles, that they may have experience of their worth and usefulness. That nothing but evil was spoken of Popery by Protestants, when they spake of it, I cannot wonder: they account nothing evil in the religion of the Romanists but Popery; which is the name of the evil of that religion. No Protestants ever denied but that the Romanists retained many good things in the religion which they profess; but those good things, they say, are no part of Popery: so that our author should not by right have been so offended that men spake no good of that which is the expression of the evil of that which in itself is good, as Popery is of the Papist's Christianity. The last parcel of that which was the matter of his trouble and offence, he displays by sundry of the contradictions which Protestants charged Popery withal. To little purpose; for either the things he mentions are not by any charged on Popery, or not in that manner he expresseth, or the contradiction between them consists not in the assertions themselves, but in some additional terms supplied by himself, to make them appear contradictions. For instance (to take those given by himself), if one say "The Papists worship stocks and stones," another say, "They worship a piece of bread," here is no contradiction. Again, if one charge them with having their consciences affrighted with purgatory, and doomsday, and penances for their sins, that they never live a quiet life; another, that they carry their top and top-gallant so high, that they will go to heaven without Christ, or (as we in the country phrase it), trust not to his merits and righteousness alone for salvation, here may be no contradiction: for all Papists are not, we know it well enough, of the same mould and form. Some may more imbibe some principles of religion, tending in appearance to mortification; some, those that lead to pride and presumption, and so be liable to several charges; but neither are these things inconsistent in themselves. Men in their greatest consternation of spirit from sense of punishment, real or imaginary, wherewith they are disquieted, may yet proudly reject the righteousness of Christ; and if our author knows not this to be true, he knows nothing of the gospel. The next instance is of the same nature. "One," he saith, "affirms that murders, adulteries, lies, blasphemies, and all sin, make up the bulk of Popery; another, that Papists are so wholly given to good works, that they place in them excessive confidence." I scarce believe that he ever heard any thus crudely charging them with either part of the imagined contradictory proposition. Taking Popery, as the Protestants do, for the exorbitancy of the religion which the Romanists profess, and considering the product of it in the most of mankind, it may be some, by a usual hyperbole, have used the words first mentioned; but if we should charge the Papists for being "wholly given to good works," we should much wrong both them and ourselves, seeing we perfectly know the contrary. The sum of both these things brought into one is but this, that many Papists, in the course of a scandalously sinful life, do place much of their confidence in good works; which is, indeed, a strange contradiction in principles between their speculation and practice, but we know well enough there is none in the charge. Let us consider one more: "One affirmed that the pope and all his Papists fall down to pictures and commit idolatry with them; another, that the pope is so far from falling down to any thing, that he exalts himself above all that is called God, and is very antichrist." If one had said, he falls down to images, another, that he falls not down to images, there had been a contradiction indeed; but our author, by his own testimony, being a civil logician, knows well enough that the falling down in the first proposition and that in the second are things of a diverse nature, and so are no contradiction. A man may fall down to images, and yet refuse to submit himself to the power that God hath set over him. And those of whom he speaks would have told him, that a great part of the pope's exalting himself against God consists in his falling down to images, wherein he exalts his own will and tradition against the will and express commands of God. The same may be showed of all the following instances, nor can he give any one that shall manifest Popery to be charged by sober Protestants with any other contradictions than what appear to every eye in the inconsistency of some of their principles one with another, and of most of them with their practice. In the particulars by himself enumerated, there is no other show of the charge of contradictory evils in Popery than what by his additions and wresting expressions is put upon them.

Weary of such preaching in England, our author addressed himself to travel beyond the seas, where what he met withal, what he observed, the weight and strength of his own conversion being laid in pretence upon it (indeed, an apology for the more generally excepted against parts of his Roman practice and worship being intended and pursued), must be particularly considered and debated.

CHAPTER XIV.

Mass.

Sect. xxii. THE title our author gives to his first head of observation is "Messach," on what account I know not, unless it be with respect to a ridiculous Hebrew etymology of the word "missa;" as though it should be the same with מִסָּה, a word quite of another signification. If this be that which his title intends, I wish him better success in his next etymologizing, for this attempt hath utterly failed him. "Missa" never came out of the east, nor hath any affinity with those tongues; being a word utterly unknown to the Syrians, and Grecians also, by whom all Hebrew words that are used in religion came into Europe. He that will trouble himself to trace the pedigree of "missa" shall find it of no such ancient stock, but a word that, with many others, came into use in the destruction of the Roman empire, and the corruption of the Latin tongue. But as it is likely our author, having not been accustomed to feed much upon Hebrew roots, might not perceive the insipidness of this pretended traduction of the word "missa," so also, on the other side, it is not improbable but that he might only by an uncouth word think to startle his poor countrymen at the entrance of the story of his travels, that they might look upon him as no small person who hath the missach, and such other hard names, at his fingers' ends; as the Gnostics heightened their disciples into an admiration of them by "Paldabaoth, Astaphæum," and other names of the like hideous noise and sound.[1]

[1] The Hebrew word "missach" signifies an offering, and the term "mass" has been derived from it by some Roman Catholic writers. The word in Latin is "missa," and it is more probable that it arose from the dismissal of the catechumens in the services of the ancient church, before the sacrament was dispensed. "Ite, missa est" were the usual words of the minister in dismissing them.—ED.

Of the discourse upon this missach, whatever it is, there are sundry parts. That he begins with, is a preference of the devotion of the Romanists incomparably above that of the Protestants. This was the entrance of his discovery. Catholics' bells ring oftener than ours; their churches are swept cleaner than ours,—yea, ours in comparison of theirs are like stables to a princely palace; their people are longer upon their knees than ours; and, upon the whole matter, they are excellent every way in their worship of God,—we every way blameworthy and contemptible: unto all which I shall only mind him of that good old advice, "Let thy neighbour praise thee, and not thine own mouth." And as for us, I hope we are not so bad but that we should rejoice truly to hear that others were better. Only, we could desire that we might find their excellency to consist in things not either indifferent wholly in themselves or else disapproved by God; which are the ways that hypocrisy usually vents itself in, and then boasts of what it hath done. Knowledge of God and his will as revealed in the gospel, real mortification, abiding in spiritual supplications, diligence in universal obedience, and fruitfulness in good works, be, as I suppose, the things which render our profession beautiful, and according to the mind of God. If our author be able to make a right judgment of these things, and find them really abounding amongst his party, I hope we shall rejoice with him, though we knew the spring of them is not their Popery, but their Christianity. [As] for the outside shows he hath as yet instanced in, they ought not in the least to have influenced his judgment in that disquisition of the truth wherein he pretends he was engaged. He could not of old have come amongst the professors and "mystæ" of those false religions, which, by the light and power of the gospel, are now banished out of the world, where he should not have met with the same wizards and appearances of devotion; so that hitherto we find no great discoveries in his missach.

From the worship of the parties compared, he comes to their preaching, and finds them as differing as their devotion. The preaching of Protestants of all sorts is sorry, pitiful stuff; inconsequent words, senseless notions, or at least rhetorical flourishes, make it up: the Catholics' grave and pithy. Still all this belongs to persons; not things. Protestants preach as well as they can, and if they cannot preach so well as his wiser Romanists, it is their unhappiness, not their fault. But yet I have a little reason to think that our author is not altogether of the mind that here he pretends to be of, but that he more hates and fears than despises the preaching of Protestants. He knows well enough what mischief it hath wrought his party, though prejudice will not suffer him to see what good it hath done the world; and therefore doubting, as I suppose, lest he should not be able to prevail with his readers to believe him in that which he would fain, it may be, but cannot, believe himself, about the excellency of the preaching of his Catholics above that of Protestants, he decries the whole work as of little or no use or concernment in Christian religion. This it had been fair for him to have openly pleaded, and not to have made a flourish with that which he knew he could make no better work of. Nor is the preaching of the Protestants, as is pretended, unlike that of the ancients. The best and most famous preacher of the ancient church, whose sermons are preserved, was Chrysostom. We know the way of his proceeding in that work was, to open the words and meaning of his text, to declare the truth contained and taught in it, to vindicate it from objections, to confirm it by other testimonies of Scripture, and to apply all unto practice in the close; and, as far as I can observe, this, in general, is the method used by Protestants, being that, indeed, which the very nature of the work dictates unto them. Wherefore, mistrusting lest he should not be able to bring men out of love with the preaching of Protestants, in comparison of the endeavours of his party in the same kind, he turns himself another way, and labours to persuade us, as I said, that preaching itself is of little or no use in Christian religion; for, so he may serve his own design, he cares not, it seems, openly to contradict the practice of the church of God ever since there was a church in the world. To avoid that charge he tells us, "That the apostles and apostolical churches had no sermons, but all their preaching was merely for the conversion of men to the faith, and when this was done, there was an end of their preaching;" and for this he instanceth in the sermons mentioned in the Acts, chap. ii. iii. v. vii. viii. x. xiii. xiv. xvi. xviii. xx. xxii. xxiv. xxvi. xxviii. I wonder what he thinks of Christ himself; whether he preached or no in the temple, or in the synagogues of the Jews; and whether the Judaical church, to whose members he preached, were not then a true, yea, the only church in the world; and whether Christ was not anointed and sent to preach the gospel to them? If he know not this, he is very ignorant; if he doth know it, he is somewhat that deserves a worse name. To labour to exterminate that out of the religion of Christ which was one of the chief works of Christ (for we do not read that he went up and down singing mass, though I have heard of a friar that conceived that to be his employment), is a work unbecoming any man that would count himself wronged not to be esteemed a Christian. But whatever Christ did, it may be, it matters not. The apostles and apostolical churches had no sermons, but only such as they preached to infidels and Jews to convert them; that is, they did not labour to instruct men in the knowledge of the mysteries of the gospel, to build them up in their faith, to teach them more and more the good knowledge of God, revealing unto them the whole counsel of his will! And is it possible that any man who hath ever read over the New Testament, or any one of Paul's epistles, should be so blinded by prejudices, and made so confident in his assertions, as to dare, in the face of the sun, whilst the Bible is in every one's hand, to utter a matter so devoid of truth and all colour or pretence of probability? Methinks men should think it enough to sacrifice their consciences to their Moloch, without casting wholly away their reputation, to be consumed in the same flames. It is true, the design of the story of the Acts being to deliver unto us the progress of the Christian faith by the ministry of the apostles, insists principally on those sermons which God in an especial manner blessed to the conversion of souls, and increase of the church thereby; but is there therefore no mention made of preaching in it to the edification of their converts? or is there no mention of preaching, unless it be said that such a one preached at such a time, so long, on such a text? When the people abode in the apostles' doctrine, Acts. ii. 42, I think the apostles taught them. And the ministry of the word, which they gave themselves unto, was principally in reference unto the church, chap. vi. 4. So Peter and John preached the word to those whom Philip had converted at Samaria, chap. viii. 25. A whole year together, Paul and Barnabas assembled themselves together with the church of Antioch, and taught much people, chap. xi. 26. At Troas Paul preached unto them who came together to break bread (that is, the church), until midnight, chap. xx. 7, 9,—which why our author calls a dispute, or what need of a dispute there was, when only the church was assembled, neither I nor he do know; and, verses 20, 27, he declares that his main work and employment was constant preaching to the disciples and churches, giving commands to the elders of the churches to do the same; and what his practice was during his imprisonment at Rome, the close of that book declares. And these, not footsteps, but express examples of and precepts concerning preaching to the churches themselves and their disciples, we have in that book purposely designed to declare their first calling and planting, not their progress and edification. Should I trace the commands given for this work, the commendation of it, the qualifications and gifts for it bestowed on men by Christ, and his requiring of their exercise, recorded in the Epistles, the work would be endless, and a good part of most of them must be transcribed. In brief, if the Lord Christ continue to bestow ministerial gifts upon any, or to call them to the office of the ministry; if they are bound to labour in the word and doctrine,—to be instant, in season and out of season, in preaching the word to those committed to their charge; if that be one of the directions given them, that they may know how to behave themselves in the church, the house of God; if they are bound to trade with the talents their Master intrusts them with, to attend unto doctrine with all diligence; if it be the duty of Christians to labour to grow and increase in the knowledge of God and his will, and that of indispensable necessity unto salvation, according to the measure of the means God is pleased to afford unto them; if their perishing through ignorance will be assuredly charged on them who are called to the care, and freedom, and instructing of them;—this business of preaching is an indispensable duty among Christians. If these things be not so indeed, for aught I know, we may do what our adversary desires us,—even burn our Bibles, and that as books that have no truth in them. Our author's denial of the practice of antiquity, conformable to this of the apostles, is of the same nature. But, that it would prove too long a diversion from my present work, I could as easily trace down the constant sedulous performance of this duty, from the days of the apostles until it gave place to that ignorance which the world was beholden to the papal apostasy for, as I can possibly write so much paper as the story of it would take up. But to what purpose should I do it? Our author, I presume, knows it well enough; and others, I hope, will not be too forward in believing his affirmations of what he believes not himself.

The main design of this discourse is to cry up the sacrifice that the Catholics have in their churches, but not the Protestants. This sacrifice, he tells us, was "the sum of all apostolical devotion, which Protestants have abolished." Strange! that in all the writings of the apostles, there should not one word be mentioned of that which was the sum of their devotion! Things, surely, judged by our author of less importance, are at large handled in them. That they should not, directly nor indirectly, once intimate that which, it seems, was the sum of their devotion is, I confess, to me somewhat strange. They must make this concealment either by design or oversight. How consistent the first is with their goodness, holiness, love to the church, the latter with their wisdom and infallibility, either with their office and duty, is easy to judge. Our author tells us, "They have a sacrifice after the order of Melchizedek." Paul tells us, indeed, that we have a High Priest "after the order of Melchisedec;" but, as I remember, this is the first time that ever I heard of a sacrifice after the order of Melchizedek, though I have read somewhat that Roman Catholics say about Melchizedek's sacrifice. Our Priest "after the order of Melchisedec" offered a sacrifice that none ever had done before, nor can do after him, even himself. If the Romanists think to offer him, they must kill him. The species of bread and wine are but a thin sacrifice, next door to nothing, yea, somewhat worse than nothing, a figment of a thing impossible, or the shadow of a dream; nor will they say they are any. It is true, which our author pleads in justification of the sacrifice of his church, that there were sacrifices among the Jews, yea, from the beginning of the world, after the entrance of sin and promise of Christ to come made to sinners; for in the state of innocency there was no sacrifice appointed, because there was no need of an atonement. But all these sacrifices, properly so called, had no other use in religion than to prefigure and represent the great sacrifice of himself to be made by the Son of God in the fulness of time. That being once performed, all other sacrifices were to cease, I mean properly so called; for we have still sacrifices metaphorical, called so by analogy, being parts of God's worship tendered unto him, and accepted with him, as were the sacrifices of old. Nor is it at all necessary that we should have proper sacrifices, that we may have metaphorical. It is enough that such there have been, and that of God's own appointment; and we have still that only one real sacrifice which was the life and soul of all them that went before. The substance being come, the light shadowing of it that was before under the law is vanished. The apostle doth expressly place the opposition that is between the sacrifice of the Christian church and that of the Judaical in this, that they were often repeated; this was performed once for all, and is a living, abiding sacrifice, constant in the church for ever, Heb. x. 1, 2: so that, by this rule, the repetition of the same or any other sacrifice, in the Christian church, can have no other foundation but an apprehension of the imperfection of the sacrifice of Christ; for, saith he, where the sacrifice is perfect, and makes them perfect that come to God by it, there must be no more sacrifice. This, then, seems to be the real difference between Protestants and Roman Catholics in this business of sacrifice:—Protestants believing the sacrifice of Christ to be absolutely perfect, so that there is no need of any other, and that it is ὁδὸς πρόσφατος καὶ ζῶσα,—"a fresh and living way,"—of going to God continually, with whom by it obtaining remission of sin, they know there is no more offering for sin; they content themselves with that sacrifice of his, continually, in its virtue and efficacy, residing in the church. Romanists, looking on that as imperfect, judge it necessary to institute a new sacrifice of their own, to be repeated every day, and that without any the least colour or warrant from the word of God or example of the apostles. But our author puts in an exception, and tells us those words of Luke, Acts xiii. 2, Λειτουργούντων δὲ αὐτῶν τῷ Κυρίῳ, are well and truly rendered by Erasmus, "Sacrificantibus illis Domino;" which one text, saith he, "gives double testimony to apostolical sacrifice and priestly ordination." And he strengthens the authority of Erasmus with reason also; for the "word can import nothing but sacrifice, since it was made τῷ Κυρίῳ: for other inferior ministries of the word and sacraments are not made to God, but the people; but the apostles were λειτουργοῦντες τῷ Κυρίῳ,—administering, liturgying, sacrificing to our Lord." For what he adds of ordination, it belongs not unto this discourse. Authority and reason are pleaded to prove, I know not what sacrifice, to be intended in these words. Erasmus is first pleaded; to whose interpretation, mentioned by our author, I shall only add his own annotations in the explication of his meaning: "Λειτουργούντων," saith he, "quod proprium est *operantium sacris.* Nullum autem sacrificium Deo gratius quam impartiri doctrinam evangelicam." So that it seems the preaching of the gospel, or taking care about it, was the sacrifice that Erasmus thought of in his translation and exposition. Yea, but the word is truly translated "sacrificantibus." But who, I pray, told our author so? The original of the word is of a much larger signification. Its common use is, to minister in any kind; it is so translated and expounded by all learned, impartial men, and is never used in the whole New Testament to denote sacrificing. Nor is זָבַח ever rendered in the Old Testament by the LXX. λειτουργία or λειτουργέω, but θυσία, θυσίασμα, θῦμα, θυμίαμα, ὁλοκαύτωμα, σφάγιον, θύω, etc. Nor is that word used absolutely in any author, profane or ecclesiastical, to signify precisely sacrificing. And I know well enough what it is that makes our author say it is properly translated "sacrificing," and I know as well that he cannot prove what he says; but he gives a reason for what he says,—it is said "to be made to the Lord, whereas other inferior ministerial acts are made to the people." I wish heartily he would once leave this scurvy trick of cogging in words to deceive his poor unwary reader; for what, I pray, makes his "made" here? what is it that is said to be "made" to the Lord? It is, "when they were ministering to the Lord;" so the words are rendered,—not, when they were making, or *making sacrifice,* or when they *made sacrificing* unto the Lord. This wild gourd, "made," puts death into his pot. And we think here in England, that in all ministerial acts, though performed towards the people, and for their good, yet men administer to the Lord in them, because performing them by his appointment, as a part of that worship which he requires at their hands.

In the close of our author's discourse he complains of the persecutions of Catholics; which, whatever they are or have been, for my part I neither approve nor justify; and do heartily wish they had never showed the world those ways of dealing with them who dissented from them in things concerning religion whereof themselves now complain, how justly I know not. But if it be for the mass that any of them have felt or do fear suffering (which I pray God avert from them), I hope they will at length come to understand how remote it is from having any affinity with the devotion of the apostolical churches, and so free themselves, if not from suffering, yet at least from suffering for that which, being not accepted with God, will yield them no solid gospel consolation in what they may endure or undergo.

CHAPTER XV.

Blessed Virgin.

Sect. xxiii. p. 267. THE 22d paragraph, concerning the blessed Virgin, is absolutely the weakest and most disingenuous in his whole discourse. The work he hath in hand is to take off offence from the Roman doctrine and practice in reference unto her. Finding that this could not be handsomely gilded over, being so rotten and corrupt as not to bear a new varnish, he turns his pen to the bespattering of Protestants for contempt of her, without the least respect to truth or common honesty. Of them it is that he says, "That they vilify and blaspheme her, and cast gibes upon her;" which he sets off with a pretty tale of "a Protestant bishop and a Catholic boy:" and lest this should not suffice to render them odious, he would have some of them thought to "taunt at Christ himself;" one of them "for ignorance, passion, and too much haste for his breakfast." Boldly to calumniate, that something may cleave, is a principle that too many have observed in their dealings with others in the world; but as it contains a renunciation of the religion of Jesus Christ, so it hath not always well succeeded. The horrid and incredible reproaches that were cast by the Pagans on the primitive Christians occasioned sundry ingenuous persons to search more into their way than otherwise they would have done; and thereby their conversion. And I am persuaded this rude charge on Protestants, as remote from truth as any thing that was cast on the first Christians by their adversaries, would have the same effects on Roman Catholics, might they meet with the same ingenuity and candour. That any Protestant should be moved or shaken in his principles by such calumnies is impossible. Every one that is so knows, that as the Protestants believe every thing that is spoken of the blessed Virgin in the Scripture or creed, or whatever may be lawfully deduced from what is so spoken, so they have all that honour and respect for her which God will allow to be given to any creature. Surely a confident accusation of incivility and blasphemy for not doing that which they know they do, and profess to all the world they do, is more like to move men in their patience towards their accusers than to prevail with them to join in the same charge against others, whom they know to be innocent as themselves. Neither will it relieve our author, in point of ingenuity and truth, that it may be he hath heard it reported of one or two brain-sick or frantic persons in England, that they have cast out blasphemous reproaches against the blessed "Mother of God." It is credibly testified that pope Leo should, before witnesses, profess his rejoicing at the advantages they had at Rome by the "fable of Christ." Were it handsome now in a Protestant to charge this blasphemy upon all Papists, though uttered by their head and guide; and to dispute against them from the confession of the Jews, who acknowledge the story of his death and suffering to be true, and of the Turks, who have a great honour and veneration for him unto this day? Well may men be counted Catholics who walk in such paths, but I see no ground or reason why we should esteem them Christians. Had our author spoken to the purpose, he should have proved the lawfulness, or, if he had spoken to his own purpose with any candour of mind or consistency of purpose in the pursuit of his design, have gilded over the practice, of giving divine honour to the holy Virgin, or worshipping her with adoration, as Protestants say, due to God alone; of ascribing all the titles of Christ unto her, turning Lord in the Psalms in most places into Lady; praying to her, not only to entreat, yea, to command her Son to help and save them, but to save them herself, as she to whom her Son hath committed the administration of mercy, keeping that of justice to himself; with many other the like horrid blasphemies, which he shall hear more of if he desire it. But instead of this difficult task, he takes up one which, it seems, he looked on as far easier,—falsely to accuse Protestants of blaspheming her. We usually smile in England at a short answer that one is said to have given Bellarmine's works; I hope I may say without offence, that, if it were not uncivil, it might suffice for an answer to this paragraph. But though most men will suppose that our author hath overshot himself, and gone too far in his charge, he himself thinks he hath not gone far enough; as well knowing there are some bounds, which when men have passed, their only course is to set a good face upon the matter, and to dare on still. Wherefore, to convince us of the truth of what he had delivered concerning Protestants reviling and blaspheming the blessed Virgin, he tells us that it is no wonder, seeing some of them, in foreign parts, have uttered words against the very honour of Jesus Christ himself. To make this good, Calvin is placed in the van, who is said "to taunt at his ignorance and passion, and too much haste for his breakfast, when he cursed the fig-tree; who, if, as is pretended, he had studied Catholic divines, they would have taught him a more modest and pious interpretation." It is quite beside my purpose and nature of the present discourse to recite the words of private men, and to contend about their sense and meaning. I shall therefore only desire the reader that thinks himself concerned in this report to consult the place in Calvin pointed unto; and if he finds any such taunts as our author mentions, or any thing delivered concerning our Lord Christ but what may be confirmed by the judgment of all the ancient fathers and many learned Romanists, I will be content to lose my reputation with him for any skill in judging at the meaning of an author. But what thoughts he will think meet to retain for this informer, I leave to himself. What Catholic divines Calvin studied, I know not; but I am sure, if some of those whom his adviser accounts so had not studied him, they had never stole so much out of his comments on the Scripture as they have done. The next primitive Protestants that are brought in to make good this charge are Servetus, Gribaldus, Lismaninus, and some other antitrinitarian heretics; in opposition to whose errors, both in their first rise and after progress, under the management of Faustus Socinus and his followers, Protestants, all Europe over, have laboured far more abundantly, and with far greater success, than all his Roman Catholics. It seems they must now all pass for primitive Protestants, because the interest of the Catholic cause requires it should be so. This is a communicable branch of papal omnipotency, to make things and persons to be what they never were. From them a return is made again to Luther, Brentius, Calvin, Zuinglius, who are said to nibble at Arianism, and shoot secret darts at the Trinity; though all impartial men must needs confess that they have asserted and proved the doctrine of it far more solidly than all the schoolmen in the world were able to do. But the main weight of the discourse of this paragraph lies upon the pretty tale in the close of it, about a Protestant bishop and a Catholic boy; which he must be a very Cato that can read without smiling. It is a little too long to transcribe, and I cannot tell it over again without spoiling of it, having never had that faculty in gilding of little stories wherein our author excelleth. The sum is, that the boy, being reproved by the bishop for saying a prayer to her, boggled at the repetition of her name when he came to repeat his creed, and cried, "My lord, here she is again; what shall I do with her now?" To whom the bishop replied, "You may let her pass in your creed, but not in your prayers;" whereupon our author subjoins, "As though we might have faith, but neither hope nor charity for her." Certainly, I suppose, my countrymen cannot but take it ill that any man should suppose them such stupid blockheads as to be imposed on with sophistry that they may feel through a pair of mittens. "Tam vacui capitis populum Phæaca putavit?" [Juv. xv. 23.] For my part, I can scarce think it worth the while to relieve men that will stoop to so naked a lure. But, that I may pass on, I will cast away one word, which nothing but gross stupidity can countenance, from heedlessness. The blessed Virgin is mentioned in the creed as the person of whom our Saviour was born, and we have therefore faith for her,—that is, we believe that Christ was born of her; but do we therefore believe in her? Certainly no more than we do in Pontius Pilate, concerning whom we believe that Christ was crucified under him. A bare mention in the creed, with reference to somewhat else believed in, is a thing in itself indifferent; and, we see, occasionally befell the best of women, and one of the worst of men: and what hope and charity should we thence conclude that we ought to have for her? We are past charitable hopes that she is for ever blessed in heaven, having full assurance of it. But if by hope for her, he means the placing of our hope, trust, and confidence in her, so as to pray unto her, as his meaning must be, how well this follows from the place she hath in the creed, he is not a man who is not able to judge.

CHAPTER XVI.

Images.

Sect. xxiv. THE next excellency of the Roman church, which so exceedingly delighted our author in his travels, is their images. It was well for him that he travelled not in the days of the apostles, nor for four or five hundred years after their decease. Had he done so, and, in his choice of a religion, would have been influenced by images and pictures, he had undoubtedly turned Pagan, or else a Gnostic (for those pretended Christians, indeed wretches worse than Pagans, as Epiphanius informs us, had got images of Christ, which, they said, were made in the days of Pontius Pilate, if not by him); their temples being richly furnished and adorned with them, whilst Christian oratories were utterly destitute of them. To forward also his inclination, he would have found them, not the representations of ordinary men, but of famous heroes, renowned throughout the whole world for their noble achievements and inventions of things necessary to human life; and those portrayed to the life, in the performance of those actions which were so useful to mankind, and by which they had stirred up just admiration of their virtue in all men. Moreover, he would have found their learned men, profound philosophers, devout priests and virgins, contemning the Christians for want of those helps to devotion towards God which in those images they enjoyed, and objecting to them their rashness, fury, and ignorance in demolishing of them. As far as I can perceive, by his good inclination to this excellency of religion (the imagery of it), had he lived in those days, he would have as easily bid adieu to Christianity as he did in these to Protestantism.

But the excellent thoughts, he tells us, that such pictures and images are apt to cast into the minds of men makes them come to our "mount Zion, the city of the living God, to celestial Jerusalem, and society of angels," and so onward, as his translation somewhat uncouthly and improperly renders that place of the apostle, Heb. xii. A man, indeed, distraught of his wits, might possibly entertain some such fancies upon his entering of a house full of fine pictures and images; but that a sober man should do so is very unlikely. It is a sign how well men understand the apostle's words, when they suppose themselves furthered in their meditation on them by images and pictures; and yet it were well if this abuse were all the use of them in the Romish church. I wish our author would inform us truly, whether many of those whom, he tells us, he saw so devout in their churches, did not lay out a good part of their devotion upon the fine pictures and images he saw them fall down before? Images began first in being ignorant people's books, but they ended in being their gods or idols. Alas, poor souls! they know little of those many curious windings and turnings of mind, through the meanders of various distinctions, which their masters prescribe to preserve them from idolatry, in that veneration of images which they teach them, when it is easy for them to know that all they do in this kind is contrary to the express will and command of God. But, that our author may charge home upon his countrymen for removing of images out of churches, he tells us that it is the judgment of all men that the violation of an image redounds to the prototype. True, provided it be an image rightly and duly destined to represent him that is intended to be injured. But suppose any man, against the express command of a king, should make an image of him, on purpose to represent him deformed and ridiculous to the people; would he interpret it an injury or dishonour done unto him if any one, out of allegiance, should break or tear such an image in pieces? I suppose a wise and just king would look on such an action as a rewardable piece of service, and would in time take care for the punishment of him that made it. The hanging of traitors in effigy is not [merely] to cast a dishonour upon the person represented, but a declaration of what he doth deserve and is adjudged unto. The psalmist, indeed, complains that they broke down the פִּתּוּחֶיהָ, or carved works, on the walls and ceiling of the temple; but that those "apertiones," or "incisuræ," were not pictures and images for the people to adore and venerate, nor were appointed for their instruction, if our author knows not, he knows whither to repair to be instructed,—namely, to any comment, old or new, extant on that psalm. And it is no small confidence, to use Scripture out of the Old Testament for the religious use of images of men's finding out and constitution, whereas they may find as many testimonies for more gods,—enough, indeed, wherein the one are denied, and the other forbidden.

Nor will the ensuing contemplation of the means whereby we come to learn things we know not,—namely, by our senses, whence images are suited to do that by the eye which sermons do by the ear, and that more effectually,—yield him any relief in his devotion for them. There is this small difference between them, that the one means of instruction is appointed by God himself; the other, that is pretended to be so, absolutely forbidden by him.

And these fine discourses of the "actuosity of the eye above the ear," and its faculty of administering to the fancy, are but pitiful, weak attempts, for men that have no less work in hand than to set up their own wisdom in the room of and above the wisdom of God.

And our author is utterly mistaken if he think the sole end of preaching the cross and death of Christ is to work out such representations to the mind as oratory may effect for the moving of corresponding affections. This may be the end of some men's rhetorical declamations about it. If he will a little attentively read over the epistles of Paul, he will discern other ends in his preaching Christ and him crucified, which the fancies he speaks of have morally little affinity withal.

But what if Catholics have nothing to say for their practice in the adoration of images, seeing the Protestants have nothing but "simple pretences" for their removal out of churches? These simple pretences are express, reiterate commands of God; which what value they are of with the Romanists, when they lie against their ways and practice, is evident. The arguments of Protestants, when they deal with the Romanists, are not directed against this or that part of their doctrine or practice about images, but the whole; that is, the making of them (some of God himself), the placing of them in churches, and giving them religious adoration: not to speak of the abominable miscarriages of many of their devotionists in teaching, or of their people in committing with them as gross idolatry as ever any of the ancient heathens did; which shall at large be proved, if our author desires it. Against this principle and whole practice one of the Protestants' "pretences," as they are called, lies in the second commandment, wherein the making of all images for any such purpose is expressly forbidden. "But the same God," say they, "commanded cherubims to be made, and placed over the ark." He did so; but I desire to know what the cherubs were images of, and that they would show he ever appointed them to be adored, or to be the immediate objects of any veneration, or to be so much as historical means of instruction, being always shut up from the view of the people, and representing nothing that ever had a real subsistence "in rerum natura." Besides, who appointed them to be made? As I take it, it was God himself, who did therein no more contradict himself than he did when he commanded his people to spoil the Egyptians, having yet forbid all men to steal. His own special dispensation of a law constitutes no general rule; so that (whoever are blind or fools) it is certain that the making of images for religious veneration is expressly forbidden of God unto the sons of men. But, alas! "They were foreign images, the ugly faces of Moloch, Dagon, Ashtaroth; he forbade not his own." Yea, but they are images or likenesses of himself that, in the first place and principally, he forbids them to make; and he enforceth his command upon them from hence, that when he spake unto them in Horeb they "saw no manner of similitude," Deut. iv. 15; which surely concerned not "the ugly face of Moloch." And it is a very pretty fancy of our author, and inferior to none of the like kind that we have met with, that they have in their Catholic churches both, "Thou shalt not make graven images," and, "Thou shalt make graven images;" because they have the image of St Peter, not of Simon Magus; of St Benedict or good St Francis, not of Luther and Calvin. I desire to know where they got that command, "Thou shalt make images?" In the original, and all the translations lately published in the "Biblia Polyglotta," it is, "Thou shalt not;" so it is in the writings of all the ancients. As for this new command, "Thou shalt make graven images," I cannot guess from whence it comes; and so shall say no more about it. Only I shall ask him one question in good earnest, desiring his resolution the next time he shall think fit to make the world merry with his witty discourses, and it is this: Suppose the Jews had not made the images of Jannes and Jambres, their Simon Maguses, but of Moses and Aaron, and had placed them in the temple and worshipped them, as Papists do the images of Peter or the blessed Virgin, whether he thinks it would have been approved of God or no? I fear he will be at a stand. But I shall not discourage him by telling him beforehand what will befall him, on what side soever he determines the question.

He will not yet have done, but tells us the precept lies in this, "That 'men shall not make to themselves:' as if he had said, 'When you come into the land among the Gentiles, let none of you make to himself any of the images he shall see there set up by the inhabitants contrary to the law of Moses, and the practice of the synagogue, which doth so honour her cherubims that she abominates all idols and their sculpture.' And thus, if any Catholic should make to himself, contrary to what is allowed, any peculiar image of the planets," etc. But that "Nil admirari" relieves me, I should be at a great loss in reading these things; for truly a man would think that he that talks at this rate had read the Bible no otherwise than he would have our people to do it; that is, not at all. I would I could prevail with him for once to read over the book of Deuteronomy. I am persuaded he will not repent him of his pains, if he be a lover of truth, as he pretends he is; at least he could not miss of the advantage of being delivered from troubling himself and others hereafter with such gross mistakes. If he will believe the author of the Pentateuch, it was the image of the true God that was principally intended in the prohibition of all images whatever to be made objects of divine adoration, and that without any respect unto the cherubims over the ark, everlastingly secluded from the sight of the people. And the images of the false gods are but in a second place forbidden, the gods themselves being renounced in the first commandment; and it is this making unto a man's self any image whatever, without the appointment of God, that is the very substance of the command. And I desire to know of our author how any image made in his church comes to represent him to whom it is assigned, or to have any religious relation to him; for instance, to St Peter rather than to Simon Magus or Judas, so that the honour done unto it should redound to the one rather than to the other? It is not from any appointment of God, nor from the nature of the thing itself, for the carved piece of wood is as fit to represent Judas as Peter; not from any influence of virtue and efficacy from Peter into the statue, as the heathens pleaded for their image-worship of old. I think the whole relation between the image and the pretended prototype depends solely on the imagination of him that made it, or him that reverenceth it. This creative faculty in the imagination is that which is forbidden to all the sons of men in the "Non facies tibi,"—"Thou shalt not make to thyself;" and when all is done, the relation supposed, which is the pretended ground of adoration, is but imaginary and fantastic,—sorry basis for the building erected on it. This whimsical termination of the worship in the prototype, by virtue of the imagination's creation of a relation between it and the image, will not free the Papists from downright idolatry in their abuse of images; much less will the pretence that it is the true God they intend to worship, that true God having declared all images of himself, set up without his command, to be abominable idols.

CHAPTER XVII.

Latin service.

Sect. xxv. p. 280. THE next thing he gilds over in the Roman practice is that which he calls their "Latin service;" that is, their keeping of the word of God and whole worship of the church (in which two all the general concernments of Christians do lie) from their understanding in an unknown tongue. We find it true, by continual experience, that great successes and confidence in their own abilities do encourage men to strange attempts; what else could make them persuade themselves that they should prevail with poor simple mortals to believe that they have nothing to do with that wherein, indeed, all their chiefest concernments do lie; and that, contrary to express direction of Scripture, universal practice of the churches of old, common sense, and the broadest light of that reason whereby they are men, they need not at all understand the things wherein their communion with God doth consist, the means whereby they must come to know his will, and way wherein they must worship him? Nor doth it suffice these gentlemen to suppose that they are able to flourish over their own practice with such pretences as may free it from blame; but they think to render it so desirable, as either to get it embraced willingly by others, or countenance themselves in imposing it upon them whether they will or no. But as they come short of those advantages whereby this matter in former days was brought about, or rather came to pass; so, to think at once to cast those shackles on men, now they are awake, which were insensibly put upon them when they were asleep, and rejected on the first beam of gospel light that shined upon them, is, I hope, but a pleasing dream. Certain I am, there must be other manner of reasonings than are insisted upon by our author, or have been by his masters as yet, that must prevail on any who are not, on the account of other things, willing to be deluded in this. That the most of Christians need never to read the Scripture, which they are commanded by God to meditate on day and night, to read, study, and grow in the knowledge of, and which by all the ancient fathers of the church they are exhorted unto; that they need not understand those prayers which they are commanded to pray with understanding, and wherein lies a principal exercise of their faith and love towards God,—"are the things which are here recommended unto us." Let us view the arguments wherewith, first, the "general custom of the western empire, in keeping the mass and Bible in an unknown tongue, is pleaded." But what is a general custom of the western empire in opposition to the command of God, and the evidence of all that reason that lies against it? Have we not an express command not to follow a multitude to do evil? Besides, what is, or ever was, the western empire unto the catholicism of the church of Christ spread over the whole world? Within a hundred years after Christ the gospel was spread to nations and in places whither the Roman power never extended itself,—"Romanis inaccessa loca,"—much less that branch of it which he calls the western empire. But neither yet was it the custom of the western empire to keep the Bible in an unknown tongue, or to perform the worship of the church in such a language. Whilst the Latin tongue was only used by them, it was generally used in other things, and was the vulgar tongue of all the nations belonging unto it. Little was there remaining of those tongues in use that were the languages of the provinces of it before they became so: so that though they had their Bible in the Latin tongue, they had it not in an unknown; no more than the Grecians had who used it in Greek. And when any people received the faith of Christ who had not before received the language of the Romans, good men translated the Bible into their own; as Jerome did for the Dalmatians. Whatever, then, may be said of the Latin, there is no pretence of the use of an unknown tongue in the worship of the church in the western empire, until it was overrun, destroyed, and broken in pieces by the northern nations, and possessed by them (most of them Pagans), who brought in several distinct languages into the provinces where they seated themselves. After those tumults ceased, and the conquerors began to take up the religion of the people into whose countries they were come,—still retaining, with some mixtures, their old dialect,—that the Scripture was not in all places (for in many it was) translated for their use, was the sin and negligence of some who had other faults besides. The primitive use of the Latin tongue in the worship of God, and translation of the Bible into it, in the western empire, whilst that language was usually spoken and read, as the Greek in the Grecian, is an undeniable argument of the judgment of the ancient church for the use of the Scripture and church liturgies in a known tongue. What ensued on, what was occasioned by, that inundation of barbarous nations that buried the world for some ages in darkness and ignorance, cannot reasonably be proposed for our imitation. I hope we shall not easily be induced either to return unto or embrace the effects of barbarism. But, saith our author, secondly, "Catholics have the sum of Scripture, both for history and dogma, delivered them in their own language, so much as may make for their salvation, good orders being set and instituted for their proficiency therein, and what needs any more? or why should they be farther permitted either to satisfy curiosity, or to raise doubts, or to wrest words and examples there recorded unto their own ruin, as we see now by experience men are apt to do?" What Catholics have or have not, is not our present dispute. Whether what they have of story and dogma in their own language be that which Paul calls "the whole counsel of God," which he declared at Ephesus, I much doubt. But the question is, whether they have what God allows them, and what he commands them to make use of? We suppose God himself, Christ and his apostles, the ancient fathers of the church, any of these, or at least when they all agree, may be esteemed as wise as our present masters at Rome. Their sense is, "That all Scripture, given by inspiration from God, is profitable for doctrine." It seems these judge not so; and therefore they afford them so much of it as may tend to their good. For my part, I know whom I am resolved to adhere to; let others do as seems good unto them. Nor, where God hath commanded and commended the use of all, do I believe the Romanists are able to make a distribution, that so much of it makes for the salvation of men,—the rest only "serves to satisfy curiosity, to raise doubts, and to occasion men to wrest words and examples;" nor, I am sure, are they able to satisfy me why any one part of the Scripture should be apt to do this more than others; nor will they say this at all of any part of their mass. Nor is it just to charge the fruits of the lusts and darkness of men on the good word of God; nor is it the taking away from men of that alone which is able to make them good and wise a meet remedy to cure their evils and follies. But these declamations against the use and study of the Scripture, I hope, come too late. Men have found too much spiritual advantage by it to be easily driven from it. Itself gives light to know its excellency and defend its use by. "But the book is sacred," he says, "and therefore not to be sullied by every hand; what God hath sanctified let not man make common." It seems, then, those parts of the Scripture which they afford to the people are more useful, but less sacred, than those that they keep away. These reasons justle one another unhandsomely. Our author should have made more room for them; for they will never lie quietly together. But what is it he means by "the book?"—the paper, ink, letters, and covering? His masters of the schools will tell him these are not sacred; if they are, the printers dedicate them. And it is a pretty, pleasant sophism that he adds, "That God having sanctified the book, we should not make it common." To what end, I pray, hath God sanctified it? Is it that it may be laid up and be hid from that people which Christ hath prayed might be sanctified by it? Is it any otherwise sanctified but as it is appointed for the use of the church,—of all that believe? Is this to make it common, to apply it unto that use whereunto of God it is segregated? Doth the sanctification of the

Scripture consist in the laying up of the book of the Bible from our profane utensils? Is this that which is intended by the author? Would it do him any good to have it granted, or further his purpose? Doth the mysteriousness of it lie in the book's being locked up? I suppose he understands this sophistry well enough; which makes it the worse.

But we have other things yet pleaded, as "the example of the Hebrew church, who neither in the time of Moses nor after translated the Scripture into the Syriac; yea, the book was privately kept in the ark or tabernacle, not touched or looked on by the people, but brought forth at times to the priest, who might, upon the Sabbath-day, read some part of it to the people, and put them in mind of their laws, religion, and duty."

I confess, in this passage, I am compelled to suspect more of ignorance than fraud; notwithstanding the flourishing made in the distribution of the Old Testament into the law, prophets, and hagiography. For, first, as to the translation of the Scripture by the Jews into the Syriac tongue, to what purpose doth he suppose should this be done? It could possibly be for no other than that for which his masters keep the Bible in Latin. I suppose he knows that at least until the captivity, when most of the Scripture was written, the Hebrew, and not the Syriac, was the vulgar language of that people. It is true, indeed, that some of the noble and chief men, that had the transaction of affairs with neighbour nations, had learned the Syriac language toward the end of their monarchy; but the body of the people were all ignorant of it, as is expressly declared, 2 Kings xviii. 26. To what end, then, should they translate the Scripture into that language which they knew not, out of that which alone they were accustomed to from their infancy, wherein it was written? Had they done so, indeed, it would have been a good argument for the Romanists to have kept it in Latin, which their people understand almost as well as the Jews did Syriac. I thought it would never have been questioned but that the Judaical church had enjoyed the Scripture of the Old Testament in their own vulgar language, and that without the help of a translation; but we must not be confident of any thing for the future. For the present this I know, that not only the whole Scripture that was given the church for its use before the captivity, was written in the tongue that they all spake and understood, but that the Lord sufficiently manifests that what he speaks unto any, he would have it delivered unto them in their own language; and therefore, appointing the Jews what they should say unto the Chaldean idolaters, he expresseth his mind in the Chaldee tongue, Jer. x. 11; where alone, in the Scripture, there is any use made of a dialect distinct from that in vulgar use, and that because the words were to be spoken unto them to whom that dialect was vulgar. And when, after the captivity, the people had learned the Chaldee language, some parts of some books then written are therein expressed; to show that it is not this or that language which, on its own account, is to confine the compass of holy writ, but that that or those are to be used which the people who are concerned in it do understand. But what language soever it was in, "it was kept privately in the ark or tabernacle, not touched, not looked upon by the people, but brought forth at times to the priest." Ὦ τᾶν ποῖόν σε ἔπος [φύγεν ἕρκος ὀδοντων;]—What book was kept in the ark? the law, prophets, and hagiography? Who told you so? A copy of the law, indeed, or Pentateuch, was by God's command put in the side of the ark, Deut. xxxi. 26. That the prophets or hagiography were ever placed there is a great mistake of our author; but not so great as that that follows,—that the book, placed in the side of the ark, "was brought forth for the priest to read in on the Sabbath-days;" when, as all men know, the ark was placed in the "sanctum sanctorum" of the tabernacle and temple, which only the high priest entered, and that once a-year, and that without liberty of bringing any thing out which was in it, for any use whatever. And his mistake is grossest of all, in imagining that they had no other copies of the law or Scripture but what was so laid up in the side of the ark, the whole people being commanded to study in it continually, and the king, in special, to write out a copy of it with his own hand, Deut. xvii. 18, out of an authentic copy; yea, they were to take sentences out of it, to write them on their fringes, and posts of their doors and houses, and on their gates; all to bind them to a constant use of them. So that this instance, on very many accounts, was unhappily stumbled on by our author, who, as it seems, knows very little of these things. He was then evidently in haste, or wanted better provision, when, on this vain surmise, he proceeds to the encomiums of his Catholic mother's indulgence to her children, in leaving of the Scripture in the hands of all that understand Greek and Latin (how little a portion of her family!) and to a declamation against the preaching and disputing of men about it, with a commendation of that reverential ignorance which will arise in men from whom the means of their better instruction is kept at a distance.

Another discourse we have annexed, to prove that "the Bible cannot be well translated, and that it loseth much of its grace and sweetness, arising from a peculiarity of spirit in its writers, by any translation whatever." I do, for my part, acknowledge that no translation is able in all things universally to exhibit that fulness of sense and secret virtue, to intimate the truth it expresseth to the mind of a believer, which is in many passages of Scripture in its original languages; but how this will further the Romanists' pretensions, who have enthroned a translation for the use of their whole church, and that none of the best neither, but in many things corrupt and barbarous, I know not. Those who look on the tongues wherein the Scripture was originally written as their fountains, if at any time they find the streams not so clear, or not to give so sweet a relish as they expected, are at liberty, if able, to repair to the fountains themselves; but those who reject the fountains, and betake themselves to one only stream, for aught I know, must abide by their own inconveniences without complaining. To say the Bible cannot be well translated, and yet to make use, principally at least, of a translation, with an undervaluing of the originals, argues no great consistency of judgment, or a prevalency of interest. That which our author in this matter sets off with a handsome flourish of words, and some very unhandsome similitudes, considering what he treats of, he sums up, p. 283, in these words:—"By all this I would say thus much, The Bible translated out of its own sacred phrase into a profane and common one, loseth both its propriety and amplitude of meaning, and is likewise divested of its peculiar majesty, holiness, and spirit; which is reason enough, if there were no other, why it should be kept inviolate in its own style and speech." So doth our author advance his wisdom and judgment above the wisdom and judgment of all churches and nations that ever embraced the faith of Christ for a thousand years; all which, notwithstanding what there is of truth in any of his insinuations, judged it their duty to translate the Scripture into their mother tongues; very many of which translations are extant even to this day. Besides, he concludes with us in general ambiguous terms; as all along in other things his practice hath been.

What means he by "the Bible's own sacred phrase," opposed to "a profane and common one?" Would not any man think that he intended the originals wherein it was written? But I dare say, if any one will ask him privately, he will give them another account, and let them know that it is a translation which he adorns with these titles; so that upon the matter he tells us, that, seeing the Bible cannot be without all the inconveniences mentioned, it is good for us to lay aside the originals, and make use only of a translation, or at least prefer a translation before them! What shall we do with those men that speak such swords and daggers, and are well neither full nor fasting,—that like the Scripture neither with a translation nor without it? Moreover, I fear he knows not well what he means by its "own sacred phrase," and "a profane, common one." Is it the syllables and words of this or that language that he intends? How comes one to be sacred, another profane and common? The languages wherein the Scriptures were originally written have been put to as bad uses as any under heaven; nor is any language profane or common, so as that the worship of God, performed in it, should not be accepted with him. That there is a frequent loss of propriety and amplitude of meaning in translations, we grant. That the Scriptures by translations, if good, true, and significant, according to the capacity and expressiveness of the languages whereinto they are translated, are divested of their majesty, holiness, and spirit, is most untrue. The majesty, holiness, and spirit of the Scriptures, lie not in words and syllables, but in the truths themselves expressed in them; and whilst these are incorruptedly declared in any language, the majesty of the word is continued. It is much that men, preferring a translation before the originals, should be otherwise minded; especially that translation being in some parts but the translation of a translation, and that the most corrupt in those parts which I know extant. And this, with many fine words, pretty allusions, and similitudes, is the sum of what is pleaded by our author, to persuade men to forego the greatest privilege which from heaven they are made partakers of, and the most necessary radical duty that in their whole lives is incumbent on them. It is certain that the giving out of the holy Scripture from God is an effect of infinite love and mercy; I suppose it no less certain that the end for which he gave it was, that men by it might be instructed in the knowledge of his will, and their obedience that they owe unto him, that so at length they may come to the enjoyment of him;—this itself declares to be its end. I think, also, that to know God, his mind and will, to yield him the obedience that he requires, is the bounden duty of every man; as well as to enjoy him is their blessedness. And can they take it kindly of those who would shut up this gift of God from them, whether they will or no? or be well pleased with them that go about to persuade them that it is best for them to have it kept by others for them, without their once looking into it? If I know them aright, this gentleman will not find his countrymen willing to part with their Bibles on such easy terms.

From the Scripture (concerning which he affirmeth, "That it lawfully may, and in reason ought, and in practice ever hath been, segregated in a language not common to vulgar ears,"—all which things are most unduly affirmed, and, because we must speak plainly, falsely) he proceeds to the worship of the church, and pleads that that also ought to be performed in such a language. It were a long and tedious business to follow him in his gilding over this practice of his church;—we may make short work with him. As he will not pretend that this practice hath the least countenance from Scripture, so if he can instance in any church in the world, that for five hundred years at least after it [*i.e.*, Scripture] set out, in the use of a worship the language whereof the people did not understand, I will cease this contest. What he affirms of the Hebrew church keeping her rites in a language differing from the vulgar, whether he intend before or after the captivity, is so untrue as that I suppose no ingenuous man would affirm it, were he not utterly ignorant of all Judaical antiquity; which I had cause to suspect before that our author is. From the days of Moses to the captivity of Babylon, there was no language in vulgar use among the people but only that wherein the Scripture was written, and their whole worship celebrated. After the captivity, though insensibly they admitted corruptions in their language, yet they all generally understood the Hebrew, unless it were the Hellenists, for whose sakes they translated the Scripture into Greek;[1] and for the use of the residue of their people, who began to take in a mixture of the Syro-Chaldean language with their own, the Targums[2] were found out. Besides, to the very utmost period of that church, the solemn worship performed in the temple, as to all the interest of words in it, was understood by the whole people attending on God therein. And in that language did the Bible lie open in their synagogues; as is evident from the offer made by them to our Saviour of their books to read in, at his first entrance into one at Capernaum.

These flourishes, then, of our orator, being not likely to have the least effect upon any who mind the apostolical advice of taking heed lest they be beguiled with enticing words, we shall not need much to insist upon them. This custom of performing the worship of God in the congregation in a tongue unknown to the assembly, "renders," he tells us, "that great act more majestic and venerable;" but why, he declares not. A blind veneration of what men understand not, because they understand it not, is neither any duty of the gospel, nor any part of its worship. St Paul tells us he would "pray with the spirit, and pray with the understanding also." Of this majestic show and blind veneration of our author, Scripture, reason, experience of

[1] Dr Owen alludes to the Septuagint—a version of the Old Testament Scriptures in Greek, executed about 285 B.C. The testimony of Aristobulus, a Jew who lived at the beginning of the second century before Christ, and who gives the earliest notice of its origin, is as follows:—"The entire translation of all things in the Law was made in the time of the king surnamed Philadelphus, Demetrius Phalereus taking the principal charge of the work." The New Testament Scriptures contain seventy-four quotations taken exactly from the Septuagint, forty-six in which the difference is extremely slight, and thirty-two in which the agreement holds in regard to meaning, while in regard to the words there is some discrepancy. These facts practically supply us with the warrant of inspiration for translating the Scriptures into the living and vernacular languages of the world. The inspired writers used and appealed to the Septuagint version; and the force of this consideration is not abated by the fact that there are eleven instances in which they seem intentionally to have renounced it. The exception sustains the general rule on which they proceeded.—ED.

[2] The principal Targums are those of Onkelos and Jonathan; the former lived about 60 B.C., the latter shortly before the birth of Christ.—ED.

the saints of God, custom of the ancient churches, know nothing. Neither is it possible to preserve in men a perpetual veneration of they know not what; nor, if it could be preserved, is it a thing that any way belongs to Christian religion. Nor can any rational man conceive wherein consists the majesty of a man's pronouncing words, in matters wherein his concernment lies, in a tongue that he understands not. And I know not wherein this device for procuring veneration in men exceeds that of the Gnostics, who fraught their sacred administrations with strange, uncouth names and terms; intended, as far as appears, for no other end but to astonish their disciples. But then the church, he saith, as "opposite to Babel, had one language all the world over, the Latin tongue being stretched as large and as wide as the catholic church: and so any priest may serve in several countries, administering presently in a place by himself or by others converted; which are conveniences attending this custom and practice." Pretty things to persuade men to worship God they know not how, or to leave that unto others to do for them which is their own duty to perform; and yet neither are they true. The church by this means is made rather like to Babel than opposite unto it. The fatal, ruining event of the division of the tongues at Babel was, that by that means they could not understand one another in what they said, and so were forced to give over that design which before they unanimously carried on. And this is the true event of some men's performing the worship of God in the Latin tongue, which others understand not,—their languages are divided, as to any use of language whatever. I believe on this, as well as on other accounts, our author, now he is warned, will take heed how he mentions Babel any more. Besides, this is not one to give one lip, one language, to the whole church, but in some things to confine some of the church unto one language, which incomparably the greatest part of it do not understand. This is confusion, not union. Still Babel returns in it. The use of a language that the greatest part of men do not understand, who are engaged in the same work whereabout it is employed, is right old Babel. Nor can any thing be more vain than the pretence that this one is "stretched as large and as wide as the catholic church;" far the greatest part of it know nothing of this tongue, nor did ever use a word of it in their church service. So that the making of the use of one tongue necessary in the service of the church is perfectly schismatical, and renders the avowers of that principle schismatics from the greatest part of the churches of Christ in the world, which are or ever were in it, since the day of his resurrection from the dead. And as for the conveniency of priests,—there where God is pleased to plant churches, he will provide those who shall administer in his name unto them, according to his mind. And those who have not the language of other places, as far as I know, may stay at home, where they may be understood, rather than undertake a pilgrimage to cant before strangers, who know not what they mean.

After an annumeration of these conveniences, he mentions that only inconvenience which, as he says, attends the solemnization of the church's worship in a tongue unknown,—namely, "that the vulgar people understand not what is said." But as this is not the only inconvenience that attends it, so it is one,—if it must be called an inconvenience, and not rather a mischievous device to render the worship of God useless,—that hath a womb full of many others, more than can easily be numbered. But we must tie ourselves to what our author pleaseth to take notice of. I desire, then, to know what are these "vulgar people" of whom he talks? Are they not such as have souls to save? Are they not incomparably the greatest part of Christians? Are they not such as God commands to worship him? Are they not such for whose sakes, benefit, and advantages, all the worship of the church is ordained, and all the administration of it appointed? Are they not those whose good, welfare, growth in grace, and knowledge, and salvation, the priests in their whole offices are bound to seek and regard? Are they not those that Christ hath purchased with his blood; whose miscarriages he will require severely at the hands of those who undertake to be their guides, if sinning through a neglect of duty in them? Are they not the church of God, the temple of the Holy Ghost? called to be saints? Or who or what is it you mean by this "vulgar people?" If they be those described, certainly their understanding of what is done in the public worship of God is a matter of importance; and your driving them from it seems to me to give a "supersedeas" to the whole work itself as to any acceptation with God. For my part, I cannot as yet discern what that makes in the church of God which this "vulgar people" must not understand. "But this," saith he, "is of no moment." Why so, I pray?—to me it seems of great weight. No; it is "of no moment, for three reasons." Which be they?—1. "They have the scope of all set down in their prayer-books, etc., whereby they may, if they please, as equally conspire and go along with the priest as if he spoke in their own tongue." But I pray, sir, tell me why, if this be good, that they should know something and give a guess at more, is it not better that they should distinctly know and understand it all? This reason plainly cuts the throat, not only of some other that went before, about the *venerable majesty* of that which is not understood, but of the whole cause itself. If to know what is spoken be good, the clearer men understand it, I think, the better. This being the tendency of this reason, we shall find the last of the three justling it, as useless, quite out of doors. Nor yet is there truth in this pretence; not one of a thousand of the people do understand one word that the priest speaks distinctly in their whole service: so that this is but an empty flourish. He tells us,—2. "Catholic people come together, not for other business at the mass, but only, with fervour of devotion, to adore Christ crucified,—in that rite he is there prefigured as crucified before them,—and, by the mediation of that sacred blood, to pour forth their supplications for themselves and others; which being done, and their good purpose of serving and pleasing that holy Lord that shed his blood for us renewed, they depart in peace. This is the general purpose of the mass; so that eyes and hands to lift up, knees to bow, and heart to melt, are there of more use than ears to hear." For his Catholic people's business at mass, I shall not much trouble myself. Christ, I know, is adored by faith and love; that faith and love, in the public worship of the church, is exercised by prayer and thanksgiving. For the "lifting up of the eyes and hands," and bowing and cringing, they are things indifferent, that may be used as they are animated by that faith and love, and no otherwise. And I desire to know what supplications they come to pour forth for themselves and others? Their private devotions? They may do that at home; the doing of it in the church is contrary to the apostle's rule. Are they the public prayers of the church? Alas! the trumpet to them, and of them, gives an uncertain sound. They know not how to prepare themselves to the work; nor can they rightly say "Amen," when they understand not what is said. So that, for my part, I understand not what is the business of Catholics at mass, or how they can perform any part of their duty to God in it or at it. But what if they understand of it nothing at all? He adds,—3. "There is no need at all for the people to hear or understand the priest, when he speaks, or prays, and sacrifices to God on their behalf. Sermons to the people must be made in the people's language; but prayers that are made to God for them, if they be made in a language that God understands, it is well enough." This reason renders the others useless, and especially shuts the first out of doors; for certainly it is nothing to the purpose that the people understand somewhat, if it be no matter whether they understand any thing at all or no. But I desire to know what prayers of the priest they are which it matters not whether the people hear or understand? Are they his private devotions for them in his closet or cell, which may be made for them as well when they are absent as present, and in some respect better too? These, doubtless, are not intended. Are they any prayers that concern the priest alone, which he is to repeat, though the people be present? No, nor these neither; at least not only these. But they are the prayers of the church, wherein the whole assembly ought to cry jointly unto Almighty God,

—part of that worship wherein all things are to be done to edification; which they are in this and the Quakers' *silent meetings* much alike. Strange! that there is no need that men should know or understand that which is their duty to perform; and which, if they do it not, is not that which it pretends to be,—the worship of the church. Again; if the people neither need hear nor understand what is spoken, I wonder what they make there. Can our author find any tradition (for I am sure Scripture he cannot) for the setting up of a dumb show in the church, to edify men by signs, and gestures, and words insignificant? These are gallant attempts. I suppose he doth not think it was so of old; for sure I am, that all the sermons which we have of any of the ancients were preached in that very language wherein they celebrated all divine worship; so that if the people understood the sermons, as he says, "they must be made to them in a language they understand." I am sure they both heard and understood the worship of the church also; but "tempora mutantur." And if it be enough that God understands the language used in the church, we full well know there is no need to use any language in it at all.

But to evidence the fertility of his invention, our author offers two things to confirm this wild assertion:—1. "That the Jews neither heard nor saw when their priest went into the 'sanctum sanctorum' to offer prayers for them; as we may learn from the gospel, where the people stood without, whilst Zacharias was praying at the altar." 2. "St Paul, at Corinth, desired the prayers of the Romans for him at that distance, who also then used a language that was not used at Corinth." These reasons, it seems, are thought of moment; let us a little poise them. For the first, our author is still the same in his discovery of skill in the rites and customs of the Judaical church; and being so great, as I imagine it is, I shall desire him in his next to inform us who told him that Zacharias entered into the "sanctum sanctorum" to pray, when the people were without. But let that pass. By the institution and appointment of God himself, the priests in their courses were to burn incense on the altar of incense, in a place separated from the people, it being no part of the worship of the people, but a typical representation of the intercession of Christ in heaven, confined to the performance of the priests by God himself; "ergo," under the gospel, there is no need that the people should either learn or understand those prayers which God requires by them and amongst them! This is civil logic. Besides, I suppose our author had forgot that the apostle Paul, in his Epistle to the Hebrews, doth purposely declare how those Mosaical distances are now removed by Christ, a free access being granted to believers, with their worship, to the throne of grace. But there is scarce a prettier fancy in his whole discourse than his application of St Paul's desiring the Romans to pray for him when he was at Corinth,—and so, consequently, the praying of all or any of the people of God for their absent friends, or the whole church,—to the business in hand; especially as it is intended, with the enforcement in the close, that they used a language not understood at Corinth. But because I write not to men who care not whether they hear or understand what is their duty in the greatest concernments of their souls, I shall not remove it out of the way, nor hinder the reader from partaking in the entertainment it will afford him.

But our author, foreseeing that even those with whom he intends chiefly to deal might possibly remember that St Paul had long ago stated this case in 1 Cor. xiv., he finds it necessary to cast a blind before them,—that if they will but fix their eyes upon it, and not be at the pains to turn to their Bibles, as it may be some will not, he may escape that sword which he knows is in the way ready drawn against him;—and therefore tells us that "if any yet will be obstinate," (and which, after so many good words spent in this business, he seems to marvel that they should,) "and object what the apostle there writes against praying and prophesying in an unknown tongue," he hath three answers in readiness for him, whereof the first is that doughty one last mentioned,—namely, "That the prayers which the apostle, when he was at Corinth, requested of the Romans for him, were to be in an unknown tongue to them that lived in Corinth;" when the only question is, whether they were in an unknown tongue to them that lived in Rome, who were desired to join in those supplications? Surely this argument,—that because we may pray for a man when and where he knows not, and in a tongue which he understands not, that therefore the worship of a church, all assembled together in one place, all to join together in it unto the edification of that whole society, may be performed in a language unknown to them so assembled,—is not of such cogency as so suddenly to be called over again. Wherefore, letting that pass, he tells us the design of the apostle in that place is "to prevent the abuse of spiritual gifts, which in those days men had received, and especially that of tongues; which he lets them know was liable to greater inconveniences than the rest there mentioned by him." But what, I pray, if this be the design of the apostle, doth it follow that in the pursuit of this design he teaches nothing concerning the use of an unknown tongue in the worship of God? Could I promise myself that every reader did either retain in his memory what is there delivered by the apostle, or would be at the pains on this occasion to read over the chapter, I should have no need to add one word in this case more; for what are the words of a poor weak man to those of the Holy Ghost speaking directly to the same purpose? But this being not from all to be expected, I shall only mind them of some few things there determined by the apostle; which, if it do but occasion him to consider the text itself, I shall obtain my purpose. The gift of speaking with strange tongues being bestowed on the church of Corinth, that they might be a sign, unto them that did not believe, of the power and presence of God amongst them, verse 22, divers of them, finding, it seems, that the use of these tongues gave them esteem and reputation in the church, did usually exercise that gift in the assembly, and that with contempt and undervaluation of prophesying in a known tongue to the edification of the whole church. To prevent this abuse, the apostle lays down this for a standing rule, that "all things are to be done in the church unto edifying;" and that this all men, as to gifts, were to seek for, that they might excel to the edifying of the church, —that is, the instructing of others in knowledge, and the exciting of the grace of God in them. And thereupon he shows them that whatever is spoken in an unknown tongue, whether it be in a way of prayer or prophesying, in the assemblies, indeed tends nothing at all to this purpose, unless it be so, that after a man hath spoken in a tongue unknown, he doth interpret what he hath so spoken in that language which they do understand. For saith he, "Distribute the church into two parts, he that speaks with a tongue (whether he pray or preach), and those that hear. He that so prays and preaches edifies and benefits himself; but he doth not benefit them that hear him: and that because they understand not what he says, nor know what he means; for," saith he, "such words as are not understood are of no more use than the indistinct noise of harps, or the confused noise of trumpets. The words, it is true, have a signification in themselves; but what is that," saith he, "to them that hear them and understand them not? They can never join with him in what he speaks, nor say Amen, or give an intelligent assent to what he hath spoken." And therefore he tells them that for his part he had rather speak five words that, being understood, might be for their profit, than a thousand in an unknown tongue, which, though they would manifest the excellency of his gift, yet would not at all profit the church whether he prayed or prophesied; with much more to the same purpose. It is hence evident to any impartial reader, that the whole strength of the apostle's discourse and reasoning in this case lies in this,—that praying or prophesying in the church in a tongue unknown, not understood by the whole church, though known and understood by him that useth it, is of no use, nor any way tends to the benefit of the church, but is a mere confusion, to be cast out from among them. The case is no other that lies before us. The priest says his prayers in a tongue that, it may be, is known to himself,—which is no great gift; the people understand nothing of what he says. This, if the apostle may be believed, is a thing of no use, practised to no purpose, wherewith the people that understand not cannot join, whereby they are not at all profited, nor can they say Amen, or give a rational assent to what he speaks. Now, saith our author, "What is all this to the service of the church?" I say, So much to that service which he pleads for, as that it is condemned by it as altogether useless, unprofitable, and not to be longer insisted on: yea, and this is so much worse than the case proposed by the apostle, inasmuch as those who prayed and prophesied with tongues received the gift and ability of so doing, in a miraculous manner, from the Holy Ghost, and therefore might with much colour of reason plead for the free liberty of the exercise of those gifts which they had so received; but our readers of the service do with much labour and pains get to read it in Latin, doing it by choice, without any intimation for such a practice from any gift that above others they have received.

If all this will not do, there is that which brings up the rear that shall make all plain,—namely, "That whatever is pretended, yet indeed Latin is no unknown tongue, being the proper language of Christians, united to the Christian faith as a garment to a body:" which he proves by many fine illustrations and similitudes, telling us withal that "this one language is not spoken in a corner, but runs quite through the earth, and is common to all, as they be ranked in the series of Christianity; wherein they are trained up by the father of the family; and which, in reference to religion, he only speaks himself." But,—because I hope there is none of my countrymen so stupid as not to have the wit of the cynic, who, when a crafty companion would prove by syllogisms that there is no such thing as motion, returned him no other answer but by rising up and walking; and will be able at least to say, notwithstanding all these fine words, "I know that Latin to the most of Christians is an unknown tongue,"—I shall not much trouble myself to return any answer unto this discourse. That there is an abstraction of Christian religion, from the persons professing it, which hath a language peculiar unto it; that the Latin tongue hath a special relation to religion above any other; that it is any other way the trade-language of religion amongst learned men, but as religion comes under the notion of the things about which some men communicate their minds one to another; that it is any way understood by the thousandth part of Christians in the world that constantly attend the worship of God; and so that it is not absolutely as unknown a tongue to them, when it is used in the service of the church, as any other in the world whatever,—are such monstrous presumptions, as I wonder a rational man would make himself guilty of by giving countenance unto them. For him whom he calls "the father of the family" of Christians, if it be God he intends, the only Father of the family, all men know he never, to any of the sons of men immediately, nor by any prophet by him inspired, communicated his mind in Latin. If it be the pope of Rome whom he ascribeth that title unto, I am sorry for the man, not knowing how well he could make himself guilty of a higher blasphemy.

CHAPTER XVIII.

Communion.

Sect. xxvi. In the next section, entitled "Table," our author seems to have lost more of the moderation that he pretends unto, and to have put a keener edge upon his spirit than in any of those foregoing; and thence it is that he falls out into some more open revilings and flourishes of a kind of a dispute than elsewhere. In the entrance of his discourse, speaking of the administration of the sacrament of the Lord's supper by Protestants, wherein the laity are also made partakers of the blessed cup, according to the institution of our Saviour, the practice of the apostles, and the universal primitive church, this civil gentleman, who complains of "unhandsome and unmannerly dealings" of others in their writings, compares it to a treatment at my lord mayor's feast, adding, scornfully enough, "For who would not have drink to their meat? and what reason can be given that they should not? or that a feast with wine should not, 'cæteris paribus,' be better than without?" If he suppose he shall be able to scoff the institutions of Christ out of the world, and to laugh men out of their obedience unto him, I hope he will find himself mistaken,—which is all I shall at present say unto him; only I would advise him to leave for the future such unseemly taunts, lest he should provoke some angry men to return expressions of the like contempt and scorn upon the transubstantiated host; which he not only fancies but adores.

From hence he pretends to proceed unto disputing; but being accustomed to a loose rhetorical sophistry, he is not able to take one smooth step towards the true stating of the matter he is to speak unto, though he says he will argue in his "plain manner,"—that is, a manner plainly his, loose, inconcluding, sophistical. The plain story is this,—Christ, instituting his blessed supper, appointed bread and wine to be blessed and delivered unto them that he invites and admits unto it. Of the effects of the blessing of these elements of bread and wine,—whether it be a transubstantiation of them into the body and blood of Christ, to be corporeally eaten; or a consecration of them into such signs and symbols as in and by the use thereof we are made partakers of the body and blood of Christ, feeding really on him by faith,—is not at all now under dispute. Of the bread and cup so blessed, according to the appointment of Christ, the priests with the Romanists only do partake; the people of the bread only. This exclusion of the people from a participation of the cup, Protestants aver to be contrary to the institution of Christ, practice of the apostles, nature of the sacrament, constant usage of them in the primitive church; and so, consequently, highly injurious to the sheep of Christ, whom he hath bought with the price of his blood, exhibited in that cup unto them. Instead of arguing plainly, as he promised to do, in justification of this practice of the church of Rome, he tells us of the wine they give their people after they have received the body; which he knows to be in their own esteem a little common drink to wash their mouths, that no crumbs of their wafer should stick by the way. What he adds, of Protestants not believing that the consecrated wine is transubstantiated into the blood of Christ (which is not the matter by himself proposed to debate), of the priest's using both bread and wine in the sacrifice (though he communicates not both unto the people), when the priest's delivering of the cup is no part of the sacrifice, but of the communion (besides, he knows that he speaks to Protestants, and so should not have pleaded his fictitious sacrifice, which, as distinct from the communion, Paul speaks of, 1 Cor. xi., neither do they acknowledge, nor can he prove it),—[is] very vain; yet with these empty flourishes, it is incredible how he triumphs over Protestants for charging the Romanists with excluding the people from the use of the cup in the sacrament, when yet it is certain they do so, nor can he deny it. "Yea, but Protestants should not say so, seeing they believe not in transubstantiation." They believe every word that Christ or his apostles have delivered concerning the nature and use of the sacrament, and all that the primitive church taught about it; if this will not enable them to say that the Romanists do that which all the world knows they do, and which they will not deny but that they do, unless they believe in transubstantiation also, they are dealt withal on more severe terms than I think our author is authorized to put upon them. But it seems the advantage lies so much in this matter on the Roman Catholics' side, that the Protestants may be for ever silent about it. And why so? "Why, Catholics do really partake of the 'animated and living body of their Redeemer. This ought to be done, to the end we may have life in us; and yet Protestants do it not.'" Who told you so? Protestants partake of his body and his blood too,—which Papists do not,—and that really and truly. Again; "Catholics have it continually sacrificed before their eyes, and the very death and effusion of their Lord's blood prefigured and set before them for faith to feed upon; this Protestants have not." I think the man is mistaken, and that he intended to say the Catholics have not, and to place Protestants in the beginning of the sentence; for it is certain that this is the very doctrine of the Protestants concerning this sacrament. They have in it the sacrifice of Christ before their eyes, and the death and effusion of his blood figured (for how that should be prefigured which is past, I know not) and set forth for faith to feed upon. This they say, this they teach and believe; when I know not how Catholics can have any thing figured unto them, nothing being the sign of itself: nor is it the feeding of faith, but of the mouth, that they are solicitous about. "But this," saith he, "they do not,"—though he had not spoken of any doing before, which is an old last that we have been now well used to,—and "yet this," saith he, "ought to be done; for so our Lord commanded, when he said to his apostles, 'Hoc facite;'—'This do ye, which you have seen me to do, and in that manner you see me do it, exercising before your eyes my priestly function according to the order of Melchizedek; with which power I do also invest you, and appoint you to do the like, even unto the consummation of the world, in commemoration of my death and passion, exhibiting and showing forth your Lord's death until he come.' This Protestants do not; and we are mad-angry that the Papist does what his Redeemer enjoined him." I fear his readers, which shall consider this odd medley, will begin to think that they are not only Protestants who used to be *mad-angry*. This kind of writing argues, I will not say both madness and anger, but one of them it doth seem plainly to do; for, setting aside a far-fetched false notion or two about Melchizedek, and the doctrine of the sacrament here expressed is that which the pope with fire and sword hath laboured to exterminate out of the world, burning hundreds (I think) in England for believing that our Lord, instituting his blessed supper, commanded his apostles to do the same that he then did, and in the same manner, even to the consummation of the world, in the commemoration of his death and passion, exhibiting and showing forth their Lord's death until he come. A man would suppose that he had taken these words out of the liturgy of the church of England, for therein are they expressly found. And why, then, have not Protestants that which he speaks of? Yea, but Christ did this in "the exercise of his priestly function; and with the same power of priesthood, according to the order of Melchizedek, invested his apostles." Both these may be granted, and the Protestants' doctrine and faith concerning this sacrament not at all impeached; but the truth is, they are both false. The Lord Christ exercised indeed his priestly function, when on the cross he offered himself to God, through the eternal Spirit, a sacrifice for the sins of the world; but it was by virtue of his kingly and prophetical power that he instituted the sacrament of his body and blood, and taught his disciples the use of it, commanding its observation in all his churches to the end of the world. And as for any others being made priests after the order of Melchizedek besides himself alone, it is a figment so expressly contrary to the words and reasoning of the apostle, that I wonder any man, not mad or angry, could once entertain any approving thoughts of it. That our author may no more mistake in this matter, I desire he would give me leave to inform him, that, setting aside his "proper sacrificing" of the Son of God, and his hideous figment of transubstantiation, both utter strangers to the Scripture and antiquity, there is nothing can by him be named concerning this sacrament, as to its honour or efficacy, but it is all admitted by Protestants.

He pretends, after this loose harangue, to speak to the thing itself, and tells us that the "consecrated chalice is not ordinarily given to people by the priest in private communion;" as though in some cases it were given amongst them to the body of the people, or that they had some public communion wherein it was ordinarily so given; both which he knows to be untrue. So impossible it seems for him to speak plainly and directly to what he treats on! But it is a thing which hath need of these artifices: if one falsity be not covered with another, it will quickly rain[1] through all. However, he tells us, that they "should do so, is neither expedient nor necessary, as to any effects of the sacrament." I wish, for his own sake, some course might be found to take him off this confidence of setting himself against the apostles and the whole primitive church at once; that he might apprehend the task too difficult for him to undertake, and meddle with it no more. All expediency in the administration of this great ordinance, and all the effects of it, depend solely on the institution and blessing of Christ; if he have appointed the use of both elements, what are we, poor worms, that we should come now, in the end of the world, and say the use of one of them is not "expedient nor necessary to any effects of communion?" Are we wiser than he? Have we more care of his church than he had? or do we think that it becomes us thus arbitrarily to choose and refuse in the institutions of our Lord and Master? What is it to us what cavils soever men can lay, that it is not necessary in the way of Protestants, nor in the way of Catholics?—we know it is necessary in the way of Christ. And if either Protestants or Catholics leave that way, for me they shall walk in their own ways by themselves. But why is it not necessary

[1] In the original edition it is printed "rain," though in reprints of the work the word "reign" has been substituted, as seemingly more intelligible. Dr Owen, however, is adopting in part an expression which seems to be a favourite with him, as it occurs more than once in his writings:—"One lie must be thatched with another, or it will quickly rain through." See vol. viii. 584.—Ed.

in the way of Protestants? "Because they place the effect of the communion in the operation of faith; and therefore, according to them, one kind is enough: nay, if we have neither kind, there is no loss but of a ceremony, which may be well enough supplied at our ordinary tables." This is pretty logic, which it seems our author learned out of Smith and Seaton. Protestants generally think that men see with their eyes, and yet they think the light of the sun necessary to the exercising of their sight; and though they believe that all saving effects of the sacrament depend on the operation of faith (and Catholics do so too, at least I am sure they say so), yet they believe also that the sacrament which Christ appointed, and the use of it as by him appointed, is necessary in its own kind for the producing of those effects. These things destroy not, but mutually assist one another, working effectually in their several kinds to the same end and purpose. Nor can there be any operation of faith, as to the special end of the sacrament, without the administration of it according to the mind and will of Christ. Besides, Protestants know that the frequent distinct proposals in the Scripture of the benefits of the death of Christ, as arising sometimes from the suffering of the body, sometimes from the effusion of the blood of their Saviour, lead them to such a distinct acting of faith upon him and receiving of him, as must needs be hindered and disturbed in the administration of the sacrament under one kind; especially if that symbol be taken from them which is peculiarly called his testament, and that blood wherewith his covenant with them was sealed: so that, according to the principles of the Protestants, the participation of the cup is of an indispensable necessity unto them that intend to use that ordinance to their benefit and comfort. And what he adds, about "drinking at our ordinary tables," because we are now speaking plainly, I must needs tell him is a profane piece of scurrility, which he may do well to abstain from for the future. What is or is not necessary, according to their Catholic doctrine, we shall not trouble ourselves, knowing that which is so called by him to be very far from being truly catholic. The Romanists' doctrine of concomitancy,[1] being a late figment to countenance their spoiling the people of the legacy of Christ, unknown to antiquity, and contrary to Scripture, and enervating the doctrine of the death of Christ, whose most precious blood was truly separated from his body,—the benefit of which separation is exhibited unto us in the sacrament by himself appointed to represent it,—we neither believe nor value.

[1] According to the Council of Trent (Catech., cap. iii. quæstio 32), the *whole* of Christ, his blood as well as his body, is contained under both species,—both the bread and the wine. This is the Romish doctrine of *concomitance;* and hence the notion that the laity, in receiving the bread as the body of Christ, do not need the wine, but receive his blood nevertheless, inasmuch as it is contained in the body.—Ed.

As the necessity of it is denied, so also that there is any precept for it. What think you, then, of Πίετε ἐξ αὐτοῦ πάντες,—"Drink ye all of it," that is, this cup? They think this to be a precept to be observed towards all those who come to this supper. What Christ did, that he commanded his apostles to do: he gives the cup to all that were present at his supper, and commands them all to drink of it. Why, I pray, are they not to do so? Why is not this part of his command as obligatory to them as any others? Alas! "They were the priests that were present; all lay people were excluded." Not one was excluded from the cup that was there at any part of the ordinance. What if they were all priests that were there (as no one of them was), —was the supper administered to them as priests, or as disciples? or is there any colour or pretence to say that one kind was given to them as priests, another as disciples? "Dic aliquem, dic, Quintiliane, colorem." Was not the whole church of Christ represented by them? Is not the command equal to all? Nay, as if on purpose to obviate this sacrilegious figment, is not this word, "Drink you all of this," added emphatically above what is spoken of the other kind? Many strange things there are which these gentlemen would have us believe about this sacrament, but none of them of a more incredible nature than this, that when Christ says to all his communicants, "Drink you all of this," and commands them to do the same that he did, his meaning was that we should say, "Drink you none of this." They had need, not of a "spatula linguæ," to let such things as these down our throats, but a bed-staff, to cram them down, or they will choke us in the swallowing, and, I am sure, will not well digest when received. He must have an iron stomach that can concoct such crude morsels.

But if this will not do, he would fain have us grant "that the whole manner of giving the communion unto the laity, whether under one or both kinds, is left to the disposition of the church." I tell you truly, I should have thought so too, had not Christ and his apostles beforehand determined it; but as the case stands, it is left so much to the disposition of the church, whether the blessed cup shall be administered to the people, as it is whether we shall have any sacraments or no, and not one jot more. And let not our author flatter himself that it was a "preconceived opinion of the arbitrariness of this business, that made men scruple it no more in former ages, when the cup was first taken from them." They scrupled it until you had roasted some of them in the fire, and shed the blood of multitudes by the sword; which was the old way of satisfying scruples.

At length our author ventures on St Paul, and hopes, if he can satisfy him, he shall do well enough, and tells us, "This indifferent use of communion amongst the ancient Christians, in either kind, sometimes the one, sometimes the other, sometimes both, is enough to verify that of St Paul, 'We are all partakers of one bread and of one cup.'" But what is this "indifferent use," and who are these "ancient Christians" he tells us of? Neither is the use of one or of both indifferent among the Papists, nor did the ancient Christians know any thing at all of this business of depriving the people of the cup, which is but a by-blow of transubstantiation. He knows they knew nothing of it, whatever he pretends. Neither doth the apostle Paul say nakedly and only, that "we are all partakers of one bread and one cup;" but, instructing the whole church of Corinth in the right use of the Lord's supper, he calls to mind what he had formerly taught them as to the celebration of it: and this, he tells them, was the imitation of the Lord himself, according as he had received it in command from him to give the blessed bread and cup to all his communicants. This he lays down as the institution of Christ,—this he calls them to the right use and practice of; telling the whole church that "as often as they eat this bread and drink this cup" (not eat the bread without the cup), they "do show forth the Lord's death until he come." And therefore doth he teach them how to perform their duty herein in a due manner: verse 28, "Let," saith he, "a man examine himself, and so let him eat of that bread and drink of that cup;" adding the reason of his caution, "for he that eateth and drinketh unworthily, eateth and drinketh," etc.; intimating, also, that they might miscarry in the use of either element, for saith he, "whosoever shall eat this bread and drink this cup unworthily." In the administration of the whole supper you may offend, unless you give heed in the participation of either element. What can possibly be spoken more fully, distinctly, plainly, as to institution, precept, practice, and duty upon all, I know not. And if we must yet dispute about this matter, whilst we acknowledge the authority of the apostle, I think there is small hope of being quit of disputes whilst this world continues. The pitiful cavils of our author against the apostle's express and often-repeated words deserve not our notice; yet, for the sake of those whom he intends to deceive, I shall briefly show their insufficiency to invalidate St Paul's authority and reasonings.

1. He says, "That we may easily see what was St Paul's opinion, from these words, 'Whosoever shall eat this bread, or drink this cup of our Lord unworthily;'" and so say I too: the meaning of them is before declared. But saith he, "Repeating the institution as our Lord delivered it, he makes him, after the consecration of the bread, say absolutely, 'Do this in commemoration of me;' but after the chalice, he speaks with a limitation, 'Do this, as oft as you shall drink it, in commemoration of me.'" What then? Pray what are the next words? Are they not, "For as often as ye eat this bread and drink this cup?" Is not the same term, "as often," annexed to the one

as well as to the other? Is it a limitation of the use of either, and not a limitation of that kind of commemoration of the Lord's death to the use of both? From these doughty observations he concludes, "That the particle 'and' in the other text must needs be taken disjunctively: 'We are all partakers of one bread, and of one cup;' that is, all of us either partake of both, or each one, at least, either of the one or other." A brave exposition! But what shall we say to the other "*and*" in the other texts so often occurring to the same purpose? Are they also to be taken disjunctively? This, it seems, is to interpret Scripture according to the sense of the fathers; to vent idle cavils, which they were never so weak or perverse as once to dream of. Had the apostle but once used that expression, "This bread and this cup," yet adjoining that expression to the institution of Christ commanding the administration of that bread and cup, it were temerarious boldness so to disjoint his words, and render them incongruous to his purpose; but, repeating the same expression so often as he doth, still with respect to the institution of the ordinance whereof he speaks, to make us believe that in all those expressions he intended quite another thing than what he says, is a wild attempt. Miserable error! what sorry shifts dost thou cast thy patrons upon? Who would love such a beast, that so claws and tears her embracers? The trivial instances of the use of the particle "and" or "et" disjunctively, as in that saying, "Mulier est domûs salus, et ruina,"—which is evidently used not of the same individual person, nor of the same actions, but only expresses the different actings of several individuals of the same species,—concern not this business, whose argument is far from being founded alone on the signification of that particle (though its use be constant enough to found an inference not to be shaken by a few anomalous instances), but from the necessary use of it in this place, arising from the context of the apostle's discourse.

2. Our author farther adds, "That sometimes the whole sacred synaxis[1] is called breaking of bread, without any mention of the chalice." And what then? I pray, is not the body of Christ sometimes mentioned without speaking of the blood, and the blood oftener without speaking of the body? Is not the whole supper called the cup, without mentioning of the bread (1 Cor. x. 21), all by the same synecdoche? I shall not insist on his gross, palpable mistakes from Luke xxiv. 30. Nothing but domineering prejudices could ever put men upon such attempts for the justifying of their errors. Upon the whole matter, we may easily discern what small cause our author hath, from such feeble premises, to erect his triumphant conclusion of the non-necessity of participation of the blessed cup by the people in the

[1] A word used in ancient times to denote the Lord's supper.—ED.

sacrament of the Lord's supper. As little cause hath he to mention antiquity and tradition from the apostles, which lie universally against him in this matter; and that there is now no such custom in the Romish church, it is because they have taken up a practice contrary to the command and practice of Christ and his apostles, and contrary to the custom, in obedience thereunto, of all the churches in the whole world.

CHAPTER XIX.

Saints.

Sect. xxvii. FROM the communion we come to saints; and these take up the longest discourse of any one subject in the book. Our author found it not an easy task to set this practice of his church, in the worship and invocating of saints, right and straight in the minds of sober men. Several ways he turns himself in his attempt; all, as far as I can perceive, to very little purpose. In all of them it is evident that he is ashamed of their practice and principles in this matter; which makes his undertakings as to Protestants so much the worse, in that he invited them to feed upon that which he himself is unwilling to taste, lest he should be poisoned. At first he would persuade us that they had only a "respectful memory and reverence for the saints departed, such as ingenuous persons will have for any worthy personages that have formerly ennobled their families." To this he adds "the consideration of their example, and the patterns they have set us in the ways of holiness, to persuade and prevail with us to imitate and follow them." And with sundry arguments doth he dispute for his honourable esteem and imitation of the saints departed. Herein, then, it may be, lies the difference between them and Protestants,—that they contend that the true saints are to be thus honoured and followed; Protestants are of the mind that neither of them is to be done. "True; for 'Luther, Wickliff, and especially Calvin, have intemperately opened their mouths against all the saints; Calvin in special against the persons renowned in the Old and New Testament, Noah, Abraham, Rebecca, Jacob, Rachel, Moses,' etc., with a great number of others." Naughty man! what hath he said of them? "It is certain, in general, that he hath said that they were all in their days sinners." Is this to be endured, that "Calvin, that holy-faced man," should say of such holy persons, that they had need to be redeemed and saved by Jesus Christ? Who can bear such intemperate "theomachy?" "Nay, but he had gone farther, 'and charged them every one with sins and miscarriages.'" If he hath spoken any thing of their sins and failings but what God hath left upon record on set purpose in his word, that they might be examples of human frailty, and testimonies of his grace and mercy in Christ towards them, for the encouragement of others that shall be overtaken in the like temptation as some of them were, let him bear his own burden. If he have said no more but what the Holy Ghost hath recorded for him and others to make use of, I envy not their cheer who triumph in falsely accusing of him. But is this indeed the difference between Papists and Protestants about the saints? Is this the doctrine of the Papists concerning them? Is their practice confined within the limits of these principles? Are these the things which in their principles and practice are blamed by Protestants? The truth is, this is the very doctrine, the very practice of Protestants. They all jointly bear a due respect to the memorial of all the saints of God, concerning whom they have assurance that they were so indeed. They praise God for them, admire his grace in them, rejoice in the fruits of their labours and sufferings for Christ, and endeavour to be followers of them in all things wherein they were followers of Christ; and hope to come to be made partakers with them of that glory and joy which they are entered into. Is this the doctrine of the Council of Trent, or of the Harmony of Confessions? Doth this represent the practice of Papists, or Protestants? It is very seldom you shall hear a sermon of a Protestant, wherein the example of one saint or other is not in one thing or other insisted on, and proposed to imitation. If this venerable esteem and sedulous imitation of saints, with praising God for his graces in them, his mercy towards them, and an endeavour to obtain the crown they have received, be the doctrine, and the whole doctrine, of the church of Rome about the saints departed, why should we contend any longer? All parties are agreed; let us contend no more about that which is not. But if it be otherwise, and that neither are these things all the things that the Papists assert and maintain in this matter, nor are these things at all opposed by the Protestants, a man may easily understand to what end our author makes a flourish with three or four leaves of his book, as though they were in difference between us. Such artifices will neither advantage his cause nor his person with sober knowing men. As to his whole discourse, then, I shall only let him know that Protestants are unconcerned in it. They bear all due reverence to the saints departed this life, and strive to follow them in their course; although I must add, also, that their example is very remote from being the chiefest incentive or rule unto and in the practice of universal obedience. The example of Christ himself, and the revealed will of God in his word, are their rule and guide; in attendance whereunto thousands amongst them (be it spoken to the praise of his glorious grace!) do instantly serve God in all good conscience day and night, and holding the Head, grow up into him who is the fulness of him that filleth all in all.

To close this discourse, and to come to that which he seems to love as a bear doth the stake,—the practice of the Romish church in the invocation and adoration of saints,—he tells us, to usher it in, two pretty stories out of antiquity; the first, of the Jews, and last, of the Pagans. 1. For the Jews, "that they accused the Christians before the Roman emperors for three things:—that they had changed the Sabbath; that they worshipped images of the saints; that they brought in a strange God named Jesus Christ." What if they did so? was all true that the Jews accused the Christians of? Besides, what is here about the invocation of saints? Somewhat, indeed, we have about pictures and images, which, it seems, are contrary to the Judaical law; not a word do we meet with about their invocation of saints. But indeed this is a pretty midnight story to be told to bring children asleep; as though the Jews durst accuse the Christians before Pagans for "having images and pictures," when the Pagans were ready every day to destroy those Jews because they would have none. A likely matter, they would admit of their complaint against them that had them, or that the Jews had no more wit than to disadvantage themselves in their contest by such a complaint! Besides, the whole insinuation is false. Neither did the Jews so accuse them, nor had the Christians admitted any religious use of pictures or images in those days. And this their defence to the accusation of the Pagans, "that they rejected all images," makes as evident as if it were written by the sunbeams to this day. Being charged by the Pagans with an imageless religion, they everywhere acknowledged it, giving their reason why they neither did nor could admit of a religious use of any image at all. I presume our author knows this to be so; and I know if he do not, he is a very unfit person to talk of antiquity.

2. Of the like nature is the story which he tells us of the things the Pagans laughed at the Christians for. Amongst these was "the worship of an ass's head: which shows," saith he, "the use and respect they had for images; for the Jews had defamed Jesus Christ our Lord, whose head and half-portrait Christians used upon their altars, even as they do at this day,—amongst other things of his great simplicity and ignorance."[1] So use men to talk, who either know not or care not what to say. I would gladly impute this story of

[1] The last clause is literally quoted from "Fiat Lux," but in such a way as to cause some misconception. It is there connected with the conduct of the Pagan who, "amongst other things of his great simplicity and ignorance," is said to have laughed at the Christians for their worship of the objects to which reference is made in the rest of the quotation. The clause, therefore, is quite irrelevant, and might have been omitted.—Ed.

the ass's head, and the Jews' accusation, to our author's simplicity and ignorance, because if I do not so, I shall be compelled to do it unto somewhat in him of a worse name; and yet that by-insinuation of the use of "the head and half-portrait of our Saviour upon altars by the old Christians," before Constantine's days, of whom he speaks, will not allow me to lay all the misadventure of this tale upon ignorance. Surely he cannot but know that what he suggests is most notoriously false, and that he cannot produce one authentic testimony, no not one, of any such thing; whereas innumerable lie expressly against it, almost in all the preserved writings of those days. For the story of the ass's head: seeing, it seems, he knows not what I thought every puny scholar to be acquainted with, I hope he will give me leave to inform him that it was an imputation laid upon the Jews, not the Christians, and that the Christians were no otherwise concerned in the fable but as they were at any time mistaken to be Jews. The figment was invented long before the name of Christians was known in the world, and divulged before and after by as great wits as any were in the world, as Apion, Tacitus, Trogus, and others; the whole rumour arising from their worshipping a golden calf in the wilderness, and afterward his imitation progeny at Dan and Bethel. The confutation of the lie by Josephus is known to all learned men, who tells Apion that "if he had not had the head of an ass, and the face of a dog, he would never have given credit unto or divulged so loud a lie." Little countenance, therefore, is our author like to obtain from this loud lie, invented against the Jews, to prove the worshipping of pictures and images among Christians; nor is that his business in hand, if he be pleased to remember himself, but the invocation of saints, which now at length he is resolved (but I see unwillingly) to speak unto.

Had he intended plain dealing, and to persuade men by reason and arguments, he should nakedly and openly have laid down the doctrine and practice of his church in this matter, and have attempted to justify the one and the other. This had been done like a man who liked and approved what his interest forced him to defend, and upon honest principles sought to draw others to share with him in their worth and excellency. But he takes quite another course, and bends his design to cover his ware, and to hoodwink his chapmen, so to strike up a blind bargain between them.

Two things he knows that, in the doctrine of his church about the veneration of saints, Protestants are offended at:—

1. "That we ought religiously to invocate and call upon them, pray unto them, flying unto them for help and assistance;" which are the very words of the Trent Council, the avowed doctrine of his church, which whosoever believes not is cursed.

2. "That we may plead for acceptance, grace, and mercy with God, for their merits and works;" which our author gilds over, but cannot deny.

If he will plainly undertake the defence of either of these, and endeavour to vindicate the first from superstition, and the latter from being highly derogatory to the mediation of Christ, both, or either, to have been known or practised in the first churches, he shall be attended unto. To tell us fine stories, and to compare their invocation of saints to the psalmist's apostrophes unto the works of the creation to set forth the praise of the Lord, which they do in what they are, without doing more, and to deny direct praying unto them, is but to abuse himself, his church, his reader, and the truth; and to proclaim to all that he is indeed ashamed of the doctrine which he owns, because it is not good or honest, as the orator charged Epicurus. In the practice of his church, very many are the things which the Protestants are offended with:—Their canonization, framed perfectly after the manner of the old heathen apotheosis; their exalting men into the throne of religious worship, some of a dubious existence, others of a more dubious saintship; their dedication of churches, altars, shrines, days to them; their composing multitudes of prayers for their people, to be repeated by them; their divulging feigned, ludicrous, ridiculous legends of their lives, to the dishonour of God, the gospel, the saints themselves; with innumerable other things of the like nature, which our author knoweth full well to be commonly practised and allowed in his church. These are the things that he ought to defend, and make good their station, if he would invite others to a fellowship and communion with him. Instead of this, he tells us that his Catholics do not invocate saints directly; when I shall undertake (what he knows can be performed) to give him a book, bigger than this of his, of prayers allowed by his church, and practised by his Catholics, made unto saints directly, for help, assistance, yea, grace, mercy, and heaven, or desiring these things for their merit, and upon their account: which, as I showed, are the two main parts of their doctrine condemned by Protestants. I can quickly send him Bonaventure's Psalter; Prayers out of the Course of Hours of the Blessed Virgin; Our Lady's Antiphonies of her Sorrows, her Seven Corporeal Joys, her Seven Heavenly Joys, out of her Rosary; Prayers to St Paul, St James, Thomas, Pancratius, George, Blase, Christopher, whom not?—all made directly to them, and that for mercies spiritual and temporal; and tell him how many years of indulgences, yea, thousands of years, his popes have granted to the saying of some of the like stamp: and all these, not out of musty legends, and the devotion of private monks and friars, but the authentic instruments of his church's worship and prayers. Let our author try whether he can justify any of these opinions or practices from the words of the Lord in Jeremiah, "Though Moses and Samuel should stand before me, yet is not my soul unto this people,"—declaring his determinate counsel for their destruction, not to be averted by Moses or Samuel, were they alive again, who in their days had stood in the gap and turned away his wrath, that his whole displeasure should not arise;—or from the words of Moses, praying the Lord to "remember Abraham, Isaac, and Jacob his servants;" which he immediately expounds, as they are also in a hundred other places, by remembering his "covenant made with them, and the oath he sware unto them." These are pitiful, poor pillars to support so vast and tottering a superstruction; and yet they are all that our author can get to give any countenance to him in his work,—which indeed is none at all.

Neither do we charge the Romanists with the particular fancies of their doctors, their "speculum trinitatis," and the like; no, nor yet with the grosser part of the people's practice in constituting their saints in special presidentships,—one over hogs, another over sheep, another over cows and cocks, like the ruder sort of the ancient heathen,—which we know our author would soon disavow: but the known doctrine and approved practice of his whole church he must openly defend, or be silent in this cause hereafter. This mincing of the matter by praying saints, not praying to them; praying to them indirectly, not directly; praying them, as David calls on sun, moon, and stars to praise the Lord; so praying to them as it is to no purpose whether they hear us or no,—is inconsistent with the doctrine and practice of his own church, to which he seemeth to draw men, and not to any private opinion of his own. And a wise piece of business it is indeed, that our author would persuade us that we may as well pray to saints in the Roman mode, as Paul desired the saints that were then alive to pray for him! We know it is the duty of living saints to pray for one another; we know a certain way to excite them to the performance of that duty in reference unto us; we have rule, precedent, and command in the Scripture to do so; the requests we make to them are no illicit acts of religion; we pray to them neither directly nor indirectly, but desire them, by virtue of our communion with them, to assist us in their prayers, as we might ask an alms or any other good turn at their hands. I wonder wise men are not ashamed thus to dally with their own and others' eternal concernments. After all this, at one breath he blows away all the Protestants as childish (just as Pyrgopolynices did the legions of his enemies): "They 'are all childish.'" Let him show himself a man, and take up any one of them as they are managed by any one learned man of the church of England, and answer it if he can. If he cannot, this boasting will little avail him with considering men. I cannot close this paragraph without marking one passage toward the close of it. Laying down three principles of the saints' invocation, whereof the first itself is true, but nothing to his purpose; the second is true in the substance of it, but false, in an addition of merit to the good works of the saints, and not one jot more to his purpose than the other; the third is, that "God cannot dislike the reflections of his divine nature diffused in the saints, out of the fulness of his beloved Son, when any makes use of them the easier to find mercy in his sight." These are good words, and make a very handsome sound. Wilt thou, reader, know the meaning of them, and withal discern how thy pretended teacher hath colluded with thee in this whole discourse? The plain English of them is this: "God cannot but approve our pleading the merits of the saints for our obtaining mercy with him;" a proposition as destructive to the whole tenor of the gospel and mediation of Jesus Christ as, in so few words, could well be stamped and divulged.

CHAPTER XX.

Purgatory.

Sect. xxviii. We are at length come to Purgatory, which is the pope's Indies, his subterranean treasure-house, on the revenues whereof he maintains a hundred thousand fighting men, so that it is not probable he will ever be easily dispossessed of it. This is the only root of *Dirges*, though our author flourishes as though it would grow on other stocks. It is their prayer for the dead which he so entitles; and in the excellency of their devotion in this particular he is so confident, that he deals with us as the orator told Q. Cæcilius, Hortensius would with him, in the case of Verres,—bid him take his option and make his choice of what he pleased, and it should all turn to his disadvantage. Hortensius, by his eloquence, would make any thing that he should fix on turn to his own end. He bids us, on the matter, choose whether to think the souls they pray for to be in heaven, hell, or purgatory. All is one; he will prove praying for them to be good and lawful. Suppose they be in heaven, what then? "What then! may we not as well pray for them as for sanctifying the name of God, which will be done whether we pray or no?" Suppose they are in hell? "Yet we know it not, and so may show our charity towards them." But suppose they be in purgatory? "It is the only course we can take to help them." (Of purgatory we shall speak anon.) If there be no other receptacle for saints departed but heaven and hell, it is but a flourish of our author, to persuade us that prayers for them in the Roman mode would be either useful or acceptable to God. Suppose them you pray for to be in hell, the best you can make of your prayers is but a vain babbling against the will and righteousness of God,—an unreasonable troubling of the Judge after he hath pronounced his sentence. "Yea, but you do not know them to be in hell." Then neither do you suppose them to be there; which yet is the case you undertake to make good, "Suppose they be in hell, yet it is well done to pray for them;" and to say they may not be there is to suppose they are not in hell,—not to suppose they are; unless you will say, suppose they are not in hell, you may pray for them, suppose they are in hell. Hereunto doth this subtilty bring us. But it is not the will of God that you should pray for any in hell, no, not for any in heaven, unless it be the will of God that you should oppose his will in the one, and exercise yourselves in things needless and unprofitable in the other; both which are far enough from his mind, and that word which, I believe, at last will be found the only true and infallible rule of worship and devotion. When we pray for the sanctifying of God's name, the coming of his kingdom, the doing of his will, we still pray for the continuance of that which is, as to outward manifestation, in an alterable condition,—for the name of God may be more or less sanctified in the world,—and for that which is future. But to pray for them that are in heaven is to pray for that for them which they are in the unalterable enjoyment of; and besides, to do and practise that in the worship of God which we have no precept, no precedent, no rule, no encouragement for in the Scripture, nor the approved examples of any holy men from the foundation of the world. Whatever charity there can be in such prayers, I am sure faith there can be none, seeing there is neither precept for them nor promise of hearing them.

But it is *Purgatory* that must bear the weight of this duty. "This," saith our author, "need not to be so condemned, being taught by Pagans and ancient rabbis, and so came down from Adam by a popular tradition through all nations;" a great many of whose names are reckoned up by him, declaring, by the way, which of them came from Shem, which from Ham, which from Japheth, to whom the Hebrews are most learnedly assigned. For the Pagans, Virgil, Cicero, and Lucretius are quoted as giving testimony to them. This testimony is true; in the first especially lies the whole doctrine of purgatory. Some Platonic philosophers, whom he followed, have been the inventors of it. That some of the Pagans invented a purgatory, and that Roman Catholics have borrowed their seat for their own turn, is granted. What our author can prove more by this argument, I know not. The names of the old Hebrew rabbins that had taught, or did believe it, he was pleased to spare; and I know his reason well enough, though he is not pleased to tell us,—and it is only this, that there are no such old rabbins, nor ever were in the world: nor was purgatory ever in the creed of the Judaical church, nor of any of the ancient rabbins. Indeed, here and there one of them seemed to have dreamed with Origen about an end of the pains of gehenna; and some of the latter masters, the cabalists especially, have espoused the Pythagorean metempsychosis: but for the purgatory of the Pagans and Papists, they know nothing of it.

On these testimonies he tells us, "that this opinion of the soul's immortality, and its detention after death in some place 'citra cœlum,' is not any new thing freshly taught, either by our Saviour or his apostles, as any peculiar doctrine of his own, but taken up as granted by the tradition of the Hebrews, and supposed and admitted by all sides as true; upon which our Lord built much of his institutions." Gallantly ventured, however! I confess, a man shall seldom meet with prettier shuffling.

Purgatory, it seems, is the doctrine of the *soul's immortality*, and detention in some place "citra cœlum." Who would ever have once dreamed of this, had not our author informed him? This it is to be learned in the Roman mystery: the doctrine of purgatory is the doctrine of the soul's immortality! Never was doctrine so foully mistaken as that hath been; but if it be not, yet it is of the "detention of the souls in some place 'citra cœlum.'" It is indeed; but yet our author knows, that in these words as bad, if not a worse fraud than under the other is couched. It was the opinion of many of the ancients that the souls of the saints that departed under the Old Testament enjoyed not the blessed presence of God, but were kept in a place of rest until the ascension of Christ. And this our author would have us to think is the doctrine of purgatory; he himself, I hope, enjoys the contentment of believing the contrary. But he tells us "that our blessed Saviour and his apostles were not the first that taught this doctrine,"—that is, of purgatory; as though they had taught it at all, or had not taught that which is inconsistent with it, and destructive of it, which is notorious that they have. And for the traditions of the Hebrew church; as that was none of them, so I believe our author knows but little what were. But he takes a great deal of pains to prove, though very unsuccessfully, that "the Jews did believe that the souls of those that departed before the resurrection of the Messiah did not enter heaven;" as though that was any thing to his purpose in hand. But he is, as I said, marvellous unsuccessful in that attempt also. The parable of Lazarus and the rich man prove only that Lazarus' soul was in Abraham's bosom; that Abraham's bosom was not in heaven, it doth not prove. Peter, in the second of the Acts, proves no more than that the whole person of David, body and soul, was not ascended into heaven; the not ascending of his soul alone being nothing to his purpose. But what he cannot evince by testimonies, he will win by dint of arguments. "The Jews," saith he, "could not believe what God had never promised; but heavenly bliss was none of the promises of Moses' law, nor were they ever put in hope of it for any good work that they should do." It seems, then, that which was promised them in Moses' law was eternal life in some place "citra cœlum," or "citra culum," until the coming of the Messiah; for this he would fain prove that they believed; and that rightly. This I confess is a rare notion, and I know not whether it be "de fide" or no; but this I am sure, that it is the first time that ever I heard of it, though I have been a little conversant with some of his great masters. But the truth is, our author hath very ill success for the most part when he talks of the Jews; as most men have when they talk of what they do not understand. Eternal life and everlasting reward, the enjoyment of God in bliss, was promised no less truly in the Old Testament than under the New, though less clearly: and our author grants it, by confessing that the estate of the saints in rest "extra cœlum," to be admitted thither upon the entrance made into it by the Messiah, was promised to them, and believed by them; though any such promise made to them, or any such belief of them, as should give us the specification of the reward they expected, he is not able to produce.

"The promise of heaven is made clear under the New Testament; yet not so," he tells us, "but that, in the execution of this promise, it is sufficiently insinuated that if any spirit issue out of his body not absolutely purified, himself may indeed, by the use of such means of grace as our Lord instituted, 'be saved, yet so as by fire,'" 1 Cor. iii. I think I know well enough what he aims at, but the sense of his words I do not so well understand. Suppose a spirit so to issue forth as he talks,—seeing we must not believe that the blood of Jesus purges us from all our sins,—who or what is it then that he means by "himself?" Is it the spirit after it is departed, or is it the person before its departure? If the latter, to what end is the issuing forth of the spirit mentioned? And what is here for purgatory, seeing the person is to be saved by the means of grace appointed by Christ? If the former, as the expression is uncouth, so I desire to know whether purgatory be an instituted means of grace or no? and whether it was believed so by Virgil, or is by any of the more learned Romanists? I think it my duty a little to retain my reader in this stumbling passage. Our author having a mind to beg some countenance for purgatory from 1 Cor. iii., and knowing full well that there is not one word spoken there about the spirits of men departed, but of their trials in this life, was forced to confound that living and dead means of grace and punishment, things present and to come, that somewhat might seem to look towards purgatory, though he knew not what. Nor doth he find any better shelter for his poor purgatory,—turned naked out of doors, throughout the whole Scripture, as injurious to the grace of God, the mediation of Christ, the tenor of the covenant of grace, and contrary to express testimonies,—in those words of our Saviour, Matt. v.; who, speaking of sinners dying in an unreconciled condition, having made no peace or agreement with God, says that, being "delivered into prison, they should not go forth until they had paid the utmost farthing." For as the persons whom he parabolically sets forth are such as die in an absolute estate of enmity with God,—which kind of persons, as I take it, Roman Catholics do not believe to go to purgatory,—so I think it is certain that those enemies of God who are or shall be cast into hell shall not depart until they have paid the uttermost farthing; and that the expression "until" doth in Scripture always denote a limitation of time to expire, and the accomplishment afterward of what is denied before, I suppose, nay, I know, he will not say: so that their lying in prison until they pay the uttermost farthing of their debts (which is not God's way of dealing with them whom he washes and pardons in the blood of Christ, who are not able to pay one farthing of them) is their lying there to eternity. And so, also, of the sins of which it is said they "shall not be forgiven in this world, nor in the world to come," in one gospel; it is said in another that they "shall never be forgiven," —that is, not really forgiven here, nor declared or manifested to be forgiven hereafter. Besides, methinks this should make very little for purgatory, however the words should be interpreted; for they are a great aggravation of the sins spoken of, as the highest and most mortal that men may contract the guilt of that can be pardoned, if they can be pardoned. That the remission of such sins may be looked for in purgatory, as yet we are not taught; nay, our own author tells us that mortal sins must be remitted before a man can be admitted into purgatory: so that certainly there is not a more useless text in the Bible to his present purpose than this is, though they be all useless enough, in all conscience.

But here a matter falls across his thoughts that doth not a little trouble him; and it is this, that St Paul, in his epistles, never makes use of "purgatory, directly at least, as a topic-place, either in his exhortations to virtue or dissuasions from vice." And, I promise you, it is a shrewd objection. It cannot but seem strange that St Paul should make no use of it, and his church make use almost of nothing else. Little, surely, did St Paul think how many monasteries and abbeys this purgatory would found, how many monks and friars it would maintain, what revenue it would bring into the church, that he passeth it by so slightly. But St Paul's business was to persuade men to virtue, and dehort them from vice; and he informs us that there is such a contemperation of heat and cold in purgatory, such an equal balance between pains and hopes, good and evil, that it is not very meet to be made a topic for these ends and purposes; that is, that indeed it is of no use in religion. The trouble and comfort of it are, by a due mixture, so allayed, as to their proper qualities, that they can have no operation upon the minds of men, to sway them one way or other. Had some of our forefathers been so far illuminated, all things had not been at the state wherein they are at this day in the Papacy; but, it may be, much more is not to be expected from it, and therefore it may now otherwise be treated than it was yerst-while, when it was made the sum and substance of religion. However, the time will come when this Platonical signet,—that hath no colour from Scripture, but is opposite to the clear testimonies of it; repugnant to the grace, truth, and mercy of God; destructive to the mediation of Christ; useless to the souls of men, serving [not] only to beget false fears in some few, but desperate presumptions, from the thoughts of an after-reserve, and second venture after this life is ended; in the most, abused to innumerable other superstitions, utterly unknown to the first churches and the orthodox bishops of them, having by various means and degrees crept into the Roman church (which shall be laid open, if called for),—shall be utterly exterminated out of the confines and limits of the church of God. In the meantime, I heartily beg of our Romanists, that they would no more endeavour to cast men into real, scorching, consuming fire, for refusing to believe that which is only imaginary and fantastical.

CHAPTER XXI.

Pope.

Sect. xxix. It is not because the Pope is forgotten all this while, that he is there placed in the rear, after images, saints, and purgatory. It is plain that he hath been borne in mind all along; yea, and so much mentioned, that a man would wonder how he comes to have a special paragraph here allotted to him. The whole book seems to be all pope from the very beginning, as to the main design of it; and now to meet pope by himself again, in the end, is somewhat unexpected. But I suppose our author thinks he can never say enough of him. Therefore, lest any thing fit to be insisted on should have escaped him in his former discourses, he hath designed this section to gather up the paralipomena, or ornaments he had forgotten before to set him forth withal. And indeed, if the pope be the man he talks of in this section, I must acknowledge he hath had much wrong done him in the world. He is one, it seems, that we "are beholding unto for all we have that is worth any thing," particularly for the "gospel, which was originally from him; for kingly authority, and his crown-land, with all the honour and power in the kingdom;—one, that we had not had any thing left us at this day either of truth or unity, humanly speaking, had not he been set over us;—one in whom Christ hath no less shown his divinity and power than in himself; in whom he is more miraculous than he was in his own person;—one that, by the only authority of his place and person, defended Christ's being God against all the world; without which, humanly speaking, Christ had not been taken for any such person as he is believed this day:" so as not only we, but Christ himself is beholding to him, that any body believes him to be God! Now, truly, if things stand thus with him, I think it is high time for us to leave our Protestancy, and to betake ourselves to the Irishman's creed, "That if Christ had not been Christ when he was Christ, St Patrick" (the pope) "would have been Christ." Nay, as he is, having the hard fate to come into the world so many ages after the ascension of Christ into heaven, I know not what is left for Christ to be or do. The Scripture tells us that the gospel is Christ's, originally from him;—now we are told it is the pope's, originally from him: that informs us that by him (the Wisdom of God) "kings reign, and princes execute judgment;"—now we are taught, "that kingly authority, with his crown-land, is from the pope:" that instructs us to expect the preservation of faith and truth in the world from Christ alone; the establishment of his throne and kingdom for ever and ever; his building, guidance, and protection of his church;—but we are now taught that for all these things we are beholding to the pope, who, by his only authority, keeps up the faith of the deity of Christ; who surely is much engaged to him, that he takes it not to himself. Besides what he is, for our better information, that we may judge aright concerning him, we may consider also what he doth, and hath been doing, it seems, a long time: —"He is one that hath never been known to let fall the least word of passion against any, nor move any engine for revenge;—one whose whole life and study is to defend innocence," etc.; that by his "general councils, all held under and by him, especially that of Nice, hath done more good than can be expressed; careful, and more than humanly happy, in all ages, in reconciling Christian princes," etc.;— "one who, let men talk what they will, if he be not an unerring guide in matters of religion and faith, all is lost." But how shall we come to know and be assured of all this? Other men, as our author knows and complains, speak other things of him. Is it meet, that in so doubtful and questionable a business, and of so great importance to be known, we should believe a stranger upon his word, and that against the vehement affirmations at least of so many to the contrary? The Scripture speaks never a word that we can find of him, nor once mentions him at all. The ancient stories of the church are utterly silent of him, as for any such person as he is here described, speaking of the bishop of Rome as of other bishops in those days. Many of the stories of after ages give us quite another character of him, both as to his personal qualifications and employment,—I mean, of the greatest part of the series of men going under that name. Instead of peace-making and reconciliation, they tell us of fierce and cruel wars, stirred up and managed by them,—of the ruin of kings and kingdoms by their means; and instead of the meekness pretended, their breathing out threatenings against men that adore them not, persecuting them with fire and sword, to the utter depopulation of some countries, and the defiling of the most of Europe with bloody cruelties. What course shall we take in the contest of assertions, that we may be able to make a right judgment concerning him? I know no better than this,—a little to examine apart the particulars of his excellency as they are given us by our author, especially the most eminent of them, and weigh whether they are given in according to truth or no.

The first that we mentioned was, that "the gospel was originally from him, and to him we are beholding for it." This we cannot readily receive; it is certainly untrue, and fearfully blasphemous to boot. The gospel was originally from Christ; and to him alone are we beholding for it, as hath been before declared. Another is, that "kingly authority amongst us, and his crown-land, is from him." This is false and seditious. Kingly authority, in general, is from God, and by his providence was it established in this land, before the pope had any thing to do here: nor doth it lean in the least on his warranty, but hath been supported without the Papacy, and against all its oppositions; which have not been a few. A third is, that, "humanly speaking, had not he been set over us, we had not had this day either truth or unity." I know not well what you mean by "humanly speaking;" but, I am sure, so to blaspheme the care and love of Christ to his church, and the sufficiency of his word and promised Spirit to preserve truth in the world without the pope, whose aid in this work he never once thought of, requested, appointed, is, if not inhuman and barbarous, yet bold and presumptuous. That "Christ hath no less showed his divinity in him than in his own person," is an expression of the same nature, or of a more dreadful, if possible it may be. I speak seriously; I do not think this is the way to make men in love with the pope. No sooner is such a word spoken but immediately the wicked bestial lives, the ignorance, atheisms, and horrid ends of many of them, present themselves to the thoughts of men, and a tremor comes over their hearts to hear men open their mouths with such blasphemies as to affirm that the Lord Christ did as much manifest his divinity and power in such beasts as in his own person. Yea, that he is "more miraculous in him than he was in himself." What proof, sir, is there of this? where is the Scripture, where the antiquity, where the reason for it? We tell you truly, we cannot believe such monstrous figments upon their bare affirmation. Yea, but this is not all: "Christ is beholding to him for all the faith of his deity that is in the world." Why so? "Why, by the 'only authority of his place and person he defended it.'" When? "When it was opposed by the Arians," and he called his Council of Nice, where he condemned them. Who would not be sick of such trifles? Is it possible that any man in his right wits should talk at such a rate? Consult the writings of those days, of Alexander of Alexandria, of Athanasius, Gregory, Basil, Chrysostom, Austin, whom not?—go over the volumes of the councils of those days: if he can once find the authority of the pope of Rome and his person pleaded as the pillar of the faith of Christ's deity, or as any argument for the proof of it, let him triumph in his discovery. Vain man, that dares to make these flourishes, when he knows how those ancient Christian heroes of those days mightily proved the deity of Christ from the Scriptures, and confounded their adversaries with their testimonies, both in their councils, disputes, and writings, which remain to this day! Was not the Scripture accounted and pleaded by them all as the bulwark of this truth? And did not some of them,—Athanasius for instance,—do and suffer for the maintaining of it more than all the bishops of Rome in those days or since? And what a trifling is it to tell us of the pope's council at Nice!—as though we did not know who called that council, who presided in it, who bare the weight of the business of it, of whom none were popes, nor any sent by popes; nay, as if we did not know that there was then no such pope in the world as he about whom we contend. Indeed, it is not candid and ingenuous for a man to talk of these things in this manner. The like must be said of the first six councils mentioned by him; in some of which the power of the bishop of Rome was expressly limited, as in that of Nice and that of Chalcedon, and in the others. Though he was ready enough to pretend to more, yet he had no more power than the bishops of other cities that had a mind to be called patriarchs. We do not then, as yet, see any reason to change our former thoughts of the pope for any thing here offered by the author; and we cannot but be far enough from taking up his, if they be those which he hath in this discourse expressed, they being all of them erroneous, the most of them blasphemous.

But yet, if we are not pleased with what he is, we may be pleased with what he does, being so excellent a well-accomplished person as he is; for he is one that was "never known to let fall a word of passion." That, for casting off his authority, [he] should procure thousands to be slain and burned, without stirring up any "engine of revenge,"—these are somewhat strange stories. Our author grievously complains of uncivil carriage toward the pope in England, in all sorts,—men, women, and children. For my part, I justify no reviling accusation in any, against any whatever; but yet I must tell him, that if he thinks to reclaim men from their hard thoughts of him (that is, not of the person of this or that pope, but of the office as by them managed), it must not be by telling him he is a fine accomplished gentleman,—that he is "a prince, a stranger, a great way off, whom it is uncivil and unmannerly to speak so hardly of;"—but labour to show that it is not his principle to impose upon the consciences of men his apprehensions in the things of God; that he is not the great proclaimer of many false opinions, heresies, and superstitions, and that with a pretence of an authority to make them receive them whether they will or no; that he hath not caused many of their forefathers to be burned to death for not submitting to his dictates, nor would do so to them had he them once absolutely in his power; that he hath never given away this kingdom to strangers, and cursed the lawful princes of it; that he pleads not a sovereignty over them and their governors, inconsistent with the laws of God and the land: "Hæc cedo, ut admoveam templis, et farre litabo."[1] For whilst the greatest part of men amongst us do look upon him as the Antichrist foretold in the Scripture, guilty of the blood of innumerable martyrs and witnesses of the truth of Christ; others, who think not so hardly of him, yet confess he is so like him, that, by the marks given of Antichrist, he is the likeliest person on the earth to be apprehended on suspicion;—all of them think that if he could get them into his power, which he endeavours continually, he would burn them to ashes; and that, in the meantime, he is the corrupt fountain and spring of all the false worship, superstition, and idolatry wherewith the faces of many churches are defiled. To suppose he can persuade them to any better respect of him than they have, by telling them how "fine a gallant gentleman" he is, and what a great way off from them, and the like stories, is to suppose that he is to deal with fools and children. For my own part, I approve no man's cursing or reviling of him; let that work be left to himself alone for me. I

[1] Pers. ii. 75. The import of the quotation in the original is, that with an unblemished character, a man may approach the temples, and make peace with no more costly offering than a handful of flour. Owen intimates that if all the statements were true, which he has supposed the Papist to make, small reason for quarrel would be left between Protestant and Papist.—Ed.

desire men would pray for him, that God would convert him and all his other enemies to the truth of the gospel; and in the meantime to deliver all his from their policy, rage, and fury.

We may easily gather what is to be thought of the other encomiums given to him by our author by what hath been observed concerning those we have passed through; as, that "his whole life and study is to defend innocency," etc. It must needs be granted that he hath taken some little time to provide for himself in the world; he had surely never arrived else to that degree of excellency as to tread on the necks of emperors, to have kings hold his stirrup, to kick off their crowns, to exceed the rulers of the earth in worldly pomp, state, and treasures, which came not to him by inheritance from St Peter: and whether he hath been such a defender of innocency and innocents, the day wherein God shall make inquisition for blood will manifest. The great work he hath done by his general councils, a summary of which is given us by our author, is next pretended:—"All this was done by him; yea, all that good that was ever done by general councils in the world was done by him: for they were all his councils, and that which was not his is none." I shall only mind our author of what was said of old unto one talking at that rate that he is pleased here to do:—

"Labore alieno magno partam gloriam
Verbis sæpe in se transmovet, qui habet salem,
Qui in te est." [Ter. Eun. iii. 1, 10.]

All the glory and renown of the old ancient councils, all their labours for the extirpation of heresies and errors, and the success that their honest endeavours were blessed withal, with the seasoning of one little word, "his," are turned over to the pope. They were "his councils;" a thing they never once dreamed of, nor any mortal man in the days wherein they were celebrated. Convened they were in the name and upon the institution of Christ, and so were "His" councils; were called together, as to their solemn external convention, by the emperors of those days, and so were not their councils, but councils held by their authority, as to all the external concernments of them. This the councils themselves did acknowledge, and so did the bishops of Rome in those days, when they joined their petitions with others unto the emperors for the convening of them; and seldom it was that they could obtain their meetings in any place they desired, though they were many of them wise at an after-game, and turned their remoteness from them into their advantage. As they were called by the emperors, so they were composed of bishops and others, with equal suffrages. How they come to be the pope's councils he himself only knows, and those to whom he is pleased to impart this secret; of other men not one. Indeed, some of them may be called his councils, if every thing is his wherein he is any way concerned. Such was the first council of Nice, as to his pretended jurisdiction; such that of Chalcedon, as to his primacy; such were sundry famous conventions in Afric, wherein his pretensions unto authority were excluded, and his unseemly frauds discovered. Nay, there is not any thing upon the roll of antiquity of greater and more prodigious scandal than the contests of popes, in some African councils, for authority and jurisdiction. Their claim was such as that the good fathers assembled wrote unto them that they would not introduce secular pride and ambition into the church of Christ. And the manner of managing their pretensions was no other but downright forgery, and that of no less than canons of the first memorable Council of Nice: which to discover, the honest African bishops were forced to send to Constantinople, Alexandria, and Antioch, for authentic copies of those canons, upon the receipt whereof they mollified the forgery with much Christian sobriety and prudence unto the bishop of Rome himself, and enacted a decree for the future, to prevent his pretensions and claims. Besides, as the good bishops aver, God himself testified against the irregular interposition of the pretended power of the bishop of Rome; for whilst they, being synodically assembled, were detained and hindered in their procedure by the Romanists' contests for superiority, Apiarius, the guilty person, being convinced in his conscience of his many notorious evils and crimes, from a just censure whereof the Roman interposition was used to shelter him, of his own accord cast himself at the feet of the assembly, confessing all his wickedness and folly. Of the six first councils, then, there is no more reason to call them the pope's, or to ascribe their achievements unto him, than there is to call them any other bishop's of any city then famous in the world. In that which he calls the "seventh general council,"—indeed a conventicle of ignorant, tumultuous, superstitious iconolaters, condemned afterward by a council held at Frankfort by the authority of Charles the Great,—he stickled to some purpose for images, which then began to be his darlings; and though we can afford that council to be his, for any concernment we have in it, yet the story of it will not allow us to do so, it being neither convened nor ruled by his authority, though the brutish monks in it were willing to shelter themselves under the splendour and lustre of his see. About those that follow we will not much contend; it matters not whose they were, unless they had been better,—especially such as laid foundations for, and stirred up princes to shed the innocent blood of the martyrs of Christ, to some of their perpetual ignominy, reproach, and ruin. But yet our author knows, or may know, what long contests there have been, even in latter ages, whether the council should be the pope's council, or the pope should be the council's pope; and how the pope carried it at last, by having more archbishoprics and bishoprics in his disposal than the councils had. And so much for the pope's councils.

Our author adds, that "he hath been more than humanly happy in reconciling Christian princes;" but yet I will venture a wager with him that I will give more instances of his setting princes together by the ears than he shall of reconciling them; and I will manifest that he hath got more by the first work than the latter. Let him begin the vie when he pleaseth; if I live, and God will, I will try this matter with him before any competent judges. "Tu dic mecum, quo pignore?" [Virg. Ecl. iii. 36.] How else to end this matter, I know not.

I see not, then, any ground my countrymen have to alter their thoughts concerning the pope, for any thing here tendered unto them by this author; yea, I know they have great reason to be confirmed in their former apprehensions concerning him: for all that truly honour the Lord Jesus Christ have reason to be moved when they hear another, if not preferred before him, nor set up in competition with him, yet openly invested with many of his privileges and prerogatives, especially considering that not only the person of Christ, but his word also, is debased to make way to his exaltation and advancement. Thence it is that it is openly averred, that were it not for his "infallibility, we should all this time have been at a loss for truth and unity." Of so small esteem with some men is the wisdom of Christ, who left his word with his church for these ends, and his word itself! All is nothing without the pope. If I mistake not, in the light and temper of my countrymen, this is not the way to gain their good opinion of him. Had our author kept himself to the general terms of a good prince, a universal pastor, a careful guide, and to general stories of his wisdom, care, and circumspection for public good,—which discourse makes up what remains of this paragraph,—he might perhaps have got some ground on their affection and esteem who know nothing concerning him to the contrary, which in England are very few. But these notes above Ela,[1] these transcendent encomiums, have quite marred his market. And if there be no medium, but men must believe the pope to be either Christ or antichrist, it is evident which way the general vogue in England will go, and that at least until fire and fagot come;—which, blessed be God! we are secured from whilst our present sovereign sways the sceptre of this land; and hope our posterity may be so under his offspring for many generations.

[1] Ela is an old term for the highest note in the scale of music. See Bailey's Dict. —Ed.

CHAPTER XXII.

Popery.

Sect. xxx. Our author hopes, it seems, that by this time he hath brought his disciples to Popery. That is the title of the last paragraph to his business, not of his book; for that which follows, being a parcel of the excellent speech of my lord chancellor, is about a matter wherein his concernment lies not: this is his close and farewell. They say there is one who, when he goes out of any place, leaves a worse savour at his departure than he gave all the time of his abode; and he seems here to be imitated. The disingenuity of this paragraph, the want of care, of truth, and of common honesty, that appears in it, sends forth a worse savour than most of those, if not than any or all of them, that went before. The design of it is to give us a parallel of some popish and protestant doctrines, that the beauty of the one may the better be set off by the deformity of the other. To this end he hath made no conscience of mangling, defacing, and defiling of the latter. The doctrines he mentions, he calls "the more plausible parts of Popery,"—such as he hath laboured in his whole discourse to gild and trick up with his rhetoric; nor shall I quarrel with him for his doting on them, only I cannot but wish it might suffice him to enjoy and proclaim the beauty of his church without open slandering and defaming of ours. This is not handsome, civil, mannerly, nor conscientious. A few instances will manifest whether he hath failed in this kind or no.

The first "plausible piece of Popery," as he calls it, that he presents us in his antithesis, is "the obligation which all have who believe in Christ to attend unto good works, and the merit and benefit of so doing:" in opposition whereunto he says Protestants "teach that there be no such things as good works pleasing unto God, but all be as menstruous rags, filthy, odious, and damnable in the sight of heaven; that if it were otherwise, yet they are not in our power to perform." Let other men do what they please, or are able: for my part, if this be a good work, to believe that a man conscientiously handles the things of religion, with a reverence of God and a regard to the account he is to make at the last day, who can thus openly calumniate and equivocate, I must confess I do not find it in my power to perform it. It may be he thinks it no great sin to calumniate and falsely accuse heretics; or, if it be, but a venial one,—such a one as hath no respect to heaven or hell, but only purgatory, which hath no great influence on the minds of men to keep them from vice or provoke them to virtue.

Do Protestants teach, "There are no such things as good works pleasing to God?" or, that "those that believe are not obliged to good works?" In which of their confessions do they so say? in what public writing of any of their churches? What one individual Protestant was ever guilty of thinking or venting this folly? If our author had told this story in Rome or Italy, he had wronged himself only in point of morality; but telling it in England, if I mistake not, he is utterly gone also as to reputation. But yet you will say, that if there be good works, yet it is not in our power to perform them. No more will Papists neither, that know what they say, or are in their right wits, that it is so without the help of the grace of God; and the Protestant never lived, that I know of, that denied them, by that help and assistance, to be in our power. "But they say, they are 'all as filthy rags,' etc." I am glad he will acknowledge Isaiah to be a Protestant, whose words they are, concerning all our righteousness, that he traduceth. We shall have him some time or other denying some of the prophets or apostles to be Protestants; and yet it is known that they all agreed in their doctrine and faith. Those other Protestants, whom he labours principally to asperse, will tell him, that although God do indispensably require good works of them that do believe; and they, by the assistance of his grace, do perform constantly those good works which, both for the matter and the manner of their performance, are acceptable to him in Jesus Christ, according to the tenor of the covenant of grace; and which, as the effect of his grace in us, shall be eternally rewarded: yet, that such is the infinite purity and holiness of the great God with whom we have to do, in whose sight the heavens are not pure, and who charges his angels with folly, that if he should deal with the best of our works according to the exigence and rigour of his justice, they would appear wanting, defective, yea, filthy in his sight; so that our works have need of acceptation in Christ no less than our persons. And they add this to their faith in this matter, that they believe that those who deny this know little of God or themselves.

My pen is dull, and the book that was lent me for a few days is called for. "Ex hoc uno," by this instance, we may take a measure of all the rest, wherein the same ingenuity and conscientious care of offending is observed as in this; that is, neither the one nor other is so. The residue of his discourse is but a commendation of his religion and the professors of it, whereof, I must confess, I begin to grow weary; having had so much of it, and so often repeated, and that from one of themselves, and that on principles which will not endure the trial and examination. Of this sort is the suffering for their religion, which he extols in them. Not what God calls them unto, or others impose upon them in any part of the world,—wherein they are not to be compared with Protestants, nor have suffered from all the world for their papal religion the hundredth part of what Protestants have suffered from themselves alone for their refusal of it, —doth he intend, but what of their own accord they undergo; not considering, that as outward affliction and persecution from the world have been always the constant lot of the true worshippers of Christ in all ages, so voluntary self-macerations have attended the ways of false worship, among all sorts of men, from the foundation of the world.

A VINDICATION

OF

THE ANIMADVERSIONS ON "FIAT LUX;"

WHEREIN THE PRINCIPLES OF THE ROMAN CHURCH AS TO MODERATION, UNITY, AND TRUTH, ARE EXAMINED; AND SUNDRY IMPORTANT CONTROVERSIES, CONCERNING THE RULE OF FAITH, PAPAL SUPREMACY, THE MASS, IMAGES, ETC., DISCUSSED.

Imprimatur,

THO. GREIG, R. in Christ. P. D. Humfr. Episc. Lond. à Sac. domesticis.

Decemb. 9, 1663.

PREFATORY NOTE.

The previous work of Owen did not pass without a reply from Cane, whose "Fiat Lux" it so smartly refutes. The latter published a letter to the author of the "Animadversions," in which he betrayed his own sense of discomfiture by wandering from the subject to assail his antagonist and direct public antipathy against him for his conduct during the time of the Commonwealth. In 1664 Dr Owen published the following work,—his chief contribution to the Popish controversy; in which, while he incidentally disposes of the political insinuations of Cane, he enters with greater fulness of detail on the leading points of the controversy, and completes the argument, which he had not time to develop in the previous treatise. The chief defect in this able work arises from the plan which Owen was constrained to adopt. It was necessary for him to review in succession the topics which his opponent had discussed in "Fiat Lux." A wish may now be felt, that, since that work has passed into merited oblivion, this masterly dissertation on the leading errors of Romanism by our author had appeared in a shape less connected with a passing dispute, and more fitted to be of general and standing value in the controversy. The exigency, however, which drew from him the publication, could not have been met, had it appeared in such a form. We would have missed the humour with which the treatise abounds, and by which Dr Owen gives buoyancy to his argument; although embarrassed sometimes by the extent and variety of his lore, he reminds us in his humour of the cumbrous gambols of the whale. All the more important subjects, too, in the controversy with Rome, are considered in the work, and some of them handled with peculiar success. Indeed, on some points, if the facts and arguments in both treatises be taken together, a more successful refutation of the claims of the Church of Rome could not be desiderated. In one respect, moreover, the author kept in view the desirableness of securing for his work a general value among Protestants, by arguing always on ground common to all Protestants, and refusing, in spite of the wily snares of his adversary, to be drawn from this ground.

Our admiration of the ability and learning in these works is increased when we remember he was all the time suffering much from a professedly Protestant government, in spite of all these services to the Protestant cause. On the Restoration, he had retired to his estate at Stadham, and lived very quietly and privately. Persecution grew so hot that he was obliged to leave it, and escape arrest by frequent removals from place to place. He came to London, and occupied himself in the publication of these treatises. In the very year when the work which follows was published, he was so harassed that he resolved to comply with an invitation from the brethren in New England, and in 1665 made preparations to leave the country. He had great difficulty even in getting his "Vindication of the Animadversions" published. The bishops appointed by act of Parliament censors of the press on theological works, refused to license the printing of it; because "upon all occasions when he mentions the evangelists and apostles, even St Peter himself, he left out the title of *Saint;*" and because "he endeavours to prove that it could not be determined that St Peter was ever at Rome." He yielded willingly to the first objection, alleging, however, that apostle and evangelist was a higher appellation than the term saint, which was applicable to all the family of God; but he declared that he would rather see his work suppressed than change his views on the other point. Most probably it would have been suppressed; on a representation, however, of Sir Edward Nicholas, one of the Secretaries of State, to the Bishop of London, it was published with the imprimatur of Thomas Greig, his lordship's domestic chaplain.

The book, when at length published, produced, like its predecessor, great effect. Lord Clarendon sent for the author by Sir Bulstrode Whitelocke, commended his work in high terms, and assured him that "he deserved the best of any English Protestant of late years."—(See Asty's Memoir, p. xxiv.) Preferment in the Church of England was also offered him; but for the particulars of this remarkable interview, we may refer to the Life of Owen, vol. i. p. lxxx.

An analysis of the work is not required. The author adopts the order of his antagonist in the discussion of the several topics. The chapters on the more important subjects are so replete with argument and learning, all flavoured with a humorous exposure of the character of Romanism, and the labyrinth of fallacies in which his opponent is entangled, that the work is yet fresh in value and interest. Considered as a whole, it has undoubtedly been superseded by other works of more enlarged design, and more adapted to the present stage of the war with Rome, but occasionally a course of admirable thinking appears, for which we may look in vain among other kindred treatises.—Ed.

TO THE READER.

CHRISTIAN READER,

ALTHOUGH our Lord Jesus Christ hath laid blessed and stable foundations of *unity, peace,* and *agreement* in judgment and affection amongst all his disciples, and given forth command for their attendance unto them, that thereby they might glorify him in the world, and promote their own spiritual advantage; yet also, foreknowing what effect the crafts of Satan, in conjunction with the darkness and lusts of men, would produce, that no offence might thence be taken against him or any of his ways, he hath forewarned all men by his Spirit what *differences, divisions, schisms,* and *heresies* would ensue on the publication of the gospel, and arise even among them that should profess subjection unto his authority and law. And, accordingly, it speedily came to pass; for what Solomon says that he discovered concerning the *first creation,*—namely, that "God made man upright, but he sought out many inventions," or immixed himself in endless questions,—the same fell out in the *new creation,* or erection of the church of Christ. The state of it was by him formed upright, and all that belonged unto it were of one heart and one soul; but this harmony and perfection of beauty, in answer to his will and institution, lasted not long among them,—many who mixed themselves with those primitive converts, or succeeded them in their profession, quickly seeking out perverse inventions. Hence, in the days of the apostles themselves, there were not only schisms and divisions made in sundry churches of their own planting, with disputes about opinions and needless impositions by those of the circumcision who believed, but also opposition was made unto the very fundamental doctrines of the deity and incarnation of the Son of God by the spirit of antichrist, then entering into the world; as is evident from their writings and epistles. But yet, as all this while our Lord Jesus Christ, according to his promise, preserved the root of love and unity amongst them who sincerely believed in him entire (as he doth still, and will do to the end), by giving the one and self-same Spirit to guide, sanctify, and unite them all unto himself; so the care and authority of the apostles, during their abode in the flesh, so far prevailed, that notwithstanding some temporary impeachments of love and union in or amongst the churches, yet no single prejudice of any long continuance befell them: for either the miscarriages which they fell into were quickly retrieved by them, the truth infallibly cleared, and provision made for peace, unity, and moderation in and about things of less concernment; or else the evil, guilt, and danger of them, remained only with and upon some particular persons, the notoriety of whose wickedness and folly cast them out, by common consent, from the communion of all the disciples of Christ.

But no sooner was that *sacred society,*—ὁ ἱερὸς ἀποστόλων χορός,—with their immediate successors, as Egesippus speaks in Eusebius, departed unto their rest with God, but that the church itself, which until then was preserved a pure and uncorrupted virgin, began to be vexed with abiding contention, and otherwise to degenerate from its primitive, original purity. From thenceforward, especially after the heat of bloody and fiery persecutions began to abate, far the greatest part of ecclesiastical records consists in relations of the divisions, differences, schisms, and heresies that fell out amongst them who professed themselves the disciples of Christ. For those failings, errors, and mistakes, which were found in men of peaceable minds, the church, indeed, of those days extended her peace and unity,—if Justin Martyr and others may be believed,—to such as the *seeming warmer zeal* and *really colder charity* of the succeeding ages could not bear withal. But yet divisions and disputes were multiplied into such an excess, as that the Gentiles fetched advantage from them, not only to reproach all Christians withal, but to deter others from the profession of Christianity. So Celsus, in his third book, deals with them; for saith he, Ἀρχόμενοι μὲν ὀλίγοι τε ἦσαν, καὶ ἓν ἐφρόνουν· ἐς πλῆθος δὲ σπαρέντες αὖθις αὖ τέμνονται καὶ σχίζονται, καὶ στάσεις ἰδίας ἔχειν ἕκαστοι θέλουσι· καὶ ὑπὸ πλήθους πάλιν διϊστάμενοι σφᾶς αὐτοὺς ἐλέγχουσιν· ἑνὸς, ὡς εἰπεῖν, ἔτι κοινωνοῦντες, εἴγε κοινωνοῦσιν ἔτι, τοῦ ὀνόματος· ὃ καὶ τοῦτο μόνον ἐγκαταλιπεῖν ὅμως αἰσχύνονται·—"At first, when there were but a few, they were of one mind, or agreed well enough; but being increased, and the multitude of them scattered abroad, they were presently divided again and again; and every one would have his own party or division; and, as a divided multitude, opposed and reproved one another; so that they had no communion among themselves but only in name, which for shame they retain." So doth he, for his purpose, as is the manner of men, invidiously exaggerate the differences that were in those early times amongst Christians; for he wrote about the days of Trajan the emperor. That others of them took the same course, is testified by Clemens, Stromat. lib. vii., Augustin. Lib. de Ovib. cap. xv., and sundry others of the ancient writers of the church. But that no just offence as to the truth, or any of the ways of Christ, might hence be taken, we are, as I said before, forewarned of all these things by the Lord himself and his apostles; as also of the use and necessity of such events and issues: whence Origen cries out,—Πάνυ θαυμασίως ὁ Παῦλος εἰρηκέναι μοι δοκεῖ,—"Most admirable unto me seems the saying of Paul,—'There must be heresies amongst you, that those who are approved may be manifest.'" Nor can any just exception be hence taken against the gospel itself; for it doth not belong unto the excellency or dignity of any thing to free itself from all opposition, but only to preserve itself from being prevailed against, and to remain victorious; as the sacred truths of Christ have done, and will do unto the end. Not a few, indeed, in these evil days wherein we live, the ends of the world, and the difficulties with which they are attended being come upon us,—persons ignorant of things past, and regardless of things to come, in bondage to their lusts and pleasures,—are ready to make use of the pretence of divisions and differences among Christians, to give up themselves unto atheism, and indulge to their pleasures like the beasts that perish: "Let us eat and drink; for to-morrow we shall die." "Quid aliud inscribi poterat sepulchro bovis!" But, whatever they pretend to the contrary, it may be easily evinced that it is their *personal dislike* of that holy obedience which the gospel requireth, not the differences that are about the doctrines of it, which alienates their minds from the truth. They will not, some of them, forego all *philosophical* inquiries after the nature and causes of things here below; they know well enough that there was never any agreement amongst the wisest and severest that at any time have been engaged in that disquisition, nor is it likely that ever there will be so. And herein they can countenance themselves with the *difficulty, obscurity,* and *importance* of the things inquired after. But as for the high and heavenly mysteries of the gospel, the least whereof is infinitely of more importance than any thing that the utmost reach and comprehension of human wisdom can attain unto, they may be neglected and despised because there are contentions about them!

—— "Hic nigræ succus loliginis, hæc est
Ærugo mera."

The truth is, this is so far from any *real ground* for any such conclusion, that it were utterly impossible that any man should believe the truth of Christian religion if he had not seen, or might not be informed, that such contention and differences had ensued in and about it; for that they should do so is plainly and frequently foretold in those sacred oracles of it, whereof, if any one be found to fail, the veracity and authority of the whole may justly be called into question. If, therefore, men will have a religion so absolutely facile and easy, that, without laying out of their rational abilities or exercising the faculties of their souls about it, without foregoing of their lusts and pleasures, without care of mistakes and miscarriages, they may be securely wrapped up in it, as it were, whether they will or no, I confess they must seek for some other where they can find it; Christianity will yield them no relief. God hath not proposed an acquaintance with the blessed concernments of his glory, and of their own eternal condition, unto the sons of men, on any such terms as that they should not need, with all diligence, to employ and exercise the faculties of their souls in the investigation of them, in the use of the means by him appointed for that purpose, seeing this is the *chiefest end* for which he hath made us those souls. And as for them who in sincerity give up their minds and consciences unto his authority and guidance, he hath not left them without an *infallible direction* for such a discharge of their own duty as is sufficient to guide and lead them in the midst of all differences, divisions, and oppositions, unto rest with himself; and the difficulties which are cast upon any in their inquiring after truth, by the error and deviation of other men from it, are all sufficiently recompensed unto them by the excellency and sweetness which they find in the truth itself, when sought out with diligence, according to the mind of Christ. And one said not amiss of old, Εἴποιμι τὸν ἐπιμελῶς ἐνιδόντα ταῖς Χριστιανισμοῦ αἱρέσεσι σοφώτατον Χριστιανὸν γενέσθαι·—"I dare say he is the wisest Christian who hath most diligently considered the various differences that are in and about Christianity," as being built in the knowledge of the truth upon the best and most stable foundations.

To this end hath the Lord Jesus given us his holy word, a perfect and sure revelation of all that he would have us to believe or do in the worship of God. This he commands us diligently to attend unto, to study, search, and inquire after, that we may know his mind and do it. It is true, in their inquiry into it, various apprehensions concerning the sense and meaning of sundry things revealed therein have befallen some men in all ages; and Origen gives this as one occasion of the differences that were in those days amongst Christians: Τοῦτο, saith he, ἠκολούθησε, διαφόρως ἐκδεξαμένων τοὺς ἅμα πᾶσι πιστευθέντας εἶναι θείους λόγους, τὸ γενέσθαι αἱρέσεις, lib. iii. Con. Cel. cap. 1;—"When many were converted unto Christianity, some of them variously understanding the holy Scripture, which they jointly believed, it came to pass that heresy ensued." For this was the whole rule of faith and unity in those days: the means for securing of us in them imposed on us of late by the Romanists was then not heard of nor thought of in the world. But, moreover, to obviate all danger that might in this matter ensue, from the manifold weakness of our minds in apprehending spiritual things, the Lord Jesus hath promised his Holy Spirit unto all them that believe in him and ask it of him, to prevent their mistakes and miscarriages in the study of his word, and to "lead them into all that truth" the knowledge whereof is necessary, that they may believe in him unto the end, and live unto him. And if they who diligently and conscientiously, without prejudices, corrupt ends or designs, in obedience to the command of Christ, shall inquire into the Scriptures, to receive from thence the *whole object* of their faith and rule of their obedience,—and who, believing his promise, shall pray for his Spirit, and wait to receive him in and by the means appointed for that end,—may not be, and are not thereby, secured from all such mistakes and errors as may disinterest them in the promises of the gospel, I know not how we may be brought unto any certainty or assurance in the truths of God, or the everlasting consolation of our own souls. Neither, indeed, is the nature of man *capable* of any farther satisfaction in or about these things, unless God should work *continual miracles*, or give continually *special revelations* unto all individuals; which would utterly overthrow the whole nature of that faith and obedience which he requires at our hands. But once to suppose that such persons, through a defect of the means appointed by Christ for the instruction and direction before mentioned, may everlastingly miscarry, is to cast an unspeakable reproach on the goodness, grace, and faithfulness of God, and enough to discourage all men from inquiring after the truth. And these things the reader will find farther cleared in the ensuing discourse, with a discovery of the weakness, falseness, and insufficiency of those rules and reliefs which are tendered unto us by the Romanists, in the lieu of them that are given us by God himself. Now, if this be the condition of things in Christian religion, as, to any one that hath with sincerity consulted the Scripture, or considered the goodness, grace, and wisdom of God, it must needs appear to be, it is manifest that men's startling at it, or being offended upon the account of divisions and differences among them that make profession thereof, is nothing but a pretence to cloak and hide their *sloth and supine negligence*, with their unwillingness to come up unto the indispensable condition of learning the truth as in Jesus,—namely, obedience unto his whole will and all his commands, so far as he is pleased to reveal them unto us. With others they are but *incentives* unto that diligence and watchfulness which the things themselves, in their nature high and arduous, and in their importance of everlasting moment, require at your hands. Farther; on those who, by the means fore-mentioned, come to the knowledge of the truth, it is incumbent, according as they are by God's providence called thereunto, and as they receive ability from him for that purpose, to contend earnestly for it;—nor is their so doing any part of the evil that attends differences and divisions, but a means appointed by God himself for their cure and removal; provided, as the apostle speaks, that they "strive or contend lawfully."

The will of God must be done in the ways of his own appointment. Outward force and violence, corporeal punishments, swords and fagots, as to any use in things purely spiritual and religious, to impose them on the consciences of men, are condemned in the *Scripture*, by all the *ancient* or first *writers* of the church, by sundry *edicts* and laws of the empire, and are contrary to the *very light of reason* whereby we are men, and all the principles of it from whence mankind consenteth and coalesceth into civil society. Explaining, declaring, proving, and confirming the truth, convincing of gainsayers by the evidence of common principles on all hands assented unto. and right reason, with prayer and supplications for success, attended with a conversation becoming the gospel we profess, is the way sanctified by God unto the promotion of the truth, and the recovery of them that are gone astray from it. Into this work, according as God hath imparted of his gifts and Spirit unto them, some in most ages of the church have been engaged; and therein have not contracted any guilt of the evils of the contentions and divisions in their days, but cleared themselves of them, and faithfully served the interest of those in their generation: and this justifies and warrants us in the pursuit of the same work, by the same means, in the same days wherein we live. And when at any time men sleep in the neglect of their duty, the envious one will not be wanting to sow his tares in the field of the Lord: which, as in the times and places wherein we live, it should quicken the diligence and industry of those upon whom the care of the preservation of the truth is, by the providence of God, in an especial manner devolved, and who have manifold advantages for their encouragement in their undertaking; so also it gives countenance even to the meanest endeavours that in sincerity are employed in the same work by others in their more private capacity,—amongst which I hope the ensuing brief discourse may, with impartial readers, find admittance. It is designed in general for the defence and vindication of the truth, and that truth which is publicly professed in this nation, against the solicitation of it, and opposition made unto it with more than ordinary vigilancy, and seeming hopes of prevalency; on what grounds I know not.

This is done by those of the Roman church; who have given in themselves as sad an instance of a degeneracy from the truth as ever the Christian world had experience of. From insensible and almost imperceptible entrances into deviations from the holy rule of the gospel,—countenanced by specious pretences of piety and devotion, but really influenced by the corrupt lusts of ambition, love of pre-eminence, and earthly-mindedness, in men ignorant or neglective of the mystery and simplicity of the gospel,—their apostasy hath been carried on by various degrees, upon advantages given unto those that made the benefit of it unto themselves, by political commotions and alterations, until, by sundry artifices and sleights of Satan and men, it is grown unto that stated opposition to the right ways of God which we behold it come unto at this day. The great Roman historian desires his reader, in the perusal of his discourses, to consider and observe, "quæ vita, qui mores fuerint: per quos viros, quibusque artibus, domi militiæque, et partum et auctum imperium sit. Labente deinde paullatim disciplina, velut desidentes primo mores sequatur animo; deinde ut magis magisque lapsi sint; tum ire cœperint præcipites: donec ad hæc tempora, quibus nec vitia nostra, nec remedia pati possumus, perventum est," [Liv. Pref.];—"What was the course of life, what were the manners of those men, both at home and abroad, by whom the Roman empire was erected and enlarged; as also how ancient discipline insensibly decaying, far different manners ensued, whose decay more and more increasing, at length they began violently to decline, until we came unto these days wherein we are able to bear neither our vices nor their remedies:" all which may be as truly and justly spoken of the present Roman ecclesiastical estate. The first rulers and members of that church, by their exemplary sanctity and suffering for the truth, deservedly obtained great renown and reputation amongst the other churches in the world; but after a while the discipline of Christ decaying amongst them, and the purity of his doctrine beginning to be corrupted, they insensibly fell from their pristine glory, until at length they precipitantly tumbled into that condition, wherein, because they fear *the spiritual remedy* would be their *temporal ruin*, they are resolved to abide, be it never so desperate or deplorable. And hence also it is, that of all the opposition that ever the disciples of Christ had to contend withal, to suffer under, or to witness against, that made unto the truth by the Roman church hath proved the longest, and been attended with the most dreadful consequents; for it is not the work of any age, or of a few persons, to unravel that web of falsehood and unrighteousness, which in a long tract of time hath been cunningly woven, and closely compacted together. Besides, the heads of this declension have provided for their security, by intermixing their concerns with the polity of many nations, and moulding the constitutions of their governments unto a subserviency to their interests and ends. But He is strong and faithful who, in his own way and time, will rescue his truth and worship from being trampled on and defiled by them. In the meantime, that which renders the errors of the fathers and sons of that church most pernicious unto the professors of Christianity is, that,—whether out of blind zeal, rooted in that obstinacy which men are usually given up unto who have refused to retain the truth in the love and power of it, or from their being necessitated thereunto in their counsels for the supportment and preservation of their present interests and secular advantages,—they are not contented to embrace, practise, and adhere unto those crooked paths that they have chosen to walk in, and to attempt the drawing of others into them by such ways and means as the light of nature, right reason, with the Scripture, direct to be used in and about the things of religion which relate to the minds and souls of men; but also, they have pursued an imposition of their conceptions and practices on other men by force and violence, until the world in many places hath been made a stage of oppression, rapine, cruelty, and war, and that which they call their church a very shambles of the slaughtered disciples of Christ. So that what the historian said of the old Romans, in reference unto the Gauls or Cimbrians,—"Usque ad nostram memoriam, Romani [aiunt] alia omnia virtuti suæ prona esse, cum Gallis pro salute non pro gloria certari,"—we may apply unto them; it is not truth only, but our temporal safety also, that we are enforced to contend with them about. And whom they cannot reach with outward violence, they endeavour to load with curses; and, by precipitate censures and determination, to eject them out of the limits of Christianity, as to the spiritual and eternal privileges wherewith it is attended. And these things make all hopes of reconciliation for the future, and of present moderation, languid and weak, as all endeavours after them hitherto have been fruitless. For whilst they contend that every proposal of their church, every way and mode in the worship of God that is in usage amongst them, is not only true and right, but of necessity to be embraced and submitted unto, and therefore impose them by all sorts of penalties on the consciences and practices of all men; is it not evident that there can be no peace nor agreement in the world but what waste and solitude, arising from an extermination of persons otherwise minded than themselves, will produce? Some of them, I confess, to serve their present supposed advantages, have of late declaimed about moderation in matters of religion; and I wish that herein that may be *sincerely* endeavoured by some, which, for sinister ends, is *corruptly* pretended by others. For mine own part, there are no sort of men from whose frame of spirit and ways I shall labour a greater distance, than theirs who set themselves against that moderation towards persons differing from them and others, in the result of their thoughts, upon an humble, sincere investigation of the truth and ways of Christ, which himself and his apostles commend unto us; or that refuse to consent unto any way of reconciliation of dissenters wherein violence is not offered unto the commands of God, as stated in their consciences. Let the Romanists renounce their principles about the *absolute necessity* of the subjection of all persons unto the pope, in answer unto that groundless and boundless authority which in things sacred and civil they assign unto him, with their resolution of imposing the dictates of their church, "per fas et nefas," upon our consciences, and we shall endeavour, with all quietness and moderation, to plead with them about our remaining differences, and to join with them in the profession of those important truths wherein we are agreed. But whilst they propose no other forms of reconciliation but our absolute submission unto their papal authority, with our assent unto, and profession of, those doctrines which we are persuaded are contrary to the Scripture, with the sense of catholic antiquity, derogatory to the glory of God, and prejudicial to the salvation of those by whom they are received, and our concurrence with them in those ways of religious worship which themselves are fallen into by degrees they know not how, and which we believe dishonourable unto God, and pernicious to the souls of men; I see no ground of any other peace with them but that only which we are bound to follow with all men, in abstaining from mutual violence, performing all offices of Christian love, and in a special praying for their repentance and coming to the acknowledgment of the truth.

On this account was it that some while since, upon the desire of some friends, I undertook the examination of a discourse entitled "Fiat Lux;" whose author, under a pretence of that moderation, which is indeed altogether inconsistent with other principles of his profession, endeavoured to insinuate a necessity of the reception of Popery for the bringing of us to peace or agreement here, and the interesting of us in any hope of eternal rest and peace hereafter. Whether that small labour were seasonable or no, or whether any service were done therein to the interest of truth, is left to the judgment of men unprejudiced. Not long after there was published an epistle, pretending a reply unto that discourse, being indeed a mere flourish of empty words, and a giving up of the cause wherein the author of "Fiat Lux" was engaged, as desperate and indefensible. However, I thought it not meet to let it pass without some consideration; partly that the design of that treatise, with others of the like nature of late published amongst us, might be farther manifested; and partly that the ends of moderation and peace being fixed between us, I might farther try and examine whose and what principles are best suited unto their pursuit and accomplishment. I have not, therefore, confined myself unto an answer unto the epistle of the author of "Fiat Lux,"—which indeed it doth not deserve, as I suppose, himself being judge,—but have only from it taken occasion to discuss those principles and usages in religion wherein the most important differences between Papists and Protestants do lie. For whereas the whole difference between them and us is branched into two general heads,—the first concerning those principles which they and we severally build our profession upon, and resolve our faith into; and the other respecting particular instances in doctrines of faith and practice in religious worship,—I have laid hold of occasion to treat of them both: of the former absolutely, and of the latter in things of most weight and concernment. And because *the judgment of antiquity* is deservedly of moment in these things, I have not only manifested it to lie plain and clear against the Romanist, in instances sufficient to impeach their pretended infallibility,—which is enough to dissolve that whole imaginary fabric that is built upon it and centres in it,—but also in most of the material controversies that are between them and us. These things, Christian reader, I thought meet to premise towards the prevention of that offence which any may really take, or for corrupt ends pretend so to do, at the *differences in general* that are amongst Christians, or those in *especial* which are between us and the Roman church; as also to give an account of the occasion, design, and end, of the ensuing consideration of them.

A VINDICATION

OF

THE ANIMADVERSIONS ON "FIAT LUX."

CHAPTER I.

SIR,

I HAVE received your epistle, and therein your excuse for your long silence; which I willingly admit of, and could have been contented it had been longer, so that you had been advantaged thereby to have spoken any thing more to the purpose than I find you have now done: "Sat cito si sat bene." Things of this nature are always done *soon* enough when they are done *well* enough, or as well as they are capable of being done. But it is no small disappointment to find ἄνθρακας ἀντὶ τοῦ θησαυροῦ, a fruitless flourish of words, where a serious debate of an important cause was expected and looked for. Nor is it a justification of any man, when he has done a thing amiss, to say he did it speedily, if he were no way necessitated so to do. You are engaged in a cause, unto whose tolerable defence, "opus est Zephyris et hirundine multa," Hor. Ep. vii. 13: though you cannot pretend so short a time to be used in it which will not by many be esteemed more than it deserves; for all time and pains taken to give countenance to error is undoubtedly misspent. Οὐ δυνάμεθά τι κατὰ τῆς ἀληθείας, ἀλλ' ὑπὲρ τῆς ἀληθείας, saith the great apostle [2 Cor. xiii. 8];—"We can do nothing against the truth, but for the truth:" which rule had you observed, you might have spared your whole time and labour in this business. However, I shall be glad to find that you have given me just cause to believe what you say, of your *not seeing the "Animadversions" on your book before February.* As I find you observant of truth in your progress, or failing therein, so shall I judge of your veracity in this unlikely story; for every man gives the best measure of himself. And though I cannot see how possibly a man could spend much time in trussing up such a fardel of trifles and quibbles as your epistle is, yet it is somewhat strange, on the other side, that you should not in eight months' space—for so long were the "Animadversions" made public before February—set eye on that which, being your own especial concernment, was, to my knowledge, in the hands of many of your party. To deal friendly with you, "Nolim cæterarum rerum te socordem eodem modo." Yea, I doubt not but you use more diligence in your other affairs; though in general the matter in debate between us seems to be your principal concernment. But now you have seen that discourse, and, as you inform me, "have read it over;" which I believe, and take not only upon the same score of present trust, but upon the evidence also which you give unto your assertion, by your careful avoiding to take any farther notice of the things that you found too difficult for you to reply unto. For any impartial reader, that shall seriously consider the "Animadversions" with your epistle, will quickly find that the main artifice wherein you confide is a pretence of saying somewhat in general, whilst you pass over the things of most importance, and which most press the cause you defend, with a perpetual silence: these you turn from, and fall upon the person of the author of the "Animadversions." If ever you debated this procedure with yourself, had I been present with you when you said with him in the poet, "Dubius sum quid faciam—Tene relinquam an rem?" I should have replied with him, "Me sodes;" but you were otherwise minded, and are gone before,—

> —— "Ego (ut contendere durum est
> Cum victore) sequar." Hor. Sat. i. 9, 42.

I will follow you with what patience I can, and make the best use I am able of what offers itself in your discourse.

Two reasons, I confess, you add why you chose "vadimonium deserere," and not reply to the "Animadversions;" which, to deal plainly with you, give me very little satisfaction. The first of them, you say, is, "because to do so would be contrary to the very end and design of 'Fiat Lux;'" which shall immediately be considered. The other is, "the threats which I have given you, that, if you dare to write again, I will make you know what manner of man I am." Sir, though it seems you dare not reply to my book, yet you dare do that which is much worse; you dare write palpable untruths, and such as yourself know to be so, as others also who have read those papers. By such things as these, with sober and ingenuous persons, you cannot but much prejudice the interest you desire to promote, as well as in yourself you wrong your *conscience* and ruin your *reputation.* Besides, all advantage springing from untruth is fading; neither will it admit of any covering but of its own kind, which can never be so increased but that it will rain through. Only, I confess thus far you have promoted your design, that you have given a new and cogent instance of *the evils attending controversies in religion,* which you declaim about in your "Fiat;" which yet is such as it had been your duty to avoid. What it is that you make use of to give countenance unto this fiction (for "malum semper habitat in alieno fundo"), I shall have occasion afterward to consider. For the present I leave you to the discipline of your own thoughts:—

> —— "Prima est hæc ultio, quod se
> Judice, nemo nocens absolvitur." Juv. xiii. 2.

And I the rather mind you of your failure at this entrance of our discourse, that I may only remit your thoughts unto this stricture when the like occasion offers itself; which I fear it will do not unfrequently. But, sir, it will be no advantage unto me or you to contend for the truth which we profess, if in the meantime we are regardless of the observance of truth in our own hearts and spirits.

Two principal heads, the discourse which you premise unto the particular consideration of the "Animadversions," is reducible unto: the first whereof is your endeavour to manifest "that I understood not the design and end of 'Fiat Lux,' a discourse" (as you modestly testify) "hard to deal with, and impossible to confute;" the other, your inquiry after the author of the "Animadversions," with your attempt to prove him one in such a condition as you may possibly hope to obtain more advantage from than you can do by endeavouring the refutation of his book. Some other occasional passages there are in it also, which, as they deserve, shall be considered. Unto these two general heads I shall give you at present a candid return, and leave you, when you are free from flies, to make what use of it you please.

The design of "Fiat Lux" I took to be the promotion of the papal interest; and the whole of it, in the relation of its parts unto one another, and the general end aimed at in it, to be a persuasive induction unto the embracement of the present Roman faith and religion. The means insisted on for this end I conceived principally to be these:—1. A declaration of the evils that attend differences in religion, and disputes about it; 2. Of the good of union, peace, love, and concord among Christians; 3. Of the impossibility of obtaining this good by any other ways or means but only by an embracement of the Roman Catholic faith and profession, with a submission to the deciding power and authority of the pope or your church; 4. A defence and illustration of some especial parts of the Roman religion, most commonly by Protestants excepted against. This was my *mistake;* unto this mistake I acknowledge my whole discourse was suited. In the same mistake are all the persons in England that ever I heard speak any thing of that discourse, of what persuasion in religion soever they were. And Aristotle thought it worth while to remember out of Hesiod, Moral. Nicom. lib. vii., that,—

> Φήμη δ' οὔ τις πάμπαν ἀπόλλυται ἥν τινα πολλοὶ
> Λαοὶ φημίζουσιν. Hesiod. Εργ. καὶ ἡμ.

That report which so many consent in is not altogether vain. But yet, lest this should not satisfy you, I shall mind you of one who is with you,—πολλῶν ἀντάξιος ἄλλων,—of as much esteem, it may be, as all the rest; and that is *yourself*. You are yourself in the same mistake: you know well enough that this was your end, this your design, these the means of your pursuing it; and you acknowledge them immediately so to have been, as we shall see in the consideration of the evidence you tender to evince that mistake in me which you surmise.

First, You tell me, p. 4, "that I mistake the drift and design of 'Fiat Lux,' whilst I take that as absolutely spoken which is only said upon an hypothesis of our present condition here in England." This were a grand mistake, indeed, that I should look on any thing proposed as an expedient for the ending of differences about religion, without a supposition of differences about religion! But how do you prove that I fell into such a mistake? I plainly and openly acknowledge that such differences there are; all my discourse proceeds on that supposition. I bewail the evil of them, and labour for moderation about them, and have long since ventured to propose my thoughts unto the world to that purpose. All that you suppose in your discourse on this account I suppose also, yea, and grant it; unless it be some such thing as is in controversy between you and Protestants, which you are somewhat frequent in the supposal of unto your advantage, and thereon would persuade them unto a relinquishment of Protestancy and embracement of Popery: which is the end of your book, and will be thought so, if you should deny it a thousand times; for "quid ego verba audiam, facta cum video?" Your protestation comes too late, when the fact hath declared your mind; neither are you now at liberty to coin new designs for your "Fiat." But this must be my mistake, which no man in his wits could possibly fall into; neither is it an evidence of any great sobriety to impute it to any man, whom we know not certainly to be distracted. But this mistake, you tell me, caused me "to judge and censure what you wrote as impertinent, impious, frivolous," etc. No such matter; my right apprehension of your hypothesis, end, or design, occasioned me to show that your discourses were incompetent to prevail with rational and sober persons to comply with your desires.

You proceed to the same purpose, p. 15, and, to manifest my mistake of your design, give an account of it, and tell us that "one thing you suppose, namely, that we are at difference." So did I also, and am not, therefore, yet fallen upon the discovery of my mistake.

Secondly, You "commend peace." I acknowledge you do, and join with you therein; neither is he worthy the name of a Christian who is otherwise minded. That is one great legacy that Christ bequeathed unto his disciples: Εἰρήνην, saith he, ἀφίημι ὑμῖν, εἰρήνην τὴν ἐμὴν δίδωμι ὑμῖν·—"Peace I leave with you, my peace I give unto you;" and he is no disciple of Christ who doth not long for it among all his disciples. This, you tell us, is the whole sum of "Fiat Lux" in few words. You will tell us otherwise immediately; and if you should not, yet we should find it otherwise. You add, therefore, "that to introduce a disposition unto peace, you make it your work to demonstrate the uselessness, endlessness, and unprofitableness of quarrels." Yet my mistake appears not. I perceived you did speak to this purpose, and I acknowledge with you that quarrels about religion are useless and unprofitable, any otherwise than as we are bound to "contend earnestly for the faith once delivered unto the saints," and to "stand fast in our liberty, not giving place to seducers," with labouring by "sound doctrine to convince and stop the mouths of gainsayers;" all which are made necessary unto us by the commands of Christ, and are not to be called quarrelling. And I know that our quarrels are not yet actually ended; that they are endless I believe not, but hope the contrary. You proceed, and grant that "you labour to persuade your countrymen of an impossibility of ever bringing our debates unto a conclusion, either by light, or spirit, or reason, or Scripture, so long as we stand separated from any superior judicative power unto which all parties will submit; and, therefore, that it is rational and Christian-like to leave these endless contentions, and resign ourselves to humility and peace." This matter will now quickly be ended, and that "ex ore tuo." Give me leave, I pray, to ask you one or two plain questions:—1. Whom do you understand by that "superior judicative power," unto whom you persuade all parties to submit? Have you not told us in your "Fiat" that it is the church or pope of Rome? or will you deny that to be your intention? 2. What do you intend by "resigning ourselves to humility and peace?" Do you not aim at our quiet submission to the determinations of the church or pope in all matters of religion? Have you not declared yourself unto this purpose in your "Fiat?" And I desire a little farther to know of you whether this be not that which formally constitutes a man a member of your church,—that he own the judicative power of the pope or your church in all matters of religion, and submit himself thereunto? If these things be so, as you cannot deny them, I hope I shall easily obtain your pardon for affirming that you yourself believed the same to be the design of your book, which I and other men apprehended to be so; for here you directly avow it. If you complain any more about this matter, pray let it be in the words of him in the comedian, "Egomet meo indicio miser, quasi sorex, hodie perii," Ter. Eun. v. 7, 23; this inconvenience you have brought upon your own self. Neither can any man long avoid such misadventures who designs to cloud his aims; which yet cannot take effect if not in some measure understood. Naked truth, managed in sincerity, whatever perplexities it may meet withal, will never leave its owners in the briers; whereas the serpentine turnings of error and falsehood, to extricate themselves, do but the more entangle their promoters. I doubt not but you hope well, that when all are become Papists again they shall live at peace; though your hope be very groundless, as I have elsewhere demonstrated. You have at best but the shadow or shell of peace; and, for the most part, not that neither. Yea, it may be easily showed that the peace you boast of is inconsistent with, and destructive of, that peace which is left by Christ unto his disciples.

But the way you propose to bring us to peace is the embracement of Popery: which is that that was fixed on by me as the design of your book; which now acknowledging, you have disarmed yourself of that imaginary advantage which you flourish withal, from "a capital mistake," as you call it, in me, in misapprehending your design. You were told before, that if by "moderation and peace" you intended a mutual forbearance of one another in our several persuasions, waiting patiently until God shall reveal unto us the precise truth in the things about which we differ, you shall have all the furtherance that I can contribute unto you. But you have another aim, another work in hand, and will not allow that any peace is attainable amongst us, but by a resignation of all our apprehensions, in matters of religion, to the guidance, determination, and decision of the pope, or your church;—a way nowhere prescribed unto us in holy writ, nor in the councils of the primitive church; and, besides, against all reason, law, and equity, your pope and church in our contests being one party litigant: yet "in this persuasion," you say, "you should abide, were there no other persons in the world but yourself that did embrace it." And to let you see how unlikely that principle is to produce peace and agreement amongst those multitudes that are at variance about these things, I can assure you that if there were none left alive on the earth but you and I, we should not agree in this thing one jot better than did Cain and Abel about the sacrifices; though I should desire you that we might manage our differences with more moderation than he did, who, by virtue of his primogeniture, seemed to lay a special claim to the priesthood. And indeed, for your part, if your present persuasion be as you sometimes pretend it to be, that your "Fiat Lux" is not a persuasive unto Popery, you have given a sufficient testimony that you can be of an opinion that no man else in the world is of, nor will be, do what you can. But the insufficiency of your principles and arguments to accomplish your design hath been in part already evinced, and shall, God willing, in our progress be farther made manifest. This is the sum of what appears in the first part of your prefatory discourse concerning my mistake of your design; which, how little it hath tended unto your advantage, I hope you begin to understand.

Your next labour consists in a pacific, charitable inquiry after the author of the "Animadversions," with an endeavour, by I know not how many reasons, to confirm your surmise that he is a person that had an interest in the late troubles in the nation, or, as you phrase it, was "a part of that dismal tempest which overbore all before it, not only church and state, but reason, right, honesty, all true religion, and even good nature too." See what despair of managing an undertaking which cannot be well deserted will drive men unto! Are you not sensible that you cry,

> —— "Vos o mihi manes
> Este boni, quoniam superis aversa voluntas?" Virg. Æn. xii. 646.

or like the Jews, who, when they were convinced of their errors and wickedness by our Saviour, began to call him "Samaritan" and "devil," and to take up stones to cast at him? or as Crescens the Cynic dealt with Justin Martyr, whom because he could not answer, after he had engaged in a dispute with him, he laboured to bring him into suspicion with the emperor and senate of Rome as a person dangerous to the commonwealth? And so also the Arians dealt with Athanasius. It were easy to manifest that the spring of all this discourse of yours is *smart*, and not *loyalty*, and that it proceeds from a sense of your own disappointment, and not zeal for the welfare of others; but how little it is to your purpose I shall show you anon, and could quickly render it as little to your advantage. For what if I should surmise that you were one of the friars that stirred up the Irish to their rebellion and unparalleled murders? Assure yourself I can quickly give as many and as probable reasons for my so doing as you have given, or can give, for your conjecture about the author of the "Animadversions" on your "Fiat Lux." You little think how much it concerns him to look to himself who undertakes to accuse another; and how easy it were to make you repent your accusation, as much as ever Crassus did his accusing of Carbo. But I was in good hope you would have left such reflections as are capable of so easy a retortion upon yourself, especially being irregular and no way subservient unto your design, and being warned beforehand so to do. Who could imagine that a man of so much piety and mortification, as in your "Fiat" you profess yourself to be, should have so little regard unto common honesty and civility? which are shrewdly intrenched upon by such uncharitable surmises. I suppose you know that the apostle reckons ὑπόνοιας πονηρὰς, whereof you have undertaken the management of one, amongst the things that are contrary to the doctrine that is according unto godliness; otherwise suspicion is in your own power, nor can any man hinder you from surmising what you please. This he knew in Plautus who cried,—

> "Ne admittam culpam ego meo sum promus pectori,
> Suspicio est in pectore alieno sita.
> Nam nunc ego te si surripuisse suspicer,
> Jovi coronam de capite e Capitolio,
> Quod in culmine astat summo, si non id feceris,
> Atque id tamen mihi lubeat suspicarier,
> Quî tu id prohibere me potes ne suspicer?" Plaut. Trin. i. 1.

And I know that, concerning all your dispute and arguings in these pages, you may say what Lucian doth about his "true story:" Γράφω τοίνυν περὶ ὧν μήτ' εἶδον, μήτ' ἔπαθον, μήτε παρ' ἄλλων ἐπυθόμην·—"You write about the things which you have neither seen nor suffered, heard nor much inquired after," Luc. Ver. Hist. i. 4. Such is the force of faction, and sweetness of revenge in carnal minds To deliver you, if it may be, from the like miscarriages for the future, let me inform you that the author of the "Animadversions" is a person who never had a hand in, nor gave consent unto, the raising of any war in these nations, nor unto any political alteration in them,—no, not to any one that was amongst us during our revolutions; but he acknowledgeth that he lived and acted under them the things wherein he thought his duty consisted, and challengeth all men to charge him with doing the least personal injury unto any, professing himself ready to give satisfaction to any one that can justly claim it. Therefore, as unto the public affairs in this nation, he is amongst them who bless God and the king for the act of oblivion; and that because he supposeth that all the inhabitants of the kingdom which lived in it when his majesty was driven out of it have cause so to do: which some priests and friars have, and that in reference unto such actings as he would scorn, for the saving of his life, to give the least countenance unto; among whom it is not unlikely that you might be one,—which yet he will not aver, nor give reasons to prove it, because he doth not know it so to be. But you have sundry reasons to justify yourself in your charge, and they are as well worthy our consideration as any thing else you have written in your epistle; and shall therefore not be neglected. The first of them you thus express, p. 12, "You cannot abide to hear of moderation; it is with you most wicked, hypocritical, and devilish, especially as it comes from me; for this one thing 'Fiat Lux' suffers more from you than for all the contents of the book put together. My reason is your passion; my moderation inflames your wrath: and you are therefore stark wild because I utter so much of sobriety." This is your first reason; which you have exactly squared to the old rule, " Calumniare fortiter, aliquid adhærebit;"—" Calumny will leave a scar." Would you were yourself only concerned in these things! But among the many woful miscarriages of men professing the religion of Jesus Christ, whereby the beauty and glory of it have been stained in the world, and itself in a great measure rendered ineffectual unto its blessed ends, there is not any thing of more sad consideration than the endeavours of men to promote and propagate the things which they suppose belong unto it by ways and means directly contrary unto, and destructive of, its most known and fundamental principles. For when it is once observed and manifest that the actings of men in the promotion of any religion are forbidden and condemned in that religion which they seek to promote, what can rationally be concluded but that they not only disbelieve themselves what they outwardly profess, but also esteem it a fit mask and cover to carry on other interests of their own which they prefer before it? And what can more evidently tend unto its disreputation and disadvantage is not easy to conceive. Such is the course here fixed on by you. It is the religion of Christ you pretend to plead for and to promote; but if there be a word true in it, the way you take for that end,—namely, by openly false accusations,—is to be abhorred; which manifests what regard unto it you inwardly cherish. And I wish this were only your *personal miscarriage*, that you were not encouraged unto it by the principles and example of your chiefest masters and leaders. The learned person who wrote the Letters discovering *the Mystery of Jesuitism* gives us just cause so to conceive; for he doth not only prove that the Jesuits have publicly maintained that " calumny is but a venial sin," nay, none at all, if used against such as you call calumniators, though grounded on absolute falsities, but hath also given us such pestilent instances of their practice, according to that principle, as Paganism was never acquainted withal.—Let. xv.[1] In their steps you set out in this your first reason, wherein there is not one word of truth. I had formerly told you that I did not think you could yourself believe some of the things that you affirmed, at which you take great offence; but I must

[1] The "Provincial Letters" by Blaise Pascal were published in this country in 1657, according to the profession on the title-page, " Faithfully rendered into English." The first of these celebrated productions appeared 13th January 1656; the last bears date 24th March 1657. It illustrates the extent of their influence, and how rapidly their fame had spread, when the same year in which the series closed should have produced a translation of them into English. The language of Owen shows that he must have seen them in this form, for the title of the volume differs from the French title prefixed to the Letters, and runs in the following terms: " Les Provinciales; or, the Mysterie of Jesuitisme Discovered in certain Letters, written upon occasion of the present differences at Sorbonne between the Jansenists and the Molinists, from January 1656 to March 1657, S. N."—Ed.

now tell you, that if you proceed in venting such notorious untruths as here you have heaped together, I shall greatly question whether seriously you believe that Jesus Christ will one day judge the world in righteousness. For I do not think you can produce a pleadable dispensation to say what you please, be it never so false, of a supposed heretic; for though, it may be, you will not keep faith with him, surely you ought to observe truth in speaking of him. You tell us, in your epistle to your "Fiat," of your "dark obscurity wherein you die daily;" but take heed, sir, lest,

> —— "Indulgentem tenebris imæque recessu
> Sedis inaspectos cœlo radiisque penates
> Servantem, tamen assiduis circumvolet alis
> Sæva dies animi, scelerumque in pectore diræ."
>
> Stat. Theb. i. 50.

Your next reason is, "Because he talks of swords and blood, fire and fagot, guns and daggers; which doth more than show that he hath not let go those hot and furious imaginations." But of what sort, by whom used, to what end? Doth he mention any of these but such as your church hath made use of for the destruction of Protestants? If you have not done so, why do you not disprove his assertions? If you have, why have you practised that in the face of the sun which you cannot endure to be told of? Is it equal, think you, that you should kill, burn, and destroy men, for the profession of their faith in Christ Jesus, and that it should not be lawful for others to say you do so? Did not yourself make the calling over of these things necessary, by crying out against Protestants for *want of moderation?* "It is one of the privileges of the pope," some say, "to judge all men, and himself to be judged by none;" but is it so also, that no man may say he hath done what all the world knows he hath done, and which we have just cause to fear he would do again had he power to his will? For my part, I can assure you, so that you will cease from charging others with that whose guilt lies heavier upon yourselves than on all the professors of Christianity in the world besides, and give any tolerable security against the like practices for the future, I shall be well content that all which is past may be put by us poor worms into perpetual oblivion; though I know it will be called over another day. Until this be done, and you leave off to make your advantages of other men's miscarriages, pray arm yourself with patience to hear sometimes a little of your own.

> Ὁπποῖόν κ' εἴπησθα ἔπος, τοῖόν κ' ἐπακούσαις,

said wise Homer of old; and another to the same purpose, "He that speaks what he will, must hear what he would not." Is it actionable with you against a Protestant, that he will not take your whole sword into his bowels without complaining? Sir, the author of the "Animadversions" doth, and ever did, abhor swords, and guns, and crusades, in matters of religion and conscience, with all violence, that may tantamount unto their usual effects. He ever thought it an uncouth sight to see men marching with *crosses* on their backs to destroy Christians, as if they had the *Alkoran* in their hearts; and therefore desires your excuse if he have reflected a little upon the miscarriages of your church in that kind, especially being called thereunto by your present contrary pretences.

"Quis tulerit Gracchos de seditione querentes?"—Juv. ii. 24.

And,—

——"Major tandem parcas insane minori."—Hor. Sat. ii. 3, 325.

It were well if your ways did no more please you, in the previous prospect you take of them than they seem to do in a subsequent reflection upon them. But this is the nature of evil,—it never comes and goes with the same appearing countenance: not that itself changeth at any time, for that which is morally evil is always so; but men's apprehensions, variously influenced by their affections, lusts, and interests, do frequently change and alter. Now, what conclusions can be made from the premises rightly stated, I leave to your own judgment, at your better leisure.

Thirdly, You add, "Your prophetic assurance, so often inculcated, that if you could but once come to whisper me in the ear, I would plainly acknowledge, either that I understand not myself what I say, or, if I do, believe it not, gives a fair character of those fanatic times wherein ignorance and hypocrisy prevailed over worth and truth, whereof, if yourself were any part, it is no wonder you should think that I or any man else should either speak he knows not what, or believe not what himself speaks." That is, a man must needs be as bad as you can imagine him, if he have not such a high opinion of your ability and integrity as to believe that you have written about nothing but what you perfectly understand, nor assert any thing, in the pursuit of your design and interest, but what you really and in cold blood believe to be true. All men, it seems, that were no part of "the former dismal tempest," have this opinion of you; "credat Apella." If it be so, I confess, for my part, I have no relief against being concluded to be whatever you please: Sosia or not Sosia, the law is in your own hands, and you may condemn all that adore you not into fanaticism at your pleasure; but as he said, "Obsecro per pacem liceat te alloqui, ut ne vapulem." If you will but grant a little truce from this severity, I doubt not but in a short time to take off from your keenness in the management of this charge; for I hope you will allow that a man may speak the truth without being a fanatic. Truth may get hatred,—I see it hath done so,—but it will make no man hateful. Without looking back, then, to your "Fiat Lux," I shall, out of this very epistle, give you to see that you have certainly failed on the one hand, in writing about things which you do not at all understand, and therefore discourse concerning them like a blind man about colours; and, as I fear, greatly also on the other,—for I cannot suppose you so ignorant as not to know that some things in your discourse are otherwise than by you represented: nay, and we shall find you at express contradictions, which, pretend what you please, I know you cannot at the same time believe. Instances of these things you will be minded of in our progress. Now, I must needs be very unhappy in discoursing of them, if this be logic and law, that for so doing I must be concluded a fanatic.

Fourthly, You add, "Your pert assertion, so oft occurring in your book, that there is neither reason, truth, nor honesty in my words, is but the overflowings of that former intemperate zeal;" whereunto may be added what in the last place you insist on to the same purpose, namely, that I "charge you with fraud, ignorance, and wickedness, when in my own heart I find you most clear from any such blemish." I do not remember where any of these expressions are used by me; that they are nowhere used thus all together, I know well enough, neither shall I make any inquiry after them. I shall therefore desire you only to produce the instances whereunto any of the censures intimated are annexed; and if I do not prove, evidently and plainly, that to be wanting in your discourse which is charged so to be, I will make you a public acknowledgment of the wrong I have done you. But if no more was by me expressed than your words, as used to your purpose, did justly deserve, pray be pleased to take notice that it is lawful for any man to speak the truth: and for my part, Ἐγὼ ὡς ὁ κωμικὸς ἔφη, ἄγροικός εἰμι, τὴν σκάφην, σκάφην λέγων, as he said in Lucian;—"I live in the country where they call a spade a spade." And if you can give any one instance where I have charged you with any failure, where there is the least probability that I had in my heart other thoughts concerning what you said, I will give up my whole interest in this cause unto you: "Mala mens, malus animus," Ter. And. i. 1, 137. You have manifested your conscience to be no just measure of other men's, who reckon upon their giving an account of what they do or say: so that you have but little advanced your charge by these undue insinuations.

Neither have you any better success in that which, in the next place, you insist upon; which yet, were it not, like the most of the rest, destitute of truth, would give more countenance unto your reflection than them all. It is, that I "give you sharp and frequent menaces, that if you write or speak again, you shall hear more, find more, feel more, more to your smart, more than you imagine, more than you would; which relish much of that insulting humour which the land groaned under." I suppose no man reads this representation of my words, with the addition of your own, which makes up the greatest part of them, but must needs think that you have been sorely threatened with some personal inconveniences which I would cause to befall you did you not surcease from writing, or that I would obtain some course to be taken with you to your prejudice. Now, this must needs savour of the spirit of our late days of trouble and mischief or at least of the former days of the prevalency of Popery amongst us, when men were not wont, in such cases, to take up at bare threats and menaces. If this be so, all men that know the author of the "Animadversions," and his condition, must needs conclude him to be very foolish and wicked: foolish, for threatening any with that which is as far from his power to execute as the person threatened can possibly desire it to be;—wicked, for designing that evil unto any individual person which he abhors "in hypothesi" to be inflicted on any upon the like account. But what if there be nothing of all this in the pretended menaces? what if the worst that is in them be only part of a desire that you would abstain from insisting on the personal miscarriages of some that profess the Protestant religion, lest he should be necessitated to make a diversion of your charge, or to show the insufficiency of it to your purpose, by recounting the more notorious failings of the guides, heads, and leaders of your church? If this be so,—as it is, in truth, the whole intendment of any of those expressions that are used by me (for the most part of them are your own figments), wherever they occur,—what conclusion can any rational man make from them? Do they not rather intimate a desire of the use of moderation in these our contests, and an abstinence from things personal (for which cause also, fruitlessly, as I now perceive, by this your new kind of ingenuity and moderation, I prefixed not my name to the "Animadversions," which you also take notice of), than any evil intention or design? This was my threatening you; to which now I shall add, that though I may not say of these papers what Catullus did of his verses on Rufus,—

> "Verum id non impune feres: nam te omnia secla
> Noscent, et, qui sis, fama loquetur anus;" Cat. lxxviii. 9.

yet I shall say, that as many as take notice of this discourse will do no less of your disingenuity and manifold falsehood, in your vain attempt to relieve your dying cause, by casting odium upon him with whom you have to do; like the bonassus that Aristotle informs us of Hist. Animal., lib. ix. cap. 24; which, being as big as a bull, but having horns turned inward and unuseful for fight, when he is pursued, casts out his excrements to defile his pursuers, and to stay them in their passage.

But what now is the end in all this heap of things, which you would have mistaken for reasons, that you aim at? It is all to show how unfit I am to defend the protestant religion, and that "I am not such a Protestant as I would be thought to be." But why so? I embrace the doctrine of the church of England, as declared in the Thirty-nine Articles, and other approved public writings of the most famous bishops and other divines thereof. I avow her rejection of the pretended authority and real errors of your church to be her duty, and justifiable. The same is my judgment in reference unto all other protestant churches in the world, in all things wherein they agree among themselves; which is in all things necessary that God may be acceptably worshipped and themselves saved. And why may I not plead the cause of Protestancy against that imputation of demerit which you heap upon it? Neither would I be thought to be any thing in religion but what I am; neither have I any sentiments therein but what I profess. But it may be you will say, in some things I differ from other Protestants. Wisely observed! and if from thence you can conclude a man unqualified for the defence of Protestancy, you have secured yourself from opposition, seeing every Protestant doth so, and must do so whilst there are differences amongst Protestants; but they are in things wherein their Protestancy is not concerned. And may I be so bold as to ask you how the case in this instance stands with yourself, who certainly would have your competency for the defence of your church unquestionable? Differences there are amongst you; and that, as in and about other things, so also about the pope himself, the head and spring of the religion you profess. Some of you maintain his *personal infallibility*, and that not only in matters of faith, but in matters of fact also; others disclaim the former as highly erroneous, and the latter as grossly blasphemous. Pray, what is your judgment in this matter? for I suppose you are not of both these opinions at once, and I am sure they are irreconcilable. Some of you mount his supremacy above a general council, some would bring him into a co-ordination with it, and some subject him unto it; though he hath almost carried the cause, by having store of bishoprics to bestow, whereas a council has none; which was the reason given of old for his prevalency in this contest. May we know what you think in this case? Some of you assert him to be, "de jure," lord of the whole world in spirituals and temporals absolutely; some in spirituals directly, and in temporals only "in ordine ad spiritualia,"—an abyss from whence you may draw out what you please; and some of you in temporals not at all: and you have not as yet given us your thoughts as to this difference amongst you. Some of you assert in him a power of deposing kings, disposing of kingdoms, transferring titles unto dominion and rule, for and upon such miscarriages as he shall judge to contain disobedience unto the see apostolic; others love not to talk at this haughty rate: neither do I know what is your judgment in this matter. This, as I said before, I am sure of, you cannot be of all these various contradictory judgments at once. Not to trouble you with instances that might be multiplied of the like differences amongst you; if, notwithstanding your adherence unto one part of the contradiction in them, you judge yourself a competent advocate for your church in general, and do busily employ yourself to win over proselytes unto her communion, have the patience to think that one who in some few things differs from some other Protestants, is not wholly incapacitated thereby to repel an unjust charge against Protestancy in general.

I have done with the two general heads of your prefatory discourse, and shall now only mark one or two incident particulars that belong not unto them, and then proceed to see if we can meet with any thing of more importance than what you have been pleased as yet to communicate unto us.

Page 5. Upon occasion of a passage in my discourse, wherein, upon misinformation, I expressed some trouble that any young men should be entangled with the rhetoric and sophistry of your "Fiat Lux," you fall into an harangue, not inferior unto some others in your epistle for that candour and ingenuity you give yourself unto.

First, you make a plea for "gentlemen" (not once named in my discourse), "that they must be allowed a sense of religion as well as ministers; that they have the body though not the cloak of religion, and are masters of their own reason." But do you consider with yourself who it is that speaks these words, and to whom you speak them? Do you indeed desire that "gentlemen" should have such a sense of religion, and make use of their reason in the choice of that which therein they adhere unto, as you pretend? Is this pretence consistent with your plea in your "Fiat Lux," wherein you labour to reduce them to a naked fanatical "credo?" or is it your interest to court them with fine words, though your intention be far otherwise? But we in England like not such proceedings:—

'Εχθρὸς γάρ μοι κεῖνος ὁμῶς ἀΐδαο πύλῃσιν,
Ὅς χ' ἕτερον μὲν κεύθει ἐνὶ φρεσίν, ἄλλο δὲ βάζει.

Nothing dislikes us more than dissimulation. And to whom do you speak? Did I, doth any Protestant, deny that gentlemen may have,—do we not say they ought to have?—their sense in religion, and their senses exercised therein? Do we deny they ought to improve their reason, in being conversant about it? Are these the principles of the church of Rome or of that of England? Do we not press them unto these things, as their principal duty in this world? Do we disallow or forbid them any means that may tend to their furtherance in the knowledge and profession of religion? Where is it that, if they do but look upon a Bible,—

—— "Furiarum maxima juxta
Accubat, et manibus prohibet contingere mensas;" Virg. Æn. vi. 605.

—the inquisitor lays hold upon them, and bids them be contented with a *rosary*, or our Lady's psalter? Do we hinder or dissuade them from any studies, or the use of books that may increase their knowledge and improve their reason? And hath not the Papacy felt the fruits and effects of these principles in the writings of kings, princes, noblemen, and gentlemen, of all sorts? And do not you yourself know all this to be true? And is it ingenuous to insist on contrary insinuations? or do you think that truly generous spirits will stoop to so poor a lure? But you proceed: "This is one difference between Catholic countries and ours,—that there the clergyman is only regarded for his virtue and the power he hath received, or is at least believed to have received, from God, in the great ministry of our reconciliation; and if he have any addition of learning besides, it is looked upon as a good accidental ornament, but not as any essential complement of his profession: so that it often happens, without any wonderment at all, that the gentleman-patron is the learned man, and the priest, his chaplain, of little or no science in comparison. But here in England, our gentlemen are disparaged by their own 'black-coats,' and not suffered to use their judgment in any kind of learning, without a gibe from them. The gentleman is reasonless, and the scribbling cassock is the only scholar; he alone must speak all, know all, and only understand." Sir, if your clergy were respected only for their virtue, they would not be overburdened with their honour, unless they have much mended their manners since all the world publicly complained of their lewdness; and which in many places the most would do so still, did they not judge the evil remediless. And if the state of things be, in your Catholic countries, between the gentry and clergy, as you inform us, I fear it is not from the learning of the one, but the ignorance of the other. And this you seem to intimate, by rejecting learning from being any essential complement of their profession: wherein you do wisely, and what you are necessitated to do; for those who are acquainted with them tell us that if it were, you would have a very thin clergy left you, very many of them not understanding the very mass-book, which they daily chant; and therefore almost every word in your "Missale Romanum" is accented, that they may know how aright to pronounce them; which yet will not deliver them from that mistake of him who, instead of "Introibo ad altare Dei," read constantly, "Introibo ad tartara Dei." Herein we envy not the condition of your Catholic countries; and though we desire our gentry were more learned than they are, yet neither we nor they could be contented to have our ministers ignorant, so that they might be in veneration for that office's sake which they are no way able to discharge. And as to what you affirm concerning England, and our usage here, in the close of your discourse, it is so utterly devoid of truth and honesty, that I cannot but wonder at your open regardlessness of them. Should you have written these things in Spain or Italy (where you have made pictures of Catholics put in bears' skins and torn with dogs in England, Eccles. Ang. Troph.) concerning England, and the manners of the inhabitants thereof, you might have hoped to have met with some so partially addicted unto your faction and interest as to suppose there were some colour of truth in what you aver; but to write these things here amongst us, in the face of the sun, where every one that casts an eye upon them will detest your confidence, and laugh at your folly, is a course of proceeding not easy to be paralleled.

I shall not insist on the particulars, there being not one word of truth in the whole, but leave you to the discipline of your own thoughts,—

"Occultum quatiente animo tortore flagellum."—Juv. xiii. 196.

And so I have done with your prefatory discourse, wherein you have made it appear with what reverence of God and love to the truth you are conversant in the great concernments of the souls of men. What, in particular, you except against in the "Animadversions," I shall now proceed to the consideration of.

CHAPTER II.

Vindication of the first chapter of the "Animadversions"—The method of "Fiat Lux"—Romanists' doctrine of the merit of good works.

In your exceptions to the first chapter of the "Animadversions," p. 20, I wish I could find any thing agreeable unto truth, according unto your own principles. It was ever granted that πολλὰ ψεύδονται ἀοιδοί· but always to fail and feign at pleasure was never allowed so much as to poets. Men may oftentimes utter many things untrue, wherein yet some principles, which they are persuaded to be agreeable unto truth, or some more general mistakes, from whence their particular assertions proceed, may countenance their consciences from a sense of guilt, and some way shield their reputation from the sharpness of censure; but willingly and often for a man practically to offend in this kind, when his mind and understanding is not imposed upon by any previous mistakes, is a miscarriage which I do not yet perceive that the subtilest of your casuists have found out an excuse for. Two exceptions you lay against this chapter,—in the first whereof, by not speaking the whole truth, you render the whole untruth; and, in the latter, you plainly affirm that which your eyes told you to be otherwise. First, you say, I proposed a dilemma unto you for saying you had concealed your method; when what I spake unto you was upon your saying, first that you had *used no method,* and afterward that you had *concealed your method;* as you also in your next words here confess. Now, both these being impossible, and severally spoken by you, only to serve a present turn, your sorry merriment about the scholar and his eggs will not free yourself from being very ridiculous. Certainly this using no method, and yet at the same time concealing your method, is part of that civil logic you have learned, no man knows where. You had far better hide your weaknesses under a universal silence, as you do to the most of them, than expose them afresh unto public contempt, trimmed up with froth and trifles. But this is but one of the least of your escapes. You proceed to downright work in your following words: "Going on, you deny" (say you) "that Protestants ever opposed the merit of good works: which at first I wondered at, seeing the sound of it hath rung so often in my own ears, and so many hundred books written in this last age so apparently witness it in all places, till I found afterward, in my thorough perusal of your book, that you neither heed what you say nor how much you deny; at last, giving a distinction of the intrinsic acceptability of our works, the easier to silence me, you say as I say." Could any man, not acquainted with you, ever imagine but that I had denied that ever Protestants opposed the merit of good works? You positively affirm I did so; you pretend to transcribe my own words; you wonder why I should say so; you produce testimony to disprove what I say: and yet all this while you know well enough that I never said so. Have a little more care, if not of your conscience, yet of your reputation; for, seriously, if you proceed in this manner, you will lose the common privilege of being believed when you speak truth. Your words in your "Fiat Lux," p. 15, second edition, are, that "Our ministers cull out various texts" (out of the Epistle of Paul to the Romans) "against the Christian doctrine of good works and their merit:" wherein you plainly distinguish between the Christian doctrine of good works and their merit; as well you may. I tell you, pp. 25, 26,[1] that no Protestant ever opposed *the Christian doctrine of good works.* Here you repeat my words, as you pretend, and say that I deny "that any Protestant ever opposed *the merit of good works;*" and fall into a feigned wonderment at me for saying that which you knew well enough I never said: for merit is not the Chris-

[1] See pp. 13, 14 of the present volume.

tian, but rather, as by you explained, the anti-christian, doctrine of good works, as being perfectly anti-evangelical. What merit you will esteem this good work of yours to have I know not, and have in part intimated what truly it doth deserve. But you add, that, "making a distinction of the intrinsic acceptability of works, you say as I say." What is that, I pray? Do I say that Protestants oppose the Christian doctrine of good works, as you say in your "Fiat?" or do I say that they never opposed the merit of good works, as you feign me to say in your epistle? Neither the one nor the other; but I say that Protestants teach the Christian doctrine of good works as revealed in the gospel, and oppose the merit of good works by you invented, and as by you explained, and now avowed. And whilst you talk at this rate, as if you were perfectly innocent, you begin your story as if you had nothing to do but to accuse another of fraud, like him that cried,

—— "Nec, si miserum fortuna Sinonem
Finxit, vanum etiam mendacemque improba finget;" Virg. Æn. ii. 79.

when you know what his business was. But the truth is, when you talk of the merit of good works you stand in a slippery place, and know not well what you would have, nor what it is that you would have me believe. Your Tridentine convention hath indeed provided a limber "cothurnus," to fit, if it were possible, your several statures and postures. But general words are nothing but the proportion of a cirque or arena for dogmatists to contend within the limits of. The ancient ecclesiastical importance of the word "merit," wherein, as it may be proved by numberless instances, it denoted no more than to "obtain," you have the most of you rejected; and do urge it in a strict legal sense, denoting working "for a reward," and performing that which is proportionable unto it, as the labour of the hireling is to his wages, according unto the strict rules of justice. See your Rhemish Annotations,[1] 1 Cor. iii., Heb. vi. 10. So is the judgment, I think, of your church explained by Suarez, tom. i. in Thom. 3, d. 41. "A supernatural work," saith he, "proceeding from grace, in

[1] In 1582, an English New Testament was printed at Rheims, for the use of the Roman Catholics in Britain, when, from the multiplication of Protestant versions, it was impossible any longer to withhold the Scriptures from the common people. It is a servile translation from the Vulgate. The annotations, to which Dr Owen refers, are most objectionable. On the words, Luke xiv. 23, "Compel them to come in," a note is appended plainly vindicating persecution. "St Augustine," it is said, "referreth this compelling to the penal laws, which Catholic princes do justly use against heretics and schismatics;" and at the close it is added, "Such are invited as the church of God hath power over, because they promised in baptism, and therefore are to be revoked not only by gentle means, but by just punishment also." The marginal title to the note is, "Heretics may by penal laws be compelled to the Catholic faith." Expressions occur in the notes referred to above, to the following effect:—"The reward of heaven is the recompense of justice;" "Good works be meritorious, and the very cause of salvation."—Ed.

itself, and in its own nature, hath a proportion unto and condignity of the reward, and is of sufficient value to be worth the same." And you seem to be of the same opinion, in owning that description of merit which Protestants reject, which I gave in my "Animadversions," —namely, "an intrinsical worth and value in works, arising from the exact answerableness unto the law and proportion unto the reward, so as on the rules of justice to deserve it." Of the same mind are most of you (see Andrad. Orthodox. Explic. lib. vi., Bagus de Merit. Op., lib. i. cap. 9), though I can assure you Paul was not, Rom. vi. 23, viii. 18: so that you must not take it ill if Protestants oppose this doctrine with testimonies out of his Epistle to the Romans, as well as out of many other portions of the holy writ; for they look upon it as an opinion perfectly destructive of the covenant of grace. Nay, I must tell you that some of your own church and way love not to talk at this high and lofty rate. Ferus speaks plain unto you on Matt. xx.: "If you desire to hold the grace and favour of God, make no mention of your own merits." Durand sticks not to call the opinion which you seem to espouse, "temerarious," yea, "blasphemous," quest. 2, d. 27. In the explication of your distinction of "congruity" and "condignity," how wofully are you divided! as also in the application of it. There is no end of your altercations about it, the terms of it being horrid, uncouth, strangers to Scripture and the ancient church, of an arbitrary signification, about which men may with probabilities contend to the world's end; and yet the very soul and life of your doctrine of merit lies in it. Some ascribe merit of *congruity* to works before grace, and of *condignity* to them done in a state of grace;—some, merit of congruity to them done by grace, and merit of condignity they utterly exclude: some give grace and the promise a place in merit;—some so explain it, that they can have no place at all therein. Generally, in your books of devotion, when you have to do with God, you begin to bethink yourselves, and speak much more humbly and modestly than you do when you endeavour to dispute subtilely, and quell your adversaries. And I am not without hope that many of you do personally believe, as to your own particular concernments, far better than when you doctrinally express yourselves when you contend with us; as when that famous emperor, Charles V., after all his bustles in and about religion, came to die, in his retirement he expressly renounced all merit of works, as a proud figment, and gave up himself to the sole grace and mercy of God in Jesus Christ, on whose purchase of heaven for him he alone relied. "Toto pectore in Deum revolutus sic ratiocinabatur," saith the renowned Thuanus, Hist. lib. xxi.: "se quidem indignum esse qui propriis meritis regnum cœlorum obtineret; sed Dominum Deum suum, qui illud duplici jure obtinuit,—et Patris hæreditate, et passionis merito,—altero contentum esse, alterum sibi donare, ex cujus dono illud sibi merito vindicet, hâcque fiduciâ fretus minime confundatur; neque enim oleum misericordiæ, nisi in vase fiduciæ poni. Hanc hominis fiduciam esse a se deficientis et innitentis Domino suo,—alioqui propriis meritis fidere non fidei esse, sed perfidiæ,—peccata remitti per Dei indulgentiam, ideoque credere nos debere, peccata deleri non posse, nisi ab eo cui soli peccavimus, et in quem peccatum non cadit, per quem solum nobis peccata condonantur." Words worthy of a lasting memory; which they will not fail of where they are recorded! "Casting himself," saith that excellent historian, "with his whole soul upon God, he thus reasoned: That for his part he was, on the account of any merits of his own, unworthy to obtain the kingdom of heaven; but his Lord and God, who hath a double right unto it,—one by inheritance of his Father, the other by the merit of his own passion,—contented himself with the one, granted the other unto him: by whose grant he rightly (or deservedly) laid claim thereunto; and, resting in this faith or confidence, he was not confounded; for the oil of mercy is not poured but into the vessel of faith. This is the faith or confidence of a man fainting or despairing in himself, and resting on his Lord,—and otherwise to trust to our own merits is not an act of faith, but of infidelity or perfidiousness,—that sins are forgiven by the mercy of God; and that therefore we ought to believe that sins cannot be blotted out or forgiven but by him against whom we have sinned, who sinneth not, and by whom alone our sins are pardoned." This, sir, is the faith of Protestants in reference unto the merit of works, which that wise and mighty emperor, after all his military actings against them, found the only safe anchor for his soul "in extremis," his only relief against crying out, with Hadrian,—

"Animula vagula, blandula,
Hospes, comesque corporis,
Quæ nunc abibis in loca?
Pallidula, frigida, nudula,
Nec, ut soles, dabis jocos."

—the only antidote against despair, the only stay of a soul when once entering the lists of eternity. And I am persuaded that many of you fix on the same principles as to your hope and expectation of life and immortality. And to what purpose, I pray you, do you trouble the world with an *opinion*, wherein you can find no *benefit*, when, if true, you should principally expect to be relieved and supported by it? But he that looks to find solid peace and consolation in this world, or a blessed entrance into another, on any other grounds than those expressed by that dying emperor, will find himself deceived. Sir, you will one day find that our *own works or merits*, purgatory, the suffrage of your church, or any parts of it, when we are dead, the surplusage of the works or merits of other sinners, are pitiful things to come into competition with the blood of Christ and pardoning mercy in him. I confess the inquisition made a shift to destroy Constantine, who was confessor to the emperor, and assisted him unto his departure. And king Philip took care that his son Charles should not live in the faith wherein his father Charles died; whereby merit, or our own righteousness, prevailed at court. But, as I said, I am persuaded that when many of you are in cold blood, and think more of God than of Protestants, and of your last account than of your present arguments, you begin to believe that mercy and the righteousness of Christ will be a *better plea,* as to your own particular concernments, at the last day. Seeing, therefore, that Protestants teach the necessity of good works, upon the cogent principles I minded you of in my "Animadversions," I suppose it might not be amiss in you to surcease from troubling them about their merit which few of you are agreed about, and which, as I would willingly hope, none of you dare trust unto. You have, I suppose, been minded before now of the conclusion made in this matter by your great champion Bellarmine, lib. v., De Justificat., cap. 7. "Propter," saith he, "incertitudinem propriæ justitiæ, et periculum inanis gloriæ, tutissimum est, fiduciam totam in sola Dei misericordia et benignitate reponere;"—"Because of the uncertainty of our own righteousness, and the danger of vain-glory, it is the safest course to place all our confidence in the alone mercy and benignity of God:" wherein, if I mistake not, he disclaimeth all that he had subtilely disputed before about the merit of works. And he appears to have been in good earnest in this conclusion, seeing he made such use of it himself, in particular, at the close of all his disputes and days; praying, in his last will and testament, that God would deal with him, not as "æstimator meriti," "a judge of his merit;" but "largitor veniæ," "a merciful pardoner;" Vit. Bell. per Sylvestr. a Pet. San. Impress. Antuerpiæ, 1631. And why is this the safest course? Certainly it must be because God hath appointed it and revealed it so to be; for on no other ground can any course towards heaven be accounted safe. And if this be the way of his appointment, that we should trust to his mercy alone in Christ Jesus,—let them that will be so minded, notwithstanding all persuasions to the contrary, as to trust to their own merit, take heed lest they find, when it is too late, that they have steered a course not so safe as they expected. And so I desire your excuse for this diversion, the design of it being only to discover one reason of your failing in morality, in affirming me to have said that which you knew well enough I did not,—which is this, that you stood in a slippery place as to the point of faith which you were asserting, being not instructed how to speak constantly and evenly unto it; and to take you off from that vain confidence which this proud opinion of the merit of works is apt to ingenerate in you: whose first inventors, I fear, did not sufficiently consider with whom they had to do; before whom sinners appearing in their own strength and righteousness will one day cry, "Who amongst us shall dwell with devouring fire? who amongst us shall inhabit with everlasting burnings?" nor the purity, perfection, and severity of his fiery law, judging, condemning, cursing every sinner for every sin, without the least intimation of mercy or compassion. If you would but seriously consider how impossible it is for any man to know all his secret sins, or to make compensation to God for the least of them that he doth know, and that the very best of his works come short of that universal perfection which is required in them, so that he dares not put the issue of his eternal condition upon any one of them singly, though all the rest of his life should be put into everlasting oblivion; and withal would diligently inquire into the end of God in giving his Son to die for sinners, with the mystery of his love and grace therein, the nature of the new covenant, the importance of the promises thereof, the weight that is laid in Scripture on the *righteousness* and *blood of Christ*, with the redemption that is purchased thereby; or to the whole work of our salvation, and the peremptory exclusion of the *merit of our works* by Paul from our justification before God;—I am persuaded you would find another manner of rest and peace unto your soul than all your own works, and your other pretended supplements of them, or reliefs against their defects, are able to supply you withal. And this I hope you will not be offended at, that I have thus occasionally minded you of.

CHAPTER III.

A defence of the second chapter of the "Animadversions"—Principles of "Fiat Lux" re-examined—Of our receiving the gospel from Rome—Our abode with them from whom we received it.

In the same page you proceed to the consideration of my second chapter, and therein of the principles which I gathered out of your "Fiat Lux," and which I affirmed to run through and to animate your whole discourse, and to be the foundation on which your superstructure is built. Concerning them all you say, p. 21, "That in the sense the words do either naturally make out, or in which I understand them, of all the whole you can hardly own any one." Pray, sir, remember that I never pretended to set down *your words*, but to express *your sense* in my own. And if I do not make it appear that there is no one of the principles mentioned which you have not, in the sense by me declared, affirmed and asserted, I will be contented to be thought to have done you some wrong, and myself much more, for want of attending unto that rule of truth which I am compelled so often to desire you to give up yourself unto the conduct of.

The first principle imputed unto your "Fiat Lux" is, "that we received the gospel first from Rome." To which you say, "We, that is, we Englishmen, received it first from thence." Well, then, this is one principle of the ten; this you own, and seek to defend. If you do so in reference unto any other, what will become of your "hardly one that you can own?" You have already one foot over the limits which you have newly prescribed yourself, and we shall find you utterly forsaking of them by-and-by. For the present you proceed unto the defence of this principle, and say, "But against this you reply that we received it not first from Rome, but by Joseph of Arimathea from Palestine; as 'Fiat Lux' himself acknowledgeth. Sir, if 'Fiat Lux' say both these things, he cannot mean them in your false, contradictory sense, but in his own true one. We, that is we Englishmen, the now actual inhabitants of this land, and progeny of the Saxons, received first our gospel and Christendom from Rome, though the Britons that inhabited the land before, differing as much from us as antipodes, had some of them been christened long before us; and yet the Christendom that prevailed and lasted among the Britons, even they also, as well as we, had it from Rome too. Mark this likewise." This matter must be called over again afterward; and therefore I shall here be the more brief upon it. In my first answer, I showed you not only that your position was not true, but also, that on supposition it were so, it would not in the least advance your intention. Here you acknowledge that the Britons at first received not the gospel from Rome, but reply two things:—First, "That belongs not unto us Englishmen or Saxons." To which I shall now only say, that if, because the Britons have been conquered, we, who are now the inhabitants of Britain, may not be thought to have received the gospel from them from whom the Britons at first received it, seeing it was never utterly extinct in Britain from its first plantation, then much less can the present inhabitants of the city of Rome, which hath been conquered oftener than Britain, be thought to have received the gospel from them by whom it was first delivered unto the old Romans: for though I confess that the Saxons, Jutes, and Angles made great havoc of the ancient Britons in some parts of this island, yet was it not comparable unto that which was made at Rome; which at length Totilas, after it had been taken and sacked more than once before, marching out of it against Belisarius, left as desolate as a wilderness, without one living soul to inhabit it. "Ipse (Totilas) cum suarum copiarum parte progreditur, Romanos qui senatorii erant ordinis secum trahens; aliâ omni urbanorum multitudine vel virilis muliebrisque sexus, et pueris in Campaniæ agros missis: ita ut Romæ nemo hominum restaret, sed vasta ibi esset solitudo," saith Procopius, Hist. Goth. i. 3. Concerning which action, saith Sigonius de Imper. Occid. lib. xix.:—"Urbs Romæ, incolis omnibus amotis, prorsus est destituta: memorandum inter pauca exempla humanæ fortunæ ludibrium, ac spectaculum ipsis etiam hostibus, quanquam ab omni humanitate remotissimis, miserandum;"—"The city of Rome, all its inhabitants being removed, was wholly desolate, an unparalleled reproach of human condition, and a spectacle of pity to the very enemies, though most remote from all humanity!" The next inhabitants of it were a mixture of Greeks, Thracians, and other nations, brought in by Belisarius. You may go now and reproach the Britons, if you please, with their being conquered by the Saxons. In the meantime, pray give me a reason why the present inhabitants of England may not date their reception of Christianity from the first planting of it in this island, as well as you suppose the present inhabitants of Rome may do theirs from the time wherein it was first preached unto the old Romans? But you except again, "That the Christendom that prevailed and lasted among the Britons before the coming of the Saxons, came from Rome too." You bid me mark that likewise. I do consider what you say, and desire you to prove it; wherein yet I will not be very urgent, because I will not put you upon impossibilities: and your incompetency to give at least colour unto this remarkable assertion shall be discovered in our farther progress. For the present I shall only mind you, that the Christianity which prevailed in Britain was that which continued among the Britons in Wales, after the conquest of these parts of the island by the Saxons: and that that came not from Rome is manifest from the customs which they observed and insisted on, differing from those of Rome, and your refusal to admit those of that church; the story whereof you have in Beda, lib. ii. cap. 2. I know it may be rationally replied that Rome might, after the time of the first preaching of the gospel in Britain, have invented many new customs which might be strange unto the Britons at the coming of Austin; for indeed so they have done: but this exception will here take no place; for the customs the British church adhered unto were such as, having their rise and occasion in the east, were never *admitted* at Rome, and so from thence could not be *transmitted* hither.

But there were also other exceptions put in unto your application of this principle unto your purpose, upon supposition that there were any truth in the matter of fact asserted by you; for, suppose that those who from beyond seas first preached the gospel to the Saxons came from Rome, yea, were sent by the bishop, or, if you please, the pope of Rome, I ask, whether it was his religion or the religion of Jesus Christ that they brought with them? Did the pope first find it out? or did they publish it in the name of the pope? You say, "It was the pope's religion, not invented but professed by him, and from him derived unto us by his missioners." Well, and what more? for all this was before supposed in my inquiry, and made the foundation of that which we sought farther after. I supposed the pope professed the religion which he sent; and your courtly expression, "Derived unto us by his missioners," is but the same in sense and meaning with my homely phrase, "They that preached it were sent by him." On this I inquire, whether it were to be esteemed his religion or no,—that is, any more his than it is the religion of every one that professeth it? or did those that were sent baptize in his name, or teach us that the pope was crucified for us? You answer, that "he sent them to preach." I see

—— "Nil opus est te
Circumagi: quendam volo visere non tibi notum;" Hor. Sat. i. 9, 16.

you understand not what I inquire after. But if that be all you have to say, as it was before supposed, so what matter is it, I pray, who planted, and who watered? it was the religion of Christ that was preached, and God that "gave the increase." Christ liveth still, his word abideth still, but the planters and waterers are dead long ago. Again: what though we received the gospel from Rome? doth it therefore follow that we received all the doctrines of *the present church of Rome* at the same time? Pope Gregory knew little of the present Roman doctrine about the pope of Rome. What was broached of it he condemned in another (even John of Constantinople, who fasted [lusted?] for a kind of popedom), and professed himself an obedient servant to his good lord the emperor. Many a good doctrine hath been lost at Rome since those old days, and many a new fancy broached, and many a tradition of men taught for a doctrine of truth.

"Hippolyte, sic est; Thesei vultus amo,
Illos priores quos tulit quondam puer,
Quum prima puras barba signaret genas,
Et ora flavus tenera tingebat rubor."

We love the church of Rome as it was in its purity and integrity, in the days of her youth and chastity, before she was deflowered by false worship; but what is that to the present Roman carnal confederacy? If, then, any in this nation did receive their religion from Rome,—as many of the Saxons had Christianity declared unto them by some sent from Rome for that purpose,—yet it doth not at all follow that they received the present religion of Rome.

> "Hei mihi qualis!——quantum mutatur ab illa," Virg. Æn. ii. 274,

which of old she professed!

> "Multa dies variusque labor mutabilis ævi,
> Rettulit in pejus." Æn. xi. 425.

And this sad alteration, declension, and change, we may bewail in her, as the prophet did the like apostasy in the church of the Jews of old: "How is the faithful city become an harlot! it was full of judgment; righteousness lodged in it; but now murderers. Thy silver is become dross, thy wine mixed with water." He admires that it should be so; was not ignorant how it became so: no more are others in reference unto your apostasy.

And what if we had received from you, or by your means, the religion that is now professed at Rome, I mean the whole of it, yet we might have received that with it,—namely, the Bible,—which would have made it our duty to examine, try, and reject any thing in it for which we saw from thence just cause so to do, unless we should be condemned for that for which the Bereans are so highly commended. So that neither is your position true, nor, if it were so, would it at all advantage your pretensions.

I added, also, "Did not the gospel come from another place to Rome, as well as to us? or was it first preached there?" This you have culled out, as supposing yourself able to say something unto it; and what is it? "Properly speaking, it came not so to Rome as it came to us; for one of the twelve fountains, nay, two of the thirteen, and those the largest and greatest, were transferred to Rome; which they watered with their blood. We had never any such standing fountain of our Christian religion here, but only a stream derived unto us from thence." It is the hard hap, it seems, of England, to claim any privilege or reputation that may stand in the way of some men's designs. No apostle nor apostolical person must be allowed to preach the gospel unto us, lest we should perk up into competition with Rome. But though Rome, it seems, must always be excepted, yet I hope you do not in general conclude our condition beneath that of any place where the gospel at first was preached, by one or two apostles, so as to cry, "Properly speaking, it came not to us at all." What think you of Jerusalem, where Christ himself and his apostles, all of them, preached the gospel? or what think you of Capernaum, that was "lifted up to heaven," in the privilege of the means of light granted for a while unto them? Do you think our condition worse than theirs? The two fountains you mentioned were opened at Antioch in Syria, as well as at other places, before they conveyed one drop of their treasures to Rome; which whether one of them ever did by his personal presence, is very questionable. And by this rule of yours, though England may not, yet every place where St Peter and St Paul preached the gospel may, contend with Rome as to this privilege. And what will you then get by your triumphing over us? "Non vides id manticæ quod in tergo est." When men are intent upon a supposed advantage, they oftentimes overlook real inconveniences that lie ready to seize upon them; as it befalls you more than once. Besides, there is nothing in the world more obscure than by whom, or what means, the gospel was first preached at Rome. By St Paul it is certain it was not; for before ever he came thither there was a great number converted to the faith, as appears from his epistle, written about the fourteenth year of Claudius, and the fifty-third of Christ. Nor yet by Peter: for, not at present to insist on the great uncertainty whether ever he was there or no, which shall afterward be spoken unto, there is nothing more certain than that, about the sixth year of Claudius, and forty-fifth of Christ, he was at Antioch, Gal. ii. (Baronius makes the third of Claudius and the forty-fifth of Christ to contemporize, but upon a mistake); and some say he abode there a good while, sundry years, and that upon as good authority as any is produced for his coming to Rome. But it is generally granted that there was a church founded at Rome that year, but by whom, ἄδηλον παντὶ πλὴν ἢ τῷ Θεῷ (as Socrates said of the preference of the condition of the living or dead),—"is known to God alone, of mortal men not to any." "Jam sumus ergo pares." For, to confess the truth unto you, I know not certainly who first preached the gospel in Britain: some say Peter, some Paul, some Simon Zelotes, most Joseph of Arimathea, as I have elsewhere showed, by whom certainly I know not; but some one it was, or more, whom God sent upon his errand, and with his message.[1] No more do you know who preached it first at Rome, though in general it appears that some of them at least were of the circumcision; whence the very first converts of that church were variously minded about the observation of Mosaical rites and ceremonies. And I doubt not but God, in his infinitely holy wisdom and providence, left the springs of Christian religion, as to matter of fact, in the first introductions of it into the nations of the world, in so much darkness as to the knowledge of aftertimes, to obviate those towering thoughts of pre-eminency which he foresaw that some men from external advantages would entertain, to the no small prejudice of the simplicity of the gospel, and ruin of Christian humility. As far as appears from story, the gospel was preached in England before any church was founded at Rome. It was so, saith Gildas, "Summo tempore Tiberii Cæsaris,"

[1] See note, page 95.

—that is, "extremo," about the end of the reign of Tiberius Cæsar, who died in the thirty-ninth year of Christ, five or six years at least before the foundations of the Roman church were laid; καὶ ταῦτα μὲν δὴ ταῦτα. These things we must speak unto, because you suppose them of importance unto your cause.

The second assertion ascribed unto your "Fiat" in the "Animadversions" is, "That whence and from whom we first received our religion, there and with them we must abide therein; to them we must repair for guidance; and return to their rule and conduct, if we have departed from them." To which you now say, "This principle, as it is never delivered by 'Fiat Lux,' though you put it upon me, so is it, in the latitude it carries, and wherein you understand it, absolutely false, never thought of by me, and indeed impossible; for how can we abide with them in any truth, who may not, perhaps, abide in it themselves? Great part of Flanders was first converted by Englishmen; and yet are they not obliged to accompany the English in our now present ways." I am glad you confess this principle now to be false: it was sufficiently proved so to be in the "Animadversions," and your whole discourse rendered thereby useless; for to what purpose will the preceding assertion, so often inculcated by you, serve, if this be false? For what matter is it from whence or whom we received the profession of religion, if there be no obligation upon us to continue in their communion, any farther than as we judge them to continue in the truth? And to what purpose do you avoid the consideration of the reasons and causes of our not abiding with you, and manage all your charge upon the general head of our *departure*, if we may have just cause, by your own concession, so to do? It is false, then, by your own acknowledgment; and I am as sure, in the sense which I understand it in, that it is yours. And you labour with all your art to prove and confirm it, both in your "Fiat," pp. 44–47, and in this very epistle, pp. 38–41, etc. On the account that the gospel came unto us from Rome, you expressly adjudge the pre-eminence over us unto Rome, and determine that her we must all hear, and obey, and abide with. But if you may say and unsay, assert and deny, avow and disclaim, at your pleasure, as things make for your advantage, and think to evade the owning of the whole drift and scope of your discourse by having expressed yourself in a loose flourish of words, it will be to no great purpose farther to talk with you.

"Quo teneam vultus mutantem Protea nodo?"—Hor. Ep. i. 1. 90.

To lay fast hold, and not startle at a new shape, was the counsel his daughter gave to Menelaus; and I must needs urge you to leave off all thoughts of evading by such changes of your hue, and to abide by what you say. I confess I believe you never intended knowingly to assert this principle in its whole latitude, because you did not, as it should seem, consider how little it would make for your advantage, seeing so many would come in for a share in the privilege intimated in it with your Roman church, and you do not in any thing love competitors. But you would fain have the conclusion hold as to your Roman church only: those that have received the gospel from her must always abide in her communion. That this assertion is not built on any general foundation of reason or authority, yourself now confess; and that you have no special privilege to plead in this cause hath been proved in the "Animadversions," whereof you are pleased to take no notice.

CHAPTER IV

Farther vindication of second chapter of the "Animadversions"—Church of Rome not what she was of old—Her falls and apostasy—Difference between idolatry, apostasy, heresy, and schism—Principles of the church of Rome condemned by the ancient church, fathers, and councils—Imposing rites unnecessary—Persecution for conscience—Papal supremacy—The branches of it—Papal personal infallibility—Religious veneration of images.

THE third assertion which you review is, "That the Roman profession of religion, and practice in the worship of God, are every way the same as when first we received the gospel from Rome; nor can they ever otherwise be." Whereunto you say, "This, indeed, though I do nowhere formally express it, yet I suppose it, because I know it hath been demonstratively proved a hundred times over. You deny it hath been proved; why do you not then disprove it? Because you decline, say you, all common-places." All that I affirmed was, that you did suppose this principle, and built many of your inferences on the supposition thereof; which you here acknowledge. And so you have already owned two of the principles whereof, in the foregoing page, you affirmed that you could hardly own any one, and that in the sense wherein by me they are proposed and understood! But what do you mean, that you "nowhere formally express it?" If you mean that you have not set it down in those syllables wherein you find it expressed in the "Animadversions," no man ever said you did: you do not use to speak so openly and plainly; to do so would bring you out of the corners, which somewhat that you pretend unto never led you into. But if you deny that you asserted and laboured to prove the whole and entire matter of it, your following discourse, wherein you endeavour a vindication of the sophism wherewith you pleaded for it in your "Fiat," will sufficiently confute you. And so you have avowed already two of the "hardly any one" principles ascribed unto you: and this you say hath been "demonstratively proved a hundred times over," and ask me why I do not disprove it, giving a ridiculous answer, as from me, unto your inquiry. But pray, sir, talk not of demonstrations in this matter: palpable sophisms, such as your masters use in this cause, are far enough from demonstrations. And if you think it enough for you to say that *it hath been proved*, why is it not a sufficient answer in me to remind you that it hath been disproved, and your pretended proofs all refuted? And according to what rules of logic do you expect arguments from me to disprove your assertion, whilst I was only answering yours that you produced in its confirmation? But that you may not complain any more, I shall make some addition of the proofs you require, by way of supererogation, when we have considered your vindication of your former arguments for the confirmation of this assertion, wherewith you closed your discourse in your "Fiat Lux." This you thus propose again, "The Roman was once a true, flourishing church; and if she ever fell, she must fall either by apostasy, heresy, or schism." So you now mince the matter: in your "Fiat" it was "a most pure, flourishing, and mother church;" and you know there are many that yet acknowledge her a true church, as a thief is a true man, who will not acknowledge her to be a pure church, much less "most pure." God be merciful to poor worms! This boasting doth not become us; it is not unlike hers who cried, "I sit as a queen, and shall see no sorrow." I wish you begin to be sensible and ashamed of it, but yet I fear it is otherwise; for whereas, in your "Fiat," you had proclaimed your Roman church and party to be absolutely innocent and unblamable, you tell us, p. 10 of your epistle, that you can make it appear that it is far more innocent and amiable than you have made it; more than absolutely innocent, it seems,—a note so high that it sounds harshly. And whereas we shall manifest your church to have lost her native beauty, we know that no painting of her (which is all you can do) will render her truly amiable unto a spiritual eye. She hath too often defiled herself to pretend now to be lovely. But to this you say I reply, "The church that then was, in the apostles' time, was indeed true,—not the Roman church that now is;" and add, "So, so; then I say that former true church must fall some time or other. When did she fall? and how did she fall,—by apostasy, heresy, or schism?" Sir, you very lamely represent my answer, that you might seem to say something unto it, when indeed you say nothing at all. I discovered unto you the equivocation you use in that expression, "The church of Rome," and showed you that the thing now so called by you had neither being nor name, neither essence nor affection, in the days of old; its very being is but the "terminus ad quem" of a church's fall. I showed you also that the church of old, that was pure, fell not whilst it was so; but that the men who succeeded in the place where they lived, in the profession of religion, gradually fell from the purity of that profession which the church at its first planting did enjoy. But all that discourse you pass by, and repeat again your former question, to which you subjoin my first answer, which was, "It was possible she might fall by an earthquake, as did those of Colosse and Laodicea;" to which you [reply,] "We speak not here of any casual or natural downfall, or death of mortals, by plague, famine, or earthquake, but a moral and voluntary lapse in faith. What do you speak to me of earthquakes?" It is well you do so now explain yourself; your former inquiry was only in general, how or by what means she ceased to be what she had been before? as though it were impossible to assign any such: neither did I exclude the sense whereunto you now restrain your words. And had I only showed you that it was possible she might fall and come to nothing, and yet not by any of the ways or means by you mentioned, without proceeding unto the consideration of them also, yet your *special* inquiry being resolved into this *general* one, from whence it is taken, how a pure, flourishing church may cease to be so? I had rendered your inquiry useless unto your present purpose, though I had not answered your intention; for certainly that which ceaseth to be, ceaseth to be pure, seeing "non-entis nullæ sunt affectiones." The church of the Britons, in this part of the island now called England, was once as pure a church as ever was the church of Rome; yet she ceased to be long since, and that neither by apostasy, heresy, nor schism, but by the sword of the Saxons. And, to tell you the truth, I do not think the old church of Rome unconcerned in this instance, then especially when Rome was left desolate by Totilas, and without inhabitant; for the church of Rome is "*urbis*," and not, as you vainly imagine, "*orbis* ecclesia."

Again: I told you she might fall by idolatry, and so neither by apostasy, heresy, or schism. To which you reply, "Good sir, idolatry is a mixed misdemeanour both in faith and manners. I speak of the single one of faith; and he that falls by idolatry, if he keep still some parts of Christianity entire, he falls by heresy,—by apostasy, if he keep none." I am persuaded you are the first that ever gave this description of idolatry, and the last that will do so: "It is a mixed misdemeanour in faith and manners." Manners you speak of in contradistinction to faith, and you so explain yourself; in which sense they relate only unto moral conversation, regulated by the second table. That idolatry hath been and is constantly attended with corruption in manners, the apostle declares, Rom. i., and I willingly grant; but how in itself or in its own nature it should come to be "a mixed misdemeanour in faith and in manners," I know not: neither can you tell me which is the fleshy, which is the fishy part of this Dagon,—what it is in it that is a misdemeanour in faith, and what in manners. According to this description of yours, an idolater should be an ill-mannered or an unmannerly heretic. But you speak of the single misdemeanour in faith; but who gave you leave so to restrain your inquiry? I allowed you before to except against one instance, whereby many a church hath fallen; but if you will except idolatry and manners also, your endeavour to provide a shelter for your guilt is shameful and vain. For what you except out of your inquiry, if you confess not to have been, yet you do that it may be or might have been. And you do wisely to let your adversary know that he is to strike you only where you suppose yourself armed, but by all means must let naked parts alone; and doubtless he must needs be very wise who will take your advice. "The church of Judah was once a pure church, in the days of David; how came she, then, to fall? by apostasy, heresy, or schism?" I answer, if you will give me leave, she fell by idolatry and corruption of manners; against both which the prophets were protestants, 2 Kings xvii. 13: וַיָּעַד יְהוָֹה,—God protested against them by his prophets. Again: the same church reformed in the days of Ezra, Nehemiah, Zerubbabel, and אַנְשֵׁי כְנֶסֶת הַגְּדוֹלָה, "the men of the great congregation," was a pure church. How did it fall? not by idolatry as formerly, but by corruption of life, unbelief, and rejecting the word of God for superstitious traditions, until it became "a den of thieves." You see, then, there are other ways of a church's falling from its pristine purity than those by you insisted on. And if you shall inquire how it may fall, you must exclude nothing out of your inquiry whereby it may do so, and whereby some churches have done so. And if you will have my thoughts in this matter, they are, that the beginning of the fall of your church and many others lay in *unbelief*, corruption of life, conformity to the world, and other sins that were found in the most of its members. And it is a fancy, to dream of the *purity* of a church in respect of its outward order, when the power and life of godliness is lost in its members; and a wicked device, to suppose a church may not be separated from Christ by unbelief, whilst it abides in an external profession of the doctrine of faith. Such a church, though it may have "a name to live," yet indeed is "dead," and dead things are unclean. We speak of its purity, and acceptation thereon in the sight of God; neither will men "dead in trespasses and sins" be "terrible" unto any "as an army with banners," unless they are like those in Lucilius, who,

> "Ut pueri infantes credunt signa omnia ahena
> Vivere et esse homines; sic isti omnia ficta
> Vera putant; credunt signis cor inesse ahenis;"

as Lactantius reports him. But you say, "If they fall by idolatry, and yet keep any parts of Christianity, they fall by heresy." But why so? Would you had thought it incumbent on you to give a reason of what you say! Are idolatry and heresy the same? Tertullian, who, of all the old ecclesiastical writers, most enlargeth the bounds of idolatry, defines it to be "Omnis circa omne idolum famulatus et servitus;"—"Any worship or service performed in reference to or about any idol." I do not remember that ever I met with your definition of idolatry in any author whatever. Bellarmine seems to place it in "Creaturam æquè colere ac Deum;"—"To worship the creature as much or equally with the Creator:" which description of it, though it be vain and groundless (for his "æquè" is neither in the Scripture nor any approved author of old required to the constituting of the worship of any creature idolatrous), yet is not this heresy neither, but that which differs from it "toto genere." We know it to be "Cultus religiosus creaturæ exhibitus,"—"Any religious worship of that which by nature is not God;" and so doth your Thomas grant it to be. Gregory de Valentia, another of your great champions, contends that "tanquam Deo," "as unto God," is to be added unto the definition; as though religious worship could be given unto any thing, and not as unto God really and indeed, though not intentionally as to the worshipper. Where a man gives religious worship, there he doth, "ipso facto," assign a divine eminency, say he what he will to the contrary. Neither will his intention of not doing it "as unto God," any more free him from idolatry than an adulteress will be free by not looking on her adulterer as her husband. I confess he adds afterward a distinction that is of great use for you, and indispensably necessary for your defence, De Idol., lib. ii. cap. 7. St Peter, he tells us, insinuates some "worship of idols,"—"cultum aliquem simulachrorum,"—to wit, that of the holy images, to be right or lawful, when he deterreth believers "ab illicitis idolorum cultibus,"—"from the unlawful worship of idols," 1 Pet. iv. 3: Ἀθεμίτοις εἰδωλολατρείαις. This were somewhat, indeed, if all epithets were distinguishing, none aggravating or declarative. When Virgil said, "Dulcia mella premes," Geor. iv., he did not insinuate that there was any bitter honey. Nor is it allowable only for poets, to use explaining and declaring epithets; but Aristotle allows it in the best orators also, so they use not μακροῖς ἢ ἀκαίροις ἢ πυκνοῖς, "long or unseasonable ones," or the same frequently: and the use of this here by Peter is free from all those vices. When the Roman orator cried out, "O scelus detestandum!"—"O wickedness to be abhorred!" he did not intend to insinuate that there was a wickedness not to be abhorred, or to be approved. But if it will follow hence that your church is guilty only of lawful idolatry, I shall not much contend about it; yet I must tell you, that as the poor woman, when the physicians in her sickness told her still that what she complained of was a good sign, cried out, Οἴμοι ὑπ' ἀγαθῶν ἀπόλλυμαι,—"Good signs have undone me,"—your lawful idolatry, if you take not better heed, will undo you. In the meantime, as to the coincidence you imagine between idolatry and heresy, I wish you would advise with your "angelical doctor," who will show you how they are contradistinct evils; which he therefore weighs in his scales, and determines which is the heaviest, 22æ q. 94, a. ad 4. The church in the wilderness fell by its μοσχοποιΐα,—its "making and worshipping a golden calf," as a representation of the presence of God. That they kept some parts of the doctrine of truth entire is evident from their proclamation of a feast to Jehovah. Do any men in their wits use to say this fall was by heresy, though all agree it was by idolatry? so that your church might fall by idolatry and not fall formally by heresy, according to the genuine importance of the word, the use of it in the Scriptures, or the definition given of it by the schoolmen, or any sober writer of what sort whatever. And here I must desire you to stay a little, if you intend to take Protestants along with you. They constantly return this answer unto you, in the first place, and tell you that your church is fallen by idolatry: it is fallen in the worship which you give unto the "consecrated host," as you call it; wherein,—if the Scriptures, which call it "bread," and the fathers, who term it the "figure of the body of Christ," if reason, and all our senses, deceive us not,—you are as plainly idolatrous as the poor wretches which fall down and worship a piece of red cloth: so your own Costerus assures us, Enchirid., cap. viii. "Tolerabilior," saith he, "est eorum error, qui pro deo colunt statuam auream, aut argenteam, aut alterius materiæ imaginem, quomodo Gentiles deos suos venerabantur, vel pannum rubrum in hastam elevatum, quod narratur de Lappis, vel viva animalia ut quondam Ægyptii, quam eorum qui frustum panis colunt;"—"Their error is more tolerable who worship a golden or silver statue, or an image of any other matter for a god, as the Gentiles worshipped their gods, or a rag of red cloth lifted upon a spear, as it is reported of the Laplanders, or living creatures, as did the Egyptians of old, than theirs who worship a piece of bread." This is that which made Averroës cry out, "Seeing the Christians eat the god whom they worship, let my soul be among the philosophers." You do the same in your worship of the cross; which the chiefest among you maintain to be the same that is due to Christ himself. And you are in the same path still in the religious adoration you give unto the blessed Virgin, your prayers to her, and invocations of her; which abound in all your books of devotion and general practice. And what need we mention any particular instances, when you have begun some of your conciliary actions, the greatest solemnities of Christianity amongst you, with invocation of her for help and assistance?

So did your council of Lateran, joining with Cardinal Cajetan, in their opening of the second session, in these words: "Quoniam nihil est quod homo de semetipso sine auxilio opeque divina possit polliceri, ad gloriosam ipsam Virginem Dei matrem primum convertam orationem meam;"—"Seeing there is nothing that a man may promise to himself, as of himself, without divine help and assistance, I will first turn my prayer unto the glorious Virgin, the mother of God." This was the doctrine, this the practice, this the idolatry, of our Lateran council. And again, in the seventh session, "Deiparæ nostræ præsidium imploremus;"—"Let us pray for the help or protection of our blessed Mother of God." And in the tenth session of the same council, Stephen, archbishop of Patras, prays, "Ut ipsa beata Virgo, angelorum domina, fons omnium gratiarum, quæ omnes hereses interimit, cujus operâ magna reformatio, concordia principum, et vera contra infideles expeditio fieri debet opem ferre dignetur;"—"That the blessed Virgin, the lady of angels, the fountain of all graces, who destroyeth all heresies, by whose assistance the great reformation, the agreement of princes, and sincere expedition against the infidels" (the business of that council), "ought to be performed, would vouchsafe to help him, that he might," etc.; and thereupon sings this hymn unto her, recorded in the acts of the council:—

"Omnium splendor, decus, et perenne
Virginum lumen, genetrix Superni,
Gloria humani generis Maria
Unica nostri.
"Sola tu Virgo dominaris astris,
Sola tu terræ maris atque cœli
Lumen, inceptis faveas rogamus
Inclyta nostris.
"Ut queam sacros reserare sensus
Qui latent chartis nimium severis;
Ingredi, et celsæ, duce te benigna,
Mænia terræ."

"O Mary! the beauty, honour, and everlasting light of all virgins, the mother of the Highest, the only glory of mankind; thou, Virgin, alone rulest the stars; thou alone art the light of earth, sea, and heaven. Do thou, O glorious lady! we entreat, prosper my endeavours, that I may unfold the sacred senses which lie hid in the too severe writings" (of the Scripture), "and kindly give me, under thy goodness, to enter the walls of the heavenly countries." I suppose it cannot be doubted whence the pattern of this *Conciliary* prayer was taken: it is but an imitation of—

"Phœbe, sylvarumque potens Diana
Lucidum cœli decus, o colendi
Semper et culti, date quæ precamur
Tempore sacro.
° ° ° °

> "Alme Sol, curru nitido diem qui
> Promis et celas, aliusque et idem
> Nasceris; possis nihil urbe Roma
> Visere majus.
> "Rite maturos aperire partus
> Lenis Ilithyia, tuere matres:
> Sive tu Lucina probas vocari,
> Seu Genitalis.
> Diva." Horat. Carm. Sæculare.

And if this be not plainly to place her in the throne of God, I know not what can be imagined so to do. Your worship of angels and of saints is of the same importance, concerning whom you do well to entitle your paragraph, "Heroes;" your doctrine and practice concerning them being the very same with those of the ancient heathen, in reference unto their demons and heroes. So your own learned Vives confesseth of many of you, in August. de Civit. Dei, lib. xxviii. cap. ult. "Multi Christiani," saith he, "divos divasque non aliter venerantur quam Deum; nec video in multis quod sit discrimen inter eorum opinionem de sanctis, et id quod Gentiles putabant de suis diis;"—"Many Christians worship he and she saints no otherwise than they do God; neither do I see, in many things, what difference there is between their opinion concerning the saints and that which the heathen thought of their gods." And it is known what Polydore Virgil before him affirmed to the same purpose. Your idolatry, in the worship of images of all sorts, shall be afterward declared. Be, then, this a single or mixed misdemeanour, it matters not; a misdemeanour it is, whereby we affirm that the Roman church is *fallen* from its pristine purity. And this we think is a full answer unto your inquiry We *need* not, you cannot compel us, to go one step farther; but our way is plain and invites us. I shall therefore proceed to let you see once again that she is fallen, by all the ways you thought meet to confine your inquiry unto.

You proceed: "Finding yourself puzzled in the third place, you lay on load. 'She fell,' say you, 'by apostasy, idolatry, heresy, schism, licentiousness, and profaneness of life.' And in this you do not much unlike the drunken youth, who, being bid to hit his master's finger with his, when he perceived he could not do it, he ran his whole fist against it." Seriously, sir, you have the worst success in your attempts for a little *wit* and merriment that ever I met with. If you would take my advice, you should not strain your genius for that which it will not afford you; you forgot the old rule,—

> "Tu nihil invitâ dices faciesve Minerva."—Hor. ad Pison., 265.

Any other diversion were better than this, which proves so successless; yet I must confess you deserve well of pastime, seeing to serve its interests you so often make yourself *ridiculous*, as you now do in this pitiful story. And I cannot tell you whether my answer have touched your finger or no, but I am sure, if it be true, it strikes your cause to the heart; and I am as sure of the truth of it as I am that I am alive. And you see how I am puzzled, even as he was who cried, "Inopem me copia fecit." Your church hath fallen so many ways, all so foully and evidently, that it is hard for any man to choose what instance to insist upon who is called on to charge her, as you, by your inquiry of them, do on your Protestant readers; and for my part, I had rather you should take your choice against which of the things mentioned you think yourself best able to defend her. And, may it please you to choose your instance, if I prove not your church to have fallen by it, I will promise you to become a Papist. You proceed to your own particulars, and ask, "Did she fall by *apostasy?*" to which you subjoin my words, "By a partial, not a total one;" with your reply, "Good sir, in this division apostasy is set to express a total relapse, in opposition to heresy, which is the partial." I see you have as little mind to be drawn to the consideration of your apostasy as of your idolatry; and would feign post off all to heresy, under a corrupt notion of which term you hope to find some shelter for yourself and your church, although in vain. But,—

> "Verte omnes tete in facies; et contrahe quicquid
> Sive animis, sive arte vales." Virg. Æn. xii. 891.

You must bear the charge of *apostasy* also; for why must that needs be the notion of these terms, in the division you made, that you now express? Is it from the strict sense and importance of the words themselves, or from the scriptural or ecclesiastical use of them, or whence is it that it *must* be so, and that it *is* so? None of these will give you any relief, or the least countenance unto your fancy. Both ἀποστασία and αἵρεσις are words ἐκ τῶν μέσων, in themselves of an indifferent signification, denoting things or acts, good or evil, according to their accidental limitations and applications. It is said of some, Ἀποστήσονται τῆς πίστεως,—"They will depart from the faith," 1 Tim. iv. 1; and the same apostle, speaking of them that name the name of Christ, says, "Let every one of them depart from iniquity," Ἀποστήτω ἀπὸ ἀδικίας, 2 Tim. ii. 19: so that the word itself signifies no more but a single and bare departure from any thing, way, rule, or practice, be it good or bad, wherein a man hath been engaged, or which he ought to avoid and fly from. And this is the use of it in the best Greek authors: Πολλὸν ἀφιστάντες are such, in Homer, who are far distant or remote on any account from any thing or place; and Τὰ πλεῖστον ἀφεστηκότα, in Aristotle, things very remote. To leave any place, company, thing, society, or rule, on any cause, is the common use of the word in Thucydides, Plutarch, Lucian, and the rest of their companions in the propriety of that language. "Apostasia," by ecclesiastical writers, is restrained unto either a backsliding in faith subjective and manners, or a causeless relinquishment of any truth before professed. So the Jews charge Paul, Acts xxi. 21, Ἀποστασίαν διδάσκεις,—"Thou teachest the apostasy" from Moses' law. Such also is the nature of αἵρεσις,—a special "option, choice," or way, in profession of any truth or error. So Paul calls Pharisaism ἀκριβεστάτην αἵρεσιν τῆς θρησκείας, Acts xxvi. 5,—"the most exact heresy," or way of religion, among the Jews. And Clemens Alexandrinus, Strom. lib. viii., calls Christian religion αἵρεσιν ἀρίστην,—the "best heresy." And the great Constantine in one of his edicts calls it αἵρεσιν καθολικήν,—"the catholic" or "general heresy;" and αἵρεσιν ἁγιωτάτην,—"the most holy heresy." The Latins, also, constantly used that word in a sense indifferent. "Cato," saith Cicero, "est in ea hæresi quæ nullum orationis florem sequitur." The words, therefore, themselves, you see, are of an indifferent signification, having this difference between them, that the one for the most part is used to signify the relinquishment of that which a man had before embraced, and the other a choice or embracing of that which a man had not before received or admitted. And this difference is constantly observed by all ecclesiastical writers, who afterward used these words in the worst or an evil sense: so that apostasy, in this appropriation of it, denotes the *relinquishment* of any important truth or way in religion; and heresy the *choice* or embracement of any new destructive opinion, or principle, or way in the profession thereof. A man, then, may be an apostate by *partial* apostasy,—that is, depart from the profession of some truth he had formerly embraced, or the performance of some duty which he was engaged in,—without being a heretic, or choosing any new opinion which he did not before embrace. Thus you signally call a monk that deserts his *monastical* profession an apostate, though he embrace no opinion which is condemned by your church, or which you think *heretical*. And a man may be a heretic,—that is, *choose* and embrace some new false opinion, which he may coin out of his own imagination,—without a *direct renunciation* of any truth which before he was instructed in. And this is that which I intended, when I told you that your church is fallen by partial apostasy, and by heresy. She hath renounced many of the important truths which the old Roman church once believed and professed, and so is fallen by apostasy; and she hath invented or coined many articles pretended to be of faith, which the old Roman church never believed, and so is fallen by heresy also. Now, what say you hereunto? Why, "Good sir, in this division apostasy is set to express a total relapse, in opposition to heresy, which is the partial."

But who gave you warrant or leave so to set them? It would, it may be, somewhat serve your turn in evading the charge of apostasy, that lies against your church, but, "good sir," will not prove that you may thus confound things for your advantage. Idolatry is heresy, and apostasy is heresy, and what not, because you suppose you have found a way to escape the imputation of heresy. I say, then, yet again, in answer to your inquiry, that your church is fallen by apostasy, in her relinquishment of many important truths, and neglect of many necessary duties, which the old Roman church embraced and performed. That these may be the more evident unto you, I shall give you some few instances of your apostasy, desiring only that you would grant me that the *primitive* church of Rome believed and faithfully retained the doctrine of truth wherein from the Scripture it was instructed:—

That church believed expressly that all they "who die in the Lord do rest from all their labours," Rev. xiv. 13;—which truth you have forsaken, by sending many of them into the flames of *purgatory.*

It believed that "the sufferings of this life are not worthy of the glory that shall be revealed in us," Rom. viii. 18;—your church is otherwise minded, asserting in our works and sufferings a *merit* of and condignity unto the glory that shall be received.

It believed that "we were saved freely, by grace, by faith, which is not of ourselves, but the gift of God; not by works, lest any one should boast," Eph. ii. 8, Tit. iii. 5; and therefore besought the Lord "not to enter into judgment with them, because in his sight no flesh could be justified," Ps. cxxx. 3, clxiii. 2;—and you are apostatized from this part of their faith.

It believed that Christ "was once only offered," Heb. x. 12; and that it could not be that "he should often offer himself, because then he must have often suffered and died," Heb. ix. 25;—which faith of theirs you are departed from.

It believed that "we have one only mediator and intercessor with God," 1 Tim. ii. 5, 1 John ii. 1;—wherein also you have renounced their persuasion; as likewise you have done in what it professed, that we may "invocate only him in whom we do believe," Rom. x. 14.

It believed that the "command to abstain from meats and marriage was the doctrine of devils," 1 Tim. iv. 1–3;—do you abide in the same faith?

It believed that "every soul," without exception, "was to be subject to the higher powers," Rom. xiii. 1;—you will not walk in the steps of their faith herein.

It believed that all "image-worship was forbidden," Exod. xx.; and whether you abide in the same persuasion we shall afterward examine. And many more instances of the like kind you may at any time be minded of.

You haste to that you would fain be at, which will be found as little to your purpose as those whose consideration you so carefully avoid. You say, "Did she fall by heresy in adhering to any error in faith contrary to the approved doctrine of the church? Here you smile seriously, and tell me, that since I take the Roman and Catholic church to be one, she could not indeed adhere to any thing but what she did adhere unto. Sir, I take them indeed to be one; but here I speak 'ad hominem,' to one that doth not take them so. And then, if indeed the Roman church had ever swerved in faith, as you say she has, and be herself as another ordinary particular church, as you say she is, then might you find some one or other more general church, if any there were, to judge her; some œcumenical council to condemn her, some fathers, either Greek or Latin, expressly to write against her, as Protestants now do; some or other grave authority to censure her; or at least some company of believers, out of whose body she went, and from whose faith she fell. None of which since you are not able to assign" (wherein you have spoken more rightly than you were aware of; for not to be able to assign none of them infers at least an ability to assign some if not all of them), "my query remains unanswered, and the Roman still as flourishing a church as ever she was."

Ans. 1. You represent my answer lamely. I desire the reader to consult it in the "Animadversions," pp. 66–68.[1] What you have taken notice of discovers only your finesse in making heresy an adherence to an error in faith, contrary to the doctrine of the church; and yourselves the church whereby you must needs be secured from heresy, though you should adhere to the most heretical principles that ever were broached in the world. But nothing of all this, as I have showed, will be allowed you. 2. As we have seen some of the reasons why you were so unwilling to try the cause of your church on the heads of idolatry and apostasy, so here you discover a sufficient reason why you have passed over your other head of schism in silence. You avow yourself one of the most schismatical principles that were ever adhered unto by any professing the name of Christ. The Roman church and the Catholic are with you one and the same. Is not this Petilianus's, in "parte Donati;" nay, Basilides's, 'Ἡμεῖς ἐσμεν οἱ ἄνθρωποι, οἱ δὲ ἄλλοι πάντες κύνες καὶ ὕες, Epiphan. Heres. iv.—"We only are men; all others are dogs and swine." "Macte virtute!" If this be not *to show moderation* and to pursue reconciliation, at once to shut out all men but yourselves from the church here, and consequently heaven hereafter, what can be thought so to be? In

[1] See pp. 28, 29, of the present volume.

earnest, sir, you may talk what you please of moderation; but whilst you avow this one wretched schismatical principle, you do your endeavour to exclude all true Christian moderation out of the world. 3. Why do you conclude that your query is not answered? Suppose one question could not be answered, doth it necessarily follow that another cannot? I suppose you take notice that this is another question, and not that at first proposed, as I told you before. Your first inquiry was about your church's *crime;* this is about her *conviction* and condemnation. And your conclusion hath no strength in it but what is built on this unquestionable maxim, that "None ever offended who was not publicly judged;" as though there were no harlots in the world but those that have been carted. It is enough, sir, that her condition is "sub judice," as it will be whether you or I will or no; and that there is not evidence wanting for her conviction, nor ever was since her fall, though it may be it hath not at all times been so publicly managed. And yet so vain is your triumphant conclusion, that we rest not here, but prove also that she hath been of old judged and condemned, as you will hear anon.

And thus I have once more given you an answer to your inquiry how your church *fell*,—namely, that she hath done so by all the ways and means by which it is possible for a church to fall. She failed, under the just hand of God, when the persons of that urbic church were extirpated, partly by others, but totally by Totilas; as the British church in England fell by the sword of the Saxons. She hath fallen by *idolatry* and corruption of life; as did the church of the Jews before the captivity. She hath fallen by her *relinquishment* of the written word as the only rule of faith and worship, and by adhering to the uncertain traditions of men; as did the church of the Jews after their return from captivity. She hath fallen by *apostasy*, in forsaking the profession of many important truths of the gospel; as the church of the Galatians did for a season, in their relinquishment of the doctrine of justification by grace alone. She hath fallen by *heresy*, in coining new articles of faith, and imposing them on the consciences of the disciples of Christ; as the Montanists did with their new Paraclete and rigid observances. She hath fallen by *schism* in herself,—as the Judaical church did when divided into Essenes, Sadducees, and Pharisees,—setting up pope against pope, and council against council, continuing in her intestine broils for some ages together; and from all others, by the wretched principle but now avowed by you; as the Donatists did of old. She hath fallen by *ambition*, in the Hildebrandine principle, asserting a *sovereignty in the pope* over the kings and potentates of the earth; whereof I can give you no precedent instance, unless it be of him who claimed the kingdoms of the world to be his own, and boasted that he disposed of them at his pleasure,

Matt. iv. And now I hope you will not take it in ill part that I have given you a plain answer unto your question; which, as I suppose, was proposed unto us for that end and purpose.

But although these things are evident and sufficiently *proved*, yet I see nothing will satisfy you unless we produce testimonies of former times, to manifest that your church hath been arraigned, judged, condemned, written against, by fathers, councils, or other churches. Now, though this be somewhat an unreasonable expectation in you, and that which I am no way bound unto by the law of our discourse to satisfy you in, yet, to prevent for the future such evasions as you have made use of on all occasions in your epistle, I shall, in a few pregnant and unquestionable instances, give you an account both when, how, and by whom, the falls of your church have been observed, reproved, condemned, and written against. Only unto what shall be discoursed unto this purpose, I desire liberty to premise these three things, which I suppose will be granted.

"Dabitur ignis tamen, etsi ab inimicis petam."

The first is, That what is by any previously condemned, before the embracing and practice of it, is no less condemned by them than if the practice had preceded their condemnation. Though you should say that your avowing of a condemned error would make it no error, yet you cannot say that it will render it not condemned; for that which is done cannot be undone, say you what you will.

Secondly, That where any opinion or practice in religion, which is embraced and used by your church, is condemned and written against, that then your church, which so embraceth and useth it, is condemned and written against. For neither do Protestants write against your church, nor condemn it on any other account, but of your opinions and practices; and you require but such a writing and condemnation as you complain of amongst them.

Thirdly, I desire you to take notice that I do not this as though it were necessary to the security and defence of the cause which we maintain against you. It is abundantly sufficient and satisfactory unto our consciences, in your casting us out from your communion, that all the ways whereby we say your church is fallen from her pristine purity are judged and condemned in the Scripture, the word of truth, whither we appeal for the last determination of the differences between us. These things being premised, to prevent such evasions as you have accustomed yourself unto, I shall, as briefly as I can, give you somewhat of that which you have now twice called for.

1. Your principle and practice, *in imposing upon all persons and churches a necessity of the observation of your rites and ceremonies, customs and traditions, casting them out of communion who refuse to submit unto this your great principle of all the schisms*

in Europe, was contradicted, written against, condemned, by councils and fathers, in the very first instance that ever you gave of it. Be pleased to consider that this concerns the very life and being of your church; for if you may not impose your constitutions, observances, and customs upon all others, "actum est," there is an end of your present church state. Let us see, then, how this was thought of in the days of old. Victor, the bishop of Rome, A.D. 96, condemns and excommunicates the churches of Asia, because they would not join with him in the celebration of Easter precisely on the Lord's day. Did this practice escape *uncontrolled?* He was written against by the great Irenæus, and reproved that he had cast out of communion τὰς ὅλας ἐκκλησίας τοῦ Θεοῦ,—"whole churches of God," for a trivial cause. His act also was condemned, in the justification of those churches, by a council in Palestine, where Theophilus presided; and another in Asia, called together for the same purpose by Polycrates, Euseb. Eccles. Hist., lib. v. cap. 22–25. This is an early instance of a considerable fall in your church, and an open opposition by councils and fathers made unto it. And do not you, sir, deceive yourself, as though the act of Victor were alone concerned in this censure of Irenæus and others. The principle before mentioned, which is the very life and soul of your church, is condemned in it. It was done also in a repetition of the same instance attempted here in England by you, when Austin, that came from Rome, would have imposed on the British churches the observation of Easter according to the custom of the Roman church. The bishops and monks of these churches not only rejected your custom, but the principle also from whence the attempt to impose it on them did proceed; protesting that they owned no subjection to the *bishop of Rome, nor other regard than what they did to every good Christian*, Concil. Anglican. p. 188.

2. Your doctrine and practice *of forcing men by carnal weapons, corporal penalties, tortures, and terrors of death, unto the embracement of your profession, and actually destroying and taking away the lives of them that persist in their dissent from you*, is condemned by fathers and councils, as well as by the Scriptures, and the light of nature itself. It is condemned by Tertullian, Apol. cap. xxiii. "Videte," saith he, "ne et hoc ad irreligiositatis elogium concurrat, adimere libertatem religionis, et interdicere optionem divinitatis, ut non liceat mihi colere quod velim, sed cogar colere quod nolim;" with the like expressions in twenty other places. All this external compulsion he ascribes unto profaneness. So doth Clemens Alexand., Stromat. viii.; so also did Lactantius: all consenting in that maxim of Tertullian, "Lex nova non se vindicat ultore gladio;"—"The law of Christ revengeth not itself with a punishing sword." The council of Sardis, Epist. ad Alexand., expressly affirms that

they dissuaded the emperor from interposing his secular power to compel them that dissented. And you are fully condemned in a canon of a council at Toledo, cap. de Judæ. distinct. 45: "Præcipit sancta synodus, nemini deinceps ad credendum vim inferre; cui enim vult Deus miseretur, et quem vult indurat;"—"The holy synod commandeth that none hereafter shall by force be compelled to the faith; for God hath mercy on whom he will have mercy, and whom he will he hardeneth." Athanasius, in his Epistle ad Solitarios, falls heavily on the Arians, that they began first to compel men to their heresy by force, prisons, and punishments; whence he concludes of their sect, "Atque ita seipsam quam non sit pia nec Dei cultrix manifestat;"—"It evidently declares itself hereby to be neither pious nor to have any reverence of God." In a book that is of some credit with you,—namely, Clemens's Constitutions,—you have this amongst other things for your comfort: Τὸ αὐτεξούσιον τῶν ἀνθρώπων ἀφῆκεν ἐλεύθερον, οὐ προσκαίρῳ θανάτῳ δικάζων ἀλλ' ἐν ἑτέρᾳ καταστάσει λογοθετῶν αὐτό·—"Christ left men the power of their wills free" (in this matter), "not punishing them with death temporal, but calling them to give an account in another world." And Chrysostom speaks to the same purpose on John vi.: Ἐρωτᾷ λέγων, Μὴ καὶ ὑμεῖς θέλετε ὑπάγειν; ὅπερ πᾶσαν ἦν ἀφαιροῦντος βίαν καὶ ἀνάγκην·—"He asked them, saying, 'Will ye also go away?' which is the question of one rejecting all force and necessity." Epiphanius gives it as the character of the semi-Arians, Τοὺς τὴν ἀλήθειαν διδάσκοντας διώκουσιν, οὐκ ἔτι λόγοις βουλόμενοι ἀνατρέπειν, ἀλλὰ καὶ ἔχθραις, καὶ πολέμοις, καὶ μαχαίραις παραδιδόντες τοὺς ὀρθῶς πιστεύοντας· λύμην γὰρ οὐ μιᾷ πόλει καὶ χώρᾳ εἰργάσαντο ἀλλὰ πολλαῖς·—"They persecute them that teach the truth, not confuting them with words, but delivering them that believe aright to hatreds, wars, and swords, having now brought destruction, not to one city or country alone, but to many." Neither can you relieve yourselves by answering that they were true believers whom they persecuted, you punish heretics and schismatics only; for they thought and said the same of themselves which you assert in your own behalf. So Salvian informs us, "Hæretici sunt, sed non scientes; denique apud nos sunt hæretici, apud se non sunt. Nam in tantum se et catholicos judicant, ut nos ipsos titulo hæreticæ pravitatis infament: quod ergo illi nobis sunt, et hoc nos illis;"—"They are heretics, but they know it not; they are heretics unto us, but not unto themselves, for they so far judge themselves to be catholic, that they condemn us for the guilt of heresy: so, then, what they are to us, that we are to them." Especially was your whole practice in this matter solemnly condemned in the case of Priscillianus, recorded by Sulpitius Severus in the end of his second book,—the only instance that Bellarmine could fix upon, in all antiquity, for the putting of any men to death upon the account of religion; for the other whom he mentions, he confesseth himself to have been a magician. Ithacius, with some other bishops his associates, procured Maximus the tyrant to put Priscillianus a Gnostic, with some others, to death, and to banish some of their followers. What saith the historian thereon? "Hoc modo," saith he, "homines luce indignissimi pessimo exemplo necati, aut exiliis mulctati;"—"On this manner were those unworthy wretches either slain or punished by banishment, by a very evil precedent." And what was the success of this zeal? "Non solum," saith he, "non repressa est hæresis, sed confirmata, latius propagata est;"—"The heresy was so far from being repressed by it, that it was the more confirmed and propagated." And what ensued hereupon in the church itself? "Inter nostros perpetuum discordiarum bellum exarserat: quod jam per quindecim annos fœdis dissensionibus agitatum nullo modo sopiri poterat. Et nunc cum maxime discordiis episcoporum turbari aut misceri omnia cernerentur, cunctaque per eos odio aut gratia, metu, inconstantia, invidia, factione, avaritia, arrogantia, somno, desidia essent depravata:—postremo plures adversum paucos bene consulentes, insanis consiliis et pertinacibus studiis certabant: inter hæc plebs Dei, et optimus quisque, probro atque ludibrio habebatur;" with which words he shuts up his ecclesiastical story. "Amongst ours, a lasting war of discord was kindled, which, after it hath now for fifteen years been carried on with shameful contentions, can by no means be allayed; and now especially, when all things appear to be troubled and perverted by the discord of the bishops, and that all things are depraved by them, through hatred, favour, fear, inconstancy, envy, faction, covetousness, pride, sleepiness, and sloth,—the most, with mad counsels and pertinacious endeavours, [were] opposing themselves to the few that are better advised. Amongst all these things the people of God, and every honest man, is become a reproach and a scorn." Thus that historian, complaining of the consequents of this proceeding. But good men left not the matter so: Martinus Turonensis presently refuseth all communion with them who had any hand in the death or banishment of the persons mentioned; so doth Ambrose declare himself to have done, Epist. xxvii.; as did the rest of the sober, godly bishops of those days. At length both Ithacius and Idacius, the promoters of this work, were solemnly excommunicated, though one of them had before, for very shame, foregone his bishopric. See Prosp. Chron. 389, and Isidore de Viris Illustribus. So that here also the judgment and practice of your church, which she is fallen into, is publicly condemned and written against thirteen hundred years ago. Should I insist on all the testimonies that of this kind might be produced,—

"Antè diem clauso componet vesper olympo," Virg. Æn. i. 378,

than I could make an end of them. I have added this instance to the former, as knowing them to be the two great pillars on which the tottering fabric of your church is raised, and which, if they were removed, the whole of it would quickly fall to the ground; and you see how long ago they were both publicly condemned.

3. Your papal œcumenical supremacy hath two main branches:—(1). *Your pope's spiritual power* over all persons and churches in the things of religion; (2.) *His power over emperors, kings, and protestants,* in reference unto religion; or, as you speak, "in ordine ad spiritualia." The first your church stumbled into by many degrees, from the days of Victor, who made the first notable halt to this purpose; the latter you stumbled into in the days of Gregory VII., or Hildebrand. It were endless to declare how this fall of your church hath been declared, written against, opposed, condemned by churches, councils, fathers, princes, and learned men in all ages. Some few evidences to this purpose, to satisfy your request, I shall direct you unto. It was written against and condemned by Cyprian, bishop of Carthage, and that in a council at Carthage, anno 258, upon an attempt made by Stephen, bishop of Rome, looking in some small degree towards that *usurped supremacy* which afterward was attained unto. You may, if you please, there see him rebuked, and the practice of your church condemned. The same Cyprian had done no less before, in reference unto some actings of Cornelius, the predecessor of Stephen, Epist. ad Cornel. Though the pretensions of Cornelius and Stephen were modest in comparison of your present vast claim, yet the churches of God in those days could not bear them. It is prejudged in the most famous council of Nice, which assigned bounds unto the jurisdiction of bishops, giving to several of them equal authority: can. 6. Τὰ ἀρχαῖα [ἔθη] κρατείτω, τὰ ἐν Αἰγύπτῳ, καὶ Λιβύῃ, καὶ Πενταπόλει, ὥστε τὸν Ἀλεξανδρείας ἐπίσκοπον πάντων τούτων ἔχειν τὴν ἐξουσίαν, ἐπειδὴ καὶ τῷ ἐν τῇ Ῥώμῃ ἐπισκόπῳ τοῦτο συνήθες ἐστίν· ὁμοίως δὲ καὶ κατὰ τὴν Ἀντιόχειαν, καὶ ἐν ταῖς ἄλλαις ἐπαρχίαις τὰ πρεσβεῖα σώζεσθαι ταῖς ἐκκλησίαις·—"Let the ancient customs be observed, that, as to Egypt, Libya, and Pentapolis, the bishops of Alexandria have power over them" (or the churches in them), "for so is the custom of the bishop of Rome" (that is, to have power over the adjoining churches); "likewise about Antioch, and in other provinces, that the ancient rights of the churches be preserved." Your great pope, whom you so frequently call "the pastor of Christendom," was here but ὁ ἐν τῇ Ῥώμῃ ἐπίσκοπος,—"the bishop in the city or church of Rome," or of the church in the city of Rome. And bounds are assigned unto the authority which he claimed by custom, as to his of Alexandria and Antioch. It is true the church of Alexandria hath some power assigned, ascribed, or granted unto it, above other churches of Egypt, Libya, and Pentapolis, for a warranty whereof the usage of the Roman church in reference unto her neighbour churches is made use of; which, to deal freely with you, and to tell you my private thoughts,

was a confirmation of a disorder by your example, which you were from that day forward seldom wanting to give plenty of. So to this purpose, Concil. Antioch. can. 13 and 15, anno 341; Concil. Constantinop. can. 2, anno 381. But this canon of the Nicene fathers openly condemneth, and is perfectly destructive of, your present claimed supremacy. Three councils together in Africa, within the space of twenty years, warned your church of her fall into this heresy, and opposed her attempts for the promotion of it:—The first at Carthage, anno 407, which *forbids all appeals unto any beyond the sea;* which Rome was to them in Africa no less than it is unto us in England. The next was the second Milevitan, anno 416, where the same prohibition is revived *with express respect* unto the see of Rome, as Binius acknowledgeth. The same order is again asserted by another council in Africa, wherein the pretensions of Boniface unto some kind of *superintendency* over other churches are sorely reproved, and his way of prosecuting his attempt, by pretended canons of the council of Nice, after great pains taken and charge disbursed in the discovery of the forgery, censured and condemned. All these testimonies of the condemnation of this fall of yours, by fathers and councils, you have gathered unto your hand in the Cod. Can. Conc. Afric., and by Binius, with others. Also the substance of all these canons of provincial synods is confirmed in the fourth chapter of the decree of the third œcumenical council at Ephesus, anno 431, can. 8: Ψῆφος· Ἔδοξε τῇ ἁγίᾳ [ταύτῃ] καὶ οἰκουμενικῇ συνόδῳ, σώζεσθαι ἑκάστῃ ἐπαρχίᾳ καθαρὰ καὶ ἀβίαστα τὰ αὐτῇ προσόντα δίκαια ἐξ ἀρχῆς ἄνωθεν, κατὰ τὸ πάλαι κρατῆσαν ἔθος·—"It seemeth good to the holy and general council that every province retain its rights pure and inviolate, which, according unto ancient custom, it had from the beginning." The decree, I confess, was purposely framed against the bishop of Antioch, who had taken on him to ordain bishops in Cyprus, out of his province; but it is built on that general reason which expressly condemns the Roman pretensions to an unlimited supremacy. The great and famous council of Chalcedon, anno 451, condemned the same heresy, and plainly overthrew the whole foundation of your papal plea, act. 15, can. 18, as the canons of that council are collected by Balsamon and Zonaras; though some of them, with intolerable partiality, would separate this and some others from the body of the canons of that council, giving them a place by themselves. The decree contains the reasons of the council's assigning privileges next unto, and equally with, the Roman, unto the Constantinopolitan church: Τῷ θρόνῳ, say they, τῆς πρεσβυτέρας Ῥώμης, διὰ τὸ βασιλεύειν τὴν πόλιν ἐκείνην, οἱ πατέρες εἰκότως ἀποδεδώκασι τὰ πρεσβεῖα·—"The fathers" (our predecessors) "granted privileges to the see of ancient Rome, because that was the imperial city." Do you see from whence proceeded all the privileges of the Roman throne?—merely from the grants and concessions of former bishops; and I wish they had been liberal only of what was their own. And what was the reason of their so doing? Because the city was "imperial:" in which one sentence, both their supremacy and the grounds of it are discarded and virtually condemned; for their pretensions are utterly inconsistent with this synodical determination. They proceed: For the same reason, Τὰ ἴσα πρεσβεῖα ἀπένειμαν τῷ τῆς νέας Ῥώμης ἁγιωτάτῳ θρόνῳ, εὐλόγως κρίναντες τὴν βασιλείᾳ καὶ συγκλήτῳ τιμηθεῖσαν πόλιν, καὶ τῶν ἴσων ἀπολαύουσαν πρεσβείων τῇ πρεσβυτέρᾳ βασιλίδι Ῥώμῃ, καὶ ἐν τοῖς ἐκκλησιαστικοῖς·—"They" (the hundred and fifty bishops) "assigned the same or equal privileges unto the holy see of new Rome; rightly determining that the city which is honoured with the empire and senate should enjoy equal privileges in things ecclesiastical with the ancient queen-Rome,"[1] or Rome-regent of old. Is not your present supremacy here sufficiently condemned, and that by as famous a council as ever the Christian world enjoyed? And it will not avail you that you fell into this heresy fully afterward, and not before the determination of this council: for he that falls into a heresy after the determination of a council is no less condemned therein than he that fell into it before, and gave occasion to the sentence; yea, his guilt is the greater of the two, because he despised the sentence which he knew, which the other, it may be, neither did nor could foresee. I gave you an instance before how it is condemned and written against by the British church here in this island, and many more instances of the same nature might be added.

The Hildebrandine branch of your supremacy,—I mean the power that you challenge over kings and potontates, "in ordine ad spiritualia,"—which, having made some progress by insensible degrees, was enthroned by Pope Gregory VII., hath as little escaped opposition, censure, and condemnation, as any heresy whereinto your church is fallen. This Gregory may be accounted the chief father of this heresy; for he licked the unshapen monster into that terrible form wherein it hath since ranged about on the earth. What this man's principles and practices were, I shall not desire you to learn of Cardinal Benno, whom yet I have reason to judge the more impartial writer of the two, but of Cardinal Baronius, who makes it his business to extol him to the skies: "Facit eum apud nos deum, virtutes narrat,"—"He makes almost a god of him;" or at least θεῖον ἄνδρα, as Socrates tells us the Lacedemonians called an excellent man, Plato in Menn. The chief kingdoms of Europe, as England and Spain, with Sicilia and Sardinia, and sundry other principalities, he claimed as his own unquestionable fee. The empire he accounted his proper care, making the deposing of emperors much of his business. The

[1] This translation is accommodated from the original terms of the canon. To give the full meaning, the Greek quotation should be completed by the addition of the following words: ὡς ἐκείνην μεγαλύνεσθαι πράγμασι.—ED.

principles he proceeded upon, the same cardinal informs us of in his Annals, ad an. 1076, n. 30. And he hath done well to record them, that they might be preserved "in perpetuam rei memoriam," that we might learn what your great father exercised himself about,—

"Dum succus pecori et lac subducitur agnis," Virg. Ec. iii. 6,

whilst the poor sheep famished for want of knowledge and instruction. They are called "Dictata Papæ," and "ex tripode" we may not doubt, being in number twenty-seven; whereof I shall mind you of a few. The first is, "Quod Romana ecclesia a solo Domino sit fundata;"—"That the Roman church was founded by the Lord alone." (2.) "Quod solus Romanus pontifex jure dicatur universalis;"—"That the Roman bishop is rightfully called universal." So some think, indeed, ever since Pope Gregory I. taught them that he who assumed that title was a forerunner of antichrist. (3.) "Quod ille solus possit deponere episcopos, vel reconciliare;"—"That he alone can depose bishops, or restore them;" which agrees well with the practice of all the councils from that of Antioch, which deposed Paulus Samosatenus. (7.) "Quod illi soli licet, pro temporis necessitate, novas leges condere;"—"That he alone, as necessity requires, can make new laws." Let him proceed. (8.) "Quod solus possit uti imperialibus insigniis;"—"He alone can use imperial ensigns." It is a great kindness in him, doubtless, to lend them to any of his neighbours, or rather subject-kings. (9.) "Quod solius papæ pedes omnes principes deosculentur;"—"That it is the pope alone whose feet all princes may or ought to kiss." Yea, and it is a kindness if he kick not their crowns from their heads with his foot, as one did our King John's; or tread upon their necks, as another did on the Emperor Frederic's." (11.) "Quod unicum est nomen in mundo,—papæ scilicet;"—"That there is only one name in the world,—to wit, that of the pope;" no other name, it seems, given under heaven. Once more, (12.) "Quod illi liceat Imperatores deponere;"—"That it is lawful for him to depose emperors." I hope you will not be offended at the calling over these heresies because the so doing is not suited to our present design. I took them out of your Cardinal Baronius, in the place above quoted, who hath placed them as on a pillar, V. D. P. L. P.,[1]—"Where they may be easily read by all men." And that you may not think that these were the heresies of Gregory alone, the same Baronius affirms that these Dictates were confirmed in a synod at Rome, whereby they became the heresies of your whole church. Did Peter thus feed the sheep of Christ? seeing "Pasce oves meas," is the great pretence for all these exorbitances. Alas,—

"Hic alienus oves custos bis mulget in hora," Virg. Ecl. iii. 5,

all this is but the shearing, milking, and slaying of a stranger, the

[1] An abbreviation for Unde De Plano Legi Possint,—"From which they can be plainly read." Siglarium Romanum.—Ed.

shepherds being driven into corners. But have these noisome heresies of your church, think you, passed without control? Was she not judged, censured, written against, and condemned in the person of her chief pastor? You must be a very stranger unto all history if you can imagine any such thing. A council assembled by the emperor at Worms, in Germany, reckons up the miscarriages of this Hildebrand, and pronounceth him deposed, with all those that adhered unto him. Another synod, anno 1080, at Brixia in Bavaria, condemns him also for the same causes. All the heroic potentates of Europe, especially the emperors of Germany, the kings of England and France, with whole assemblies of their clergy, have always opposed and condemned this branch of your supremacy. And to this purpose hundreds of their laws, decrees, edicts, and declarations, are at this day extant.

4. Your *pope's personal infallibility*, with the requisite qualifications, is another heretical opinion that your church hath fallen by. And herein you are αὐτοκατάκριτοι,—"condemned of yourselves,"—and we need no farther witness against you; you have been often taken ἐπαυτοφώρῳ,—"in the very fact." I know there is an opinion secretly advancing amongst some of you, whereby you would cast out of the bounds of your defence this personal infallibility of your pope; but we have no more reason to esteem that opinion the doctrine of your church than we have to conclude that the Jesuits' new position, asserting him infallible in matter of fact, is so. And though I know not perfectly what your opinion is in this matter, yet I may take a time to show how utterly unserviceable unto your purpose the new way of the explication of infallibility is. For it hath but these two general inconveniences attending it,—first, That it is not the opinion of your church; secondly, If that be the *only* infallibility we are to rest on, the whole claim of your church, and its interest therein, falls to the ground;—both which I hope to have an opportunity to manifest. In the meantime, we take that for the doctrine of your church which is declared by itself so to be, which is explained and defended by her most famous champions. And, indeed, you in your "Fiat" assert, as I have showed, the pope personally to be an unerring guide; which is that we inquire after. Bellarmine tells us that all Catholics agree in these two things:—(1.) "Pontificem, cum generali concilio, non posse errare in condendis decretis fidei, vel generalibus præceptis morum;"—"That the pope, with a general council, cannot err in making decrees of faith, or general precepts concerning manners." (2.) "Pontificem solum, vel cum suo particulari concilio, aliquid in re dubia statuentem, sive errare possit sive non, esse ab omnibus fidelibus obedienter audiendum;"—"All believers must willingly obey the pope, either alone or with his particular council, determining in doubtful matters, whether he may err or no."

I confess, if this be so, and he must be obeyed, whether he do right or wrong, whether he teacheth truly or falsely, it is to no great purpose to talk of his infallibility; for follow him we must whither ever he leads us, though it should be to hell. And the Catholic proposition that he asserts himself is, that, "Summus pontifex, cum totam ecclesiam docet in his quæ ad fidem pertinent, nullo casu errare potest;"—"The pope, when he teacheth the whole church, can in no case err in those things which appertain unto faith," De Rom. Pontif., lib. iv. cap. 2, 3. What a blind that is "of teaching the whole church," children can see. The pope can no way *teach the whole church* but as he declares his opinion or judgment; which may be divulged unto *many*, as that of another man. Let us see, then, how well they have made good this their infallibility, and how well their judgment hath been approved of by the church of old. I will not here mind you of the decree fathered on Clemens, wherein he determines that "all things among Christians ought to be common; and among them, wives;"—because I know it is *falsely* imposed on him, though you may be *justly* charged with it, who are the authors of those forgeries whereof that is a part. Nor shall I rake the epistles which you ascribe unto divers of the ancient bishops of Rome, that are full of ignorance, errors, and pitiful nonsense, because they are, questionless, pseudepigraphal, though you who own them may be justly charged with their follies. Nor will I much insist on the testimony of Tertullian in his book against Praxeas, that the bishop of Rome owned the *prophecies of Montanus*, until Praxeas persuaded him to the contrary; because, it may be, you will say that perhaps Tertullian spake partially in favour of a sect whereunto he was himself addicted,—though, for aught I know, he is as sufficient a witness in *matter of fact* as any one man upon the roll of antiquity. But what say you to Marcellinus? Did he not *sacrifice to idols?* which, according unto you, is "a mixed misdemeanour in faith and manners" (Con. tom. i., Vita Marcel.), and therefore certainly a shrewd impeachment of his *infallibility;* and was he not judged for it? What think you of Liberius? did he not subscribe to *Arianism?* Sozomen tells you expressly that he did so, lib. iv. cap. 15; and so doth Athanasius, Epist. ad Solitarios, giving the reason why he did so,—namely, out of fear; and so doth Jerome, both in Script. Ecclesiast. Fortunat. and in Euseb. Chron. Pope Honorius was solemnly condemned for a *Monothelite heretic* in the sixth general council, act. 12, 13; which sentence was afterward ratified by your own darling, the second of Nice, act. 3, 7, and is mentioned in a decretal epistle of Pope Leo II. So infallible was he during his life, so infallible was he thought to be when he was dead,—whilst he lived he taught heresy, and when he was dead he was condemned for a heretic; and with him the principle which is the hinge of your present faith.

Neither did Vigilius behave himself one jot better in his chair. The council of Pisa deposed Gregory XII. and Benedict XIII. for *schismatics* and *heretics.* The council of Constance accused John XXIII. of *abominable heresy*, sess. 11. And that of Basil condemned Eugenius as one "a fide devium et pertinacem hæreticum," sess. 34;— "an erroneous person and obstinate heretic." Other instances of the like nature might be called over, manifesting that your popes have erred, and been condemned as persons erroneous; and therein the principle of their infallibility.

I would be unwilling to tire your patience, yet, upon your reiterated desire, I shall present you with one instance more; and I will do it but briefly, because I must deal with you again about the same matter.

5. Your church is fallen by *idolatry*, as otherwise, so in that religious *veneration of images* which she useth; whereunto you have added heresy, in teaching it for a doctrine of truth, and imposing the belief of it by your Tridentine determination on the consciences of the disciples of Christ. I know you would fain mince the matter, and spread over the corrupt doctrine of your church about it with *ῥήμασι βυσσίνοις*, "silken words," as you do the posts that they are made of with gold, when, as the prophet speaks of your predecessors in that work, you lavish it out of the bag for that purpose. But to what purpose? Your *first* council, the second of Nice (which yet was not wholly yours neither, for it condemns Honorius, calls Tharasius the *œcumenical patriarch*, and he expounds in it the rock on which the church was built to be Christ, and not Peter); your last council, that of Trent; your angelical doctor, Thomas of Aquine; your great champions, Bellarmine and Baronius, Suarez, Vasquez, and the rest of them; with the Catholic practice and usage of your church in all places,—declare sufficiently what is your faith, or rather misbelief, in this matter. Hence Azorius, Institut. lib. ix. cap. 6, tells us that "Constans est theologorum sententia, imaginem eodem honore et cultu coli, quo colitur id cujus est imago;"—"It is the constant judgment of divines, that the image is to be worshipped with the same honour and worship wherewith that is worshipped whose image it is." The Nicene council, by the instigation of Pope Adrian, anathematizeth every one who doth but doubt of the adoration of images, act. 7. Thomas contendeth that the cross is to be worshipped with "latria," p. 3, q. 25, a. 4; which is a word that he and you suppose to express religious worship of the highest sort. And your council of Trent, in their decree about this matter, confirmed the doctrine of that *lestrical*[1] *convention at Nice*, whose frauds and impostures were

[1] An epithet, *λῃστρικός*, *plundering* or *piratical*,—applied to characterize a council whose acts, according to Gibbon, are "a curious monument of superstition and ignorance, of falsehood and folly."—Decline and Fall of the Roman Empire, chap. xlix.—Ed.

never paralleled in the world but by itself. And do you think that a few ambiguous flourishing words of you, an unknown person, shall make the world believe that they understand not the doctrine and practice of your church, which is proclaimed unto them by the fathers and masters of your persuasion herein, and expressed in practices under their eyes every day? Do you think it so easy for you, "Cornicum oculos, configere," as Cicero tells us an attorney, one Cn. Flavius, thought to do, in going beyond all that the great lawyers had done before him, Orat. pro Muræna, 11. We cannot yet be persuaded that you are so great an interpreter of the Roman oracles as to believe you before all the sages before mentioned, to whom hundreds may be added. And what do you think of this doctrine and practice of your church? Hath it been opposed, judged, and condemned, or no? The first writers of Christianity, Justin Martyr, Irenæus, Origen, Tertullian, Arnobius, Lactantius, utterly abhorred the use of all images, at least "in sacris." The council held at Eliberis in Spain, twelve or thirteen years before the famous assembly at Nice, positively forbid all use of pictures in churches: Can. 36, "Placuit, picturas in ecclesia esse non debere; ne quod colitur et adoratur in parietibus depingatur;"—"The council resolved that pictures ought not to be in churches; that that which is worshipped and adored be not painted on walls." Cyprian condemns it, Epist. ad Demetriad. And so, generally, do all the fathers, as may be gathered in the pitiful endeavours and forgeries of the second Nicene council, endeavouring to confirm it from them. Epiphanius reckons it among the errors of the Gnostics; and himself brake an image that he found hanging in a church, Epist. ad Johan. Hierosol. Austin was of the same judgment, see Lib. de Morib. Eccles. Cathol. cap. xxxiv. Your adoration of them is expressly condemned by Gregory the Great, in an epistle to Serinus, lib. vii. epist. 111, and lib. ix. epist. 9. The Greek church condemned it, in a synod at Constantinople, anno 754. And one learned man in those days undertaking its defence (and, indeed, the only man of learning that ever did so until of late), they *excommunicated* and cursed him. This was Damascenus; concerning whom they used those expressions, repeated in the second Nicene council: Μανσοὺρ τῷ κακωνύμῳ καὶ Σαῤῥακηνόφρονι ἀνάθεμα· τῷ εἰκονολάτρῃ καὶ φαλσογράφῳ Μανσοὺρ ἀνάθεμα· τῷ τοῦ Χριστοῦ ὑβριστῇ καὶ ἐπιβούλῳ τῆς βασιλείας Μανσοὺρ ἀνάθεμα· τῷ τῆς ἀσεβείας διδασκάλῳ καὶ παρερμηνευτῇ τῆς θείας γραφῆς Μανσοὺρ ἀνάθεμα·—"Unto Mansour,[1] of an evil name, and in judgment consenting with Saracens, anathema; to Mansour, a wor-

[1] Johannes Damascenus flourished during the first half of the eighth century, and died at the monastery of St Saba in A.D. 756. He wrote extensively on philosophical and religious questions, and his works, exclusive of manuscripts still extant, fill two folio volumes. On account of his oratorical powers, he was named Chrysorrhoas; but, according to Bayle, he called himself Mansour, "the redeemed," while his opponents termed him Manser, "the bastard."—ED.

shipper of images and writer of falsehood, anathema; to Mansour, contumelious against Christ and traitor to the empire, anathema; to Mansour, a teacher of impiety and perverse interpreter of Scripture, anathema," Synod. Nic. ii. Act. 6. For that it was Johannes Damascenus that they intended, the Nicene fathers sufficiently manifest in the answer following, read by Epiphanius the deacon. And this reward did he meet withal, from the seventh council at Constantinople, for his pains in asserting the veneration of images; although he did not, in that particular, pervert the Scripture as some of you do, but laid the whole weight of his opinion on tradition; wherein he is followed by Vasquez among yourselves. Moreover, the western churches, in a great council at Frankfort in Germany, utterly condemned the Nicene determination, which in your Tridentine convention you approve and ratify, anno 794. It was also condemned here by the church of England, and the doctrine of it fully confuted by Albinus, Hoveden Annal. anno 791. Never was any heresy more publicly and solemnly condemned than this, whereby your church is fallen from its pristine purity. But hereof more afterward.

It were no difficult matter to proceed unto all the chief ways whereby your church is fallen, and to manifest that they have been all publicly disclaimed and condemned by the better and sounder part of professors; but the instances insisted on may, I hope, prove sufficient for your satisfaction. I shall therefore proceed to consider what you offer unto the remaining principles which I conceived to animate the whole discourse of your "Fiat Lux."

CHAPTER V.

Other principles of "Fiat Lux" re-examined—Things not at quiet in religion, before reformation of the first reformers—Departure from Rome no cause of divisions—Returnal unto Rome no means of union.

You proceed unto the fourth assertion gathered out of your "Fiat," which you thus lay down: "'It is,' say you, 'frequently pleaded by our author that all things, as to religion, were ever quiet and in peace before the Protestants' relinquishment of the Roman see.' That 'ever' is your own addition, but let it pass; what say you hereunto? This principle you pretend is drawn out of 'Fiat Lux,' not because it is there, but only to open a door to yourself to expatiate into some wide general discourse about the many wars, distractions, altercations, that have been aforetime up and down in the world, in some several ages of Christianity. And you therefore say, it is frequently pleaded by me, because indeed I never spake one word of it, and it is in truth a false and fond assertion; though neither you nor I can deny that such as keep unity of faith with the church can never, so long as they hold it, fall out upon that account." Sir, I take you to be the author of "Fiat Lux;" and if you are so, I cannot but think you were asleep when you talked at this rate. "The assertion is false and fond; you speak not one word of it!" Pray, sir, take a little advice of your son, "Fiat," not to talk on this manner; and you will wonder yourself how you came to swallow so much confidence as in the face of the world to vent such things as these. He tells us from you, pp. 234–236, chap. iv., second edition, that "After the conversion of this land by the children of blessed St Bene't, notwithstanding the interposition of the Norman conquest, that all men lived peaceably together, without any the least disturbance upon the account of religion, until the end of King Henry VIII.'s reign, about five hundred years after the conquest." See also what in general you discourse of all places to this purpose, pp. 221, 222. And, p. 227, you do in express terms lay down the position which here you so exclaim against as "false and fond;" but you may make as bold with it as you please, for it is your own. "Never had this land," say you, "for so many hundred years as it was Catholic, upon the account of religion any disturbance at all; whereas, after the exile of the Catholic belief in our land, from the period of King Henry VIII.'s reign to these days, we have been in actual disquiet, or at least in fears." "Estne hæc tunica filii tui?" Are not these your words? Doth not your son "Fiat" wear this livery? And do you not speak to this purpose in twenty other places? Is it not one of the main suppositions you proceed upon in your whole discourse? You do well now, indeed, to acknowledge that what you spake was "fond and false," and you might do as much for the most that you have written in that whole discourse; but now openly to deny what you have asserted, and that in so many places, that is not so well done of you. There are, sir, many ways to free yourself from that damage you feel or fear from the "Animadversions." When any thing is charged on you or proved against you which you are not able to defend, you may ingenuously acknowledge your mistake, and that without any dishonour to you at all: good men have done so; so may you or I when we have just occasion. It is none of your tenets that you are all of you infallible, or that your personal mistakes or miscarriages will prejudice your cause. Or you might pass it by in silence, as you have done with the things of the most importance in the "Animadversions;" and so keep up your reputation that you could reply to them if you would, or were free from flies. And we know Πολλοῖς ἀπόκρισις ἡ σιωπὴ τυγχάνει, as Menander speaks;—"Silence is with many the best answer." Or you might attempt to disprove or answer, as the case requires. But this that you have fixed upon, of denying your own words, is the very worst course that you could have chosen, upon the account either of conscience or reputation. However, thus much we have obtained,—one of the chief pretences of your "Fiat" is, by your own confession, "false and fond." It is indeed no wonder that it should be so; it was fully proved to be so in the "Animadversions: but that you should acknowledge it to be so is somewhat strange; and it would have been very welcome news had you plainly owned your conviction of it, and not renounced your own offspring. But I see you have a mind to the benefit you aimed at by it, though you are ashamed of the way you used for the obtaining of it; and therefore add, "That neither you nor I can deny that such as keep the unity of faith with that church can never, so long as they hold it, fall out on that account." But this, on the first consideration, seems to me no very singular privilege; methinks a Turk, a Jew, an Arian, may say the same of their societies: it being no more but this,—"So long as you agree with us, you shall be sure to agree with us!" They must be very unfriendly minded towards you that will call these κυρίας δόξας into question. Yet there remains still one scruple on my mind in reference unto what you assert. I am not satisfied that there is in your church any such *unity of faith* as can keep men from falling out or differing in and about the doctrines and opinions they profess. If there be, the children of your church are marvellous morose, that they have not all this while learned to be quiet, but are at this very day writing volumes against one another,[1] and procuring the books of one another to be prohibited and condemned; which the writings of one of the most learned of you in this nation have lately not escaped. I know you will say sometimes, that though you *differ*, yet you differ not in things belonging unto the *unity of faith*. But I fear this is but a blind, an *apron of fig-leaves*. What you cannot agree in, be it of never so great importance, you will agree to say that it belongs not unto the unity of faith; when things no way to be compared in weight and use with them, so you agree about them, shall be asserted so to do. And in what you differ, whilst the scales of interest on the part of the combatants hang even, all your differences are but in school and disputable points;—but if one party prevail in interest and reputation, and render their antagonists inconsiderable as to any outward trouble, those very points that before were disputable shall be made necessary, and to-belong to the unity of faith; as it lately happened in the case of the Jansenists. And here you are safe again: the unity of the faith is that which you agree in; and that which you cannot agree about belongs not unto it, as you tell us, though you talk at another rate among yourselves. But we must think that the unity of faith

[1] The allusion must be to the disputes at this time prevailing between the Jansenists and Jesuits.—Ed.

is bounded by the confines of your wranglements, and your agreement is the rule of it. This, it may be, you think suits your turn: but whether it be so well suited unto the interest of the gospel and of truth, you must give men leave to inquire, or they will do it "ingratiis," whether you will or no. But if by the unity of faith you intend the substantial doctrines of the gospel proposed in the Scripture to be believed on necessity unto salvation, it is unquestionably among all the churches in the world, and might possibly be brought forth into some tolerable communion in profession and practice, did not your schismatical interest and principles interpose themselves to the contrary.

The fifth supposition in your "Fiat," observed in the "Animadversions," is, "That the first reformers were most of them contemptible persons, their means indirect, and their ends sinister;" to which you reply, "Where is it, sir, where is it, that I meddle with any men's persons, or say they are contemptible? What and how many are those persons? and where did they live? But this you add of your own is in a vast universal notion, to the end you may bring in the apostles and prophets, and some kings, into the list of persons by me surnamed 'contemptible,' and liken my speech, who never spake any such thing, to the sarcasms of Celsus, Lucian, Porphyry, Julian, and other Pagans." So you begin; but "ne sævi, magne Sacerdos!" Have a little patience, and I will direct you to the places where you display in many words that which in a few I represented. They are in your "Fiat," chap. iv., sect. 18, second edition, from p. 239, unto sect. 20, p. 251. Had you lost your "Fiat," that you make such an outcry after that which in a moment he could have supplied you withal? "Calvin, and a tailor's widow,—Luther and Catharine Bore,—pleased with a naked unicorn,—swarms of reformers as thick as grasshoppers,—fallen priests and votaries,—ambitious heads, emulating one another,—if not the worst, yet none of the best that ever were,—so eagerly quarrelling among themselves, that a sober man would not have patience to hear their sermons or read their books;" with much more to the same purpose, you will find in the places which I have now directed you unto. But I see you love to say what you please, but not to hear of it again. But he that can, in no more words, more truly express the full and genuine sense of your 18th and 19th chapters than I have done, in the assertion you so cry out against, shall have my thanks for his pains; only, I must mind you that you have perverted it, in placing the last words as if they referred unto the reformers you talk of, that they did their work for "sinister ends," when I only said that "their doctrine, according to your insinuations, was received for sinister ends;" wherein I comprised your foul reflections upon King Henry VIII., and

Queen Elizabeth his daughter,—not placing them, as you now feign, among the number of them whom I affirmed to be reported by you as a company of contemptible persons. But now, upon a confidence that you have shifted your hands of a necessity to reinforce this assertion, which you find, it may be, in yourself an incompetency for, you reflect back upon some former passages in the "Animadversions," wherein the general objections that you lay against Protestancy are observed to be the same for substance that long ago were by Celsus objected unto Christianity, and say, "So likewise, in the very beginning of this your second chapter, you spend four leaves in a parallel betwixt me and the pagan Celsus; whereof there is not any member of it true. 'Doth Fiat Lux,' say you, 'lay the cause of all the troubles, disorders, tumults, wars, within the nations of Europe, upon Protestants? doth he charge the Protestants, that by their schisms and seditions they make a way for other revolts? doth he gather a rhapsody of insignificant words? doth he insist upon their divisions? doth he manage the arguments of the Jews against Christ, etc.?—so doth Celsus, who is confuted by Origen.' Where does 'Fiat Lux,' where does, does he, does he any such thing? Are you not ashamed to talk at this rate? I give a hint, indeed, of the divisions that be amongst us, and the frequent argumentations that are made to embroil and puzzle one another, with our much evil, and little appearance of any good in order unto unity and peace; which is the end of my discourse. But must I therefore be Celsus? Did Celsus any such thing to such an end? It is the end that moralizeth, and specifies the action. To diminish Christianity, by upbraiding our frailties, is paganish; to exhort to unity, by representing the inconvenience of faction, is a Christian and pious work. When honest Protestants in the pulpit speak ten times more full and vehemently against the divisions, wars, and contentions that be amongst us, than ever came into my thoughts, must they therefore every one of them be a Celsus, a pagan Celsus? What stuff is this? But it is not only my defamation you aim at; your own glory comes in the rear. If I be Celsus, the pagan Celsus, you then, forsooth, must be Origen that wrote against him, honest Origen; that is the thing. Pray, sir,—it is but a word,—let me advise you, by the way, that you do not forget yourself in your heat, and give your wife occasion to fall out with you. However you may, yet will not your wife like it perhaps so well that her husband should be Origen." Such trash as this must he consider who is forced to have to do with you. These, it seems, are the meditations you are conversant with in your retirements. What little regard you have in them unto truth or honesty shall quickly be discovered unto you. 1. Do I compare you with Celsus, or do I make you to be Celsus? I had certainly been very much mistaken if I had done so, ὗς τὴν ᾽Αθηνᾶν; to compare a person of so small abilities in literature, as you discover yourself to be, with so *learned a philosopher*, had been a great mistake. And I wish you give me not occasion to think you as much inferior unto him in morals as I know you are in your intellectuals. But, sir, I nowhere compare you unto him; but only show a coincidence of your objections against Protestancy with some of his against Christianity; which the likeness of your cause and interest cast you upon. 2. I did not say, "You had the same end with him:" I expressed my thoughts to the contrary; nor did compare your act and his in point of morality, but only showed, as I said before, a coincidence in your reasonings. This you saw and read; and now, in an open defiance of truth and ingenuity, express the contrary. Celsus would not have done so. But I must tell you, sir, you are mistaken, if you suppose that the end doth so absolutely moralize an action that it of itself should render it good or evil. Evil it may, but good of itself it cannot; for, "Bonum oritur ex integris causis, malum ex quolibet defectu." Rectifying the intention will not secure your morality. And yet, also, on second thoughts, I see not much difference between the *ends* that Celsus proposed unto himself upon his general principle, and those that you propose to yourself upon your own; as well as the *way* whereby you proceed is the same. But yet, upon the accounts before mentioned, I shall free you from your fears of being thought like him. 3. When Protestants preach against our divisions, they charge them upon the *persons* of them that are guilty, whereas you do it on the *principles* of the religion that they profess; so that although you may deal like Celsus, they do not. 4. The scurrilous sarcasm wherewith you close your discourse is not meet for any thing but the entertainment of a friar and his concubine; such as in some places, formerly, men have by public edicts forced you to maintain, as the only expedient to preserve their families from being defiled by you. 5. Let us now pass through the instances that you have culled out of many charged upon you, to be the same with those of Celsus, concerning which you make such a trebled outcry, "Does he, does he, does he?" The first is, "Doth 'Fiat Lux' lay the cause of all tumults and disorders on Protestants?" "Clames licet, et mare cœlo Confundas," Juv. vi. 282. "Fiat Lux" doth so, chap. iv., sect. 17, p. 237, sect. 18, pp. 242, 243, sect. 20, p. 255, and in sundry other places. You add, "Doth he charge Protestants, that by their schisms and seditions they make way for other revolts?" He doth so, and that frequently, chap. iii., sect. 14, p. 187, etc. "Doth he," you add, "gather a rhapsody of insignificant words, as did Celsus?" I say he doth, in the pretended plea that he insists on for Quakers, and for Presbyterians also, chap. iii., sect. 13, pp. 172, 173, etc. Again, "Doth he manage the arguments of the Jews against Christianity, as was done by Celsus?" He doth directly, expressly, and at large, chap. iii., sect. 12, p. 158, etc. I confess, because it may be you know it not, you might have questioned the truth of my parallel on the side that concerned Celsus, which yet I am ready at any time, if you shall so do, to give you satisfaction in; but that you would question it on your own part, when your whole discourse, and the most of the passages in it, make it so evident, I could not foresee. But your whole defence is nothing but a noise or an outcry, to deter men from coming nigh you to see how the case stands with you. It will not serve your turn, ἐῤῥίφθη κύβος· you must abide by what you have done, or fairly retract it. In the meantime, I am glad to find you ashamed of that which elsewhere you so much boast and glory in.

With the sixth and seventh principles mentioned by me you deal in like manner. You deny them to be yours; which is plainly to deny yourself to be the author of "Fiat Lux." And surely every man that hath once looked seriously into that discourse of yours will be amazed to hear you saying that you never asserted "Our departure from Rome to be the cause of the evils among Protestants;" or that "There is no remedy for them but by a returnal thither again;" which are the things that now you deny to be spoken or intended by you. For my part, I am now so used unto this kind of confidence, that nothing you say or deny seems strange unto me. And whereas unto your denial you add not any thing that may give occasion unto any useful discourse, I shall pass it by, and proceed unto that which will afford us some better advantage unto that purpose.

CHAPTER VI.

Farther vindication of the second chapter of the "Animadversions"—Scripture sufficient to settle men in the truth—Instance against it, examined, removed—Principles of Protestants and Romanists in reference unto moderation compared and discussed.

THE eighth principle, which way soever it be determined, is of great importance as to the cause under debate. Here, then, we shall stay a while, and examine the difficulties which you labour to entangle that assertion withal; which we acknowledge to be the great and fundamental principle of our profession, and you oppose. The position I laid down as yours is, "That the Scripture, on sundry accounts, is insufficient to settle us in the truth of religion, or to bring us to an agreement amongst ourselves." Hereunto I subjoined the four heads of reasons which, in your "Fiat," you insisted on to make good your assertion. These you thought meet to pass by without reviving them again to your farther disadvantage. You are acquainted, it seems, with the old rule,

—— "Et quæ
Desperat tractata nitescere posse, relinquit." Hor. ad. Pis. 150.

The position itself you dare not directly deny; but you seek what you can to waive the owning of it, contrary to your express discourse, chap iii. sect. 15, pp. 199, 200, etc.; as also in sundry other places, interwoven with expressions exceedingly derogatory to the authority, excellency, efficacy, and fulness of the Scripture; as hath been showed in the "Animadversions." But let us now consider what you plead for yourself. Thus, then, you proceed: "You speak not one word to the purpose, or against me at all, if I had delivered any such principle. God's word is both the sufficient and only necessary means of both our conversion and settlement, as well in truth as virtue. But the thing you heed not, and unto which I only speak, is this, that the Scripture be in two hands; for example, of the Protestant church in England, and of the Puritan, who with the Scripture rose up and rebelled against her. Can the Scripture alone of itself decide the business? How shall it do it? Has it ever done it? Or can that written word, now solitary and in private hands, so settle any in a way that neither himself, nor present adherents, nor future generations, shall question it, or with as much probability dissent from it, either totally or in part, as himself first set it? This is the case unto which you do neither here nor in your whole book speak one word; and what you speak otherwise of the Scripture's excellency, I allow it for good."

1. Because you are not the *only* judge of what I have written, nor indeed any competent judge of it at all, I shall not concern myself in the censure which your interest compels you to pass on it. It is left unto the thoughts of those who are more impartial. 2. Setting aside your instance, pitched on "ad invidiam" only, with some equivocal expressions, as must needs be thought μάλα ἐντέχνως, "very artificially," to be put into the state of a question, and that which you deny is this, "That where any persons or churches are at variance or difference about any thing concerning religion or the worship of God, the Scripture is not sufficient for the umpirage of that difference, so that they may be reconciled and centre in the profession of the same truth." I wish you would now tell me what discrepancy there is between the assertion which I ascribed unto you, and that which yourself here avow. I suppose they are in substance the same, and as such will be owned by every one that understands any thing of the matters about which we treat. And this is so spoken unto in

the "Animadversions," that you have no mind to undertake the examination of it; but labour to divert the discourse unto that which may appear something else, but indeed is not so. 3. For your distinction between Protestants and Puritans in England, I know not well what to make of it. I know no Puritans in England that are not Protestants, though all the Protestants in England do not absolutely agree in every "punctilio" relating to religion, nor in all things relating unto the outward worship of God; no more than did the churches in the apostles' days, or than your Catholics do. You give us, then, a distinction like that which a man may give between the church of Rome and the Jesuits or Dominicans; or the sons of St Bene't or of St Francis of Assisi;—a distinction or distribution of the genus into the genus and one species comprehended under it, as if you should have said, "That 'animal' is either 'animal' or 'homo.'" 4. Though I had rather, therefore, that you had placed your instance between the church of Rome and Protestants, yet because any instance of persons that have different apprehensions about things belonging to the worship of God will suffice us as to the present purpose, I shall let it pass: only I desire you once more, that when you would endeavour to render any thing, way, or acting of men odious, that you would forbear to cast the Scripture into a copartnership therein; which here you seem to do. "The Puritan," you say, "with the Scripture rose up and rebelled." Rebellion is the name of an outrageous evil, such as the Scripture giveth not the least countenance unto; and therefore when you think meet to charge it upon any, you may do well not to say that "they do it with the Scripture." It will not be to your comfort or advantage so to do. This is but my advice; you may do as you see cause.

—— "Tales casus Cassandra canebat."—Virg. Æn. iii. 183.

5. The differences you suppose and look upon as undeterminable by the Scripture, are about things that in themselves really and in truth belong unto Christian religion, or such as do not so indeed, but are only fancied by some men so to do. If they are of this latter sort, as the most of the controversies which we have with you are,—as about your mass, purgatory, the pope,—we account that all differences about them are sufficiently determined in the Scriptures, because they are nowhere mentioned in them. And this must needs be so, if the word of God be, as you here grant, "the sufficient and only means both of our conversion and settlement, as well in truth as in virtue." Sir, I had no sooner written these words, in that haste wherein I treat with you, but I suspected a necessity of craving your pardon for supposing my inference confirmed by your concession; for whereas you had immediately before set down the assertion supposed to be yours about

the Scriptures, you add the words now mentioned, "God's word is the sufficient and only means of our conversion and settlement in the truth." I did not in the least suspect that you intended any legerdemain in the business, but that the Scripture and God's word had been only various denominations with you of the same precise thing, as they are with us: only, I confess, at the first view, I wondered how you could reconcile this assertion with the known principles of your church; and, besides, I knew it to be perfectly destructive of your design in your following inquiry. But now I fear you play hide-and-seek in the ambiguity your church hath put upon that title, "God's word;" which it hath applied unto your unwritten traditions as well as unto the written word, as the Jews apply the same term unto their oral law. And therefore, as I said before, I crave your pardon for supposing my inference confirmed by your concession, wherein I fear I was mistaken, and only desire you that for the future you would speak your mind plainly and candidly, as it becomes a Christian and lover of truth to do. But my assertion I esteem never the worse, though it have not the happiness to enjoy your approbation; especially considering that, in the particular instances mentioned, there are many things delivered in Scripture inconsistent with and destructive of your notions about them, sufficient to exterminate them from the confines of the city of God. 6. Suppose the matters in difference do *really* belong unto religion and the worship of God, and that the difference lies only in men's various conception of them, you ask, "Can the Scripture alone of itself decide the business?" What do you mean by "alone of itself?" If you mean, without men's *application* of themselves unto it, and *subjecting* of their consciences unto its authoritative decisions, neither it nor any thing else can do it. The matter itself is perfectly stated in the Scripture, whether any men take notice of it or no; but their various apprehensions about it must be regulated by their applications unto it in the way mentioned. On this only supposition, that those who are at variance about things which really appertain unto the religion of Jesus Christ will refer the determination of them unto the Scripture, and bring the conceptions of their minds to be regulated thereby, standing unto its arbitrament, it is able alone and of itself to end all their differences, and settle them all in the truth. This hath been proved unto you a thousand times, and confirmed by most clear *testimonies* of the Scripture itself, with *arguments* taken from its nature, perfection, and the end of its giving forth unto men; as also from the *practice* of our Lord Jesus and his apostles, with their directions and commands given unto us for the same purpose; from the *practice* of the first churches, with innumerable testimonies of the ancient fathers and doctors. Neither can this be denied without that horrible derogation from its perfection and plenitude, so reverenced by them of old, which is objected unto you for your so doing. Protestants suppose the Scripture to be given forth by God, to be unto the church *a perfect rule* of that faith and obedience which he requires at the hands of the sons of men. They suppose that it is such a revelation of his mind or will as is intelligible unto all them that are concerned to know it, if they use the means by him appointed to come unto a right understanding of it. They suppose that what is not taught therein, or not taught so clearly as that men who humbly and heartily seek unto him may know his mind therein as to what he requireth of them, cannot possibly be the necessary and indispensable duty of any one to perform. They suppose that it is the duty of every man to search the Scriptures with all diligence, by the help and assistance of the means that God hath appointed in his church, to come to the knowledge of his mind and will in all things concerning their faith and obedience; and firmly to believe and adhere unto what they find revealed by him. And they, moreover, suppose that those who deny any of these suppositions are therein, and so far as they do so, injurious to the grace, wisdom, love, and care of God towards his church, to the honour and perfection of the Scripture, the comfort and establishment of the souls of men, leaving them no assured principles to build their faith and salvation upon. Now, from these suppositions, I hope you see that it will unavoidably follow that the Scripture is able every way to effect that which you deny unto it a sufficiency for; for where, I pray you, lies its defect? I am afraid, from the next part of your question, "Has it ever done it?" that you run upon a great mistake. The defect that follows the failings and miscarriages of men, you would have imputed unto the want of sufficiency in the Scripture. But we cannot allow you herein. The Scripture in its place, and in that kind of cause which it is, is as sufficient to settle men, all men, in the truth, as the sun is to give light to all men to see by; but the sun that giveth light doth not give eyes also. The Scripture doth its work as a *moral rule;* which men are not necessitated or compelled to attend unto or follow. And if, through their neglect of it, or not attendance unto it, or disability to discern the mind and will of God in it,—whether proceeding from their *natural impotency* and blindness in their lapsed condition, or some *evil habit of mind* contracted by their giving admission unto corrupt prejudices and traditional principles,—the work be not effected, this is no impeachment of the Scripture's sufficiency, but a manifestation of their weakness and folly. Besides, all that unity in faith that hath been at any time, or is in the world, according to the mind of God; every decision that hath been made at any time of any difference in or about religion, in a right way and order,—hath been by the Scripture, which God hath sanctified unto these ends and purposes. And it is impossible that the miscarriages or defects of men can reflect the least blame upon it, or make it esteemed insufficient for the end now inquired after. The pursuit, then, of your inquiry which now you insist upon, is in part vain, in part already answered. In vain it is that you inquire "whether the written word can settle any man in a way that neither himself, nor present adherents, nor future generations shall question?" for our inquiry is not after what may be, or what shall be, but what ought to be. It is able to settle a man in a way that none ought to question unto the world's end: so it settled the first Christians. But to secure us that none shall ever question the way whereinto it leads us, *that* it is not designed for, nor is it either needful or possible that it should be so. The oral preaching of the Son of God and of his apostles did not so secure them whom they taught. The way that they professed was everywhere questioned, contradicted, spoken against; and many, after the profession of it, again renounced it. And I wonder what feat you have to settle any one in a way that shall never be questioned. The *authority of your pope and church will not do it:* themselves are things as highly questioned and disputed about as any thing that was ever named with reference unto religion. If you shall say, "But yet they ought not to be so questioned, and it is the fault of men that they are so," you may well spare me the labour of answering your question, seeing you have done it yourself. And whereas you add, "Or with as much probability dissent from it, either totally or in part, as himself first set it,"—when the very preceding words do not speak of a man's own setting, but of the Scripture's settling, the man only embracing what that settleth and determineth,—it is answered already, that what is so settled by the Scripture, and received as settled, cannot justly be questioned by any. And you insinuate a most irrational supposition, on which your assertion is built,—namely, that error may have as much probability as truth. For I suppose you will grant that what is settled by the Scripture is true, and therefore that which dissents from it must needs be an error; which, that it may be as probable indeed as truth (for we speak not of appearances, which have all their strength from our weaknesses), is a new notion, which may well be added to your many other of the like rarity and evidence. But why is not the Scripture able to settle men in unquestionable truth? When the people of old doubted about the ways of God wherein they ought to walk, himself sends them to "the law and to the testimony" for their instruction and settlement, Isa. viii. 20; and we think the counsel of him who cannot deceive nor be deceived is to be hearkened unto, as well as his command to be obeyed. Our Saviour assures us that if men will not hear Moses and the prophets, and take direction from them for those ways wherein they may please God, they will not do it, whatsoever they pretend, from any other means which they rather approve of, Luke xvi. 29, 31. Yea, and when the great fundamental of Christian religion, concerning the person of the Messiah, was in question, he sends men for their settlement unto the Scriptures, John v. 39. And we suppose that that which is sufficient to settle us in the foundation is so to confirm us also in the whole superstructure; especially considering that it is able "to make the man of God perfect, and to be thoroughly furnished unto all good works," 2 Tim. iii. 16, 17. What more is required unto the settlement of any one in religion we know not, nor what can rationally stand in competition with the Scripture to this purpose, seeing that is expressly commended unto us for it by the Holy Ghost; other ways are built on the conjectures of men. Yea, the assurance which we may have hereby is preferred by Peter before that which any may have by an immediate voice from heaven, 2 Pet. i. 19. And is it not an unreasonable thing, now, for you to come and tell us that the Scripture is not sufficient to give us an unquestionable settlement in religion? "Whether it be meet to hearken unto God or men, judge you." For our part, we seek not for the foundation of our settlement in long uncertain discourses, dubious conclusions and inferences, fallible conjectures, sophistical reasonings, such as you would call us unto, but in the express direction and command of God. Him we can follow and trust unto, without the least fear of miscarriage. Whither you would lead us we know not, and are not willing to make desperate experiments in things of so high concernment. But since you have been pleased to overlook what hath been discoursed unto this purpose in the "Animadversions," and, with your usual confidence, to affirm "that I nowhere at all speak one word to the case that you proposed," I shall, for your farther satisfaction, give you a little enlargement of my thoughts as to the principles on which Protestants and Romanists proceed in these matters, and compare them together, that it may be seen whether of us builds on the most stable and adequate foundation as to the superstruction aimed at by us both.

Two things you profess, if I mistake not, to aim at in your "Fiat;" at least you pretend so to do:—1. *Moderation* in and about our differences whilst they continue; 2. The *reduction* of all dissenters unto a *unity in faith* and profession;—things, no doubt, great and excellent. He can be no Christian that aims not at them, that doth not earnestly desire them. You profess to make them your design; Protestants do so also. Now, let us consider whether of the two, you or they, are fitted with principles, according unto the diversity of professions wherein you are engaged, for the regular accomplishment and effecting of these ends. And in the consideration of the latter of them, you will find your present case fully and clearly resolved.

1. For the first,—of moderation,—I intend by it, and I think so do you also, the mutual forbearance of one another as to *any effects of hatred*, enmity, or animosities of any kind, attended with offices of love, charity, kindness, and compassion, proceeding from a frame of heart or gracious habit of mind naturally producing such effects, with a quiet, peaceable deportment towards one another, during our present differences in or about any thing in religion. Certainly, this moderation is a blessed thing; earnestly commended unto us by our Lord Jesus Christ and his apostles; and as necessary to preserve peace among Christians as the sun in the firmament is to give light unto the world. The very heathen could say, Πάντων μέτρον ἄριστον,—"Moderation is the life of all things;" and nothing is durable but from the influence which it receives from it. Now, in pressing after moderation, Protestants proceed chiefly on two principles, which, being once admitted, make it a duty indispensable. And I can assure you that no man will long follow after moderation but only he that looks upon it as his duty so to do; incident provocations will quickly divert them in their course who pursue it for any other ends or on any other accounts.

The first principle of the Protestants disposing them to moderation, and indispensably exacting it of them as their duty, is, that amongst all the professors of the name of Christ, who are known by their relation unto any church, or way of note or mark in the world, not actually condemned in the primitive or apostolical times, there is so much saving truth owned and taught, as, being received with faith and submitted unto with sincere obedience, is *sufficient* to give them that profess it an interest in Christ and in the covenant of grace and love of God, and to secure their salvation. This principle hath been openly defended by them, and I profess it to be mine. It is true, there are ways whereby the truth mentioned may be rendered ineffectual; but that hinders not but that the principle is true, and that the truth so received is *sufficient* for the producing of those effects in its kind and place. And let men pretend what they please, the last day will discover that that faith which "purifieth the heart," and renders the person in whom it is accepted with God by Jesus Christ, may have its *objective truths* confined in a very narrow compass; yet it must embrace all that is indispensably necessary to salvation. And it is an unsufferable tyranny over the souls and consciences of men, to introduce and assert a necessity of believing whatever this or that church, any, or indeed all churches, shall please to propose; for the proposal of all the churches in the world cannot make any thing to be *necessary* to be believed that was not so antecedently unto that proposal. Churches may help the faith of believers; they cannot burden it, or exercise any dominion over it. He that believeth that whatever God reveals is true, and that the holy Scripture is a perfect revelation of his mind and will (wherein almost all Christians agree), need not fear that he shall be burdened with multitudes of particular articles of faith, provided he do his duty in sincerity, to come to an acquaintance with what God hath so revealed. Now, if men's common interest in Christ their head, and their participation of the same Spirit from him, with their union in the bond of the covenant of grace, and an equal sharing in the love of God the Father, be the principles, and, upon the matter, the only grounds and reasons of that *special love,* without dissimulation, which Christians ought to bear one towards another,—from whence the moderation pleaded for must proceed, or it is a thing of no use in our present case, at least no way generally belonging to the gospel of Jesus Christ,—and if all these things may be obtained by virtue of that truth which is professed in common among all known societies of Christians, doth it not unavoidably follow that we ought to exercise moderation towards one another, however differing in or about things which destroy not the principles of love and union? Certainly we ought, unless we will resolvedly stifle the actings of that love which is implanted in all the disciples of Christ, and, besides, live in an open disobedience unto his commands. This, then, indispensably exacts moderation in Protestants towards them that differ from them; and that not only within the lines of Protestancy, because they believe that, notwithstanding that dissent, they have, or may have, for aught they know, an interest in those things which are the only reasons of that love which is required in them towards the disciples of Christ. There is a moderation proceeding from the principles of reason in general, and requisite unto our common interest in humanity, which is good, and an especial ornament unto them in whom it is, especially if they are persons exalted above others in place of rule and government. Men fierce, implacable, revengeful, impatient, treading down all that they dislike under their feet, are the greatest defacers of the image of God in the world, and, upon the matter, the only troublers of human society. But the moderation which the gospel requireth ariseth and proceedeth from the principles of union with Christ before mentioned; which is that that proves us disciples of Christ indeed, and will confirm the mind in suitable actings against all the provocations to the contrary which, from the infirmities and miscarriages of men, we are sure to meet withal. Neither doth this at all hinder but that we may contend earnestly for the truth delivered unto us, and labour, by the ways of Christ's appointment, to reclaim others from such opinions, ways, and practices, in and about the things of religion and worship of God, as are injurious unto his glory, and may be destructive and pernicious to their own souls. Neither doth it, in the least, put any discouragement upon endeavours to oppose the impiety and profaneness of men in their corruption in life and conversation; which certainly and unquestionably are inconsistent with and destructive of the profession of the gospel, let them on whom they are found be of what party, church, or way of religion they please. And if those in whose hearts are the ways of God, however diversified among themselves by various apprehensions of some doctrines and practices, would sincerely, according to their duty, set themselves to oppose that profaneness, wickedness of life, or open viciousness of conversation, which is breaking in like a flood upon the world,—and which, as it hath already almost drowned the whole glory of Christian religion, so it will undoubtedly, if not prevented, end in the woful calamity and final ruin of Christendom,—they would have less mind and leisure to wrangle fiercely among themselves, and breathe out destruction against one another for their mistakes and differences about things which, by their own experience, they find not to take off from their love to Christ, nor weaken the obedience he requires at their hands. But whilst the whole power of Christianity is despised, conversion to God and separation from the ways of the perishing world are set at nought, and men think they have nothing to do in religion but to be zealously addicted to this or that party amongst them that profess it, it is no wonder if they think their chiefest duty to consist in destroying one another. But for men that profess to be leaders and guides of others in Christian religion, openly to pursue carnal and worldly interests, greatness, wealth, outward splendour and pomp, to live in luxury and pride, to labour to strengthen and support themselves by the adherence of persons of profane and wicked lives, that so they may destroy all that in any opinion differ from themselves, is vigorously to endeavour to drive out of the world that religion which they profess, and, in the meantime, to render it so uncomely and undesirable that others must needs be discouraged from its embracement. But these things cannot spring from the principles of Protestants, which, as I have manifested, lead them unto other manner of actings. And it is to no purpose to ask, why then they are not all affected accordingly? for they that are not so do live in an open contradiction to their own avowed principles; which, that it is no news in the world, the vicious lives of many, in all places professing Christianity, will not suffer us to doubt. For though that religion which they profess teacheth them to "deny all ungodliness and worldly lusts, to live soberly, and righteously, and godly, in this present world," if they intend the least benefit by it, yet they hold the profession of it on a contrary practice. And for this self-deceiving, attended with eternal ruin, many men are beholding unto such notions as yours about your church, securing salvation within the pale of its external communion, laying little weight on the things which, at the last day, will only stand them in stead. But for Protestants, setting aside their occasional exasperations, when they begin to bethink themselves, they cannot satisfy their own consciences in a resolution not to love them, because of some differences, whom they believe *that God loves or may love,* notwithstanding those differences from them; or to renounce all union with them who, they are persuaded, are united unto Christ; or not to be moderate towards them in this world with whom they expect to live for ever in another. I speak only of them, on all sides, who have received into their hearts, and do express in their lives, the scriptural power and energy of the gospel, who are begotten unto Christ by the word of truth, and have received of his Spirit, promised in the covenant of grace unto all them that believe on him; for, not to dissemble with you, I believe all others, as to their *present state*, to be in the same condition before God, be they of what church or way they will, though they are not all in the same condition in respect of the means of their spiritual advantage which they enjoy or may do so, they being much more excellent in some societies of Christians than others. This then, to return, is the principle of Protestants, derived down unto them from Christ and his apostles; and hereby are they eminently furnished for the exercise of that moderation which you so much and so deservedly commend. And more fully to tell you *my private judgment*, which whether it be my own only I do not much concern myself to inquire, but this it is:—Any man in the world who receiveth the Scripture of the Old and New Testament as the word of God, and on that account assents in general to the whole truth revealed in them, worshipping God in Christ, and yielding obedience unto him answerable unto his light and conviction,—not contradicting his profession by any practice inconsistent with true piety, nor owning of any opinion or persuasion destructive to the known fundamentals of Christianity,—though he should have the unhappiness to dissent, in some things, from all the churches that are at this day in the world, may yet have an *internal, supernatural*, saving principle of his faith and obedience, and be undoubtedly saved. And I am sure it is my duty to exercise moderation towards every man concerning whom I have, or ought to have, that persuasion.

2. Some Protestants are of that judgment that *external force ought to have no place at all in matters of faith*, however laws may be constituted with penalties for the preservation of public outward

order in a nation; most of them, that "hæreticidium," or putting men to death for their misapprehensions in the things of God, is absolutely unlawful; and all of them, that faith is the gift of God, for the communication whereof unto men he hath appointed certain means, whereof external force is none;—unto which two last positions, not only the greatest Protestant but the greatest potentate in Europe hath lately, in his own words, expressive of a heavenly benignity towards mankind in their infirmities, declared his royal assent.[1] And I shall somewhat question the Protestancy of them whom his authority, example, and reason doth not conclude in these things. For my part, I desire no better, I can give no greater warrant to assert them as the principles of Protestants than what I have now acquainted you with. And it is no small satisfaction unto me to contemplate on the *heavenly principle* of gospel peace planted in the noble soil of *royal ingenuity and goodness;* whence fruit may be expected to the great profit and advantage of the whole world. Nor is it easy to discover the natural and genuine tendency of these principles towards moderation. Indeed, in acting according unto them, and in a regular consistency with them, consists the moderation which we treat about. Wherever, then, Protestants use not that moderation towards those that dissent from them, if otherwise peaceable, which the Lord Jesus requires his disciples to exercise towards all them that profess the same common hope with them, the fault is solely in the persons so offending, and is not countenanced from any principles which they avow. Whether it be so with those of your church shall now be considered.

1. You have no one principle that you more pertinaciously adhere unto, nor which yields you greater advantage with weak, unstable souls, than that whereby *you confine all Christianity within the bounds of your own communion.* The Roman church and the catholic are with you one and the same. No privilege of the gospel, you suppose, belongs unto any soul in the world who lives not in your communion, and in professed subjection unto the pope. Union with Christ, saving faith here, with salvation hereafter, belongs to no other,—no, not one. This is the moderation of your church, whereunto your outward actings have, for the most part, been suited. Indeed, by this one principle, you are utterly incapacitated to exercise any of that moderation towards those that dissent from you which the gospel

[1] In December 1662, Charles II., with the ulterior view of abetting the Papists, and asserting, at the same time, the royal prerogative entitled "the dispensing power," issued a declaration, in which, says Burnet, "the king expressed his aversion to all severities on the account of religion, but more particularly to all sanguinary laws, and gave hopes both to Papists and Nonconformists that he would find out such ways for tempering the severities of the laws, that all his subjects would be easy under them."—"History of His Own Times," i. 194. Probably it is to this declaration our author refers.—Ed.

requires. You cannot love them as the disciples of Christ, nor act towards them from any such principles. It is possible for you to show moderation towards them as men; but to show any moderation towards them as those [who are] partakers of the same precious faith with you, that is impossible for you to do. Yet this is that which we are inquiring after,—not the moderation that may be amongst men as men, but that which ought to be among Christians as Christians. This is gospel moderation; the other is common unto us with Turks, Jews, and Pagans, and not at all of our present disquisition. And I wish that this were found amongst you, as proceeding from the principles of reason, with ingenuity and goodness of nature, more than it is; for that which proceedeth from, and is regulated by, interest, is *hypocritical*, and not thankworthy. As occasion offers itself, it will turn and change; as we have found it to do in most kingdoms of Europe. Apparent, then, it is, that this fundamental principle of your profession, " Subesse Romano pontifici," etc.,—that it is of " indispensable necessity unto salvation unto every soul to be subject unto the pope of Rome,"—doth utterly incapacitate you for that moderation towards any that are not of you which Christ requires in his disciples towards one another; seeing you judge none to be so but yourselves. Yet I assure you withal that I hope, yea, I am verily persuaded, that there are many, very many amongst you, whose minds and affections are so influenced by common ingrafted notions of God and his goodness, with a sense of the frailties of mankind, and weakness of the evidence that is rendered unto them for the eviction of that indispensable necessity of subjection to the pope which their masters urge, as also with the beams of truth shining forth in general in the Scriptures, and what they know or have heard of the practices of primitive times, as that, being seasoned with Christian charity and candour, they are not so leavened with the sour prejudice of this principle as to be rendered unmeet for the due exercise of moderation. But for this they are not beholding to your church, nor this great principle of your profession.

2. It is the principle of your church, whereunto your practice hath been suited, that *those who dissent from* you in things determined by your church, being heretics, if they continue so to do after the application of the means for their reclaiming which you think meet to use, ought to be *imprisoned, burned, or one way or other put to death.* This you cannot deny to be your principle, in being the very foundation of your *Inquisition,*—the chief corner-stone in your ecclesiastical fabric, that couples and holds up the whole building together. And it hath been asserted in your *practice* for sundry ages, in most nations of Europe. Your councils, as that of Constance, have *determined* it, and practised accordingly with John Huss and Jerome; your doctors *dispute* for it; your church *lives* upon it. That you are

destitute of any colour from antiquity in this your way, I have showed before. Bellarmine, De Laic., cap. xxii., could find no other instance of it but that of Priscillianus, which what entertainment it found in the church of God, I have declared; with that of one Basilius, out of Gregory's Dialogues, lib. i. cap. 4, whom he confesseth to have been a magician; and of Bogomilus, in the days of Alexius Comnenus, 1100 years after Christ, whose putting to death notwithstanding was afterward censured and condemned in a synod of more sober persons than those who procured it. Instances of your avowing this principle in your dealing with the Albigenses of old, the inhabitants of Merindol and Cabrieres in France, with the Waldenses in the valleys of Piedmont, formerly and of late; of your judiciary proceedings against multitudes of persons of all sorts, conditions, ages, and sexes, in this and most other nations of Europe, you are not pleased with the mention of; I shall therefore pass them by: only, I desire you would not question whether this be the principle of your church or no, seeing you have given the world too great assurance that so it is; and yourself, in your "Fiat," commend the wisdom of Philip, king of Spain, in his rigour in the pursuit of it, p. 243. These things being so, I desire to know what foundation you have to stand upon in pressing for moderation amongst dissenters in religion. I confess it is a huge argument of your good nature that you are so inclinable unto it; but when you should come to the real exercise of it, I am afraid you would find your hands tied up by these principles of your church, and your endeavours thereupon become very faint and evanid. Men in such cases may make great pretences,—

> "At velut in somnis oculos ubi languida pressit
> Nocte quies, nequicquam avidos extendere cursus
> Velle videmur, et in mediis conatibus ægri
> Succidimus." Virg. Æn. xii. 908.

Being destitute of any real foundation, your attempts are but like the fruitless endeavours of men in their sleep, wherein great workings of spirits and fancy produce no effects. I confess, notwithstanding all this, others may be moderate towards you; I judge it their duty so to be, I desire they may be so; but how you should exercise moderation towards others, I cannot so well discern. Only as unto the former, so much more am I relieved as unto this principle, from the persuasion I have of the candour and ingenuity of many individual persons of your profession, which will not suffer them to be captivated under the power of such corrupt prejudices as these. And for my part, if I could approve of external force in any case in matters of religion, it would be against the promoters of the principle mentioned.

> —— "Cogendus" ——
> "In mores hominemque Creon." Statius, Theb. xii. 165.

When men, under pretence of *zeal for religion*, depose all sense of the *laws of nature* and humanity, some earnestness may be justified in unteaching them their untoward catechisms, which lie indeed not only against the design, spirit, principles, and letter of the gospel, but " terrarum leges et mundi fœdera,"—the very foundations of reason on which men coalesce into civil society. But, as we observed before, out of one of the ancients, "Force hath no place in or about the law of Christ," one way or other.

That which gave occasion unto this discourse was your insinuation of the Scripture's insufficiency for the settlement of men in the unity of faith, the contrary whereof being the great principle of Protestancy, I was willing a little to enlarge myself unto the consideration of your principles and ours,—not only with reference unto the unity of faith, but also as unto that moderation which you pretend to plead for, and the want whereof you charge on Protestants, premising it unto the ensuing discourse, wherein you will meet with a full and a direct answer unto your question.

CHAPTER VII.

Unity of faith, wherein it consists—Principles of Protestants as to the settling men in religion and unity of faith, proposed and confirmed.

THE next thing proposed as a good to be aimed at, is *unity in faith*, and settlement or infallible assurance therein. This is a good desirable for itself; whereas the moderation treated of is only a medium of relief against other evils until this may be attained. And therefore, though it be, upon supposition of our differences, earnestly to be endeavoured after, yet it is not to be rested in, as though the utmost of our duty consisted in it, and we had no prospect beyond it. It is a *catholic unity* in faith which all Christians are to aim at; and so both you and we profess to do, only we differ both about the nature of it and the proper means of attaining it. For the nature of it, you conceive it to consist in the " explicit or implicit belief of all things and doctrines determined on, taught, and proposed by your church [to] be believed, and nothing else (with faith supernatural) but what is so taught and proposed." But this description of the unity of faith we can by no means admit of:—1. Because it is *novel*. It hath no footstep in any writings of the apostles, nor of the first fathers or writers of the church, nor in the practice of the disciples of Christ for many ages. That the determination of the Roman church, and its proposal of things or articles to be believed, should be the adequate rule of faith unto all believers, is a matter as foreign unto all antiquity as that the prophecies of Montanus should be so. 2. Because it makes the unity of faith, after the full and last revelation of the will of God, *flux, alterable, and unstable,* liable to increase and decrease; whereas it is uniform, constant, always the same in all ages, times, and places, since the finishing of the canon of the Scriptures. For we know, and all the world knows, that your church hath determined many things lately—some χθὲς καὶ πρώην, as it were but yesterday—to be believed, which itself had never before determined, and so hath increased the rule of faith, moved its centre, and extended its circumference; and what she may farther determine and propose to-morrow, no man knows. And your duty it is to be ready to believe whatever she shall so propose; whereby you cannot certainly know unto your dying day whether you do believe all that may belong to the unity of faith or no. Nay,—3. Your church hath determined and proposed to be believed *express contradictions:* which determinations abiding on record, you are not agreed which of them to adhere unto; as is manifest in your conciliary decrees about the power of the Pope and the Council, unto which of them the pre-eminence is due. Now, this is a strange rule of the unity of faith, that is not only capable of increase, changes, and alterations, so that that may belong unto it one day which did not belong unto it another,—as is evident from your Tridentine decrees, wherein you made many things necessary to be believed which before were esteemed but probable, and were the subjects of sophistical altercations in your schools,—but also compriseth in itself express contradictions; which cannot at all belong unto faith, because both of them may be false, one of them must be so; nor to unity, because contrary and adverse. 4. Whereas holding "the unity of the Spirit in the bond of peace," or the unity of faith, is so great and important a duty unto all Christians, that they can no way discharge their consciences unto God without a well-grounded satisfaction that they live in the performance of it, this description of its nature renders it *morally impossible* for any man explicitly to know (and that only a man knows which he knows explicitly) that he doth answer his duty herein. For, (1.) The determinations of your church of things to be believed are so *many and various,* that it is not within the compass of an ordinary diligence and ability to search and find them out. Nor, when a man hath done his utmost, can he obtain any tolerable security that there have not other determinations been made, that he is not as yet come to an acquaintance with all, or that he ever shall so do; and how in this case he can have any satisfactory persuasion that he keeps the unity of faith, is not as yet made evident. (2.) In the determinations he may meet withal, or by any means come to the knowledge of, he is to receive and believe the things determined and proposed unto him *in the sense intended by the church*, or else he is never the nearer to his end: but what that sense is in the most of your church's proposals, your doctors do so endlessly quarrel among themselves, that it is impossible a man should come unto any great certainty in his inquiry after it; yet a precise meaning in all her proposals your church must have, or she hath none at all. What shall a man do, when he comes unto one of your *great masters* to be acquainted with the genuine sense of one of your church's proposals? this being the way that he takes for his satisfaction:—First, he speaks unto the *article* or question to be considered in *general;* then gives the *different senses* of it according to these and those famous masters, the most of which he confutes,—who yet all of them professed themselves to explain and to speak according to the sense of your church; and, lastly, gives his own *interpretation* of it, which, it may be, within a few months is confuted by another. (3.) Suppose a man have attained a knowledge of all that your church hath determined and proposed to be believed, and to a right understanding of her precise sense and meaning in all her determinations and proposals,—which I believe never yet man attained unto,—yet what assurance can he have, if he live in any place remote from Rome, but that your church may have made *some new determinations* in matters of faith, whose embracement, in the sense which she intends, belongs unto his keeping the unity of faith, which yet he is not acquainted withal? Is it not simply impossible for him to be satisfied at any time that he believes all that is to be believed, or that he holds the unity of faith? Your late pontifical determination in the case of the Jansenists and Molinists is sufficient to illustrate this instance. For I suppose you are equally bound not to believe what your church condemneth as heretical, as you are bound to believe what it proposeth for Catholic doctrine. (4.) I desire to know when a man who lives here in England *begins* to be obliged to believe the determinations of your church that are made at Rome. It may be he first hears of them in a "Mercury" or weekly news-book; or it may be he hath notice of them by some private letters, from some who live near the place; or it may be he hath a knowledge of them by common report; or it may be they are printed in some books, or that there is a brief of them published somewhere under the name of the pope; or they are put into some volume written about the councils; or some religious person, on whom he much relies, assures him of them. I know you believe that your church's proposition is a sufficient means of the revelation of any article, to make it necessary to be believed; but I desire to know what is necessary to cause a man to receive any dictate or doctrine as your church's proposition?—not only upon this account, that you are not very well agreed upon the "requisita" unto the making of such a proposition, but also because, be you as infallible as you please in your proposals, the means and ways you use to communicate those proposals you make unto individuals in whom alone the faith whereof we treat exists are all of them fallible. Now, that which I desire to know is, What is or what are those certain means and ways of communicating the propositions of your church unto any person, wherein he is bound to acquiesce, and upon the application of them unto him to believe them, "fide divina cui non potest subesse falsum?" Is it any one thing, or way, or means, that [forms] the hinge upon which his assent turns? or is it a complication of many things concurring to the same purpose? If it be any one thing, way, or medium, that you fix upon, pray let us know it, and we shall examine its fitness and sufficiency for the use you put it unto. I am sure we shall find it to be either *infallible* or *fallible.* If you say the *former*, and that *that* particular upon which the assent of a man's mind unto any thing to be the proposal of your church depends, must, in the testimony it gives and evidence that it affords, be esteemed infallible, then you have as many infallible persons, things, or writings, as you make use of to acquaint one another with the determinations of your church; that is, upon the matter, you are all so, though I know in particular that you are not. If the *latter*, notwithstanding the first pretended infallible proposition, your faith will be found to be resolved immediately into a fallible information; for what will it advantage me that the proposal of your church cannot deceive me, if I may be deceived in the communicating of that proposal unto me? And I can with no more firmness, certainty, or assurance, believe the thing proposed unto me, than I do believe that it is the proposal of the church wherein it is made. For you pretend not unto any *self-evidencing efficacy* in your church's propositions, or things proposed by it; but all their authority, *as to me*, turns upon the assurance that I have of their relation unto your church, or that they are the proposals of your church, concerning which I have nothing but very fallible evidence, and so cannot possibly believe them with faith divine and supernatural. If you shall say that there are many things concurring unto this communication of your church's proposal unto a man, as the *notoriety of the fact, suitable proceedings upon it, books* written to prove it, *testimonies* of good men, and the like, I cannot but mind you that all these being "sigillatim," every one apart fallible, they cannot in their conspiracy improve themselves into an infallibility. Strengthen a probability they may; testify infallibly they neither do nor can. So that, on this account, it is not only impossible for a man to know whether he holds the unity of faith or no, but, indeed, whether he believe any thing at all with faith supernatural and divine, seeing he hath no infallible evidence for what is proposed unto him to believe, to build his faith upon.

5. Protestants are not satisfied with your general *implicit assent* unto what your church teacheth and determineth, which you have invented to solve the difficulties that attend your description of the unity of faith. Of what use it may be unto other purposes, I do not now dispute; but as to this, of the preservation of the unity of faith, it is certainly of none at all. The unity of faith consists in all men's express believing all that all men are bound expressly to believe, be it what it will. Now, you would have this preserved by men's not believing what they are bound to believe: for what belongs to this keeping the unity of faith, they are bound to believe expressly; and what they believe implicitly, they do indeed no more but not expressly disbelieve,—for if they do any more than not disbelieve, they put forth some act of their understanding about it, and so far expressly believe it: so that, upon the matter, you would have men to keep the unity of faith by a not believing of that which, that they may keep the unity of faith, they are bound expressly to believe; nor can you do otherwise whilst you make all the propositions of your church of things to be believed to belong to the unity of faith. Lastly, The *determinations* of your church you make to be the *next efficient cause* of your unity. Now these, not being absolutely infallible, leave it, like Delos, flitting up and down in *the sea of probabilities* only. This we shall manifest unto you immediately; at least, we shall evidence that you have no cogent reasons nor stable grounds to prove your church infallible in her determinations. At present, it shall suffice to mind you that she hath determined contradictions, and that in as eminent a manner as it is possible for her to declare her sense by,—namely, by councils confirmed by popes; and an infallible determination of contradictions is not a notion of any easy digestion in the thoughts of a man in his right wits. We confess, then, that we cannot agree with you in your rule of the unity of faith, though the thing itself we press after as our duty. For, (2.) Protestants do not conceive this unity to consist in a precise determination of all questions that are or may be raised in or about things belonging unto the faith, whether it be made by your church or any other way. Your Thomas of Aquine,[1] who without question is the best and most sober of all your school doctors, hath in one book given us five hundred and twenty-two articles of religion, which you esteem miraculously stated: "Quot articuli, tot miracula." All these have at least five questions, one with another, stated and determined in explication of them; which amount unto two thousand six hundred and ten conclusions in matters of religion. Now, we are far from think-

[1] Aquino, anciently Aquinum, is a city, now decayed, within the kingdom of Naples. Our author invariably gives the word a French termination, and there seemed no necessity to change it into the modern form.—Ed.

ing that all these determinations, or the like, belong unto the unity of faith, though much of the religion amongst some of you lies in not dissenting from them. The questions that your Bellarmine hath determined and asserted, the positions in them *as of faith*, and necessary to be believed, are, I think, near forty times as many as the articles of the ancient creed of the church, and such as it is most evident that, if they be of the nature and importance pretended, it is impossible that any considerable number of men should ever be able to discharge their duty in this business of holding the unity of faith. That a man believe in general that the holy Scripture is given by inspiration from God, and that all things proposed therein for him to believe are therefore infallibly true, and to be as such believed; and that, in particular, he believe every article or point of truth that he hath sufficient means for his instruction in, and conviction that it is so revealed; they judge to be necessary unto the holding of the unity of faith. And this also they know, that this sufficiency of means unto every one that enjoys the benefit of the Scriptures, extends itself unto all those articles of truth which are necessary for him to believe, so as that he may yield unto God the obedience that he requireth, receive the Holy Spirit of promise, and be accepted with God. Herein doth that unity of faith which is amongst the disciples of Christ in the world consist, and ever did; nor can do so in any thing else. Nor doth that variety of apprehensions that in many things is found among the disciples of Christ, and ever was, render this unity, like that you plead for, various and uncertain; for the rule and formal reason of it,—namely, God's revelation in the Scripture,—is still one and the same, perfectly unalterable. And the several degrees that men attain unto in their apprehensions of it do no more reflect a charge of variety upon it than the difference of seeing, as to the several degrees of the sharpness or obtuseness of our bodily eyes, doth upon the light given by the sun. The truth is, if there was any common measure of the assents of men, either as to the *intension* of it, as it is subjectively in their minds, or *extension* of it, as it respecteth truths revealed, that belonged unto the unity of faith, it were impossible there should be any such thing in the world, at least that any such thing should be known to be. Only this I acknowledge, that it is the duty of all men to come up to the full and explicit acknowledgment of all the truths revealed in the word of God, wherein the glory of God and the Christian's duty are concerned; as also to a joint consent in faith objective, or propositions of truth revealed, at least in things of most importance,—though their faith subjective, or the internal assent of their minds, have, as it will have in several persons, various degrees, yea, in the same persons, it may be, at different seasons. And in our labouring to come up unto this joint acknowledgment of the same sense and intendment of God in all revealed truths consists our endeavour after that perfection in the unity of faith which in this life is attainable; as our moderation doth in our walking in peace and love with and towards others, according to what we have already attained. We may distinguish, then, between that *unity of faith* which an interest in gives union with Christ unto them that hold it, and communion in love with all equally interested therein; and that *accomplishment of it* which gives a sameness of profession, and consent in all acts of outward communion in the worship of God. The first is found in and amongst all the disciples of Christ in the world, wherever they are; the latter is that which, moreover, it is your duty to press after. The former consists in an assent in general unto all the truths of God revealed in the Scripture, and in particular unto them that we have sufficient means to evidence them unto us to be so revealed. The latter may come under a double consideration: for either there may be required unto it, in them who hold it, the joint perception of and assent unto every truth revealed in the Scripture, with an equal degree of certainty in adherence and evidence in perception,—and it is not in this life, wherein the best of us know but in part, attainable; or only such a concurrence in an assent unto the necessary propositions of truth as may enable them to hold together that outward communion in the worship of God which we before mentioned. And this is certainly attainable by the ways and means that shall immediately be laid down; and where this is, there is the unity of faith in that completeness which we are bound to labour for the attainment of. This the apostolical churches enjoyed of old, and unto the recovery whereof there is nothing more prejudicial than your new stating of it upon the account of your church's proposals.

This unity of faith we judge good and necessary, and that it is our duty to press after it; so also in general do you. It remains, then, that we consider what is the way, what are the means and principles, that Protestants propose and insist upon for the attainment of it; that is, in answer to your question, "What it is that can settle any man in the truth of religion, and unite all men therein?" And then, because you object this unto us, as if we were at some loss and uncertainty therein, and yourselves very secure, I shall consider what are the grounds and principles that you proceed upon for the same ends and purposes,—namely, to "settle any man in the truth of religion, and to bring all men to a harmony and consent therein."

Now, I shall herein manifest unto you these two things:—1. That the principles which the Protestants proceed upon, in the improvement whereof they obtain themselves assured and infallible settlement in the truth, and labour to reduce others unto the unity of faith, are such as are both *suited unto, and sufficient for*, the end and work which they design to effect by them, and also in themselves of such unquestionable truth, certainty, and evidence, that either they are all granted by yourselves, or cannot be denied without shaking the very foundations of Christianity. 2. That those which you proceed upon are some of them *untrue*, and most of them *dubious* and *questionable*, none of them able to bear the weight that you lay upon them; and some of them such as the admission of would give just cause to question the whole truth of Christian religion. And both these, sir, I crave leave to manifest unto you, whereby you may the better judge whether the Scripture or your church be the best way to bring men unto settlement in religion, which is the thing inquired after.

I. Protestants lay down this as the ἡ ἀρχὴ τῆς ὑποστάσεως καὶ ὁμολογίας,—as "the very beginning and first principle of their confidence and confession,"—that *all Scripture is given by inspiration of God*, as the Holy Ghost teacheth them, 2 Tim. iii. 16; that is, that the books of the Old and New Testament were all of them written by the immediate guidance, direction, and inspiration of God;—"the hand of the LORD," as David speaks, 1 Chron. xxviii. 19, being upon the penmen thereof in writing; and his Spirit, as Peter informs us, speaking in them, 1 Pet. i. 11: so that whatever is contained and delivered in them is given out from God, and is received on his authority. This principle I suppose you grant to be true. Do you not? If you will deny it, say so, and we will proceed no farther until we have proved it. I know you have various ways laboured to undermine the αὐτοπιστία of the holy Scriptures; many queries you put unto men, how they can know it to be from God, to be true, from heaven, and not of men?—many scruples you endeavour to possess them with against its authority. It is not my present business to remove them; it is sufficient unto me,—1. That you yourselves, who differ from us in other things, and with whom our contest about the best way of coming to settlement in the truth alone is, do acknowledge this principle we proceed upon to be true. And,—2. That ye cannot oppose it without setting yourselves to dig up the very foundations of Christian religion, and to open a way to let in an inundation of atheism on the world. So our first step is fixed on the grand fundamental principle of all the religion and acceptable worship of God that is in the world.

II. They affirm that this Scripture *evidenceth itself by many infallible* τεκμήρια *to be so given by inspiration from God;* and, besides, is witnessed so to be by the testimony of the church of God from the days of Moses, wherein it began to be written, to the days wherein we live,—our Lord Christ and his apostles asserting and confirming the same testimony; which testimony is conveyed unto us by uninterrupted catholic tradition. The first part of this position, I confess, some of you deny; and the latter part of it you generally all of you pervert, confining the testimony mentioned unto that of your present church; which is a very inconsiderable part of it, if any part at all. But how groundlessly, how prejudicially to the verity and honour of Christian religion in general, you do these things, I shall briefly show you.

Some of you, I say, deny the first part of this assertion; so doth Andradius, Defens. Concil. Trident. lib. iii. "Neque enim," saith he, "in ipsis libris quibus sacra mysteria conscripta sunt, quicquam inest divinitatis, quod nos ad credendum quæ illis continentur, religione aliquâ constringat;"—"Neither is there in the books themselves, wherein the holy mysteries are written, any thing of divinity that should constrain us, by virtue of any religious respect thereunto, to believe the things that are contained in them." Hence Cochlæus, lib. ii. De Authoritate Eccles. et Script., gathers up *a [great] many instances* out of the book of the Scripture, which he declares to be altogether incredible, were it not for the authority of the church. I need not mention any more of your leaders concurring with them; you know who is of the same mind with them, if the author of "Fiat Lux" be not unknown to you. Your resolving universal tradition into the authority of your present church, to which end there is a book written not long since by a Jesuit, under the name of Vincentius Severinus, is no less notorious. Some of you, I confess, are more modest, and otherwise minded, as to both parts of our assertion. See Malderus, Episcop. Antwerp. De Object. Fidei, qu. 1; Vaselius Groningen. De Potestat. Eccles. et Epist. ad Jacob. Hock. Alliacens. in lib. i. Sentent. Artic. 3; Gerson Exam. Doc. part. 2, consid. i. tom. i. fol. 105; and in twenty other places. But when you come to deal with Protestants, and consider well the tendency of this assertion, you use, I confess, a hundred tergiversations, and are most unwilling to come to the acknowledgment of it; and, rather than suffer from it, deny it downright, and that with scurrilous reflections and comparisons, likening it, as to any characters of God's truth and holiness upon it, unto Livy's story, yea, Æsop's Fables, or a piece of poetry. And when you have done so, you apply yourselves to the canvassing of stories in the Old Testament, and to find out appearing contradictions; and tell us of the uncertainty of the authors of some particular books,—that the whole is of itself a dead letter, which can prove nothing at all; inquiring, Who told us that the penmen of it were divinely inspired, seeing they testify no such thing of themselves? and if they should, yet others may do, and have done so, who, notwithstanding, were not so inspired; and ask us, Why we receive the Gospel of Luke, who was not an apostle, and reject that of Thomas, who was one? with many the like cavilling exceptions.

But,—1. That must needs be *a bad cause* which stands in need of such a defence. Is this the voice of Jacob, or Esau? Are these the expressions of Christians, or Pagans? From whose quiver are these arrows taken? Is this fair, sober, candid, Christian dealing? Have you no way to defend the authority of your church but by questioning the authority of the Scripture? Did ever any of the fathers of old, or any in the world before yourselves, take this course to plead their interests in any thing they professed? Is this practice Catholic, or, like many of your principles, singular, your own, Donatistical? Is it any great sign that you have an interest in that *living child*, when you are so ready he should be destroyed, rather than you would be cast in your contest with Protestants? 2. Do you think that this course, of proclaiming to Atheists, Turks, and Pagans, that the Scripture, which all Christians maintain against them to be the word of the living God, given by inspiration from him,—and on which the faith of all the martyrs who have suffered from their opposition, rage, and cruelty, and of all others that truly believe in Jesus Christ, was and is founded, and whereinto it is resolved,—hath no arguments of its divine original implanted on it, no lines of the excellencies and perfections of its author drawn on it, no power or efficacy towards the consciences of men, evidencing its authority over them, no ability of itself to comfort and support them in their trials and sufferings with the hope of things that are not seen;—is this, think you, an acceptable service unto the Lord Christ, who will one day judge the secrets of all hearts according unto that word? or is it not really to expose Christian religion to scorn and contempt? And do you find so much sweetness in "dolus, an virtus, quis in hoste requirat?" Virg. Æn. ii. 390, as to cast off all reverence of God and his word, in the pursuit of the supposed adversaries of your earthly interests? 3. If your arguments and objections are *effectual* and *prevalent* unto the end for which you intend them, will not your direct issue be the utter overthrow of the very foundation of the whole profession of Christians in the world? And are you, like Samson, content to pull down the house that must fall upon yourselves also, so that you may stifle Protestants with its fall? It may be it were well you should do so, were it a house of Dagon, a temple dedicated unto idols; but to deal so with that *wherein dwells the majesty of the living God* is not so justifiable. It is true, evert this principle and you overthrow the foundation on which the faith of Protestants is built; but it is no less true that you do the same to the foundation of the Christian faith in general, wherein we hope your own concernment also lies. And this is the thing that I am declaring unto you,—namely, that either you acknowledge the principles on which Protestants build their faith and profession, or by denying them you open a door unto atheism, at least to the extirpation of Christian religion out of the world. I confess you pretend a relief against the present instance, in the authority of your church, sufficient, as you say, to give a credibility unto the Scripture, though its own self-evidencing power and efficacy, with the confirmation of it by Catholic tradition, exclusive to your present suffrage, be rejected. Now, I suppose you will grant that the prop you supply men withal, upon your casting down the foundations on which they have laid the weight of their eternal salvation, had need be firm and immovable. And remember that you have to do with them who, though they may be otherwise inclinable unto you,

"Non tamen ignorant quid distent æra lupinis," Hor. Ep. i. 7, 23;

and must use their own judgment in the consideration of what you tender unto them. And they ask you,—1. What will you do if it be as you say with them who absolutely reject the authority of your church; which is the condition of more than a moiety of the inhabitants of the world, to speak sufficiently within compass? And,—2. What will you advise us to say to innumerable other persons that are pious and rational, who, upon the mere consideration of the lives of many, of the most, of the guides of your church, your bloody, inhuman practices, your pursuit of worldly, carnal designs, your visible, secular interest, wherein you are combined and united, cannot persuade themselves that the testimony of your church, in and about things that are invisible, spiritual, heavenly, and eternal, is at all valuable, much less that it is sufficient to bear the weight you would lay upon it? 3. Was not this the way and method of Vaninus for the introduction of his atheism,—first, to question, slight, and sophistically except against the old approved arguments and evidences manifesting the being and existence of a divine, self-subsisting power; substituting in their room, for the confirmation of it, his own sophisms, which himself knew might be easily discussed and disproved? Do you deal any better with us, in decrying the Scripture's self-evidencing efficacy, with the testimony given unto it by God himself, substituting nothing in the room thereof but the authority of your church? A man, certainly, can take up nothing upon the sole authority of your church, until, contrary to the pretensions, reasons, and arguments of far a greater number of Christians than yourselves, he acknowledge you to be a true church at least, if not the only church in the world. Now, how, I pray, will you bring him into that state and condition that he may rationally make any such judgment? How will you prove unto him that there is any such thing as a *church* in the world; that a church hath *any authority;* that its testimony can make any thing credible, or meet to be believed? You must prove these things to him, or whatever assent he gives unto what you say is from fanatical credulity. To suppose that he should believe you upon your word, because you are the church, is to suppose that he believes that which you are yet but attempting to induce him to believe. If you persist to press him, without other proof, not only to believe what you first said unto him, but also even this, that whatever you shall say to him hereafter, that he must believe it because you say it, will not any rational man nauseate at your unreasonable importunity, and tell you that men who have a mind to be befooled may meet with such alchymistical pretenders all the world over? Will you persuade him that *you are the church*, and that the church is furnished with the authority mentioned, by rational arguments? I wish you would inform me of any one that you can make use of that doth not include a supposition of something unproved by you, and which can never be proved but by your own authority, which is the thing in question; or the immediate authority of God, which you reject. A number, indeed, of pretences, or, it may be, probabilities, you may heap together; which yet upon examination will not be found so much neither, unless a man will swallow amongst them that which is destitute of all probability but what is included in the evidence given unto it by divine revelation, which is not yet pleaded unto him. It may be, then, you will work *miracles* to confirm your assertions. Let us see them; for although very many things are requisite to manifest any works of wonder that may be wrought in the world to be real miracles, and good caution be required to judge unto what end miracles are wrought, yet, if we may have any tolerable evidence of your working miracles in confirmation of this assertion, that you are the true and only church of God, with the other inferences depending thereon, which we are in the consideration of, you will find us very easy to be treated withal. But herein also you fail. You have, then, no way to deal with such a man as we first supposed, but as you do with us, and producing testimonies of Scripture to prove and confirm the authority of your church; and then you will quickly find where you are, and what snares you have cast yourselves into. Will not a man who hears you proving *the authority of your church* by the Scripture ask you, "And whence *hath this Scripture its authority?*" yea, that is supposed to be the thing in question, which, denying unto it an *αὐτοπιστία*, you yet produce to confirm the authority of that by whose authority alone itself is evidenced to have any authority at all. Rest in the authority of God, manifesting itself in the Scripture, witnessed unto by the catholic tradition of all ages, you will not. But you will prove the Scripture to be the word of God by the testimony of your church; and you will prove your church to be enabled sufficiently to testify the Scriptures to be of God, by the testimonies of the Scripture. Would you know where to begin and where to end? But you are, indeed, in a circle which hath neither beginning nor ending. I know not when we shall be enabled to say,—

"Inventus, Chrysippe, tui finitor acervi."—Pers. vi. 80.

Now, do you think it reasonable that we should leave our stable and immovable firm foundations to run round with you in this *endless circle*, until, through giddiness, we fall into unbelief or atheism? This is that which I told you before,—you must either acknowledge our principle in this matter to be firm and certain, or open a door to atheism and the contempt of Christian religion, seeing you are not able to substitute any thing in the room thereof that is able to bear the weight that must be laid upon it, if we believe. For how should you do so? Shall man be like unto God, or equal unto him? The testimony we rest in is divine, fortified from all objections by the strongest human testimony possible,—namely, catholic tradition. That which you would supply us with is merely human, and no more. And, 4. Your importunity in opposing this principle is so much the more marvellous unto us, because therein you openly oppose yourselves to express testimonies of Scripture and the full suffrage of the ancient church. I wish you would a little weigh what is affirmed, 2 Pet. i. 19, 20; Ps. cxix. 152; John v. 34–36, 39; 1 Thess. ii. 13; Acts xvii. 11; 1 John v. 6, 10, ii. 20; Heb. xi.; 1 Tim. i. 15; Acts xxvi. 22. And will you take with you the consent of the ancients? Clemens Alexand. Strom. vii., speaks fully to our purpose; as he doth also, lib. iv., where he plainly affirms that the church proved the *Scripture by itself;* and *other things*, as the unity of the Deity, *by the Scripture.* But his own words in the former place are worth the recital:—Ἔχομεν, saith he, τὴν ἀρχὴν τῆς πίστεως,[1] τὸν Κύριον, διά τε τῶν προφητῶν, διά τε τοῦ εὐαγγελίου, καὶ διὰ τῶν μακαρίων ἀποστόλων πολυτρόπως καὶ πολυμερῶς ἐξ ἀρχῆς εἰς τέλος ἡγούμενον τῆς γνώσεως. Τὴν ἀρχὴν δ' εἴ τις ἑτέρου δεῖσθαι ὑπολάβοι, οὐκέτ' ἂν ὄντως ἀρχὴ φυλαχθείη·—"For the beginning of faith, or principle of what we teach, we have the Lord; who in sundry manners, and by divers parts, by the prophets, gospel, and holy apostles, leads us to knowledge. And if any one suppose that a principle stands in need of another" (to prove it), "he destroys the nature of a principle," or "it is no longer preserved a principle." This is that we say,—the Scripture, the Old and New Testament, is the principle of our faith. This is *proved by itself* to be of the Lord, who is its author; and if we cause it to depend on any thing else, it is no longer the principle of our faith and profession. And a little after, where he hath showed that a principle ought not to be disputed, nor to be the τὸ κρινόμενον of any debate, he adds, Εἰκότως τοίνυν πίστει περιλαβόντες ἀναπόδεικτον τὴν ἀρχὴν, ἐκ περιουσίας καὶ τὰς ἀποδείξεις παρ' αὐτῆς τῆς

[1] Διδασκαλίας, ex editione Oxoniensi, A.D. 1715.—Ed.

ἀρχῆς λαβόντες, φωνῇ Κυρίου παιδευόμεθα πρὸς τὴν ἐπίγνωσιν τῆς ἀληθείας·—"It is meet, then, that receiving by faith the most absolute principle without other demonstration, and taking demonstrations of the principle from the principle itself, we be instructed by the voice of the Lord unto the knowledge of the truth;" that is, we believe the Scripture for its own sake, and the testimony that God gives unto it, in it and by it, and do prove every thing else by it; and so are confirmed in the faith or knowledge of the truth. So he farther explains himself, Οὐ γὰρ ἁπλῶς ἀποφαινομένοις ἀνθρώποις προσέχομεν, οἷς καὶ ἀνταποφαίνεσθαι ἐπ' ἴσης ἔξεστιν·—"For we do not simply or absolutely attend or give heed unto men determining or defining; against whom it is equal that we may define or declare our judgments." So it is; whilst the authority of man, or men, any society of men in the world, is pleaded, the authority of others may by as good reason be objected against it; as, whilst you plead your church and its definitions, others may on as good grounds oppose theirs unto you therein. And therefore Clemens proceeds: Εἰ δ' οὐκ ἀρκεῖ μόνον ἁπλῶς εἰπεῖν τὸ δόξαν, ἀλλὰ πιστώσασθαι δεῖ τὸ λεχθὲν, οὐ τὴν ἐξ ἀνθρώπων ἀναμένομεν μαρτυρίαν, ἀλλὰ τῇ τοῦ Κυρίου φωνῇ πιστούμεθα τὸ ζητούμενον, ἢ πασῶν ἀποδείξεων ἐχεγγυωτέρα, μᾶλλον δ' ἣ μόνη ἀπόδειξις οὖσα τυγχάνει· καθ' ἣν ἐπιστήμην οἱ ἀπογευσάμενοι μόνον τῶν Γραφῶν, πιστοί·—"For if it be not sufficient merely to declare or assert that which appears to be truth, but also to make that credible or fit to be believed which is spoken, we seek not after the testimony that is given by men, but we confirm that which is proposed or inquired about with the voice of the Lord; which is more full than any demonstration, or rather is itself the only demonstration; according to the knowledge whereof they that have tasted of the Scriptures are believers." Into the voice, the word of God alone, the church then resolved their faith; this only they built upon, acknowledging *all human testimony* to be too weak and infirm to be made a foundation for it; and this voice of God, in the Scripture evidencing itself so to be, is the only demonstration of faith which they rested in: whereupon, a little after, he adds, Οὕτως οὖν καὶ ἡμεῖς ἀπ' αὐτῶν τῶν Γραφῶν τελείως ἀποδεικνύντες, ἐκ πίστεως πειθόμεθα ἀποδεικτικῶς·—"So we, having perfect demonstrations out of the Scriptures, are by faith demonstratively assured or persuaded of the truth of the things proposed." This was the profession of the church of old; this the resolution of their faith; this is that which Protestants in this case adhere unto. They proved the Scripture to be from God,—as he elsewhere speaks, ἐξ αὐθεντείας παντοκρατορικῆς,—as we also do; Strom. iv. To this purpose speaks Salvianus de Gub., lib. iii., "Alia omnia (id est, humana dicta) argumentis et testibus egent; Dei autem sermo ipse sibi testis est, quia necesse est ut quicquid incorrupta veritas loquitur, incorruptum sit testimonum veritatis;"—"All other sayings stand in need of arguments and witnesses to confirm them: the word of God is witness to itself; for whatever the truth incorrupted speaks, must of necessity be an incorrupted testimony of truth." And although some of them allowed the testimony of the church as a motive unto believing the gospel, or things preached from it, yet as to the belief of the Scripture, with faith divine and supernatural, to be the word of God, they required but these two things:—1. That *self-evidence* in the Scripture itself which is needful for an indemonstrable principle, from which and by which all other things are to be demonstrated. And that self-evidence Clemens puts in the place of all demonstrations. 2. The *efficacy of the Spirit* in the heart, to enable it to give a saving assent unto the truth proposed unto it. Thus Austin, in his Confessions, lib. vi. cap. 5, "Persuasisti mihi, o Domine Deus, non qui crederent libris tuis, quos tantâ in omnibus fere gentibus authoritate fundasti, sed qui non crederent esse culpandos; nec audiendos esse, siqui mihi forte dicerent, 'Unde scis illos libros unius [veri et] veracissimi Dei Spiritu esse, humano generi ministratos?' id ipsum enim maxime credendum erat;"—"O Lord God, thou hast persuaded me, that not they who believe thy books, which with so great authority thou hast settled almost in all nations, were to be blamed, but those who believe them not; and that I should not hearken unto any of them who might chance say unto me, 'Whence dost thou know those books to be given out unto mankind from the Spirit of the true God?' for that is the thing which principally was to be believed." In which words the holy man hath given us full direction what to say, when you come upon us with that question, which some used, it seems, in his days;—a great testimony of the antiquity of your principles. Add hereunto what he writes in the 11th book and 3d chapter of the same treatise, and we have the sum of the resolution and principle of his faith. "Audiam," saith he, "et intelligam quomodo fecisti cœlum et terram. Scripsit hoc Moses; scripsit et abiit, transivit hinc ad te; neque enim nunc ante me est. Nam si esset, tenerem eum, et rogarem eum, et per te obsecrarem ut mihi ista panderet; et præberem aures corporis mei sonis erumpentibus ex ore ejus. At si Hebræâ voce loqueretur, frustra pulsaret sensum meum, nec inde mentem meam quidquam tangeret: si autem Latine, scirem quid diceret. Sed unde scirem an verum diceret? quod si et hoc scirem, num et ab illo scirem? Intus utique mihi, intus in domicilio cogitationis, nec Hebræa, nec Græca, nec Latina, nec barbara, veritas, sine oris et linguæ organis, sine strepitu syllabarum, diceret, 'Verum dicit;' et ego statim certus confidenter illi homini tuo dicerem, 'Verum dicis.' Cum ergo illum interrogare non possim, te, quo plenus vera dixit, veritas, rogo te, Deus meus, rogo parce peccatis meis; et qui illi servo tuo dedisti hæc dicere, da et mihi hæc intelligere;"—"I would hear and understand, O Lord, how thou hast made the heavens and the earth. Moses wrote this; he wrote it and is gone, and he is gone to thee; for now he is not present with me. If he were, I would lay hold on him, and ask him, and beseech him, for thy sake, that he would unfold these things unto me; and I would cause the ears of my body to attend unto the words of his mouth. But if he should speak in the Hebrew tongue, he would only in vain strike upon my outward sense, and my mind within would not be affected with it. If he speak in Latin, I should know what he said. But whence should I know that he spake the truth? should I know this also from him? The truth, that is neither Hebrew, Greek, Latin, nor expressed in any barbarous language, would say unto me inwardly, in the dwelling-place of my thoughts, without the organs of mouth or tongue, or noise of syllables, 'He speaks the truth;' and I with confidence should say unto him, thy servant, 'Thou speakest the truth.' Seeing, therefore, I cannot inquire of him, I beseech thee, that art truth, with whom he being filled spake the truth, I beseech thee, O my God, pardon my sins; and thou who gavest unto him, thy servant, to speak these things, grant unto me to understand them." Thus this holy man ascribes his assent unto the unquestionable principle of the Scripture, as to the effecting of it in himself, to the work of God's Spirit in his heart. As Basil also doth on Ps. cxv.: Πίστις ἡ ὑπὲρ τὰς λογικὰς μεθόδους τὴν ψυχὴν εἰς συγκατάϐασιν ἕλκουσα, ἡ πίστις οὐχ' ἡ γεωμετρικαῖς ἀνάγκαις, ἀλλ' ἡ ταῖς τοῦ Πνεύματος ἐνεργείαις ἐγγινομένη·—"Faith, which draws the soul unto consent above the efficacy of all ways or methods of persuasion; faith, that is wrought and begotten in us, not by geometrical enforcements or demonstrations, but by the effectual operations of the Spirit." And both these principles are excellently expressed by one amongst yourselves, even Baptista Mantuanus, Lib. de Patientia, cap. 32, 33. "Sæpenumero," saith he, "mecum cogitavi, unde tam suadibilis esset ista Scriptura, ut tam potenter influat in animos auditorum; unde tantum habeat energiæ, ut non ad opinandum, sed ad solide credendum, omnes inflectat;"—"I have often thought with myself, whence the Scripture is so persuasive; whence it doth so powerfully influence the minds of the hearers; whence it hath so much efficacy, that it should incline and bow all men, not to think as probable, but solidly to believe, the things it proposeth." "Non," saith he, "est hoc imputandum rationum evidentiæ quas non adducit; non artis industriæ et verbis suavibus et ad persuadendum accommodatis, quibus non utitur;"—"It is not to be ascribed unto the evidence of reasons, which it bringeth not; neither to the excellency of art, sweet words, and accommodated unto persuasion, which it makes no use of." "Sed vide an id in causa sit, quod persuasi sumus eam a Prima Veritate fluxisse;"—"But see if this be not the cause of it, that we are persuaded that it proceeds from the Prime Verity." He proceeds, "Sed unde sumus ita persuasi nisi ab ipsa? quasi ad ei credendum non sua ipsus trahat authoritas. Sed unde quæso hanc sibi authoritatem, vindicavit? Neque enim vidimus nos Deum conscionantem, scribentem, docentem; tamen ac si vidissemus, credimus et tenemus a Spiritu Sancto fluxisse quod legimus. Forsitan fuerit hæc ratio firmiter adhærendi, quod in ea veritas sit solidior, quamvis non clarior. Habet enim omnis veritas vim inclinativam; et major majorem, maxima maximam. Sed cur ergo omnes non credunt evangelio? Respondeo, Quod non omnes trahuntur a Deo." And again, "Inest ergo Scripturis sacris nescio quid naturâ sublimius; id est, inspiratio facta divinitus et divinæ irradiatonis influxus certus." "But whence are we persuaded that it is from the First Verity but from itself? its own authority draws us to believe it. But whence obtains it this authority? We see not God preaching, writing, teaching; but yet, as if we had seen him, we believe and firmly hold that which we read to have come from the Holy Ghost. It may be that this is a reason of our firm adhering unto it, that the truth in it is more solid, though not more clear" (than in any other way of proposal.) "And all truth hath a power to incline unto belief; the greater the truth, the greater its power, and the greatest truth must have the greatest power so to incline us. But why, then, do not all believe the gospel? I answer, Because all are not drawn of God." "There is, then, in the holy Scripture somewhat more sublime than nature; that is, the divine inspiration from whence it is, and the divine irradiation wherewith it is accompanied." This is the principle of Protestants. The sacred Scripture is credible, as proceeding from the First Verity; this it manifests by *its own light and efficacy;* and we are enabled to believe it by the effectual working of the Spirit of God in our hearts. Whence our Saviour asks the Jews, John v. 47, "If ye believe not the writings of Moses, how shall ye believe my words?" They who will not believe the written word of the Scripture upon the authority that it hath in itself, would not believe if Christ should personally speak unto them. So saith Theophylact on the place: Οὐ πιστεύετε τοῖς γεγραμμένοις· καὶ πῶς πιστεύσετε τοῖς ἐμοῖς ἀγράφοις ῥήμασι;

III. Protestants believe and profess that the *end wherefore God gave forth his word by inspiration was, that it might be a stable, infallible revelation of his mind and will* as to that knowledge which he would have mankind entertain of him, with that worship and obedience which he requireth of them, that so they may please him in this world, and come unto the fruition of him unto all eternity. God, who is the formal object, is also the prime cause of all religious worship. What is due unto him as the first cause, last end, and sovereign

Lord of all, as to the substance of it, and what he farther appoints himself as to the manner of its performance, suited unto his own holiness, and the condition wherein in reference unto our last end we stand and are, making up the whole of it,—that he hath given his word to reveal these things unto us, to be our rule, guide, and direction in our ways, walkings, and universal deportment before him, is, as I take it, a fundamental principle of our Christian profession. Neither do I know that this is denied by your church, although you startle at the inferences that are justly made from it. I shall not need, therefore, to add any thing in its confirmation, but only mind you again that the calling of it into question is directly against the very heart of all religion, and the unanimous consent of all that in the world are called Christians, or ever were so. Yea, and it must be granted, or the whole Scripture esteemed a fable, because it frequently declares that it is given unto us of God for this end and purpose. And hence do Protestants infer two other conclusions, on which they build their persuasion concerning the unity of faith, and the proper means of their settlement therein:—

1. That therefore *the Scripture is perfect and every way complete,*—namely, with respect unto that end whereunto of God it is designed; a perfect and complete revelation of the will of God as to his worship and our obedience. And we cannot but wonder that any who profess themselves to believe that it was given for the end mentioned, should not have that sacred reverence for the wisdom, goodness, and love of its Author unto mankind, as freely to assent unto this inference and conclusion: "He is our Rock, and his work is perfect." And lest any men should please themselves in the imagination of contributing any thing towards the effecting of the end of his word by a supply unto it, he hath strictly forbidden them any such addition, Deut. iv. 2, xii. 32, Prov. xxx. 6; which, if it were not complete in reference unto its proper end, would hold no great correspondency with that love and goodness which the same word everywhere declares to be in him. I suppose you know with how many *express testimonies* of Scripture itself this truth is confirmed; which, added unto that light and evidence which, as a deduction from the former fundamental truth, it hath in itself, is very sufficient to render it unquestionable. You may at your leisure, besides those fore-named, consult Ps. xix. 8; Isa. viii. 20; Ezek. xxxvi. 27; Matt. xv. 6; Luke i. 3, 4, xvi. 29, 31, xxiv. 25–27; John v. 39, xx. 9; Acts i. 16, xvii. 2, 3, xx. 27, xxvi. 22; Rom. x. 17, xv. 4; 1 Cor. xiv. 6; Gal. i. 8; Eph. ii. 19, 20; 2 Tim. iii. 16, 17; Heb. i. 1; 2 Pet. i. 19; Rev. xxii. 18. For though texts of Scripture are not appointed for us to "throw at one another's heads," as you talk in your "Fiat," yet they are for us to use and insist on in the confirmation of the

truth, if we may take the example of Christ and all his apostles for our warrant. And it were endless to recite the full and plain testimonies of the ancient fathers and councils to this purpose; neither is that my present design, though I did somewhat occasionally that way upon the former principle. It shall suffice me to show that the denial of this assertion also, as it is inferred from the foregoing principle, is prejudicial, if not pernicious, to Christian religion in general. The whole of our faith and profession is resolved into the known excellencies and perfections of the nature of God. Amongst these there are none that have a more immediate and quickening influence into them than his wisdom, goodness, grace, care, and love towards them unto whom he is pleased to reveal himself; nor is there any property of his nature that in his word he more frequently gives testimony unto. And all of them doth he declare himself to have exalted and glorified in a signal manner, in that revelation which he hath made of himself, his mind and will therein. I suppose this cannot be denied by any who hath the least sense of the importance of the things revealed. Now, if the revelation made for the end before proposed be not perfect and complete,—that is, *sufficient* to enable a man to know so much of God, his mind and will, and to direct him so in his worship and obedience unto him, as that he may please him here and come to the fruition of him hereafter,—it must needs become an evident means of deceiving him and ruining him, and that to all eternity. And the least fear of any such event overthrows all the notions which he had before entertained of those blessed properties of the divine nature; and so, consequently, disposeth him unto atheism. For if a man hath once received the Scripture as the word of God, and that [as] given unto him to be his guide unto heaven by God himself, if one shall come to him and tell him, "Yea, but it is not a perfect guide; but though you should attend sincerely to all the directions that it gives you, yet you may come short of your duty and expectation; you may neither please God here nor come to the fruition of him hereafter;"—in case he should assent unto this suggestion, can he entertain any other thoughts of God but such as our first parents did, when, by attendance unto the false insinuations of the old serpent, they cast off his sovereignty and their dependence on him? Neither can you relieve him against such thoughts by your pretended traditional supply, seeing it will still be impossible for him to look on this revelation of the will of God as imperfect and insufficient for the end for which it plainly professeth itself to be given forth by him, without some intrenchment on those notions of his nature which he had before received; for it will presently occur unto him, that, seeing this way of revealing himself for the ends mentioned is good, and approved of himself so to be, if he hath not made it complete for that end, it was either because he could not; and where, then, is his *wisdom?* or because he would not; and where, then, is his *love*, care, and goodness? and seeing he saith he hath done what you would have him to believe that he hath not done, where is his *truth* and veracity? Certainly, a man that seriously ponders what he hath to do, and knows the vanity of an irrational, fanatical "credo," will conclude that either the Scripture is to be received as perfect or not to be received at all.

2. Protestants conclude hence, *That the Scripture, given of God for this purpose, is intelligible unto men using the means by God appointed to come to the understanding of his mind and will therein.* I know many of your way are pleased grievously to mistake our intention in this inference and conclusion. Sometimes they would impose upon us to say that all places of Scripture, all words and sentences in it, are plain, and of an obvious sense, and easy to be understood. And yet this you know, or may know if you please, and, I am sure, ought to know before you talk of these things with us, that we absolutely deny. It is one thing to say that *all necessary truth* is plainly and clearly revealed in the Scripture, which we do say; and another, that *every text and passage* in the Scripture is plain and easy to be understood, which we do not say, nor ever thought, as confessing that to say so were to contradict our own experience and that of the disciples of Christ in all ages. Sometimes you feign as though we asserted *all the things that are revealed* in the Scripture to be plain and obvious to every man's understanding; whereas we acknowledge that the things themselves revealed are many of them mysterious, surpassing the comprehension of any man in this world, and only maintain that the propositions wherein the revelation of them is made are plain and intelligible unto them that use the means appointed of God to come to a right understanding of them. And sometimes you would commit this with another principle of ours, whereby we assert that the *supernatural light of grace*, to be wrought in our hearts by the Holy Ghost, is necessary to give unto us a saving perception and understanding of the mind of God in the Scripture; for what needs such special assistance in so plain a matter? as though the asserting of the perspicuity in the object made ability to discern in the subject altogether unnecessary, or that he who affirms the sun to give *light* doth at the same time affirm also that men have no need of *eyes* to see it withal. Besides, we know there is a vast difference between a notional speculative apprehension and perception of the meaning and truth of the propositions contained in the Scripture,—which we acknowledge that every reasonable, unprejudiced person may attain unto,—and a gracious, saving, spiritual perception of them, and assent unto them with faith divine

and supernatural; and this, we say, is the especial work of the Holy Ghost in the hearts of the elect. And I know not how many other exceptions you make to keep yourselves from a right understanding of our intention in this inference; but, as yourself elsewhere learnedly observe, "Who so blind as he that will not see?" I shall therefore once more, that we may proceed, declare unto you what it is that we intend in this assertion;—it is, namely, that the things which are revealed in the Scripture, to the end that, by the belief of them and obedience unto them, we may please God, are so proposed and declared that a man, any man, free from prejudices and temptations, in and by the use of the means appointed him of God for that purpose, may come to the understanding (and that infallibly) of all that God would have him know or do in religion, there being no defect or hinderance in the Scripture, or manner of its revealing things necessary, that should obstruct him therein. What are the means appointed of God for this purpose we do not now inquire, but shall anon declare. What defect, blindness, or darkness there is, may be, in and upon the minds of men in their depraved, lapsed condition,—what disadvantages they may be cast under by their prejudices, traditions, negligences, sins, and profaneness,—belongs not unto our present disquisition. That which we assert concerns merely the manner of the proposal of the truths to be believed which are revealed in the Scripture; and this, we say, is such as that there is no impossibility, no, nor great difficulty, but that a man may come to the right understanding of them,—not as to the comprehension of the things themselves, but the perception of the sense of the propositions wherein they are expressed. And this assertion of ours is, as the former, grounded on the Scripture itself. See, if you please, Deut. xxx. 11; Ps. xix. 8, cxix. 105; Prov. vi. 23; 2 Cor. iv. 3; 2 Pet. i. 19. And to deny it is to pluck up all religion by the roots, and to turn men loose unto scepticism, libertinism, and atheism; and that with such a horrid reproach unto God himself, as that nothing more abominable can be invented. The devil of old, being not able to give out certain answers unto them that came to inquire about their concernments at his oracles, put them off a long time with dubious, enigmatical, unintelligible sophisms; but when once the world had, by experience, study, and observation, improved itself into a wisdom beyond the pitch of its first rudeness, men began generally to despise what they saw could not be certainly understood. This made the devil pluck in his horns, as not finding it for the interest of his kingdom to expose himself to be scoffed at by them with whose follies and fanatical credulity, in esteeming highly of that which could not be understood, he had for many generations sported himself. And do they not blasphemously expose the oracles of the true, holy, and living God to no less contempt, who, for their own sinister ends, would frighten men from them with the ugly scarecrow of *obscurity*, or their not being intelligible unto every man by the use of means, so far as he is concerned to know them, and the mind of God in them? And herein also Protestants stand as firmly as the fundamentals of Christianity will bear them.

IV. Protestants believe that *it is the duty of all men who desire to know the will of God, and to worship him according unto his mind, to use diligence, in the improvement of the means appointed for that end*, to come unto a right and full understanding of all things in the Scripture wherein their faith and obedience are concerned. This *necessarily* follows from the principles before laid down; nor is it possible it should be otherwise. It is doubtless incumbent on every man to study and know his duty. That cannot be a man's duty which he is not bound to know, especially not such a duty as whereon his eternal welfare should depend; and I suppose a man can take no better course to come to the knowledge of his duty than that which God hath appointed for that purpose. His commands and exhortations, which we have given us in the Scripture, for our diligence in this matter, with the explications and improvements of them in the writings of the fathers, are so obvious, trite, and known, that it were mere loss of time to insist on the repetition of them. I suppose I should speak within compass if I should say that one Chrysostom doth, in a hundred places, exhort Christians of all sorts to the diligent study and search of the Scriptures, and especially of the epistles of Paul,—not the most plain and easy part of them. I know the practice of your church lies to the contrary, and what you plead in the justification of that practice; but I am sorry both for her and you,—both for the contrivers of, and consenters unto, this abomination; and I fear what your account will be as to this matter at the last day. God having granted the inestimable benefit of his word unto mankind, revealing therein unto them the only way by which they may attain unto a blessed eternity, is it not the greatest ingratitude that any man can possibly contract the guilt of, to neglect the use of it? What, then, is your condition, who, upon slight and trivial pretences, set up your own wisdom and authority against the wisdom and authority of God; advising and commanding men, upon the pain of your displeasure in this world, not to attend unto that which God commands them to attend unto, on pain of his displeasure in the world to come? So that though I confess that you deny this principle, yet I cannot see but that you do so, not only upon the hazard of your own souls and the souls of them that attend unto you, seeing that "if the blind lead the blind, both must fall into the ditch;" but also that you do it to the great prejudice of Christian religion in the very foundations of it. For what can a man rationally conclude, that shall see you driving all persons, and that on no small penalties, excepting yourselves who are concerned in the conspiracy, and some few others whom you suppose sufficiently initiated in your mysteries, from the reading and study of those books wherein the world knows, and yourselves confess, that the arcana of Christian religion are contained, but that there are some things in them, like the hidden "sacra" of the old pagan hierophants, which may not be disclosed, because, however countenanced by a remote veneration, yet are [they] indeed "turpia" or "ridicula,"—things to be ashamed of or scorned? And the truth is, some of your doctors have spoken very suspiciously this way, whilst they justify your practice in driving the people from the study of the Scripture, by intimations of things and expressions not so pure and chaste as to be fit for the knowledge of the promiscuous multitude; when, in the meantime, themselves or their associates do publish unto all the world, in their rules and directions for confession, such abominable filth and ribaldry as, I think, was never by any other means vented amongst mankind.

V. Protestants say that *the Lord Christ hath instituted his church, and therein appointed a ministry to preside over the rest of his disciples in his name, and to unfold unto them his mind and will as recorded in his word;* for which end he hath promised his presence with them by his Spirit unto the end of the world, to enable them, in an humble dependence on his assistance, to find out and declare his commands and appointments unto their brethren. This position, I suppose, you will not contend with us about; although I know that you put another sense upon most of the terms of it than the Scripture will allow, or we can admit of.

These are the principles of Protestants; this is the progress of their faith in coming unto settlement and assurance. These are the foundations, which are as unquestionable as any thing in Christianity; the *most* of them, yourselves being judges. And from them one of these two things will necessarily follow,—either, That all men, unto whom the word of God doth come, will come to *an agreement* in the truth, or the unity of faith; or, secondly, That it is their *own fault* if they do not so do: for what, upon these principles, should hinder them from so doing? All saving truth is revealed by God in the Scripture, unto the end that men may come to the knowledge of it. It is so revealed by him that it is possible, and, with his assistance, easy, for men to know aright his mind and will about these things so revealed; and he hath appointed *regular ways* and *means* for men to wait upon him in and by, for the obtaining of his assistance. Now, pray, revive your *question* that gave occasion unto this discourse,—However men may differ in religion, why is not the Scripture *sufficient* to bring them unto an agreement and settlement? Take heed that in your answer you deny not some principle that will involve the whole interest of Christianity in its ruin. Where is the defect? where the hinderance why all men, upon these principles, however differing at present, may not come to a full settlement and agreement? I hope you will find none but what are in themselves; and for them, "ipsi viderint," the Scripture is blameless. Here is certainty of revelation from God,—fulness of that revelation as to our duty, clearness and perspicuity for our understanding of it,—means appointed and sanctified for that end; what, I pray, is wanting? All truths wherein it is the duty of men to agree are fixed and stated, so that it can never be lawful for any man, in any generation, to call any of them into question;—plain and evident, that no man can mistake the mind of God in them in things wherein his duty is concerned, without his own crime and guilt. You will say, then, it may be, "But why, then, do not men agree? why do you not agree among yourselves?" But I would hope that it is scarcely possible for any man to be so ignorant of the condition of mankind, and amongst them of the best of men, as seriously to ask this question. Are not all men naturally blind in the things of God? Do not the best of men know only in part? Have not the different tempers, constitutions, and educations of men a great influence upon their understandings and judgments? Besides, do not lust, corruptions, carnal interests, and respect unto worldly things, bear sway in the minds of many that profess Christian religion? Are not many prepossessed with prejudices, traditions, customs, and usages against the truth? And are not these things, and the like, sufficient to keep up variance in the world, without the least suspicion of any disability in the Scripture to bring them to a holy agreement and immovable settlement? Neither is there any other way for men to come unto settlement and agreement in religion, according to the mind of God, but that only which hath been now proposed; and this they will come unto when all men shall be persuaded to captivate their understandings to the obedience of faith. I deny not that by *outward force* and compulsion, by *supine negligence* of their own concernments, by refusing to bethink themselves, and such other ways and means, some men may come to some agreement amongst themselves in the things of religion. But this agreement, we say, is not of God, it is not built upon τὸ θεμέλιον τῆς πίστεως ἐπὶ Θεόν,—"the foundation of faith towards God;" and so is of no esteem with him. That such is all the unity which, on your principles, you are able to bring men unto, we shall manifest in our next discourse. For the present, I dare challenge you, or any man in the world, to question or oppose any one of the principles before laid down; and which, whilst they stand firm, it is evident unto all how the Scripture is able to settle men unquestionably in the truth, and that for ever, ὅπερ ἔδει δεῖξαι. I shall close this discourse with a passage out of Chrysostom, which fully confirms all that I have asserted; it is in Homil. 33, in Act. Apost. cap. xv. Τί οὖν, saith he, ἂν εἴπωμεν πρὸς τοὺς Ἕλληνας; Ἔρχεται Ἕλλην, καὶ λέγει ὅτι βούλομαι γενέσθαι Χριστιανὸς, ἀλλ' οὐκ οἶδα τίνι προσθῶμαι.—"What shall we say unto the Gentiles? A Gentile cometh and saith, 'I would be a Christian, but I know not unto whom amongst you I should adhere.'" Let us hear the reasons of his hesitation. Saith he, Μάχη παρ' ὑμῖν πολλὴ καὶ στάσις, πολὺς θόρυβος· ποῖον ἕλωμαι δόγμα; τί αἱρήσομαι; ἕκαστος λέγει ὅτι ἀληθεύω· τίνι πεισθῶ; μηδὲν ὅλως εἰδὼς ἐν ταῖς γραφαῖς·—"There are many contentions, seditions, and tumults amongst you: what opinion to choose I know not. Every one says, I am in the truth; [whom shall I believe?] I am utterly ignorant of what is in the Scripture about these things." Do you know whose objections these are, and by whom they have been lately managed? Will you hear what Chrysostom answers? Saith he, Πάνυ γε τοῦτο ὑπὲρ ἡμῶν· εἰ μὲν γὰρ λογισμοῖς ἐλέγομεν πείθεσθαι, εἰκότως ἐθορυβοῦ· εἰδὲ ταῖς γραφαῖς λέγομεν πιστεύειν, αὗται δὲ ἁπλαῖ καὶ ἀληθεῖς, εὔκολόν σοι τὸ κρινόμενον· εἴ τις ἐκείναις συμφωνεῖ, οὗτος Χριστιανός· εἴ τις μάχεται, οὗτος πόῤῥω τοῦ κανόνος τούτου·—"This makes wholly for us; for if we should say that we believe on probable reasonings, thou mayst justly be troubled; but seeing we profess that we believe in the Scriptures, which are plain and true, it is easy for thee to judge and determine. He that yields his consent unto them, he is a Christian; and he that contends against them is far from the rule of Christianity." And in the process of his discourse, which is well worth the perusal before you write any more familiar epistles, he requires no more of a man to settle him in the truth, but that he receive the Scripture, and have νοῦν καὶ κρίσιν, "a mind and judgment," to use in the consideration of it.

It remaineth now that we consider what it is that you propose unto men to bring them unto a settlement in religion, and all Christians to the unity of faith, with the principles that you proceed upon to that purpose; which, because I would not too far lengthen out this discourse, I shall refer to the next chapter.

CHAPTER VIII.

Principles of Papists, whereon they proceed in bringing men to a settlement in religion and the unity of faith, examined.

YOUR plea to this purpose is blended with a double pretence of pope and church. Sometimes you tell us of the pope and his succession to St Peter, and sometimes of the church and its authority. Sometimes you speak as if both these were one and the same; and sometimes you seem to distinguish them. Some of you lay most weight upon the *papal succession* and *infallibility;* and some on the *church's jurisdiction* and *authority.* I shall crave leave to take your pleas asunder, and first to consider what force they have in them, as unto the end whereunto they are applied, severally and apart; and then see what, in their joint concurrence, they can contribute thereunto. And whatever you think of it, I suppose this course of proceeding will please ingenuous persons and lovers of truth, because it enables them to take a distinct view of the things whereon they are to give judgment; whereas in your handling of them, something you suppose, something you insinuate, something you openly aver, yet so confound them with other heterogeneous discourses, that it can hardly be discerned what grounds you build upon;—a way of proceeding which, as it argues a secret guilt and fear of bringing forth your principles to light, so a gross kind of sophistry exploded by all masters of reason whatsoever. They would not have us "fumum ex fulgore, sed ex fumo dare lucem,"—"darken things clear and perspicuous in themselves, but to make things dark and confused perspicuous." And the orator tells us that Epicurus's discourse was ambiguous, because his "sententia" was "inhonesta,"—"his opinion shameful." And to what purpose should any one contend with you about such general ambiguous expressions, ὥσπερ ἐν νυκτομαχίᾳ? I shall, then, begin with the pope and his *infallibility*, because you seem to lay most weight thereon, and tell us plainly, p. 379 of your "Fiat," second edition, "That if the pope be not an unerring guide in affairs of religion, all is lost;" and that "a man once rid of his authority may as easily deride and as solidly confute the incarnation as the sprinkling of holy water:" so resolving our faith of the incarnation of Christ into his authority or testimony. Yea, and in the same page, "That if it had not been for the pope, Christ himself had not been taken in the world for any such person as he is believed this day;" and p. 378, to the same purpose, "The first great fundamental of Christian religion, which is the truth and divinity of Christ, had it not been for him, had failed long ago in the world;" with much more to the same purpose. Hence it is evident that, in your judgment, all truth and certainty in religion depends on the pope's authority and infallibility; or, as you express it, "his unerring guidance." This is your principle, this you propose as the only medium to bring us unto that settlement in religion which you suppose the Scripture is not able to do. What course should we now take? would you have us believe you at the first word, without farther trial or examination? would you have a man to do so who never before heard of pope or church? We are commanded to "try all things, and to hold fast that which is good;" to try pretending spirits. And the Bereans are commended for examining by the Scripture what Paul himself preached unto them. An implicit credulity given up to such dictates is the height of fanaticism. Have we not reason, then, to call you and your co-partners in this design to an account how you prove that which you so strenuously assert and suppose, and to examine the principles of that authority whereunto you resolve all your faith and religion? If, upon mature consideration, these prove solid, and the inferences you make from them cogent, it is good reason that you should be attended unto. If they prove otherwise, if the first be false and the latter sophistical, you cannot justly take it ill of him that shall advise you to take heed that, whilst you are gloriously displaying your colours, the ground that you stand upon do not sink under your feet. And here you are forced to go many a step backward to fix your first footing (until you leave your pope quite out of sight), from whence you advance towards him by several degrees, and so arrive at his supremacy and infallibility; and so we shall have "reditum Diomedis ab interitu Meleagri."[1]

I. Your first principle to this purpose is, "That Peter was the prince of the apostles, and that in him the Lord Jesus founded a monarchy in his church." So, p. 360, you call him "The head and prince of the whole congregation." Now, this we think no meet principle for any one to begin withal, in asserting the foundation of faith and religion; nor do we think that if it were meet so to be used, that it is any way subservient unto your design and purpose.

1. *A principle, fundamental, or first entrance into any way of settlement in faith or religion, it cannot possibly be,* because it presupposeth the knowledge of, and assent unto, many other great fundamental articles of Christian religion, yea, upon the matter, all that are so: for before you can rationally talk with a man about Peter's principality, and the monarchical state of the church hereon depending, you must suppose that he *believes the Scripture* to be the word of God, and all things that are taught therein concerning Jesus Christ, his person, nature, offices, work, and gospel, to be certainly and infallibly true; for they are all supposed in your assertion, which without the knowledge of them is uncouth, horrid, insignificant, and foreign to all notions that a man can rationally entertain of God or religion; nay, no attempt of proof or confirmation can be given unto it but by and from Scripture, whereby you fall directly into the principle which you seek so carefully to avoid,—namely, that the Scripture is the only way and means of settling us in the truth, since you cannot settle any man in the very first proposition which you make to lead him into another way but by the Scripture. So powerful is truth, that those who will not follow it *willingly*, it will lead them *captive* in triumph, whether they will or no.

2. *It is unmeet for any purpose, because it is not true.* No one

[1] Hor. ad Pisones, 146.

word from the Scripture can you produce in its confirmation; where yet if it be not revealed, it must pass as a very uncertain and frivolous conjecture. You can produce no suffrage of the ancient church unto your purpose; which yet if you could, would not presently render any assertion so confirmed infallibly certain, much less fundamental. Some, indeed, of the fourth century call Peter "Principem apostolorum;" but explain themselves to intend thereby τὸν πρῶτον, "the first," or leader, not τὸν ἄρχοντα, "the prince," or ruler. And when the ambiguity of that word began to be abused unto pretensions of pre-eminence, the council of Carthage expressly condemned it, allowing none to be termed "Princeps sacerdotum." Many in those days thought Peter to be among the apostles like the "Princeps senatus," or "Princeps civitatis," the chief in their assemblies, or principal in dignity, how truly I know not: but that he should be amongst them and over them *a prince in office*, a monarch as to rule and power, is a thing that they never once dreamed of; and the asseveration of it is an open untruth. The apostles were equal in their call, office, place, dignity, employments: all the difference between them was in their labours, sufferings, and success, wherein Paul seems to have had the pre-eminence; who, as Peter and all the rest of the apostles, every one singly and for himself, had the care of all the churches committed unto him, though it may be, for the better discharge of their duty ordinarily they divided their work, as they found it necessary for them to apply themselves unto it in particular. See 2 Cor. xi. And this equality between the apostles is more than once insinuated by Paul, and that with special reference unto Peter, 1 Cor. i.; Gal. i. 18, 19, ii. 9. And is it not wonderful, that if this assertion should not only be true, but such a truth as on which the whole faith of the church was to be built, that the Scripture should be utterly silent of it, that it should give us no rules about it, no directions to use and improve it, afford us no one instance of the exercise of the power and authority intimated, no, not one; but that, on the contrary, it should lay down principles exclusive of it? Matt. xx. 25, 26; Luke xxii. 25, 26; and when it comes to make an enumeration of all the offices appointed by Christ in his church, Eph. iv. 11, should pass over the prince and his office in silence, on which all the rest were to depend? You see what a foundation you begin to build upon,—a mere imagination and groundless presumption, which hath not the least countenance given unto it by Scripture or antiquity. What a perplexed condition must you needs cast men into, if they shall attend unto your persuasions to rest on the pope's unerring guidance for all their certainty in religion, when the first motive you propose unto them, to gain their assent, is a proposition so far destitute of any cogent evidence of its truth or innate credibility, that it is *apparently false*, and easily manifested so to be!

3. Were it never so true, as it is notoriously false, yet it *would not one jot promote your design.* It is about Peter the apostle, and not the pope of Rome, that we are discoursing. Do you think a man can easily commence, "per saltum," from the imaginary principality of Peter, unto the infallibility of the *present pope* of Rome? "Quid papæ cum Petro?" what relation is there between the one and other? Suppose a man have so good a mind unto your company as to be willing to set out with you in this ominous stumbling at the threshold, what will you next lead him into? You say,—

II. "That St Peter, besides his apostolical power and office (wherein, setting aside the prerogative of his princedom before mentioned, the rest of the apostles were partakers with him), had also an œcumenical episcopal power invested in him, which was to be transmitted unto others after him." His office purely apostolical you have no mind to lay claim unto. It may be you despair of being able to prove that your pope is immediately called and sent by Christ; that he is furnished with a power of working miracles, and such other things as concurred to the constitution of the office apostolical. And perhaps himself hath but little mind to be exercised in the discharge of that office, by travelling up and down, poor, despised, persecuted, to preach the gospel. *Monarchy, rule, supremacy, authority, jurisdiction, infallibility,* are words that better please him; and therefore have you mounted this notion of Peter's episcopacy, whereunto you would have us think that all the fine things you so love and dote upon are annexed. Poor, labouring, persecuted Peter the *apostle,* may die and be forgotten; but Peter the *bishop,* harnessed with power, principality, sovereignty, and vicarship of Christ, this is the man you inquire after: but you will have very hard work to find him in the Scripture, or antiquity, yea, the least footstep of him. And do you think, indeed, that this episcopacy of Peter, distinct from his apostleship, is a meet stone to be laid in the foundation of faith? It is a thing that plainly overthrows his apostleship: for if he were a *bishop,* properly and distinctly, he was no *apostle,*—if an *apostle,* not such a *bishop;* that is, if his care were confined unto any one church, and his residence required therein, as the case is with a proper bishop, how could the care of all the churches be upon him? how could he be obliged to pass up and down the world in pursuit of his commission of preaching the gospel unto all nations, or to travel up and down as the necessity of the churches did require? But you will say that he was not bishop of this or that particular, but of the church universal; but I supposed you had thought him bishop of the church of Rome, and that you will plead him afterward so to have been. And I must assure you that he that thinks the church of Rome, in the days of Peter and Paul, was the same with the church catholic, and not looked on [as being] as particular a church as that of Jerusalem, or Ephesus, or Corinth, is a person with whom I will have as little to do as I can in this matter. For to what purpose should any one spend time to debate things with men absurd and unreasonable, and who will affirm that it is midnight at noon-day? I know the apostolical office did include in it the power of all other offices in the church whatever, as the less are included in the greater; but that he who was an apostle should formally also be a bishop, though an apostle might exercise the whole power and office of a bishop, is ἐκ τῶν ἀδυνάτων,—somewhat allied unto impossibilities. Do you see what a quagmire you are building upon? I know if a man will let you alone, you will raise a structure, which, after you have painted and gilded, you may prevail with many harbourless creatures to accept of an habitation therein: for when you have laid your foundation out of sight, you will pretend that all your building is on a rock; whereas, indeed, you have nothing but the rotten posts of such suppositions as these to support it withal. But suppose that Peter was thus a prince, monarch, apostle, bishop,—that is, a catholic, particular officer,—what is that to you? Why,—

III. "This Peter came and preached the gospel at Rome." Though you can by no means prove this assertion so as to make it "de fide," or necessarily to be believed of any one man in the world, much less to become meet to enjoy a place among those fundamentals that are tendered unto us to bring us unto settlement in religion, yet, being a matter very uncertain and of little importance, I shall not much contend with you about it. Witnesses merely human and fallible you have for it a great many; and exceptions almost without number may be put in against your testimonies, and those of great weight and moment. Now, although that which you affirm might be granted you without any real advantage unto your cause, or the enabling of you to draw any lawful inferences to uphold your papal claim by, yet, to let you see on what sorry, uncertain presumptions you build your faith and profession, and that in and about things which you make of indispensable necessity unto salvation, I shall in our passage remind you of some few of them, which, I profess seriously unto you, make it not only questionable unto me whether or no, but also somewhat improbable, that ever Peter came to Rome.[1] 1. Though those

[1] It may be useful to the general reader if we indicate briefly the present state of the controversy in regard to Peter's residence in Rome. *The opinions in regard to his connection with it* may be reduced under three divisions. Some ascribe to him a lengthened residence in Rome, during which he acted not merely as bishop of the church in that city, but exercised a species of primacy over the rest of the apostles. This view, which the church of Rome generally is disposed to uphold, is exhibited by the following writers:—Baronius, in his "Annales," A.D. 44–46, 56, 69; Bellarmine, "De Rom. Pontif.," lib. ii.; and Cortesius, "De Romano itinere gestisque Principis Apostolorum."

There are authorities, again, who deny that Peter ever was at Rome. It would appear that the Waldenses held this view, and that they have been followed in it by Mat. Flacius, Claude Salmasius, Fred. Spanheim ("De Fictâ Profectione Petri Apostoli

that follow and give their assents unto this story are *many*, yet it was taken up upon the credit and report of *one* or *two* persons; as Eusebius manifests, lib. ii. cap. 25. Whether Dionysius Corinthius or Papias first began the story I know not; but I know certainly that both of them manifested themselves, in other things, to be a little too credulous. 2. That which many of them built their credulity upon is very uncertain, if not certainly false,—namely, that Peter *wrote his first epistle from Rome*, which he calls Babylon in the subscription of it. But wherefore he should then so call it, no man can tell. The Apocalypse of John, who prophesied what Rome should be in after ages, and thereon what name should be accommodated unto it for its false worship and persecution, was not yet written. Nor was there any thing yet spoken of or known among the disciples, whence they might conjecture Rome to be intended by that appellation. So that, according unto this supposition, St Peter, intending to acquaint them unto whom he wrote where he was when he wrote unto them, and to present them with the respects of

in Urbem Romam," 1679), Eichhorn (in his "Introduction to the New Testament"), De Wette (in his "Introduction to the New Testament"), and Baur (in a work entitled "Der Apostel Paulus").

The middle opinion,—which rejects the traditions about Peter having been the founder of the church at Rome, and having presided as bishop over it for the space of twenty-five years, but admits the fact that he visited it shortly before his death, and suffered martyrdom in it,—has been entertained even by some Roman Catholic authors, such as Hug (in his "Introduction to the New Testament"). Several Protestant writers have yielded this modified credence to the old tradition:—Salom. Van Til ("De Petro Romæ Martyre, non Pontifice," 1710), Barrow (in his "Treatise on the Pope's Supremacy"), Credner ("Introduction," i. 628), Gieseler ("Eccles. Hist.," i. 78), Olshausen ("Introduction to the Epistle to the Romans"), Guerike ("Introduction"), and Wieseler ("On the Chronology of the Gospel and the Apostolic Age"). A translation of Wieseler's discussion of this question appeared in vol. v. of Dr Kitto's "Journal of Sacred Literature," and we refer to it as containing in detail several facts and references at which we can only hint in the compass of a note.

The substance of the *ancient testimony* may be briefly given:—CLEMENS ROMANUS (Epist. i. cap. 5) affirms that Peter suffered martyrdom, but does not specify the place; and it is only by inference we learn from Clemens that the martyrdom of the apostle took place at Rome. In the PRÆDICATIO PAULI, the conclusion of a work entitled "Prædicatio Petri," and referred, on good evidence, to the beginning of the second century, it was affirmed that Peter and Paul, "having come to an arrangement as to the method of conducting their labours, *at last*, as if then for the first time, became acquainted *in the City*" (Rome). That such a statement was contained in the "Prædicatio," appears from a treatise, "De Rebaptismate," printed commonly among the works of Cyprian. The author of the treatise, however, alludes to the tradition of such a meeting between Paul and Peter as among "quædam alia hujuscemodi absurde ac turpiter confecta" in the "Prædicatio." The testimonies of three writers have been preserved by Eusebius ("Hist. Eccles.," ii. 15 and 25):—PAPIAS, who is represented as affirming that Peter composed his first Epistle at Rome; DIONYSIUS of Corinth (A.D. 170), who makes Peter and Paul to have preached in Italy together, and to have suffered martyrdom about the same time; and CAIUS ROMANUS (A.D. 200), who declares that the graves of these two apostles were pointed out at the Vatican and on the Ostian road. IGNATIUS ("Epist. ad Rom.," cap. iv.) merely says, "I do not, like Peter and Paul, give you directions;" which words are understood to imply that Peter and Paul, in the belief of Ignatius, had at one time instructed and governed the church at Rome. IRENÆUS ("Adv. Haer.," iii. 1) speaks of Peter and Paul having preached and founded the church in Rome." TERTULLIAN ("De Præs. Haer.," cap. xxxvi.)

the church in that place, had, by an enigmatical expression, rather amused than informed them. Besides, he had before this agreed with and solemnly engaged himself unto Paul to take care of the Circumcision; unto whom, after he had preached a while in Palestine, it is more than probable that he betook himself unto Babylon in Assyria,—the principal seat of their residence in their first and most populous dispersion,—from whence he wrote unto all their colonies scattered abroad in the neighbouring nations. So that although I will not, because of the consent of many of the ancients, deny that Peter went to Rome and preached there, yet I am fully satisfied that this foundation of the story told by them is a perfect mistake, consisting in an unwarrantable, causeless wresting of a plain expression unto a mystical sense and meaning. 3. Your witnesses agree not at all in their story; neither as to the time of his going to Rome nor as to the occasion of it, nor as to the season of his abode there. Many of them assign unto him twenty-five years for his residence there, which is evidently false, and easily disproved. This computa-

specifies the nature of their death at Rome:—"Ubi Petrus passioni Dominicæ adæquatur, ubi Paulus Johannis (Baptistæ) exitu coronatur." These quotations and references embody the amount of information conveyed to us by the original and ancient testimony, on which succeeding writers have relied in affirming that Peter visited Rome, and suffered there. Arnobius ("Adv. Gentes," lib. ii.) and Cyril of Jerusalem ("De Hæres.," cap. xv.) also concur in stating that Peter was in Rome; but these authors belong to the fourth century.

The authority of *Scripture* in this question comes in to determine when it is most likely that Peter arrived at Rome; and this point is fully discussed by our author. According to the "Chronicon" of Eusebius, he reached it about A.D. 42, and was put to death about twenty-five years afterwards, or A.D. 67. But, by a reference to Acts xv., Gal. ii. 1, 9, 11, it will be found that Peter was at Jerusalem and Antioch, and had been chiefly labouring among the Circumcision, up to A.D. 54; facts which make it impossible that he could have been residing *constantly* at Rome, and very improbable that up to that period he ever had seen Rome at all. There is, farther, no allusion to Peter in the Epistle to the Romans, A.D. 58; and this circumstance is the more remarkable, when the conclusion of it is filled with affectionate salutations to several members of the Roman church. Paul is understood to have been brought to Rome about the spring of A.D. 61; and while Luke records no interview with Peter, he also uses language as if, almost for the first time, the gospel had been unfolded to the Jews in Rome through the instrumentality of Paul, Acts xxviii. 17–31. If Peter was at Rome during the imprisonment of Paul, how are we to account for the absence of any allusion to him in all the epistles written by Paul at Rome—the Epistles to the Colossians, Philippians, Philemon, and Timothy? In the Second Epistle to Timothy,—the last which Paul wrote,—there is nothing which indicates the presence of Peter at Rome; or, if he were at Rome, he must have been in the number of those who deserted Paul in his extremity, 2 Tim. iv. 16; an inference, however, which must be rejected on other grounds than the discredit it reflects on one who, according to the Romish church, was the first of the popes. By the Second Epistle to Timothy we are brought to A.D. 63; and if he suffered in A.D. 67, this allows but four years for his residence in Rome. Ancient tradition makes the martyrdom of Paul and Peter simultaneous, and the date of Paul's martyrdom varies, according to different authorities, from A.D. 64 to A.D. 68. If the former date be assumed as correct, the time during which Peter was in Rome fell short of a year; if the latter be correct, he might have been there for four or five years. But it cannot be ascertained when he reached Rome; and the length of the interval between his arrival in it and his martyrdom involves a question for the determination of which no materials in the shape of authentic history remain to us.—ED.

tion is ascribed to Eusebius in Chron. lib. i.; but it is evidently an addition of Jerome's, in whose days the tradition was increased, for there is no such thing in the original Greek copy of Eusebius, nor doth it agree with what he had elsewhere written concerning him. And it is very well worth while to consider how Onuphrius Panvinus, a very learned antiquary of your own party, makes up these twenty-five years of Peter's episcopacy at Rome, Annotat. in Plat. in Vit. B. Petr. "Ex novem primis annis," saith he, "post Christi mortem, usque ad initium secundi anni Imperii Claudii, Petrum Judæâ nunquam excessisse, ex Actis Apostolorum, et Pauli Epistola ad Galatas, apertissime constat. Si igitur, ut inter omnes authores convenit, eo tempore Romam venit, illud certe necessarium videtur eum ante ad urbem adventum Antiochiæ septem annis non sedisse; sed hanc ejus Antiochenam cathedram alio tempore fuisse. Quam rem ex vetustissimorum authorum testimonio sic constitui: Secundo Imperii Claudii anno Romam venit; a quo tempore usque ad illius obitum, anni plus minus viginti quinque intersunt, quibus, etsi eum Romæ sedisse veteres scribunt, non tamen præterea sequitur, ipsum semper in urbe commoratum esse: nam, quarto anno ejus ad urbem adventus, Hierusolymam reversus est, et ibi concilio apostolorum interfuit; inde Antiochiam profectus, septem ibidem annis usque ad Neronis Imperium permansit, cujus initio Romam reversus Romanam dilabentem reparavit ecclesiam. Peregrinatione inde per universam fere Europam suscepta, Romam rediens novissimo Neronis Imperii anno, martyrium crucis passus est;"—"For the first nine years after the death of Christ, unto the beginning of the second year of Claudius, it is most evident, from the Acts, and Epistle to the Galatians, that Peter went not out of Palestine. If therefore, as all agree, he came at that time to Rome, it is certain that he had not abode at Antioch seven years before his coming thither (which yet all the witnesses agree in); but this his Antiochian chair fell out at some other time. Wherefore, I thus order the whole matter from the testimony of most ancient authors" (not that any one before him ever wrote any such thing, but this he supposeth may be said to reconcile their contradictions): "In the second year of Claudius he came to Rome. From thence unto his death were twenty-five years, more or less: which space of time, although the ancients write that he sat at Rome, yet it doth not follow thence that he always abode in the city; for, in the fourth year after his coming, he returned unto Jerusalem to be present at the council of the apostles; thence going unto Antioch, he continued there seven years, unto the reign of Nero. In the beginning of his reign, he returned unto Rome, to repair the decaying church there. From thence, passing almost through all Europe, he returned again to Rome in the last year of Nero, and underwent martyrdom by the cross." You may easily discern the uncertainty, at least, of that story, which this learned man can give no countenance unto but by multiplying improbable imaginations to shelter one another. For,—(1.) Who ever said that Peter came from Rome to come up to the council at Jerusalem, when it is most manifest, from the story of the Acts, that he had never before departed out of Judea? And this council being granted to have been in the sixth year of Claudius, as here it is by Onuphrius, quite overthrows the tradition of his going to Rome in his second. (2.) The abode of twenty-five years at Rome, as thus disposed, is no abode indeed; for he continued almost twice as long at Antioch as he did at Rome. (3.) Here is no time at all allowed unto him for preaching the gospel in Galatia, Cappadocia, Asia, and Bithynia, which certainly are not provinces of Europe; in which places Eusebius, Hist. lib. iii. cap. 1, Origen, and all the ancients, agree that he did attend unto his apostleship towards the Jews, and his epistles make it evident. (4.) Nor is there any time left for him to be at Babylon, where yet we know he was. So that this fancy can have no countenance given it without a full rejection of all that we know to be true in the story. 4. The Scripture is *utterly silent* of any such thing *as Peter's going to Rome.* Other journeyings of his it records, as to Samaria, Lydda, Joppa, Cæsarea, Antioch. Now, it was no way material that his coming unto any of these places should be known but only in reference unto the things done there by him, and yet they are recorded; but this his going to Rome, which is supposed to be of such huge importance in Christian religion, and that, according to Onuphrius, falling out in the midst of his other journeyings, as it must do if ever it fell out, is utterly passed by in silence. If it had been to have such an influence into the very being of Christianity as now is pretended, some men will be apt to think that the mention of it would not have been omitted. 5. *Paul,* in his Epistle to the Romans, written a good while after this imaginary going of Peter to Rome, makes no mention of him, when yet he saluted by name those of chief note and dignity in the church there; so that, undoubtedly, he was not then come thither. 6. *The same apostle being at Rome in the reign of Nero,* in the midst of the time allotted unto the abode of Peter there, *never once mentions him* in any of the epistles which from thence he wrote unto the churches and his fellow-labourers, though he doth remember very many others that were with him in the city. 7. He asserts that, in one of his epistles from thence, which, as I think, sufficiently proves that Peter was not then there: for he says plainly that in his trial *he was forsaken by all men,* that no man stood by him; which he mentions as their sin, and prays for pardon for them. Now, no man can reasonably think that Peter was amongst the number of them whom he complained of. 8. The story is not consistent with what is *expressly written of Peter by Luke* in the Acts, and Paul in his Epistle to the Galatians. Paul was converted unto the faith about the thirty-eighth year of Christ, or fifth after his ascension. After this he continued three years preaching the gospel about Damascus and in Arabia. In the fortieth or forty-first year of Christ he came to Jerusalem, to confer with Peter, Gal. i.; which was the first of Claudius. As yet, therefore, Peter was not removed out of Judea. Fourteen years after,—that is, either after his first going up to Jerusalem, or rather fourteen years after his first conversion,—he went up again to Jerusalem, and found Peter still there; which was in the fifty-second year of Christ, and the thirteenth of Claudius. Or if you should take the date of the fourteen years mentioned by him shorter by five or six years, and reckon their beginning from the passion and resurrection of Christ, which is not improbable, then this going up of Paul to Jerusalem will be found to be the same with his going up to the council from Antioch, about the sixth or rather seventh year of Claudius. Peter was then yet certainly at Jerusalem,—that is, about the forty-sixth year of Christ; some while after you would have the church to be founded by him at Rome. After this, when Paul had taken a long progress through many countries, wherein he must needs spend some years, returning unto Antioch, Acts xviii. 22, he there again met with Peter, Gal. ii. 11, Peter being yet still in the east, towards the end of the reign of Claudius. At Antioch, where Paul found him, if any of your witnesses may be believed, he abode seven years. Besides, he was now very old, and ready to lay down his mortality, as our Lord had showed him; and, in all probability, after his remove from Antioch, spent the residue of his days in the eastern dispersion of the Jews. For,—9. Much of the apostle's work in Palestine among the Jews was now drawing to an end; the elect being gathered in, troubles were growing upon the nation: and Peter had, as we observed before, agreed with Paul to take the care of the Circumcision, of whom the greatest number by far, excepting only Judea itself, was in Babylon, and the eastern nations about it. Now, whether these and the like observations out of the Scripture, concerning the course of St. Peter's life, be not sufficient to outbalance the testimony of your disagreeing witnesses, impartial and unprejudiced men may judge. For my part, I do not intend to conclude peremptorily from them that Peter was never at Rome, or never preached the gospel there; but that your assertion of it is improbable, and built upon very questionable grounds, that I suppose I may safely conclude. And God forbid that we should once imagine the present faith of Christians, or their profession of Christian religion, to be built upon such uncertain conjectures, or to be concerned in them, whether they be true or false. Nothing can be spoken with more reproach unto it than to say that it stands in need of such supportment. And yet, if this one supposition fail you, all your building falls to the ground in a moment. Never was so stupendous a fabric raised on such imaginary foundations. But, that we may proceed, let us suppose this also, that Peter was at Rome, and preached the gospel there, what will thence follow unto your advantage? what towards the settlement of any man in religion, or bringing us unto the unity of faith,—the things inquired after? He was at, he preached the gospel at, Jerusalem, Samaria, Joppa, Antioch, Babylon, and sundry other places; and yet we find no such consequences pleaded from thence as you urge from his coming to Rome. Wherefore you add,—

IV. "That St Peter was bishop of the Roman church; that he fixed his seat there, and there he died." In gathering up your principles I follow the footsteps of Bellarmine, Baronius, and other great champions of your church, so that you cannot except against the method of our proposals of them. Now, this conclusion is built on these three suppositions:—1. That Peter had an *episcopal office* distinct from his apostolical; 2. That *he was at Rome;* 3. That he *fixed his episcopal see there;*—whereof the second is very questionable, the first and last are absolutely false: so that the conclusion itself must needs be a notable fundamental principle of faith. It is true, and I showed it before, that the apostles, when they came into any church, did exercise all the power of bishops in and over that church; but not as bishops, but as apostles: as a king may, in any of the cities of his dominions where he comes, exercise all the authority of the mayor or particular governor of that place where he is, which yet doth not make him become the mayor of the place, which would be a diminution of his royal dignity. No more did the apostles become local bishops, because of their exercising episcopal power in any particular church by virtue of their authority apostolical, wherein that other was included, as hath been declared. And "cui bono?" to what purpose serves this fictitious episcopacy? All the privileges that you contend for the assignation of unto Peter were bestowed upon him as an apostle, or as a believing disciple of Christ; as such he had those peculiar grants made unto him. The keys of the kingdom of heaven were given unto him as an apostle (or, according to St Austin, as a believer); as such was he commanded to feed the sheep of Christ. It was unto him as an apostle, or a professing believer, that Christ promised to build the church on the faith that he had professed. You reckon all these things among the privileges of Peter the apostle; who as such is said to be ὁ πρῶτος, or first in order. As an apostle he had the care of all the churches committed unto him; as an apostle he was divinely inspired and enabled infallibly to reveal the mind of Christ. All these things belonged unto him as an apostle. And what privilege he could have besides as a bishop, neither you nor I can tell, no more than you can when, how, or by whom he was called and ordained unto any such office; all which we know well enough concerning his apostleship. If you will, then, have any to succeed him in the enjoyment of any or of all these privileges, you must bespeak him to succeed him in his apostleship, and not in his bishopric. Besides, as I said before, this imaginary episcopacy, which limits and confines him unto a particular church, as it doth if it be an episcopacy properly so called, is destructive of his apostolical office, and of his duty in answering the commission given him of preaching the gospel to every creature, following the guidance of God's providence and conduct of the Holy Ghost in his way. Many of the ancients, I confess, affirm that Peter sat bishop of the church of Rome: but they all evidently use the word in a large sense, to imply that during his abode there (for that there he was they did suppose) he took upon him the especial care of that church; for the same persons constantly affirm that Paul also was bishop of the same church at the same time, which cannot be otherwise understood than in the large sense mentioned. And Rufinus, Præfat. Recog. Clement. ad Gaudent., unriddles the mystery. "Linus," saith he, "et Cletus fuerunt ante Clementem episcopi in urbe Roma, sed superstite Petro; videlicet, ut illi episcopatus curam gererent, iste vero apostolatus impleret officium;"—"Linus and Cletus were bishops in the city of Rome before Clemens, but whilst Peter was yet alive; they performing the duty of bishops, Peter attending unto his office apostolical." And hereby doth he utterly discard the present new plea of the foundation of your faith; for though he assert that Peter the apostle was at Rome, yet he denies that he ever sat bishop there, but names two others that ruled that church at Rome jointly during his time, either in one assembly or in two,—the one of the Circumcision, the other of the Gentile converts. And if Peter were thus bishop of Rome, and entered, as you say, upon his episcopacy at his first coming thither, whence is it that you are forced to confess that he was so long absent from his charge? *Five* years, saith Bellarmine; but that will by no means salve the difficulty. *Seven*, saith Onuphrius, at once, and abiding at one place; the most part of his time, besides, being spent in other places, and yet allowing him no time at all for those places where he certainly was. *Eighteen*, saith Cortesius. Strange, that he should be so long absent from his especial cure, and never write one word to them for their instruction or consolation, whereas, in the meantime, he wrote two epistles unto them who, it seems, did not in any special manner belong unto his charge! I wish we could once find our way out of this maze of uncertainties. This is but a sad disquisition after principles of faith, to settle men in religion by them; and yet, if we should suppose this also, we are far enough from our journey's end. The present bishop of Rome is as yet behind the curtain, neither can he appear upon the stage until he be ushered in by one pretence more of the same nature with them that went before. And this is,—

V. "That some one must needs succeed Peter in his episcopacy." But why so? why was it not needful that one should succeed him in his apostleship? Why was it not needful that Paul should have a successor as well as Peter? and John as well as either of them? "Because," you say, "that was necessary for the church; not so these." But who told you so? Where is the proof of what you aver? Who made you judges of what is necessary and what is not necessary for the church of Christ, when himself is silent? And why is not the succession of an apostle necessary as well as of such a bishop as you fancy? Had it not been better to have had one still residing in the church of whose infallibility there could have been no doubt or question,—one that had the power of working miracles, that should have no need to scare the people by shaking fire out of his sleeve, as your Pope Gregory VII. was wont to do, if Cardinal Benno may be believed? But you have now carried us quite off from the Scripture, and story, and probable conjectures, to attend unto you whilst you give the Lord Jesus prudential advice about what is necessary for his church. "It must needs be so, it is meet it should be so," is the best of your proof in this matter; only, your "Fratres Walenburgici" add, "that never any man ordained the government of a community more weakly than Christ must be supposed to have done the government of his church, if he have not appointed such a successor to Peter as you imagine." But it is easy for you to assert what you please of this nature, and as easy for any one to reject what you so assert, if he please. These things are without the verge of Christian religion,—chimeras, towers and palaces in the air. But what must St Peter be succeeded in? "His episcopacy." And what therewithal? "His authority, power, jurisdiction over all churches in the world, with an unerring judgment in matters of faith." But all these belonged unto Peter, as far as ever they belonged unto him, as he was an apostle, long before you fancy him to have been a bishop: as, then, his episcopacy came without these things, so, for aught you know, it might go without them. This is a matter of huge importance in that system of principles which you tender unto us to bring us unto settlement in religion and the unity of faith. Would you would consider a little how you may give some tolerable appearance of proof unto that which the Scripture is so utterly silent in; yea, which lies against the whole economy of the

Lord Jesus Christ in his ordering of his church, as delivered unto us therein. "Dic aliquem, dic, Quintiliane, colorem." But we come now to the pope, whom here we first find "latentem post principia," and coming forth μετὰ πολλῆς φαντασίας with his claim. For you say,—

VI. "That the bishop of Rome is the man that thus succeeds Peter in his episcopacy; which, though it were settled at Rome, was over the whole catholic church." So you *say*, and so you profess yourselves to *believe*. And we desire that you would not take it amiss, if we desire to know upon what grounds you do so; being unwilling to cast away all consideration, that we may embrace a fanatical "credo" in this unlikely business. We desire therefore to know who appointed that there should be any succession? who, that the bishop of Rome should be this successor? Did Jesus Christ do it? We may justly expect you should say he did; but if you do, we desire to know when, where, how, seeing the Scripture is utterly silent of any such thing. Did St Peter himself do it? Pray, manifest unto us that by the appointment of Jesus Christ he had power so to do; and that, secondly, he actually did so. Neither of these can you prove, or produce any testimony worth crediting in confirmation of it. Did it necessarily follow from hence, because that was the place where Peter died? But this was accidental, a thing that Peter thought not of; for you say that a few days before his death, he was leaving that place. Besides, according to this insinuation, why did not every apostle leave a successor behind him in the place where he died, and that by virtue of his dying in that place? Or produce you any patent granted to Peter in especial, that where he died, there he should leave a successor behind him? But it seems the whole weight of your faith is laid upon a matter of fact accidentally fallen out, yea, and that very uncertain whether ever it fell out or no. Show us any thing of the will and institution of Christ in this matter; as that Peter should go to Rome, that he should fix his seat there, that he should die there, that he should have a successor, that the bishop of Rome should be his successor, that unto this successor I know not what nor how many privileges should be conveyed. All these are arbitrary εὑρήματα, inventions, that men may multiply "in infinitum" at their pleasure; for what should set bounds to the imaginations of men when once they cast off all reverence of Christ and his truth? Once more: Why did not Peter fix a seat and leave a successor at Antioch, and in other places, where he abode, and preached, and exercised episcopal power without all question? Was it because he *died* at Rome? This is to acknowledge that the whole Papacy is built, as was said, upon an accidental matter of fact, and that supposed, not proved. Farther: if he must be supposed to succeed

Peter, I desire to know *what that succession* is, and wherein he doth succeed him. Doth he succeed him *in all that he had and was,* in reference unto the church of God? Doth he succeed him *in the manner of his call* to his office? Peter was called immediately by Christ in his own person: the pope is chosen by the conclave of cardinals; concerning whom, their office, privileges, power, right to choose the successor of Peter, there is not one iota in the Scripture, or any monuments of the best antiquity; and how, in their election of popes, they have been influenced by the interest of powerful strumpets, your own Baronius will inform you. Doth he succeed him in the *way and manner of his personal discharge* of his office and employment? Not in the least. Peter, in the pursuit of his commission, and in obedience unto the command of his Lord and Master, travelled up and down the world preaching the gospel, planting and watering the churches of Christ in patience, self-denial, humility, zeal, temperance, meekness; the pope reigns at Rome in ease, exalting himself above the kings of the earth, without taking the least pains in his own person for the conversion of sinners or edification of the disciples of Christ. Doth he succeed him in his *personal qualifications,* which were of such extraordinary advantage unto the church of God in his days,—his faith, love, holiness, light, and knowledge? You will not say so. Many of your popes, by your own confession, have been ignorant and stupid; many of them flagitiously wicked, to say no more. Doth he succeed him in *the way and manner of his exercising his care* and *authority* towards the churches of Christ? As little as the rest. Peter did it by his prayers for the churches, personal visitation, and instruction of them, writing by inspiration, for their direction and guidance, according to the will of God: the pope by bulls, and consistorial determinations, executed by intricate legal processes and officers, unknown not only to Peter, but all antiquity; whose ways, practices, orders, terms, St Peter himself, were he upon the earth again, would very little understand. Doth he succeed him in his *personal infallibility?* Agree among yourselves if you can, and give an answer unto this inquiry. Doth he succeed him in his *power of working miracles?* You do not so much as pretend thereunto. Doth he succeed him in the *doctrine* that he taught? It hath been proved unto you a thousand times that he doth not; and we are still ready to prove it again, if you call us thereunto. Wherein, then, doth this succession consist that you talk of? In his power, authority, jurisdiction, supremacy, monarchy, with the secular advantages of riches, honour, and pomp that attend them; things sweet and desirable unto carnal minds. This is the succession you pretend to plead for. And are you not therein to be commended for your wisdom? In the things that Peter really enjoyed, and which were of singular spiritual advantage unto the church of God, you disclaim any succession unto him, and fix it on things wherein he was no way concerned, that make for your own secular advantage and interest. You have certainly laid your design very well, if these things would hold good to eternity; for hence it is that you draw out the monarchy of your pope, direct and absolute in ecclesiastical things over the whole church; indirect at least, and "in ordine ad spiritualia," over the whole world. This is the Diana, in making of shrines for whom your occupation consists; and it brings no small gains unto you. Hence you wire-draw his cathedral infallibility, legislative authority, freedom from the judgment of any; whereby you hope to secure him and yourselves from all opposition, endeavouring to terrify them with this Medusa's head that approach unto you. Hence are his titles, "The Vicar of Christ, Head and Spouse of his Church, Vice-Deus, Deus alter in Terris," and the like, whereby you keep up popular veneration, and preserve his majestic distance from the poor disciples of Christ. Hence you warrant his practices, suited unto these pretensions and titles, in the deposing of kings, transposing of titles unto dominion and rule, giving away of kingdoms, stirring up and waging mighty wars, causing and commanding them that dissent from him, or refuse to yield obedience unto him, to be destroyed with fire and sword. And who can now question but that you have very wisely stated your succession?

This is the way, this the progress, whereby you pretend to bring us unto the unity of faith. If we will submit unto the pope, and acquiesce in his determinations (whereunto to induce us we have the cogent reasons now considered), the work will be effected. This is the way that God hath, as you pretend, appointed to bring us unto settlement in religion. These things you have told us so often, and with so much confidence, that you take it ill we should question the truth of any thing you aver in the whole matter, and look upon us as very ignorant or unreasonable for our so doing. Yea, he that believes it safer for him to trust the everlasting concernments of his soul unto the goodness, grace, and faithfulness of God in his word, than unto these principles of yours, is rejected by you out of the limits of the catholic church,—that is, of Christianity, for they are the same. To make good your judgment and censure, then, you vent endless cavils against the authority, perfection, and perspicuity of the Scriptures, pretending to despise and scorn whatever is offered in their vindication. This rope of sand, composed of false suppositions, groundless presumptions, inconsequent inferences, in all which there is not one word of infallible truth, at least that you can any way make appear so to be, is the great bond you used to gird men withal into the unity of faith. In brief, you tell us that if we will all submit to the pope, we shall be sure all to agree. But this is no more but, as I have before told you, what every party of men in the world tender us, upon the same or the like condition. It is not a mere agreement we aim at, but an agreement in the truth; not a mere unity, but a unity of faith;—and faith must be built on principles infallible, or it will prove in the close to have been fancy, not faith; carnal imagination, not Christian belief: otherwise we may agree in Turcism, or Judaism, or Paganism, as well as in Christianity, and to as good purpose. Now, what of this kind do you tender unto us? Would you have us to leave the sure word of prophecy, more sure than a voice from heaven; the light shining in the dark places of this world, which we are commanded to attend unto by God himself; the holy Scripture given by inspiration, which is able to make us wise unto salvation; the word that is perfect, sure, right, converting the soul, enlightening the eyes, making wise the simple,—whose observation is attended with great reward,—to give heed, yea, to give up all our spiritual and eternal concernments, to the credit of old, groundless, uncertain stories, inevident presumptions, fables invented for and openly improved unto carnal, secular, and wicked ends? Is your request reasonable? Would we could prevail with you to cease your importunity in this matter; especially considering the dangerous consequence of the admission of these your principles unto Christianity in general. For if it be so that St Peter had such an episcopacy as you talk of, and that a continuance of it in a succession by the bishops of Rome be of that indispensable necessity unto the preservation of Christian religion as is pretended, many men, considering the nature and quality of that succession,—how the means of its continuation have been arbitrarily and occasionally changed,—what place formerly popular suffrage and the imperial authority have had in it,—how it came to be devolved on a conclave of cardinals,—what violence and tumults have attended one way, what briberies and filthy respects unto the lusts of unclean persons, the other,—what interruptions the succession itself hath had, by vacancies, schisms, and contests for the place, and uncertainty of the person that had the best right unto the popedom, according to the customs of the days wherein he lived,—and that many of the persons who have had a place in the pretended succession have been plainly men of the world, such as cannot receive the Spirit of Christ, yea, open enemies unto his cross,—would find just cause to suspect that Christianity were utterly failed many ages ago in the world; which certainly would not much promote the settlement in truth and unity of faith that we are inquiring after. And this is the first way that you propose to supply that defect which you charge upon the Scripture, that it is insufficient to reconcile men that are at variance about religion, and settle them in the truth. And if you are able, by so many uncertainties and untruths, to bring men unto a certainty and settlement in the truth, you need not despair of compassing any thing that you shall have a mind to attempt.

But you have yet another plea, which you make no less use of than of the former; which must therefore be also (now you have engaged us in this work) a little examined. This is the CHURCH, its *authority* and *infallibility*. The truth is, when you come to make a practical application of this plea unto your own use, you resolve it into and confound it with that foregoing of the pope, in whom solely many of you would have this authority and infallibility of the church to reside. Yet because, in your management of it, you proceed on other principles than those before mentioned, this pretence also shall be apart considered. And here you tell us,—

I. "That the church was before the Scripture, and giveth authority unto it." By the Scriptures you know that we understand the word of God, with this one adjunct, of its being written by his command and appointment. We do not say that it belongs unto the essence of the word of God that it be written: whatever is spoken by God we admit as his word, when we are infallibly assured that by him it was spoken; and that we should do so before, himself doth not require at our hands, for he would have us use our utmost diligence not to be imposed upon by any in his name. Therefore we grant that the word of God was given out for the rule of men in his worship two thousand years before it was written; but it was so given forth as that they unto whom it came had infallible assurance that from him it came, and his word it was. And if you, or any man else, can give us *such assurance* that any thing is or hath been spoken by him besides what we have *now written* in the Scripture, we shall receive it with the same faith and obedience wherewith we receive the Scripture itself. Whereas, therefore, you say "that the church was before the Scripture,"—if you intend no more but that there was a church in the world before the word of God was written, we grant it true, but not at all to your purpose. If you intend that "the church is before the word of God," which at an appointed time was written, it may possibly be wrested unto your purpose, but is far from being true, seeing the church is a society of men called to the knowledge and worship of God by his word. They become a church by the call of that word which, it seems, you would have not given until they are a church: so effects produce their causes, children beget their parents, light brings forth the sun, and heat the fire; so are the prophets and apostles built upon the foundation of the church, whereof the pope is the corner-stone; so was the Judaical church before the law of its constitution, and the Christian before the word of promise whereon it was founded, and the word of command by which it was edified.

In brief, from the day wherein man was first created upon the earth, to the days wherein we live, never did a person or church yield any obedience, or perform any acceptable worship unto God, but what was founded on and regulated by his word, given unto them antecedently unto their obedience and worship, to be the sole foundation and rule of it. That you have no concernment in what is or may be truly spoken of the church, we shall afterward show; but it is not for the interest of truth that we should suffer you, without control, to impose such absurd notions on the minds of men, especially when you pretend to direct them unto a settlement in religion. Alike *true* is it that "the church gives authority unto the Scripture." Every true church, indeed, gives witness or testimony unto it; and it is its duty so to do. It holds it forth, declares and manifests it, so that it may be considered and taken notice of by all; which is one main end of the institution of the church in this world. But the church *no more gives authority to the Scripture than it gives authority to God himself.* He requires of men the discharge of that duty which he hath assigned unto them, but stands not in need of their suffrage to confirm his authority. It was not so, indeed, with the idols of old, of whom Tertullian said rightly, "Si deus homini non placuerit, deus non erit." The reputation of their deity depended on the testimony of men, as you say that of Christ's doth on the authority of the pope. But I shall not farther insist upon the disprovement of this vanity, having showed already that the Scripture hath all its authority, both in itself and in reference unto us, from him whose word it is; and we have also made it appear that your assertions to the contrary are meet for nothing but to open a door unto all irreligiousness, profaneness, and atheism; so that there is οὐδὲν ὑγιές,—"nothing sound or savoury,"—nothing which a heart careful to preserve its loyalty unto God will not nauseate at,—nothing not suited to oppugn the fundamentals of Christian religion in this your position. This ground well fixed, you tell us,—

II. "That the church is infallible, or cannot err in what she teacheth to be believed." And we ask you what church you mean, and how far you intend that it is infallible? The *only known* church which was then in the world was in the wilderness, when Moses was in the mount. Was it infallible when it *made the golden calf,* and danced about it, proclaiming a feast unto Jehovah before the calf? Was the same church afterward infallible in the days of the judges, when it *worshipped Baalim* and Ashtaroth? or in the days of Jeroboam, when it *sacrificed before the calves* at Dan and Bethel? or in the other branch of it in the days of Ahaz, when the high priest set up an altar in the temple for the king to *offer sacrifice unto the gods of Damascus?* or in the days of Jehoiakim and Zedekiah, when the high priest, with the rest of the priests, *imprisoned and would have slain Jeremiah* for preaching the word of God? or when they preferred the worship of the *queen of heaven* before that of the God of Abraham? Or was it infallible when the high priest, with the whole council or sanhedrim of the church, *judicially condemned*, as far as in them lay, their own Messiah, and rejected the gospel that was preached unto them? You must inform us what other church was then in the world, or you will quickly perceive how ungrounded your general maxim is of the church's absolute infallibility. As far, indeed, as it attends unto the infallible rule given unto it it is so, but not one jot farther. Moreover, we desire to know *what church* you mean in your assertion, or, rather, what is it you mean by *the church?* Do you intend the *mystical church*, or the whole number of God's elect in all ages, or in any age, militant on the earth, which principally is the church of God? Eph. v. 25; or do you intend the whole diffused body of the disciples of Christ in the world, separated to God by baptism and the profession of saving truth, which is the *church catholic visible?* or do you mean any *particular church*, as the Roman or Constantinopolitan, the French, Dutch, or English church? If you intend the first of these, or the church in the first sense, we acknowledge that it is thus far infallible,—that no true member of it shall ever totally and finally renounce, lose, or forsake that faith without which they cannot please God and be saved: this the Scripture teacheth, this Austin confirmeth in a hundred places. If you intend the church in the second sense, we grant that also so far unerring and infallible, as that there ever was and ever shall be in the world a number of men making profession of the saving truth of the gospel, and yielding professed subjection unto our Lord Jesus Christ according unto it; wherein consists his visible kingdom in this world, that never was, that never can be, utterly overthrown. If you speak of a church in the last sense, then we tell you that no such church is, by virtue of any promise of our Lord Jesus Christ, freed from erring, yea, so far as to deny the fundamentals of Christianity, and thereby to lose the very being of a church. Whilst it continues a church it cannot err fundamentally, because such errors destroy the very being of a church; but those who were once a church, by their failing in the truth, may cease to be so any longer. And a church as such may so fail, though every person in it do not so; for the individual members of it, that are so also of the mystical church, shall be preserved in its apostasy. And so the mystical church and the catholic church of professors may be continued, though all particular churches should fail. So that no person, the church in no sense, is absolutely freed in this world from the danger of all errors: that is the condition we shall attain in heaven; here, where we know but in part, we are incapable of it. The church of the elect, and every member of it, shall eventually be preserved by the power of the Holy Ghost from any such error as would utterly destroy their communion with Christ in grace here, or prevent their fruition of him in glory hereafter; or, as the apostle speaks, they shall assuredly be "kept by the power of God through faith unto salvation." The general church of visible professors shall be always so far preserved in the world, as that there shall never want some, in some place or other of it, that shall profess all needful saving truths of the gospel, in the belief whereof, and obedience whereunto, a man may be saved; but for particular churches, as such, they have no security but what lies in their diligent attendance unto that infallible rule, which will preserve them from all hurtful errors, if, through their own default, they neglect not to keep close unto it. And your flattering yourselves with an imagination of any other privilege is that which hath wrought your ruin. You are deceived if, in this matter, you are of Menander's mind, who said, Αὐτόματα τὰ πράγματ' ἐπὶ τὸ συμφέρον ῥεῖ κἂν καθευδήσῃ,—"All will, of its own accord, fall out well with you though you sleep securely." As for all other churches in the world besides your own, we have your concession not only that they were and are fallible, but that they have actually erred long since; and the same hath been proved against yours a thousand times; and your best reserve against particular charges of error lies in this impertinent general pretence, that you cannot err. It may be you will ask, for you use so to do, and it is the design of your "Fiat" to promote the inquiry,—"If the *church* be *fallible* (that is, to propose unto us the things and doctrines that we are to believe), how can we with *faith infallible* believe her proposals?" And I tell you truly, I know not how we can, if we believe them only upon her authority, or she propose them to be believed solely upon that account; but when she proposeth them unto us to be believed on the authority of God speaking in the Scriptures, we both can and do believe what she teacheth and proposeth, and that with faith infallible, resolved into the veracity of God in his word. And we grant every church to be so far infallible as it attends unto the only infallible rule amongst men. When you prove that any one church is, by any promise of Christ, any grant of privilege expressed or intimated in the Scripture, placed in an unerring condition, any farther than as, in the use of the means appointed, she attends unto the only rule of her preservation; or that any church shall be necessitated to attend unto that rule whether she will or no, whereby she may be preserved; or can give us an instance of any church, since the foundation of the world, that hath been actually preserved, and absolutely, from all error (other than that of your own, which you know we cannot admit of),—as you will do μέγα καὶ περιβόητον ἔργον, "a great and memorable work," so we shall grant as much as you can reasonably desire of us, upon the account of the assertion under consideration. But until you do some one or all of these, your crying out, "The church, the church, the church cannot err," makes no other noise in our ears than that of the Jews, "The temple of the Lord, the temple of the Lord, the law shall not fail," did in the ears of the prophets of old. Neither do we speak this of the church, or any church, as though we were concerned to question or deny any just privileges belonging unto it, thereby to secure ourselves from any pretensions of yours, but merely for the sake of truth. For we shall manifest anon unto you that you are as little concerned in the privileges of the church, be they what they will, more or less, as any society of the professors of Christianity in the world, if so be that you are concerned in them at all. So that if the truth would permit us to agree with you in all things that you assign unto the church, yet the difference between you and us were never the nearer to an end; for we should still differ with you about your share and interest therein, and for ever abhor your frowardness in appropriating of them all unto yourselves. And herein, as I said, hath lain a great part of your ruin: whilst you have been sweetly dreaming of an infallibility, you have really plunged yourselves into errors innumerable; and when any one hath jogged you to awake you out of your fatal sleep, by minding you of your particular errors, your dream hath left such an impression upon your imagination as that you think them *no errors*, upon this only ground, because *you cannot err*. I am persuaded, had it not been for this one error, you had been freed from many others. But this perfectly disenables you for any candid inquisition after the truth; for why should he once look about him, or, indeed, so much as take care to keep his eyes open, who is sure that he can never be out of his way? Hence you inquire not at all whether what you profess be truth or not; but to learn what your church teacheth, and defend it, is all that you have to do about religion in this world. And whatever absurdities or inconveniencies you find yourselves driven unto in the handling of particular points, all is one; they must be right, though you cannot defend them, because your church, which cannot err, hath so declared them to be! And if you should chance to be convinced of any truth in particular that is contrary to the determination of your church, you know not how to embrace it, but must shut your eyes against its light and evidence, and cast it out of your minds, or wander up and down with a various assent between contradictions. Well said he of old,—

> Εὐήθειά μοι φαίνεται δηλουμένη
> Τὸ νοεῖν μὲν ὅσα δεῖ, μὴ φυλάττεσθαι δ' ἃ δεῖ.

This is flat folly,—namely, for a man to live in rebellion unto his own light. But you add,—

III. "That yourselves,—that is, the pope, with those who in matters of religion adhere unto him, and live in subjection unto him,—are this church, in an assent unto whose infallible teachings and determinations the unity of faith doth consist." Could you prove this assertion, I confess it would stand you in good stead. But before we inquire after that, we shall endeavour a little to come unto a right understanding of what you say. When you affirm that the Roman church is the church of Christ, you intend either that it is the *only church* of Christ,—all the church of Christ,—and so, consequently, the catholic church; or you mean that it is a church of Christ, which hath an *especial prerogative,* enabling it to require obedience of all the disciples of Christ.

1. If you say the former, we desire to know, First, *When* it became so to be. It was not so when all the church was together at Jerusalem, and no foundation of any church at all laid at Rome, Acts i. 1–5. It was not so when the first church of the Gentiles was gathered at Antioch, and the disciples first began to be called Christians; for as yet we have no tidings of any church at Rome. It was not so when Paul wrote his epistles, for he makes express mention of many other churches in other places, which had no relation unto any church at Rome more than they had one to another, in their common profession of the same faith, and therein enjoyed equal gifts and privileges with it. It was not so in the days of the primitive fathers of the first three hundred years, who all of them, not one excepted, took the Roman to be a local particular church, and the bishop of Rome to be such a bishop as they esteemed of all other churches and bishops. Their persuasion in this matter is expressed in the beginning of the Epistle of Clemens, or church of Rome, unto the church of Corinth: Ἡ ἐκκλησία τοῦ Θεοῦ ἡ παροικοῦσα Ῥώμην, τῇ ἐκκλησίᾳ τοῦ Θεοῦ παροικούσῃ Κόρινθον·—"The church [of God] that is at Rome to the church [of God] that is at Corinth;" both local churches, both equal. And such is the language of all the writers of those times. It was not so in the days of the fathers and councils of the next three centuries, who still accounted it a particular church,—diocesan or patriarchal, but all of them particular; never calling it *catholic* but upon the account of its holding the *catholic faith,* as they called all other churches that did so, in opposition to the errors, heresies, and schisms of any in their days. We desire, then, to know *when* it became the only or absolutely catholic church of Christ; as also, secondly, by *what means* it became so to be. It did not do so by virtue of any institution, warrant, or command of Christ. You were never able to produce the least intimation of any such warrant out of any writing of divine inspiration,

nor approved catholic writer of the first ages after Christ, though it hugely concern you so to do, if it were possible to be done; but they all expressly teach that which is inconsistent with such pretences. It did not do so by any decree of the first general councils, which are all of them silent as to any such thing; and some of them, as those of Nice, Ephesus, and Chalcedon, expressly declare and determine the contrary,—at least that which is contrary thereunto. We can find no other way or means whereby it can pretend unto this vast privilege, unless it be the grant of Phocas unto Boniface that he should be called the Universal Bishop; who, to serve his own ends, was very liberal of that which was not at all in his power to bestow. And yet neither is this, though it be a means that you have more reason to be ashamed than to boast of, sufficient to found your present claim, considering how that name was in those days no more than a name, —a mere airy, ambitious title,—that carried along with it no real power, and "stet magni nominis umbra."

Secondly, We cannot give our assent unto this claim of yours, because we should thereby be necessitated to cut off from the church, and consequently *all hope of salvation*, far the greatest number of men in the world who in this and all foregoing ages have called and do "call upon the name of our Lord Jesus Christ, their Lord and ours." This we dare not do, especially considering that many of them have spent, and do spend, their days in great affliction, for their testimony unto Christ and his gospel; and many of them every day seal their testimony with their blood,—so belonging, as we believe, unto that "holy army of martyrs" which continually praiseth God. Now, as herein we dare not concur with you, considering the charge given unto Timothy by Paul, Μὴ κοινώνει ἁμαρτίαις ἀλλοτρίαις,—"Be not partaker of other men's sins;" so indeed we are persuaded that your opinion, or rather presumption, in this matter, is extremely injurious to the grace of Christ, the love and goodness of God, as also to the truth of the gospel. And therefore,—

Thirdly, We suppose this the most *schismatical principle* that ever was broached under the sun, since there was a church upon the earth; and that because,—(1.) It is the most *groundless;* (2.) The most *uncharitable* that ever was; and, (3.) Of the most *pernicious* consequence, as having a principal influence into the present irreconcilableness of differences among Christians in the world; which will one day be charged on the authors and abettors of it. For it will one day appear that it is not the various conceptions of the minds of peaceable men about the things of God, nor the various degrees of knowledge and faith that are found amongst them, but groundless impositions of things as necessary to be believed and practised beyond Scripture warrant, that are the springs and causes of all, or at least the most blamable and sinful, differences among Christians.

Fourthly, We know this pretence, should it take place, would prove extremely *hazardous unto the truth of the promises of Christ* given unto the catholic church. For suppose that to be one and the same with the Roman, and whatever mishap may befall the one must be thought to befall the other; for on our supposition they are not only like Hippocrates's twins, that, being born together, wept and joyed together, and together died, but like Hippocrates himself, as the same individual person or thing, being both the same,—one church that hath two names, Catholic and Roman; that is, universal-particular: no otherwise two than as Julius Cæsar was, when, by his overawing his colleague from the execution of his office, they dated their acts at Rome, "Julio et Cæsare consulibus;" for, as thev said,—

> "Non Bibulo quicquam nuper sed Cæsare factum est;
> Nam Bibulo fieri consule nil memini."

Now, besides the *failings* which we know your church to have been subject unto, in point of faith, manners, and worship, it hath also been at least in danger of destruction in the time of the prevalency of the Goths, Vandals, Huns, and Longobards, especially when Rome itself was left desolate and without inhabitant by Totilas. And what yet farther may befall it before the end of the world, Θεοῦ ἐν γούνασι κεῖται. Only this I know, that many are in expectation of a sad catastrophe to be given unto it, and that on grounds not to be despised. Now, God forbid that the church unto which the promises are made should be once thought to be subject unto all the dangers and hazards that you wilfully expose yourselves unto. So that as this is a very groundless presumption in itself, so it is a very great aggravation of your miscarriages also, whilst you seek to entitle the catholic church of Christ unto them which can neither contract any such guilt as you have done, nor be liable to any such misery or punishment as you are.

Fifthly, We see not the promises made unto the catholic church *fulfilled unto you*, as we see that to have befallen your church which is contrary unto the promises that ever it should befall the catholic. The conclusion, then, will necessarily on both instances follow, that either you are not the catholic church, or that the promises of Christ have failed and been of none effect; and you may easily guess which part of the conclusion it is best and most safe for us to give assent unto. I shall give you one or two instances unto this last head. Christ hath promised his Spirit unto his church,—that is, his catholic church,—to "abide with it for ever," John xiv. 16. But this promise hath not been made good unto your church at all times, because it hath not been so unto the head of it. Many a time the head of your church hath not received the Spirit of Christ, for our Saviour tells us in the next words that "the world cannot receive him,"—that is, men of the world, carnally-minded men, cannot do so; for he is the peculiar inheritance of those that are called, sanctified, and do believe. Now, if ever there was any "world" in the world, any of the "world" in the earth, some, many, of your popes have been so; and therefore, by the testimony of Christ, could not receive the Spirit that he promised unto his church. Again, it is promised unto the church mystical or catholic, in the first and chiefest notion of it, "that all her children shall be holy, all taught of God;" and all that are so taught, as our Saviour informs us, "come to him" by saving faith. You will not, I am sure, for shame, affirm that this promise hath been made good to all, either children or fathers, of your church. Innumerable other promises made to the catholic church may be instanced in, which you can no better or otherwise apply unto your church than one of your popes did that of the psalmist to himself, "Thou shalt tread on the lion and the basilisk," when he set his foot on the neck of Frederick the emperor. But the arguments are endless whereby the vanity of this pretence may be disproved. I shall only add,—

Sixthly, That it is contrary to all *story*, reason, and common sense; for it is notorious that far the greatest part of Christians that belong to the catholic church of Christ, or have done so from the days that Christianity first entered the world, successively in all ages, never thought themselves any otherwise concerned in the Roman church than in any other particular church of name in the world: and is it not a madness to exclude them all from being Christians, or belonging to the catholic church, because they belonged not to the Roman? This I could easily demonstrate throughout all ages of the church successively. But we need not insist longer on the disproving of that assertion which implies a flat contradiction in the very terms of it. If any church be the catholic, it cannot therefore be the Roman; and if it be the Roman properly, it cannot therefore be the catholic.

2. If you shall say that you mean only that you are a particular church of Christ, but yet that or such a particular church *as hath the great privileges of infallibility and universal authority* annexed unto it, which make it of necessity for all men to submit unto it, and to acquiesce in its determinations, I answer,—(1.) I fear you will not say so; you will not, I fear, renounce your claim unto catholicism. I have already observed that yourself in particular affirm the Roman and catholic church to be one and the same. It is not enough for you that you belong any way to the church of Christ, but you plead that none do so but yourselves. (2.) Indeed you do not own yourselves in this very assertion to be a particular church; your claim of

universal authority and jurisdiction, which you still carry along with you, is inconsistent with any such concession. (3.) To make the best of it that we can, what ground have you to give us this difference between the churches of Christ, that one is fallible, another infallible; that one hath power over all the rest; that one depends on Christ, all the rest on that one? Where is the least intimation given of any such thing in the *Scripture?* where or by whom is it expressly asserted amongst the *ancient writers* of the church? Was this principle pleaded or once asserted in any of the *ancient councils?* Some ambiguous expressions of particular persons, most of them bishops of Rome in the declining days of the church, you produce, indeed, unto this purpose; but can any rational man think them a sufficient foundation of that stupendous fabric which you endeavour to erect upon them? I suppose you will not find any such persons hasty in their so doing: those who are already engaged will not be easily recovered. For new proselytes unto these principles, you have small ground to expect any; unless it be of persons whose lives are either tainted with sensuality, which they would gladly have a refuge for against the accusations of their consciences, or whose minds are entangled with worldly, secular advantages, suited to their conditions, tempers, and inclinations.

Thus I have, with what briefness I could, showed you the uncertainty, indeed falseness, of those general principles from which you educe all your other pleas and reasonings, into which they must be resolved. And now, I pray, consider the groundwork you lay for the bringing of men unto a settlement in the truth, and unto the unity of faith, in opposition to the Scripture, which you reject as insufficient unto this purpose. The sum of it is, an acquiescency in the proposals and determinations of your church, as to all things that concern faith and the worship of God; the two main principles that concur unto it we have apart considered, and have found them every way insufficient for the end proposed. Neither have they one jot more of strength when they are complicated and blended together, as they usually are by you, than they have in and of themselves, as they stand singly on their own bottoms A thousand falsehoods put together will be far enough from making one truth. A multiplication of them may increase a sophism, but not add the least weight or strength to an argument. An army of cripples will not make one sound man. And can you think it reasonable that we should renounce our sure and firm word of prophecy to attend unto you in this chase of uncertain conjectures and palpable untruths? Suppose this were a way that would bring you and us to an agreement, and take away the evil of our differences, I can name you twenty that would do it as effectually; and they should none of them have any evil in them but only that which yours also is openly guilty of,—namely, the relinquishment of our duty towards God and care of our own souls, to come to some peace amongst ourselves in this world: which would be nothing else but a plain conspiracy against Jesus Christ, and rejection of his authority. At present, I shall say no more but that he who is led into the truth by so many errors, and is brought unto establishment by so many uncertainties, hath singular success, and such as no other man hath reason to look for; or he is like Robert, duke of Normandy, who, when he caused the Saracens to carry him into Jerusalem, sent word unto his friends in Europe that he was "carried into heaven on the backs of devils."

It may also, in particular, be easily made to appear how unsuited your means of bringing men unto the unity of faith are unto that supposition of the present differences in religion between you and us which you proceed upon; for suppose a man be convinced that many things taught by your church are false, and contrary to the mind of God, as you know the case to be between you and us, what course would you take with him to reduce him unto the unity of faith? Would you tell him that your church cannot err? or would you endeavour to persuade him that the particulars which he instanceth in as errors are not so indeed, but real truths, and necessarily by him to be believed? The former, if you would speak it out downright and openly, as becometh men who distrust not the truth of their principles (for he that is persuaded of the truth never fears its strength), would soon appear to be a very wise course indeed. You would persuade a man in general that you cannot err, whilst he gives you instances that you have actually erred. Do not think you have any sophisms against motion in general that will prevail with any man to assent unto you whilst he is able to rise and walk to and fro. Besides, he that is convinced of any thing wherein you err, believes the opposite unto it to be true; and that on grounds unto him sufficiently cogent to require his assent. If you could now persuade him that you cannot err, whilst he actually believes things to be true which he knows to be contrary to your determination, what a sweet condition should you bring him into! Can you enable him to believe contradictions at the same time? or, when a man, on particular grounds and evidences, is come to a settled, firm persuasion that any doctrine of your church (suppose that of transubstantiation) is false and contradictory unto Scripture and right reason, if you should, abstracting from particulars, in general puzzle him with sophisms and pretences for your church's infallibility, do you think it is an easy thing for him immediately to forego that persuasion in particular which his mind, upon cogent, and to him unavoidable, grounds and arguments, was possessed withal, without a rational removal of those grounds and arguments? Men's belief of things never pierces deeper into their souls than their imagination, who can take it up and lay it down at their pleasure. I am persuaded, therefore, you would take the latter course, and strive to convince him of his mistakes in the things that he judgeth erroneous in the doctrine of your church. And what way would you proceed by for his conviction? Would you not produce *testimonies of Scripture*, with arguments drawn from them, and the *suffrage of the Fathers* to the same purpose? Nay, would you not do so, if the error he charge you withal be that of the authority and infallibility of your church? I am sure all your controversy-writers of note take this course. And do you not see, then, that you are brought, whether you will or no, unto the use of that way and means for the reducing of men unto the unity of faith which you before rejected, which Protestants avow as sufficient to that purpose?

CHAPTER IX.

Proposals from protestant principles tending unto moderation and unity.

YOU may, from what hath been spoken, perceive how, upon your own principles, you are utterly disenabled to exercise any true moderation towards dissenters from you; and that which you do so exercise we are beholding for it, as Cicero said of the honesty of some of the Epicureans, to the goodness of their nature, which the illness of their opinions cannot corrupt; neither are you any way enabled by them to reduce men unto the unity of faith: so that you are not more happy in your proposing of good ends unto yourself than you are unhappy in choosing mediums for the effecting of them. It may be, for your own skill, you are able, like Archimedes, to remove the earthly ball of our contentions; but you are like him again that you have nowhere to stand whilst you go about your work. However, we thank you for your good intentions: "In magnis voluisse," is no small commendation. Protestants, on the other side, you see, are furnished with firm, stable principles and rules in the pursuit both of moderation and unity; and there are some things in themselves very practicable, and naturally deducible from the principles of Protestants, wherein the complete exercise of moderation may be obtained, and a better progress made towards unity than is likely to be by a rigid contending to impose different principles on one another; or by impetuous clamours of "Lo here, and lo there," which at present most men are taken up withal. Some few of them I shall name unto you, as a pacific coronis to the preceding critical discourse; and

> —— "Si quid novisti rectius istis
> Candidus imperti; si non, his utere mecum." Hor. Ep. i. 6, 68.

And they are these:—

I. Whereas our Saviour hath determined that our happiness consisteth not in the *knowing* the things of the gospel, but in *doing* of them; and seeing that no man can expect any benefit or advantage from or by Christ Jesus but only they that yield obedience unto him, to whom alone he is a "captain of salvation;" the first thing wherein all that profess Christianity ought to agree and consent together is, jointly to obey the commands of Christ,—"to live godly, righteously, and soberly in this present world," following after "holiness, without which no man shall see God." Until we all agree in this, and make it our business, and fix it as our end, in vain shall we attempt to agree in notional and speculative truths; nor would it be much to our advantage so to do. For as I remember I have told you before, so I now on this occasion tell you again, it will at the last day appear that it is all one to any man what party or way in Christian religion he hath been of, if he have not personally been born again, and, upon mixing the promises of Christ with faith, have thereupon yielded obedience unto him unto the end. I confess men may have many advantages in one way, that they may not have in another,—they may have better means of instruction, and better examples for imitation; but as to the event, it will be one and the same with all unbelievers, all unrighteous and ungodly persons; and men may be very zealous believers in a party who are in the sight of God unbelievers as to the whole design of the gospel. This is a principle wherein, as I take it, *all Christians agree*,—namely, that the profession of Christianity will do no man the least good as to his eternal concernments that lives not up to the *power* of it; yea, it will be an aggravation of his condemnation: and the want hereof is that which hath lost all the lustre and splendour of the religion taught by Jesus Christ in the world. Would Christians of all parties make it their business to retrieve its reputation, wherein also their own bliss and happiness is involved, by a universal obedience unto the precepts of it, it would insensibly sink a thousand of their differences under ground. Were this attended unto, the world would quickly say with admiration,—

> "Magnus ab integro seclorum nascitur ordo:
> Jam nova progenies cœlo demittitur alto." Virg. Ecl. iv. 5, 7.

The old, glorious, beautiful face of Christianity would be restored unto it again; which many deform more and more every day by painting a dead carcase instead of the living spouse of Christ. And if ever we intend to take one step towards any agreement or unity, it must be by fixing this principle in the minds of all men,—that it is of no advantage to any man whatever church or way in Christian religion he be of, unless he personally believe the promises, and live in obedience unto all the precepts of Christ; and that for him who doth so, that it is a trampling of the whole gospel under foot to say that his salvation could be endangered by his not being of this or that church or way, especially considering how much of the world hath immixed itself into all the known ways that are in it. Were this once well fixed on the minds of men, and did they practically believe that men shall not be dealt withal at the last day *by gross*, as of this or that party or church, but that every *individual* person must stand upon his own bottom, *live by his own faith, or perish for want of it*, as if there had been no other persons in the world but himself, we should quickly find their keenness in promoting and contending for their several parties taken off, their heat allayed, and they will begin to find their business and concernment in religion to be utterly another matter than they thought of. For the present, some Protestants think that when the Roman power is by one means or other broken, which they expect, that then we shall agree and have peace; Romanists, on the other side, look for and desire the extirpation of all that they call heresy or heretics, by one way or other. Some, pretending highly to moderation on both sides, especially among the Protestants, hope that it may be attained by mutual condescension of the parties at variance, contemperation of opinions and practices unto the present distant apprehensions and interests of the chief leaders of either side: what issue and event their desires, hopes, and attempts will have, time will show to all the world. For my part, until, by a fresh pouring out of the Spirit of God from on high, I see Christians in profession agreeing in pursuing the end of Christianity, endeavouring to be followers of Jesus Christ in a conversation becoming the gospel, without trusting to the parties wherein they are engaged, I shall have very little hopes to see any unity amongst us that shall be one jot better than our present differences. To see this, if any thing, would make me say,—

"O mihi tam longæ maneat pars ultima vitæ!"—Virg. Ecl. iv. 53.

The present face of Christianity makes the world a wearisome wilderness; nor should I think any thing a more necessary duty than it would be for persons of piety and ability to apologize for the religion of Jesus Christ, and to show how unconcerned it is in the ways and practices of the most that profess it, and how utterly another thing it is from what in the world it is represented to be,—so to put a stop unto that atheism which is breaking in upon us from the contempt that men have of that idea of Christian religion which they have taken from the manner of its profession and lives of its professors,—were it not that I suppose it more immediately incumbent on them and us all to do the same work in a real expression of its power and excellency, in such a kind of goodness, holiness, righteousness, and heavenliness of conversation, as the world is only as yet in secret acquainted withal. When this is done, the way for a farther agreement will be open and facile; and until it be so, men will fight on,—

> —— "Ipsique, nepotesque
> Et nati natorum, et qui nascentur ab illis;"

we shall have no end of our quarrels. Could I see a heroic temper fall on the minds of men of the several parties at variance, to bid adieu to the world, its customs, manners, and fashions, which are all vain and perishing;—not in a local, corporeal retirement from the men and lawful businesses of it, or a relinquishment of the necessary callings and employments in it, but in their spirits and affections; could I see them taking up the cross of Christ,—not on their backs in its *figure*, but on their hearts in its *power*,—and in their whole conversation conforming themselves unto his blessed example, so teaching all others of their parties what it is that they build upon for a blessed eternity, that they may not please and deceive themselves with their conceited orthodoxy in the trifling differences which they have with other Christians; I should hope the very name of persecution, and every thing that is contrary to Christian moderation, would quickly be driven out of Christendom, and that error, and whatever is contrary to the unity of faith, would not be long-lived after them. But whilst these things are far from us, let us not flatter ourselves as though a windy flourish of words had any efficacy in it to bring us to moderation and unity. At variance we are, and at variance we must be content to be; that being but one of the evils that at this day triumph in the world over conquered Christianity. This being supposed,—

II. Whereas the doctrine of God is a mystery, in the knowledge whereof men attain unto wisdom according to that measure of light and grace which the Spirit, who divides unto every man as he will, is pleased to communicate unto them, if men would not frame *any other rule* or standard unto that wisdom, and the various degrees of it, but only that which God himself hath assigned thereunto, the fuel would, upon the matter, be wholly taken away from the fire of our contentions. All men *have not*, nor, let men pretend what they please to the contrary, *ever had*, nor ever will have, the same light, the same knowledge, the same spiritual wisdom and understanding, the same degree of assurance, the same measure of comprehension, in the things of God. But whilst they have the same rule, the same *objective revelation*, the use of the same means to grow spiritually wise in the knowledge of it, they have all the agreement that God hath appointed for them, or calls them unto. To frame for them all, in rigid confessions, or systems of supposed credible propositions, a Procrustes' bed to stretch them upon, or crop them unto the size of, so to reduce them to the same opinion in all things, is a vain and fruitless attempt, that men have for many generations wearied themselves about, and yet continue so to do. Remove out of the way anathemas upon *propositions* arbitrarily composed and expressed, *philosophical conclusions, rules of faith* of a mere human composure, or use them no otherwise but only to testify the voluntary consent of men's minds in expressing to their own satisfaction the things which they do believe, and let men be esteemed to believe and to have attained degrees in the faith according as they are taught of God, with an allowance for every one's measure of means, light, grace, gifts, which are not things in our own power, and we shall be nearer unto quietness than most men imagine. When Christians had any unity in the world, the Bible alone was thought to contain their religion, and every one endeavoured to learn the mind of God out of it, both by their own endeavours and as they were instructed therein by their guides; neither did they pursue this work with any other end but only that they might be strengthened in their faith and hope, and learn to serve God and obey him, that so they might come to the blessed enjoyment of him. Nor will there ever, I fear, be again any unity among them until things are reduced to the same state and condition. But among all the vanities that the minds of men are exercised with in this world, there is none to be compared unto that of their hoping and endeavouring to bring all persons that profess the religion of Jesus Christ, to acquiesce in the same opinions about all particulars which are any way determined to belong thereunto, especially considering how endlessly they are multiplied and branched into instances; such, for aught appears, the first churches took little or no notice of, nay, neither knew nor understood any thing of them, in the sense and terms wherein they are now proposed as a "tessera" of communion among Christians. In a word, leave Christian religion unto its primitive liberty, wherein it was believed to be revealed of God, and that revelation of it to be contained in the Scripture, which men searched and studied, to become themselves, and to teach others to be, wise in the knowledge of God and living unto him, and the most of the contests that are in the world will quickly vanish and disappear. But whilst every one hath a *confession*, a *way*, a *church*, and its *authority*, which must be imposed on all others, or else he cries to his nearest relations,—

> "Lupis et agnis quanta sortito obtigit
> Tecum mihi discordia est;"

we may look for peace, moderation, and unity, when we are here no more, and not sooner. So that,—

III. If those theological determinations that make up at this day amongst some men the greatest part of those assertions, positions, or propositions, which are called *articles of faith* or truth,—which are not delivered in the words that the Spirit of God teacheth, but in terms of art, and in answer unto rules and notions which the world might haply, without any great disadvantage, [have] been unacquainted withal unto this day had not Aristotle found them out or stumbled on them,—might be eliminated from the city of God and communion of Christians, and left for men to exercise their wits about who have nothing else to do, and the doctrine of truth which is according unto godliness left unto that noble, heavenly, spiritual, generous amplitude, wherein it was delivered in the Scripture and believed in the first churches, innumerable causes of strife and contentions would be taken away: but, "ferri video mea gaudia ventis," small hopes have I to see any such impression and consent to befall the minds of concerned men; and yet, I must confess, I have not one jot more of the reuniting the disciples of Christ in love and concord. But most men that profess any thing of divinity have learned it as an art or human science, out of the road, compass, and track whereof they know nothing of the mind of God; nay, many scarce know the things in themselves, and as they are to be believed, which they are passing skilful in as they are expressed in their arbitrary terms of art, which none almost understand but themselves. And is it likely that such men, who are not a few in the world, will let go their skill and knowledge, and with them their reputation and advantage, and sacrifice them all to the peace and agreement that we are seeking after? Some learn their divinity out of the *late* and *modern* schools, both in the Reformed and Papal church; in both which a science is proposed under that name, consisting in a farrago of credible propositions, asserted in terms suited unto that philosophy that is variously predominant in them. What a kind of theology this hath produced in the Papacy, Agricola, Erasmus, Vives, Jansenius, with innumerable other learned men of your own, have sufficiently declared. And that it hath any better success in the Reformed churches, many things, which I shall not now instance in, give me cause to doubt. Some boast themselves to learn their divinity from the fathers, and say they depart not from their sense and idiom of expression in what they believe and profess. But we find by experience that, what for want of wisdom and judgment in themselves, what for such reasons taken from the writings which they make their oracles, which I shall not insist upon, much of the divinity of some of these men consists in that which, to avoid provocation, I shall not express. Whilst men are thus pre-engaged, it will be very hard to prevail with them to think that the greatest part of their divinity is such that Christian religion, either as to the matter, or at least as to that mode wherein alone they have imbibed it, is little or not at all concerned in: nor will it be easy to persuade them that it is a mystery laid up in the Scripture, and all true divinity a wisdom in the knowledge of that mystery, and skill to live unto God accordingly; without which, as I said before, we shall have no peace or agreement in this world. "Nobis curiositate opus non est post Jesum Christum, nec inquisitione post evangelium," says Tertullian;—"Curiosity after the doctrine of Christ, and philosophical inquisitions" (in religion) "after the gospel, belong not unto us." As we are,—

IV. It were well if Christians would but seriously consider what and *how many things they are wherein their present apprehensions of the mind and will of God do centre and agree*,—I mean as to the substance of them, their nature and importance, and how far they will lead men in the ways of pleasing God, and coming to the enjoyment of him. Were not an endeavour to this purpose impeded by many men's importunate cries of "*All* or *none*," "As good nothing at all as not every thing," and that in this or that way, mode, or fashion, it might not a little conduce to the peace of Christendom. And I must acknowledge unto you that I think it is prejudice, carnal interest, love of power, and present enjoyments, with other secular advantages, joined with pride, self-will, and contempt of others, that keep the professors of Christianity from conspiring to improve this consideration. But, God help us, we are all for *parties*, and our own exact being in the right, and therein the *only church* of Christ in the earth,—at least, that others are so only so far as they agree with us, we being ourselves the rule and standard of all gospel church state, laying weight upon what we *differ* from others in, for the most part exceedingly above what it doth deserve. Were "the same mind in us that was in Christ Jesus," the same frame of spirit that was in his blessed apostles, we should be willing to try the effects of his love and care towards all that profess his name, by a sedate consideration, at least, how far he hath instructed them in the knowledge of his will, and what effects this learning of him may produce. And to tell you truly, I do not think there is a more horrid monster in the earth than that opinion is, which, in the great diversity that there is among Christians in the world, includes happiness and salvation within the limits and precincts of any party of them, as though

Christ and the gospel, their own faith, obedience, and sufferings, could not possibly do them any good in their station and condition. This is that Alecto,

> —— "Cui tristia bella,
> Iraque, insidiæque, et crimina noxia cordi.
> Odit et ipse pater Pluton; odêre sorores
> Tartareæ monstrum: Tot sese vertit in ora,
> Tam sævæ facies, tot pullulat atra colubris." Virg. Æn. vii. 325.

Wherever this opinion takes place, which indeed bids defiance to the goodness of God and the blood of Christ with a gigantic boldness, for men to talk of moderation, unity, and peace, is to mock others, and to befool themselves in things of the greatest importance in the world. "Altera manu ostentant panem, altera lapidem ferunt." For my own part, I have not any firmer persuasion in and about these things, nor that yields more satisfaction and contentment unto my mind in reflections upon it, than this,—that if a man sincerely believe all that, and only that, wherein all Christians in the world agree, and yield obedience unto God according to the guidance of what he doth so believe, not neglecting or refusing the knowledge of any one truth that he hath sufficient means to be instructed in, he need not go unto any church in the world to secure his salvation. "Hic murus aheneus esto," Hor. Ep. i. 1, 60. It is true it is the duty of such a man to join himself unto some church of Christ or other, which walks in professed subjection unto his institutions, and in the observation of his appointments; but to think that his not being of, or joining with, this or that society, should cut him off from all hopes of a blessed eternity, is but to entertain a *viper* in our minds, or to act suitably to the principles of the *old serpent*, and to put forth the venom of his poison. Some of the ancients, indeed, tell us that out of the catholic church there is no salvation; and so say I also, but, withal, that the belief mentioned of the truths generally embraced by Christians in their present divisions in the world (I still speak of the most famous and numerous societies of them), and its profession, do so constitute a man a member of the catholic church, that whilst he walks answerably to his profession, it is not in the power of this or that, no, not of all the churches in the world, to divest him of that privilege. Nor can all these cries that are in the world, "We are the church, and we are the church; you are not the church, and you are not the church," persuade me but that as every assembly in the general notion of it is a church, so every assembly of Christians that ordinarily meet to worship God in Christ according to his appointment is a church of Christ,—

> —— "Hæc, mi pater,
> Te dicere æquom fuit, et id defendere." Ter. Adel. iv. 5, 40.

When you talked of moderation and unity, such principles as these had better become you than those which you either privately couched in your discourse or openly insisted on. Men that think of reducing unity among Christians, upon the precise terms of that truth which they suppose themselves "in solidum" possessors of, "ipsi sibi somnia fingunt," do but entertain themselves with pleasant dreams, which a little consideration may awake them from. Charity, condescension, a retrenchment of opinions, with a rejection of secular interests, and a design for the pursuit of general obedience,—without any such respect to the particular enclosures which diversity of opinions, and different measures of light and knowledge, have made in the field of the Lord, as should confine the effects of any duty towards the disciples of Christ unto those within them,—with the like actings of minds suited unto the example of Jesus Christ, must introduce the desired unity, or we shall expect it in vain.

These are some of my hasty thoughts upon the principles of Protestants before mentioned, which you and others may make use of as you and they please. In the meantime, I shall pray that we may, amidst all our *differences*, love one another, pray for one another, wait patiently for the communication of farther light unto one another, leave evil surmises, and much more the condemning and seeking the ruin of those that dissent from us, which men usually do on various pretences, most of them false and coined for the present purpose. And when we can arrive thereunto, I shall hope that from such general principles as before mentioned somewhat may be advanced towards the peace of Christians; and that there will be so when the whole concernment of religion shall, in the providence of God, be unravelled from that worldly and secular interest wherewith it hath been wound up and entangled for sundry ages; and when men shall not be engaged, from their cradles to their graves, in a precipitate zeal for any church or way of profession, by outward advantages inseparably mixed and blended with it before they came into the world. In the meantime, to expect unity in profession, by the reduction of all men to a precise agreement in all the doctrines that have been and are ventilated among Christians, and in all acts and ways of worship, is to refer the supreme and last determination of things evangelical to the sword of secular power and violence, and to inscribe "Vox ultima Christi" upon great guns and other engines of war, seeing otherwise it will not be effected;—and what may be done this way I know not.

"Sponte tonat; coeunt ipsæ sine flamine nubes."

CHAPTER X.

Farther vindication of the second chapter of the "Animadversions"—The remaining principles of "Fiat Lux" considered.

It is time to return and put an end unto our review of those principles which I observed your discourse to be built upon. The next, as laid down in the "Animadversions," p. 103,[1] is, "That the pope is a good man, one that seeks nothing but our good, that never did us harm, but hath the care and inspection of us committed unto him by Christ." In the repetition hereof you leave out all the last part, and express no more but "The pope is a good man, and seeks nothing but our good;" and therein aim at a double advantage unto yourself,—first, That you may, with some colour of truth, though *really* without it, deny the assertion to be yours, when the latter part of it, which, upon the matter, is that which gives the sense and determines the meaning of the whole, is expressly contended for by you, and that frequently and at large; secondly, That you may vent an empty cavil against that expression, "Seeks nothing but our good," whereas had you added the next words, "And never did us harm," every one would have perceived in what sense the former were spoken, and so have prevented the frivolous exception. Your words are, "This also I nowhere aver, for I never saw him, nor have any such acquaintance with him as to know whether he be a good man or no; though, in charity, I do not use to judge hardly of any body, much less could say that he whom I know to have a general solicitude for all churches seeks nothing but our good. Sir, if I had pondered my words in 'Fiat Lux' no better than you heed yours in your 'Animadversions' upon it, they might even go together, both of them, to lay up pepper and spices, or some yet more vile employment."

For what you have said of the pope, I desire the reader to consult your paragraph so entitled; and if he find not that you have said *ten times more* in the commendation of him than I intimated in the words laid down for your principle, I am content to be esteemed to have done you wrong. You have, indeed, not only set him out *as a good man*, but have made him *much more than a man*, and have ascribed that unto him which is not lawful to be ascribed unto any man whatever. Some of your expressions I have again reminded you of, and many others of the same nature might be instanced in; and what you can say more of him than you have done, unless you would "exalt him above all that is called God, and is worshipped," unless you should set him "in the temple of God, and show him that

[1] See p. 42 of the present volume.

he is God," I know not. Let the reader, if he please, consult your expressions where you have placed them; I shall stain paper with them no more. And you do but trifle with us, when you tell us that "you know not the pope, nor have any such acquaintance with him as to know whether he be a good man or no,"—as though your personal acquaintance with this or that pope belonged at all to our question; although I must needs say that it seems very strange unto me that you should hang the weight of religion and the salvation of your own soul upon one of whom you know not so much as whether he be a good man or no. For my part, I am persuaded there is no such hardship in Christian religion, as that we should be bound to believe that all the safety of our faith and salvation depends on a man, and he such a one as concerning whom we know not whether he be a good man or no. The apostle lays the foundation of our hope on better ground, Heb. i. 1–3. And yet, whatever opinion you may have of your present pope, you are forced to be at this indifferency about his honesty, because you are not able to deny but that very many of his predecessors, on whose shoulders the weight of all your religion lay, no less than you suppose it doth on his who now sways the papal sceptre, were very brutes,—so far from being good men as that they may be reckoned amongst the worst in the world. Protestants, as I said, are persuaded that their faith is laid up in better hands. With the latter part of my words, as by you set down, you play sophistically, that you might say something to them (as to my knowledge, I never observed any man so hard put to it to say somewhat, were it right or wrong); which seems to be the utmost of your design. You feign the sense of my words to be, "That the pope doth no other thing in the world but seek our good;" and confute me by saying, "That he hath a general solicitude for all churches." But, sir, I said not, "He doth nothing but seek our good;" but only, "He seeks nothing but our good, and never did us harm." And you may quickly see how causelessly you fall into a contemplation of your accuracy in your "Fiat," and of the looseness of my expressions in the "Animadversions;" for although I acknowledge that discourse to have been written in greater haste than perhaps the severer judgments of learned men might well allow of, as is also this return unto your epistle, being both of them proportioned rather unto the merits of your discourse than that of the cause in agitation between us, yet I cannot see that you or any man else hath any just cause to except against this expression of my intention, which yet is the only one that in that kind falls under your censure. For whereas I say that the pope seeks nothing but our good, and that he never did us harm, would any man living but yourself understand these words any otherwise but with reference unto them of whom I speak?—that is, as to us, he seeks nothing but *our* good, whatever he doth in the world besides. And is it not a wild interpretation that you make of my words, whilst you suppose me to intimate that "absolutely the pope doth nothing in the world," or hath no other business at all that he concerns himself in, but only the seeking of our good in particular? If you cannot allow the books that you read the common civility of interpreting things indefinitely expressed in them with the limitations that the subject-matter whereof they treat requires, you had better employ your time in any thing than study, as being not able to understand many lines in any author you shall read. Nor are such expressions to be avoided in our common discourse. If a man, talking of your "Fiat," should say that you do nothing but seek the good of your countrymen, would you interpret his words as though he denied that you say mass, and hear confessions, or to intimate that you do nothing but write "Fiats?" And you know with whom lies both "jus et norma loquendi."

The tenth and last principle is, "That the devotion of Catholics far transcends that of Protestants." So you now express it; what you mention being but one part of three that the "Animadversions" speak unto. Hereunto you reply, "But, sir, I never made in 'Fiat Lux' any comparisons between your devotions; nor can I say how much the one is, or how little the other. But you are the maddest commentator that I have ever seen: you first make the text, and then animadversions upon it." Pray, sir, have a *little patience*, and learn from this instance not to be too confident upon your memory for the future. I shall rather think that fails you at present than your conscience: but a failure I am sure there is, and you shall take the liberty to charge it where you please; which is more than every one would allow you. I would, indeed, desirously free myself from the labour of transcribing aught that you have written to this purpose in your "Fiat," and only refer you to the places, which you seem to have forgotten; but because this is the last instance of this kind that we are to treat about, and you have by degrees raised your confidence in denying your own words, to that height as to accuse them of madness who do but remind you of them, I shall represent unto you once again what you have written to this purpose: and I am persuaded, upon your review of it, you will like it so well as to be sorry that ever you disowned it. I shall instance only in one place, which is sect. xxii., pp. 270, 271, where your words are these:—"When I beheld" (in the Catholic countries) "the deep reverence and earnest devotion of the people, the majesty of their service, the gravity of their altars, the decency of their priests, 'Certainly,' said I within myself, 'this is the house of God, the gate of heaven.' Alas!, our churches in England, as they be now, be as short of those, either for decency, use, or piety, as stables to a princely palace! There they be upon their knees all the week long at their prayers, many of them constantly an hour together in the morning, and half an hour he that is least. And, 'My house,' said God, 'is the house of prayer:' but our churches are either shut up all the week, or, if they be open, are wholly taken up with boys shouting, running, and gamboling all about. On Sundays, indeed, our people sit quiet, and decently dressed, but to bow the knee is quite out of fashion; and if any one chance to do it, as it is rare to behold, so he is very nimble at it, and as soon up as down, as if he made a courtship with his knees, and only tried if his nerves and sinews were as good to bow as to stand upright. And our whole religious work here is to sit quietly whilst the minister speaks upon a text, ... and that we spend all our days, ever learning and teaching," etc. If this discourse must be esteemed text, I pray tell me whose it is, yours or mine; or whether it doth not contain a comparison between the devotion of your Catholics and Protestants; and whether that of the former be not preferred above the other: and when you have done so, pray also tell me whether you suppose it an honest and candid way of handling matters of this importance, or, indeed, of any sort whatever, for a man to say and unsay at his pleasure according unto what he apprehends to be for his present advantage; and whether a man may believe you that you so accurately pondered the words of your "Fiat" as you seem to pretend, seeing you dare not abide by what you have written, but disclaim it. And yet I confess this may fall out, if your design in the weighing of your words was so to place them as to deceive us by them; which, indeed, it seems to have been. But it is your unhappiness that your words are brought unto other men's scales after they had so fairly passed your own. For the devotion itself (by the way) of Catholics, which you here paint forth unto us, it looks very suspiciously to be painted. The piety of your churches, wherein they exceed ours, I confess I understand not; and your people's frequenting public places to perform their private devotions leans much to the old Pharisaism, which our Saviour himself hath branded to all eternity for hypocritical, and carried on with little attendance unto his precept of making the closet, and that with the door shut upon the devotionists, the most proper seat of private supplications. Besides, if their prayers consist, as for the most part they do, in going over by tale a set number of sayings which they little understand, you may do well to commend your devotion to them that understand not one word of gospel, for those that do will not attend unto it. And so I have once more passed through the principles of your work, with a fresh discussion of some of them,—which I tell you again I suppose sufficient to satisfy judicious and ingenuous persons in the sophistry and inconclusiveness of the whole; my farther procedure being intended for the satisfaction of yourself and such others as have imbibed the prejudices which you endeavour to forestall your minds withal, and thereby have given no small impeachment unto your judgment and ingenuity.

CHAPTER XI.

Judicious readers—Schoolmen the forgers of Popery—Nature of the discourse in "Fiat Lux."

YOUR ensuing discourses are such as might well be passed by, as containing nothing serious or worth a review.

> "An passim sequerer corvum?"

Ludicrous similitudes, with trifling exceptions to some words in the "Animadversions," cut off from that coherence wherein they are placed, are the chief ingredients of it. With these you aim, with your wonted success, to make sport:—

> —— "Venite in ignem
> Pleni ruris et inficetiarum
> Annales Volusî."

I wish we had agreed beforehand,

> "Ut faceres tu quod velles; nec non ego possem,
> Indulgere mihi,"

that I might have been freed from the consideration of such trifles: as the case stands, I shall make my passage through them with what speed I can.

First, You except against the close of the consideration of your principles, namely, "That I would do so to my book also, if I had none to deal with but ingenuous and judicious readers;" and tell me, "that it seems what follows is for readers neither judicious nor ingenuous." But why so, I pray? That which is written for the information of them who want either judgment or ingenuity, may be also written for their use who have both. Neither did I speak absolutely of them that were ingenuous and judicious, but added also, that they were such as had an acquaintance with the state of religion of old and at this day in Europe, with the concernment of their own souls in these things. With such as these, I supposed then, and do still, that a discovery of the sophistry of your discourse, and the falseness of the principles you proceeded on, was sufficient to give them satisfaction as to the usefulness of the whole, without a particular ventilating of the flourishes that you made upon your sandy foundations. But because I know there were some that might, by the commendation of your friends, light upon your discourse, that either, being prepossessed by prejudices, might want the ingenuity to examine particularly your assertions and inferences, or, through unacquaintedness with the stories of some things that you referred unto, might be disenabled to make a right judgment of what you averred, I was willing to take some farther pains also for your satisfaction; and what was herein done or spoken amiss, as yet I cannot discern. But I am persuaded that if you had not supposed that you had some of little judgment and less ingenuity to give satisfaction unto, you would never have pleased yourself with the writing of such empty trifles in a business wherein you pretend so great a concernment.

Page 31. You observe that I say, "The schoolmen were the hammerers and forgers of Popery;" and add, "Alas, sir, I see that anger spoils your memory: for in the 11th and 12th chapters you make Popery to be hammered and forged not a few hundreds of years before any schoolmen were extant; and therefore tell me that I hate the schoolmen as the Frenchmen do Talbot, for having been frightened with them formerly,—

'Sed risu inepto res ineptior nulla est.'"

I confess the language of your schoolmen is so corrupt and barbarous,—many of the things they sweat about so vain, curious, unprofitable,—their way of handling things, and expressing the notions of their minds, so perplexed, dark, obscure, and oftentimes unintelligible,—divers of their assertions and suppositions so horrid and monstrous,—the whole system of their pretended divinity so alien and foreign unto the mystery of the gospel,—that I know no great reason that any man hath much to delight in them. These things have made them the sport and scorn of the learnedest men that ever lived in the communion of your own church. What one said of old of others may be well applied unto them:—

"Statum lacessunt omnipotentis Dei
 Calumniosis litibus.
Fidem minutis dissecant ambagibus
 Ut quisque est lingua nequior.
Solvunt ligantque quæstionum vincula
 Per Syllogismos plectiles."

Indeed, to see them come forth harnessed with syllogisms and sophisms; attended with *obs* and *sols;* speaking part the language of the Jews, and part the language of Ashdod; fighting and contending among themselves as if they had sprung from the teeth of Cadmus' serpent; subjecting all the properties, decrees, and actions of the holy God to their profane babblings,—might perhaps beget some fear in the minds of men not much guilty of want of constancy, as the sight of the harpies did of old to Æneas and his companions, of whom they gave that account,—

> "Tristius haud illis monstrum, nec sævior ulla
> Pestis et ira Deum Stygiis sese extulit undis.
> Vidimus, et subita gelidus formidine sanguis
> Diriguit; cecidere animi." Virg. Æn. iii. 214, 259.

But the truth is, there is no real cause of fear of them: they are not like to do mischief to any, unless they are resolved aforehand to give up their faith in the things of God to the authority of this or that philosopher, and forego all solid, rational consideration of things, to betake themselves to sophistical canting, and the winding up of subtilty into plain nonsense,—which oftentimes befalls the best of them; whence Melchior Canus, one of yourselves, says of some of your learned disputes, "Puderet me dicere non intelligere, si ipsi intelligerent qui tractârunt;"—"I should be ashamed to say I did not understand them, but that they understood not themselves." Others may be entangled by them, who, if they cannot untie your knots, may break your webs, especially when they find the conclusions, as oftentimes they are, directly contrary to Scripture, right reason, and natural sense itself. For they are the genuine offspring of the old sophisters whom Lucian talks of in his "Menippus," or Νεκυομαντεία, and tells us that, in hearing the disputations, Τὸ πάντων δεινῶν ἀτοπώτατον, ὅτι περὶ τῶν ἐναντιωτάτων ἕκαστος αὐτῶν λέγων, σφόδρα νικῶντας καὶ πιθανοὺς λόγους ἐπορίζετο, ὥστε μήτε τῷ θερμὸν τὸ αὐτὸ πρᾶγμα λέγοντι, μήτε τῷ ψυχρόν, ἀντιλέγειν ἔχειν, καὶ ταῦτα, εἰδότα σαφῶς ὡς οὐκ ἄν ποτε θερμόν τι εἴη καὶ ψυχρὸν ἐν ταυτῷ χρόνῳ·—"That," saith he, "which seemed the most absurd of all was, that when they disputed of things absolutely contrary, they yet brought invincible and persuasive reasons to prove what they said, so that I durst not speak a word against him that affirmed hot and cold to be the same, although I knew well enough that the same thing could not be hot and cold at the same time." And therefore he tells us, that in hearing of them he did, like a man half asleep, sometimes nod one way and sometimes another; which is certainly the deportment of the generality of them who are conversant in the wrangles of your schoolmen. But whatever I said of them or your church is perfectly consistent with itself and the truth. I grant that before the schoolmen set forth in the world, many unsound opinions were broached in, and many superstitious practices admitted into your church, and a great pretence raised unto a superintendency over other churches; which were parts of that mass out of which your Popery is formed: but before the schoolmen took it in hand, it was "rudis indigestaque moles,"—a heap, not a house. As Rabbi Juda Hakkadosh gathered the passant traditions of his own time among the Jews into a body or system, which is called the "Mishna," or duplicate of their law,—wherein he composed a new religion for them, sufficiently distant from that which was professed by their forefathers,—so have your schoolmen done also. Out of the passant traditions of the days wherein they lived, blended with sophistical, corrupted notions of their own, countenanced and gilded with the sayings of some ancient writers of the church, for the most part wrested or misunderstood, they have hammered out that *system of philosophical-traditional divinity* which is now enstamped with the authority of the Tridentine council; being as far distant from the divinity of the New Testament as the farrago of traditions collected by Rabbi Juda, and improved in the Talmuds, is from that of the Old.

Pages 33–35. Having nothing else to say, you fall again upon my pretended mistake of considering that as "spoken absolutely by you which you spake only upon supposition;" and talk of "metaphysical speculations in your 'Fiat,' which you conceive me very unmeet to deal withal; and direct me to Bellarmine's catechism, as better suiting my inclination and capacity." But, sir, we are not wont here in England to account cloudy, dark, sophistical declamations, to be metaphysical speculations; nor every feigned supposition to be a philosophical abstraction. I wish you would be persuaded that there is not the least tincture of any solid metaphysics in your whole discourse. It may be, indeed, you would be angry with them that should undeceive you, and cry out,—

> —— "Pol, me occidistis, amici,
> Non servastis;"

as he did,—

> "Cui demptus per vim mentis gratissimus error."

You may perhaps please yourself with conceits of your metaphysical achievements; but your friends cannot but pity you to see your vanity. The least youth in our universities will tell you, that to make a general supposition, true or false, and to flourish upon it with words of a seeming probability, without any cogency or proof, belongs to rhetoric, and not at all to metaphysics; and this is the very nature of your discourse. Nor do I mistake your aim in it, as you pretend. I grant in the place you would be thought to reply unto, though you speak not one word to the purpose, that your inquiry is after a means of settling men in the truth, upon supposition that they are not yet attained thereunto; and you labour to show the difficulty that there is in that attainment, upon the account of the insufficiency of many mediums that may be pretended to be used for that end. In answer unto your inquiry, I tell you directly, that the only means of settling men in the truth of religion is divine revelation, and that this revelation is entirely and perfectly contained in the Scripture; which, therefore, is a sufficient means of settling all men in the truth. Suppose them "rasæ tabulæ;" suppose them utterly ignorant of truth; suppose them prejudiced against it; suppose them divided amongst themselves about it;—the only safe, rational, secure way of bringing them all to settlement is their belief of the revelation of God contained in the Scripture. This I manifested unto you in the "Animadversions;" whereunto you reply by a commendation of your own metaphysical abilities, with the excellencies of your discourse, without taking the least notice of my answer, or the reasons given you against that fanatical, groundless "credo" which you would now again impose upon us.

CHAPTER XII.

False suppositions, causing false and absurd consequences—Whence we had the gospel in England, and by whose means—What is our duty in reference unto them by whom we receive the gospel.

Page 36. You insist upon somewhat in particular that looks towards your purpose, which shall therefore be discussed; for I shall not willingly miss any opportunity that you will afford me of examining whatever you have to tender in the behalf of your dying cause. You mind me, therefore, of my answer unto that discourse of yours, "If the Papist or Roman Catholic, who first brought us the news of Christianity, be now become so odious, then may likewise the whole story of Christianity be thought a romance. You speak with the like extravagancy, and mind not my hypothetics at all, to speak directly to my inference, as it becomes a man of art to do; but, neglecting my consequence, which in that discourse is principally and solely intended, you seem to deny my supposition, which, if my discourse had been drawn into a syllogism, would have been the minor of it. And it consists of two categories,—First, That the Papist is now become odious; secondly, That the Papist delivered us the first news of Christianity. The first of these you little heed; the second you deny. 'That the Papist,' say you, 'or Roman Catholic, first brought Christ and his Christianity into this land, is most untrue. I wonder,' etc. And your reason is, 'Because if any Romans came hither, they were not Papists; and indeed our Christianity came from the east.' And this is all you say to my hypothetic, or conditional ratiocination, as if I had said nothing at all but that one absolute category, which, being delivered before, I now only suppose. You used to call me a civil logician, but I fear a natural one, as you are, will hardly be able to justify this notion of yours as artificial. A conditional hath a verity of its own, so far differing from the supposed category, that this being false, that may yet be true. For example, if I should say thus, 'A man who hath wings as an eagle, or if a man had the wings of an eagle, he might fly in the air as well as another bird;' and such an assertion is not to be confuted by proving that a man hath not the wings of an eagle."

The substance of this whole discourse is no more but this, That because the inference upon a supposition may be a consequence *logically* true, though the supposition be false or feigned, therefore the *consequent*, or thing inferred, also is really true, and a man must fly in the air, as you say, "like another bird." But, sir, though every consequence be true logically,—that is, lawfully inferred from its premises, be they true or false, and so must in disputation be allowed,—yet, where the consequent is the thing in question, to suppose that if the consequence be lawfully educed from the premises, that it also must be true, is a fond surmise. And therefore they know "qui nondum ære laventur," that the way to disappoint the conclusion of an hypothetic syllogism is to disprove the category included in the supposition, when reduced into an assumption from whence it is to be inferred. For instance, if the thing in question be, Whether a man can fly in the air, as you say, "like another bird," and to prove it, you should say, "If he has wings he can do so;" the way, I think, to stop your progress is to deny that he hath wings; and if you should continue to wrangle that your inference is good, "If he hath wings he may fly like another bird," you would but make yourself ridiculous. But if you may be allowed to make false and absurd suppositions, and must have them taken for granted, you are very much to blame if you infer not conclusions unto your own purpose. And this in general is your constant way of dealing. Unless we will allow you to suppose yourselves to be the church, and that all the excellent things which are spoken of the church belong unto you alone, with the like groundless presumptions, you are instantly mute, as if there had appeared unto you

"Harpocrates digito qui significat St."[1]

But if, in the case in agitation between us, I should permit you without control to make what suppositions you please, and to make inferences from them which must be admitted for truth because logically following upon your suppositions, what man of art I might have appeared unto *you* I know not; I fear with others I should scarcely have preserved the reputation of common sense or under-

[1] God of silence; commonly represented with his finger on his mouth, as if hushing to silence, and saying "St."—Ed.

standing. And I must acknowledge unto you that I am ignorant of that logic which teacheth men to suffer their adversaries to proceed and infer upon absurdities and false suppositions, to oppose the truth which they maintain. And yet I know well enough what Aristotle hath taught us concerning *τὸ λαμϐάνειν τὸ ἐν ἀρχῇ, καὶ τὸ ἀναίτιον ὡς αἴτιον τιθέναι·* in which part of his logic you seem to have been most conversant.

But let us once again consider your ratiocination as here you endeavour to reinforce it. Your supposition, you say, "includes these two categories,—first, That the Papists are become odious unto us; secondly, That the Papists delivered us the first news of Christianity." Well, both these propositions I deny. Papists are not become odious unto us, though we love not their Popery; Papists did not bring us the first news of Christianity. This I have proved unto you already, and shall yet do it farther Will you now be angry and talk of logic, because I grant not the consequent of these false pretensions to be true? as if every syllogism must of necessity be true materially which is so in form. But yet farther to discover your mistake, I was so willing to hear you out unto the utmost of what you had to say, that in the "Animadversions," after the discovery of the falsity of the assertions that it arose from, I suffered your supposition to pass, and showed you the weakness of your inference upon it. And the reason of my so doing was this, that because though the Papists brought not the gospel first into England, yet I do not judge it impossible but that they may be the means of communicating it unto some other place or people; and I would be loath to grant that they who receive it from them must either always embrace their Popery or renounce the gospel. I confess a great entanglement would be put on the thoughts and minds of such persons by the principle of the *infallibility* of them that sent your teachers; whereinto it may be also they would labour to resolve your belief. But yet if withal you shall communicate unto them the gospel itself, as the great repository of the mysteries of that religion wherein you instruct them, there is a sufficient foundation laid for their reception of Christianity and the rejection of your Popery; for when once the gospel hath evidenced itself unto their consciences that it is from God, as it will do if it be received unto any benefit or advantage at all, they will or may easily discern that those who brought it unto them were themselves in many things deceived in their apprehensions of the mind of God therein revealed, especially as to your pretence of the infallibility of any man or men, any farther than his conceptions agree with what is revealed in that gospel which they have received, and now for its own sake believe to be from God. And once to imagine that when the Scripture is received by faith, and hath brought the soul into subjection to the authority of God, exerting itself in it and by it, that it will not warrant them in the rejection of any respect unto men whatever, is "to err, not knowing the Scripture, nor the power of God." In this condition of things, men will bless God for any means which he was pleased to use in the communicating the gospel unto them; and if those who were employed in that work shall persist in obtruding upon their faith and worship things that are not revealed, they will quickly discover such a contradiction in their principles as that it is utterly impossible that they should rationally assent unto and embrace them all, but either they must renounce the gospel which they have brought them, or reject those other principles which they would impose upon them that are contrary thereunto. And whether of these they will do, upon a supposition that the gospel hath now obtained that authority over their consciences and minds which it claims in and over all that receive it, it is no hard matter to determine. Men, then, who have themselves mixed the doctrine of the gospel with many abominable errors of their own, may in the providence of God be made instrumental to convey the gospel unto others. At the first tender of it they may, for the truth's sake, which they are convinced of, receive also the errors that are tendered unto them, as being as yet not able to discern the chaff from the wheat; but when once the gospel is rooted in their minds, and they begin to have their senses exercised therein to discern between good and evil, and their faith of the truth they receive is resolved into the authority of God himself, the author of the gospel, they have their warrant for the rejection of the errors which they had before imbibed, according as they shall be discovered unto them. For though they may first consider the gospel on the proposition of them that first bring them the tidings of it, as the Samaritans came to our Saviour upon the information of the woman, yet when they come to experience themselves its power and efficacy, they believe it for its own sake, as those did also in our Lord Jesus Christ upon his own account; when this is done they will be enabled to distinguish, as the prophet speaks, "between a dream and a prophecy, between chaff and wheat," between error and truth. And thus if we should grant that the first news of Christianity was brought into England by Papists, yet it doth not at all follow that if we reject Popery we must also reject the gospel, or esteem it a romance; for if we should have received Popery, we should have received it only upon the credit and authority of them that brought it, but the truth of Christianity we should have received on the authority of the gospel which was brought unto us: so that our entertainment of Popery and Christianity standing not on the same bottom or foot of account, we might well reject the one and retain the other. But this consideration as to us is needless;

they were not Papists which brought Christianity first into this land. Wherefore, well knowing that the whole strength of your reasoning depends on the supposition that they were so, you proceed to confirm it in your manner; that is, by saying it over again. But we will hear you speaking your own words:—

"We had not our Christianity immediately from the east, nor from Joseph of Arimathea, we Englishmen had not; for as he delivered his Christianity unto some Britons when our land was not called England, but Albion or Brittany, and the inhabitants were not Englishmen, but Britons or Cimbrians, so likewise did that Christianity and the whole news of it quite vanish, being suddenly overwhelmed by the ancient deluge of Paganism. Nor did it ever come from them to us; nay, the Britons themselves had so forgot and lost it, that they also needed a second conversion; which they received from Pope Eleutherius. And that was the only news of Christianity which prevailed and lasted even amongst the very Britons: which seems to me a great secret of divine Providence in planting and governing his church, as if he would have nothing to stand firm and lasting but what was immediately fixed by and seated upon that rock;—for all other conversions have variety, and the very seats of the other apostles failed, that all might the better cement in the unity of one head; nay, the tables which God wrote with his own hand were broken, but the others written by Moses remained, that we might learn to give a due respect unto him whom God hath set over us as our head and ruler under him, and none exalt himself against him. I know you will laugh at this my observation; but I cannot but tell you what I think. When I speak, then, of the news of Christianity being first brought to this land, I mean not that which was first brought upon the earth or soil of this land, and spoken to any body then dwelling here, but that which was delivered to the forefathers of the now present inhabitants, who were Saxons or Englishmen. And I say that we, the now present inhabitants of England, offspring of the Saxons or English, had the first news of our Christianity immediately from Rome, and from Pope Gregorius, the Roman patriarch, by the hands of his missioner, St Austin. Since, then, the categoric expressions are both clear,—namely, That the Papists first brought us the news of Christianity; and, secondly, That the Papist is now become odious unto us,—what say you to my consequent, That the whole story of Christianity may as well be deemed a romance as any part of that Christianity we at first received is now judged to be a part of a romance? This consequence of mine it behoved a man of those great parts you would be thought to have to heed attentively, and yet you never minded it."

Some few observations upon this discourse of yours will farther manifest the absurdity of that consequence which you feign not to have been taken notice of in the "Animadversions;" for which you had no cause, but that you might easily discern that you did not deserve it. First, then, you grant that the gospel came out of the east into this land: so, then, we did not first receive the gospel from Rome, much less by the means of Papists. "But the land was then called Albion or Brittany, and the people Britons or Cimbrians, not Englishmen." What then? though the names of places or people are changed, the gospel, wherever it is, is still the same. "But the Britons lost the gospel until they had a new conversion from Rome, by the means of Eleutherius." But you fail, sir, and are either ignorant in the story of those times or else wilfully pervert the truth. All the fathers and favourers of that story agree that Christianity was well rooted and known in Britain when Lucius, as is pretended, sent to Eleutherius for assistance in its propagation. Your own Baronius will assure you no less, ad an. 183, n. 3, 4. Gildas, De Excid. will do it more fully. Virunnius tells us that the Britons were then "strengthened in the faith," not that they then received it; strengthened in what they had, not newly converted, though some, as it is said, were so. And the days of Lucius are assigned by Sabellicus as the time wherein the whole province received the name of Christ "publicitus cum ordinatione,"—"by public decree." That it was received there before, and abode there, as in other places of the world, under persecution, all men agree. In this interval of time did the British church bring forth Claudia, Ruffina, Elvanus, and Meduinus; whose names, amongst others, are yet preserved. And to this space of time do the testimonies of Tertullian adv. Judæos, and of Origen, Hom. 4, in Ezek., concerning Christianity in Britain, belong. Besides, if the only prevalent religion in Brittany were, as you fancy, that which came from Rome, how came the observation of Easter, both amongst the Britons, as Beda manifests, and the Scots, as Petrus Cluniacensis declares, to be answerable to the customs of the Eastern church, and contrary to those of the Roman? Did those that came from Rome teach them to do that which they judged their duty not to do? But what need we stay in the confutation of this figment? The very epistle of Eleutherius manifests it abundantly so to be. If there be any thing of truth in that rescript, it doth not appear that Lucius wrote any thing unto him about Christian religion, but about the imperial laws to govern his kingdom by; and Eleutherius, in his answer, plainly intimates that the Scripture was received amongst the Britons, and the gospel much dispersed over the whole nation. And yet this figment of your own you make the bottom of a most strange contemplation,—namely, that God in his "providence would have all that Christianity fail which came not from Rome." That is the meaning of those expressions, "He would have nothing stand firm or lasting but what was immediately fixed by and seated on that rock; for all other conversions have vanished." Really, sir, I am sorry for you, to see what woful shelves your prejudicate opinions do cast you upon, who in yourself seem to be a well-meaning, good-natured man. Do you think, indeed, that those conversions that were wrought in the world by the means of any persons not coming from Rome, which were Christ himself and all his apostles, were not fixed on the rock? Can such a blasphemous thought enter into your heart? If those primitive converts that were called unto the faith by persons coming out of the east were not built on the rock, they all perished everlastingly, every soul of them; and if the other churches planted by them were not immediately fixed and seated on the rock, they went all to hell, —the gates of it prevailed against them. Do you think, indeed, that God suffered all the churches in the world to come to nothing, that all Christians might be brought into subjection to your pope? which you call "cementing in a unity of one head." If you do so, you think, wickedly, that he is altogether like unto yourself; but he will reprove you, and set your faults in order before your eyes. Such horrible, dismal thoughts do men allow themselves to be conversant withal, who are resolved to sacrifice truth, reason, and charity unto their prejudices and interest! Take heed, sir, lest the rock that you boast of prove not seven hills, and deceive you. In the pursuit of the same consideration you tell me, "that I will laugh at your observation, that the tables written by God's own hand were broken, but those written by Moses remained, that we may learn to give a due respect to him whom God hath set over us." But you do not well to say so; I do not laugh at your observation, but I really pity you that make it. Pray, sir, what were those tables that were written by Moses, when those written by God were broken? Such mistakes as these you ever and anon fall into, and I fear for want of being conversant in holy writ; which it seems your principles prompt you unto a neglect of. Sir, the tables prepared by Moses were no less written with the finger of God than those were which he first prepared himself, Exod. xxxiv. 1, 28; Deut. x. 1, 2, 4. And if you had laid a good ground for your notion, that the tables prepared by God were broken, and those hewed by Moses preserved, and would have only added, what you ought to have done, that there was nothing in the tables delivered unto the people by Moses but what was written by the finger of God, I should have commended both it and the inference you make from it. As it is built by you on the sand, it would fall with its own weight, were it no heavier than a feather. But you lay great stress, I suppose, on that which follows,—namely, "That the Britons being expelled by the Saxons, the Saxons first received their Christianity from Rome." You may remember what hath been told you already in answer to this case, about Rome's being left without inhabitants by Totilas. Besides, if we that are now inhabitants of England must be thought to have first received the gospel then when it was first preached unto our own progenitors, in a direct line ascending, this will be found a matter so dubious and uncertain as not possibly to be a thing of any concernment in Christian religion; and, moreover, will exempt most of the *chief families* of England from your enclosure, seeing one way or other they derive themselves from the ancient Britons. Such pitiful trifles are you forced to make use of to give countenance unto your cause! But let it be granted that Christianity was first communicated unto the Saxons from Rome in the days of Pope Gregory,—which yet, indeed, is not true neither; for queen Bertha, with her bishop Luidhardus, had both practised the worship of Christ in England before his coming, and so prepared the people, that Gregory says in one of his epistles, "Anglorum gentem voluisse fieri Christianam,"—what will thence ensue? "Why, plainly, that we must all be Papists, or atheists, and esteem the whole gospel a romance." But why so, I pray? "Why, *the categoric assertions are both clear*,—namely, that the Papists first brought us the news of Christianity, and that Papists are now odious." But how comes this about? We were talking of Gregory, and some that came from Rome in his days; and if you take them for Papists you are much deceived. Prove that there was one Papist at Rome in the days of that Gregory, and I will be another,—I mean such a Papist as your present pope is, or as yourself are. Do you think that Gregory believed the Catholic supremacy and infallibility of the pope? the doing whereof in an especial manner constitutes a man a Papist. If you have any such thoughts, you are an utter stranger to the state of things in those days, as also to the writings of Gregory himself: for your better information you may do well to consult him, lib. iv. epist. 32, 36, 38; and sundry other instances may be given out of his own writings, how remote he was from your present Popery. Irregularities and superstitious observations were, not a few in his days, crept into the church of Rome, which you still pertinaciously adhere unto;—as you have the happiness to adhere firmly unto any thing that you once irregularly embrace; but that the main doctrines, principles, practices, and modes of worship which constitute Popery, were known, admitted, practised, or received at Rome in the days of Gregory, I know full well that you are not able to prove. And by this you may see the truth of your first assertion, "That Papists brought us the first news of Christianity;" which you do not in the least endeavour to prove, but take it, hand over head, to be the same with this, "That some from Rome preached the gospel to the Saxons in the days of Gregory," which it hath no manner of affinity withal. Your second true assertion is, "That the Papist is now become odious unto us;" but yet neither will this be granted you. *Popery* we dislike; but that the *Papists* are become odious unto us we absolutely deny. Though we like not the Popery they have admitted, yet we love them for the Christianity which they have retained. And must not that needs be a doughty consequence that is educed out of principles wherein there is not a word of truth? Besides, I have already in part manifested unto you, that supposing both of them to be true, as neither of them is, yet your consequence is altogether inconsequent, and will by no means follow upon them. And this will yet more fully appear in an examination of your ensuing discourse.

That which you fix upon to except against is towards the close of my discourse to this purpose, in these words, as set down by you, p. 40: "Many things delivered us at first with the first news of Christianity, may be afterward rejected for the love of Christ, and by the commission of Christ." The truth of this assertion I have newly proved again unto you, and have exemplified it in the instance of Papists bringing the first news of Christianity to any place; which is not impossible but they may do, though to this nation they did not. I had also before confirmed it with such reasons as you judged it best to take no notice of; which is your way with things that are too hard for you to grapple withal. I must, I see, drive these things through the thick obstacles of your prejudices with more instances, or you will not be sensible of them. What think you, then, of those who received the first news of Christianity by believers of the Circumcision, who at the same time taught them the necessity of being circumcised, and of keeping Moses's law? Were they not bound afterward, upon the discovery of the mistake of their teachers, to retain the gospel, and the truth thereof taught by them, and to reject the observation of Mosaical rites and observations? or were they free, upon the discovery of their mistake, to esteem the whole gospel a romance? What think you of those that were converted by Arians? which were great multitudes, and some whole nations. Were not those nations bound for the love of Christ, by his word, to retain their Christianity, and reject their Arianism? or must they needs account the whole gospel a fable, when they were convinced of the error of their first teachers, denying Christ Jesus in his divine nature to be of the same substance with his Father, or essentially God? To give you an instance that, it may be, will please you better: There are very many Indians in New England, or elsewhere, converted unto Christianity by Protestants; without whose instruction they had never received the least rumour or report of it. Tell me your judgment: if you were now amongst them, would you not endeavour to persuade them that

Christian religion indeed was true, but that their first instructors in it had deceived them as to many particulars of it; which you would undeceive them in, and yet keep them close to their Christianity? And do you not know that many who have in former days been by heretics converted to Christianity from Paganism, have afterward, from the principles of their Christianity, been convinced of their heresy, and retaining the one, have rejected the other? It is not for your advantage to maintain an opposition against so evident a truth, and exemplified by so many instances in all ages. I know well enough the ground of your pertinaciousness in your mistake; it is, that men who receive the gospel do resolve their faith into the authority of them that first preach it unto them. Now, this supposition is openly false, and universally, as to all persons whatever not divinely inspired, yea, as to the apostles themselves, but only with respect unto their working of miracles, which gave testimony unto the doctrine that they taught. Otherwise, God's revelation contained in the Scriptures is that which the faith of men is formally and ultimately resolved into; so that, whatever propositions that are made unto them they may reject, unless they do it with a "non obstante" for its supposed revelation, the whole revelation abides unshaken, and their faith founded thereon. But as to the persons who first bring unto any the tidings of the gospel, seeing the faith of them that receive it is not resolved into their authority or infallibility, they may, they ought, to examine their proposals by that unerring word which they ultimately rest upon, as did the Bereans, and receive or reject them, at first or afterward, as they see cause; and this without the least impeachment of the truth or authority of the gospel itself, which, under this formal consideration, as revealed of God, they absolutely believe. Let us now see what you except hereunto. First, you ask, "What love of Christ's dictates, what commission of Christ, allows you to choose and reject at your own pleasure?" *Ans.* None; nor was that at all in question, nor do you speak like a man that durst look upon the true state of the controversy between us. You proclaim your cause desperate by this perpetual tergiversation. The question is, Whether, when men preach the gospel unto others as a revelation from God, and bring along with them the Scripture, wherein they say that revelation is comprised, when that is received as such, and hath its authority confirmed in the minds of them that receive it, whether are they not bound to try all the teaching in particular of them that first bring it unto them, or afterward continue the preaching of it, whether it be consonant to that rule or word wherein they believe the whole revelation of the will of God relating to the gospel declared unto them to be contained, and *to embrace what is suitable thereunto*, and to reject any thing that in particular may be, by the mistakes of the teachers, imposed upon them? Instead of "believing what the Scripture teacheth, and rejecting what it condemns," you substitute "*choosing or rejecting at your own pleasure*,"—a thing wherein our discourse is not at all concerned. You add, "What heretic was ever so much a fool as not to pretend the love of Christ and commission of Christ for what he did?" What then, I pray? May not others do a thing really upon such grounds as some pretend to do them on falsely? May not a judge have his commission from the king because some have counterfeited the great seal? May not you sincerely seek the good and peace of your country upon the principles of your religion, though some, pretending the same principles, have sought its disturbance and ruin? If there be any force in this exception, it overthrows the authority and efficacy of every thing that any man may falsely pretend unto; which is to shut all order, rule, government, and virtue out of the world. You proceed, "How shall any one know you do it out of any such love or commission, since those who delivered the articles of faith now rejected pretended equal love to Christ and commission of Christ for the delivery of them as any other?" I wonder you should proceed with such impertinent inquiries. How can any man manifest that he doth any thing by the commission of another, but by his producing and manifesting his commission to be his? And how can he prove that he doth it out of love to him, but by his diligence, care, and conscience in the discharge of his duty? as our Saviour tells us, saying, "If ye love me, keep my commandments," which is the proper effect of love unto him, and open evidence or manifestation of it. Now, how should a man prove that he doth any thing by the commission of Christ, but by producing that commission; that is, in the things about which we treat, by declaring and evidencing that the things he proposeth to be believed are revealed by his Spirit in his word, and that the things which he rejects are contrary thereunto? And whatever men may pretend, Christ gives out no adverse commissions; his word is every way and every where the same, at perfect harmony and consistency with itself: so that if it come to that, that several persons do teach contrary doctrines, either before or after one another, or together, under the same pretence of receiving them from Christ,—as was the case between the Pharisees of old that believed and the apostles,—they that attend unto them have a perfect *guide* to direct them in their choice, a perfect *rule* to judge of the things proposed. As in the church of the Jews, the Pharisees had taught the people many things as from God,—for their traditions or *oral law* they pretended to be from God,—our Saviour comes, really a teacher from God, and he disproves their false doctrines which they had prepossessed the people withal; and all this he doth by the Scripture, the word of truth, which they had before received. And this example hath he left unto his church unto the end of the world. But you yet proceed: "Why may we not at length reject all the rest for love of something else, when this love of Christ, which is now crept into the very outside of our lips, is slipped off from thence? Do you think men cannot find a cavil against him as well as his law delivered unto us with the first news of him, and as easily dig up the root as cut up the branches?" You are the pleasantest man at a disputation that ever I met withal; "haud ulli veterum virtute secundus," you outgo your masters in palpable sophistry. If we may and ought, for the love of Christ, reject errors and untruths taught by fallible men, then we may reject him also for the love of other things! Who doubts it but men may if they will, if they have a mind to do so? They may do so physically, but may they do so morally? may they do so upon the same or as good grounds and reasons as they reject errors and false worship for the sake of Christ? With such kind of arguing is the Roman cause supported. Again, you suppose the *law* of Christ to be rejected, and therefore say that his *person* may be so also; but this contains an application of the general thesis unto your particular case, and thereupon the begging of the thing in question. Our inquiry was general, whether things at first delivered by any persons that preach the gospel may not be rejected, without any impeachment of the authority of the gospel itself? Here, that you may insinuate that to be the case between you and us, you suppose the things rejected to be the law of Christ, when, indeed, they are things rejected because they are contrary to the law of Christ, and so affirmed in the assertion which you seek to oppose; for nothing may be rejected by the commission of Christ but what is contrary to his law. The truth is, he that rejects the law of Christ, as it is his, needs no other inducement to reject his person; for he hath done it already in the rejection of his law. But yet it may not be granted, though it belong not unto our present discourse, that every one that rejects any part of the law of Christ must therefore be in a propensity to reject Christ himself, provided that he do it only because he doth not believe it to be any part of his law; for whilst a man abides firm and constant in his faith in Christ and love unto him, with a resolution to submit himself to his whole word, law, and institutions, his misapprehensions of this or that particular in them is no impeachment of his faith or love. Of the same importance is that which you add,—namely, "Did not the Jews, by pretence of their love to the immortal God, whom their forefathers served, reject the whole gospel at once? and why may we not possibly by piecemeal?" You do only cavil at the expression I used, of doing the thing mentioned "for the love of Christ:" but I used it not alone, as knowing how easy a thing it was to pretend it, and how unwarrantable a ground of any actings in religion such a pretence would prove; wherefore I added unto it his "commission,"—that is, his word. And so I desire to know of you whether the Jews, out of love to God, and by the direction of his word, did reject the gospel or no. This you must assert if you intend by this instance to oppose my assertion. Besides, indeed, the Jews did scarce pretend to reject the gospel out of love to God, but to their old church-state and traditions; on which very account yourselves at this day reject many important truths of it. But it is one thing vainly to pretend the love of God; another so to love him indeed as to keep his commandments, and in so doing to cleave unto the truth, and to reject that which is contrary thereunto. You add, as the issue of these inquiries: "Let us leave cavils; grant my supposition, which you cannot deny; then speak to my consequence, which I deem most strong and good, to infer a conclusion which neither you nor I can grant." *Ans.* I wish you had thought before of leaving cavils, that we might have been eased of the consideration of the foregoing queries, which are nothing else, and those very trivial. Your supposition,—which is, "That Papists first brought the gospel into England,"—you say I cannot deny; but, sir, I do deny it, and challenge you or any man in the world to make it good, or to give any colour of truth unto it. Then your consequence you say you "deem strong and good." I doubt not but you do so: so did Suffenus of his poems; but another was not of the same mind, who says of him,—

—— "Qui modo scurra,
Aut si quid hac re tritius, videbatur,
Idem inficeto est inficetior rure,
Simul poemata attigit; neque idem unquam
Æque est beatus, ac poema cum scribit:
Tam gaudet in se, tamque se ipse miratur." Catull. xxii. 12–17.

You may, for aught I know, have a good faculty at some other things; but you very unhappily please yourself in drawing of consequences, which, for the most part, are very infirm and naught, as, in particular, I have abundantly manifested that to be which you now speak of. But you conclude: "I tell you plainly, and without tergiversation, before God and all his holy angels, what I should think if I descended unto any conclusion in this affair. And it is this,—either the Papist, who holds at this day all these articles of faith which were delivered at the first conversion of this land by St Austin, is unjustly become odious amongst us; or else, my honest parsons, throw off your cassocks, and resign your benefices and glebe-lands into the hands of your neighbours, whose they were aforetime. My consequence is irrefragable." And I tell you plainly that I greatly pity you for your discourse, and that on many accounts:—1. That, in the same breath wherein you so solemnly protest before God and his holy angels, you should so openly prevaricate as to intimate that you *descend unto no conclusions* in this affair, wherein, notwithstanding your pretences, you really *dogmatize*, and that with as much confidence as it is possible, I think, for any man to do. And, 2. That you cast "before God and his holy angels" the light froth of your scoffing expressions, "My honest parsons," etc.,—a sign with what conscience you are conversant in these things. And, 3. That, undertaking to write and declare your mind in things of the nature and importance that these are of, you should have no more judgment in them or about them than so solemnly to entitle such a trifling sophism by the name of "Irrefragable consequence." As also, 4. That, in the solemnity of your protestation, you forgot to express your mind in sober sense; for, aiming to make a disjunctive conclusion, you make the parts of it not at all *disparate*, but *coincident* as to your intention, the one of them being the direct consequent of the other. 5. That you so much make naked your *desires after benefices and glebe-lands*, as though they were the great matter in contest amongst us; which reflects no small shame and stain on Christian religion and all the professors of it. 6. Your "irrefragable consequence" is a most pitiful piece of sophistry, built upon I know not how many false suppositions; as,—(1.) "That Papists are become odious unto us;" whereas we only reject your Popery, love your persons, and approve of your Christianity. (2.) "That Papists brought us the first tidings of the gospel;" which hath been sufficiently before disproved. (3.) "That Papists hold all things in religion that they did, and as they did, who first brought us the news of Christianity;" which we have also manifested to be otherwise, in the signal instance of the opinion of Pope Gregory about your papal power and titles. (4.) "That we have no occasion of exception against Papists but only their holding the things that those did who first preached the gospel here;" when that is no cause at all of our exceptions, but their multitude of pretended articles of faith, and idolatrous superstitious practices in worship, superadded by them since that time, are the things they stand charged withal. Now, your consequent being built on all these suppositions, fit to hold a principal place in Lucian's "Vera Historia," must needs be irrefragable.

What you add farther on this subject is but a repetition in other words of what you had said before, with an application of your false and groundless supposition unto our present differences; but yet, lest you should flatter yourself, or your disciples deceive themselves with thoughts that there is any thing of weight or moment in it, it shall also be considered. You add, then, "That if any part, much more if any parts, great substantial parts, of religion brought into the land with the first news of Christianity, be once rejected (as they are now amongst us) as Romish or Romanical, and that rejection or reformation be permitted, then may other parts, and all parts, if the gap be not stopped, be looked upon at length as points of no better a condition."

I have given you sundry instances already, undeniably evincing that some opinions of them who first bring the news of Christian religion unto any may be afterward rejected, without the least impeachment of the *truth* of the whole or of our faith therein; yea, men may be necessitated so to reject them, to keep entire the truth of the whole. But the rejection supposed is of *men's* opinions that bring Christian religion, and not of any parts of Christian religion itself; for the *mistakes* of any men whatever, whether in speculation or practice about religion, are no parts of religion, much less substantial parts of it. Such was the opinion of the necessity of the observation of Mosaical rites, taught, with a suitable practice, by many believers of the Circumcision, who first preached the gospel in sundry places in the world; and such were the rites and opinions brought into England by Austin that are rejected by Protestants,—if any such there were, which as yet you have not made to appear. There is no such affinity between truth and error, however any men may endeavour to blend them together, but that others may separate between them, and reject the one without any prejudice unto the other: "Male sarta Gratia nequicquam coit," Hor. Ep. i. 3,31. Yea, the truth and light of the gospel is of that nature, as that, if it be once sincerely received in the mind and embraced, it will work out all those false notions which by any means together with it may be instilled, as "rectum" is "index sui et obliqui." Whilst, then, we know and are persuaded that in any system of religion which is proposed unto us it is only error which we reject, having an infallible rule for the guidance of our judgment therein, there is no danger of weakening our assent unto the truth which we retain. Truth and falsehood can never stand upon the same bottom, nor have the same evidence, though they may be proposed at the same time unto us, and by the same persons; so that there is no difficulty in apprehending how the one may be received and the other rejected. Nor may it be granted (though your concernment lie not therein at all), that if a man reject or disbelieve any point of truth that is delivered unto him in an entire system of truths, that he is thereby made inclinable to reject the rest also, or disenabled to give a firm assent unto them; unless he reject or disbelieve it upon a notion that is common to them all. For instance, he that rejects any truth revealed in the Scripture on this ground, that the Scripture is not an infallible revelation of divine and supernatural truth, cannot but, in the pursuit of that apprehension of his, reject also all other truths therein revealed, at least so far as they are knowable only by that revelation; but he that shall disbelieve any truth revealed in the Scripture, because it is not manifest unto him to be so revealed, and is in a readiness to receive it when it shall be so manifest, upon the authority of the author of the whole, is not in the least danger to be induced by that disbelief to question any thing of that which he is convinced so to be revealed. But, as I said, your concernment lies not therein, who are not able to prove that Protestants have rejected any one part, much less "substantial part" of religion; and your conclusion, upon a supposition of the rejection of errors and practices of the contrary to the gospel or principles of religion, is very infirm. The ground of all your sophistry lies in this, that men who receive Christian religion are bound to resolve their faith into the authority of them that preach it first unto them; whereupon, it being impossible for them to question any thing they teach without an impeachment of their *absolute infallibility*, and so far the authority which they are to rest upon, they have no firm foundation left for their assent unto the things which as yet they do not question; and consequently, in process of time, may easily be induced so to do. But this presumption is perfectly destructive to all the certainty of Christian religion; for whereas it proposeth the subject-matter of it to be believed with divine faith and supernatural, it leaves no formal reason or cause of any such faith, no foundation for it to be built upon, or principle to be resolved into: for how can divine faith arise out of human authority? For acts being specificated by their objects, such as is the authority on which a man believes, such is his faith;—human, if that be human; divine, if it be divine. But resolving, as we ought, all our faith into the authority of God revealing things to be believed, and knowing that revelation to be entirely contained in the Scriptures, by which we are to examine and try whatever is, by any man or men, proposed unto us as an object of our faith,—they proposing it only upon this consideration, that it is a part of that which is revealed by God in the Scripture for us to believe, without which they have no ground nor warrant to propose any thing at all unto us in that kind,—we may reject any of their proposals which we find and discern not to be so revealed, or not to be agreeable to what is so revealed, without the least weakening of our assent unto what is revealed indeed, or making way for any man so to do. For whilst the *formal reason* of faith remains absolutely unimpeached, different apprehensions about particular things to be believed have no efficacy to weaken faith itself; as we shall farther see in the examination of your ensuing discourse:—

"The same way and means that lopped off some branches will do the like to others, and the root too." (But the errors and mistakes of men are not branches growing from the root of the gospel.) "A vilification of that church wherein they find themselves who have a mind to prevaricate, upon pretence of Scripture and power of interpreting it, light, Spirit, or reason, adjoined with a personal obstinacy that will not submit, will do it roundly and to effect. This first brought off the Protestants from the Roman Catholic church; this lately separated the Presbyterians from the English Protestant church, the Independent from the Presbyterian, and the Quakers from the other Independent. And this left good, maintains nothing of Christian religion but the moral part, which in deed and truth is but honest Paganism. This speech is worthy of all serious consideration."

That which this discourse seems to amount unto is, that if a man question or reject any thing that is taught by the church whereof he is a member, there remains no way for him to come unto any certainty in the remaining parts of religion, but that he may, on as good grounds, question and reject all things as any. As you phrase the matter, by "men's vilifying a church who have a mind to prevaricate, upon pretence of Scripture," etc., though there is no consequence in what you say, yet no man can be so mad as to plead in justification of such a proceeding; for it is not much to be doubted but that he who layeth such a foundation, and makes such a beginning of a separation from any church, will make a progress suitable thereunto. But if you will speak unto your own purpose, and so as they may have any concernment in what you say with whom you deal, you must otherwise frame your hypothesis: Suppose a man to be a member of any church, or to find himself in any church-state with others, and that he doth at any time, by the light and direction of the Scripture, discover any thing or things to be taught or practised in that church whereof he is so a member which he cannot assent unto, unless he will contradict the revelation that God hath made of himself, his mind and will, in that complete rule of all that religion and worship which are pleasing unto him, and therefore doth suspend his assent thereunto, and therein dissent from the determination of that church; then you are to assert, for the promotion of your design, that all the consequents will follow which you expatiate upon. But this supposition fixes immovably, upon the penalty of forfeiting their interest in all saving truth, all Christians whatever, Greeks, Abyssines, Armenians, Protestants, in the churches wherein they find themselves, and so makes frustrate all the attempts for their reconciliation to the church of Rome; for do you think they will attend unto you, when you persuade them to a relinquishment of the communion of that church wherein they find themselves to join with you, when the first thing you tell them is, that if they do so they are undone, and that for ever? And yet this is the sum of all that you can plead with them, if there be any sense in the argument you make use of against our relinquishment of the opinions and practices of the church of Rome, because we or our forefathers were at any time members thereof, or lived in its communion. But you would have this the special privilege of your church alone. Any *other* church a man may leave, yea, *all other churches* besides: he may relinquish the principles wherein he hath been instructed: yea, it is his duty to renounce their communion. Only your church of Rome is wholly sacred; a man that hath once been a member of it must be so for ever; and he that questions any thing taught therein may, on the same grounds, question all the articles of faith in the Christian religion. And who gave you leave to suppose the only thing in question between us, and to use it as a medium to educe your conclusion from? Is it your business to take care,

> —— "Bullatis ut tibi nugis
> Pagina turgescat, dare pondus idonea fumo?" Pers. v. 19.

We know the condition of your Roman church to be no other than that of other churches, if it be not worse than that of any of them. And, therefore, on what terms and reasons soever a man may relinquish the opinions and renounce the communion of any other church, upon the same may he renounce the communion and relinquish the opinions of yours; and if there be no reasons sufficiently cogent so to deal with any church whatever, I pray on what grounds do you proceed to persuade others to such a course, that they may join with you?

> —— "Dicisque facisque quod ipse
> Non sani esse hominis non sanus juret Orestes." Pers. iii. 117.

To disentangle you out of this labyrinth whereinto you have cast yourself, I shall desire you to observe, that if the Lord Christ by his word be the *supreme revealer* of all divine truth, and the church (that is, any church whatever) be only the *ministerial proposer* of it, under and from him, being to be regulated in all its propositions by his revelation; if it shall chance to propose that for truth which is not by him revealed,—as it may do, seeing it hath no security of being preserved from such failures, but only in its attendance unto that rule, which it may neglect or corrupt,—a man in such a case cannot discharge his duty to the *supreme revealer* without dissenting from the *ministerial proposer*. Nay, if it be a truth which is proposed, and a man dissent from it because he is not convinced that it is revealed, he is in no danger to be induced to question other propositions which he knows to be so revealed, his faith being built upon and resolved into that revelation alone. All that remains of your discourse lies with its whole weight on this presumption: Because some men may either wilfully prevaricate from the truth, or be mistaken in their apprehensions of it, and so dissent from a church that teacheth the truth, and wherein she so teacheth it, without cause; therefore no man may or ought to relinquish the errors of a church, which he is really and truly convinced by Scripture, and solid reason suitable thereunto, so to be;—an inference so wild and so destructive of all assurance in every thing that is knowable in the world, that I wonder how your interest could induce you to give any countenance unto it! for if no man can certainly and infallibly know any thing, by any way or means, wherein some or other are ignorantly or wilfully mistaken, we must bid adieu for ever to the certain knowledge of any thing in this world. And how slightly soever you are pleased to speak of Scripture, light, Spirit, and reason, they are the proper names of the ways and helps that God hath graciously given to the sons of men to come to the knowledge of himself. And if the Scripture, by the assistance of the Spirit of God, and the light in it communicated unto men by him, be not sufficient to lead them, in the use and improvement of their reason, unto the saving knowledge of the will of God, and that assurance therein which may be a firm foundation of acceptable obedience unto him, they must be content to go without it, for other ways and means of it there are none. But this is your manner of dealing with us. All other churches must be slighted and relinquished, the means appointed and sanctified by God himself to bring us unto the knowledge of and settlement in the truth must be rejected, that all men may be brought to a fanatical, unreasonable resignation of their faith to you and your church. If this be not done, men may with as good reason renounce truth as error, and after they have rejected one error, be inclined to cast off all that truth for the sake whereof that error was rejected by them! And I know not what other inconveniences and mischiefs will follow. It must needs be well for you that you are,

—— "Gallinæ filius albæ;"

seeing all others are,

—— "Viles pulli nati infelicibus ovis."

Your only misadventure is, that you are fallen into somewhat an unhappy age, wherein men are hard-hearted, and will not give away their faith and reason to every one that can take the confidence to beg them at their hands.

But you will now prove by instances that if a man deny any thing that your church proposeth, he may with as good reason deny every truth whatever. I shall follow you through them, and consider what, in your matter or manner of proposal, is worthy that serious perusal of them which you so much desire. To begin: "See if the Quakers deny not as resolutely the regenerating power of baptism as you the efficacy of absolution. See if the Presbyterians do not with as much reason evacuate the prelacy of Protestants as they the Papacy." All things it seems are alike, truth and error, and may with the same reason be opposed and rejected. And because some men renounce errors, others may on as good grounds renounce the truth, and oppose it with as solid and cogent reasons! The Scripture, it seems, is of no use to direct, guide, or settle men in these things that relate to the worship and knowledge of God! What a strange dream hath the church of God been in from the days of Moses, if this be so! Hitherto it hath been thought that what the Scripture teacheth in these things turned the scales, and made the embracement of it reasonable, as the rejection of them the contrary. As the woman said to Joab, "They were wont to speak in old time, saying, They shall surely ask counsel at Abel; and so they ended the matter." They said in old time concerning these things, "To the law, and to the testimony; search the Scriptures;" and so they ended the matter. But it seems "tempora mutantur," and that now truth and falsehood are equally probable, having the same grounds, the same evidences. "Quis leget hæc? mîn' tu istud ais?" Do you think to be believed in these incredible figments, fit to bear a part in the stories of Ulysses unto Alcinous? Yet you proceed: "See if the Socinian arguments against the Trinity be not as strong as yours against the eucharist." But where did you ever read any arguments of ours against the eucharist? Have you a dispensation to say what you please for the promotion of the Catholic cause? Are not the arguments you intend indeed rather *for* the eucharist than *against* it,—arguments to vindicate the nature of that holy eucharistical ordinance, and to preserve it from the manifold abuses that you and your church do put upon it? that is, they are arguments against your transubstantiation and proper sacrifice that you intend. And will you now say that the arguments of the Socinians against the Trinity, the great fundamental article of our profession, plainly taught in the Scripture, and constantly believed by the church of all ages, are of equal force and validity with those used against your transubstantiation and sacrifice of the mass,—things never mentioned, no not once, in the whole Scripture, never heard of nor believed by the church of old, and destructive in your reception unto all that reason and sense whereby we are, and know that we are, men and live? But suppose your prejudice and partial addiction unto your way and faction may be allowed to countenance you in this monstrous comparing and coupling of things together, like his who

"Mortua jungebat corpora vivis;"

is your inference from your inquiry any other but this, that the Scripture, setting aside the authority of your church, is of no use to instruct men in the truth, but that all things are alike uncertain unto all? And this you farther manifest to be your meaning in your following inquiries. "See," say you, "if the Jew do not with as much plausibility deride Christ, as you his church." And would you could see what it is to be a zealot in a faction, or would learn to deal candidly and honestly in things wherein your own and the souls of other men are concerned. Who is it amongst us that derides the church of Christ? Did Elijah deride the temple at Jerusalem when he opposed the priests of Baal? or must every one presently be judged to deride the church of Christ, who opposeth the corruptions that the Roman faction have endeavoured to bring into that part of it wherein for some ages they have prevailed? What plausibility you have found out in the Jews' derision of Christ, I know not. I know some that are as conversant in their writings, at least, as you seem to have been, who affirm that your arguings and revilings are utterly destitute of all plausibility and tolerable pretence. But men must have leave to say what they please, when they will be talking of they know not what; as is the case with you when by any chance you stumble on the Jews or their concernments. This is that which, for the present, you would persuade men unto,—that the arguments of the Jews against Christ are as good as those of Protestants against your church. "Credat Apella." Of the same nature with these is the remainder of your instances and queries. You suppose that a man may have as good reasons for the denial of hell as purgatory; of God's providence and the soul's immortality as of any piece of Popery; and then may not want appearing incongruities, tautologies, improbabilities, to disenable all holy writ at once! This is the condition of the man who disbelieves any thing proposed by your church; nor in that state is he capable of any relief,—fluctuate he must in all uncertainties. Truth and error are all one unto him; and he hath as good grounds for the one as the other. But, sir, pray what serves the Scripture for all this while? will it afford a man no light, no guidance, no direction? Was this quite out of your mind? or did you presume your reader would not once cast his thoughts towards it for his relief in that maze of uncertainties which you endeavour to cast him into? or dare you manage such an impeachment of the wisdom and goodness of God, as to affirm that that revelation of himself which he hath graciously afforded unto men to teach them the knowledge of himself, and to bring them to settlement and assurance therein, is of no use or validity to any such purpose? The Holy Ghost tells us that "the Scripture is profitable for doctrine and instruction, able to make the man of God perfect, and us all wise unto salvation;" that the "sure word of prophecy," whereunto he commands us to attend, is "a light shining in a dark place;" directs us to search into it, that we may come to the acknowledgment of the truth, sending us unto it for our settlement; affirming that they who speak not "according to the law and the testimony have no light in them." He assures us that the word of God "is a light unto our feet; and his law perfect, converting the soul;" that it is "able to build us up, and to give us an inheritance among all them that are sanctified;" that the things in it are "written that we might believe that Jesus is the Christ, the Son of God, and that believing we may have life through his name." See also Luke xvi. 29, 31; Ps. xix. 7, 8; 2 Pet. i. 19; John v. 39; Rom. xv. 4; Heb. iv. 12. Is there no truth in all this, and much more that is affirmed to the same purpose? or are you surprised with this mention of it, as Cæsar Borgia was with his sickness at the death of his father Pope Alexander, which spoiled all his designs, and made him cry that he had never thought of it, and so had not provided against it? Do you not know that a volume might be filled with testimonies of *ancient fathers*, bearing witness to the *sufficiency* and *efficacy* of the Scripture for the settlement of the minds of men in the knowledge of God and his worship? Doth not the experience of all ages, of all places in the world, render your sophistry contemptible? Are there not, were there not, millions of Christians always, who either knew not, or regarded not, or openly rejected, the authority of your church, and disbelieved many of her present proposals, who yet were and are steadfast and immovable in the faith of Christ, and willingly seal the truth of it with their dearest blood? But if neither the testimony of God himself in the Scriptures, nor the concurrent suffrage of the ancient church, nor the experience of so many thousands of the disciples of Christ, is of any moment with you, I hope you will not take it amiss if I look upon you as one giving in yourself as signal an instance of the power of prejudice, and partial addiction to a party and interest, as a man can well meet withal in the world. This discourse, you tell me in your close, you have bestowed upon me in a way of *supererogation;* wherein you deal with us as you do with God himself. The *duties* he expressly, by his commands, requireth at your hands, you *pass by* without so much as taking notice of some of them; and others, as those of the *second command*, you openly reject, offering him somewhat of your own that he doth not require, by the way, as you barbarously call it, of *supererogation:* and so here you have passed over in silence that which was incumbent on you to have replied unto, if you had not a mind "vadimonium deserere," to give over the defence of that cause you had undertaken, and in the room thereof substitute this needless and useless diversion, by the way, as you say, of supererogation. But yet, because you were so free of your charity, before you had paid your debts, as to bestow it upon me, I was not unwilling to requite your kindness, and have therefore sent it you back again, with that acknowledgment of your favour wherewith it is now attended.

CHAPTER XIII.

Faith and charity of Roman Catholics.

YOUR following discourse, pp. 44, 45, is spent partly in the commendation of your "Fiat Lux," and the metaphysical, abstracted discourses of it; partly in a repetition, in other words, of what you had before insisted on. The former I shall no farther endeavour to disturb your contentment in. It is a common error,—

—— "Neque est quisquam
Quem non in aliqua re videre Suffenum
Possis." Catull. xxii. 19.

I am not your rival in the admiration of it, and shall therefore leave you quietly in the embracements of your darling. And for the latter, we have had enough of it already; and so, by this time, I hope you think also. The close only of your discourse is considerable, and therefore I shall transcribe it for your second thoughts; and it is this:—

"But, sir, what you say here, and so often up and down your book, of Papists' contempt of the Scripture, I beseech you will please to abstain from it for the time to come. I have conversed with the Roman Catholics of France, Flanders, and Germany; I have read more of their books, both histories, contemplative and scholastical divines, than I believe you have ever seen or heard of; I have seen the colleges of sacred priests, and religious houses; I have communed with all sort of people, and perused their counsels;—and after all this I tell you, and out of my love I tell you, that their respect to Scripture is real, absolute, and cordial, even to admiration. Others may talk of it, but they act it, and would be ready to stone that man that should diminish holy writ. Let us not wrong the innocent. The Scripture is theirs, and Jesus Christ is theirs, who also will plead their cause when he sees time."

What you mention of your own diligence and achievements, what you have *done*, where you have *been*, what you have seen and discoursed, I shall not trouble you about. It may be, as to your soul's health,

—— "Tutior, poteras esse domi."

But yet, for all the report that you are pleased to make of yourself, it is not hard to discern that you and I

—— "Nec pondera rerum
Nec momenta sumus."

And notwithstanding your writings, it would have been very difficult for any man to have guessed at your great reading, had you not satisfied us by this your own information of it. It may be, if you had spared some of the time which you have spent in the reading of your Catholic books unto the study of the Scripture, it had not been unto your disadvantage. In the meantime, there is an hyperbole in your confidence a little too evident; for it is possible that I may, and true that I have seen more of your authors in half an hour than you can read, I think, in a hundred years; unless you intend always to give no other account of your reading than you have done in your "Fiat" and "Epistola." But we are weary of this περιαυτολογία,—

"Quin tu alium quæras quoi centones farcias."—Plaut. Epist. iii. 4, 18.

But to pass by this boasting; there are two parts of your discourse,—the one concerning the *faith*, the other expressing the *charity* of the Roman Catholics. The first contains what respect you would be thought to have for the Scripture; the latter, what you really have for all other Christians besides yourselves. As to the former, you tell me that I speak of the "Papists' contempt of the Scripture," and desire me to abstain from it for the time to come. Whether I have used that expression anywhere of contempt of the Scripture, well I know not. But whereas I look upon you as my *friend*,—at least, for the good advice I have frequently given you, I have deserved that you should be so,—and therefore shall not deny you any thing that I can *reasonably grant;* and whereas I cannot readily comply with you in your present request, as to the alteration of my mind in reference unto the respect that Papists bear unto the Scriptures, I esteem myself obliged to give you some account of the reasons why I persist in my former thoughts: which I hope, as is usual in such cases, you will be pleased to take in friendly part. For besides, sir, that you back your request with nothing but some over-confident asseverations, subscribed with "Teste meipso," I have many reasons, taken from the practice and doctrine of your church, that strongly induce me to abide in my former persuasion; as,—1. You know that in these and the neighbouring nations, Papists have *publicly burned* the Scriptures, and destroyed more copies of them than ever Antiochus Epiphanes did of the Jewish law. And if you should go about to prove unto me that Protestants have no great regard to the sacred images that have been worshipped, because in these and the neighbouring nations they brake and burned a great number of them, I should not readily know what to answer you; nor can I entertain any such confidence of your abilities as to expect from you a satisfactory answer unto my instance of the very same nature, manifesting what respect Papists bear unto the Scriptures. 2. You know that they have *imprisoned and burned* sundry persons for keeping the Scriptures in their houses, or some parts of them, and reading them for their instruction and comfort. Nor is this any great sign of respect unto them; no more than it is of men's respect to treason or murder, because they hang them up who are guilty of them. And, 3. Your church *prohibiteth the reading of them* unto laymen, unless, in some special cases, some few of them be licensed by you so to do; and you study and sweat for arguments to prove the reading of them needless and dangerous, putting them, as translated, into the catalogue of books prohibited. Now, this is the very mark and stamp that your church sets upon those books which she disapproves, and discountenanceth as pernicious to the faithful. 4. Your council of Trent hath decreed that your *unwritten traditions* are to be received with the same faith and veneration as the Scriptures, constituting them to be one part of the word of God, and the Scriptures another: than which nothing could be spoken more in contempt of it or in reproach unto it; for I must assure you Protestants think you cannot possibly contract a greater guilt, by any contempt of the Scripture, than you do by reducing it into order with your unwritten traditions. 5. You have *added books*, not only written with a human and fallible spirit, but farced with *actual mistakes* and falsehoods, unto the canon of the Scripture, giving just occasion unto them who receive it from *you only* to question the authority of the whole. And, 6. You teach *the authority of the Scripture*, at least in respect of us (which is all it hath, for authority is ἐκ τῶν πρός τί, and must regard some in relation unto whom it doth consist), depends on the *authority of your church*;—the readiest way in the world to bring it into contempt with them that know what your church is, and what it hath been. And, 7. You plead that *it is very obscure and unintelligible of itself*, and that in things of the greatest moment and of most indispensable necessity unto salvation; whereby you render it perfectly useless, according to the old rule, "Quod non potest intelligi, debet negligi,"—it is fit "that should be neglected which cannot be understood." And, 8. There is a book lately written by one of your party, after you have been frequently warned and told of these things, entitled "Fiat Lux," giving countenance unto many other hard reflections upon it; as hath been manifested in the "Animadversions" written on that book. 9. Your *great masters* in their writings have spoken very contemptuously of it; whereof I shall give you a few instances. *The council of Trent*, which is properly yours, determines, as I told you, that their traditions are to be received and venerated, "pari pietatis affectu et reverentia,"—"with an equal affection of piety and reverence,"—as the Scriptures of the Old and New Testament; which is a setting up of the altar of Damascus with that of God himself in the same temple, sess. 4, dec. 1. And *Andradius*, no small part of that convention, in his defence of that decree, tells us that, "Cum Christus fragilitati memoriæ evangelio scripto succurrendum putavit, ita breve compendium libris tradi voluit, ut pars maxima, tanquam magni precii thesaurus, traditionibus intimis ecclesiæ visceribus infixis, relicta fuerit;"—"As our Lord Christ thought meet to relieve the frailty of memory by the written gospel, so he would have a short compendium or abridgment committed unto books, that the greatest part, as a most precious treasure, might be left unto traditions, fixed in the very inward bowels of the church." This is that "*cordial* and *absolute* respect, even unto *admiration*," that your Catholics bear unto the Scripture,—and he that doth not admire it seems to me to be very stupid, —It contains some *small part* of the mysteries of Christian religion, the *great treasure* of them lying in your traditions! And thereupon he concludes, "Canonem seu regulam fidei exactissimam non esse Scripturam, sed ecclesiæ judicium;"—"That the canon or most exact rule of faith is not the Scripture, but the judgment of the church;" much to the same purpose as you plead in your "Fiat" and "Epistola." *Pighius*, another champion of your church (Ecclesiast. Hierarch., lib. i. cap. 4), after he hath given many reasons to prove the obscurity of the Scripture, with its flexibility to every man's sense, as you know who also hath done and referred all things to be determined by the church, concludes, "Si hujus doctrinæ memores fuissemus, hæreticos scilicet non esse informandos vel convincendos ex Scripturis, meliore sane loco essent res nostræ; sed dum ostentandi ingenii et eruditionis gratia cum Luthero in certamen descenditur Scripturarum, excitatum est hoc quod, proh dolor! nunc videmus incendium;"—"Had we been mindful of this doctrine, that heretics are not to be instructed nor convinced out of the Scriptures, our affairs had been in a better condition than now they are; but whilst some, to show their wit and learning, would needs contend with Luther out of the Scriptures, the fire which we now with grief behold was kindled and stirred up." And it may be you remember who it was that called the Scripture "Evangelium nigrum" and "Theologiam atramentariam," seeing he was one of the most famous champions of your church and cause. But before we quite leave your council of Trent, we may do well to remember the advice which the fathers of it, who upon the stirs in Germany removed unto Bononia, gave to the pope, Julius III., which one that was then amongst them afterward published. "Denique," say they in their letters to him, "quod inter omnia consilia quæ nos hoc tempore dare possumus omnium gravissimum, ad extremum reservavimus. Oculi hic aperiendi sunt; omnibus nervis adnitendum erit ut quam minimum evangelii poterit (præsertim vulgari lingua) in iis legatur civitatibus quæ sub tua ditione et potestate sunt, sufficiatque tantillum illud quod in missa legi solet, nec eo amplius cuiquam mortalium legere liceat. Quamdiu enim pauculo illo homines contenti fuerunt, tamdiu res tuæ ex sententia successêre, eædemque in contrarium labi cœperunt ex quo ulterius legi vulgo usurpatum est. Hic ille, in summa, est liber qui præter cæteros hasce nobis tempestates ac turbines conciliavit quibus prope abrepti sumus. Et sane siquis illum diligenter expendat, deinde quæ in nostris fieri ecclesiis consueverunt, singula ordine contempletur, videbit plurimum inter se dissidere, et hanc doctrinam nostram ab illa prorsus diversam esse, ac sæpe contrariam etiam. Quod simul atque homines intelligant, a docto scilicet aliquo adversariorum stimulati, non ante clamandi finem faciunt, quam rem plane omnem divulgaverint, nosque invisos omnibus reddiderint. Quare occultandæ pauculæ illæ chartulæ sed adhibitâ quadam cautione et diligentia, ne ea res majores nobis turbas ac tumultus excitet;"—"Last of all, that which is the most weighty of all the advices which at this time we shall give unto you, we have reserved for the close of all. Your eyes are here to be opened; you are to endeavour, with the utmost of your power, that as little as may be of the gospel (especially in any vulgar tongue) be read in those cities which are under your government and authority, but let that little suffice them which is wont to be read in the mass" (of which mind you also know who is): "neither let it be lawful for any man to read any more of it; for as long as men were contented with that little, your affairs were as prosperous as heart could desire, and began immediately to decline upon the custom of reading any more of it. This is, in brief, that book which above all others hath procured unto us those tempests and storms wherewith we are almost carried away headlong. And the truth is, if any one shall diligently consider it, and then seriously ponder on all the things that are accustomed to be done in our churches, he will find them to be very different the one from the other, and our doctrine to be diverse from the doctrine thereof, yea, and oftentimes plainly contrary unto it. Now this when men begin to understand, being stirred up by some learned men or other amongst the adversaries, they make no end of clamouring until they have divulged the whole matter, and rendered us hateful unto all. Wherefore those few sheets of paper are to be hid; but with caution and diligence, lest their concealment should stir us up greater troubles." This is fair and open, being a brief summary of that admiration of the Scriptures which so abounds in Catholic countries. That Hermannus, one of some account in your church, affirmed that the Scriptures could be of no more authority than Æsop's Fables, were they not confirmed by the testimony of your church, we are informed by one Brentius; and we believe the information to be true, because the saying is defended by Hosius, De Authoritat. Script., lib. iii., who adds unto it of his own: "Revera nisi nos authoritas ecclesiæ doceret hanc Scripturam esse canonicam, perexiguum apud nos pondus haberet;"—"The truth is, if the authority of the church did not teach us that this Scripture is canonical, it would be of very light weight unto us." Such cordial respect do you bear unto it! And the forementioned Andradius, Defens. Con. Trid. lib. ii., to the same purpose: "Neque enim in ipsis libris, quibus sacra mysteria conscripta sunt, quicquam inest divinitatis quæ nos ad credendum quæ in illis continentur religione aliqua constringat. Sed ecclesiæ, quæ codices illos sacros esse docet, et antiquorum patrum fidem et pietatem commendat, tanta inest vis et amplitudo, ut illis nemo sine gravissima impietatis nota possit repugnare;"—"Neither is there in those books, wherein the divine mysteries are written, any thing or any character of divinity or divine original which should, on a religious account, oblige us to believe the things that are contained in them. But yet such is the force and authority of the church, which teacheth those books to be sacred, and commendeth the faith and piety of the ancient fathers, that no man can oppose them without a grievous mark of impiety." How, by what means, from whom, should we learn the sense of your church, if not from your council of Trent, and such mighty champions of it? Do you think it equitable that we should listen to the suggestions of every *obscure* friar, and entertain thoughts from them about the sense of your church contrary to the plain assertion of your *councils* and great rabbis? And if this be the respect that, in Catholic countries, is given to the Scripture, I hope you will not find many of your countrymen rivals with them therein. It is all but "Hail" and "Crucify." "We respect the Scriptures, but there is *another part* of God's word besides them; we respect the Scriptures, but *traditions* contain more of the doctrine of truth; we respect the Scriptures, but think it not meet that Christians be suffered to read them; we respect the Scripture, but do not think that it hath any character in it of its own divine original for which we should believe it; we respect the Scripture, but yet we would not believe it were it not commended unto us by our church; we respect the Scripture, but it is dark, obscure, not intelligible but by the interpretation of our church." Pray, sir, keep your respects at home; they are despised by the Scripture itself, which gives testimony unto its own authority, perfection, sufficiency to guide us to God, perspicuity, and certainty, without any respect unto your church or its authority; and we know its testimony to be true. And for our part, we fear that whilst these Joab's kisses of respect are upon your lips, you have a sword in your right hands to let out the vitals of divine truth and religion. Do you think your general expressions of respect, and that unto "admiration," are a covering long and broad enough to hide all this contempt and reproach that you continually pour upon the Scriptures? Deal thus with your ruler, and see whether he will accept your person. Give him some good words in general, but let your particular expressions of your esteem of him come short of what his state and regal dignity do require, will it be well taken at your hands? Expressions of the same nature with these instanced in might be collected of your chiefest authors sufficient to fill a volume; and yet I never read nor heard that any of them were ever "stoned" in your Catholic countries, whatever you intimate of the boiling up of your zeal into a rage against those that should go about to diminish it. Indeed, whatever you pretend, this is your faith about the Scripture; and therefore I desire that you would accept of this account why I cannot comply with your wish, and not speak any more of Papists slighting the Scripture, seeing I know they do so in the sense and way by me expressed, and other ways I never said they did so.

From the account of your faith we may proceed to your charity, wherewith you close this discourse. Speaking of your Roman Catholics, you say, "The Scripture is theirs, and Jesus Christ is theirs, who will one day plead their cause." What do you mean, sir, by "theirs?" Do you intend it exclusively to all others? so theirs as not to be the right and portion of any other? It is evident that this is your sense, not only because, unless it be so, the words have neither sense nor emphasis in them; but also because, suitably unto this sense, you elsewhere declare that the Roman and the catholic church are with you one and the same. This is your *charity*, fit to accompany and to be the fruit of the faith before discoursed of. This is your catholicism, the empaling of Christ, Scripture, the church, and consequently all acceptable religion, to the Roman party and faction;—downright Donatism, the wretchedest schism that ever rent the church of God; which makes the wounds of Christendom incurable, and all hope of coalition in love desperate.

St Paul, directing one of his epistles unto "All that in every place call upon the name of Jesus Christ our Lord," that no countenance from that expression of "Jesus Christ our Lord" might be given unto any surmise of his appropriating unto himself and those with him a peculiar interest in Jesus Christ, he adds immediately, "Both their Lord and ours,"—the Lord of all that in every place call upon his name, 1 Cor. i. 2. This was the old catholicism, which the new hath as much affinity unto as darkness hath to light, and not one jot more. "The Scripture is ours, and Christ is ours, and what have any else to do with them? What though in other places you call on the name of Jesus Christ, yet he is our Lord, not yours." This, I say, is that wretched schism which, clothed with the name of Catholicism (which, after it had slain, it robbed of its name and garments), the world for some ages hath groaned under, and is like to do so whilst it is supported by so many secular advantages and interests as are subservient unto it at this day.

CHAPTER XIV.

Of reason—Jews' objections against Christ.

Page 47. You proceed to vindicate your *unreasonable* paragraph about *reason*, or rather against it. What reason we are to expect in a dispute against the use of reason in and about the things which are the highest and most proper object of it, is easy for any one to imagine; for by reason in religion we understand not merely the ratiocination of a man, upon and according to the inbred principles of his nature, but every acting of the understanding of a man about the things of God, proceeding from such principles, or guided by any such rule, as no way impeach its rationality. To vindicate your discourse in your "Fiat" upon this subject, you make use of two mediums:—1. You pretend that to be the whole subject of your discourse about reason which is but a part of it; and, 2. You deny that to be the design and aim of your book which you yourself know, and all other men acknowledge, so to be.

On the first head you tell me that your discourse concerned "reason to be excluded from the employment of framing articles of religion." It is true you talk somewhat to that purpose; and you were told that Protestants were no way concerned in that discourse. And it is no less true that you dispute against the use and exercise of reason in our choice of, or adhering unto, any religion, or any way or practice in religion; that is, the liberty of a man's rational judgment in determining what is right and what is wrong, what true, what false, in the things that are proposed unto him as belonging unto religion, guided, bounded, and determined by the only rule, measure, and last umpire in and about such things. This you oppose and that directly, and that to this end,—to show unto Protestants that they can come unto no certainty in religion by this exercise of their reason in and about the things of God. That men should, by the use of reason, endeavour to find out and frame a religion, is fond to imagine. They who ever attempted any such thing knew it was not religion, but a pretence to some other end, that they were coining. To make the reason of a man, proceeding and acting upon its own light and inbred principles, the absolute and sovereign judge of the things that are proposed to be believed or practised in religion, so as that it should be free for him to receive or reject them, according as they answer and are suited thereunto, is no less absurd and foolish: and whoever will assert it must build his assertion on this supposition, that a man is capable of comprehending fully and clearly whatsoever God can reveal of himself; which is contrary to the prime dictates of reason, in reference unto the simplicity and infiniteness of God's being, and so would imply a contradiction in its first admission. It is no less untrue that a man, in the lapsed, depraved condition of nature, can, by the light thereof, and the utmost improvement of his reason, come to a saving, sanctifying perception of the things themselves that God hath revealed concerning himself, his will, and worship; which is the peculiar effect of the Spirit and grace of Christ. But to say that a man is not to use his reason in finding out the sense and meaning of the propositions wherein the truths of religion are represented unto him, and in judging of their truth and falsehood by the rule of them, which is the Scripture, is to deny that indeed we are men, and to put a reproach upon our mortality, by intimating that men do not, cannot, nor ought to do, that which they not only know they do, but also that they cannot but do: for they do but vainly deceive themselves who suppose, or rather dream, that they make any determination of what is true or false in religion without the use and exercise of their reason; it is to say they do it as beasts, and not as men,—than which nothing can be spoken more to the dishonour of religion, nor more effectual to deter men from the entertainment of it. For our part we rejoice in this, that we dare avow the religion which we profess to be *highly rational*, and that the *most mysterious articles* of it are proposed unto our belief on grounds of the most unquestionable reason, and such as cannot be rejected without a contradiction to the most sovereign dictates of that intellectual nature wherewith of God we are endued. And it is not a few trifling instances of some men's abuse of their reason, in its prejudicate exercise about the things of God, that shall make us ungrateful to God that he hath made us men, or to neglect the laying out of the best that he hath intrusted us with by nature in his service in the work of grace. And what course do you yourself proceed in? When any thing is proposed unto you concerning religion, do you not *think* upon it? doth not your mind exercise about it those first acts of reason or understanding which prepare and dispose you to *discourse and compute* it with yourself? do you not consider whether the thing itself be good or evil, and whether the propositions wherein it is made unto you are true or false? do you not call to mind the rule and measure whereby you are to make a judgment whether they be so or no? We talk not now *what that rule is*, but only whether you do not make a judgment of the propositions that are made unto you by some rule or other; and whether, with that judgment, your mind do not assent unto them or dissent from them. Yea, is not your judgment, which you so make, the *assent* or *dissent* of your mind? or what course do you take? I wish you would inform us of your excellent expedient to teach a man to cry "Credo," without the use or exercise of his reason to bring him thereunto. But when you have done so, I know it is no other way but that by which you may teach a parrot or starling to say as much, or the crow that cried of old, "Εσται πάντα καλῶς. But you would evade all concernment in this discourse, by denying that your "Fiat Lux" "was written unto any such concernment against Protestants." I know not well what you mean by your "Unto any such concernment against Protestants." That the main design of your discourse is to bring Protestants unto an uncertainty in their profession, by everting the principles which you apprehend them to build upon, and thereon to persuade them unto Popery, I was in hope you would have no more denied. It hath been evidenced unto you, with as needless a labour as ever any man was put unto; but it is done because you would needs have it so, and shall not now be done again.

Your ensuing discourse, wherein you attempt to say something unto the ninth chapter of the "Animadversions," is not unlike the preceding; and therefore I shall cast them under one head. Your business in it is to cast a fresh dishonour upon Christian religion, by questioning the *defensibility* of its principles against Jewish objections any otherwise than by an irrational "credo." Let us hear you speak in your own language. "Your vaunting flourishes," you say, "about Scripture, which you love to talk on, will not, without the help of your 'credo' and humble resignation, solve the argument; which, that you may the easilier be quit of, you never examine, but only run on in your usual flourishes about the use and excellency of God's word. I told you in 'Fiat Lux' what the Jew will reply to all such reasonings; but you have the pregnant wit not to heed any thing that may hinder your flourishes. But if you were kept up in a chamber with a learned Jew, without bread, water, and fire, till you had satisfied him in that objection, I am still well enough assured, for all your vaunts, that if you do not make use of your 'credo,' which here you contemn, you might there stay till hunger and cold have made an end of you." The meaning of this discourse is, that the Jews' pretence of rejecting Christ upon the authority and tradition of their church, was not, nor is to be, satisfied by testimonies given in the Scripture unto the person, doctrine, and work of the Messiah. The sum of the objection laid down in your "Fiat Lux" is that which I have now mentioned. It was the plea of the Jews against Christ and his doctrine, managed from the *authority* and *tradition* of their church. That Christ and his apostles gave the answer unto this objection which I have now intimated,—namely, the testimony of God himself in the Scripture to the truth of that which they objected against, which was to be preferred unto the authority and testimony of their church,—I have undeniably proved unto you in the "Animadversions;" and it is manifest to every one that hath but read the New Testament with any consideration or understanding. The same way was persisted in by the ancient fathers; as all their writings against the Jews do testify. And I must now tell you, that your calling *the validity of this answer* into question is highly injurious unto the honour of Christianity, and blasphemous against Christ himself. The best interpretation that I can give unto your words is, that you are a person wholly ignorant of the controversies that are between the Jews and Christians, and the way that is to be taken for their satisfaction or confutation. You tell us, indeed, in your "Fiat," that the Jews will reply to those testimonies of Scripture which are alleged as giving witness to our Lord Jesus Christ and his doctrine, and contend about the interpretation of them; and this you tell me "I have the wit to take no notice of;"—which, by the way, is unduly averred by you, and contrary to your own *science* and *conscience*, seeing you profess that you have read over my "Animadversions;" and probably the very place wherein I do take notice of what you said to that purpose, and replied unto it, was not far from your eye when you wrote the contrary. And as I showed you what was the opinion of the *ancients* of that reply of the Jews which you mention, so I shall now add that nothing but gross ignorance in these things can give countenance to an imagination that there is any thing but folly and madness in the rabbinical evasions of the testimonies of the Old Testament given unto our Lord Christ and his gospel. And your substitution of a *naked fanatical "credo,"* not resolved into the testimony of the holy writ, in the room of that *express witness* which is given in holy Scripture unto the person and doctrine of our Lord Jesus Christ, to oppose therewith the Judaical plea from their church, state, power, and authority, is an engine fit to undermine the very root of Christianity, and to render the whole gospel highly questionable. Besides, it is so absurd as to the conviction of the Jews, such a mere "petitio principii," or begging of what is in controversy between Christians and them, that I challenge you to produce any one learned man that hath made use of it to that purpose. To think that your "credo," built on principles which he despiseth, which you cannot prove unto him, will convince another man of the truth of what you believe, can have no other ground but a magical fancy that the fixing of your imagination shall affect his, and conform it unto your apprehension of things. Such is your course in telling the Jews of the authority of your church, and your "credo" thereupon; which cannot be supposed to have any existence "in rerum natura," unless it be first supposed that their church was failed, which supposal that it was not is the sole foundation of their objection. What end you can propose herein, but to expose yourself and your profession unto their scorn and contempt, I know not. Sir, the Lord Christ confirmed himself to be the Son of God and Saviour of the world by the miracles which he wrought; and the doctrine which he taught was testified to be divine by signs and express words from heaven. He proved it also by the testimonies out of the law and prophets; all which was confirmed by his resurrection from the dead. This coming of the promised Messiah, the work that he was to perform, and the characteristical τεκμήρια of him, in application unto the person of Jesus of Nazareth, the apostles and evangelists proved out of the Scripture, to the conviction and conversion of thousands of the Jews, and the confusion of the rest. And if you know not that the ancient fathers, and learned men of succeeding ages, have undeniably proved against the Jews, out of the Scripture of the Old Testament, and by the testimony thereof, that the promised Messiah was to be God and man in one person; that he was to come at the time of the appearance of our Lord Jesus Christ in the flesh; that the work which he was to perform was the very same and no other than what was wrought and accomplished by him, with all the other important concernments of his person and office,—so that they have nothing left to countenance them in their obstinacy but mere senseless trifles;—you are exceedingly unmeet to make use of their objections, or the condition of the controversy between them and Christians. For what you add in reference unto myself, I shall need only to mind you that the question is not about any *personal ability* of mine to satisfy a Jew,—which, whatever it be, when I have a mind to increase it, for somewhat that I know of, and which I have learned out of their writings, I will not come unto you for assistance,—but concerning the sufficiency of that principle for the confronting of Judaical objections, taken from the authority of their church; which I have formerly proved unto you that our Lord Jesus Christ and his apostles made use of unto that purpose. And I will not say that it was from *the pregnancy of your wit*, that, whatever heed you took unto the stating of the case between you and Protestants in the "Animadversions," parallel unto that between the Jews and the apostles (seeing a very little wit will suffice to direct a man to let that alone which he finds too heavy for him to remove out of his way), you speak not one word unto it: yet I will say that it is a thing of that kind whereof there are frequent instances in your whole discourse; and for what reason is not very difficult for any man to conjecture.

CHAPTER XV.

Pleas of Prelate Protestants—Christ the only supreme and absolute head of the church.

Page 49. YOU take a view of the 10th chapter of the "Animadversions," opposed unto the 13th and 14th paragraphs of your "Fiat Lux," wherein you pretend to set forth the various pleas of those that are at difference amongst us in matters of religion. These you there distribute into Independents, Presbyterians, and Protestants. Here, omitting the consideration of the two former, you apply yourself unto what was spoken about "Prelate Protestants," as you call them. "You endeavour," say you, "to disable both what I have set down to make against the prelate Protestant, and also what I have said for him. I said in 'Fiat Lux,' that it made not a little against our Protestants, that after the prelate Protestancy was settled in England, they were forced, for their own preservation against the Puritans, to take up some of those principles again which former Protestants had cast down for popish; as is the authority of the visible church, efficacy of ordination, difference between clergy and laity. Here, first, you deny that these principles are popish; but, sir, there are some Jews, even at this day, who will deny any such man as Pontius Pilate to have ever been in Jewry. I have other things to do than to fill volumes with useless texts, which here I might easily do out of the books both of the first reformers, and Catholic divines and councils."

What acquaintance you have with the Jews we have in part seen already, and shall have occasion hereafter to examine a little farther. In the meantime, you may be pleased to take notice that men who know what they say are not easily affrighted from it by a show of such mormoes, as he in the comedian was from his own house by his servant's pretence that it was haunted by sprites, when there were none in it but his own debauched companions. I denied those opinions to be popish, and should do so still, were I accused for so doing before a Roman judge as corrupt and wicked as Pontius Pilate; for I can prove them to be more ancient than any part of Popery, in the sense explained in the "Animadversions," and admitted generally by Protestants. We never esteem every thing popish that Papists hold or believe. Some things in your profession belong unto your *Christianity;* some things to your *Popery.* And I am persuaded you do not think this proposition, "Jesus Christ is the Son of God," to be heretical, because those whom you account heretics do profess and believe it. Prove the principles you mention to be invented by yourselves, without any foundation in the Scripture or constant suffrage of the ancient churches, and you prove them to be popish, to be your own. If you cannot do so, though Papists profess them, yet they may be Christian. This is spoken as to the principles themselves, not unto your explanation of them, which in sundry particulars is popish, which was never owned by prelate Protestants. You proceed: "You challenge me to prove that these principles were ever denied by our prelate Protestants; and this you do wittily and like yourself. You therefore bid me prove that those principles were ever denied by our prelate Protestants, because I say that our prelate Protestants here in England, as soon as they became such, took up again those forenamed principles, which Protestants, their forefathers, both here in England and beyond seas, before our prelacy was set up, had still rejected. When I say, then, that our prelate Protestants affirmed and asserted those principles which former Protestants denied, you bid me prove that our prelate Protestants ever denied them." But whatever you can prove or cannot prove, you have made it very easy for any man to prove that you have very little regard unto truth and sobriety in what you aver, so that you may acquit yourself from that which presseth you, and which, according to the rules of them, you cannot stand before. You tell us, in the entrance of this discourse, that you said "that prelate Protestants, for their own preservation, took up some of those principles again which former Protestants had cast down for popish;" and here expressly, that you "said not that they took up the principles which themselves had cast down, but only those which other before them had so dealt withal." Now, pray take a view of your own words, whereby you express yourself in this matter, chap. iii. sect. 14, p. 189, second edition. Are they not these: "The prelate Protestant, to defend himself against them" (the Presbyterians and Independents), "is forced to make use of those very principles which himself aforetime" (not other Protestants but himself), "when he" (not others) "first contended against Popery, destroyed. So that upon him falls most heavily, even like thunder and lightning from heaven, utterly to kill and cut him asunder, that great oracle delivered by St Paul, 'If I build up again the things I'" (not another) "'formerly destroyed, I make myself a prevaricator, an impostor, a reprobate?'" What think you of these words? Do you charge the prelate Protestant with building up what others had pulled down, or what he had destroyed himself? Is your rule out of St Paul applicable unto him upon any other account but that he himself was both the *builder* and *destroyer?* Sir, such miscarriages as these Protestants know to be mortal sins; and if, without contrition for them, you have celebrated any sacrament of your church, it cannot be avoided but that you have brought a great inconvenience on some of your disciples. Besides, suppose you had spoken as you now feign yourself to have done, I desire to know who they are whom you intend when you say, "Our prelate Protestants, so soon as they became such;" as though they were first Protestants at large, and destroyed those principles which afterward they built up when they became prelate Protestants; seeing all men know that our reformation was begun by prelates themselves, and such as never disclaimed the principles by you instanced in.

But you tell me, "I do not only reject what you object against prelate Protestants, but also what you allege in their behalf." I do so indeed,—though I laugh not at you or it, as you pretend,—and so must any man do, who, pleading for Protestancy, hath not a mind openly to prevaricate; for your plea for them is such as, if admitted, would not only overthrow your prelacy, which you pretend to assert, but also destroy your Protestancy, which you will not deny but that you seek to oppose. Nay, it is no other but what was contradicted in the very council of Trent by the Spanish prelates, as that which they conceived to have been an engine contrived for the ruin of episcopacy under a pretence of establishing it, and which, instead of asserting them to be bishops in the church, would have rendered them all curates to the pope. You would have us believe that Christ hath appointed *one episcopal monarch* in his church, with plenitude of power, to represent his own person, which is the pope; and from him all other bishops to derive their power, being substituted by him, and unto him, unto their work. And must not this needs be an *acceptable defensative* or plea unto prelate Protestants; which, if it be admitted, they can be no longer supposed to be made overseers of their flocks by the Holy Ghost, but by the pope, which forfeits their *prelacy;* and, besides, asserts his *supremacy*, which destroys their *Protestancy?*

Upon this occasion you proceed to touch upon somewhat of great importance concerning the head of the church, wherein you know a great part of the difference between yourself and those whom you oppose to consist. In your passage you mention the use of true logic; but I fear we shall find that in your discourse "laudatur et alget." I should have been glad to have found you making what use you were able of that which you commend. It would, I suppose, have directed you to have stated plainly and clearly what it is that you assert, and what it is that you oppose, and to have given your arguments *catasceuastical* of the one, and *anasceuastical*[1] of the other. But either you knew not that way of procedure, or you con-

[1] Catasceuastical and anasceuastical are old logical terms, equivalent to *constructive* and *destructive;* and the clause means, "arguments in support of the one, and in refutation of the other."—Ed.

sidered how little advantage unto your end you were like to obtain thereby; and therefore you make use only of that part of logic which teacheth the nature and kinds of sophisms, in particular that of confounding things which ought to be distinguished. However, your discourse, such as it is, shall be examined, and that by the rules of that logic which yourself commend.

You say, p. 51, "The church says, 'I must have a bishop,' or otherwise she will not have such a visible head as she had at first. This that you may enervate, you tell me 'that the church hath still the same head she had, which is Christ, who is present with his church by his Spirit and his laws, and is man-God still as much as ever he was, and ever the same will be; and if I would have any other visible bishop to be head, then it seems I would not have the same head, and so would have the same, and not the same.'"

This is but one part of my answer, and that very lamely and imperfectly reported. The reader, if he please, may see the whole of it, chap. ix. p. 223,[1] etc., and therewithal take a specimen of your ingenuity in this controversy. It were very sufficient, to render your following exceptions against it useless unto your purpose, merely to repeat what you seek to oppose; but because you shall not have any pretence that any thing you have said is passed over undiscussed, I shall consider what you offer in way of exception to so much of my answer as you are pleased yourself to express, and, as may be supposed, thought yourself qualified to deal withal. Thus, then, you proceed:—

"I cannot in reason be thought to speak otherwise, if we would use true logic, of the identity of the head, than I do of the identity of the body, of the church. This body is not numerically the same; for the men of the first age are long ago gone out of the world, and another generation come, who yet are a body of Christians of the same kind, though not numerically the same. So do I require, that since Jesus Christ as man, the head immediate of other believing men, is departed hence to the glory of his Father, that the church should still have a head of the same kind, as visibly now present, as she had in the beginning; or else, say I, she cannot be completely the same body, or a body of the same kind visible, as she was. But this she hath not, this she is not, except she have a visible bishop, as she had in the beginning, present with her, guiding and ruling under God. Christ our Lord is indeed still man-God, but his manhood is now separate; nor is he visibly present as man, which immediately headed his believers under God, on whose influence their nature depended. His Godhead is still the same in all things, not only in itself, but in order to his church also, as it was before equally invisible,

[1] See pages 86, 87 of this volume.

and in the like manner believed; but the nature delegate under God, and once ruling visibly amongst us by words and examples, is now utterly withdrawn. And if a nature of the same kind be not now delegate with a power of exterior government, as at the first there was, then hath not the church the same head now which she had then. 'Qui habet aures audiendi audiat.'"

How you have secured your logic in this discourse shall afterward be considered; your divinity seems, at the first view, liable unto just exceptions. For,—1. You suppose Christ in his human nature only to have been the head of his church; and therefore the absence of that to necessitate the constitution of another. Now, this supposition is openly false, and dangerous to the whole being of Christianity. It is the Son of God who is the head of the church; who as he is man, so also is he "over all, God blessed for ever;" and as God and man in one person is that head, and ever was since his incarnation, and ever will be to the end of the world. To deny this is to overthrow the foundation of the church's faith, preservation, and consolation, it being founded and built on this, that he was "the Son of the living God," Matt. xvi. And yet into this supposition alone is your imaginary necessity of *the substitution of another head* in his room resolved. 2. You plainly confess that the present church hath not the same head that the church had when our Lord Christ conversed with them in the days of his flesh. That, you say, was his "human nature, delegate under God; which being now removed and separate, another person so delegate under God is substituted in his place:" which not only deprives the church of its *first head*, but also *deposeth the human nature* of Christ from that office of headship to his church which you confess that for a while it enjoyed, leaving him nothing but what belongs unto him as God, wherein alone you will allow him to be that unto his church which formerly he was. Confessing, I say, the human nature of Christ to have been the head of the church, and now denying it so to be, you do what lies in you to depose him from his office and throne, allowing his human nature, as far as I can perceive, to be of little other use than to be eaten by you in the mass. 3. You make your intention yet more evident, by intimating that the human nature of Christ is now no more head of the church than the present church is made up of the same numerical members that it was constituted of in the days of his flesh. What change you suppose in the church, the body, the same you suppose and assert in the head thereof; and as that change excludes those former members from being present members, so this excludes the former head from being the present head. Of old the head of the church was the human nature of Christ, delegate under God; now that is removed, and another person in the same nature is so delegated unto the same office. Now, this is not a head under Christ, but in distinction from him, in the same place wherein he was, and so exclusive of him; which must needs be *Antichrist*, one pretending to be in his room and place, to his exclusion,—that is, one set up against him. And thus also what you seek to avoid doth inevitably follow upon your discourse,—namely, that "you would have the church, for the preservation of its oneness and sameness, to have the same head she had;" which is not the same, unless you will say that the pope is Christ. These are the principles that you proceed upon:—First, You tell us "That the human nature of Christ, delegate under God, was the visible head of the church." Secondly, "That this nature is now removed from us, and ceaseth so to be;" that is, not only to be visible, but the visible head of the church, and is no more so than the present church is made up of the same individual members as it was in the days of his flesh, which, as you well observe, it is not. Thirdly, "That a nature of the same kind in another person is now delegate under God to the same office of a visible head, with that power of external government which Christ had whilst he was that head." And is it not plain from hence that you exclude the Lord Christ from being that head of his church which he was in former days? And, substituting another in his room and place, you at once depose him, and assign another head unto the church; and that in your attempt to prove that her head must still be the same, or she cannot be so. Farther: the human nature of Christ was personally united unto the Son of God; and if that head which you now fancy the church to have be not so united, it is not the same head that that was; and so, whilst you seek to establish, not indeed a sameness in the head of the church, but a likeness in several heads of it as to *visibility*, you evidently assert a change in the nature of that head of the church which we inquire after. In a word, Christ and the pope are not the same; and therefore if it be necessary, to maintain that the church hath the same head that she had, to assert that in the room of Christ she hath the pope, you prove that she hath the same head that she had, because she hath one that is not the same she had; and so, "Qui habet aures audiat." 4. You vainly imagine the whole catholic church any otherwise visible than with the eyes of faith and understanding. It was never so; no, not when Christ conversed with it in the earth; no, not if you should suppose only his blessed mother, his twelve apostles, and some few more, only to belong unto it. For though all the members of it might be seen, and that at once, by the bodily eyes of men, as might also the human nature of him who was the head of it, yet *as he was Head of the church*, and in that his whole person wherein he was so and is so, he was never visible unto any; "for no man hath seen God at any time." And therefore you, substituting a head in his room who in his whole person is visible, seeing he was not so, do change the head of the church as to its visibility also (for one that is in his whole person visible and another that is not so are not alike visible), wherein you would principally place the identity of the church. 5. Let us see whether your *logic* be any better than your *divinity*. The best argument that can be formed out of your discourse is this: "If the church hath not a head visibly present with her, as she had when Christ, in his human nature, was on the earth, she is not the same that she was: but according to their principles she hath not a head now so visibly present with her; therefore she is not the same, according unto them." I desire to know how you prove your inference. It is built on this supposition,—that the *sameness* of the church depends upon the *visibility* of its head, and not on the sameness of the head itself; which is a fond conceit, and contrary to express Scripture, Eph. iv. 3–7, and not capable of the least countenance from reason. It may be you will say that though your argument do not conclude that on our supposition the church is not the same absolutely as it was, yet it doth that it is not the same as to visibility. Whereunto I answer,—(1.) That there is no necessity that the church should be always the same as to visibility, or always visible in the same manner, or always equally visible as to all concernments of it. (2.) You mistake the whole nature of the visibility of the church, supposing it to consist in its being seen with the bodily eyes of men; whereas it is only an affection of its public profession of the truth, whereunto its being seen in part or in whole by the eyes of any or all men doth no way belong. (3.) That the church, as I said before, was indeed never absolutely visible in its head and members, he who was the head of it being never in his whole person visible unto the eyes of men; and he is yet, as he was of old, visible to the eyes of faith, whereby we see him that is invisible. So that to be visible to the bodily eyes of men, in its head and members, was never a property of the church, much less such a one as that thereon its sameness in all ages should depend. 6. You fail also in supposing that the numerical sameness of the church as a body depends absolutely on the sameness of its members; for whilst in succession it hath all things the same that concur unto its constitution, order, and existence, it may be still the same body corporate, though it consist not of the same individual persons or bodies natural,—as the kingdom of England is the same kingdom that it was two hundred years ago, though there be not now one person living that then it was made up of: for though the *matter* be the same only *specifically*, yet the *form* being the same *numerically*, that denominates the body to be so. But that I may the better represent unto you the proper genius and design of your discourse, I shall briefly mind you of the principles which you oppose in it and seek to evert by it; as also of those which you intend to compass your purpose by. Of the first sort are these:—1. "That the Lord Christ, God and man in one person, is, and ever continues to be, the only absolute monarchical head of his own church." I suppose it needless for me to confirm this principle by testimonies of Scripture, which, it being a matter of pure revelation, is the only way of confirmation that it is capable of. That he is the head of his church is so frequently averred, that every one who hath but read the New Testament will assent unto it, upon the bare repetition of the words, with the same faith whereby he assents unto the writing itself, whatever it be; and we shall afterward see that the notion of a head is absolutely exclusive of competition in the matter denoted by it. A head, properly, is singly and absolutely so; and therefore the substitution of another head unto the church in the room of Christ, or with him, is perfectly exclusive of him from being so. 2. "That Christ as God-man, in his whole person, was never visible to the fleshly eyes of men;" and whereas as such he was head of the church, as the head of the church he was never absolutely visible. His human nature was seen of old, which was but something of him as he was and is the head of the church; otherwise than by faith no man hath seen him at any time: and it changeth the condition of the church to suppose that now it hath a head who, being a mere man, is in his whole person visible, so far as a man may be seen. 3. That the visibility of the church consisteth in its public profession of the truth, and not in its being objected to the bodily eyes of men. It is a thing that faith may believe, it is a thing that reason may take notice of, consider, and comprehend, the eyes of the body being of no use in this matter. When a church professeth the truth, it is "the ground and pillar" of it, a city on a hill,—that is, visible, though no man see it, yea, though no man observe or contemplate on any thing about it; its own profession, not other men's observation, constitutes it visible. Nor is there any thing more required to a church's visibility but its profession of the truth, unto which all the outward advantages which it hath, or may have, of appearing conspicuously or gloriously to the consideration of men, are purely accidental, which may be separated from it without any prejudice unto its visibility. 4. That the sameness of the church in all ages doth not depend on its sameness in respect of *degrees* of visibility. That the church be the same that it was, [it] is required that it profess the same truth it did, whereby it becomes absolutely visible; but the degrees of this visibility, as to conspicuousness and notoriety, depending on things accidental unto the being, and consequently visibility, of the church, do no way affect it as unto any change. Now, from hence it follows,—1. That the presence or absence of the human nature of Christ with or from his church on earth doth not belong unto the visibility of it; so that the absence of it doth no way infer a necessity of substituting another visible head in his stead. Nor was the presence of his human nature with his church any way necessary to the visibility of it, his conversation on the earth being wholly for other ends and purposes. 2. That the presence or absence of the human nature of Christ not varying his headship, which under both considerations is still the same, the supposition of another head is perfectly destructive of the whole headship of Christ, there being no vacancy possible to be imagined for that supply but by the removal of Christ out of his place. For he being the head of his church as God and man, in his whole person invisible, and the visibility of the church consisting solely in its own profession of the truth, the absence of his human nature from the earth neither changeth his own headship nor prejudiceth the church's visibility, so that either the one or the other of them should induce a necessity of the supply of another head. Consider now what it is that you oppose unto these things. You tell us,—1. "That Christ was the head of the church in his human nature, delegated by and under God to that purpose." You mean he was so absolutely, and as man, exclusively to his divine nature. This your whole discourse, with the inferences that you draw from this supposition, abundantly manifests. If you can make this good, you may conclude what you please. I know no man that hath any great cause to oppose himself unto you, for you have taken away the very foundation of the being and safety of the church in your supposition. 2. You inform us, "That Christ by his ascension into heaven ceased to be that head that he was, so that of necessity another must be substituted in his place and room;" and this we must think to be the pope. He is, I confess, absent from his church here on earth as to his bodily appearance amongst us; which, as it was not necessary as to his headship, so he promised to supply the inconvenience which his disciples apprehended would ensue thereupon, so that they should have great cause to rejoice at it, as that wherein their great advantage would lie, John xvi. 7. That this should be by giving us a pope at Rome in his stead, he hath no way intimated. And unto those who know what your pope is, and what he hath done in the world, you will hardly make it evident that the great advantage which the Lord Christ promised unto his disciples upon his absence is made good unto them by his supervisorship. 3. You would have the "visibility of the church depend on the visibility of its head, as also its sameness in all ages." And no one, you are secure, who is now visible, pretends to be the head of the church but the pope alone, and therefore of necessity he it must be. But, sir, if the Lord Jesus Christ had had no other nature than that wherein he was visible to the eyes of men, he could never have been a meet head for a church dispersed throughout the whole world, nor have been able to discharge the duty annexed by God unto that office. And if so, I hope you will not take it amiss if on that supposition I deem your pope, of whom millions of Christians know nothing but by *uncertain* rumours, nor he of them, to be very unmeet for the discharge of it. And for the visibility of the church, I have before declared wherein it doth consist. Upon the whole matter, you do not only come short of proving the identity and oneness of the church to depend upon one visible bishop as its monarchical head, but also the principles whereby you attempt the confirmation of that absurd position are of that nature that they exclude the headship of Christ, and infer no less change or alteration in the church than that which must needs ensue thereon, and the substitution of another in his room; which destroys the very essence and being of it.

Let us now consider what you farther reply unto that which is offered in the "Animadversions" unto the purpose now discoursed of. Your ensuing words are,—

"And here, by the way, we may take notice what a fierce English Protestant you are, who labour so stoutly to evacuate my argument for episcopacy, and leave none of your own behind you, nor acquaint the world with any, though you know far better; but would make us believe, notwithstanding those far better reasons for prelacy, that Christ himself, as he is the immediate head of invisible influence, so is he likewise the only and immediate head of visible direction and government amongst us, without the interposition of any person, delegate in his stead, to oversee and rule under him in his church on earth; which is against the tenor both of sacred gospel and St Paul's epistles, and all antiquity, and the present ecclesiastical polity of England, and is the doctrine not of any English Protestant, but of the Presbyterian, Independent, and Quaker."

How little cause you have to attempt an impeachment of my Protestancy, I hope I have in some measure evidenced unto you; and shall yet farther make it manifest, as you give me occasion so to do. In the meantime, as I told you before that I would not plead the particular concernment of any party amongst Protestants, no more than you do that of any party among yourselves, so I am sure enough that I have delivered nothing prejudicial unto any of them, because I have kept myself unto the defence of their Protestancy, wherein they all agree. Nor have I given you an answer unto any argument that tends in the least to the confirmation of such a prelacy as by any sort of Protestants is admitted; but only showed the emptiness and pernicious consequences of your sophism, wherewith you plead in pretence for prelacy, indeed for a papal supremacy, and that on such principles as are absolutely destructive of that Protestant prelacy which you would be thought to give countenance unto. And your ensuing discourse, wherein you labour to justify your reflection on me, is a pitiful piece of falsehood and sophistry. For,—1. This *double head* of the catholic church,—one of influence, the other of direction and government,—which you fancy some Protestants to admit of, is a thing that they declare against as injurious to the Lord Christ, and that which would render the church "biceps monstrum,"—horrid and deformed. It is Christ himself; who as by his Spirit he exercises the office of a head by invisible influence, so by his word that of visible direction and rule: he is, I say, the only head of visible direction to his church, though he be not a visible head to that purpose; which that he should be is to no purpose at all. 2. If by the "interposition of any person under Christ, delegate in his stead," you understand any one single person delegated in his stead to oversee and rule the *whole catholic church*, such a one as you now plead for in your "Epistle," it is intolerable arrogancy to intimate that he is designed either in the gospel, or St Paul's epistles, or antiquity, whereas you are not able to assign any place, or text, or word in them, directly or by fair consequence, to justify what you assert. And for the present ecclesiastical polity of the church of England, if you yet know it not, let me inform you that the very foundations of it are laid in a direct contrary supposition,—namely, that there is no such single person delegated under Christ for the rule of the whole catholic church; which gives us a new evidence of your conscientious care in what you say and write. 3. If you intend (that which is not at all to your purpose) "persons to rule under Christ in the church," presiding, according to his direction and institution, in and over the particular churches whereunto they do relate, governing them in his name, by his authority, and according to his word, I desire you to inform me wherein I have said, or written, or intimated any thing that may give you the least countenance in your affirming that by me it is denied; or where it was ever denied by any Protestant whatever, prelatical, presbyterian, or independent. Neither doth this concession of theirs in the least impeach the sole sovereign monarchy of Christ, and single headship over his church to all ends and purposes. A monarch may be, and is, the sole supreme governor and political head of his kingdom, though he appoint others to execute his laws, by virtue of authority derived from him, in the several provinces, shires, and parishes of it. And Christ is the only head of his church, though he have appointed others to preside and rule in his name, in those distributions of his disciples whereinto they are cast by his appointment.

But you proceed: "Christ, in their way, is immediate head not only of subministration and influence, but of exterior derivation also and government, to his church." *Ans.* He is so,—the supreme and only head of the church catholic, in the one way and other, though the means of conveying influences of grace and of exterior rule be various. "Then," say you, "is he such a head to all believers, or no?" To all; the whole body in general, and every individual member thereof in particular. "If he be so to all," you say, "then no man is to be governed in affairs of religion by any other man." But why so, I pray? Can no man govern, in any sense or place, but he must be a supreme head? The king is immediate head unto all his subjects; he is king not only to the whole kingdom, but to every individual person in his kingdom;—doth it thence follow that they may not be governed by officers subordinate, delegated under him to rule them by his authority according to his laws? or that if they may be so, he is not the only immediate king and supreme head unto them all? The apostle tells us expressly that the "head of every man is Christ," 1 Cor. xi. 3; and that a head of rule, as the husband is the head of the wife, Eph. v. 23; as well as he is a head of influence unto the whole body, and every member of it in particular, 1 Cor. xii. 12, Col. ii. 19. And it is a senseless thing to imagine that this should in the least impeach his appointment of men to rule under him in his church according to his law; who are thereupon not *heads*, but in respect of him *servants*, and in respect to the particular churches wherein they serve him rulers or guides, yea, their servants for his sake,—not lords over the flocks, but ministers of their faith. By these are the flocks of Christ governed, as by shepherds appointed by him, the great "shepherd and bishop of their souls," according to the rules by him prescribed for the rule of the one and obedience of the other. But if by "Governed by another man," you mean *absolutely, supremely*, at his will and pleasure, then we deny that any disciple of Christ is in the things of God so to be governed by any man; and affirm that to assert it is to cast down Jesus Christ from his throne. But you say, "If he be not immediate head unto all, but ministers head the people, and Christ heads the ministers, this in effect is nothing but to make every minister a bishop. Why do you not plainly say what it is more than manifest you would have? All this while you heed no more the laws of the land than constitutions of the gospel." *Ans.* I have told you how Christ is the immediate head unto all, and yet how he hath appointed others to preside in his churches under him; and that this should infer an equality in all that are by him appointed to that work is most senseless to imagine. Nor did I in the least intimate any such thing, but only that therefore there was no need of any one supreme head of the whole catholic church, nor any place or room left for such a one, without the deposition of Christ himself. Because the king is the only supreme head of all his people, doth it therefore follow that if he appoint constables to rule in every parish, with that allotment of power which, by his laws, he gives unto them, and justices of peace to rule over them in a whole county, that therefore every constable in effect is a justice of peace, or that there is a sameness in their office? Christ is the head of every man that is in the church, be he bishop, or minister, or private man; and when the ministers are said to head the people, or the bishops to head them, the expression is improper,—an inferior, ministerial, subordinate rule being expressed by the name of that which is supreme and absolute; or, they head them not absolutely, but in some respect only, as every one of them dischargeth the authority over and towards them wherewith he is intrusted. This assertion of Christ's sole, absolute headship, and denial of any monarchical state in the church catholic but what ariseth from thence, doth not, as every child may see, concern the difference that is about the superiority of bishops to ministers or presbyters: for, notwithstanding this, there are degrees in the ministry of the church, and several orders of men are engaged therein; and whatever there are, there might have been more, had it seemed good to our Lord Christ to appoint them. And whatever order of men may be supposed to be instituted by him in his church, he must be supposed to be the head of them all, and they are all to serve him in the duties and offices that they have to discharge towards the church and one another. This headship of Christ is the thing that you are to oppose, and its exclusiveness to the substitution of an absolute head over the whole catholic church in his place, because of his bodily absence from the earth. But this you cast out of sight, and instead thereof fall upon the equality of bishops and ministers, which no way ensues thereon, both bishops and presbyters agreeing well enough in the truth we assert and plead for. "This," you say, "is contrary to the gospel, and the law of the land." What is, I pray? that "Christ is the only absolute head of the catholic church?" "No; but 'that bishops and ministers are in effect all one.'" But what is that to your purpose? will it advantage your cause what way ever that problem be determined? Was any occasion offered you to discourse upon that question? Nay, you perceive well enough yourself that this is nothing at all to your design, and therefore in your following discourse you double and sophisticate, making it evident that either you understand not yourself what you say, or that you would not have others understand you, or that you confound all things with a design to deceive: for when you come to speak of the *gospel*, you attempt to prove the appointment of one supreme pastor to the whole catholic church, and, by the *law of the land*, the superiority of bishops over ministers, as though these things were the same, or had any relation one to another; whereas we have showed the former, in your sense, to be destructive to the latter. Truth never put any man upon such subterfuges; and I hope the difficulties that you find yourself perplexed withal may direct you at length to find that there is a "deceit in your right hand." But let us hear your own words:—

"As for the gospel, the Lord, who had been visible governor and pastor of his flock on earth, when he was now to depart hence, as all the apostles expected one to be chosen to succeed him in his care, so did he, notwithstanding his own invisible presence and providence over his flock, publicly appoint one. And when he taught them that he who was greatest among them should be as the least, he did not deny but suppose one greater, and taught, in one and the same breath, both that he was over them, and for what he was over them,—namely, to feed, not to tyrannize; not to domineer and hurt, but to direct, comfort, and conduct his flock in all humility and tenderness, as a servant of all their spiritual necessities. And if a bishop be otherwise affected, it is the fault of his person, not his place."

And what is it that you would prove hereby? Is it that bishops are above ministers? which, in the words immediately foregoing, you asserted, and in those next ensuing confirm from the law of the land. Is there any tendency in your discourse towards any such purpose? Nay, do not yourself know that what you seek to insinuate,—namely, the institution of one supreme pastor of the whole catholic church, one of the apostles to be above and ruler over all the rest of the apostles, and the whole church besides,—is perfectly destructive of the hierarchy of bishops in England as established by law; and also at once casting down the main if not only foundation that they plead for their station and order from the gospel? For all "prelate Protestants," as you call them, assert an equality *in all the apostles*, and a superiority in them to the seventy disciples; whence, by a parity of reason, they conclude unto the superiority of bishops over ministers to be continued in the church. And are you not a fair advocate for your cause, and well meet for the reproving of others for not consenting unto them? But, waiving that which you little care for, and are not at all concerned in, let us see how you prove that which we know you greatly desire to give some countenance unto; that is, a universal visible pastor over the whole catholic church, in the place and room of Christ himself. First, you tell us that "the apostles expected one to be chosen to succeed Christ in his care." But to have one *succeed* another in his care infers that that other *ceased* to take and exercise the care which formerly he had and exercised; which in this case is highly *blasphemous* once to imagine.

I wish you would take more care of what you say in things of this nature, and not suffer the impetuous bias of your interest to cast you upon expressions so injurious to the honour of Christ and safety of his church. And how do you prove that the apostles had any such expectation as that which you mention? Our Saviour gave them *equal commission* to teach all nations; told them that as his Father had sent him so he sent them; that he had chosen them twelve, but that one of them was a *devil*,—never that one of them should be *pope*. Their institution, instruction, privileges, charge, calling, were all equal. How, then, should they come to have this expectation, that one of them should be chosen to succeed Christ in his care, when they were all chosen to serve under him in the continuance of his care towards his church? That which you obscurely intimate from whence this expectation of yours might arise, is the contest that was amongst them about pre-eminence: Luke xxii. 24, "There was a strife amongst them which of them should be accounted the greatest." This, you suppose, was upon their persuasion that one should be chosen in particular to succeed the Lord Christ in his care; whereupon they fell into difference about the place. But,—1. Is it not somewhat strange unto yourself how they should contest about a succession unto Christ in his absence, *who had not once thought that he would ever be absent* from them, nor could bear the mention of it without great sorrow of heart when afterward he began to acquaint them with it? 2. How should they come in your apprehension to quarrel about that which, as you suppose and contend, was *some while before determined?* for this contest of yours was some while after the promise of the keys to Peter, and the saying of Christ that he "would build his church on the rock." Were the apostles, think you, as stupid as Protestants, that they could not see the supremacy of Peter in those passages, but must yet fall at variance who should be pope? 3. How doth it appear that this strife of theirs who should be greatest did not arise from their apprehension of an earthly kingdom, a hope whereof, according to the then current persuasion of the Judaical church, to be erected by their master, whom they believed in as the true Messiah, they were not delivered from until after his resurrection, when they were filled with the Spirit of the New Testament? Acts i. Certainly from that root sprang the ambitious desire of the sons of Zebedee after pre-eminence in his kingdom; and the designing of the rest of them in this place, from the manner of its management, by *strife*, seems to have had no better a spring. 4. The stop put by our Lord Jesus unto the strife that was amongst them makes it manifest that it arose from no such expectation as you imagine; or that at least if it did, yet your expectation was irregular, vain, and groundless: for, —(1.) He tells them that there should be *no such greatness* in his church as that which they contended about, being like to the sovereignty exercised by and in the nations of the earth: from which he that can show a difference in your papal rule, "erit mihi magnus Apollo." (2.) He tells them that his Father had equally provided a kingdom,—that is, heavenly and eternal,—for all them that believed; which was the *only greatness* that they ought to look or inquire after. (3.) That as to their privilege in his kingdom, it should be *equal* unto them all; for they "should all sit on thrones, judging the twelve tribes of Israel:" so ascribing equal power, authority, and dignity unto them all; which utterly overthrows the figment of the supremacy of any one of them over the rest, Luke xxii. 30, Matt. xix. 28. And, (4.) Yet farther to prevent any such conceit as that which you suppose them to have had concerning the prelation of any one of them, he tells them that "one was their Master, even Christ, and that all they were brethren," Matt. xxiii. 8; so giving them to understand that he had designed them to be perfectly and every way equal among themselves. So ill have you laid the foundation of your plea, as that it guides us to a full determination of the contrary to your pretence, and that given by our Saviour himself, with many reasons persuading his disciples of the equity of it and unto an acquiescency in it. And what you add, that he presently appointed one to the pre-eminency you imagine, is altogether inconsistent with what you would conclude from the strife about it; for the appointment you fancy *preceded this contention*, and had it been real, and to any such purpose, would certainly have prevented it. Thus you do neither prove from the gospel what you *pretend* unto, namely, that bishops are above ministers,—so well do you plead your cause! nor what you *intend*, namely, that the pope is appointed over them all. Only you wisely add a caution about what a bishop ought to be and do "de jure," and what any one of them may do or be "de facto;" because it is impossible for any man to find the least difference between the domination which our *Saviour* expressly *condemns* and that which your *pope* doth *exercise*, although I know not whether you would think meet to have him divested of that authority on the pretence whereof he so domineers in the world.

Finding yourself destitute of any countenance from the gospel, you proceed to the laws of the land. To what purpose?—to prove that Christ appointed "one amongst his apostles to preside with plenitude of power over all the rest of them," and consequently over the whole catholic church succeeding him in his care? Certainly you will find little countenance in our laws to this purpose. But let us hear your own words again. "As for the laws of the land," say you, "it is there most strongly decreed, by the consent and authority of the whole kingdom, not only that bishops are our ministers, but that the king's majesty is head of the bishops also in the line of hierarchy, from whose hand they receive both their places and jurisdiction. This was established not only by one, but by several parliament acts, both in the reign of King Edward and Queen Elizabeth." What will hence follow?—that there is one universal bishop appointed to succeed Christ in his care over the church catholic, the thing you attempted to prove in the words immediately foregoing? Do not the same laws which assert the order you mention exclude that which you would introduce? Or would you prove that bishops by the law of this land have a jurisdiction superior unto ministers? Who ever went about to deny it? or what will the remembrance of it advance your pretensions? And yet neither is this fairly expressed by you. For as no Protestants assert the king to be in his power and office interposed between Christ and bishops or ministers, as to their *ministerial office*, which is purely spiritual; so the power of supreme jurisdiction which they ascribe unto him is not, as you falsely insinuate, granted unto him by the laws of King Edward and Queen Elizabeth, but is an inseparable privilege of his imperial crown, exercised by his royal predecessors, and asserted by them against the intrusions and usurpations of the pope of Rome, only declared by those and other laws. But I perceive you have another design in hand. You are entering upon a discourse wherein you compare yourselves not only with Presbyterians and Independents, but prelate Protestants also, in what you ascribe unto kings in ecclesiastical affairs, preferring yourselves before and above them all. What just cause you have so to do, we shall afterward consider. Your confidence in it at first view presents itself unto us. For whereas there was not in the "Animadversions" any occasion of it administered unto you, and yourself confess that your whole discourse about it is beside your purpose, p. 66; yet, waiving almost every thing that was incumbent upon you to have insisted on, if you would not plainly have appeared "vadimonium deseruisse," and to have given up your "Fiat" as indefensible, you divert into a long harangue about it. The thesis you would by various flourishes give countenance unto is this, That Papists in their deference unto kings, even in ecclesiastical matters, and in their principles of their obedience unto them, do excel Protestants of all sorts. That this is not to our present purpose, yourself cannot but see and acknowledge. However, your discourse, such as it is, relating to one special head of difference between us, shall be apart considered by itself in our next chapter.

CHAPTER XVI.

The power assigned by Papists and Protestants unto kings in matters ecclesiastical —Their several principles discussed and compared.

YOUR discourse on this head is not reducible by logic itself unto any method or rules of argument. For it is in general,—1. So *loose*, ambiguous, and metaphorically expressed; 2. So *sophistical* and inconclusive; 3. So *inconsistent* in sundry instances with the principles and practices of your church, if you speak intelligibly; 4. So *false* and untrue in many particulars,—that it is scarcely, for these excellent qualifications, to be paralleled with any thing either in your "Fiat" or your "Epistola." First, It is *loose* and ambiguous:—(1.) Not stating what you intend by "*the head of the church,*" which you discourse about. (2.) Not *determining* whether the king be such a head of execution in matters of religion as may use the liberty of his own judgment as to what he puts in execution, or whether he be not bound to execute your pope's determinations on the penalty of the forfeiture of his Christianity; which I doubt we shall find to be your opinion. (3.) Not declaring wherein the power which you assign unto him is founded (whether *in God's immediate institution* or the *concession of the pope*), whereon it should solely depend, unto whom it is in all things to be made subservient. Secondly, *Sophistical:*—(1.) In playing with the ambiguity of that expression, "Head of the church," and by the advantage thereof imposing on Protestants contradictions between their profession and practice, as though in the one they acknowledged the king to be head of the church, and not in the other (whereas there is a perfect consonancy between them in the sense wherein they understand that expression); shrouding your own sense and opinion in the meantime under the same ambiguity. (2.) In supposing an absolute universal head of the whole catholic church, and then giving reasons why no king can be that head; when you know that the whole question is, whether there be any such head of the catholic church on earth or no. (3.) In supposing the principles and practices of the primitive church to have been the same with those of the present Roman, and those of the present Roman to have been all known and allowed of old,—which begs all that is in controversy between us; and sundry other instances of the like nature may be observed in it. Thirdly, *Inconsistent* with the principles and practices of your own church, both—(1.) In what you ascribe unto kings; and, (2.) In your stating of the power and jurisdiction of your pope,—if the ambiguity of your words and expressions will allow us to conclude what you intend or aim at. Fourthly,

False:—(1.) In matter of fact, as to what you relate of the obedience of your church unto kings; (2.) In the principles and opinions which you impose on your adversaries; (3.) In the declaration that you make of your own; and, (4.) In many particular assertions, whose consideration will afterward occur.

This is a business I could have been glad you had not necessitated me to the consideration of; for it cannot be truly and distinctly handled without some such reflections upon your church and way as may, without extraordinary indulgence, redound unto your disadvantage. You have by your own voluntary choice called me to the discussion of those principles which have created you much trouble in these nations, and put you oftentimes upon attempting their disquiet. Now, these are things which I desire not. I am but a private man, and am very well contented you should enjoy all that peace and liberty which you think not meet in other nations, where the power is at your disposal, to grant unto them that dissent from you. "Lex talionis" should be far from influencing the minds of Christians in this matter, however the equity of it may at any time be pleaded or urged to relieve others in other places under bondage and persecution. But I am sure, if I judge your proceedings against other men dissenting from you in conscience to be unjustifiable by the Scripture, or light of nature, or suffrage of the ancient church, as I do, I have no reason to desire that they should be drawn into precedent against yourselves, in any place in the world. And therefore, sir, had you provided the best colour you could for your own principles, and palliated them to the utmost, so to hide them from the eyes of those who it may be are ready to seek their disturbance and trouble from an apprehension of the evil that may ensue upon them, and had not set them up in comparison with the principles of Protestants of all sorts, and, for the setting off your own with the better grace and lustre, untruly and invidiously reported theirs, to expose them unto those thoughts and that severity from supreme powers which you seek yourselves to waive, I should have wholly passed by this discourse, unto which no occasion was administered in the "Animadversions." But now, as you have handled the matter, unless I would have it taken for granted that the principles of the Roman church are more suited unto the establishment and promotion of the interest and sovereignty of kings and other supreme magistrates, and in particular the kings of these nations, than those of Protestants, which in truth I do not believe, I must of necessity make a little farther inquiry into your discourse. And I desire your pardon if in my so doing any thing be spoken that suits not so well your interest and designs, neither expecting nor desiring any, if aught be delivered by me not according to truth.

To make our way the more clear, some of the ambiguous expressions which you make use of to cloud and hide your intention in your inquiry after the head of the church, must be explained:—

1. By the *church* you understand not this or that particular church, not the church of this or that nation, kingdom, or country, but *the whole catholic church* throughout the world. And when you have explained yourself to this purpose, you endeavour, by *six arguments* no less (pp. 67, 68), to prove that no king ever was or can be head of it. He said well of old,—

> "In causa facili cuivis licet esse diserto."—Ov. Trist. iii. 11, 21.

I wonder you contented yourself to give us six reasons only, and that you proceeded not at least unto the high hills of *eighteenthly* and *nineteenthly* that you talk of in your "Fiat Lux," where you scoff at the preaching of Presbyterians. It may be you will scarcely ever obtain such another opportunity of showing the fertility of your invention. So did he flourish who thought himself secure from adversaries,—

> —— "Caput altum in prælia tollit,
> Ostenditque humeros latos, alternaque jactat
> Brachia protendens, et verberat ictibus auras." Virg. Æn. v. 375.

But you do like him,—you only beat the air. Do you think any man was ever so distempered as to dream that any king whatever could be "the absolute head of the whole catholic church of Christ?" We no more think any king, in any sense, to be the head of the catholic church than we think the pope so to be. The Roman empire was at its height and glory when first Christianity set forth in the world, and had extended its bounds beyond those of any kingdom that arose before it, or that hath since succeeded unto it; and yet, within a very few years after the resurrection of Christ, the gospel had diffused itself beyond the limits of that empire, among the Parthians and Indians, and unto "Britannorum Romanis inaccessa loca," as Tertullian calls them. Now, none ever supposed that any king had power or authority of any sort in reference unto the church, or any members of it, without or beyond the precise limits of his own dominions. The inquiry we have under consideration about the power of kings, and the obedience due unto them in ecclesiastical things, is limited absolutely unto their own kingdoms, and unto those of their subjects which are Christians in them. And thus,—

> "Hi motus animorum atque hæc certamina tanta
> Pulveris exigui jactu compressa quiescunt." Virg. Georg. iv. 87.

A little observation of this one known and granted principle renders not only your six reasons altogether useless, but supersedes also a great part of your rhetoric, which, under the ambiguity of that expression, you display in your whole discourse.

2. You pleasantly lead about your unwary reader with the ambiguity of the other term, "The head." Hence, p. 58, you fall into a great exclamation against Protestants, "That, acknowledging the king to be the head of the church, they do not supplicate unto him and acquiesce in his judgment in religious affairs;"—as if ever any Protestant acknowledged any king, or any mortal man, to be such a head of the church as you fancy to yourselves, in whose determinations in religion all men are bound spiritually, and as to their eternal concernments, to acquiesce, and that not because they are true according to the Scripture, but because they are his. Such a head you make the pope; such a one on earth all Protestants deny: which evacuates your whole discourse to that purpose, pp. 58, 59. It is true, in opposition unto your papal claim of authority and jurisdiction over the subjects of this kingdom, Protestants do assert the king to be so head of the church within his own realms and dominions, as that he is, by God's appointment, the sole fountain and spring amongst men of all authority and power to be exercised over the persons of his subjects in matters of external cognizance and order; being no way obnoxious to the direction, supervisorship, and superintendency of any other,—in particular, not of the pope. He is not the "only striker," as you phrase it, in his kingdoms; but the only protector under God of all his subjects, and the only distributer of justice, in rewards and punishments, unto them, not depending in the administration of the one or other on the determinations or orders of your pope or church. Not that any of them do use absolutely that expression of "Head of the church;" but that they ascribe unto him all authority that ought or can be exercised in his dominions over any of his subjects, whether in things civil or ecclesiastical, that are not merely spiritual, and to be ministerially ordered in obedience unto Christ Jesus. And that you may the better see what it is that Protestants ascribe unto the king, and to every king that is absolutely supreme, as his majesty is in his own dominions, and withal how exceeding vain your unreasonable reproach is, which you cast upon them for not giving themselves up unto an absolute acquiescency in human determinations, as merely such, on pretence that they proceed from the head of the church, I shall give you a brief account of their thoughts in this whole matter:—

1. They say that the king is the *supreme governor over all persons* whatever within his realms and dominions, none being exempted on any account from subjection unto his regal authority. How well you approve of this proposition in the great assignations you pretend unto kingly power, we shall afterward inquire. Protestants found their persuasion in this matter on the authority of the Scripture, both Old Testament and New, and the very principles constituting

sovereign power amongst men. You speak fair to kings, but at first dash exempt a considerable number of their born subjects, owing them indispensable natural allegiance, from their jurisdiction. Of this sort are the clergy. But the kings of Judah of old were not of your mind. Solomon certainly thought Abiathar, though high priest, subject to his royal authority, when he denounced against him a sentence of death, and actually deposed him from the priesthood. The like course did his successors proceed in. For neither had God, in the first provision he made for a king amongst his people, Deut. xvii., nor in that prescription of the manner of the kingdom which he gave them by Samuel, once intimated an exemption of any persons, priests or others, from the rule or authority of the prince which he would set over them. In the New Testament we have the rule, as the practice in the Old, Rom. xiii. 1, "Let every soul be subject to the higher powers,"—the power that bears the sword, "the striker." And we think that your clergymen have souls (at least "pro sale"), and so come within the circumference of this command and rule. Chrysostom, in his comment on that place, is of our mind, and prevents your pretence of an exception from the rule by special privilege, giving us a distribution of the universality of the persons here intended into their several kinds. Δεικνὺς, saith he, *ὅτι ταῦτα διατάττεται καὶ ἱερεῦσι καὶ μοναχοῖς οὐχὶ τοῖς βιωτικοῖς μόνον· ἐκ προοιμίων αὐτὸ δῆλον ἐποίησεν, οὕτω λέγων, Πᾶσα ψυχὴ ἐξουσίαις ὑπερεχούσαις ὑποτασσέσθω, κᾂν ἀπόστολος ἦς, κᾂν εὐαγγελιστὴς, κᾂν προφήτης, κᾂν ὁστισοῦν· οὐδὲ γὰρ ἀνατρέπει τὴν εὐσέβειαν αὕτη ἡ ὑποταγὴ, καὶ οὐχ' ἁπλῶς εἶπε πιθέσθω, ἀλλ' ὑποτασσέσθω·*—"He showeth that these things are commanded unto all, unto priests and monks, and not to secular persons only; which he declareth in the very entrance of his discourse, saying, 'Let every soul be subject to the higher powers,' whether thou be an apostle, or an evangelist, or a prophet, or whatever thou be; for subjection overthrows not piety. And he saith not simply, 'Let him obey,' but, 'Let him be subject.'" The very same instances are given by Theodoret, Oecumenius, and Theophylact. Bernard, Epist. 42, ad Archiepisc. Senonens., meets with your exception, which in his days began to be broached in the world, and tells you expressly that it is a delusion. In conformity unto this rule of St Paul, Peter exhorts all Christians, none excepted, to "submit themselves unto the king, as supreme," 1 Epist. ii. 13. And whatever we conclude from these words in reference unto the king, I fear that if, instead of the *king*, he had said the *pope*, you would have thought us very impudent if we had persisted in the denial of your monstrous imaginary headship; but in this principle, on these and the like grounds, do all Protestants concur. And, indeed, to fancy a sovereign monarch with so great a number of men as your clergy consists of in many kingdoms exempted from his regal authority, is to lay such an axe unto the root of his government, as whereby with one stroke you may hew it down at your pleasure.

2. Protestants affirm that "Rex in regno suo," every king in his own kingdom, is the supreme dispenser of justice and judgment unto all persons, *in all causes* that belong unto or are determinable "in foro exteriori," in any court of judicature, whether the matter which they concern be civil or ecclesiastical. No cause, no difference determinable by any law of man, and to be determined by coercive umpirage or authority, is exempted from his cognizance. Neither can any man, on any pretence, claim any jurisdiction over any of his subjects not directly and immediately derived from him. Neither can any king who is a sovereign monarch, like the kings of this land, yield or grant a power in any other to judge of any ecclesiastical causes among his subjects, as arising from any other spring, or growing on any other root but that of his own authority, without an impeachment and irreparable prejudice to his crown and dignity; neither doth any such concession, grant, or supposition, make it indeed so to be, but is a mere fiction and mistake, all that is done upon it being "ipso facto" null, and of none effect. Neither, if a king should make a pretended legal grant of such power unto any, would any right accrue unto them thereby; the making of such a grant being a matter absolutely out of his power, as are all things whereby his regal authority, wherein the majesty of his kingdom is inwrapped, may be diminished: for that king who hath a power to diminish his kingly authority never was intrusted with absolute kingly power. Neither is this power granted unto our kings by the acts of parliament, which you mention, made in the beginning of the Reformation, but was always inherent in them, and exercised in innumerable instances, and often vindicated with a high hand from papal encroachments, even during the hour and power of your darkness; as hath been sufficiently proved by many, both divines and lawyers. Things of mere spiritual order, as preaching the word, administration of the sacraments, and the like, we ascribe not unto kings, nor the communicating of power unto any for their performance. The sovereign power of these things is vested in Christ alone, and by him committed unto his ministers; but religion hath many concernments that attend it, which must be disposed of by forensical, juridical process and determinations. All these, with the persons of them that are interested in them, are subject immediately to the power and authority of the king, and none other; and to exempt them, or any of them, or any of the like nature which may emerge amongst men in things relating unto conscience and religion, whose catalogue may be endlessly extended, from royal cognizance, is to make mere properties of kings, in things which in

a very special manner concern the peace and welfare of their subjects, and the distribution of rewards and punishments among them. Of this sort are all things that concern the authoritative public conventions of church officers, and differences amongst them about their interests, practices, and public profession of doctrines; collations of legal dignities and benefices, by and with investitures legal and valid; all ecclesiastical revenues with their incidences; the courts and jurisdictions of ecclesiastical persons for the reglement of the outward man by censures and sentences of law, with the like. And as this whole matter is sufficiently confirmed by what was spoken before of the power of kings over the persons of all their subjects, and (for to what end should they have such a power, if in respect of many of them, and that in the chief concernments of their rule and government, it may never be exerted?) so I should tire your patience if I should report one half of the laws, instances, and pleas, made, given, and used by the ancient Christian kings and emperors in the pursuit and for the confirmation of this their just power. The decrees and edicts of Constantine the Great, commanding, ruling, and disposing of bishops in cases ecclesiastical; the laws of Justinian, Charles the Great, Ludovicus his son, and Lotharius his successor, with more innumerable to the same purpose, are extant and known unto all. So also are the pleas, protestations, and vindications of most of the kingdoms of Europe, after once the pretensions of Papacy began to be broached to their prejudice. And, in particular, notable instances you might have of the exercise of this royal power in the first Christian magistrate invested with supreme authority, both in the case of Athanasius, Socrat. lib. i. cap. 28, and cap. 34, Athan. Apol. 2, as also of the Donatists, Euseb. lib. x. cap. 5, August. Epist. 162, 166, and Advers. Crescon. lib. iii. cap. 17; whereunto innumerable instances in his successors may be added.

3. Protestants teach unanimously that it is *incumbent* on kings to find out, receive, embrace, and promote the truth of the gospel, and the worship of God appointed therein, confirming, protecting, and defending of it by their regal power and authority; as also, that in their so doing they are to use the liberty of *their own judgments*, informed by the ways that God hath appointed for that end, independently of the dictates, determinations, and orders of any other person or persons in the world, unto whose authority they should be obnoxious. Heathen kings made laws for God, Dan. iii. vi.; Jonah iii. And the great thing that we find any of the good kings of Judah commended for is, that they commanded the worship of God to be observed and performed according unto his own appointment. For this end were they then bound to write out a copy of the law with their own hands, Deut. xvii. 18, and to study in it continually.

To this purpose were they warned, charged, exhorted, and excited by the prophets; that is, that they should serve God as kings. And to this purpose are there innumerable laws of the best Christian kings and emperors still extant in the world.

In these things consists that supremacy or headship of kings which Protestants unanimously ascribe unto them, especially those in England to his royal majesty. And from hence you may see the frivolousness of sundry things you object unto them,—

As, *first*, of the scheme or series of ecclesiastical power which you ascribe to prelate Protestants and the laws of the land, from which you say the Presbyterians dissent; which you thus express:—

"By the laws of our land, our series of government ecclesiastical stands thus:	"The Presbyterian predicament is thus:
God,	God,
Christ,	Christ,
King,	Minister,
Bishop,	People.
Ministers,	
People.	

"So that the minister's head, in the Presbyterian predicament, toucheth Christ's feet immediately, and nothing intervenes. You pretend, indeed, that hereby you do exalt Christ. But this is a mere cheat, as all men may see with their eyes; for Christ is but where he was: but the minister indeed is exalted, being now set in the king's place, one degree higher than the bishops, who by law is under king and bishops too."

If I mistake not in my guess, you greatly pleased yourself with your scheme, wherein you pretend to make, forsooth, an ocular demonstration of what you undertook to prove; whereas, indeed, it is as trivial a fancy as a man can ordinarily meet withal. For,—1. Neither the law, nor prelates, nor Presbyterians, ascribe any place at all unto the king's majesty in the series of *spiritual order;* he is neither bishop, nor minister, nor deacon, or any way authorized by Christ to convey or communicate power merely spiritual unto any others. No such thing is *claimed* by our kings, or *declared* in law, or asserted by *Protestants* of any sort. But in the series of exterior government, both prelate Protestants and Presbyterians assign a supremacy over all persons in his dominions, and that in all causes that are inquirable and determinable by or in any court exercising jurisdiction and authority, unto his majesty. All sorts assign unto him the supreme place under Christ in external government and jurisdiction. None assign him any place in spiritual order, and merely spiritual power. 2. If you place bishops on the series of exterior government, as appointed by the king and confirmed by the law of the land, there is yet no difference with respect unto them. 3. The question, then, is solely about the series of spiritual order, and thereabout it is confessed there are various apprehensions of Protestants; which is all you prove, and so do, "magno conatu nugas agere." Who knows it not? I wish there were any need to prove it. But, sir, this difference about the superiority of bishops to presbyters, or their equality or identity, was agitated in the church many and many a hundred year before you or I were born, and will be so probably when we are both dead and forgotten; so that what it makes in this dispute is very hard for a sober man to conjecture. 4. Who they are that pretend to exalt Christ, *by a mere asserting ministers* not to be by his institution subject to bishops, which you call a "cheat," I know not, nor shall be their advocate. They exalt Christ who love him and keep his commandments, and no other.

Secondly, You may also as easily discern the frivolousness of your exclamation against Protestants for not giving up their differences in religion to the *umpirage of kings,* upon the assignment of that supremacy unto them which hath been declared. When we make the king such a head of the catholic church as you make the pope, we shall seek unto him as the fountain of our faith; as you pretend to do unto the pope. For the present, we give that honour to none but Christ himself; and for what we assign in profession unto the king, we answer it wholly in our practical submission. Protestants never thought nor said that any king was appointed by Christ to be supreme, *infallible proposer* of all things to be believed and done in the worship of God; no king ever assumed that power unto himself. It is Jesus Christ alone who is *the supreme and absolute lawgiver* of his church, "the author and finisher of our faith;" and it is the honour of kings to serve him, in the promotion of his interest, by the exercise of that authority and duty which we have before declared. What, unto the dethroning and dishonour as much as in you lieth of Christ himself, and of kings also, you assign unto the pope, in making him the supreme head and fountain of your faith, hath been already considered. This is the substance of what you except against Protestants, either as to opinion or practice, in this matter of deference unto kingly authority in things ecclesiastical. What is the sense of your church, which you prefer unto your sentiments herein, I shall, after I have a little examined your present pretensions, manifest unto you (seeing you will have it so) from those who are full well able to inform us of it:—

> "Fas mihi *pontificum* sacrata resolvere jura;
> ——— atque omnia ferre sub auras,
> Siqua tegunt; teneor *Romæ* nec legibus ullis." Virg. Æn. ii. 157.

For your own part, you have expressed yourself in this matter so loosely, generally, and ambiguously, that it is very hard for any man to collect from your words what it is that you assert or what you deny. I shall endeavour to draw out your sense by a few inquiries; as,—1. Do you think the king hath *any authority* vested in him, *as king,* in ecclesiastical affairs and over ecclesiastical persons? You tell us, "That Catholics observe the king in all things, as well ecclesiastic as civil," p. 59; "That in the line of corporeal power and authority the king is immediately under God," p. 61; with other words to the same purpose, if they are to any purpose at all. I desire to know whether you grant in him an authority derived immediately from God in and over ecclesiastical affairs, as to convene synods or councils, to reform things amiss in the church, as to the outward administration of them? or do you think that he hath such power and authority to make, constitute, or appoint laws, with penal sanctions, in and about things ecclesiastical? And, 2. Do you think that in the work which he hath to do for the church, be it what it will, he may use *the liberty of his own judgment,* directed by the light of the Scripture, or that he is precisely to follow the declarations and determinations of the pope? If he have not this authority, if he may not use this liberty, the good words you speak of Catholics, and give unto him, signify, indeed, nothing at all. If, then, he hath and may, you openly rise up against the bulls, briefs, and interdicts of your popes themselves, and the universal practice of your church for many ages. And, therefore, I desire you to inform me, 3. Whether you do not judge him *absolutely* to be *subject and accountable* to the pope for whatever he doth in ecclesiastical affairs in his own kingdoms and dominions? If you answer suitably to the principles, maxims, and practice of your church, you must say he is: and if so, I must tell you that whatever you ascribe unto him in things ecclesiastical, he acts not about them as king, but in some other capacity; for to do a thing as a king, and to be accountable for what he doth therein to the pope, implies a contradiction. 4. Hath not the pope a power over his subjects, many of them at least, to convent, censure, judge, and punish them, and to exempt them *in criminal cases* from his jurisdiction? And is not this *a fair supremacy,* that it is meet he should be contented withal, when you put it into the power of another to exempt as many of his subjects as he pleaseth and are willing from his regal authority? 5. When you say, "That, in matters of faith, kings for their own ease remit their subjects to their papal pastor," p. 57, whether do you not collude with us, or, indeed, do at all think as you speak? Do you think that kings have *real power* in and about those things wherein you depend on the pope, and only remit their subjects to him for their own ease? You cannot but know that this one concession would ruin the whole Papacy, as being expressly destructive of all the foundations on which it is built. Nor did ever any pope proceed on this ground in his interposures in the world about matters of faith,—that such things, indeed, belonged unto others, and were only by them remitted unto him for their ease. 6. Whether you do not include kings themselves in your general assertion, p. 55, "That they who after papal decisions remain contumacious forfeit their Christianity?" and if so, whether you do not at once overthrow all your other splendid concessions, and make kings absolute dependants on the pope for all the privileges of their Christianity; and whether you account not among them their very regal dignity itself?—whereby it may easily appear how much Protestant kings and potentates are beholding unto you, seeing it is manifest that they live and rule in a neglect of many papal decisions and determinations. 7. Whether you do not very fondly pretend to prove your Roman Catholics' acknowledgment of the power of princes to make laws, in cases ecclesiastical, from the laws of Justinian, p. 59; whereas they are instances of regal power, in such cases plainly destructive of your present Hildebrandine faith and authority? and whether you suppose such laws to have any force or authority of law without the papal sanction and confirmation? 8. Whether you think, indeed, that *confession unto priests* is such an effectual means of securing the peace and interest of kings as you pretend, p. 59? and whether Queen Elizabeth, King James, Henry III. and IV. of France, had cause to believe it? and whether you learned this notion from Parry, Ravaillac, Mariana, Clement, Parsons, Allen, Garnet, Gerard, Oldcome, with their associates? 9. Whether you forget not yourself when you place "Aaron and Joshua in government together," p. 64? 10. Whether you really believe that the pope hath power only to "*persuade* in matters of religion," as you pretend, p. 65? and if so, from what topics he takes the *whips, wires,* and *racks* that he makes use of in his Inquisition? and whether he hath not a right even to destroy kings themselves, who will not be his executioners in destroying of others? I wish you would come out of the clouds, and speak your mind freely and plainly to some of these inquiries. Your present ambiguous discourse, in the face of it, suited unto your interest, gives no satisfaction whilst these snakes lie in the grass of it. Wherefore, leaving you a little to your second thoughts, I shall inquire of your masters and fathers themselves what is the true sense of your church in this matter; and we shall find them speaking it out plainly and roundly. For they tell us,—

1. That *the government of the whole catholic church is monarchical,*—a state wherein all power is derived from one fountain, one and the same person. This is the first principle that is laid down by all your writers, in treating of the church and its power, and that which your great Cardinal Baronius lays as the foundation on which he builds the huge structure of his ecclesiastical annals.

2. That *the pope is this monarch of the church,*—the person in whom alone the sovereign rule of it is originally vested; so that it is absolutely impossible that any other person should have, enjoy, or

use any ecclesiastical authority but what is derived from him. I believe you suppose this sufficiently proved by Bellarmine and others. Yourself own it, nor can deny it without a disclaimure of your present Papacy. And this *one principle* perfectly discovers the vanity of your pretended attributions of power in ecclesiastical things to kings and princes; for to suppose a monarchical estate, and not to suppose all power and authority in that state to be derived from the monarch in it and of it alone, is to suppose a perfect contradiction, or a state monarchical that is not monarchical. Protestants place the monarchical state of the catholic church in its relation unto Christ alone; and therefore it is incumbent on them to assert that no man hath, nor can have, a power in the church, as such, but what is derived from and communicated unto him by him. And you, placing it in reference unto the pope, must of necessity deny that any power can be exercised in it but what is derived from him; so that whatever you pretend in this kind to grant unto kings, you allow it unto them only by concession or delegation from the pope. They must hold it from him in chief, or he cannot be the chief, only, and absolute head and monarch, of the catholic church; which you would persuade us to believe that he is. Kings then may, even in church affairs, be "strikers" under him,—be the servants and executioners of his will and pleasure; but authority from God, immediately in and about them, they have none, nor can have any whilst your imaginary monarchy takes place. This one fundamental principle of your religion sufficiently discovers the insignificancy of your flourish about kingly authority in ecclesiastical things, seeing, upon a supposition of it, they can have none at all. But you stay not here; for,—

3. *You ascribe unto your popes a universal dominion, even in civil things, over all Christian kings and their subjects.* In the explanation of this dominion, I confess you somewhat vary among yourselves; but the thing itself is generally asserted by you, and made a foundation of practice. Some of you maintain that the pope, by divine right and constitution, hath an absolute supreme dominion over the whole world. This opinion, Bellarmine, lib. v., De Pont. cap. 1, confesseth to be maintained by Augustinus Triumphus, Alvarus, Pelagius, Hostiensis, and Panormitanus. And himself, in the next words, condemns the opinion of them who deny the pope to have any such temporal power as that he may command secular princes, and deprive them of their kingdoms and principalities, not only as false, but as downright heresy. And why doth he name the first opinion as that of four or five doctors, when it is the common opinion of your church, as Baronius sufficiently manifests in the life of Gregory VII.? That great preserver of your pontifical omnipotency, in his bull against Henry the German emperor, affirms that he

hath "power to take away empires, kingdoms, and principalities, or whatever a mortal man may have;" as Platina records it in his life. As also, Pope Nicholas II., in his Epistle ad Mediolanens., asserts that the rights both of the heavenly and earthly empires are committed unto him. And he that hath but looked on the Dictates of the forenamed Gregory, confirmed in a council at Rome, and defended by Baronius, or into their Decretals, knows that you give both swords to the pope, and that over and over; whence Carerius, lib. i. cap. 9, affirms that it is the common opinion of the school divines that the pope hath "plenissimam potestatem," plenary power, over the whole world, both in ecclesiastical and temporal matters. And you know the old comparison made by the Canonists, cap. de Major. et Obed., between the pope and the emperor,—namely, that "he is as the sun, the emperor as the moon," which borrows all its light from the other. Bellarmine, and those few whom he follows, or that follow him, maintain that the pope "hath this power only indirectly, and in order unto spiritual things." The meaning of which assertion, as he explains himself, is, that besides that *direct power* which he hath over those countries and kingdoms which, on one pretence or other, he claims to be *feudatory* to the Roman see, which are no small number of the chiefest kingdoms of Europe, he hath a power over them all, to *dispose* of them, their kings and rulers, according as he judgeth it to conduce to the good and interest of the church;—which as it really differs very little from the former opinion, so Barclay tells us that Pope Sixtus was very little pleased with that seeming depression of the papal power, which his words intimate. But the stated doctrine of your church in this matter is so declared by Hosius, Augustinus Triumphus, Carerius, Schioppius, Marca, and others, all approved by her authority, that there can be no question of it. Moreover, to make way for the putting of this indirect power into direct execution, you declare,—

4. *That the pope is the supreme judge of faith, and his declarations and determinations so far the rule of it, as that they are to be received, and finally submitted unto.* Not to do so, is that which you express *heresy*, or *schism*, or *apostasy*. About this principle also of your profession there have been, as about most other things amongst you, great disputes and wranglings between the doctors and props of your church. Much debate there hath been whether this power be to be attributed unto the pope without a council, or above a council, or against one. About these chimeras are whole volumes filled with keen and subtile argumentations. But the pope's *personal*, or at least *cathedral* determination, hath at length prevailed. For whatever some few of you may whisper, unto your own trouble and disadvantage, to the impeachment of his personal infallibility, you are

easily decried by the general voice of your doctors; and, besides, those very persons themselves, wherever they would place the infallibility of the church that they fancy, are forced to put it so far into the pope's hand and management, as that whatever he determines, with the necessary solemnities, in matters of faith, is ultimately at least to be acquiesced in. So yourself assure us, averring that he who doth not so "forfeits his Christianity," and consequently all the privileges which thereby he enjoys; and we have reason sufficient, from former experience, to believe that [if] the pope have the ability unto his will, [he] is ready enough to take the forfeiture. Whether upon a prince's falling into heresy, in not acquiescing in your papal determinations, his subjects are discharged, "ipso facto," from all obedience unto him, as Dominicus Bannes and others maintain, or whether there needs the denunciation of a sentence against him by the pope for their absolution, you are not agreed. But yet,—

5. You affirm *that in case of such disobedience unto the pope, he is armed with power to depose kings and princes, and to give away and bestow their kingdoms and dominions on others.* Innumerable are the instances whereby the popes themselves have justified their claim of this power in the face of the world; and it were endless to recount the emperors, kings, and free princes that they have attempted to ruin and destroy (in the pursuit of some whereof they actually succeeded), with the desolations of nations that have ensued thereon. I shall mention but one, and that given us in the days of our fathers, and it may be in the memory of some yet alive. Pope Pius V. takes upon him, contrary to the advice and entreaties of the Emperor of Germany and others, to depose Queen Elizabeth, and to devote her to destruction. To this end he *absolved all her subjects from their allegiance*, and gave away her kingdoms and dominions to the Spaniard, assisting him to his utmost in his attempt to take possession of his grant; and all for refusing obedience to the see of Rome! You cannot, I presume, be offended with my mention of that which is known unto all; for these things were not done in a corner. And is it not hence evident that all the power which you grant unto kings is merely precarious, which they hold of your pope as tenants at will? and should they not appear to do so, were his force, wit, and courage answerable to his will and pretence of authority? But be it that because you cannot help it, you suffer them to live at peace and quietness in the main of their rule; yet you still curb them in their own dominions; for,—

6. *You exempt all the clergy from under their rule and power.* See your Bellarmine sweating to prove that they are not bound to their laws, so as to be judged by them without their leave, if they transgress, or to pay any tribute, De Cleric. lib. i. cap. 28. They

are all reserved to the power and jurisdiction of the pope. And he that shall consider into what a vast and boundless multitude, by reason of the several disorderly orders of your *city monks* and friars, your clergy is swelled into in most places of Europe, will easily perceive what your interest is in every kingdom of it. I am persuaded there is scarce a considerable nation wherein the profession of your religion is enthroned, in which the pope hath not a hundred thousand able fighting men, that are his peculiar subjects, exempted from the power and jurisdiction of kings themselves; which you must needs conceive to be a blessed interpretation of that of the apostle, "Let every soul be subject to the higher powers." And,—

7. You extend *the papal power to things as well as persons* in the dominions of all kings and commonwealths; for the lands and possessions that are given unto any of the pope's especial subjects, you will have to be exempted from tributes and public burdens of the state. And you farther contend, that it is not in the power of any kings or rulers to hinder such alienations of lands and possessions from their dominions. By this means no small part of the territories of many princes is subduced from under their power. The dreadful consequences of which principles so startled the wise state of Venice, that you know they disputed it to the utmost with your vice-god Paul V. In dealing with them, as I remember, their attempt was successless; for, notwithstanding the defence made of the papal process against them by Baronius, Bellarmine, and others, yet the actings of that sober state in forbidding such alienation of lands and fees from their rule and power without their consent, with their plea for the subjection of ecclesiastics unto them in their own dominions, was so vindicated by Dr Paul Suave,[1] Marsilius of Padua, and others, that *the horns of the bull,* which had been thrust forth against them unto so great a length, were pulled in again.

I told you, in the entrance of this discourse, how unwilling I should have been to have given you the least disquietment in your way, had you only attempted to set off your own respects unto royal power unto the best advantage you could; but your setting up your principles and practices in competition with those of Protestants of any sort whatever, and preferring them before and above them, as unto your deference unto kings, and that in matters ecclesiastical, hath made these few instances, expressive of the real sense of your church in this matter, as I suppose, necessary and equal.

[1] The common form of the name is Paul Sarpi. The History of the Council of Trent by the learned doctor was published under the assumed name of Pietro Soave Polano; an anagram of his real name, Paolo Sarpi Veneto,—Paul Sarpi of Venice.—Ed.

CHAPTER XVII.

Scripture—Story of the progress and declension of religion vindicated—Papal artifices for the promotion of their power and interest—Advantages made by them on the Western Empire.

YOU proceed, p. 70, unto the animadversions on your 13th paragraph, entitled "Scripture," wherein how greatly and causelessly it is by you undervalued is fully declared; but whatever is offered in it for the discovery of your miscarriage and your own conviction, you wisely pass over without taking notice of it at all, and only repeat again your case to the same purpose, and almost in the very same words you had done before. Now, this I have already considered and removed out of our way, so that it is altogether needless to divert again to the discussion of it. That which we have to do, for the answering of all your cavils and objections in and about the case you frame and propose, is, to declare and manifest the Scripture's sufficiency for the revelation of all necessary truths, therein affording us a stable rule of faith, every way suited to the decision of all differences in and about religion, and to keep Christians in perfect peace, as it did of old; and this we have already done. Why this proper work of the Scripture is not in all places and at all times effected, proceeds from the lusts and prejudices of men; which when, by the grace of God, they shall be removed, it will no longer be obstructed.

Your next attempt, p. 72, is upon my "story of the progress and corruption of Christian religion in the world," with respect unto that of your own. Yours, you tell us, "is serious, temperate, and sober;" every way as excellent as Suffenus thought his verses. Mine, you say, "is fraught with defamation and wrath against all ages and people." Very good! I doubt not but you thought it was fit you should say so, though you knew no reason why, nor could fix on any thing in it for your warrant in these intemperate reproaches. Do I say any thing but what the *stories* of all ages and the *experience* of Christendom do proclaim? Is it now a defamation, to report what the learned men of those days have recorded, what good men bewailed, and the sad effects whereof the world long groaned under, and was at length ruined by? What "wrath" is in all this? May not men be warned to take heed of falling into the like evils, by the miscarriages of them that went before them, without "wrath and defamation?" Are the books of the Kings, Chronicles, and Prophets "fraught with wrath and defamation," because they report, complain of, and reprove, the sad apostasies of the church in those days, with the wickedness of the kings, priests, and people that it was composed of, and declare the abomination of those ways of false worship, licentiousness of life, violence, and oppression, whereby they provoked God against them to their ruin? If my story be not true, why do you not disprove it? if it be, why do you exclaim against it? Do I not direct you unto authors of unquestionable credit, complaining of the things which I report from them? And if you know not that many others may be added unto those by me named, testifying the same things, you know very little of the matter you undertake to treat about. But we need go no farther than yourself to discover how devoid of all pretence your reproaches are, and that by considering the exceptions which you put in to my story; which may rationally be supposed to be the most plausible you could invent, and directed against those parts of it which you imagined were most obnoxious to your charge. I shall, therefore, consider them in the order wherein they are proposed, and discover whether the keenness of your assault answer the noise of your outcry at its entrance.

First, You observe that I say, "Joseph of Arimathea was in England, but that he taught the same religion that is now in England." Unto which you reply, "But what is that religion?" and this inquiry I have observed you elsewhere to insist upon. But I told you before that I intend the Protestant religion, and that as confirmed and established by law in this kingdom. And the advantage you endeavour from some differences that are amongst us is little to your purposes, and less to the commendation ot your ingenuity. For besides that there are differences of as high a nature, and, considering the principles you proceed upon, of greater importance among yourselves, and those agitated with as great animosities and subtilties as those among any sort of men at variance about religion in the world, you, that so earnestly seek and press after a forbearance for your profession besides and against the established law, should not, methinks, at the same time be so forward in reproaching us that there are dissenters in the kingdom from some things established by law, especially considering how utterly inconsiderable for the most part they are, in comparison of the things wherein you differ from us all. This, I fear, is the reward that they have cause to expect from many of you, who are inclined to desire that you, amongst others, might be partakers of indulgence from the extremity of the law; though from others of you, for whose sakes they are inclined unto those desires, I hope they may look for better things, and such as accompany charity, moderation, and peace. So that your first exception gives a greater impeachment unto your own candour and ingenuity, than unto the truth or sobriety of my story.

You proceed and say, "That I tell you that the story of Fugatius and Damianus, missioners of Pope Eleutherius, is suspected by me for many reasons;" and reply, "Because you assign none, I am therefore moved to think they may be all reduced unto one; which is, that you will not acknowledge any good thing ever to have come from Rome." But see what it is for a man to give himself up unto vain surmises! You know full well that I plead that you are no way concerned in what was done at Rome in the days of Eleutherius, who was neither Pope nor Papist, nor knew any thing of that which we reject as Popery; so that I had no reason to disdain or deny any good thing that was then done at Rome, or by any from thence. Besides, I can assure you that to this day I would willingly own, embrace, and rejoice in any good that is or may be done there, may I be truly and impartially informed of it; and should be glad to hear of more than unprejudiced men have been able of late ages to inform us of. I am far from making an *enclosure* of all goodness unto any *party* of men in the world, and far from judging or condemning all of any party, or supposing that no good thing can be done by them or proceed from them. Such conceits are apt to flow from the high towering thoughts of *infallibility and supremacy,* and the confining of Christianity to some certain company of men, in some parts of the world; which I am a stranger unto. I know no party among Christians that is in all things to be admired, nor any that is in all things to be condemned; and can perfectly free you, if you are capable of satisfaction, from all fears of my dislike of any thing because it came or comes from Rome. For to me it is all one from whence *truth* and *virtue* come; they shall be welcome for their own sakes. But you seem to be guided in these and the like surmises by your own humour, principles, and way of managing things in religion,—a Lesbian rule, which will suffer you to depart from the paths of truth and charity no oftener than you have a mind so to do. To deliver you from your mistake in this particular, I shall now give you some of those reasons which beget in me a suspicion concerning the truth of that story about Fugatius and Damianus, as it is commonly told, only intimating the heads of them with all possible brevity.

First, then, I suppose the whole story is built on the authority of the epistle of Eleutherius unto Lucius, which is yet extant: other foundation of it, that I know of, is neither pleaded or pretended. Now, there want not reasons to prove that epistle, as the most of those fathered on the old bishops of Rome, to be supposititious. For, —1. The author of that epistle condemneth the *imperial laws,* and rejecteth them as unmeet to be used in the civil government of this nation; which Eleutherius neither ought to have done, nor could safely do. 2. It supposeth Lucius to have the Roman law sent unto him, which had been long before exercised in this nation, and was well known in the whole province, as he witnesseth of days before these:

"Gallia causidicos docuit facunda Britannos."—Juv. xv. 111.

Secondly, The *first reporters* of this story agree not in the time wherein the matter mentioned in it should fall out. Beda, lib. i. cap. 4, assigns it unto the year 156, which was twenty-two years before Eleutherius was bishop, as Baronius manifests. Henricus de Erfordia ascribes it unto the nineteenth year of the reign of Verus the emperor, who reigned not so many years at all. Ado refers it unto the time of Commodus, with some part of whose reign the episcopacy of Eleutherius did indeed contemporate. 2. Geoffrey of Monmouth, the chief promoter of this report, joineth it with so many lies and open fictions, as may well draw the truth of the whole story into question. So that divers would have us believe that some such thing was done at one time or other, but when they cannot tell. 3. Both the epistle of Eleutherius and the reporters of it do suppose that Lucius, to whom he wrote, was *an absolute monarch* in England, king over the whole kingdom, with supreme authority and power, ruling his subjects by the advice of his nobles, without being obnoxious unto or dependent in his government on any others. But this supposition is so openly repugnant to the whole story of the state of things in the province of England in those days, that it is beyond the wit of man to make any reconciliation between them; for besides that Cæsar and Tacitus do both plainly affirm that in the days of the Romans' entrance upon this island, there was no such king or monarch among the Britons, but that they were all divided into several toparchies, and those at mortal feuds and variance among themselves (which made for the conquest of them all), it was now become a presidiary province of the Roman empire, and had been so from the days of Claudius; as Suetonius, Tacitus, and Dio inform us. Especially was it reduced into and settled in that form by Pub. Ostorius in the days of Nero, upon the conquest of Boadicea, queen of the Iceni; and fully subjected in its remainders unto the Roman yoke and laws, after some strugglings for liberty, by Julius Agricola, in the days of Vespasian; as Tacitus assures us in the life of his father-in-law. In this estate Britain continued under Nerva and Trajan; the whole province being afterward secured by Adrian from the incursion of the Picts, and other barbarous nations, with the defence of his famous walls; whereof Spartianus gives us an account. In this condition did the whole province continue unto the death of Commodus, under the rule of Ulpius Marcellus; as we are informed by Dio and Lampridius. This was the state of affairs in Britain when the epistle of Eleutherius is supposed to be written. And for my part, I cannot discover where this Lucius should reign with all that sovereignty ascribed unto him. Baronius thinks he might do so beyond the Picts' wall; which utterly overthrows the whole story, and leaves the whole province of Britain utterly unconcerned in the coming of Fugatius and Damianus into this island. These are some, and many other reasons of my suspicion I could add, manifesting it to be far more just than yours,—"That I had no reason for it but only because I would not acknowledge that any good could come from Rome."[1]

Let us now see what you farther except against the account I give of the progress and declension of religion in these and other nations. You add, "'Then,' say you, 'succeeded times of luxury, sloth, pride, ambition, scandalous riots, and corruption both of faith and manners, over all the Christian world, both princes, priests, prelates, and people.'" But you somewhat pervert my words, so to make them liable unto your exception; for as by me they are laid down, it seems you could find no occasion against them. I tell you, p. 253, [p. 99], "That after these things a sad decay in faith and holiness of life befell professors, not only in this nation, but, for the most part, all the world over. The stories of those days are full of nothing more than the oppression, luxury, sloth of rulers; the pride, ambition, and unseemly, scandalous contests for pre-eminence of sees and extent of jurisdiction, among bishops; the sensuality and ignorance of the most of men." Now, whether these words are not agreeable to truth and sobriety, I leave to every man to judge who hath any tolerable acquaintance with history, or the occurrences of the ages respected in them. Your reply unto them is: "Not a grain of virtue or goodness, we must think, in so many Christian kingdoms and ages!" But why must you think so? Who induceth you thereunto? When the church of Israel was professedly far more corrupted than I have intimated the state of the Christian church in any part of the world to have been, yet there was more than "a grain of virtue or goodness," not

[1] On page 98 of this volume the reader will find a note, in which the leading facts in regard to Lucius are mentioned. Our author, of course, had a perfect right to devolve the burden of proof upon his opponent, and to insist upon historical evidence of the correspondence between the British prince and Eleutherius. He does not venture upon an unqualified denial of all the tradition, contenting himself with indicating his "suspicion," on various weighty grounds, that the story had much of the fabulous about it. That no author worthy of credit, before the days of Bede, should have recorded this alleged second conversion of our island to the Christian faith; and that among all the Latin authors—by one reckoning twenty-six, and by another fifty in number—who subsequently, up to the time of Usher, have endorsed the story, there should be a discrepancy in regard to the chronology of the events in question, so great as to cover nearly a century between the earliest and latest dates assigned; are the main difficulties which impede our unhesitating reception of the narrative, even when carefully sifted and stripped of the accessories with which monkish fiction has invested it. Among Protestant authors, however, who have investigated the subject, a decided impression seems to prevail that some degree of credit is due to the substance of the ancient tradition. This view has been held by some, who reject as spurious the epistle of Eleutherius to which Dr Owen takes just exception, on several other grounds besides those which are urged in the text above. The epistle speaks as if *all* Britain were under the sway of Lucius, whereas but a small part of it was subject to him; and several expressions in it betray a strong trace of English law and Norman idiom, indicative of a far later origin

only in Elijah, but in the meanest of those seven thousand who, within the small precincts of that kingdom, had not bowed the knee to Baal. I never in the least questioned but that in that declension of Christianity which I intimated, and remission of the most from their pristine zeal, there were thousands and ten thousands that kept their integrity, and mourned for all the abominations that they saw practised in the world. Pray, reflect a little upon the condition of the Asian churches mentioned in the Revelation. The discovery made of their spiritual state by Christ himself, chap. ii. iii., was within less than forty years after their first planting; and yet you see most of them had left their "first love," and were decayed in their faith and zeal. In one of them there were but "a few names" remaining that had any life or integrity for Christ,—the body of the church having only "a name to live," being truly and really "dead" as to any acts of spiritual life, wherein our communion with God consists. And do you make it so strange, that whereas the churches that were planted and watered by the apostles themselves, and enriched with many excellent gifts and graces, should, within the space of less than *forty years*, by the testimony of the Lord Christ himself, so decay and fall off from their first purity, faith, and works, other churches, who had not their advantages, should do so within the space of four hundred years, of which season I speak? I fear your vain conceit of being "rich and wanting nothing," of infallibility and impossibility to stand in need of any reformation, of being as good as ever any church was, or as you need to be, is that which hath more prejudiced your church in particular than you can readily imagine. And what I affirmed of those other churches, I know well enough how to prove out of the best and most approved authors of those days. If, besides

than is claimed for it. The external evidence is equally decisive. The epistle is found in no author for a thousand years after the age of Eleutherius; it is not known under whose auspices it first came to light; and the learned antiquarian Spelman pronounced the only manuscript copy of it extant, and preserved first in the archives of the London Guild, and latterly in the Cotton library, to be in his day not more than two centuries old. The main facts of the story, however, are not dependent upon the authenticity of this document, nor is their credibility seriously shaken by the argument that the existence of a native king in any part of Britain, at the time referred to, cannot be reconciled with the fact that the island was then but a province of the Roman empire. Tacitus speaks of Prasutagus and Cogidunus as British kings, retaining some shadow of royal state and dignity, while subject, nevertheless, to the imperial yoke, ("Annal.," lib. xiv. cap. 31, and "Vit. Agric.," cap. 14). The case of Herod in Judea supplies another analogy. The strength of our author's reply to the Romish plea, which he is engaged in rebutting, lies in the fact that Britain in those days must have received Christianity, not Romanism, from Eleutherius; while, even according to the tenor of the tradition itself, in every form in which it has been preserved, Christianity previously existed in the island. It is safe enough to conclude, with an old writer, that the tradition about Lucius contains "multa falsa, alia incerta, nonnulla etiam vera vel saltem probabilia!" These words are quoted from the "Prælectiones Ecclesiasticæ" of John Richardson of Cambridge, 1725 (vol. i. p. 251), to which the reader may be referred for a judicious and comprehensive discussion of this interesting historical question.—Ed.

historians, which give sufficient testimony unto my observation, you will please to consult Chrysostom, Hom. iii. De Incomprehens. Dei Natur., Hom. xix. in Ac. 9, Hom. xv. in Heb. 8, and Augustin. Lib. de Fid. et Bon. Op. cap. xix., you will find that I had good ground for what I said. And what if I had minded you of the words of Salvian, De Provid. lib. iii.: "Quemcunque invenies in ecclesia non aut ebriosum, aut adulterum, aut fornicatorem, aut raptorem, aut ganeonem, aut latronem, aut homicidam, et quod omnibus potius est, prope hæc cuncta sine fine?"—should I have escaped your censure of giving you "a story false and defamatory, loaden with foul language against all nations, ages, and conditions, that none can like who bear any respect either to modesty, religion, or truth?" "Ne sævi, magne sacerdos." What ground have you for this intemperate railing? What instance can you give of any thing of this nature? what expression giving countenance unto this severity? If you will exercise yourself in writing "Fiats," you must of necessity arm yourself with a little patience to hear sometimes things that do not please you, and not presently cry out, "Defamation, false, wrath, foul language," etc. I suppose you know that not long after the times wherein I say religion, as to the power and purity of it, much decayed in the world, God brought an overflowing scourge and deluge of judgments upon most of the nations of Europe that made profession of Christianity. What, in sadness, do you think might be the cause of that dispensation of his providence? Do you think that all things were well enough amongst them, and that in all things their ways pleased God? Is such an apprehension suitable to the goodness, mercy, love, and faithfulness of God? or must he lose the glory of all his properties in the administration of his righteous judgments, rather than you will acknowledge a demerit in them whom he took away as with a flood? So, indeed, the Jews would have had it of old under their sufferings; but he pleaded and vindicated the equality and righteousness of his ways against their proud repinings. Pray, be as angry with me as you please, but take heed of justifying any against God: the task will prove too hard for you. And yet to this purpose are your following contemptuous expressions; for unto my observation, that after these times the Goths and Vandals, with others, overflowed the Christian world, you subjoin, "Either to punish them, we may believe, or to teach them how to mend their manners." Sir, I know not what you believe, or do not believe, or whether you believe any thing of this kind or no: but I will tell you what I am persuaded all the world believes, who know the story of those times, and are not atheists; and it is, that though the Goths and Vandals, Saxons, Huns, Franks, and Longobards, with the rest of the barbarous nations who divided the provinces of the western empire amongst them, had, it may be, no more thought to punish the nations professing Christianity for their sins, wickedness, and superstition (though one of their chief leaders proclaimed himself "the scourge of God" against them), than had the king of Babylon to punish Judah for her sins and idolatry in especial, yet that God ordered them no less than he did him in his providence, for those ends which you so scorn and despise,—that is, either to punish them for their sins, or to provoke them to leave them by repentance. Take heed of being a scoffer in these things, lest your bands be made strong. God is not unrighteous who exerciseth judgment. The Judge of all the world will do right. Nor doth he afflict any people, much less extirpate them from the face of the earth, without a cause. Many wicked, provoking, sinful, idolatrous nations, he spareth in his patience and forbearance, and will yet do so; but he destroys none without a cause And all that I intended by the remembrance of the sins of those nations which were exposed unto devastation was but to show that their destruction was of themselves.

You leap unto another clause which you rend out of my discourse, "That these Pagans took at last unto Christianity;" and say, "Haply because it was a more loose and wicked life than their own Pagan profession." But are you not ashamed of this trifling? Doth this disprove my assertion? Is it not true? Did they not do so? Did not the above-mentioned nations, when they had settled themselves in the provinces of the empire, take upon them the profession of the Christian religion? Did not the Saxons do so in Brittany, the Franks in Gaul, the Goths and Longobards in Italy, the Vandals in Africa, the Huns in Pannonia? I cannot believe you are so ignorant in these things as your exceptions bespeak you. Nor do I well understand what you intend by them, they are so frivolous and useless; nor, surely, can any man in his right wits suppose them of any validity to impeach the evidence of the known stories which my discourse relates unto.

But you lay more weight on what you cull out in the next place, which as you have laid it down is, "That these now christened Pagans advanced the pope's authority, when Christian religion was now grown degenerate;" and say, "Now we come to know how the Roman bishop became a patriarch above the rest,—by means, namely, of the new-converted Pagans." But I wonder you speak so nicely in their chief affair; as though that were the question, whether the bishop of Rome, according unto some ecclesiastical constitutions, were made a patriarch or no? and that, whether he were not esteemed to have some kind of pre-eminence in respect of those other bishops who upon the same account were so styled? When we have occasion to speak of the question we shall not be backward to declare our thoughts on it. For the present, you represent the pope unto us as the *absolute head of the church catholic*, the supreme judge of all controversies in religion, the sole fountain of unity, and spring of all ecclesiastical jurisdiction, etc. Nor did I say that your pope was by these nations, after their conversion, advanced unto the height you labour now to fix him in; but only that his authority was signally advanced by them: which is so certain a truth, that your own historians and annalists openly proclaim it; and you cannot deny it unless you would be esteemed the most ungrateful person in the world. But this is your way and manner: all that is done for you is mere duty; which when it is done you will thank no man for. Are all the grants of power, privileges, and possessions made unto your papal see by the kings of this nation, both before and since the Conquest, by the kings of France, and emperors of the posterity of Charles the Great, by the kings of Poland, Denmark, and Sweden, by the Longobards in Italy, not worth your thanks? It is well you have got your ends;—the net may be cast away when the fish is caught.

"But an odd chance," you say, "it was, that they should think of advancing him to what they never heard either himself or any other advanced unto before among Christians." But yet this was done, and no such "odd chance" neither. Your popes had for a season before been aspiring to greater heights than formerly they had attained unto, and used all ways possible to commend themselves and their authority,—not what truly it was, but what they would have it to be,—unto all with whom they had to do; and thereupon, by sundry means and artifices, imposed upon the nations some undue conceits of it; though it was not fully nor so easily admitted of as it may be you may imagine. But in many things they were willing to gratify him in his pretensions, little knowing the tendency of them; many things he took the advantage of their straits and divisions to impose upon them; many things he obtained from them by flattery and carnal compliances;—until, by sundry serpentine advances, he had brought them all unto his *bow,* and some of the greatest of them to his *stirrup.*

"It was yet more odd," say you, "and strange, that all Christendom should calmly submit unto a power set up anew by young converted Pagans; no prince or bishop, either here or of any other Christian kingdom, either then or ever after to this day, excepting against it. Had not all the bishops and priests of Africa, Egypt, Syria, Thrace, Greece, and all the Christian world, acknowledged, by a hundred experiments, the supreme spiritual authority of the Roman patriarch in all times before this deluge of Goths and Vandals? But why do I expostulate with you, who write these things not to judicious readers, but to fools and children, who are not more apt to tell a truth than to believe a lie?" But, sir, you shall quickly see whose discourse, yours or mine, stands in need of weak and credulous readers. That which you have in this place to oppose is only this, "That your papal authority received a signal advancement by and among the northern nations, who, after long wars, divided the provinces of the western empire among them." Now, this is so broad a truth, that nothing but brutish ignorance or obstinate perverseness can possibly cause any man to call it into question. It was not absolutely the setting up of the Papacy, but an accession unto the papal power and authority, which I ascribed unto that original; and this if you dare to deny, it were easy, out of your own annalists, to overwhelm you with instances in the confirmation of it. But yet neither were your concessions made nor his assumptions carried on in that silence which you fancy when you imagine that his aspirings were neither taken notice of nor opposed, but that all Christendom should calmly submit unto them. Where do you think you are, that you talk at this rate? Did you never read of any opposition made in former days unto your pretended papal power? none at all? from no kings, no princes, no bishops, no parts of Christendom? Happy man, who hath lived so quietly as you seem to have done, and so little concerned in things past or present! Did you never read or hear of the *declarations* and *edicts* of emperors and kings, of *determinations* of councils, *writings* of learned men, in all ages, against your papal usurpations? Did you never hear how, before the times that we now talk of, Irenæus reproved Victor; how Cyprian opposed Cornelius and Stephen; how the councils of Africa admonished Celestine and Boniface of their miscarriages in their claims of power and jurisdiction? Are you an utter stranger unto the opposition made by the German emperors unto your Hildebrandine supremacy, with the books written against your pretensions to that purpose? Have you not read your own Baronius, a great part of whose voluminous annals consists in his endeavours to vindicate your papal power from the open opposition that was made to its introduction in every age? You must needs sleep quietly, seeing you lie so far from noise. I have already in part let you see the fondness of this dream, that your papal supremacy was ever calmly submitted unto, and have manifested that it was publicly condemned before it was born. But because I then confined myself unto more ancient times than those which are now under discourse, I shall mind you of a few instances of the opposition made unto it, either about or presently after that signal advancement which I affirmed that it received from the newly-converted nations of the west.

About the year 608, presently after the Saxons had received Christianity, and therewithal contributed their power, some of them at least, to the furtherance of your papal claim,—which was then set on foot, though in a much inferior degree unto what you have since promoted it unto,—it was publicly excepted against and disclaimed by a convention or synod of the British clergy, who denied *that they owed any subjection* unto the see of Rome, or any respect but such as Christians ought to bear one towards another, and would not give place unto its authority in things of very small weight and amount. Bed. Hist. lib. ii. cap. 2, Concil. Anglic. p. 188. The sixth general council, that *condemned Pope Honorius* for a heretic, anno 681, with the second Nicene, anno 787, which confirmed the same sentence, do shrewdly impeach your present supremacy. In the fourth council of Constantinople, anno 870, the Epanagnosticum of Basilius the emperor to the synod, approved by them all, begins thus: "Cum divina et benignissima Providentia nobis gubernacula universalis navis commisit, omne studium arripuimus, et ante publicas curas, ecclesiasticas contentiones dissolvendi;"—"Whereas the gracious divine Providence has committed unto us the government of the universal ship, we have taken all occasion, before other public cares, to dissolve or compose ecclesiastical dissensions." How suitable these expressions of the emperor are unto your present pretensions yourself may judge. And having mentioned that synod, which you call the eighth general council, because of its opposition to the learned Photius, I shall only ask of you, whether you think there was no exception made to your supremacy by that Photius, with the emperors and bishops of the east who consulted with him, and afterward justified him against the censures procured against him by Popes Nicholas and Hadrian? Do not all your writers to this day complain of this opposition made unto you by Photius? What think you of the council of Frankfort, assembled by Charles the Great, which so openly condemned that doctrine which Pope Hadrian, and the Roman clergy with him, laboured so earnestly to promote, as we shall afterward show? In the same order you may place the councils that deposed their popes, as did one at Rome, under Otho the emperor, John XII., a sweet bishop, anno 963; another at Sutrinum, anno 1046, when Cerberus, as Baronius himself confesseth, ruled at Rome, anno 1044, n. 5, three popes at once domineering there. "Uno contra duos," saith Sigibert, "et duobus contra unum, de papatu contendentibus, rex contra eos vadit, eosque canonica et imperiali censura deponit;"—"One against two, and two against one, contending about the papacy, the king went against them all, and deposed them by canonical and imperial censure." Or, as Platina, Vit. Greg. VI.: "Henricus habita synodo, tria ista teterrima monstra abdicare se magistratu coegit;"—"Henry calling a synod, compelled those three filthy monsters" (Benedict, Sylvester, and Gregory) "to renounce their magistracy or papacy." Have you not heard how many synods and councils were convened against the usurpations and innovations of Gregory VII., as at Worms, Papia, Brixia, Mentz, and elsewhere? What think you of the assembly at Clarendon here in England, anno 1164, where it was decreed, saith Matth. Paris, "Juxta antiquas regni consuetudines non licere vel archiepiscopis, vel episcopis, vel aliis personis, exire regnum absque licentia regis;"—"That, according to the ancient customs of the kingdom, it was not lawful for any archbishops, bishops, or other persons, to depart the kingdom without the leave of the king,"—that is, to go to Rome; and that in all appeals, "Ultimo perveniendum ad regem ita ut non debeat ulterius procedi sine assensu domini regis;"—"The last is to be made unto the king, without whose assent no farther process ought to be made?" For opposition unto which decree, Thomas à Becket had the hap to become a *traitor* and a *saint.* The stories of the patriarchs of Ravenna in times more remote, and in those of the council of Constance and Basil in latter ages, are too well known to be particularly again insisted on. Were princes more silent than synods? Reconcile, if you are able, the laws of Charles the Great and his son Lewis with their pope's now claimed authority. Henry II. of Germany both deposed popes and limited their power; Henry III. attempted no less, though with less success. See Sigibert Chron. anno 1046; Platina, Vit. Greg. VI.; Sigon. de Reg. lib. viii. From that time forward until the Reformation, no one age can be instanced in wherein great, open, and signal opposition was not made unto the papal authority, which you seek again to introduce. The instances already given are sufficient to convince the vanity of your pretence, that never any opposition was made unto it.

Of the same nature is that which you nextly affirm, of "all the bishops and priests of Africa, Egypt, Syria, Thrace, Greece, and all the Christian world, by a hundred experiments, acknowledging the supreme spiritual authority of the Roman patriarch." I must, I see, still mind you of what it is that you are to speak unto. It is not the patriarchate of your pope, with the authority, privileges, and pre-eminences which by virtue thereof he lays claim unto, but his singular succession to Christ and Peter in the absolute headship of the whole catholic church, that you are treating about. Now, supposing you may be better skilled in the affairs of the eastern church than, for aught as I can yet perceive you are in those of the western, let me crave this favour of you, that you would direct me unto one of those hundred experiments whereby the acknowledgment you mention, preceding the conversion of the northern nations, may be confirmed. It will, I confess unto you, be a singular kindness, seeing I know not where to find any one of that nature within the time limited, nor, to tell you the truth, since unto this day; for I suppose you will not imagine that the feigned professions of subjection, which poverty and hopes of supplies from the court of Rome hath extorted of late from some few mean persons, whose titles only were of any consideration in the world, will deserve any place in this disquisition. Until you are pleased, therefore, to favour me with your information, I must abide in my ignorance of any such experiments as those which you intimate.

The artifices, I confess, of your popes in former days to draw men, especially in the eastern church, to an acknowledgment of that authority which in their several seasons they claimed, have been many, and their success various. Sometimes they obtained a seeming compliance in some, and sometimes they procured their authors very shrewd rebukes. It may not be amiss to recount some of them:—

1. Upon all occasions they set forth themselves *the dignity and pre-eminence of your see,* with swelling encomiums and titles, asserting their own primacy and power. Such self-assumings are many of the old papal epistles stuffed withal. A sober, humble Christian cannot but nauseate at the reading of them; for it is easily discernible how anti-evangelical such courses are, and how unbecoming all that pretend themselves to be disciples of Jesus Christ. From these are their chiefest testimonies in this case taken; and we may say of them all, they bear witness to themselves, and that contrary to the Scripture, and their witness is not true.

2. *When and wherever such letters and epistles as proclaimed their privileges have been admitted, through the inadvertency or modesty of them to whom they were sent, unwilling to quarrel with them about the good opinion which they had of themselves* (which kind of entertainment they yet sometimes met not withal), the next successors always took for granted and pleaded what their predecessors had presumptuously broached, as that which of right and unquestionably belonged unto them. And this they made sure of, that they would never lose any ground, or take any one step backwards from what any of them had advanced unto.

3. Wherever they heard of any difference among bishops, *they were still imposing their umpirage upon them;* which commonly, by the one or other of the parties at variance, to balance thereby some disadvantages that they had to wrestle withal, was admitted: yea, sometimes they would begin to take part with them that were openly in the wrong, even heretics themselves, that they might thereby procure an address to them from others, which afterward they would interpret as an express of their subjection. And wherever their umpirage was admitted, they were never wanting to improve their own interest by it; like the old Romans, who, being chosen to determine a controversy between other people about some lands, adjudged them unto themselves.

4. *If any person that was really injured*, or pretended so to be, made any address unto them for any kind of relief, immediately they laid hold of their address as an appeal to their authority, and acted in their behalf accordingly; though they were sometimes chidden for their pains, and advised to meddle with what they had to do withal.

5. Did *any bishops of note write them letters of respect*, presently in their rescripts they return them thanks *for their profession of subjection* to the see apostolic; so, supposing them to do that which in truth they did not, they promise to do for them that which they never desired, and by both made way for the enlargement of the confines of their own authority.

6. Where *any prince or emperor* was entangled in his affairs, they were still ready to crush them into that condition of trouble from whence they could not be delivered but by their assistance, or to make them believe that their adherence unto them was the only means to preserve them from ruin; and so procured their suffrage unto their authority.

Unto these and the like heads of corrupt and sinful artifices may the most of the testimonies commonly pleaded for the pope's supremacy be referred. By such ways and means hath it been erected; yet far enough from any such prevalency, for seven hundred years, as to afford us any of the experiments which you boast of.

The next thing you except against in my story is my affirming "That Austin the monk, who came hither from Rome, was a man, as far as appears by the story, little acquainted with the gospel." In the repetition of which words, to keep your hand in ure,[1] you leave out that expression, "As far as appears by the story," which is the evidence whereunto I appeal for the truth of my assertion, and add, to aggravate the matter, the words "Very, very little;" and then add, "Here is the thanks that good St Austin hath, who, out of his love and kindness, entered upon the wild forest of our Paganism, with great hazards and inexpressible sufferings of hunger, cold, and other corporal inconveniencies!" But in the place you except against, I acknowledge that God made him a special instrument in bringing the Scripture or gospel amongst us, which I presume also he declared, according to the light and ability which he had. But you are your own mother's son; nothing will serve your turn but "Absolute, most pure, and perfect." For what I have farther intimated of him, there are sundry things in the history of his coming hither, and proceedings here, that warrant the suggestion. The questions that he sent for resolution unto Gregory at Rome discover what manner of man he was. Let a man be never so partially addicted unto him and his work, he must acknowledge that their frivolousness and impertinency,

[1] An obsolete term for *use*.—ED.

considering the work he had in hand, discover somewhat besides learning and wisdom in him. So also did his driving of ten thousand men, besides an innumerable company of women and children, all together, into the river Swale in Yorkshire, and there causing them to baptize one another. His contest with the British bishops about the time of the observation of Easter, breaking the peace for a circumstance of a ceremony that hath cost the church twenty times more trouble than it is worth, is of the same nature. And I desire to know whence you have *your story of his inexpressible suffering* here amongst us. All that I can find informs us that he was right meetly entertained by King Ethelbert, at his first landing, by the means of Bertha, his wife, a Christian before his coming, with all plentiful provision for himself and his companions. The next news we hear of him is about his archiepiscopacy, his pall, and his throne, from whence he would not rise to receive the poor Britons that came to confer with him! Farther of his sufferings, as yet, I can meet with nothing.

And these are the things which you thought yourself able to except against in my story of the progress and declension of religion. The sum of it I shall now comprise in some few assertions; which you may do well to consider, and get them disproved:—

1. The first is, That the *gospel was preached in this island, in the days of the apostles,* by *persons coming from the east,* directed by the providence of God for that purpose,—most probably by Joseph of Arimathea in chief,—without any respect to Rome or mission from thence.

2. That the doctrine preached then by them was the *same* that is now publicly *professed in England,* and not that taught by the church of Rome, where there is a discrepancy between us.

3. That the story of the coming of Fugatius and Damianus into the province of Britain, sent by Eleutherius unto Lucius, is uncertain, improbable, and not to be reconciled unto the state and condition of the affairs in these nations at the time supposed for its accomplishment.

4. That about the fourth, fifth, and sixth centuries, *the generality of the professors of Christian religion* in the world were wofully declined from the primitive zeal, piety, faith, love, and purity in the worship of God, which their predecessors in the same profession glorified God by; and that in particular the British church was much degenerated.

5. That the bishops of Rome for five hundred years never laid claim unto that sovereign power and infallibility which they have challenged since the days of Pope Gregory VII.

6. That the bishops of Rome in that space of time, pretending

unto some *disorderly supremacy* over other bishops and churches, though incomparably short of their after and present pretences, were rebuked and opposed by the best and most learned men of those days.

7. That the distraction of the provinces of the western part of the empire by Goths, Vandals, Huns, Saxons, Alans, Franks, Longobards, and their associates, was no less just, in the holy providence of God, upon the account of the moral evils and superstitions of the professors of Christianity amongst them, than was that which afterward ensued of the eastern provinces by the Saracens and Turks.

8. That these nations having planted themselves in the provinces of the empire, together with Christianity, either *received* anew or *retained* many paganish customs, ceremonies, rites, and opinions therewithal.

9. That their kings, by *grants* of privileges, donations, and concessions of power, made partly out of blind zeal, partly to secure some interests of their own, exceedingly advanced the papal power, and confirmed their formerly rejected pretensions.

10. That when they began to perceive and feel the *pernicious effects* and consequences of their own facility, their grants being made a ground of farther encroachments, they opposed themselves, in their laws, and edicts, and practices, against them.

11. That there was on all hands *a sad declension*, in the western church, in doctrine, worship, and manners, continually progressive, unto the time of reformation.

These are the principal assertions on which my story is built, and which it supposeth. If you have a mind to get them, or any of them, called to an account and examined, I shall, if God will and I live, give them their confirmation from such undoubted records as you have no just cause to except against.

CHAPTER XVIII.

Reformation of religion—Papal contradictions—"Ejice ancillam."

Some of your following leaves are such as admit of no useful consideration. Wilful mistakes, diversions from the cause under debate, with vain flourishes, make up both pages in them. I shall pass through them briefly, and give you some account from them of yourself, and your prevarication in the cause whose defence you have undertaken. Page 75, you undertake the 12th chapter of the

"Animadversions," which discusseth the story of the reformation of religion, which you took up on common fame,—

> "Fama, malum quo non aliud velocius ullum."—Virg. Æn. iv. 174.

And that you may be able to say somewhat to the discourse before you, or to make a pretence of doing so, you wholly pass by every thing that is contained in it, and impose upon me that which is not in it at all, which you strenuously exagitate. For whereas, a little to take off your edge in reflecting on the persons whom you supposed instrumental in the Reformation, especially King Henry VIII., I minded you how easy a thing it was to deprive you of your pretended advantage, by giving you an account of the wicked lives, with the brutish and diabolical practices, of many of your popes, whom you account the heads of your church, and the very centre wherein all the lines of your profession meet, you feign as though I had imposed all the crimes I intimated them to be guilty of, and many more whose names you heap together, upon Popery, or the religion that you profess; yea, that I should say that it is nothing else but only a heap of the wickednesses by you enumerated. Now this I did not do; but you feign it of your own head, that you may have somewhat to speak against, and a pretence of intimating in the close of your discourse that you have considered the chapter about Reformation, whereas in truth you have not spoken one word unto it, nor unto any thing contained in it. And yet when you have done, as if you had been talking about any thing wherein I am in the least measure concerned, you come in, in the close, with your grave advice, "That I should take heed of blaspheming that innocent Catholic flock, which the angels of God watch over to protect them." As though a man could not remember the wicked crimes of your nocent popes, but he must be thought to blaspheme the innocent flock of Christ, which never had greater enemies in this world than some of them have been. If this be to blaspheme, then some of your own councils, all your historians, many of the most learned men of your church, are notorious blasphemers. But you wilfully mistake, and beg that *their schismatical papal faction* may be esteemed the innocent *catholic church* of Christ; without a concession whereof, your inferences and persuasions are very weak and feeble.

Of the like nature unto this is your ensuing discourse about the *contradictions* which you fancied in your "Fiat Lux" to be imposed on Papists, p. 77. Two things you insist upon, waiving those that you had formerly mentioned, as finding them in their examination unable to yield you the advantage you thought to make of them. You feign a "new contradiction," which you say is imposed on Papists. "For," say you, "while our kings reign in peace, then the Papist religion is persecuted as contrary to monarchy; when we have destroyed that government then is the Papist harassed, spoiled, pillaged, murdered, because their religion is wholly addicted unto monarchy, and Papists are all for kings. These are contradictions. Is there not somewhat of the power of darkness in this?" But you again mistake; and that, I fear, because you will do so. There was no persecution of Papists in this land at any time but what was in pursuit of some laws that were made against them. Now, not one of those laws intimate any such thing as that they were "opposite unto monarchy," but rather their design to promote a double monarchy on different accounts in this nation;—the one of the pope, and the other of him to whom the kingdom was given by the pope, and who for many years in vain attempted to possess himself of it. And on that account were you charged with an opposition to our monarchs, but not unto monarchy itself. And yet I must say, that if what hath been before discoursed of your faith and persuasion concerning the papal sovereignty be well considered, it will be found that if not your religion, yet the principles of some of the chief professors of it do carry in their womb a great impeachment of imperial power. Nor can I gather that in the times of our confusion you suffered as Papists for your friendship and love to monarchy, whatever some individual persons amongst you might do; seeing some of you would have been contented with its everlasting seclusion, so that your interest in the land might have been secured. And whether your popes themselves be not of that mind, I leave to all men to judge who know how much they are wont to prefer their own interest before the rights of other men. In the meantime, you may take notice, that whilst men are owned to pursue one certain end, they may at several times fix on mediums for the compassing of it opposite and contrary one to another. "Hæc non successit, alia aggrediamur via;"—"When one way fails, another quite contrary unto it may be fixed on." And whilst it is supposed that their end is the promotion of the papal interest, it is not improbable but that at several times you may make use of several ways and means, opposite and contrary one to another, and that this may be imputed unto you without the charge of contradictions upon you. But you may, if you please, omit discourses of this nature. I am none of those that would charge any thing upon you to your disadvantage in this world; neither do I desire your trouble any more than mine own. My aim is only to defend the truth, which you oppose.

Your next attempt is to vindicate yourself from any such intention in your application of "Ejice ancillam cum puero suo," as I apprehended. Whether what you say to this purpose will satisfy your reader or no I greatly question. For my part, as I shall speak nothing but what I believe to be according unto truth, so if I am, or have been at any time, mistaken in my apprehension of your sense and mind, I am resolved not to defend any thing because I have spoken it. "Homo sum," and therefore subject to mistakes; though I am not in the least convinced that I was actually mistaken in my conceptions of your sense and meaning in your "Fiat." But that we may not needlessly contend about words, yours or mine, I shall put you into a way whereby you may immediately determine this difference, and manifest that I mistook your intention, if I did so indeed. And it is this, Do but renounce those principles,—which if you maintain, you constantly affirm all that in those words I supposed you to intimate,— and this strife will be at an end. And they are but these two:—1. That all those who *refuse* to believe and worship God according to the propositions and determinations of your church are *heretics*. 2. That *obstinate heretics* are to be *accursed*, *persecuted*, *destroyed*, and *consumed* out of the world. Do but renounce these principles, and I shall readily acknowledge myself mistaken in the intention of the words you mention. If you will not so do, to what purpose is it to contend with you about one single expression, ambiguously, as you pretend, used by you, when in your avowed principles you maintain whatever is suggested to be intimated in it? Thus easily might you have saved your longsome discourse on this matter. And as for the emblem which you close it with, of the "rod of Moses,"—which, as you say, "taken in the right end was a walking-staff, in the wrong a serpent,"—it is such a childish figment, as you have no cause to thank them that imposed it upon your credulity.

CHAPTER XIX.

Of preaching—The mass, and the sacrifice of it—Transubstantiation—Service of the church.

WE are arrived at length unto the consideration of those particulars in your Roman faith which in your "Fiat" you chose out either to adorn and set off the way in religion which you invite your countrymen to embrace, or so to gild it as that they may not take any prejudice from them against the whole of what you profess. The first of these is that which you entitled "Messach," which you now inform us to be a Saxon word, the same with "Mass." But why you make use of such an obsolete word to amuse your readers withal, you give us no account. Will you give me leave to guess? for, if I mistake not, I am not far from your fancy. Plain, downright "Mass" is a thing that hath gotten a very ill name amongst your countrymen, especially since so many of their forefathers were burned to death for refusing to resort unto it. Hence, it may be, you thought meet to waive that name, which both the thing known to be signified by it in its own nature, and your procedure about it, had rendered obnoxious to suspicion. So you call it by a *new old name*, or an *old new name*, that men might not at first know what you intended, upon your invitation, to entertain them withal; and yet, it may be, that they would like it under a new dress, which the old name might have startled them from the consideration of. But "Mass," or "Messach," let it be as you please, we shall now consider what it is that you offer afresh concerning it, and hear you speak out your own words. Thus you say, p. 81:—

"Having laughed at my admiration of Catholic service, you carp at me for saying that the first Christians were never called together to hear a sermon; and to convince me you bring some places out of St Paul's epistles and the Acts, which commend the ministry of the word. This, indeed, is your usual way of refuting my speeches. You flourish copiously in that which is not at all against me, and never apply it to my words, lest it should appear, as it is, impertinent. I deny not that converts were farther instructed, or that the preaching of God's word is good and useful; but that which I say is, that the primitive Christians were never called together for that end as the great work of their Christianity. This I have clearly proved."

Well, sir, without retortion, which just indignation against this unhandsome management of a desperate cause is ready to suggest, be pleased to take a little view of your own words once more. Page 279, you tell us that "the apostles and apostolical Christians placed their religion not in hearing or making sermons, *for they had none*, but in attending to their Christian liturgy; and the sermons mentioned in the Acts were made to the Jews and Pagans for their conversion, not to any Christians at all." Could I now take any other course to confute these false and impious assertions than what I did in the "Animadversions?" I proved unto you that sermons were made unto Christians by the apostles for their edification; that order is given by them for the instant preaching of the word, in and unto the churches, unto the end of the world; and that those are by them signally commended who laboured in that work: and what can be spoken more directly to the confutation of your assertion? You would now shroud yourself under the ambiguity of that expression, "The great work of their Christianity," which yet you make no use of in your "Fiat." The words there from which you would get countenance unto your present evasion are these: "Nowhere was ever sermon made to formal Christians, either by St Peter or Paul, or any other, as the work of their religion that they came together for; nor did the Christians ever dream of serving God after their conversion by any such means, but *only* by the eucharist or liturgy." Here is somewhat of the " work of their religion which they came together for;" nothing of the " great work of their Christianity." Now, that preaching was a work of their religion that they came together for, though not the only work of it, nor only end for which they so convened, which no man ever dreamed that it was; and that the primitive Christians did, by and in that work, serve God; hath been proved unto you from the Scripture. And all antiquity, with the whole story of the church, gives attestation to the same truth. Sir, it were far more honourable for you to renounce a false and scandalous assertion when you are convinced that such it is, than to seek to palliate it, and to secure yourself by such unhandsome evasions. " Preaching of the word unto believers" is an ordinance of Christ, and that of indispensable necessity unto their edification, or growth in grace and knowledge, which he requireth of them. In the practice of this ordinance were the apostles themselves sedulous, and commanded others so to be. So were they in the primitive following times, as you may learn from the account given us of church meetings by Justin Martyr and Tertullian in their Apologies, and all that have transmitted any thing unto posterity concerning their assemblies. For this end, to hear the word preached, Christians came together; *not only, or solely,* or exclusively to the administration of other ordinances, but as to a part of that worship which God required at their hands, and wherein no small part of their spiritual advantage was inwrapped. To deny this, as you do in your " Fiat," is to deny that the sun shines at noon-day, and to endeavour to dig up the very roots of piety, knowledge, and all Christianity; to what ends and purposes, and for the enthroning of what other thing in their room, let all indifferent men judge. And I shall take leave to say, that, to my best observation, I never met with an assertion in any author, of what religion soever, more remote from truth, sobriety, and modesty, than that of yours in your " Fiat," p. 275: " Nor did the primitive Christians for three hundred years ever hear a sermon made unto them upon a text; but merely flocked together, at their priests' appointment, unto their messachs." This, I say, is so loudly and notoriously untrue, and so known to be so to all that have ever looked into the stories of those times, that I am amazed at your confidence in the publishing of it. It may be you will hope to shelter yourself under the ambiguity of that expression, " Made unto them upon a text;" supposing that an instance cannot be given of that mode of preaching, wherein some certain text is read at the entrance of a sermon, and principally insisted upon. But this *fig-leaf* will not cover you from the just censure of knowing men; for,—1. The following adversative. "But merely," is perfectly exclusive of all preaching, be it of what mode it will. 2. The reading of "one certain text" before preaching is not necessary unto it, but all preaching is, and ever was, upon some text or texts; that is, it consisted in the explication and application of the word of God,—that is, some part or portion of it. 3. Whereas it is certain that our Saviour himself *preached on a text*, Luke iv. 17–21, as also did his apostles, Acts viii. 35, and the fathers of the following ages, it is sufficient y evident that that was also the constant mode of preaching in the first three hundred years, as may be made good in the instance of Origen, and sundry others.

You go on, and except against me for saying, "That we hear nothing of your sacrifice of the mass in the Scripture," and say, "You will neither hear nor see. Say you, the passion of our Lord is our Christian sacrifice?—do not I say so too? but that this incruent sacrifice was instituted by the same Lord before his death, to figure out daily before our eyes that passion of his which was then approaching, in commemoration of his death, so long as the world should last."

I must desire you to stay here a little. This sacrifice you make the main of Christian religion. Protestants, for the want of it, you esteem to have no religion at all. We must, therefore, consider what it is that you intend by it, for I suppose you would not have us accept of we know not what; and you seem both in your "Fiat" and in your "Epistola" to obscure it as much as you are able. 1. You call it an "incruent sacrifice;" which, (1.) Shows only *what it is not*, and that in only one instance, which is a very lame description of any thing; and this also may be affirmed of any metaphorical sacrifice whatever, as "offering unto God the calves of our lips,"—it is an "incruent sacrifice." (2.) Your expression implies a *contradiction*. Every proper propitiatory sacrifice was bloody; and an incruent proper sacrifice, such as you would have this to be, is a proper improper propitiatory sacrifice! 2. You say it "was instituted by our Lord to figure out his passion." (1.) This is a weighty proof of what you have in hand, being the *only thing* to be proved. (2.) I suppose, in the examination of it, it will appear that you sacrifice *that very body and blood of Christ*, in your own conceits, which himself offered unto God; and how you can make any thing to be a figure of itself, as yet I do not perfectly understand. (3.) That the Lord Christ appointed the sacrament of his body and blood, and our eucharistical sacrifice therein, to be a commemoration of his death and passion, is the doctrine of Protestants, wherewith your sacrifice hath a perfect inconsistency, as we shall find in the consideration of it. This is the substance of what you are pleased to acquaint us with about this "great business of our religion." But because you shall perceive that it was not without good grounds and reasons that I affirmed the Scripture to be utterly silent of this that you make the great work of Christianity, I shall a little farther inquire after the nature of it,—that, I mean, which by you it is fancied to be; for it is a mere creature of your own imagination.

1. You always contend that it is "a proper sacrifice" which you intend. The first canon of your council accurseth them who deny it to be "verum et proprium sacrificium," a "true and proper sacrifice;" wherein, as they say before, "Christus immolatur," "Christ is sacrificed." Many things in the New Testament, in respect of their analogy unto the institutions of the Old, are called "sacrifices," even almost all spiritual actions that are acceptable unto God in Christ. The preaching of the gospel unto the conversion of sinners is termed "sacrificing," Rom. xv. 16; so is faith itself, Phil. ii. 17; so prayers and thanksgiving are an oblation, Heb. v. 7, xiii. 15; and good works are called "sacrifices," Heb. xiii. 16, Phil. iv. 18; and our whole Christian obedience is intimated by Peter so to be. In the sacrament of the eucharist it is that you seek for your sacrifice. And if you would be contented to call it and esteem it so, upon the account of its comprising some of the things before mentioned, or merely as a spiritual action appointed by God, and acceptable unto him, there would be an end of this contest. But you must have it "a proper sacrifice," like those of Aaron of old; not a "remembrance" of the sacrifice of Christ, but a "sacrifice of Christ himself," wherein "Christus immolatur," "Christ is sacrificed," as the council speaks.

2. The sacrifices of old were of two sorts:—(1.) *Eucharistical*, or oblations of the fruits of the earth or other things, whereby the sacrificers acknowledged God as the Lord and author of all good things and mercies, with thanksgiving. (2.) *Propitiatory*, for the atoning of God, the reconciling him unto sinners, for the turning away of his wrath, and the impetration of the pardon of sin. This was done typically and sacramentally, by virtue of their respect unto the oblation of Christ, by the old bloody sacrifices of the law; really and effectually by that bloody sacrifice which the Lord Jesus Christ once offered for all. Now because, in the sacrament of the eucharist, it is our duty to offer up unto God our thankful prayers for his unspeakable love in sending his only Son to die for us, we do not contend with any who on that account, and with respect unto that peculiar act of our duty in it, shall call it a eucharistical sacrifice, yea, affirm it so to be. But you will have it a "propitiatory sacrifice;" a sacrifice of atonement, like that made by Christ himself; "a sacrifice for the sins of the living and the dead," making reconciliation with God, obtain-

ing pardon of sin, and eternal life;—things peculiar to the *one sacrifice* of Christ in his death and passion.

3. Though you usually exclude the *communion* from it,—wherein you do wisely, that it may have no affinity with the institution of Christ,—yet you do not precisely determine your sacrifice unto any one act or action in your mass, but make it comprise the whole, with the manner of its celebration, from the first setting forth of the elements of bread and wine mixed with water, unto the end of the offertory, after their transubstantiation and religious adoration thereupon, and their offering up unto God the body and blood of Christ under the accidents of bread and wine. The *presentation* of the bread and wine you would prove to belong unto your sacrifice from the example of Melchizedek. Your *transubstantiation* is also of the *essence* of it; for "it is required in a sacrifice," says your Bellarmine, "that the sensible thing to be offered unto God be changed and plainly destroyed," De Miss., lib. i. cap. 2: which you esteem the substance of your bread and wine to be in your transubstantiation. Your religious adoration of the consecrated host belongs also unto it, for that in the canon of the mass immediately ensues your transubstantiating consecration before the oblation itself, and so must necessarily be a part of your sacrifice. Your "offering up unto God of Jesus Christ," praying him to accept of him at the priest's hands ("supra quæ propitio et sereno vultu respicere digneris et accepta habere"), belongs also unto it. So doth your direction of it to the propitiating of God, and the expiation of the sins of the quick and the dead; the ceremonies also wherewith your mass is celebrated, as I suppose, most of them belong to your sacrifice. And those who believe them not to be duties of piety are accursed by your council of Trent. The priest's eating of the host belongs to the sacrifice; yea, saith Bellarmine, it is "pars essentialis sacrificii," though not "tota essentia,"—an *essential part* of the sacrifice, though *the whole essence* of it doth not consist therein. I know you are at a great loss and variance among yourselves to find out what it is that is properly your sacrifice, or wherein the essence of it doth consist. Some of your discrepant opinions are given us by your Azorius, lib. x. cap. 19: "Sunt," saith he, "qui putant rationem sacrificii totam constitui in verbis, precibus, ceremoniis, et ritibus, qui in consecratione adhibentur, eo quod sacrificii ratio, inquiunt, nequit in ipsa consecratione consistere, quin e contrario consecratio ad rationem sacramenti potius quam ad naturam sacrificii pertinet. Alii existimant sacrificii rationem tribus sacerdotis actionibus constare, consecratione, oblatione, et sumptione. Alii quidem sensêre ad rationem hujus sacrificii quatuor imo quinque actiones concurrere, consecrationem, oblationem, fractionem, sumptionem. Alii rationem sacrificii ponunt in duobus actibus, consecra-

tione et oblatione. Alii constituunt totam rationem sacrificii in una actione, viz., consecratione;"—"There are who think the nature of the sacrifice to consist in the words, prayers, ceremonies, and rites which are used in the consecration, because, they say, the nature of the sacrifice cannot consist in the consecration itself, which rather belongs unto the nature of a sacrament than of a sacrifice. Others think that the sacrifice consists in three actions of the priest,—consecration, oblation, and sumption, or receiving of the host. Others in four or five,—as consecration, oblation, fraction, sumption. Others in two,—consecration and oblation; and some in one,—consecration." And is not this a brave business, to impose on the consciences of all men, when you know not yourselves what it is that you would so impose! A sacrifice must be believed, and they are all accursed by you that believe it not; but what the sacrifice is, and wherein it doth consist, you cannot tell! And an easy matter it were to manifest that all the particulars which you assign as those that either belong necessarily unto the integrity of a sacrifice, or those wherein some of you, or any of you, would have its essence to consist, are indeed of no such nature or importance; but that is not my present business. I am only inquiring what your sacrifice is, according unto your own sense and imagination; and that we may not mistake, I shall set down such a general description of it as the canon of the mass, the general rubric of the missal, the rites and cautels of its celebration, will afford unto us. Now, in these it is represented as a sacred action, wherein a proper priest or sacrificer, arrayed with various consecrated attire, standing at the altar, taketh bread and wine,—about which he useth great variety of postures and gestures, inclinations, bowings, kneelings, stretching out and gathering in his arms, with a multitude of crossings at the end and in the midst of his pronunciation of certain words of Scripture,—turns them into the real natural body and blood of Christ the Son of God; worshipping them so converted with religious adoration, showing them to the people for the same purpose; and then offering the body and blood unto God, praying for his acceptance of them so offered, and that it may be available for the living and the dead, for the pardoning of their sins and saving of their souls: after which he takes that body of Christ, so made, worshipped, and offered, and eats and devours it! By all which Christ is truly and properly sacrificed!

This is the sacrifice of your church, wherein, as you inform us, the main of your devotion and worship doth consist. Of this sacrifice I told you formerly the *Scripture* is silent; and I now add, that so also is *antiquity*. You cannot produce any one approved writer, for the space of six hundred years, that gives testimony to this your sacrifice; for, whatever flourish you may make with the ambiguity of the word "sacrifice," which we cleared before, your transubstantiation, and other things asserted by you to belong unto the integrity if not the essence of your sacrifice, are strangers unto antiquity, as hath been lately proved unto you, and will, no doubt, be yet farther confirmed so to be.

I told you, as you observe, that this sacrifice is an utter stranger to Scripture, as also that it is inconsistent with what is therein delivered. The apostle, in the Epistle to the Hebrews, plainly affirms that the sacrifice of the church of the Christians is but one, and that "once offered for all," whereas those of the Jews, by reason of their imperfection, were often repeated; which you choose out to reply unto, and say, "It is true, the sacrifice of our Lord's passion, of which the apostle, in that whole discourse, intends only to treat in opposition unto that of bulls and goats, was so done but once,—that it could not be done twice; but as the sacrifices of the old law were instituted by Almighty God, to be often iterated, before the passion of the Messias, for a continual exercise of religion, so did the same Lord, for the very same purpose, institute another, to be iterated after his death, unto which it was to have reference when it should be past, as the former had to the same death when it was to come." So you.

But,—1. This *begs the question;* for you only repeat and say that such a sacrifice was instituted by Christ, which you know is by us utterly denied. 2. It plainly *contradicts the apostle,* and overthrows his whole argument and design. (1.) It contradicts him in express terms; for whereas he says not only that "Christ once offered" himself, but also that he was "once offered" for all,—that is, "no more to be offered,"—you affirm that he is often offered, and that every day. (2.) His design is to demonstrate the excellency of the condition of the church of the New Testament, and the worship of God therein above that of the Old. And this he proves to consist herein in a special manner, that they had *many sacrifices,* which were of necessity to be reiterated because they could not take away sin. "For," saith he, "if they could, then should they not have been repeated, nor would there have been need of any other sacrifice. But now," saith he, "this is done by the *one sacrifice* of Christ, which hath so taken away sin as that it hath made the repetition of itself, or the institution of any other sacrifice, needless; and therefore we have no more but that *one,* and that one *once* performed." Now, unless you will deny the apostle's assertions, either,—(1.) That if one sacrifice can take away sin, there is no need of another; or, (2.) That the one sacrifice of Christ did perfectly take away sin as to atonement; and also, (3.) Assert that the condition of the gospel church is still the same with that of the Jews, and that we have need of a sacrifice to be repeated, not only as theirs was, year by year, from whence he argues the imperfection of the greatest solemn sacrifice of expiation, but day by day, with a farther and greater weakness (repetition, in the judgment of the apostle, being an evidence thereof),—there will be no place left for your sacrifice; that is, your main worship belongs not to the church of God at all. (4.) You pretend that in this worship Christ himself is sacrificed unto God, but "incruenter," and without suffering; but the apostle plainly tells us that if he be often offered he must "often suffer," Heb. ix. 26. And the sacrifice of Christ without his passion, his offering without suffering, evacuates both the one and the other.

But what of all this? If the apostles used the sacrifice you talk of, that of the mass, is it meet we should do so also? Hereof you say, "Were not the apostles according to this rite λειτουργοῦντες τῷ Κυρίῳ, 'sacrificing to our great Lord God,' when Paul was, by imposition of hands, segregated from the laity to his divine service, as I clearly in my paragraph evinced out of the history of the Acts of the Apostles? 'No,' say you, 'the apostles were not then about any sacrifice, but only preaching God's word, or some such thing, to the people, in the name and behalf of God.' But, sir, is this to be in earnest, or jest? The sacred text says they were sacrificing to our Lord, liturgying and ministering unto him; you say they were not sacrificing to God, but only preaching to the people. And now the question is, whether you or I more rightly understand that apostolical book? For my sense and meaning I have all antiquity, as well as the plain words of the sacred text; you have neither."

How empty and vain this discourse of yours is, wherein you seem greatly to triumph, will quickly be discovered. And you are a merry man, if you think by such arguments as these to persuade us that the apostles sacrificed to God according to the rite of your mass; as though we did not know by whom the chief parts of it, particularly those wherein you place your sacrifice, were invented, many hundreds of years after they fell asleep. 1. You say they were λειτουργοῦντες τῷ Κυρίῳ, "sacrificing to our great Lord God," as though it were God the Father, or God absolutely, that is intended in that expression, τῷ Κυρίῳ, "To the Lord." Ὁ Κύριος, "The Lord," is, sir, peculiarly denotative of the person of the mediator, Jesus Christ, God and man, according to that rule given us by the apostle, 1 Cor. viii. 6, "To us there is one God, the Father; καὶ εἷς Κύριος, and one Lord Jesus Christ." And this is the constant denotation of the word when used absolutely, as here it is, throughout the whole New Testament. To Christ the mediator were the churches ministering, Acts xiii. 2; that is, in his name and authority, according to his appointment, and unto his service. And this one observation sufficiently discovers the vanity of your argument; for you will not say that they offered sacrifice to the Lord Christ emphatically and reduplicatively, seeing, if you may be believed, it is he whom they offered in sacrifice. Of such force is the sophism wherein you boast! And, 2. You wisely observe that Paul, by the imposition of hands there mentioned, was segregated from the laity; whereas he tells you that he was "an apostle" (wherein certainly he was segregated from the laity), "neither of men, nor by men, but by Jesus Christ, and God the Father," Gal. i. 1; that is, there was no intimation or interposition of the ministry or authority of any man in his call to that office, which he had for sundry years exercised before this his peculiar separation to the work of preaching anew to the Gentiles. So well are you skilled in the sense of that apostolical book! 3. And not to insist on the repetition of my former answer, which in your wonted manner you lamely and unduly represent, could you by other arguments, and on other testimonies, prove that the sacrifice you plead for was instituted by Christ and offered by the apostles, there might possibly be some colour for a man to think that they performed that duty also when they were said λειτουργεῖν in the service of God; but from that general expression, intimating any kind of public ministry whatever, and never used in any author, sacred or profane, precisely and absolutely to signify sacrificing, to conclude that they were offering sacrifice, and to use no other testimony to prove they had any such sacrifice, is such a fondness as nothing but insuperable prejudice can persuade a man in his right wits to give countenance unto. St Paul tells us that the magistrate is λειτουργὸς Θεοῦ,—doth he mean that he is God's sacrificer, or his minister? And he says of himself that he was λειτουργὸς τοῦ Χριστοῦ,—doth he intend that he was Christ's sacrificer, or his servant? Rom. xv. 16, 27, he says that it was the duty of the Gentiles, λειτουργῆσαι ἐν τοῖς σαρκικοῖς,—doth he mean to sacrifice in your carnal things, or to minister of them to the Jews? But you will, it may be, except that they were not said λειτουργεῖν τῷ Κυρίῳ, as those here (that is, the prophets of the church of Antioch, and not the apostles, as you mistake) are said to do, "to liturgy to the Lord;" it must needs be sacrificing, because it was "to the Lord." But, (1.) I have showed you how this pretence is perfectly destructive of your own intendment, in that it is the Lord Christ that is especially meant, unto whom distinctly you will not say they were sacrificing. And, (2.) Were it not so, yet the expression would not give you the least colour of advantage. What think you of 1 Sam. iii. 1, Καὶ τὸ παιδάριον Σαμουὴλ ἦν λειτουργῶν τῷ Κυρίῳ ἐνώπιον Ἡλί—"And the child Samuel was liturgying" (seeing you will have it so) "unto the LORD before Eli?" Do you think that the child, which was not of the family of Aaron, nor yet called to be a prophet, was offering sacrifice to God, and the high priest looking on? Do you not see the fondness of your pretension? (3.) I told you before, but now begin to fear that you are too old to learn what you do not like, that the LXX. never translated זָבַח, "sacrifice," or to sacrifice, by λειτουργία or λειτουργῶ, nor intimate any sacrifice anywhere by that word. And you may, if you please, now learn, by the instance of Samuel, that what men perform in the worship of God according to his command, they may be said therein to "minister unto or before the Lord in." (4.) The note of your own Cajetan upon the place is worth your consideration: "Non explicatur species ministerii; sed ex eo quod dixerant (prophetæ et doctores) insinuatur quod ministrabant Domino, docendo et prophetando;"—"What kind of ministry is spoken of is not explained; but by saying they were prophets and teachers (that were employed in it), it is insinuated that they ministered unto the Lord by teaching and prophesying." What have prophets and teachers to do with sacrifice? If as such they administered unto the Lord, they did it by prophesying and teaching, which were accompanied by prayer. Here is no mention of sacrifice nor work for priests; so that the context excludes your sense. The same is the interpretation of Erasmus. (5.) Your vulgar Latin [the Vulgate] reads the words, "administrantibus Domino," as they were "ministering unto the Lord," excluding their notion of sacrificing. And, (6.) The Syriac transposeth the words, and interprets the sacrifice intended in them וכד הנון צימין הוו ומתכשפין לאלהא,—and when they "were fasting and praying unto the Lord." Praying (together with prophesying and preaching) was their ministry, not sacrificing. To the same purpose all ancient translations, not one giving countenance unto your fancy. So well have you the plain words of the sacred text for you! (7.) Are you not ashamed to boast that you have all antiquity for your sense and meaning? Produce any one ancient author, if you can, that gives the least countenance unto it. This boasting is uncomely, because untrue. Bellarmine, out of whom you took your plea from this place, and your quotation of Erasmus in your "Fiat," cannot produce the suffrage of any one of the ancients for your interpretation of the words; no more can any of your commentators. The homilies of Chrysostom on that passage are lost. Œcumenius is quite blank against you; so is Cajetan, Erasmus, and Vatablus of your own. And do you not now see what is become of your boasting? And are not your countrymen beholding unto you, for endeavouring so industriously to draw them off from the institution of Christ, to place their confidence and devotion in that which hath not the least footstep in Scripture or antiquity, but is expressly condemned by them both? But, to tell you my judgment, you will prevail with very few of them to answer your desires. Will they judge it meet and equal, think you, to change a blessed sacrament that Christ hath appointed, to embrace a sacrifice that you have invented? to leave calling upon God, according to the sense of their wants, with understanding, as they do in that celebration of the eucharist which now they enjoy, to attend unto a priest sometimes *muttering*, sometimes *saying*, sometimes *singing* a deal of Latin, whereof they understand never a word? to forego that internal humility, self-abasement, and prostration of soul unto God, which they are inured unto in that sacrament, to become spectators of the theatrical gestures of your sacrificers? Besides, they are not able to comply with your request, and to make your mass the sum of their devotion and worship of God, without offering the highest violence to their faith as they are Christians, their reason as they are men, and that sense which they have in common with other creatures. And what are you, or what have you done for them, that you should at once expect such a profuse largeness at their hands?

I. For your faith, if it be grounded in the Scripture, as every true Protestant's is, your sacrifice, if admitted, will unquestionably evert it.

1. To accept of a worship pretended to be of such huge importance as to be available for the impetration of grace, mercy, pardon of sins, removal of punishment, life eternal for the living and the dead, destitute of all foundation in or countenance from the Scripture, [is] absolutely inconsistent with their faith.

2. It is no less, to have a *sacrament*, which is given unto us of God as a pledge and token of his love and grace, turned into a *sacrifice*, which is a thing by us offered unto God and accepted by him; so that they differ, as in other things, so in their terms, "a quo," and "ad quem," from what they proceed, and by whom they are accepted.

3. Besides, they will quickly discover your pretensions to be contrary unto what the Scripture teacheth them, both concerning the sacrifice of Christ and also his institution of his last supper, which is your rule, and compriseth the whole of your duty in the administration of it. They do not find that therein Christ offered himself unto his Father, but to his disciples: not to him, to be accepted of him; but to them, to be by faith received.

4. And whereas the apostle expressly affirms that "he offered himself but once," if he offered himself a sacrifice in his last supper, you must maintain that he offered himself twice, unless you will deny his sacrifice on the cross.

5. Moreover, it is greatly opposite to your countrymen's faith about the priesthood of Christ and his real sacrifice; which are to them things of that moment, that whosoever shakes their faith in and about them shakes the very foundations of their hope, consolation, and salvation. They have been taught that Christ remains a high

priest for ever; and the multiplication of priests in succession arising merely from the mortality and death of them that preceded, they believe that no priest can be substituted unto him in his office to offer a proper sacrifice unto God, the same which he offered himself, without a supposition of an insufficiency in him for his work. It is true, there are persons who, in his name and authority, as he is the great prophet of the church, do minister unto it, whom some of them, either as the word may be an abbreviation of presbyter, or out of analogy unto them who of old served at the altar, do call priests: but that any should intervene between God and Christ in sacrificing, or the discharge of his priestly office, you will not find your countrymen ready to believe; for they are persuaded there are as many mediators and sureties as priests or sacrificers of the new covenant.

6. Moreover, they believe that the sacrifice of the mass is a high derogation from the virtue and efficacy of the sacrifice of Christ on the cross, and to be set up in competition with it.

7. They are at a stand at the whole matter,—to see you turning bread and wine into that very body and blood of Christ which suffered on the cross, and then to worship them, and then to pray to God to accept at your hands that Christ which you have made, and then to eat him! But when they consider that by so doing you suppose yourselves to effect that which they believe to be wrought only by the blood of the cross of Christ, once offered for all, and therein fancy a sacrifice of Christ, wherein he dieth not, contrary to so many express testimonies of Scripture, they are utterly averse from it: for whereas they look for redemption, forgiveness of sins, and reconciliation with God, by the one sacrifice of Christ upon the cross (wherein consists the foundation of their hope and consolation; because it, being absolutely perfect, was every way able and sufficient, without any repetition, as the apostle teacheth them, to take away sin, and for ever to consummate them that are sanctified), you teach them now to look for the same things from this sacrifice of yours; which would make them question the validity and perfection of that of Christ.

8. And when they have so done, yet they would still be forced to question the validity of yours, because it is a pretended sacrifice of Christ without his death, which they know to have been indispensably required to render his sacrifice valid and effectual.

9. And they cannot but think that this repeated sacrifice, being pretended to be for the very same ends and purposes with that of Christ himself, is very apt to take off the minds and confidence of men from that one sacrifice performed so long ago, which they have not seen, and to fix them on that which their eyes daily look upon, as the "præsens numen" that they can immediately apply themselves unto. Thus they fear that insensibly all faith of the true propitiation

wrought by Christ is obliterated, and that which they think an idol set up in the room of it.

10. And, which farther troubles them, they are jealous that by this your fiction you quite overthrow the testament of Christ, which certainly no man ought to endeavour the disannulling of; for whereas in this sacrament believers come to receive from him the great legacy of his body and blood, with all the fruits of his death and passion, you direct them to be offering and sacrificing of them unto God: which quite alters the will of our great testator. And very many other things there are wherein your countrymen affirm that your sacrifice is contrary to the faith wherein from Scripture they have been instructed, and that in things of the greatest importance to their consolation here and salvation hereafter.

II. Neither is this all: your request also lies cross to your *reason* no less than to your *faith;* for your sacrifice cannot be performed without a supposition of a change of the substance of the bread and wine into the substance of the body and blood of Christ, and the substance of that body and blood in every consecrated host, under the species of bread and wine, Christ himself alive being in every host and every particle of it. Hence many things, they say, ensue which no man can possibly admit of without offering violence unto the main principles of that reason whereby we are distinguished from the beasts that perish. Some few of them may be instanced in:—

1. *Accidents subsisting without a subject* follows hence necessarily, in the first place: so that there should be whiteness, and nothing white; length, and nothing long; breadth, and nothing broad; weight, and nothing heavy,—for all these accidents of bread remain, when you would have them say that the bread is gone,—so that there is left a white, sweet, long, broad, heavy nothing! This your countrymen cannot understand.

2. Besides, they say, you hereby teach them that *one and the same body of Christ which is in heaven is also on the altar;* not by an impletion of the whole space between heaven and earth, that some part of it should be in heaven and some on earth, but that the one body which is in heaven, and whilst it is there, is also on the altar, in the accidents of bread; which upon the matter is, that one and the same body is two, yea, a hundred or a thousand, according as in the mass you are pleased to multiply it. Now, that one and the same body should be locally divided or separated from itself,—that whilst that one body is on the altar, that other one body, which is the same, should be in heaven,—your countrymen think to imply a contradiction.

3. And so, also, they do that a *body* should be in *any place*, and yet not as a *body*, but as a *spirit.* For whereas you say that whole

Christ is contained under each species of bread and wine, and under every the most minute part of either species, as your council speaks, you make the body of Christ to be whole in the whole, and whole in every part; when the very nature of a body requires that it have "partes extra partes,"—its parts distinct from one another, and those occupying their distinct particular places. But you make the body of Christ neither to be compassed in nor to fill the place wherein it is; that is, *to be in a place* and *not to be in a place.* For if it be a body, and be under the species of bread and wine upon the altar, it is in a place; and if it be not comprehended in that space where it is, and doth fill it, it is not in a place: and therefore is there and is not there at the same time.

4. And, moreover, we all know that the *consecrated wafer* bears no proportion to the *true natural body* of Christ; and yet this is said to be contained under that: so that the body contained is much greater and farther extended than the body that contains it or the space wherein it is; for it is so under the host as not to be elsewhere, unless in another host.

5. Nay, it is in every *minute part* of the host; which multiplies contradictions in your assertion.

6. Of the same nature is it that you are forced to feign the same body in ten thousand *distant* places at the same time, and that with all *contradictory adjuncts* and *affections.* Now, your countrymen think that these and innumerable other consequences of your transubstantiation, which you presuppose to your sacrifice, or rather make a principal part thereof, are such as overthrow the whole order of nature and being of things, and leave nothing certain among the sons of men.

III. Their *sense* is equally engaged against you with their *reason.* Your host is visible, tangible, gustable. When they *see it*, they see bread; when they *feel* it, they feel bread; when they *taste* it, they taste bread; and yet you tell them it is not bread. Whom shall they believe? If things be not as they see them, feel them, taste them, it may be they are not men, nor do go on their feet, but are deceived in all these things, and suppose they see, perceive, and understand what they do not. You tell them, indeed, that the bread is changed into the body of Christ, that body that was born of the blessed Virgin, and was crucified at Jerusalem; that all taste, length, breadth, weight is taken away from it; and that the taste and weight of the bread is continued, which are the things they see, feel, and taste. But they likewise tell you that your persuasion is an inveterate prejudice, which you have blindly captivated your minds unto, and that if you would but give yourselves the liberty of exercising any reflex thoughts upon your own acts, you would find that, upon the suppositions you proceed on, you have not any just grounds to conclude yourselves to be living men; for you teach men to deny and question all that from reason or sense you can insist upon to prove that so you are. On these and the like accounts, the encomiums you give of your sacrifice will scarce prevail with your countrymen to relinquish all the worship of God, wherein they find daily comfort and advantage to their souls, for the embracement of it

---

CHAPTER XX.

Of the blessed Virgin.

UNTO the 15th chapter of the "Animadversions," directed to your paragraph of the blessed Virgin, you can find, it seems, nothing to say, and therefore betake yourself to clamorous revilings. All that you say in your "Fiat" on this head is but a heap of false accusations against Protestants for dishonouring her; and all that you say in your epistle in its vindication is railing at me for minding you of your miscarriage. My whole book, you say, is nothing but "calumnies, a bundle of slanders, a mere quiver of sharp arrows of desolation." I am not sorry that you are sensible that it hath arrows in it, tending to the desolation of your abominations; but I challenge you to give an instance of any one calumny or slander in it, from the beginning to the end. If you do not do so, I here declare you to be really and highly guilty of that which you would falsely impose upon another. Free yourself by some one instance if you can; if you cannot, your reputation will follow your conscience whither it will be hard for you to find them again. The substance of that chapter is this, which is all that I shall now say to your nothing against it:—Protestants yield to the blessed Virgin all the honour that the Scripture allows them or directs them unto, or that the primitive church did ascribe unto her; and the Papists give her the honour due to God alone, whereby they horribly dishonour God and her.

CHAPTER XXI.

Images—Doctrine of the council of Trent—Of the second Nicene—The arguments for the adoration of images—Doctrine of the ancient church—Of the chief doctrine of the Roman church—Practice of the whole—Vain foundations of the pretences for image-worship examined and disproved.

YOUR next procedure is to your discourse of figures or images, and my animadversions upon it. And here you say, "you will come up close unto me;"—you mean, in replying unto what I delivered about it. But, sir, I thought this had been contrary to your design; you professed, at the beginning of your epistle, that it was so, and have made good use of that declaration of yourself by avoiding every thing in my discourse that you found yourself pressed with, and too difficult a task for you to deal withal. Why do you now begin to forget yourself, and to cast off the pretence you have hitherto shadowed yourself under, and excused yourself by, from tergiversation? Surely you think you are upon this head able to say *somewhat to the purpose,* which you despaired of doing upon others of as great importance; and therefore now you may argue and dispute, which before the design of your "Fiat" would not permit you to do. As far as I can observe, you speak nothing at any time but what you think is at present for your turn; but whether it have any consistency with that which elsewhere you have delivered, you make it not much your concernment to inquire. But we shall quickly see whether you had any just ground of encouragement to harness yourself, and to come up, as you speak, "close to me" in this business or no. It may be, before the close of our discourse, you will begin to think it had been as well for you to have persisted in your former avoidance, as to make this profession of a close dispute. And, whatever you pretend to the contrary, really you have done so. You hide the opinion and practice of your church about the worship of images, which you seem to be ashamed of, instead of defending them; and except against some passages in my "Animadversions," instead of answering the whole, which you seem to pretend unto. I shall, therefore, declare what is the true judgment of your church in this matter, and then vindicate the passages of my discourse which you take notice of in your exceptions; and under both heads declare the abomination of your faith and practice in your doctrine about images and worship of them.

The doctrine of your church in this matter I suppose we may be acquainted with from the determinations of your *councils,* the explication of your most famous *doctors,* the practice of your *people,* and the distinctions used by you to quit yourselves from idolatry in your doctrine and practice. And you will thereby learn, or may, at least, to what purpose it is for you to seek to palliate and hide the deformity of that which your mother and her wise men have made naked to all the world.

Your council of Trent is very wary in this matter, as it was in most of its other affairs; and, indeed, seeing it was resolved not to give place to the truth, it became it so to be, that it might keep any footing in the minds of men, and not tumble headlong into contempt and reproach. Many difficulties it had to wrestle withal. It saw the practice of their church, which was not totally to be deserted, lest the great mystery of its infallibility should be impaired, and its nakedness laid open; the general complaint, on the other side, of learned and sober men, that, under a pretence of image-worship, as horrible idolatry was brought into the church of God as ever was practised amongst the heathen, did not a little perplex it. It had also the various and contradictory opinions of the great doctors of your church and masters of your faith about the kind of worship which is due to images; all which had great followers ready to dispute endlessly in the maintenance of their several conceits. Amidst these rocks and oppositions, the fathers found no way to sail safely, but by the help of general and ambiguous words,—a course which, in the like difficulties, had frequently before stood them in good stead: wherefore they so expressed themselves, that no party at variance among them might think their opinions condemned, that the general practice of their church might be countenanced, and yet no particular asserted that was most obnoxious to the exceptions of the Lutherans. Thus, then, they speak: "Imagines porro Christi, Deiparæ Virginis et aliorum sanctorum in templis præsertim habendas et retinendas; eisque debitum honorem et venerationem impertiendam, non quod credatur,[1]—quoniam honos qui eis exhibetur refertur ad prototypa, quæ illæ representant;" with much more to that purpose. And we may observe, that the decree speaks only of the images of Christ, the blessed Virgin, and other saints, not expressly mentioning the images of God the Father, of the Trinity, and of the Holy Ghost, nor of angels, which they knew to be made, and to be had in veneration in their church. Nor do they anywhere reject the use, making, or worshipping of them; yea, in their following words they do plainly allow of the figuring of the Deity. "Quod," say they, "si aliquando historias et narrationes sacræ Scripturæ, quum id indoctæ plebi expediet, exprimi et figurari contigerit, doceatur populus, non propterea divinitatem figurari quasi corporeis oculis conspici, vel coloribus aut figuris exprimi possit." The words are, as most of the rest in this particular, as ambiguous as the oracles of Delphi. This cannot be denied to be in them, however,—1. "That the unlearned people are to be taught that the Deity is not painted or figured, as though it could be seen or expressed by colours, but for some other end," as it seems for their instruction: which, indeed, is honest and fair dealing; for they plainly tell them that by their pictures they teach them lies, the language of the picture being that God may be

[1] The words are extracted from Can. et Dec. Conc. Trid. sess. 25. The sentence is obscure, as it stands above, from the omission of the following words after "credatur:"—"inesse aliqua in iis divinitas vel virtus, propter quam sint colendæ, vel quod ab eis sit aliquid petendum, vel quod fiducia in imaginibus sit figenda veluti olim fiebat a gentibus quæ in idolis spem suam collocabant; sed ——."—Ed.

so pictured, whereby all your pictures and images of God the Father as an old man, of the Trinity as one person with three faces, and the Holy Ghost as a dove, are approved. 2. Religious worship of images is confirmed. "Due honour and veneration," or worship, "is to be given unto them," saith the council. Now, it is not mutual compliment they are discoursing about. There is no such intercourse between their images and them ordinarily, though sometimes civil salutations have passed between them; nor is it any token of civil subjection, for images have no eminency or authority of that kind: but it is divine or religious veneration and worship which they affirm is to be assigned unto them. 3. They say that "due honour and veneration," that is religious, is to be assigned unto them, but what in especial that honour and worship is, they do not determine: whether it be the same that is due to the sampler, as some, the most of your divines think, or whether it be an honour of some inferior nature, as others contend, "pugnant ipsi nepotesque," the synod leaves them where it found them, sufficiently at variance among themselves. 4. They farther assert the worship that is given by them to images to be religious or divine, in that they affirm the honour done to the image is referred unto the prototype which it doth represent. Now, suppose this be Jesus Christ himself: I suppose that they will grant that all the honour we yield to him by any way or means is divine or religious; and therefore so, consequently, that which they would have to be given unto his image (that is, a stock or stone, which they fancy so to be) must be so also. Now, sir, you may see from hence what it is that you are to speak unto and to defend, or else to hold your peace in this matter. And I shall yet make it a little more plain unto you. Your Trent council approves and commends the second council of Nice, as that which taught and confirmed that doctrine and practice about images and their worship which your church allows. I shall, therefore, briefly let you know what was the judgment of that council, and what was the doctrine and practice confirmed in it, under many dreadful anathematisms.

This second of Nice, or pseudo-synod of the Greeks, as it is called by the council of Frankfort, whereunto we are sent by the Tridentine fathers to be instructed in the due worship of images, was assembled by the authority of Irene the empress, a proud imperious woman, and her son Constantine, whose eyes she afterward put out, and thrust him into a monastery, in the year 490. Tharasius was then patriarch of Constantinople, and Hadrian the first bishop or pope of Rome. This man, most zealously or superstitiously addicted unto the worship of images, and that contrary to the judgment of most of the western churches, as soon afterward appeared in the council holden at Frankfort by the authority of Charles the Great, had a particular advantage both over the empress and the patriarch of Constantinople. The eastern empire being then greatly weakened by its own intestine divisions, and pressed on all sides by the Saracens, the empress began to entertain some hopes of relief from the French in the west, whose power was then grown very great; and to that end solicited a marriage for her son with the daughter of Charles the Great, and supposed that she might be helped therein by the mediation of Hadrian,—the bishops of Rome having no small hand in the promotion of the attempt of Pepin and Charles the Great for the crown of France, and afterward for the conquest of Italy and Germany. And, besides, she was a woman herself zealously addicted to that kind of superstition which Hadrian had espoused, as having in the time of Leo her husband kept her images in private, contrary unto what she had solemnly sworn unto her father, as Credenus relates in his annals. As for Tharasius, he was, contrary to all ecclesiastical canons, of a mere layman, at once, "per saltum," made patriarch of Constantinople; which Hadrian, upon his first hearing of, greatly exclaimed against, and refused to receive him into the society of patriarchs upon his sending of his significatory epistle. This is fully declared in the epistle of Hadrian, extant in the acts of the council. But yet afterward, bethinking himself how useful this man might be unto his design in getting the worship of images established in the east, he declares that if he will use means to get the "heresy," as he called it, of the image-opposers extirpated, and their veneration established, he would consent to his election and consecration, or else not. Finding how the matter was like to go with him, this lay-patriarch undertakes the work, and effectually prosecutes it in this synod, assembled at Nice by the authority of Irene the empress and her son Constantine. But by the way, when the council was assembled, he omitted not the opportunity of improving his own interest, getting himself styled Oecumenical or Universal Patriarch; which Anastasius Bibliothecarius, in his dedication of his translation of the Acts of this Convention unto John VIII., bewails, and ascribes it unto the flattery of the Greeks. The frauds, forgeries, and follies of this council, and ignorance and dotage of the fathers of it, have been sufficiently by others discovered. Our present concernment is only to inquire,—first, *What they taught* concerning image-worship; and, secondly, *How they proved* what they taught; seeing unto them we are sent by the Tridentine decree to be instructed in your faith in this matter.

First, They make the having and use of images in the worship of God of indispensable necessity; so that they anathematize and cast out of the communion of the church all that refuse to receive and use them according to their prescript. Yea, they proceed so far in their approbation of the confession of Theodosius, the bishop of Ammoria, as to denounce an anathema against them that do but doubt of their reception: Τοῖς ἀμφίβολον ἔχουσι τὴν διάνοιαν καὶ μὴ ἐκ ψυχῆς ὁμολογοῦσι προσκυνεῖν τὰς σεπτὰς εἰκόνας ἀνάθεμα (so he closeth his confession, which they all approve as orthodox);—"Anathema to them that are ambiguous or doubtful in their minds, and do not confess with their hearts" ("ex animo") "that sacred images are to be worshipped;" wherein they, and you with them, add schism to their idolatry, casting out of the churches those who offend neither against the gospel nor the determination of any general council of old; making the rule of your communion to consist in a sorry piece of will-worship of your own invention; which doubles the crime of your superstition, and lays an intolerable entanglement upon the consciences of men which are persuaded from the Scripture that they shall be accursed of God if they do receive images into his worship, after the manner of your prescription.

Secondly, They affirm, a hundred times over, that "images are religiously to be adored and worshipped;" that is, with divine worship. So, in the confession of the same Theodosius: Ὁμολογῶ καὶ συντίθεμαι καὶ δέχομαι καὶ ἀσπάζομαι, καὶ προσκυνῶ τὴν εἰκόνα τοῦ Κυρίου ἡμῶν Ἰησοῦ Χριστοῦ, (and so of the rest);—"I confess, consent unto, receive, embrace or salute, I worship or adore, the image of our Lord Jesus Christ, and of the blessed Virgin, and of the apostles and martyrs." The same is affirmed in the epistle of Hadrian, recited in the second act of the synod, which they all approve, and afresh curse all them that dogmatize or teach any thing against that worship of images. And Gregory the monk, no small man amongst them, affirms that he hoped by his confession of this doctrine he believed, he "should obtain the forgiveness of his sins," act. 2. And John, who falsely pretended himself to be delegated from the oriental patriarchs, when he was sent only by a few ignorant monks of Palestine, prefers images above the word itself, act. 4: Ὥστε μείζων ἡ εἰκὼν τοῦ λόγου·—"An image is greater than the word." And again, Ἰσοδυναμοῦσι αἱ τίμιαι εἰκόνες τῷ εὐαγγελίῳ·—"Honourable images are equivalent to the gospel." And they prove the worship they intend to be divine by their wise explication of that text, "The Lord thy God shalt thou worship, and him only shalt thou serve." Ἐπὶ μὲν τοῦ λατρεύσεις προσέθηκε τὸ μόνον, ἐπὶ δὲ τοῦ προσκυνήσεις οὐδαμῶς, ὥστε προσκυνεῖν μὲν ἔξεστι, λατρεύειν δὲ οὐδαμῶς·—"Unto the words, 'Thou shalt serve,' '*only*' is subjoined; but not unto the word 'worship:' so that it is lawful to worship (images), but not to serve them." A wise business! but it discovers sufficiently what is the worship which they ascribe unto images, even the same that is given unto God; for, if we may believe them, other things are not excluded from communion with God in this matter of worship and adoration. Whence the council of

Frankfort doth expressly charge them that they taught that images were to be adored with the honour due to God, act. 4. And so much weight do they lay upon this devotion, that they approve the counsel given by Theodorus the abbot unto the monk whom the devil vexed with temptations for worshipping the image of Christ; who told him that " He had better resort to all the stews in the town than cease worshipping of Christ in his image;"—Συμφέρει σοι μὴ καταλιπεῖν εἰς τὴν πόλιν ταύτην πορνεῖον εἰς ὃ μὴ εἰσέλθῃς, κ. τ. λ. It seems it was uncleanness that the devil tempted him unto, as well knowing that spiritual and corporeal fornication commonly go together.

Thirdly, In every *session* they instance in some particulars wherein the adoration of images which they professed did consist; as, in particular, in religious *saluting* of them, *kissing* of them, *bowing* before them, and so *adoring* of them. To this purpose their words are very express. Now all these were ever esteemed tokens, pledges, and expressions of religious or divine worship, and were the very ways whereby the heathen of old expressed their veneration of their images and idols. Job, intimating the way whereby they worshipped the sun, moon, and host of heaven,—which crime he denies himself to be guilty of,—tells us, " that when he considered the sun and the moon, his heart did not seduce him that he should put his hand to his mouth;" that is, to salute them: " For this," saith he, " had been to deny God above," Job xxxi. 26–28. As Catulus,—

> " Constiteram, exorientem auroram forte salutans,
> Quum subito a lævâ Roscius exoritur." Cic. N. D., i. 28.

He stood saluting or worshipping the rising sun. And that also was their meaning in kissing of them, or kissing their hands in saluting of them. Hos. xiii. 2, " Let them kiss the calves;" that is, worship them, express their religious adoration of them, by that outward sign. As Cicero, in Verr. vi. 43: " Herculis simulacrum non solum venerari, sed etiam osculari soliti fuerunt." So Minutius Felix tells us that his companion Cæcilius coming where the image of Serapis was set up, " admovit manum ori et osculum labris pressit,"—" put his hand to his mouth and kissed it," as worshipping of it. And for creeping, kneeling, or bowing, it is so certain an evidence of divine worship, that all worship, both false and idolatrous or true, is oftentimes expressed thereby. So the worshipping of Baal is called, " Bowing the knee to Baal." They that bowed the knee unto him or his image, in their so doing worshipped him, 1 Kings xix. 18; Rom. xi. 4. And where God promiseth to bring all nations to the worship of himself, he says, " They shall bow the knee to him," Rom. xiv. 11. So that these are all expressions of religious worship; and they are all accursed over and over by the council, who do not by these means express their worship of images. This is the doctrine, this is the practice, which the Tridentine decree approves of, and sends us to learn of the second synod of Nice. And this they express, in most places, in those very terms that were used by the Pagans in the worship of their idols; making, indeed, no distinction, but that whereas the Pagans worshipped the images of Jupiter and Minerva, and the like, they in the like manner worshipped the images of Christ and his apostles. And therefore in the Indies, the Catholic Spaniards took away the zemes, or images of their idols, that the poor natives had before, and gave them the images of Christ and his mother in their stead.

This being the doctrine of the council, it may not be amiss to consider a little how they proved and confirmed it. Two things they principally insisted on:—1. *Testimonies of Scripture;* 2. *Miracles.* Some sayings also they produced out of some ancient writers of the church, but all of them either perverted or forged. The Scriptures they insisted on were all of them gathered together in the epistle of Pope Hadrian, which was solemnly assented unto by the whole council. And they were these:—"God made man of the dust of the earth, after his own image," Gen. i. "Abel, by his own choice, offered a sacrifice unto God of the firstlings of his flock," Gen. iv. "Adam, of his own mind, called all the beasts of the field by their proper names," Gen. ii. "Noah, of his own accord, built an altar unto the Lord," Gen. viii. "Abraham, of his own free will, erected an altar to the glory of God," Gen. xii. "Jacob, having seen in his sleep the angels of God ascending and descending by the ladder, set up the stone on which his head lay for a pillar," Gen. xxviii.; and again, "He worshipped on the top of his staff," Gen. xlvii. 31. "Moses made the brazen serpent and the cherubims." Isaiah saith, "In those days there shall be an altar unto the Lord, and it shall be for a sign and a testimony," chap. xix. David the psalmist says, "Confession and beauty are before him;" and again, "Lord, I have loved the beauty of thine house;" and again, "Thy face, Lord, will I seek," Ps. xxvi.; and again, "The rich among the people shall bow themselves before thy face," Ps. xliv.; and again, "The light of thy countenance is signed or lifted up upon us," Ps. iv.[1] "Si hoc non sit testimoniorum satis, ego nescio quid sit satis." He must be very refractory, and deserve a world of anathematisms, that is not convinced by all these testimonies that images ought to be worshipped. But, "Quod non dant proceres, dabit histrio;"—"If the Scripture will not do it, miracles shall." Of these we have an endless number heaped up by the good fathers, to prove their doctrine and justify their practice. The worst is, that Tharasius almost spoils the market, by acknowledging that the images in their days would work none of the miracles they talked of, so that they had them all upon hear-say.

[1] These numerals are according to the Douay version.—ED

Act. 4, Ἀλλὰ, saith he, μήτις εἴπῃ τίνος ἕνεκεν αἱ παῤ ἡμῖν εἰκόνες οὐ θαυματουργοῦσι· πρὸς ὃν ἀποκρινούμεθα, ὅτι καθὼς ὁ ἀπόστολος εἴρηκεν, ὅτι τὰ σημεῖα τοῖς ἀπίστοις οὐ τοῖς πιστεύουσι—"But if any should say, 'Why do our images work no miracles?' to them we answer, 'Because,' as the apostle saith, 'signs are for *unbelievers*, not for *them that believe*.'" And yet the misadventure of it is, that the most of the miracles which they report and build their faith upon were wrought as by, so amongst, their chiefest believers. And what were the miracles themselves they boasted of? Such a heap of trash, such a fardel of lies, as the like were scarce ever heaped together, unless it were in the golden legend. Hadrian insists on the leprosy and cure of Constantine,—as loud a lie as any in the Talmud or Alkoran. Theodorus of Myra tells us of a deacon that "dreamed he saw one in his sleep whom he took to be St Nicholas," act. 4. Another tells us a tale of one that "struck a nail in the forehead of an image, and was troubled with a pain in his head until it was pulled out." Another dreamed "that the blessed Virgin brought Cosma and Damiana to him, and commanded them to cure him of his distemper." One man's daughter, another's wife, is helped by those images. And they all consent in the story of the image of Christ, made without hands or human help, by God alone (Θεοπετής), that he sent to Abgarus, king of the Edessenes,—as bellowing a lie as any in the herd. So true was it, that the council of Frankfort affirmed of this idolatrous conventicle, that they endeavoured to confirm their superstition by feigned wonders and old wives' tales.

1. Sir, this is the doctrine, this the confirmation of it, which we are directed unto and enjoined to embrace by your *Tridentine decree*. This is that, yea, and more also, as you will hear by-and-by, that you are bound to maintain and make good, if you intend to say any thing to the purpose about figures or images; for you must not think, by your sleight flourishes, to blind the eyes of men in these days, as you have done formerly. Own your own doctrine and practice, or renounce it. This tergiversation is shameful. And you will yet find yourself farther pressed with the doctrine of chiefest pillars of your church, and the public practice of it; for though this superstitious conventicle at Nice departed from the faith of the ancient church, and was quickly reproved and convinced of folly by persons of more learning, sobriety, and modesty than themselves, in the very age wherein they lived, yet it rose not up unto the half of the abominations in the filth and guilt whereof your church hath since rolled itself. And yet, because I presume you are well pleased with these Nicenians, who gave so great a lift to the setting up of your idols, I shall give you a brief account, both what was the judgment and practice of them that went before them in this matter, as also of some that followed after them, with joint consent detesting your folly

and superstition. You tell us somewhere in your "Fiat," that the primitive Christians had the picture or half-portraiture of Christ upon their altars. I suppose you did not invent it yourself. I wish you had told us of the legend that suggested it unto you; for you seem, in point of story, to be conversant in such learned authors as few can trace you in. If you please to have a little patience, I shall mind you of some that give us another account of things in those days.

(1.) Some there are of the first Christians who give us an account of *the whole worship of God,* with the manner and form of it which was observed in their assemblies in their days. So doth Justin Martyr in his Apologies, Tertullian in his, Origen against Celsus, with some others. Now, in none of these is there any one word concerning images, their use, or their worship in the service of God, although they descend to describe very minute particulars and circumstances of their way and proceeding.

(2.) Some there are who give an account of *the persecutions of several churches,* with the outrages of the Pagans against their assemblies, the Scriptures, all the ordinances and worship (as do those golden fragments of the first and best antiquity, the epistles of the churches of Vienne and Lyons to the parishes of Asia; of the church of Smyrna about the martyrdom of Polycarpus, preserved and recorded by Eusebius), and yet make no mention of any *figures,* pictures, or images of Christ, the blessed Virgin, or his apostles, or of any rage of their adversaries against them, or of any spite done unto them; which they would not have omitted had there been any such in use amongst them.

(3.) There are, besides these, some unquestionable remnants of the conceptions that the wisest and soberest of the heathen had concerning the Christians and their worship,—as in the epistles of Pliny about their assemblies, and the rescript of Trajan, as also in Lucian's Philopatris,[1]—in none of which is any intimation of the Nicene images or their adoration. It may be you will undervalue this consideration, because built upon testimony negatively, when it doth not follow that because such and such mentioned them not, therefore they were not then in use or being; but, sir, an argument taken from the absolute silence of all approved authors, concerning any thing of importance supposed to be or happen in their days, and who would have had just occasion to make mention of it had any such thing then been "in rerum natura," is as great an evidence, and of as full a certainty, as the monuments of times are capable of. Is it possible for any rational man to conceive, that if there had been such a use and veneration of images in the primitive churches as is now in the Roman, or that the reception and veneration of them was made the

[1] See note, vol. viii. p. 641.

"tessera" of church communion, as it is by the Nicene conventicle, that all the first writers of Christianity, treating expressly and purposely of the assemblies of the Christians, and the worship of God in them, with the manner and circumstances thereof, would have been utterly silent of them? or that those who set down and committed to record all the particularities of the Pagans' rage in scattering their assemblies, would not drop one word of any indignity showed to any of their sacred images, when they pass not by their wrath against their houses, goods, and cattle? Such things are fond to imagine.

(4.) Many of the ancients do note it as an *abomination* in some of the first heretics, that they had introduced the use of images into their worship, with the adoration of them. Theodoret. Hæret. sub. lib. i., tells us that Simon Magus gave his own image and that of Selene to be worshipped by his followers. And Irenæus, lib. i. cap. 23, that the followers of Basilides used images and invocations: and cap. 24, that the Gnostics had images, both painted ones and carved, and that of Christ, which they said was made originally by Pontius Pilate; and this they adored. And so doth Epiphanius also, tom. ii. lib. 1, Hær. 27. Carpocrates procured the images of Christ and Paul to be made, and adored them; and the like is recorded of others. Now, do you think they would have observed and reproved this practice as an abomination in the heretics, if there had been any thing in the church's usage that might give countenance thereunto? or, at least, that they would not have distinguished between that abuse of images which they condemned in the heretics and that use which was retained and approved among themselves? But they are utterly silent as unto any such matter, contenting themselves to report and reprove the superstition and idolatry of the heretics in their adoration of them. But this is not all.

(5.) They positively *deny that they had any images*, or made any use of them, and defend themselves against the charge of the Pagans against them for professing an imageless religion. Clemens Alexand., Strom. lib. vi., plainly and openly confesseth and testifieth that Christians had no images in the world; and in his Adhortat. ad Gent. he positively asserts that the arts of painting and carving, as to any religious use, were forbidden to Christians; and that in the worship of God they had no sensible image made of any sensible matter, because they worshipped God with the understanding. What was the judgment of Tertullian is known from his book, De Idololatria; from whence if we should transcribe what is argumentative against image-worship, very little would be remaining. But of all the ancients Origen doth most clearly manifest what was the doctrine and practice of the church of God in his days; as in other places, so in his seventh book against Celsus he directly handles this matter. Celsus charged the Christians that they made use of no images in the worship of God, telling them that therein they were like the Persians, Scythians, Numidians, and Seres; all which impious nations hated all images, as the Turks do at this day. To which discourse of his, Origen, returning answer, grants that the Christians had no images in their sacred worship, no more than had the barbarous nations mentioned by Celsus; but withal adds the difference that was between those and these, and tells you that their abstinence from image-worship was on various accounts. And after he hath showed wherefore those nations received them not, he adds, "That Christians and Jews abstained from all sacred use of images, because of God's command, 'Thou shalt fear' (as he reads the text) 'the Lord thy God, and him only shalt thou serve;' and, 'Thou shalt not make to thyself any graven image, nor the likeness of any thing that is in heaven above, or in the earth beneath:" and adds, that they were so far from praying to the images, as the Pagans did, that, saith he, Οὐ τιμῶμεν τὰ ἀγάλματα· (a thing expressly commanded in the Nicene conventicle);—"We do not give any honour at all to images, lest we should give countenance to the error of ignorant people, that there were somewhat of Divinity in them;" with very much more to the same purpose, expressly condemning all the use of images in the worship of God, and openly testifying that there was no such usage among the Christians in those days heard of in the world. Arnobius or Minutius Felix acknowledgeth the same: "Cruces nec colimus nec optamus;"—"We do no more worship crosses than desire them;" and grants that Christians had "nulla nota simulachra," because no image could be made to or of Him whom alone they worshipped. What was the judgment of the Eliberine council I have before told you. Lactantius, in his Institut. ad Constant., lib. ii., by a happy anticipation, answers all the arguments that you use to this day in defence of your image-worship, and concludes peremptorily, that "where there are any images, there is no religion;" showing how perverse a thing it is that the image of a dead man should be worshipped by a living image of God. The time would fail me to relate the words of Eusebius, Athanasius, Hilarius, Ambrosius, Cyrillus, Chrysostom, Epiphanius, Jerome, Austin, and others, to the same purpose. I cannot but think that it is fully evident, to any one that consults antiquity, that the image use and worship, which is become the "tessera" of your church communion, by your espousing the canons and determinations of the second Nicene synod, was in part utterly unknown unto, and in part expressly condemned by, the whole primitive church for six hundred years after Christ; and that you have plainly, by your Tridentine decree and Nicene anathematisms, cut off yourselves from the communion of the catholic church of Christ, and all particular assemblies that worship him in sincerity, for the space of some hundreds of years in the world.

Thus things went in the church of God before your Nicene convention. How did they succeed afterward? Did image-worship presently prevail upon their determinations? or was that then the faith of the generality of the church of Christ which was declared by the fathers of that convention? Nothing less. No sooner was the rumour of this horrible innovation in Christian religion spread abroad in the world but than upon it there was a full assembly of three hundred bishops of the western provinces assembled at Frankfort in Germany, wherein the superstition and folly of the Nicene assembly was laid open, their arguments confuted, their determinations rejected, and image-worship absolutely condemned as forbidden by the word of God, and contrary to the ancient, constant, known practice of the whole church of God.

And now, sir, as I said, you may begin to see what you have to do, if you intend to speak any thing to the purpose concerning your figures and images. You must take the decree of your council of Trent, and the Nicene canons therein confirmed, and prove, confirm, and vindicate them from the opposition made to them by Tertullian, Arnobius, Origen, Lactantius, the synod of Frankfort, and others of the ancients innumerable, by whom they are rejected and condemned; and yet, when you have done so, if you are able so to do, your work is not one quarter at an end. You can make nothing of this business until you have confuted or burned the Scripture itself, wherein your image-making and image-worship is as fully condemned as it is possible any superstition or idolatry should be. Your present loose discourses, whereby you endeavour to possess the minds of unwary men that you do not do that which indeed you do every day, and which almost all the world know that you do, and which you curse others for not doing, will not, with considering persons, redound at all unto your advantage.

2. That you may the better also discern what is incumbent on you, and expected from you the next time you talk of figures, I shall make bold to mind you of what is the doctrine of the chief *masters* and instructors of your church; from whence, certainly, we may better learn what the doctrine and practice of it is, than from one who discovers enough in what he says and writes to keep us from laying any great weight on his authority. Now, I confess that you do in this, as in sundry other points of your religion, give us an egregious specimen of that consent and unity among yourselves which you so frequently boast of. Raphael de Torre, in his Sum. Relig., quæst. 94, artic. 2, disput. 6, dub. 5, gives us an account of five several opinions maintained by your doctors in this matter; of all which he rejects

that only of Durand and some others, affirming that images are not worshipped properly but only improperly and abusively, as rash and savouring of heresy. The same doth Bellarmine also; and the truth is, that that opinion of Durand, Gerson, and some others, is plainly condemned by the Tridentine decree, as hath been already declared. The authors of the other four opinions, though they differ among themselves, and have several digladiations about some expressions and distinctions, framed merely in their own imaginations, agree well enough that "images are religiously to be worshipped." Worshipped religiously they ought to be; but whether "per se" and *absolutely, directly* and *ultimately*,—whether with the *same kind* of worship wherewith that is to be worshipped which they represent,—they are not so fully agreed as might be desired in a matter of this importance: for it is justly to be feared that, whilst your doctors are wrangling, your people are committing as gross idolatry as any of the heathen were guilty of. In the meantime, the most prevalent opinion of your doctors is that of Thomas and his followers, "That images are to be adored with the same kind of worship wherewith that which they represent is to be worshipped." And, therefore, whereas the Lord Christ is to be worshipped with "latria,"—that which is peculiar, in your judgment, to God alone,—"it follows," saith he, "that his image is to be worshipped with the same worship also." And as some of your learned men do boast that this indeed is the only approved opinion in this matter in your church, so the truth is, if you will speak congruously, and at any consistency with yourselves, it must be so; for whereas you lay the foundation of all your worship of them, be it of what sort it will, in that figment, that the honour which is done to the image redounds unto him whose image it is, if the honour done to the image be of an inferior sort and kind unto that which is due unto the exampler of it, by referring that honour thereunto, you debase and dishonour, it by ascribing less unto it than is its due. If, then, you intend to answer just expectation in this matter, the next time you speak of figures, pray consider what your Thomas teacheth as the doctrine of your church, 3 p. q. 25, æ. 3, which Azorius says is the constant judgment of divines, lib. ix. cap. 6; as also the exposition of the Tridentine decree by Suarez, tom. i. d. 54, sect. 4; Vasquez, Costerus, Bellarmine, and others. And,—

3. You may do well to consider the practice and usage of your *Catholic people* all the world over, especially in those places where you have preserved them from being disturbed in their devotion by the arguments and exceptions of Protestants; as also the direction that is given them for the exercise of their devotion in that prescription of rites and prayers which is afforded unto them. Is not your bowing, kneeling, creeping, kissing, offering, singing, praying to the

cross and images, notorious? yea, your placing your trust and confidence in them? yea, have you omitted any abominations of the heathen that you have not acted over again, to provoke the Lord to anger? And,—

4. Do you think to relieve them from the guilt of idolatry by a company of distinctions, which neither they nor you understand? The next time you see one of your Catholics worshipping an image upon his knees, I pray go to him and tell him that he must worship the image with "dulia" or "superdulia," but not with "latria;" or if with "latria," yet not by *itself* and *simply*, but after a sort *analogically* and *reductively*,—or that he is about a double worship, one terminated on the image, and the other passing by it unto the exemplar of it,—and you will find what thanks he will give you for your good instruction. And how small a portion are these of that mass of distinctions which you have coined, to free them from idolatry who worship images, who all the while understand not one word of what you intend by them! Nor can any rational man reduce them unto any thing intelligible.

Sir, in this matter of images you talk of coming up close to your business, and I was willing to take a little pains with you to direct you in your way, that, having a mind to your work, as you seem to pretend, you may not mistake and wander away from your duty, but address yourself unto that which you undertake, and which is expected from you. You are to prove,—1. That there is *a necessity of receiving* the use of images in the worship of the church, so that whosoever doth not admit them is to be cast out of the communion thereof; and, 2. That these images so received are to be *worshipped and adored* with religious veneration,—if not with the very same worship that is due to the persons represented by them, yet with that which redounds unto them,—and that not only by the outward gesture of the body, but the inward motions of the mind. And when you shall have proved that the doctrine and practice of your church, in this matter of making and worshipping images, is not contrary to the Scripture, or was ever received or approved by the primitive church for six hundred years, I will promise you, setting aside all other considerations, immediately to become a Papist: for the present, I see no cause so to do, and shall therefore return to consider what you here say for the farther adorning of your pictures.

The first thing you reflect upon is my censure of that passage in your "Fiat," that "the sight of images in the church is apt to cast the minds of men on that meditation of the apostle, Heb. xii., 'You are come to mount Sion, to the city of the living God, to the heavenly Jerusalem, the society of angels, and church of the first-born, written in heaven, to God the judge of all, to the spirits of just men made perfect, to Jesus the mediator of the new covenant:'"—"These, I tell you, upon the sight of a house full of images, may be the thoughts of a man distracted of his wits, not of any that are sober and wise." To which you reply, "Madmen, it seems, can tell what figures represent; sober and wise men cannot." But who told you that your images represent the things mentioned by the apostle,—for instance, "God the judge of all, the spirits of just men, angels, and the church of the first-born?" or can any man, unless he be greatly distempered in his imagination, fancy any such thing? The house of Micah, Judges xvii., was notably furnished with images of all sorts. Judges xvii., he had בֵּית אֱלֹהִים, "a house full of gods," or a chapel adorned with images; for there was in it פֶּסֶל, "a carved image," and אֵפוֹד, a "sacred ornament" for it, and תְּרָפִים, "lesser portable images," and מַסֵּכָה, a "molten statue," Judges xviii. Would it not, think you, notwithstanding the gaiety of all this provision, have been a mad thought in the Danites if, upon their entrance into this house, they had apprehended themselves to be come to the communion of the catholic church, and therein to the invisible God, to angels, and saints departed? The truth is, there is "aliquid dementiæ," a tincture of madness, in all idolatry, whence the Scripture testifies that men are "mad upon their idols;" but yet we do not find that these Danites, though resolved upon false worship, were so mad as to entertain such vain thoughts as you imagine the chapel full of images might have suggested unto them. Or do you think Ezekiel had any such thoughts when God showed him in vision the imagery of the house of Israel, with all the deities "pourtrayed on the wall," and the elders worshipping before them? Ezek. viii. God and the prophet discover other thoughts in reference unto them. Besides, sir, the Holy Ghost tells us that "a graven image is a teacher of lies," Hab. ii. 18; and how likely it is that a man should learn any truth from that whose work it is only to teach lies, I do not as yet understand.

You proceed to another exception. "'The violation of an image,' say you, 'redounds to the prototype, if it be rightly and duly represented, not else.'" To which you reply, "And when, then, for example, is Christ crucified rightly and duly represented? Are you one of those that can tell what figures represent or not?" 1. You do not rightly report my words, though you might as easily have done it as set down those you have made use of. My words were, "That the violation of an image redounds to the prototype, provided it be an image rightly and duly destined to represent him that is intended to be injured;" which is so cleared by an instance there expressed, as turns your exception out of doors as altogether useless. For, first, I require that the image be *rightly and duly destined to the representation of the prototype,*—that is, by him or by them who have power so to do, and by the express consent and will of him whose image it is, who otherwise is not concerned in it. Now, nothing of all this can you affirm concerning your images. 2. I require *an intention of doing injury* or contumely unto the person represented by the image, without which whatever is done to the image reflects not at all upon him: and so a man may break an image of a king, which he finds formed against his will, in some ugly shape, to expose him to contempt and scorn, as I suppose out of loyalty unto him, without the least violation of his honour; which is the very condition of your images and those that reject them. And this also may suffice to what you add about *hanging of traitors in effigy*, which is a particular instance of your general assertion, that the violation of an image redounds to the prototype: which we grant it doth when the image is rightly designed to that purpose, by them who have just authority so to do, and when there is an intention of casting contempt upon it; the first whereof is not found amongst your images, nor the latter among them who reject them.

Besides, if all that were granted you which you express, yet what you aim at would not ensue. For though it should be supposed that the violation of an image would redound unto the injury of the prototype, upon a mere intention of reflecting upon him, without which it is a foolish conceit to apprehend any such thing, yet it doth not thence follow that the honour done to an image redounds unto him that is represented by it, provided that the intention of them that give the honour be so to do; for besides our intention in the worship of God, we have a rule to attend unto, without the observation whereof the other will stand us in little stead. And if this might be admitted, the grossest idolatry that ever was in the world might easily be excused. That, for instance, of the Israelites setting up a golden calf, and worshipping it, must needs be esteemed excellent, seeing they thought to give honour to Jehovah thereby. When the things mentioned, then, are wanting, images may be dealt withal as false money, which his majesty causeth every day to be broken, though it have his own image and superscription upon it, because stamped without his warrant.

You proceed, and add as my words, "Where the psalmist complains of God's enemies breaking down his sculptures, he means not thereby any images or figures, but only wainscot or carved ceilings." Would you could find in your heart rightly to report my words! The reason is evident why you do not,—namely, because then you had not been able to make any pretence of a reply unto them. But yet this ought not to have prevailed with you to persist in such unhandsome dealing. My words are, "The psalmist, indeed, complains that they broke down the פִּתּוּחִים, or 'carved works,' Ps. lxxiv. 6, on the walls and ceilings of the temple" (though the Greeks render פִּתּוּחִים, τὰς θύρας αὐτῆς, "her doors," the verb signifying principally "to open"); "but that those 'apertiones' or 'incisuræ' were not pictures and images for the people to adore and venerate, or appointed for their instruction, you may learn." You see, sir, I grant that the word may denote "carved works;" and if so, I think they must be either on the walls or ceiling. That which only I deny was, that these פִּתּוּחִים, or "carved works," were proposed to the people to be adored or venerated. This you should have confuted, or held your peace. But you take another course: having misreported my words, to gain some countenance thereby unto what you had to except against them, you add, "Surely the prophet wanted a word then to express himself, or translators to express the prophet. If we must guess at his meaning without heeding his words, one might think it as probable that the house of God was adorned with sculptures of cherubims and other angels, to represent his true house that is above, as with the circles, etc. of wainscot." Sir, the prophet wanted not a word rightly to express his meaning and intention. פָּתַח is originally "aperire," to "open," and "solvere," to "loose," and because engravings are made by opening the matter engraved with incisions. It signifies also to "engrave," as 2 Chron. iii. 7, וּפִתַּח כְּרוּבִים,—"he graved cherubims" (and thence is פִּתֻּחָהּ, Zech. iii. 9, "engraving," or "work engraving"); the word here used by the psalmist expressing the effect of what is affirmed, 2 Chron. iii. 7, and elsewhere. And this is well enough expressed by sundry translators. And you speak very faintly when you talk of the guessing at the psalmist's meaning about the temple's being adorned with engraven cherubims, as though you knew not certainly that it was so, or as though it were a thing at all questionable. Sir, the text is express for it, both in the Kings, Chronicles, and Ezekiel; neither was it ever called in question. But withal, the same places inform us that there were as many palm-trees as cherubims, and those attended with flowers and pomegranates; and the cherubims in Ezekiel's vision had each one two faces,—the one of a man, the other of a young lion,—the one face looking towards "one palm-tree, the other towards another:" all which we grant were used for ornament in that wonderful and magnificent structure; but so to imagine that they were proposed to the people to adore and venerate is a little flowing, if not foaming, of the madness we lately discoursed of. That cherubims were not images I shall show you by-and-by. And I desire to be informed of you what palm-trees and flowers, or angels with two faces, one of a man, another of a lion, you think there are in heaven, that you should suppose them represented by these below? You may easily discern how well you have evinced the conclusion manifested before, to expect some proof at your hands, by faintly intimating that the walls of the temple were engraven with cherubims, palm-trees, and flowers, and therefore, doubtless, he that will not worship images deserves to be anathematized.

You add nextly, as my words, "The eye may not have her species as well as the ear; because God hath commanded the one and not the other." You know full well that you do not express my words nor meaning as you ought. But I shall now cease to expect better dealing from you, and make the best that I may of what you are pleased to set down. Speaking in general, I do not nor did deny that the eye might have its use, and the species of it, to help and further our faith and devotion in the worship of God,—it hath so in the sacraments by him instituted: but I tell you it can have no use to these ends in things which God hath forbidden, as he hath done the making of images for religious adoration. But you say, "'Fiat Lux' makes it appear that God commands both, and the nature of man requireth both; nor can I give any reason why I may not look upon him who was crucified, as well as hear him." Pray, sir, talk not of "Fiat Lux" making it appear; the design of "Fiat Lux" is rather to *hide* than to make any thing *appear*. And you might have done well to direct us unto that place in your "Fiat" where you fancied that you had made it appear that God commands that use of images in his worship which you plead for; and as for what the nature of man requireth, we suppose God knows as well at least as the pope, and is as careful to make suitable provision for its relief and help in the duties he calls us to the performance of. And it is an easy thing to give you a reason why you may not look on him that was crucified (that is, with your bodily eyes), as well as hear him by the preaching of the word; and it is because you cannot. You yourself tell us, when you think it for your purpose, that "Christ as to his human nature is now invisible;" and that is it I think you intend. Now, how you will look with your bodily eyes on that which unto you and us is at present invisible, I cannot understand. I know that one of the great fathers of your second Nicene faith publicly affirmed in the council, with the approbation of his associates, that Christ is so present with or related unto his image, that he that should speak of it and should say, "This is Christ," should not err. But I know also he did it with as much wisdom as he whom the prophet derides for carving a stock into the likeness of a man, and then saying unto it, "Thou art my god." So, sir, you *may not* with your *bodily eyes* look on him that was crucified, because you cannot; and as looking on the *picture* of him which, you mean, is nothing of that which we contend about, so I fear it is unto you only a means of taking you from looking after his *person* in a way of *believing*, which he so earnestly calls us unto.

Your next progress is to some words of mine about *the end of preaching*, which you set down: "Nor is the sole end of preaching, as 'Fiat Lux' would have it, only to move the mind of hearers unto corresponding affections;" whereas, indeed, they are, "He is mistaken if he think the sole end of preaching the cross and death of Christ is to work out such representations to the mind as oratory may effect for the moving of corresponding affections;"—which if you know not to differ very much from what you have expressed, I wish you would let these matters alone, and talk of what you understand. However, your reply unto what you are pleased to express is such a piece of ridiculous scurrility as I shall not stain paper with a recital of. In sum, you deny there is any other end of preaching, and excuse yourself that you thought not of those other ends which you suppose I might have in my heart, but yet conceal; and then instance in such a rabblement of foolish, wicked fancies as I wonder how your thoughts came to be conversant about. As to the thing itself, I must tell you, sir, whether you are willing to hear it or no, that if you know no other end of preaching the cross and death of Christ but merely to work upon the minds of men so as to stir up their affections, you are a person better skilled in the mass-book than the gospel, and much fitter to be employed in sacrificing according to the order of that than in preaching of the mystery and doctrine of this. Did never any man inform you that one end of preaching the word was to *regenerate the whole souls* of men, and to beget them anew unto God? that it was also to open their eyes, and to illuminate them with the saving knowledge of God in Christ? that it was to beget and increase faith in them? that it was to be a means of their growth in grace, and in the knowledge of God? that the word preached is "profitable for reproof, correction, doctrine, and instruction in righteousness?" that it is appointed as the great means of working the souls of men into a likeness and conformity unto the Lord Jesus, or the changing of them into his image? that it is appointed for the refreshment of the weary, and consolation of the sorrowful, and making wise of the simple? Did you never hear that the word preached hath its effect upon the understanding and will as well as upon the affections, and upon these consequentially only unto its efficacy on them, if they are not deluded? Is growth in knowledge, faith, grace, holiness, conformity unto Christ, communion with God,—for which end the word is commanded to be preached,—nothing at all with you? Is being made wise in the mystery of the love of God in Christ, to have an insight into, and some understanding of, the unsearchable treasures of his grace, and by all this the building up of souls in their most holy faith, of no value with you? Are you a stranger unto these things, and yet think yourself a meet person to persuade your countrymen to forsake the religion they have long professed, and to follow you they know not whither? or do you know them, and yet dare to thrust in your scurrility to their exclusion? Plainly, sir, the most charitable judgment that I can make of this discourse of yours is, that it proceeds from ignorance of the most important truths and most necessary works of the gospel.

You next proceed to your plea from the *cherubims* set up by Moses in the holy place over the ark; and thence you will needs wrest an argument for your images and the worship of them, although your Vasquez is ashamed of it, and hath cashiered it long ago, and that worthily, as not at all belonging unto this matter. For,—1. The cherubims were not *images;* to which you say, " Since the real cherubims are not made of beaten gold, those set up by Moses must be only figures." But it is of images that we are speaking precisely, and not in general of figures. Figures may include types and hieroglyphics, and any representation of things: images represent persons,—and such alone are those about which we treat; and if a person be not represented by an image, it is not his image. Now, I pray, tell me what personal subsistences these cherubims, with their various wings and faces, did represent? Do you believe that they give you the shape and likeness of angels? It is true, John the bishop of Thessalonica, in your synod of Nice, with the approbation of the rest of his company, affirms that it was the opinion of the catholic church that angels and archangels were not altogether " incorporeal and invisible, but to have a slender body of air or fire," act. 5. But are you of the same mind? or do you not rather think that the catholic church was belied and abused by the synod? And if they are absolutely incorporeal and invisible, how can an image be made of them? Should a man look on the cherubims as images of angels, would not the first thing they would teach him be a lie,—namely, that angels are like unto them; which is the first language of any image whatever? The truth is, the Mosaical cherubims were mere hieroglyphics, to represent the constant tender love and watchfulness of God over the ark of his covenant and the people that kept it, and had nothing of the nature of images in them. 2. I say, suppose of them what you please, yet they were not set up to be *adored,* as your images are. To which you reply, " It is not to my purpose or yours that they were not set up to be adored; for images in Catholic churches are not set up for any such purpose, nor do I anywhere say so. No man alive hath any such thought; no tradition, no council, hath delivered it; no practice infers it." And do you think meet to talk at this rate? Have you no tradition amongst you that you plead for the adoration of images? hath no council amongst you determined it? doth not your practice speak it? Were you awake when you wrote these things? Did you never read your Tridentine decrees, or the Nicene canons commended by them? is not the adoration of images asserted a hundred times expressly in it? Hath no man alive such thoughts? Are not only Thomas and Bonaventure, but Bellarmine, Gregory de Valentia, Baronius, Suarez, Vasquez, Azorius, with all the rest of your great champions, now utterly defeated, and have not one man left to be of their judgment? I would be glad to hear more of this matter. Speak plainly. Do you renounce all adoration and worship of images? is that the doctrine of your church? Prove it so, and I shall publicly acknowledge myself to have been a long time in a very great mistake. But it was for this cause that I gave you a little image of the doctrine and practice of your church in this matter, at the entrance of our discourse, foreseeing how you would prevaricate in our progress. Come, sir, if image-worship be such a shameful thing that you dare not avow it, deal ingenuously, and acknowledge the failings of your church in this matter, and labour to bring her to amendment. If you think otherwise, and, in truth, yet like it well enough, deal like a man, and dare to defend it at least as well as you can; and more no man can look for at your hands. You mention somewhat of the different opinions of your schoolmen in this matter; which you slight. But, sir, I tell you again, that you and all your masters are agreed that images are to be adored and venerated,—that is, worshipped; and their disputes about that honour that rests absolutely on the image, and that which passeth on to the prototype, with the kind of the one and the other, are such as neither themselves nor any other do understand. You tell us, indeed, "All catholic councils and practice declare such sacred figures to be expedient assistants to our thoughts in our divine meditations and prayers; and that is all you know of it." But if you intend councils and practice truly catholic or primitive, you can give no instance of allowing so much to images as here you ascribe unto them; no, not one council can you produce to that purpose for some hundreds of years, but a constant current of testimonies for the rejection of such pretended expediencies and assistances, the first beginning of their use arising from heathens, as Eusebius declares, lib. vii. cap. 18. But if you intend your Roman Catholic councils and practice, your assertion is as devoid of truth as any thing you can possibly utter. What kind of assistance in devotion these your sacred figures do yield, we shall anon consider.

It is added in the "Animadversions," "That it was God who appointed these cherubims to be made, and placed where they were never seen of the people: and that his special dispensation of a law constitutes no general rule; so he commanded his people to spoil the Egyptians, though he forbid all men to steal." This was said on supposition that they were images, or adored, both which I showed to be false; and it is the answer given by Tertullian, when he was pleading against all making up of pictures, which we do not. Now, do you produce God's special command for the making, use, and veneration of your images, and this contest will soon be at an end. But whereas God, who commanded these cherubims to be made, hath severely interdicted the making of images, as to any use in his worship unto us, what conclusion you can hence draw I see not. To this you reply in a large discourse, wherein are many things *atheological.* I shall briefly pass through what you say. Thus, then, you begin: "We must know, you as well as I, that God, who forbids men to steal, did not then command to steal, as you say he did, when he bade his people spoil the Egyptians under the species of a loan." "Malum omen!" You stumble at the threshold. Did I say that God "commanded men to steal?" "Porrige frontem." The words of the "Animadversions" lay before you when you wrote this, and you could not but know that you wrote that which was not true. This immorality doth not become any man, of what religion soever he be. Stealing denotes the pravity of taking that which is another man's. This God neither doth nor can command; for the taking of that which formerly belonged to another is not stealing if God command it, for the reason which yourself have stumbled on, as we shall see afterward. The Egyptians were spoiled by God's command, but the people did not steal: for his command, who is the sovereign Lord of all things, the great possessor of heaven and earth, dispensed with his law of one man's taking that which before belonged unto another, as to that particular whereunto his command extended, in reference whereunto stealing, or the pravity of that act of alienation, consists; and so it is in other cases. It is murder for a father to slay his son; neither can God command a man to murder his son: and yet he commanded Abraham to slay his. To so little purpose is your following attempt to prove that the Hebrews did not steal, and that God did not command them to steal; which you fancied, or rather feigned, to be asserted in the "Animadversions," that you might make a pretence of saying something: so that it had been much better to have passed over this whole matter with your wonted silence, which relieves you against the things which you despair of returning a reply unto. You say, "The Hebrews might have right to those few goods they took in satisfaction for their long oppression, and it may be their own allowance was not paid them." But this right, whatever it may be pretended, was only "ad rem," a general equity, which they had no warrant to put in execution by any particular instance; and therefore you add, secondly, "Because it is a thing of danger that any servant should be allowed to right himself by putting his hand to his master's goods, though his case of wrong be never so clear, therefore did the command of God intervene to justify their action." But why do you call this "a thing of danger" only? is it not of more than *danger*, even expressly *sinful?* Then is a thing morally dangerous, when there *may* be sin in it, not when unavoidably there *is;* then, indeed, there is danger of punishment, or rather certainty of it, without repentance; but we do not say then there is danger of sinning. It may be you do it to comply with your casuists, who have determined that in some cases it is lawful for a servant himself to make up his wrongs out of his master's goods; which caused your friends some trouble, as you know in the case of John de Alva.[1] You proceed, and insist upon the command of God, proceeding from his sovereignty and lordship over all, warranting the Hebrews to take the Egyptians' goods, and so spoil them; and that rightly. "But this," say you, "can no way be applied unto images; nor could God command the Hebrews to make any images if he had absolutely forbidden to have any at all made." Sir, this is not our case. God forbade the Hebrews to make any images, so as to bow down to them in a way of religious worship, and yet might command them to make hieroglyphical representations of his care and watchfulness, and to set them up where they might not be worshipped. But let us suppose that you speak "ad idem," and pertinently; let us see how you prove what you say. "For this," say you, "concerns not any affair between neighbour and neighbour, whereof the supreme Lord hath absolute dominion, but the service only and adoration due from man to his Maker; which God, being absolutely good and immutably true, cannot alter or dispense with. Nor doth it stand with his nature and deity to change, dispense, or vary the first table of his law concerning himself, as he may the second, which concerns neighbours, for want of that dominion over himself which he hath over any creature, to take away its right, to preserve or destroy it, as himself pleaseth; and therefore you conclude, that if God had commanded his people to set up no images, he could not have commanded them to set up any, because this would imply a contra-

[1] John de Alva was a servant in the Jesuit College of Clermont, who pilfered from his masters, and, on his examination before the civil court, quoted in his defence the maxim of a Jesuit, Father Bauny, who held it lawful for a servant to purloin from his master, if the theft were simply to make amends for any insufficiency in his wages. The story is humorously given in the "Provincial Letters," (Let. VI.) There is a singular parallel to be found in the history of another Alva, famous for his atrocities in the Low Countries. When he was recalled from the disgrace which he had incurred for them, to reduce Portugal under the Spanish crown, he seized an immense treasure at Lisbon, and refused to give any account of it, holding it as the reward due to him for his services, and compensation for his four years' disgrace and imprisonment. "If the king," said he, "ask me for an account, I will make him a statement of kingdoms preserved and conquered, of signal victories, of successful sieges, and of sixty years' service." No farther inquiries were made.—ED.

diction in himself." A very profound theological discourse, which might become one of the *angelical* or *seraphical* doctors of your church! But who, I pray, told you that there was the same reason of *all the commands* of the first table? Vows and oaths are a part of the worship of God prescribed in the third commandment; yet, whatever God can do, your pope takes upon himself to dispense with them every day. He so dispensed with the oath of Ladislaus, king of Hungary, made in his peace with the Turks, to the extreme danger of his whole kingdom, the irreparable loss and almost ruin of all Christendom. So he dispensed with the oath of Henry II. of France, which ended in his expulsion out of Italy, his loss of the famous battle of St Quentin, and the danger of his whole kingdom. The strict observation of the Sabbath by the Jews was commanded unto them in a precept of the first table, and was not a matter between neighbours, but belonged immediately to the worship of God himself: according to your divinity, God could not dispense with them to do any labour that day; but our Lord Jesus Christ hath taught us, that by his command the priests were to labour on that day in killing the sacrifices, by virtue of an after-exception. And your book of Maccabees will inform you that the whole people judged themselves dispensed withal in case of imminent danger. The whole fabric of Mosaical worship was a thing that belonged immediately to God himself, and was not a matter between neighbours, which had its foundation in the second commandment; and yet I suppose you will grant that God hath altered it, changed it, and taken it away. So excellent is your rule as to all the precepts of the first table, which indeed holds only in the first command! Things that naturally and necessarily belong to the dependence of the rational creature on God, as the first cause, last end, and supreme Lord of all, are absolutely indispensable; which are in general all comprised, as to their nature, in the first precept, wherein we are commanded to receive him alone as our God, and consequently to yield him that obedience of faith, love, honour, which is due to him as God: but the outward modes and ways of expressing and testifying that subjection and obedience which we owe unto him, depending on his arbitrary institution, are changeable, dispensable, and liable to be varied at his pleasure; which they were at several seasons, before the last hand was put to the revelation of his will by his Son. And then, though God did absolutely forbid his people the making of images, as to any use of them in his worship and service, he might, by particular exception, have made some himself, or appointed them to be made, and have designed them to what use he pleased; from whence it would not follow in the least, that they who were to regulate their obedience by his command, and not by that instance of his own particular exception unto his institution, might set up any other images for the same end and purpose, no more than they might set up other altars for sacrifice besides that appointed by him, when he had commanded that they should not do so. Supposing, then, that which is not true, and which you can give no colour of proof to, namely, that the "cherubims were images properly so called," and set up by God's command to be adored, yet they were no less still under the force of his prohibition against the making of images, than if he had never appointed any to be made at all. It was no more free for them to do so than it is for you now, under the New Testament, to make five sacraments more, of your own heads, because he hath appointed *two*. So unhappy are you in the confirmation of your own supposition, which yet, as I have showed you, is by no means to be granted. And this is the substance of your plea for this practice and usage of your church; which, whether it will justify you in your *open transgression* of so many express commands that lie against you in this matter, the day that shall discover all things will manifest.

You proceed to the vindication of another passage in your "Fiat," from the animadversions upon it, with as little success as the former you have attempted. "'Fiat Lux' says, 'God forbade foreign images, such as Moloch, Dagon, and Ashtaroth, but he commanded his own'" (sir, Moloch and Ashtaroth were not images properly so called, whatever may be said of Dagon,—the one was the sun, the other the host of heaven, or the moon and stars); "but the 'Animadversions' say, 'that God forbade any likeness of himself to be made.'" They do so, and what say you to the contrary? Why, "You may know and consider that the statues and graven images of the heathen, towards whose land Israel, then in the wilderness, was journeying, were ever made by the Pagans to represent God, and not any devils, although they were deluded in it." But,—1. Your good friends will give you little thanks for this concession, whose strongest plea to vindicate themselves and you from idolatry in your image-worship is, that the images of the heathen were not made to represent God, but that an idol was really and absolutely nothing. 2. God did not forbid the people in particular the making images unto Moloch, Dagon, or Ashtaroth, but prohibits the worshipping of the idols themselves in any way; but he forbids the making of any images and similitudes of himself in the first place, and of all other things, to worship them. But what of all this? "Why then," say you, "there was good reason that the Hebrews, who should be cautioned from such snares, should be forbidden to make to themselves any similitude or likeness of God." Well, then, they were so forbidden; this is that which the "Animadversions" affirmed before, and "Fiat Lux" denied, affirming that they were the "ugly faces of Moloch" that were forbidden. "Moses," say you, p. 294, "forbade profane and foreign images, but he commanded his own;" but here you grant that God forbade the making of any similitude or likeness of himself,—the reason of it we shall not much dispute whilst the thing is confessed, though I must inform you that himself insists upon another, and not that which you suggest, which you will find if you will but peruse the places I formerly directed you unto. But say you, "What figure or similitude the true God hath allowed his people, that let them hold and use until the fulness of time should come, when the figure of his substance, the splendour of his glory, and only image of his nature, should appear; and now, since God hath been pleased to show us his face, pray give Christians leave to keep and honour it." I presume you know not that your discourse is sophistical and atheological, and I shall therefore give you a little light into your mistakes:—1. What do you mean by "figure or similitude" that the true God had allowed his people? Was it any figure or similitude of himself, not of Moloch, which you were speaking of immediately before, and which your following words interpret your meaning of, where you affirm that in the "fulness of time" he hath given us the "image of himself?" have you not denied it in the words last mentioned? Have you no regard how you jumble contradictions together, so you may make a show of saying something? Do you intend any other likeness or similitude? why then do you deal sophistically in using the same expression to denote diverse things? 2. It is atheological, that you affirm Christ to be the "image of the nature of God." He is, and is said to be, the "image of his Father's person," Heb. i. 3. And when he is said to be the "image of the invisible God," the term God is to be taken ὑποστατικῶς for the person of the Father, and not οὐσιωδῶς for the nature, or substance, or essence of God. 3. Christ is the *essential image* of the Father in his divine nature, inasmuch as he is partaker with him of all the same divine properties and excellencies, and morally in his whole person God and man, as mediator, in that the love, grace, will, and wisdom of the Father are in him fully represented unto us, and not in the outward lineaments of his human nature, Isa. lii. liii. And what is all this to your images that give us the shape and form of a man, and of what individual person neither you nor we know? 4. And is it not a fine business, to talk of seeing the "face of God," which shone forth in Christ, in a carved image, or a painted figure? Is not this to confess plainly that your images are teachers of lies? 5. Your *logic* is like your divinity. Inartificial argument or testimony you use none in this place, and I desire you would draw your discourse into a syllogism: "'Christ is the brightness of the glory of God; God shows us his face in him:' therefore we ought to make images of wood and stone, carved and painted, and set them up in churches to be adored." Ὅπερ ἔδει δεῖξαι; And hereby you may also discern what is to be judged of your defence of what you had affirmed in your "Fiat,"—namely, "That we had a command that we should have images, and a command that we should not have images;" which I never imagined that you would put upon a various lection of the text, and thought it sufficient to manifest your failing to intimate unto you the express preciseness of the prohibition, with which your fancied command for images is wholly inconsistent. God hath strictly forbidden us to make any image, either of himself or of any other person or thing, to adore or worship it, or to put it unto use purely religious: this is an everlasting rule of our obedience. His "own making of cherubims," and placing them in the most holy place, whilst the Judaical economy continued, gives us no dispensation as to the obedience which we owe to that command and rule whereby we must be judged at the last day.

Your last exception is laid against what I affirmed concerning the *relation* you fancy between the *image* and its *prototype*, whereby you would excuse the honour and worship which you give unto it, which I said is a *mere effect of your own imagination.* To which you reply, that, "speaking of a formal representation or relation, and not of the efficient cause of it, you cannot but wonder at this illogical assertion." But, sir, this your "formal representation or relation," which you fancy, must have an efficient cause, and hath so,—a real one if it be real, an imaginary one if it be fictitious,—and this I inquired after; and I think it is not illogical to affirm that the relation you pretend is fictitious, because it hath no cause but your own imagination, on which alone it depends. A divine institution constituting such a relation you have none, nor doth it ensue on the nature of the thing itself; for the carving of a stock into the likeness of a man gives it no such relation to this or that individual man, as that which is done unto the one should have any respect unto the other. But you add, "Is the picture made by the spectator's imagination to represent this or that thing, or the imagination rather guided to it by the picture? By this rule of yours, the image of Cæsar, did not my imagination help it, would no more represent a man than a mouse." But you quite mistake the matter. The relation you fancy includes two things:—First, that this image represents not a man in general, but this or that individual man in particular, and that exclusively to all others; for instance, Simon Peter, and not Simon Magus, who was a man no less than he or any other man whatever. Now, though herein the imagination may be assisted when it hath any certain grounds of discerning a particular likeness in an image unto one man when he was living more than to another, yet you in most of your images are destitute of any such assistance. You know not at all that your images represent any thing peculiar in the persons whereof you pretend them to be the images; which sufficiently appears by the variety that is in the images whereby you represent the same person, even Christ himself, in several places: so that though every man in his right wits may conceive that an image is the image of a man and not of a mouse, yet that it should be the image of this or that man, of Christ himself or Peter, he hath no ground to imagine but what is suggested unto him by his imagination, directed by the circumstances of its place and title. When Clodius had thrust Cicero into banishment, to do him the greater spite he demolished his house, and dedicated it as a devoted place to their gods, setting up in it the image of the goddess Libertas. The orator, upon his return, in his Oration ad Pontifices for the recovery of his house, to overthrow this pretended dedication and devotion of it, pleads two things:—First, that the image pretended by Clodius to be the image of Libertas was indeed the image of a famous or rather infamous whore that lived at Tanager. Had this dedication passed, I wonder how this image could have had any relation unto Libertas but by virtue of the imagination of its worshippers, when in very deed it was the image of a Tangræan whore. And the same orator tells us of a famous painter, who, making the picture of Venus and her companions for their temples, still drew them by some strumpet or other that he kept company withal. And whether you have not been so imposed upon sometimes or no I very much question; in which case nothing but your imagination can free you from the worship of a quean when you aim your devotion another way. Again: he pleads that the dedication of that image was not regularly religious, nor according to that institution which they esteemed divine; whence no sacredness in it could ensue. And want of institution which may be so esteemed is that also which we object against your dedication of images; for, besides a relation to this or that individual person,—which, as I have showed, the most of your images have not, but what in your fancy you give unto them, which is natural or civil,—you fancy also a religious relation, a sacred conjunction, between the image and prototype, so that the worship yielded to the one should redound to the other in a religious way. And this, I say, is also the product of your own fancy. If it be not, I pray, will you assign some other cause of it? for, to tell you the truth, excluding divine institution, which you have not, other I can think of none. And if you could pretend divine institution constituting a sacred relation between images and their prototypes, yet it would not presently follow that they were to be worshipped, no, not supposing the prototypes themselves to be the proper objects of religious adoration, which as to the most of them you know we deny, unless you have also a command to warrant you:

for there is, by the institution of God himself, a *sacramental relation* between the water in baptism and the blood of Christ; and yet I do not know that you plead that the water is to be worshipped. And thus is it as to your wooden cross: you put two sticks across, and worship them; you take them asunder, and burn them. It is the very instance of your Nicene council, for so they repeat the words of Leontius, and approve them, act. 4: Ἕως μὲν ἐστι συμπεπεδημένα τὰ δύω ξύλα τοῦ σταυροῦ προσκυνῶ τὸν τύπον διὰ Χρίστὸν τὸν ἐν αὐτῷ σταυρωθέντα, ἐπὰν δὲ διαιρεθῶσιν ἐξ ἀλλήλων ῥίπτω αὐτὰ καὶ κατακαίω·—"Whilst the two sticks of the cross are put together or compacted, I adore that figure for Christ's sake, who suffered thereon; but when they are separated, I cast them away and burn them." A pretty course, whereby a man may keep a sacred fire, and worship all his wood-pile before he burns it! And all this you are beholding unto your imagination for.

We have done with your exceptions and pleas; and I dare leave it to the conscience and judgment of any man fearing God, and not captivated under the power of prejudices and a vain conversation received by tradition from his fathers, whether your pretences are sufficient to warrant us to break in upon those many and severe interdictions of God, lying expressly in the letter against this usage and practice, and so apprehended in their intention by the whole primitive church. In the command itself, we are forbidden to make to ourselves,—that is, in reference unto the worship of God treated of in that precept,—not only פֶּסֶל, γλυπτόν, "sculptile," a "graven image," but also כָּל־תְּמוּנָה, πᾶν ὁμοίωμα, "any kind of likeness" of any thing in heaven, earth, or sea; so as that a man should הִשְׁתַּחוֹת, προσκυνεῖν, "bow down," adore, or venerate them, or עָבוֹד, δουλεύειν, "serve them" with any sacred veneration. And the natural equity of this precept was understood by the wisest of the heathen; for not only doth Tacitus witness that the ancient Germans had no images of their gods, but it is known that Numa Pompilius, the Roman Solon, admitted not the use of them. Seneca decries them, Epist. 33; and Macrobius denies that antiquity made any image to the most high God. What Silius, Persius, and Statius observed to the same purpose, I have showed elsewhere. And from this principle Paul pleads with the Athenians that the τὸ Θεῖον was not to be represented with images of gold and silver or carved stones. Neither doth God leave us under this interdiction as proceeding from his sovereign authority, but frequently also shows the *reasonableness* of his will by asserting the *incomprehensibility* of his nature, and minding us that, in the great manifestation of his glory unto the people, they saw no manner of likeness or similitude; which should have been showed unto them had he been by any sensible means or matter to be represented.

And yet, sir, all this will not deter you from making images, and various pictures of God himself and the blessed Trinity. Indeed, you say you do not do it to represent the essence and nature of the invisible God, but only some *divine manifestations of his excellency or presence;* so that those images are only metaphorical. But you venture too boldly on the commands of God with your *cobweb distinctions;* nor do you difference yourselves hereby from the more sober heathen, who openly professed that in their many names and images of God they had no design to teach a multiplication of the divine essence, but only to represent the various properties and excellencies of that one Deity which they adored, as Lactantius will inform you. Neither, I fear, do you consider aright, or sufficiently esteem, the scandal that by this means you cast before the Jews and Turks, who abhor the worship of God amongst you upon the account of your images; and Christians also kept from participating in their "sacra" by this means. Lampridius tells us, in the Life of Alexander Severus, that Hadrian the emperor erected temples in sundry cities without images in them, until he was forbidden by the soothsayers, affirming that this was the only way to make all men become Christians; as though the weight of the controversy between Christians and Pagans had turned on this hinge, whether God were to be worshipped in images or no? As for other images and pictures, which may as to a civil use be made, which you set up in your churches to be adored and venerated, is not your doctrine and practice a mere ἐθελοθρησκεία, "a will-worship," condemned by the apostle, Col. ii. 23, —a worship destitute of institution, promise, command, or any ground of acceptance with God; a worship wherein you do what is right in your own eyes, like the people in the wilderness, and not that only which is commanded you, which God complains of and reproves, Deut. xii. 8, 28? And, besides, you are conversant in a will-worship of a most dangerous importance, wherein you ascribe the honour that is due unto God alone unto that which by nature is not God; which is downright idolatry. I know how you turn and wind yourselves into various forms, and multiply unintelligible distinctions to extricate yourselves out of the snare that you wilfully cast yourselves into: but you all agree well enough in this, if your Nicene and Trent councils, your Baronius, Vasquez, Suarez, and other great masters of your "sacra" may be believed, that they are to be adored and worshipped,—that is, with adoration religious; which, whatever you may talk of its modes, or distinguish about its kind, is to give the honour due to God alone unto stocks and stones. And the best security you have to free you from the horrible guilt of idolatry lies in the pretended conjunction and religious relation that is between the image and its prototype; which is plainly imaginary and fictitious. And now, sir, I hope I shall obtain your excuse for having drawn forth this discourse unto a length beyond my intention, yourself having given me the occasion so to do, by pretending that you would, upon this head of images, *come up close unto me;* which caused me to give you a little taste of what entertainment you are to expect if you shall think meet to continue in the same resolution.

CHAPTER XXII.

Of Latin service.

THE 17th chapter of the "Animadversions," about tongues and Latin service, is your next task. Of this you say, that "it hath some colour of plausibility; but because I neither do nor will understand the customs of that church which I am so eager to oppose, all my words are but wind." *Ans.* No such thing as "plausibility" was aimed at in any part of that discourse. It was the promotion or defence of truth which was designed throughout the whole, and nothing else: for that are all things to be done, and nothing against it. What you are able to except against in that discourse will speedily appear. In the meantime, pray take notice that I have no eagerness to oppose either you or your church; so you will let the truth alone, I shall for ever let you alone, without opposition. It was the defence of *that*, and not an opposition to *you*, that I was engaged in. In the same design do I still persist, in the vindication of what I had formerly written, and shall assure you that you shall never be opposed by me, but only so far and wherein I am fully convinced that you oppose the truth. Manifest that to be on your side, and I shall be ready to embrace both you and it; for I am absolutely free from all respects unto things in this world that should or might retard me in so doing. But that I may hereafter speak somewhat more to the purpose in opposition unto you, or else give my consent with understanding unto what you teach, pray inform me how I may come to the knowledge of the customs of your church, which, you say, "I neither do nor will understand." I have read your councils, those that are properly yours; your mass-book and rituals; many of your annalists or historians; with your writers of controversies and casuists: all of the best note, fame, and reputation amongst you. Can none of them inform us what the customs of your church are? If you have such Egyptian or Eleusinian mysteries as no man can understand before he be initiated amongst you, I must despair of coming unto any acquaintance with them; for I shall never engage into the belief of *I know not what.* For the present, I shall declare you my apprehension as to that custom of your church, as you call it, which we have now under consideration, and desire your charity in my direction if I understand it not aright. It is your custom to keep the Scriptures from the people in an unknown tongue. Somewhat contrary to this your former custom, in this last age you have made some *translations* out of a *translation*, and that none of the best: the use whereof you permit to very few, by virtue of special dispensation; pleading that the use of it in the church, among the body of its members, is useless and dangerous. Again: it is the custom of your church to celebrate all its public worship in Latin, whereof the generality of your people understand nothing at all; and you forbid the exercise of your church-worship in a vulgar tongue, understood by the community of your church or people. These I apprehend to be the customs of your church; and, to the best of my understanding, they are directly contrary,—1. To the *end of God* in granting unto his church the inestimable benefit of his word and worship; and, 2. To the *command of God*, given unto all, to read, meditate, and study his word continually; and, 3. *Prejudicial to the souls of men*, in depriving them of those unspeakable spiritual advantages which they might attain in the discharge of their duty, and which others, not subject unto your authority, have experience of; and, 4. *Opposite unto, yea, destructive of, that edification* which is the immediate end of all things done or to be done in public assemblies of the church; and, 5. *Forbidden expressly* by the apostle, who enforceth his prohibition with many cogent reasons, 1 Cor. xiv.; and, 6. *Contrary to the express practice* of the primitive church, both Judaical and Christian, all whose worship was performed in the same language wherein the people were instructed by preaching and exhortations,—which I presume you will think it necessary they should well understand; being, 7. *Brought into use gradually and occasionally*, through the stupendous negligence of some who presided in the churches of those days, when the languages wherein the Scripture was first written, and whereinto, for the use of the whole church, it had been of old translated,—as the Old Testament into Greek, and the whole into Latin,—through the tumults and wars that fell out in the world, became corrupted, or were extirpated; and, 8. *A means of turning the worship of Christ*, from a rational way of strengthening faith and increasing holiness, into a dumb *histrionical* show, exciting brutish and irregular affections; and, 9. Were the great *cause of that darkness and ignorance* which spread itself in former days over the whole face of your church, and yet continueth in a great measure so to do; and, in sum, are as great an instance of the power of inveterate prejudices and carnal interests against the light of the truth as I think was ever given in the world.

These are my apprehensions concerning the customs of your church in this matter, with their nature and tendency. I shall now try whether you, who blame my misunderstanding of them, can give me any better information, or reason for the change of my thoughts concerning them. But "carbones pro thesauro;" instead of either farther clearing or vindicating your customs and practice, you fall into encomiums of your church, a story of a Greek bishop, with some other thing as little to your purpose.

> "Fur es, ait Pedio. Pedius quid? crimina rasis
> Librat in antithetis. Doctas posuisse figuras
> Laudatur." Pers. i. 85.

You are accused to have robbed the church of the use of the Scripture, and the means of its edification in the worship of God; and when you should produce your defensative, you make a fine discourse quite to other purposes. Such as it is, we must pass through it.

First, you say, "I have heard many grave Protestant divines ingenuously acknowledge that divine comfort and sanctity of life requisite unto salvation, which religion aims at, may with more perfection and less inconvenience be attained by the customs of the Roman church than that of ours. For religion is not to sit perching upon the lips, but to be got by heart; it consists not in reading, but doing: and in this, not in that, lives the substance of it; which is soon and easily conveyed. Christ our Lord drew a compendium of all divine truths in two words; which our great apostle again abridged into one." *Ans.* First, I hope you will give me leave a little to suspend my assent unto what you affirm;—not that I question your *veracity* as to the matter of fact related by you, that some persons have told you what you say, but I suppose you are mistaken in them; for whereas the gospel is the doctrine of truth according unto godliness, and the promotion of holiness and consolation (which cannot at all be promoted but in ways and by means of God's appointment) is the next end of all religion, they can be no Protestant divines who acknowledge this end to be better attainable in your way than their own, because such an acknowledgment would be a virtual renunciation of their Protestancy. The judgment of this church, and all the real grave divines of it, is perfectly against you; and, should you condescend unto them in other things, [they] would not embrace your communion whilst you impose upon them a necessity of celebrating the worship of God in a tongue unknown unto them amongst whom and for whose sake it is publicly celebrated. The reasons you subjoin to the concession you mention I presume are your own; they are like to many others that you make use of. The best sense of the entrance of your words that I can make is in that description they afford us of the worship of your church, as to the people's concernment in it. The words of it may sit *perching upon your lips*, as on the tongue of a parrot, or, it may be, may be *got by heart*, or as we say, without book, when the sense of them affects not your minds nor understandings at all. If in these vain, loose expressions you design any thing else, it seems to be an opposition between reading and studying the Scriptures, or joining with understanding in the prayers of the church,—the things under consideration,—and the getting of the power of the word of God to dwell in the heart; which is skilfully to oppose the means and the end, and those placed in that relation not only by their natural aptitude, but also by God's express appointment and command. So wisely, also, do you oppose *reading* and *doing* in general, as though *reading* were not *doing*, and a part of that obedience which God requires at our hands, and a blessed means of helping and furthering us in the remainder of it; for certainly that we may do the will of God, it is required that we know it. And what better way there is to come to the knowledge of the will of God, than by reading and meditating in and upon the word of truth wherein he hath revealed it, with the advantage of the other means of his appointment for the same end, in the public preaching or proposition of it, I am not as yet informed. And I wish you had acquainted us with those two words of our Saviour, and that one of the apostle, wherein they give us a compendium of all divine truths; for if it be so, I am persuaded you will be to seek for your warrant in imposing your *long creeds*, and almost *volumes* of propositions, to be believed as such. But you cannot avoid mistakes in things that you might omit as not at all to your purpose. Our Saviour, indeed, gives us the two general heads of those duties of obedience which are required at our hands towards God and our neighbours, and the apostle shows the perfection of it to consist in love, with its due exercise; but where in two or three words they give us the compendium of all divine truths which we are to believe, that we may acceptably perform the obedience that in general they describe, we are yet to seek, and shall be so, for any information you are able to give us.

In your following discourse you make a flourish with what your church hath in gospels, epistles, good books, anniversary observations, and I know not what besides. But, sir, we discourse not about what you have, but what you have not, nor will have, though God command you to have it, and threaten you for not having it. You have not the Scripture ordinarily in a language that they can understand who, if they are the disciples of Christ, are bound to read, study, and meditate in it continually; which are therefore hindered by you in the discharge of their duty, whilst you "neither enter into the kingdom of heaven yourselves, nor suffer them that would." Nay, you have *burned* men and their Bibles together for attempting to discharge that duty which God requireth of them, and wherein so much of their spiritual advantage is inwrapped. Neither have you the entire worship of God in a tongue known to the people, whereby they might join in it, and pray with understanding, and be edified by what they hear (which the apostle makes the end of all things done or to be done in public assemblies); but are left to have their brutish affections led up and down by dumb shows, postures, and gestures, whereunto the Scripture and antiquity are utter strangers. These things you have not; and, which renders your condition so much the worse, you refuse to have them, though you may, though you are entreated by God and man to make use of them; yea, where great and populous nations under your power have humbly petitioned you that by your leave and permission they might enjoy the Bible, and that service of God which they could understand, you have chosen rather to run all things into confusion, and to fall upon them with fire and sword, than to grant them their request.

"O curvæ in terras animæ, et cœlestium inanes!"

But you add, "Besides what you mention, what can promote your salvation?" for say you, "What farther good may it do to read the letter of St Paul's Epistles, to the Romans, for example, or Corinthians, wherein questions and cases and theological discourses are treated, that vulgar people can neither understand nor are at all concerned to know? And, I pray you, tell me ingenuously and without heat, what more of good could accrue to any by the translated letter of a book, whereof I will be bold to say that nine parts in ten concern not my particular either to know or practise, than by the conceived substance of God's will unto me, and my own duty towards him?" Sir, I shall deal with you without any blamable heat, yet so as he deserves to be dealt withal who will not cease to "pervert the right ways of the Lord." And,—1. Who taught you to make your apprehensions the *measure* of other men's faith and practice? If you know not of any thing needful to promote salvation but what you reckon up in the usage of your church, hinder not them that do. It is not so much your own practice as your imposition of it on others that we are in the consideration of. Would it worth suffice you to reject, as to your own interest, the means appointed of God for the furtherance of our salvation, and that you would not compel others to join with you in the refusal of them! Is it possible that a man professing himself a *divine* and a *priest* of the Catholic church, an *instructor* of the ignorant, an undertaker to persuade whole nations to relinquish the way of religion wherein they are engaged, to follow him in his ways that they have not known, should profess that he "knows not of what use, unto the promotion of the salvation of the souls of men, the use of the whole Scripture given by inspiration of God is?" Be advised not to impose these conceptions of your fancy and mind, as it seems unexercised in that heavenly treasury, on those who have αἰσθητήρια γεγυμνασμένα, "senses exercised" therein, so as to be able to discern between good and evil. If no other reason can prevail with you, I hope experience may give you such a despair of success as to cause you to surcease. 2. This *vulgar people* that you talk of (as the Pharisees did of them that were willing to attend unto the preaching of Christ, Ὁ ὄχλος οὗτος ὁ μὴ γινώσκων τὸν νόμον, John vii. 49;—"This vulgar rout that know not the law"), if they are Christians, they are such as to whom the epistles were originally written, and for whose sakes they are preserved; such as Christ hath redeemed and sanctified in his own blood, and given the anointing unto, whereby they may know all things; and are partakers of the promise that they "shall be taught of God." The gospel takes not away the outward differences and distinctions that are, on other accounts, amongst the children of men; but in the things of the gospel itself there are none vulgar or common, nor as such to be despised, but believers are "all one in Christ Jesus," Col. iii. 11; James ii. 1–6. How it is now I know not, but I am sure that at the beginning of the preaching of the gospel, the poor principally received it; and the greatest number of them that were effectually called was of those whom you speak so contemptuously of, as the apostle testifies, 1 Cor. i. 26. And the same is made good in all ancient story. Neither are these vulgar people such ignoramuses as you imagine, unless it be where you make and keep them such, by detaining from them the means of knowledge, and who perish for the want of it, as the prophet complained of old. I speak not of them who continue willingly ignorant under the most effectual means of light; but of such as, being really "born of God," and becoming thereby "a holy nation, a royal priesthood," as they are called, yea, "kings and priests unto God," do conscientiously attend unto his teachings. Of these there are thousands, yea, ten thousands in England, who are among the vulgar sort as to their outward and civil condition, that, if occasion were administered, would farther try your divinity than you are aware, and give you another manner of account of Paul's epistles than I perceive you suppose they would. You are mistaken if you imagine that either greatness, or learning, or secular wisdom will give a man understanding in the mysteries of the gospel, or make him wise therein. This wisdom is from above,—is wrought by the Spirit of God, in the use of spiritual means by himself appointed for that purpose; and we know not that men of any condition are excepted from his dispensations of light and grace. 3. To whom, and for whose instruction, were those epistles of Paul written? Were they not to the churches of those days: "to all that were at Rome, called to be saints," Rom. i. 7; and "to the church of God that was at Corinth, sanctified in Christ Jesus, with all that everywhere call on his name?" 1 Cor. i. 2. And why, I pray, may not the churches of these days be concerned to know the things that the Spirit of God thought meet to instruct the former churches in? Are believers now grown unconcerned in the doctrine of the law and gospel, of sin and grace, of justification, sanctification, adoption, the obedience of faith, and duties of holiness, which St Paul reveals and declares in his epistles? What would you make of them? or what would you make of the apostle, to write things for the standing use of the church, wherein so few were like to be concerned? or do you think that there are but few things in the Scripture wherein the souls of the people are concerned, and that all the rest are left for learned men to dispute and wrangle about? But you say there are "particular cases in them, that belonged, it may be, only to them unto whom their resolution was directed." But are you such a stranger in the Israel of the church as not to know that in the same cases, or others of a very near alliance unto them, determinable by the apostolical rules delivered in them, the consciences of your vulgar people are still concerned? 4. Those epistles of Paul wherein you instance were written by *divine inspiration*, and given out, by the direction of the Holy Ghost, for the use of the church of God in all ages. This, I suppose, you will not deny. If so, why do you set up your wisdom, built on frivolous cavils, against the will, wisdom, love, and care of God? I fear you are a stranger unto that benefit, strength, supportment, light, knowledge, grace, wisdom, and consolation, which true believers, the disciples of Christ, do every day receive by reading, studying, and meditating on Paul's epistles. I wish you would mind some of old Chrysostom's exhortations unto all sorts of persons to the reading and study of them; they are so interwoven in all his expositions and sermons on them, that it were lost labour to direct you unto any place in particular. 5. The latter part of your discourse would make me suspect that your converse with the Quakers, that you talked of in your "Fiat," had a little tainted your judgment, but that I can ascribe the rise of it unto another cause. Your preferring "the conceived substance of God's will before the letter of the Scripture" is their very opinion. But what do you mean by "the conceived substance of God's will?" Is it the doctrine concerning the will of God delivered in the Scripture, or is it somewhat else? If some other thing, why do you not declare it? If it be no other, why do you distinguish it from itself, and prefer it above itself? or do you conceive there is a "conceived substance of God's will" that is taught, or may be, by men, better than by God himself? (6.) Somewhat you intimate, it may be to this purpose, in the close of this discourse, p. 96, where you say, "The question between us is not, whether the people are to have God's word or no? but, whether that word consist in the letter left to the people's disposal, or in the substance urgently imposed upon the people for their practice? And this because you understand not, but mistake the whole business, all your talk in this your seventeenth chapter vades into nothing." Truly, sir, I never heard before that this was the state of the controversy between us, nor do I now believe it so to be. For,—(1.) We say not that the letter of the Scripture is to be left unto the *people's disposal;* but that the Scripture is to be commended unto their reverent use and meditation: which we think cannot be ingenuously denied by any man that hath read the Scripture, or knows aught of the duty of the disciples of Christ. (2.) The "conceived substance of the word of God," as by any man conceived and proposed, is no otherwise the word of God but as it answers what is written in the Scripture, and by virtue of its analogy therewith. (3.) If by "urging the substance of the word of God" on the people, you understand their instruction in their duty out of the word of God, by catechising, preaching, admonitions, and exhortations, as you must if you speak intelligibly, why do you oppose these things as inconsistent? May not the people have the use of the Scripture, and yet have the word preached unto them by their teachers? Did not Paul preach the substance of the word unto the Bereans? and yet they are commended that they tried what he delivered unto them by the Scripture itself, which they enjoyed. And, (4.) Why do you appropriate this "urging of the substance of the word of God" unto your usage and practice, giving out as ours the leaving of the letter of the Scripture to "the people's disposal," when we know the former to be done far more effectually among Protestants than among you, and yourself cannot deny it to be done more frequently? (5.) You reproach the Scripture, by calling it "the letter," in opposition to your "conceived substance of the word of God:" for though the literal sense of metaphorical expressions (by you yet adhered unto) be sometimes called "the flesh," John vi. 63, and the carnal sense of the institutions of the Old Testament be termed "the letter," 2 Cor. iii. 6, Rom. ii. 27, yet the covenant of God is, that his Spirit and word shall ever accompany one another, Isa. lix. 21; and our Saviour tells us that "his words are spirit and life," John vi. 63, and the apostle, "that the word of God is living and powerful, and sharper than any two-edged sword," Heb. iv. 12. There is in the written word a living and life-giving power and efficacy, which believers have experience of, and which I should be sorry to conclude you to be unacquainted withal. "It is the power of God unto salvation," the immortal seed whereby we are begotten unto God, and the food whereby our souls are nourished. And all this is so not only as to the τὸ γραπτόν, "that which is written," but the ἡ γραφή, "the writing," or Scripture itself, which is given by inspiration from God; for though the things themselves written are the will of God, and intended in the writing, yet the writing itself, being given out by inspiration, is the word of God, and only original means of communicating the other unto us, or the word of God wherein his will is contained,—formally so, as the other is materially. (6.) I find you are not well pleased when you are minded of the contemptuous expressions which some of your friends have used concerning the holy Scripture; but I am now enforced to tell you, that you yourself have equalled, in my apprehension, the very worst of them, in affirming that "nine parts in ten of it concern not your particular either to know or practise:" for I presume you make the instance only in yourself, intending all other individual persons no less than yourself. The apostle tells us that "all Scripture is given by inspiration of God, and is profitable for doctrine, for reproof, for correction, for instruction in righteousness:" you, that "nine parts in ten of it do not concern us to know or practise;" that is, not at all. He informs us, that "whatsoever things were written aforetime were written for our learning, that we through patience and comfort of the Scriptures might have hope:" not above one part of ten of what is so written, if you may be believed, is useful to any such purpose. Do you consider what you say? God hath given us his whole word for our use and benefit. "Nine parts in ten of it," say you, "do not concern us. Can possibly any man break forth into a higher reflection upon the wisdom and love of the holy God? or do you think you could have made a more woful discovery of your unacquaintedness with your own duty, the nature of faith and obedience evangelical, than you have done in these words? You will not make thus bold with the books that Aristotle hath left us in philosophy, or Galen in medicine. But the wisdom of God, in that writing which he hath given us for the revelation of his will, it seems, may be despised. Such fruit, in the depraved nature of man, will ἀμετρία τῆς ἀνθολκῆς produce. The *practice* we blame in you is not worse than the *reasonings* you use in its confirmation. I pray God neither of them may be ever laid unto your charge.

Your following words are a commendation of the zeal and piety of the days and times before the Reformation, with reflections upon all things amongst us since; and this I shall pass by, so to avoid the occasion of representing unto you the true state of things, both here and elsewhere, in the ages you so much extol. Neither, indeed, is it to any great purpose to lay open anew that darkness and wickedness which the world groaned under, and all sober men complained of. You proceed to other exceptions, and say:—

"Where 'Fiat Lux' says that the Pentateuch or hagiography was never, by any high priest among the Jews, put into a vulgar tongue, nor the gospel or liturgy out of Greek in the eastern part of the Christian church, or Latin in the western, you slight this discourse of mine, because Hebrew, Greek, and Latin were vulgar tongues in themselves. I know this well enough; but when, and how long ago, were they so? Not for some thousand years, to my knowledge. And was the Bible, Psalms, or Christian liturgy, then put into vulgar tongues when those they were first written in ceased to be vulgar? This you should have spoken unto if you had meant to say any thing or gainsay me. Nor is it to purpose to tell me that St Jerome translated the Bible into Dalmatian. I know well enough it hath been translated by some special persons into Gothish, Armenian, Ethiopian, and other particular dialects; but did *the church*, either of the Hebrews or the Christians, either Greek or Latin, ever deliver it so translated to the generality of people, or use it in their service, or command it so to be done, as a thing of general concernment and necessity? So far is it from that, that they would never permit it."

I thought you would as little have meddled with this matter again as you have done with other things of the like disadvantage unto you. For,—1. I told you sufficiently before what a vanity it was to inquire after a *translation* of the Old Testament out of the Hebrew before the Babylonish captivity, there being no other language but that understood amongst the generality of the Jewish people; and I then manifested unto you, and shall do so farther immediately, that the translation of the Scripture into Syriac, which you inquire after, could have had no other design amongst the Jews in those days than your keeping of it in Latin hath,—namely, that the people might not understand it: for if you shall persist to think that the Jews, before the Babylonish captivity at least, had any other vulgar language but the Hebrew, you will make all men of understanding smile at you at an extraordinary rate. Some while after the return of the people from their captivity, they began to lose the purity of their own tongue, and most of them understood the Syro-Chaldean, wherein about that time some small parts of the Scripture also were written. In no long process of time a great portion of them living scattered in the provinces of the Macedonian empire, and therefore called Hellenists, used and spake the Greek tongue, their own ceasing to be vulgar unto them. All these, both in private and in their public synagogue worship, made use of a translation of the Scripture into Greek, which was now become their vulgar tongue, and that made either by the Seventy-two elders sent from Jerusalem to Ptolemy Philadelphus, or, which is more probable, by the Jews of Alexandria, unto which city multitudes of them repaired, the nation being made free of it by its founder; or, it may be, some while after, by the priest Onias, who led a great colony of them into Egypt, and there built them a temple for their worship. So did these Hebrews make use of a translation when their own tongue ceased to be vulgar unto them. The monster of serving God by rational men with a tongue whereof they understand never a word, was not yet hatched. The other portion of the people, who either lived in Palestine or those parts of the east where the Greek tongue never prevailed into common use, so soon as their language began to be mixed with the Syro-Chaldean, and the purity of it to grow into disuse, made use constantly of their Targums, or translations into that tongue. Neither can it be proved but that the Jerusalem Jews understood the Hebrew well enough until the destruction of the city and temple by Titus. So that from the church of the Jews you cannot obtain the least countenance to your practice. And there lies in God's dealing with them a strong argument and testimony against it; for if God himself thought meet to intrust his oracles unto his people in that language which was common unto them all, hath he not taught us that it is his will they should still be so continued? And is there not still the same reason for it as there was at first? 2. Farther: the practice of *the Latin church* is unavoidably against you; for whereas the Scripture was no part of it written in Latin, which was their vulgar tongue, it was immediately, both Old Testament and New, turned thereinto, and therein used, as in their public worship, so by private persons of all sorts, upon the encouragement of the rulers of it. And no reason of their translation of it, which they made and had from time immemorial, can possibly be imagined, but only the indispensable necessity which they apprehended of having the Scripture in a language which the people did generally speak and understand. 3. The case was the same in *the ancient Greek church*. The New Testament was originally written in their own vulgar tongue, which they made use of accordingly; and as for the Old, they constantly used a translation of it into the same dialect. So that it is impossible that we can obtain a clearer suffrage from the ancient churches, both Jews and Christians, and these both of Latins and Greeks, in any thing, than we have against this custom of your church. "But these languages," you say, "have ceased to be vulgar for some thousand years to your knowledge." "Bona verba!" You know much, I perceive, yet not so much but that it is possible you may sometimes fail in your chronological faculty. Pray, how many thousand years is it, think you, since Christ's birth, now this year 1663; or since the ruin of the Greek or Latin empire, and therein the corruption of their languages? I believe you will not find it above three or four thousand at the most, upon your next calculation; though I can assure you an ingenious person told me he thought, from the manner of your speaking, you might guess at some nine or ten. What then? "Was the Bible," say you, "put into other vulgar tongues when they ceased to be vulgar?" Yes, by some they were: Jerome translated it into the Dalmatian tongue; Ulphilas into the Gothish; Beda a great part of it into the Saxon; and the like, no doubt, was done by others. The eastern countries, also, to whom the Greek was not so well known, had translations of their own from the very beginning of their Christianity. And for the rest, shall the wretched negligence of men in times of confusion and ignorance,—such as those were wherein the Greek and Latin tongues ceased to be vulgar,—prescribe a rule and law unto us of practice in the worship of God contrary to his own *direction*, the *nature* of the thing itself, and the *example* of all the churches of Christ for five hundred years? For besides that in the empire it was always used and read in the vulgar tongues, those nations that knew not the two great languages that were commonly spoken therein, from the time that they received the Christian faith, took care to have the Scriptures translated into their own mother-tongue. So Chrysostom tells us that the Gospel of John, wherein occasionally he especially instanceth, was in his days translated into the Syrian, Egyptian, Indian, Persian, and Ethiopian languages, Hom. i. on John. But you say, "Did *the church*, either of the Hebrews or Christians, Greek or Latin, ever deliver it translated to the generality of the people, or use it in their service, or command it so to be done, as a thing of general concernment? So far is it from that, that they would never permit it." But you do not sufficiently consider what you say. The *Hebrew* church had no need so to do. God gave the Scripture unto it in their own mother-tongue, and that only; and they had no reason to translate it out of their knowledge and understanding. The *Greek* church had the New Testament in the same manner, and the Old they translated, or delivered it so translated by others, unto the generality of the people, and used it in their service. The *Latin* church did so also. The Scriptures, both of the Old and New Testament also, being originally written in languages unknown vulgarly unto them, they had them translated into their own common tongue for the generality of the people, and used that translation in their public service. The same was the practice of the Syrians and all other nations of old that had a language in common use peculiar to themselves. All your plea ariseth from the practice of some who, through ignorance or negligence, provided not for the good and necessity of the churches of Christ, when, through the changes and confusions that happened in the world, the Greek and Latin tongues ceased to be vulgar; which how many thousand years ago it was, you may calculate at your next leisure. This is that which in them we blame, and in you much more, because you will follow them after you have been so frequently admonished of your miscarriage therein; for you add to your sin by making that which was *neglect* in them *wilful choice* in you, commanding that not to be done which they only omitted to do.

But you will not leave this matter. You told us in your "Fiat" that "neither Moses, nor any after him, did take care to have the Scripture turned into Syriac." I desired to know why they should, seeing Hebrew was their vulgar tongue, and the Syriac unknown unto them; which I proved from the saying of the princes of Hezekiah, when they desired Rabshakeh to "speak unto them in Syriac, which they understood, and not in the Jews' language in the hearing of the people," to affright and trouble them. This I did for your satisfaction, the thing itself being absolutely out of question, and not in the least needing any proof amongst those who understand any thing of this business. But you yet attempt to revive your first mistake, and to say somewhat unto the instance whereby it was rectified; but with your usual success. Will you, therefore, be pleased to hear yourself talk, you know not what, in this matter once more? Thus, then, you proceed:—"Sir, you are mistaken; for the tongue the princes persuaded Rabshakeh to speak was the Assyrian, his own language,—which was learned by the gentry in Palestine, as we in England learn the French,—which, although by abbreviation it be called Syriac, yet it differed as much from the Jews' languago which was spoken by Christ and his apostles (whereof "Eli, Eli, lama sabachthani" is a part), and was ever since that time called Syrian or Syriac, as French differs from English. And if you would read attentively, you may suspect, by the very words of the text, that the Jews' language even then was not the Hebrew: for it had been a shorter and plainer expression, and more answerable to their custom so to call it, if it had been so, than, by a paraphrase, to name it 'The Jews' language;' which if then it was called Syrian, as afterward it was, then had the princes reason to call it rather the Jews' language than Syrian, because that and the Assyrian differed more in nature than appellation, though some difference doubtless there was in the very word and name, although translators have not heeded to deliver it. Shibbolet and Sibbolet may differ more in signification than sound; nor is British and brutish so near in nature as they are in name. And who knows not that Syria and Assyria were several kingdoms, as likewise were the languages?"

I had much ado at first to understand what it is that you would have in this discourse; and no wonder, for I am sure you do not understand yourself. And I am persuaded that if you knew how many prodigies you have poured out in these few lines, you would be amazed at the product of your own imagination. For,—1. You yet again suppose Syriac to have been the vulgar language of the Jews in the days of Hezekiah, a thing that never fell upon the fancy of any man before you, being contrary to express Scripture in the testimony before recited, and all the monuments of those days, wherein the sermons of the prophets unto the people are recorded in the purest Hebrew; neither had the people as yet been carried captive out of their own land, or been mixed with strangers, so as to have lost their language, as you imagine, unless you think that indeed the Hebrew was never their vulgar tongue. 2. You suppose the Syrian and Assyrian at that time to have been different languages, whereof those who understood the one understood not the other, when they were but one and the same, called לָשׁוֹן אֲרַמִּי, "The tongue of Aram;" neither was there ever any other difference between the language of the Assyrians or Chaldeans, and that which was afterward peculiarly called Syriac, but in some few words and various terminations: and how far this differed from the Jews' language you have an instance in the names given by Jacob and Laban to the same heap of witness, Gen xxxi. 47, the one calling it גַּלְעֵד, "Galeed," the other, יְגַר שָׂהֲדוּתָא, "Jegar-sahadutha;" neither was it at all understood by the common people of the Jews, Jer. v. 15. 3. You suppose that in the language wherein Rabshakeh and the princes conferred, their Syriac was an abbreviation of Assyriac, because in sound it was so near the other that they would have him speak in; so that the Jews, speaking Syriac, when the princes desired Rabshakeh to speak Syriac, they meant another language, as much differing from that as French from English. But you are in the dark, and know not how you wander up and down to no purpose. There is nothing of the words that you pretend to be an abbreviation the one of the other in the text; nor is there any such relation between them as you imagine, that they should be near in sound, though not in nature. Eliakim entreats Rabshakeh that he would speak אֲרָמִית, "Aramith, Aramice;" that is, as the Greeks and Latins express that people and language "Syriace," in Syriac,—that he would speak the language of Aram; which language was spoken also by אַשּׁוּר, the king and people of Assyria. And truly אֲרָם, "Aram, "is no abbreviation of אַשּׁוּר, "Ashur," as I suppose. 4. You talk of the length of that expression, "In the Jews' language," when there is nothing in the text but יְהוּדִית, "Jehudith, Judaice," that is, "In Hebrew." 5. Some difference you suppose there was between the Assyrian and Syrian in "sound and name, though translators have not heeded to deliver it," when there was no agreement at all between them; but you say there was "more in nature," when there was none at all. לָשׁוֹן אֲרַמִּי, "Lashon Arami, the tongue of Aram," was the language of Assyria, Ashur being but a colony of Aram. 6. So you think that Shibboleth and Sibboleth may differ more in "signification than sound." But, pray, what do you think is the signification of סִבֹּלֶת, as the Ephraimites pronounced שִׁבֹּלֶת? Just as much as a word falsely pronounced signifieth, and no more,—that is, of itself just nothing at all; for סִבֹּלֶת, "Sibboleth," is no Hebrew word, but merely שִׁבֹּלֶת, "Shibboleth," falsely pronounced. 7. You imagine that the language spoken by Christ and his apostles was the same that was spoken in the days of Hezekiah; and this you would prove, from those words, "Eli, Eli, lama sabachthani," to be that which is now commonly called Syriac, and fancy an Assyrian tongue, as much differing from it as French differs from English: which manifests your skill in the oriental languages; for want whereof I do not blame you, for what is that to me? But I cannot take it well that you should choose me out to trouble me with talking about that which you do not understand; for here you give us two languages, the Syriac and Assyriac, which names in the original differed but little in sound, but the languages themselves did as much in nature as French and English. And the Syriac, you tell us, was that which is now so peculiarly called; but what the Assyriac was you tell us not, but only that when the princes persuade Rabshakeh to speak אֲרָמִית, "Aramith," they intended an Assyrian language that was not Syrian. The boys that grind colours in our grammar schools laugh at these "mormoes." 8. Neither do you know well what you say when you affirm that the language of Christ and his apostles was the same that was ever since called the Syriac; for the very instance you give manifests it to have been a different dialect from it,—the words, as recorded by the evangelists, being absolutely the same neither with the Hebrew, nor Targum, nor Syriac translation of the Old Testament; that wherein we have the translation of the Scripture, and which prevailed in the eastern church, being a peculiar Antiochian dialect of the old Aramean tongue. And that whole language called the Syriac peculiarly now, and whereof there were various dialects of old, seems to have had its beginning after the Jews' return from their captivity, being but a degenerate mixture of the Hebrew and Chaldee; whereinto, also, after the prevalency of the Macedonian empire, many Greek words were admitted, and some Latin ones also afterward. 9. You advantage not yourself by affirming that Assyria and Syria were several kingdoms; for, as Strabo will inform you, they were both originally called Syrian, and, indeed, were one and the same until the more eastern provinces about Babylon obtaining their peculiar denominations, that part of Asia which contains Comagena, Phœnicia, Palestina, and Cœlo-syria became to be especially called Syria. Originally they were all Aramites, as every one knows that can but read the Scripture in its original language.

And now I suppose you may see how little you have advantaged yourself or your cause by this maze of mistakes and contradictions; for no error can be so thick covered with others but that it will rain through. The Jews you suppose to have lost their own language in the days of Hezekiah, and to have spoken Syriac; the Syrian and Assyrian to have been languages as far distant as French and English; that when the princes entreated Rabshakeh to speak the Syrian language, אֲרָמִית, they intended not the Syrian language, which was indeed the Jews', but the Assyrian, quite differing from it; and so, when they desired him not to speak יְהוּדִית, but אֲרָמִית, you suppose them to have desired him not to speak in the Jews' language, but to speak in the Jews' language, which you say was the Syriac. And sundry other no less unhappy absurdities have you amassed together.

But you will retrieve us out of this labyrinth by a story of what a Greek bishop did and said at Paris in the presence of Dr Cousins, now bishop of Durham; how he refused the articles of the English church, and did all things according to the Roman mode; asserting the use of liturgies in the vulgar Greek. Unto which I shall say no more but that it was at Paris, and not at Durham.

"**Græculus esuriens, in cœlum jusseris, ibit.**"—Juv. iii. 78.

I have myself known some eminent members of that church in England, two especially,—one many years ago, called Conopius, who, if I mistake not, upon his return obtained the honour of a patriarchate, being sent hither by the then patriarch of Constantinople; the other not many years ago, called Anastatius Comnenus, archimandrite, as his testimonials bespake him, of a monastery on mount Sinai. Both these, I am sure, made it their business to inveigh against your church and practices, having the arguments of Nilus against your supremacy at their fingers' ends. And if the Greek church and you are so well agreed as you pretend, why do you censure them as heretics and schismatics, and receive only some few of them who are runagates from their own tents? What may those whom you proclaim to be your enemies expect from you, when you deal thus severely with those whom you give out to be your friends? But as for this matter of the Scripture, and prayers in an unknown tongue, they transgress not with so high a hand as you do, the old Greek being not so absolutely remote from the present vulgar as the Latin is from our English and the languages of divers other nations whom you compel to your church-service in that tongue; and, besides, they have the Scripture translated into their present vulgar tongue for the use of private persons: yet we approve not their practice, but look upon it as a great means of continuing that ignorance and darkness which is unquestionably spread over the major part of that church; which in some places, as in Russia, is to such a degree as to dispose the people unto barbarism. We know, also, that herein they are gone off from the constant and catholic usage of their forefathers, who for some centuries of years, from the days of the apostles themselves, who planted churches amongst them, both had the Bible in their own vulgar tongue, and made no use of any other in the public service of their assemblies. And that their example, in their present degenerate condition, which in some things you as little approve of as we do in others, should have any great power upon us, I know as yet little reason to judge.

Your last attempt in this matter is to vindicate what you have said in your "Fiat," as you now affirm, "That the Bible was kept in an ark or tabernacle, not touched by the people, but brought out at times to the priest, that he might instruct the people out of it." To which you say I answer, "That the ark was placed in the 'sanctum sanctorum,' which was not entered into but by the priest, and that only once a year;" and reply, "But, sir, I speak not there of any 'sanctum sanctorum,' or of any ark in that place. Was there, or could there be, no more arks but one? If you had been only, in these latter days, in any synagogue or convention of the Jews, you might have seen even now how the Bible is still kept with them in an ark or tabernacle, in imitation of their forefathers, when they have no 'sanctum sanctorum' amongst them. You may also discern how, according to your custom, they cringe and prostrate at the bringing out of the Bible; which is the only solemn adoration left amongst them. There be more arks than that in the 'sanctum sanctorum.' If I had called it a box, or a chest, or a cupboard, you had let it pass; but I used that word, as more sacred."

The oftener that you touch upon this string, the harsher is the sound that it yields. I would desire you to free yourself from the unhappiness of supposing that it tends unto your disreputation to be esteemed unacquainted with the Jews' language and customs. If you cannot do so, you will not be able to avoid suffering from your own thoughts, especially if you cannot forbear talking about them. This was all that in your former discourse you were obnoxious unto, but this renewal of it hath rendered your condition somewhat worse than it was; for failures in skill and science are not in demerit to be compared with those in morality, which are voluntary, and of choice. Your words in your "Fiat," after you had learnedly observed that the Bible was never in Moses' time, nor afterward by any high priest, translated into Syriac for the use of the people, are: "Nay, it was so far from that, that it was not touched nor looked upon by the people, but kept privately in the ark or tabernacle, and brought forth at times by the priest, who might upon the Sabbath-day read some part of it to the people." I confess, your expression, "In the ark or tabernacle," was somewhat uncouth, and discovered that you did but obscurely guess at the thing you ventured to discourse about. But I took your words in that only sense they were capable of,—namely, that the Bible was kept in the ark, or at least in the tabernacle; that is, some part of it, whereunto the people had no access. And he must be a man devoid of reason and common sense who could imagine that you intended any thing but the sacred ark and tabernacle, when you said that it was kept in the ark or tabernacle; for not only, by all rules of interpretation, is the word used indefinitely to be taken "in sensu famosiori," but also your manner of expression will admit of no other sense or intention. Now, herein, in the "Animadversions," I minded you of your failure, and told you that not the *whole Bible*, as you imagined, but only the Pentateuch, was placed, not *in*, but *at the sides* of the ark; that the ark was kept in the sanctuary; that no priest went in thither but only the high priest, and that but once a year; that the book of the law was never brought forth from thence to be read to the people; and, lastly, that whatever of this kind you might fancy, yet it would not in the least conduce to your purpose, it being openly evident that, besides the public lections out of the law, that people had all of them the Scripture in their houses, and were bound by the command of God to read and meditate in them continually. What say you now to these things?—1. You change your words, and affirm that you said it was kept "in an ark or tabernacle;" as though you meant any ark or chest. But you too much wrong yourself. Your words are, as before represented, "In *the* ark or tabernacle:" and you remembered them well enough to be so, which so perplexeth you in your attempt to rectify what you said; for after you have changed the first word, the addition of the next leaves you in the briers of nonsense, "In an ark *or* tabernacle," as though they were terms convertible,—a chest or a tent. I wish you would make an end of this fond shooting at rovers. 2. You apply that to the practice of the *present Jews* in their synagogues which you plainly spake of the *ancient Jews* whilst their temple and church-state continued; wherein again you intrench upon morality for an evasion. And, besides, you cast yourself upon new mistakes; for,—(1.) The book kept in a chest by them, and brought forth with the veneration you speak of, is not the *whole Bible*, as you imagine, but only the Pentateuch, which was read in their synagogues on the Sabbath-days, ἐκ γενεῶν ἀρχαίων, as James tells us, Acts xv. 21; only, whereas their law was particularly sought after to be destroyed by Antiochus Epiphanes, they supplied the room of it with the other parts of the Scripture divided into chapters, answerable unto the sections of the law. Nor, (2.) Is that brought out *to* or *by* a priest, but to any rabbi that presides in their synagogue worship; for they have no priest amongst them, nor certain distinction of tribes: so that if you yourself have been in any synagogue or convention of the Jews, it is evident that you understood little of what you saw them do. (3.) For their *prostration* at the bringing out of the book, which you seem to commend as a solemn adoration, it is downright *idolatrous;* for in it they openly worship the *material* roll or book that they keep.

But what is it that you would from hence conclude? Is it that which you attempted in your "Fiat,"—namely, that the people amongst the Jews had not the Bible in their own language, and in common use among them? You may as easily prove that the sun shines not at noon-day. The Scripture was committed unto them in their own mother-tongue, and they were commanded of God to read and study it continually, the psalmist pronouncing them blessed who did accordingly; and the present Jews make the same duty of indispensable necessity unto every one amongst them after he comes to be "filius præcepti," or liable to the keeping of any command of God. The rules they give for all sorts of persons, high and low, rich and poor, young and old, sick and in health, for the performance of this duty, are known to all who have any acquaintance with their present principles, practices, state, and condition; and you shall scarcely meet with a *child* amongst them of nine years old who is not exercised to the reading of the Bible in Hebrew;—and yet, though they all generally learn the Hebrew tongue for this purpose in their infancy, lest they should neglect it, or through trouble be kept from it, they have translated the whole Old Testament into all the languages of the nations amongst whom in any numbers they are scattered. The Arabic translation of the Mauritanian Jews, the Spanish of the Spaniards and Portuguese, I can show you if you please. Upon the whole matter, I wish you knew how great the work is wherein you are engaged, and how contemptible the engines are whereby you hope to effect it. But such positions and such confirmations are very well suited. And this is the sum of what you plead afresh in vindication of your Latin service, and keeping the Scripture from the use of the people. If you suppose yourself armed hereby against the express *institution* of Christ by his apostles, the *example* of God's dealing with his people of old, the *nature* of the things themselves, and *universal practice* of the primitive church, I really pity you, and shall continue to pray for you, that you may not any longer bring upon yourself the blood of souls.

CHAPTER XXIII.

Communion.

THE defence of your paragraph about communion in one kind is totally deserted by you. I know no other cause of your so doing but a sense of your incompetency for its defence, seeing you expend words enough about things of less importance. But you please yourself with the commendation of what you had written on this subject in your "Fiat," as full of "Christian reason, convincing reason and sobriety, and how it would have prevailed upon your own judgment had you been otherwise minded." You seem to dwell far from neighbours, and to be a very easy man to be entreated unto what you have a mind unto. But you might not have done amiss to have waited a little for the praise of others; this out of your own mouth is not very comely. And I shall only take leave once more to inform you, that an opposition to the *institution* of Christ, the *command* of the apostle, the *practice* of the primitive church, with the *faith and consolation* of believers, such as is your paragraph about communion in one kind, whatever *overweening thoughts* you may have of the product of your own fancy, cannot, indeed, have any one grain in it of sobriety or Christian reason.

CHAPTER XXIV.

Heroes—Of the ass's head, whose worship was objected to Jews and Christians.

YOUR last endeavour consists in an exception to somewhat affirmed in the 19th chapter of the "Animadversions," directed unto your paragraph about *saints* and *heroes;* and I am sorry that I must close with the consideration of it, because I would willingly have taken my leave of you upon better terms than your discourse will allow me to do. But I shall as speedily represent you unto yourself as I am able, and then give you my "salve æternumque vale."

You tell us in your "Fiat" that the "Pagans defamed the Christians for the worship of an ass's head;" and you give this reason of it, "Because the Jews had defamed our Lord Jesus Christ, whose head and half-portraiture Christians used upon their altars, even as they do at this day, of his great simplicity and ignorance." Two things you suppose,—1. That the Christians placed the head and half-portraiture of our Saviour in those days on their altars; which is alone to your purpose. 2. That this gave occasion to the Pagans to defame them with the worship of an ass's head, because the Jews had so blasphemed the Lord Christ, as you say. These things I told you are fond and false, and destitute of all colour of testimony from antiquity; that the worship of an ass's head was originally charged on the Jews themselves, and on Christians no otherwise but as they were accounted a sect of them, or their offspring; and that what in the same place you assert, of "the Jews accusing the Christians for the worship of images," or "the Christians using the picture of Christ's head or his half-portraiture on their altars," are monsters that none of the ancients ever dreamed of. What plead you now in your vindication? Quite omitting that wherein alone you are concerned, you only undertake to prove that the worship of an ass's head was imputed to the Christians as well as to the Jews, which you say "I deny, and say that it was not charged on the Jews at all." And the reason of this charge, you say, was, "Because they were reckoned among the Jews 'in odiosis,' and accounted of them." So well do you mind what you had said before of the rise of that imputation on the Christians, from the blasphemy of the Jews! So,—1. In your "Fiat" you say nothing of the Jews at all, but only that by their calumnies the Pagans took occasion to slander the Christians; being now *better instructed by the "Animadversions,"* in the rise of that foolish calumny, you change your note, and close in with what is in them asserted. 2. You unduly affirm that "I deny this to have been charged on the Christians," when I grant it was, and that in the very same manner and on the same account that yourself now, contrary to what you had written before, acknowledge it to have been. He must be as much unacquainted with these things as somebody else whom I shall not name, "honoris gratia," seems to be, who knows not that this foolish impiety was imputed, in process of time, to the Christians by the Pagans, among a litter of other follies, as well as unto the Jews. Cæcilius, in Minucius, tells us, "Audio eos ineptissimæ pecudis caput asini consecratum inepta nescio qua persuasione venerari;"—"I hear that by a foolish persuasion they worship the head of an ass, a vile beast." And Tertullian, Apol., cap. xvi., "Nam quidam somniastis caput asininum esse Deum nostrum;"—"Some of you dream that an ass's head is our God;"—

presently declaring thereon, that this imputation was derived on them from the Jews, who first suffered under that fable. And if any thing gave new occasion unto it among the Christians, it was not the picture of Christ despised by the Jews, as you imagine, but the report of his riding on an ass; which Athanasius takes notice of, Homil. ad Pagan. They said, "Ὅτι ὁ Θεὸς Χριστιανῶν ὁ καλούμενος Χριστὸς εἰς ὀνάριον ἐκάθισε·—"That the God of the Christians, who is called Christ, sat on an ass." But you will prove what you say out of Tertullian. Say you, "The same Tertullian, in his Apologetic, adds these words: 'The calumnies (saith he) invented to cry down our religion grew to such an excess of impiety, that not long ago, in this very city, a picture of our God was shown, by a certain infamous person, with the ears of an ass, and a hoof on one foot, clothed with a gown, and a book in his hand, with this inscription, 'Onochoetes, the God of the Christians.'' And he adds, 'That the Christians in the city, as they were much offended with the impiety, so did they not a little wonder at the strange, uncouth name the villain had put upon our Lord and Master. Onochoetes, forsooth! he must be called Onochoetes!'" In this testimony of you know not what, you triumph, and conclude, "Are you not a strange man, to tell me that what I speak of this business is notoriously false, nay, and that I know it is false, and that I cannot produce one authentic testimony, no not one, of any such thing? But this is your ordinary confidence." Seriously, sir, I wonder where you got this quotation out of Tertullian. Let me desire you to be wary in receiving any thing hereafter from the same hand, out of authors that you want the confidence to venture upon yourself. The words of Tertullian, which your translator hath abused you in, are these:—"Sed nova jam Dei nostri in ista civitate proxime editio publicata est, ex quo quidam in frustrandis bestiis mercenarius noxius picturam proposuit cum ejusmodi inscriptione, 'Deus Christianorum Ononychites.' Is erat auribus asininis, altero pede ungulatus, librum gestans et togatus. Risimus et nomen et formam. Sed illi debebant adorare statim biforme numen qui canino et leonino capite commistos deos receperunt;"—"Lately in that city" (that is, Rome) "there was a public show made of our God, wherein a guilty person hired to fight with wild beasts, and to cozen their rage, proposed a picture with this inscription, 'Ononychites, the God of the Christians.' He had ass's ears, hoofed on one foot, carrying a book, and in a gown. We laughed at the name and shape. But they ought immediately to have adored this double-shaped deity, who have received gods mingled with dogs' and lions' heads." You see how well you have given us the words of Tertullian, which you pretend to do, saying, "He adds these words." But I confess, though he says no such matter, it is like enough he would have wondered at the name of Onochoetes, had the villain given it unto his picture; for neither he nor any man else knows what it should mean. He knew well enough what Ononychites signified, and laughed at it. It is but Asinungulus; which, it may be, comes nearer their understanding. I confess some would read it Onochoerites, as if it were compounded of ὄνος and χοῖρος, because of these words of Epiphanius concerning the Gnostics, Φασὶ δὲ τὸν Σαϐαὼθ, οἱ μὲν ὄνου μορφὴν ἔχειν, οἱ δὲ χοίρου·—"Some say their Sabaoth had the form of an ass, some of a hog." But Tertullian, in the description of the picture, mentions no part of a hog, nor rejects the abomination of the Gnostics, as was the manner of the Christians when charged with their silliness and folly, as may be seen abundantly in Origen against Celsus. But who or what your Onochoetes should be, no man knows. But see your farther unhappiness. You prove not by your quotation that which no man denies, namely, that the Christians also were charged with the worship of an ass's head; which, if you had but looked into Tertullian himself, you must have found him expressly affirming it in the beginning of that chapter from whence your story is taken. Much less do you prove any thing of the Christians placing the head and half-portraiture of our Saviour upon their altars before or in the days of Constantine; which was that alone that was incumbent on you to have done. And now, to give a brief view of that whole portraiture that you have drawn of yourself in your epistle, I shall only mind you that those words of mine, "That your assertions were notoriously false, and that you could not produce so much as one testimony of any such thing," were not by me used at all in reference unto the Pagans' charge upon the Christians for worshipping an ass's head, but unto what you said about the use of the picture of Christ on the altars of Christians, with the rise of the charge mentioned from thence. This you know to be so, for my words must needs lie before you in your attempt for a reply unto them; and finding them to be true, and that you were not able to "produce one testimony, no not one," in the confirmation of what you had written, you pretend them now to be spoken in reference unto that whereunto you know they did not at all relate, the thing itself being acknowledged by me. This dealing becomes not any man pretending to ingenuity or professing Christianity.

What remains of your epistle is *personal*. Men are busy, and not so far concerned, I am sure, in me, nor (I am almost persuaded) in you, as to trouble themselves with the perusal of what belongs unto us personally. For my part, I know it is my duty in *all things*, especially in those that are of such near concernment unto his glory as are all his truths and worship, to commend my conscience unto God, and to be conversant in them in *simplicity* and godly sincerity, and not in *fleshly wisdom*, not corrupting the word of truth, nor lying in wait with any subtle sleights to deceive. And this, through his grace, I shall attend unto, whatever reward I may meet withal in this world; for "I know in whom I have believed, who is able to keep that which I desire to commit unto him." And for your part, I desire your prosperity as my own, I rejoice in your quiet, and shall never envy you your liberty, and do pray that you may receive grace, truth, and peace from Him who alone is able to bestow them on you.

THE

CHURCH OF ROME NO SAFE GUIDE;

OR,

REASONS TO PROVE THAT NO RATIONAL MAN, WHO TAKES DUE CARE OF HIS OWN ETERNAL SALVATION, CAN GIVE HIMSELF UP UNTO THE CONDUCT OF THAT CHURCH IN MATTERS OF RELIGION.

"Trust ye not in lying words, saying, The temple of the LORD, The temple of the LORD, The temple of the LORD, are these. Will ye steal, murder, and commit adultery, and swear falsely, and burn incense unto Baal, and walk after other gods whom ye know not; and come and stand before me in this house, which is called by my name?"—JER. vii. 4, 9, 10.

Imprimatur,

March 5, 1679.

PREFATORY NOTE.

When Dr Owen published the three following pamphlets, the nation was in a state of great alarm lest Popery should be re-established in Britain. Parliament had become suspicious, so early as 1673, that some project of this nature was entertained; and accordingly it passed the Test Act, condemned the marriage of the Duke of York with the Princess of Modena, and resolved to grant no supplies till security was obtained against the restoration of Popery. The same jealous mood continued till the Popish plot of 1678 produced an outburst of excitement and horror throughout the country. The House of Commons, having passed a resolution affirming that such a plot had been contrived by Popish recusants for the subversion of the government, and the destruction of the Protestant religion as by law established, adopted stringent measures in defence of the threatened liberties of the nation. The Roman Catholic Lords were excluded from Parliament; a Secretary of State was imprisoned for commissioning gentlemen whose Protestantism was suspected; the Duke of York was expelled from the Privy Council; and the Lord Treasurer Danby was impeached of high treason. In the midst of these proceedings, the House of Commons was suddenly dissolved. The fears of the nation were increased; a Parliament was returned even more zealous for the interests of Protestantism; and as soon as it met, the bill to exclude the Duke of York from succession to the crown was proposed.

Even were it conceded that the stories of Titus Oates were altogether unworthy of credit, it was no groundless panic that now agitated the nation. Charles, however destitute of any fixed principles, had betrayed leanings in the direction of Rome. He was under the influence of the French monarch, who was doing his utmost at the time, by means of an atrocious persecution, to fulfil his marriage-contract with the Infanta of Spain, in which it was stipulated that the Huguenots should be rooted out of France. A great multitude, as we learn from the following pamphlet, influenced by the court or by the reigning fashion of the day, had passed into the communion of the Romish Church. The Duke of York was publicly committed to the interests of the Papacy; and it was natural to expect, from the bigoted obstinacy of his character, that he would stake even his crown itself in an effort to make his creed again the religion of the State.

Accordingly, both in the Established Church and among the Nonconformists, every exertion was made to rouse a spirit adequate to the emergency, by exposing the errors of Popery, and fostering a healthful antipathy to its despotism and superstition. Several treatises appeared, marked by the brief-spoken earnestness of men in actual conflict. The divines of the Church of England contributed to the discussion in works which leave nothing to be desired in close logic and vigorous statement. Most of these works ran to no great length, and were chiefly such tracts and pamphlets as Bishop Gibson has treasured up in his "Preservative against Popery." There was no time to indite such bulky treatises as "Barrow on the Supremacy of the Pope." There would have been less time to read them. The vessel was boarded, and, quitting the heavier ordnance, the crew had to fight hand to hand for the possession of the deck.

The Nonconformists delivered and published their "Morning Exercises against Popery." Their leading divines all took part in the controversy, in productions not so remarkable for the acumen, clearness, and vivacity which adorn the pages of such writers as Stillingfleet, Tillotson, and Tenison;—equal, however, in the resources of learning, real strength of argument, and knowledge of human nature, and superior perhaps in the skill with which divine truth was made to bear on the conscience.

Dr Owen in this crisis wrote several sermons and treatises. In the tract which follows, his aim is to show that the Church of Rome is no safe guide to the enjoyment of implicit certainty in religious convictions; and that the Scriptures, with the promised aid of the Holy Spirit, furnish the sole guidance upon which the awakened soul, in its pursuit of truth and salvation, must depend. He assigns as a reason for discussing the pretended infallibility of Rome, that its wary advocates, accounting this dogma their stronghold, "declined all particular controversies, and betook themselves to this alone." He reviews the causes by which Popery gains accessions to its ranks:—ignorance of spiritual religion, loose morals, secular interest, strong delusion sent on men that they should believe a lie, and the terrors of persecution. The main part of the treatise is occupied with nine different grounds on account of which the guidance of the Church of Rome is to be distrusted and rejected. All of them deserve serious consideration. A peculiar shrewdness distinguishes the treatise, occasionally the diction rises into an animation rare with our author, and everywhere the spiritual sagacity is apparent, which gives a crowning value to his views on such a topic as he now handles.—Ed.

PREFACE.

THE ensuing discourse was the subject and substance of two sermons preached unto a private congregation. The author of them had no design or purpose ever to have made them public. The importunity of many, who judged they might be of use unto others, because they found them so unto themselves, gave occasion unto this publication of them;—yet had they not so prevailed, but that he judged it was neither unmeet for him nor unseasonable for others. "In publico discrimine omnis homo miles est;"—no man is to be forbidden to bring his bucket to help to allay the flames of a raging fire. And it is the pretence of the church of Rome to be the only guide of all Christians in religion which is here examined,—a work which a concurrence of all sorts of circumstances renders seasonable. For as this pretence is the sole foundation of the whole Papacy, with all the power and secular advantages that it hath obtained unto itself, so it is that alone which gives countenance and warranty unto the factors and agents of that church to design and perpetrate such things as are destructive of all that is praiseworthy or desirable among mankind, and unspeakably scandalous unto Christian religion. Remove the sand or rubbish hereof, and the whole fabric will dissolve of itself and fall to the ground. This small discourse is an attempt unto that end, whose success is humbly recommended unto the care of God over his church. If there seem to be any severities of expression used towards some of the church of Rome, the reader is to consider that hard things cannot well be represented in soft and pliant words. And if there be nothing of this nature found, but what hath the appearance of severity from the things themselves which are expressed, there is no blamable excess. However, the author is one who heartily desires and prays for the outward peace and tranquillity of all men in this world, whose principles will allow them to live peaceably with others.

THE

CHURCH OF ROME NO SAFE GUIDE.

THE foundation of the small ensuing discourse shall be laid in a position wherein, as I suppose, persons of all sorts who are concerned in the things treated about are agreed,—namely, that it is the duty of every man who taketh care of his own eternal salvation, to betake himself unto some guide or conduct that may safely lead him unto the knowledge of the truth, and the practice of Christian obedience. The nature of religion, the state of our own minds in this world, with the eternal importance of a safe, unerring guidance in things spiritual and supernatural, do require that the utmost of our diligence and prudence be used in the discharge of this duty, in the choice of this guide. No man of himself is sufficient, by his *own reason alone*, to be his own guide. They who, thinking themselves wise, have attempted so to be, "have waxed vain in their imaginations, and their foolish hearts have been darkened," Rom. i. 21. The warning and instruction given by Solomon do principally respect this case: "He that trusteth in his own heart is a fool; but whoso walketh wisely, he shall be delivered," Prov. xxviii. 26. But the knowledge of and adherence unto such a guide are eminently necessary when there are great differences and divisions amongst men about religion, especially if they are managed in ways and by means not only scandalous unto religion itself, but pernicious unto human society in their consequence. When men not only say and contend that "Here is Christ, and lo, there is Christ," Matt. xxiv. 23, but also, on the account of these differences, engage into ways and practices ruinous unto the souls of men, and destructive unto all that is praiseworthy in this world, those who are not careful to choose and adhere unto a faithful guide and conduct are no less defective in wisdom than negligent in their duty.

Were a man in a wilderness where are a multitude of cross paths all pretending to lead unto an inhabited city, whither he must go or perish; if he see men not only contending some for one way, some for another, but killing and destroying one another about the preference of the several ways they esteem best and safest, he deserves to wander and perish if he refuse a guide that is tendered unto him with sufficient evidence of his truth and faithfulness. That there is such a one ready in our present case shall be immediately evinced.

The differences in religion that are at present among us are of two sorts:—First, Such as, comparatively, are of *small moment* as unto the principal ends of the life of God. The measure of these differences is, that which way soever they are determined in the minds of men, they neither overthrow the foundation nor obstruct the due exercise of faith and love; for this is our great duty, with respect unto doctrines in religion, that we "hold fast the form of sound words, in faith and love which is in Christ Jesus," 2 Tim. i. 13. And if any of them are so small as that it cannot be pretended that they overthrow the foundations of faith and love, yet if they hinder them in their operations and due exercise according unto the rule of the gospel, they are pernicious unto the souls of them in whom they have that effect. But such differences which comply with this measure tend unto nothing in themselves that is obstructive unto the glory or power of religion, whatever they may be pressed and wrested unto by the lusts, prejudices, and carnal interests of men; for there is no ground to be taken from them for *severe thoughts* concerning the state and condition of them who so differ, as unto their interest in present grace and future glory. To live in a neglect of love, in all the effects and fruits of it, towards such on any pretences, to design their hurt and evil, is to live in open contradiction unto all the rules of the gospel.

Such severe thoughts are the principal causes and occasion of all pernicious evils in religion, especially those which are most scandalous unto it, and most inconsistent with that good of mankind which Christian religion is designed to promote; for things are come to that pass among the generality of Christians, that when once persons begin to damn others in their minds for their dissent from them, they judge themselves at liberty, and count that it is their duty, to do them all the mischief they can in this world. They first make themselves their judges that they must go to hell, and then would be their executioners, to send them thither as fast as they can. Whether this be a representation of Christ or of the devil is not hard to determine. Sure I am, it is not compliant with the advice given unto all guides of the church, of an attendance whereunto they must give an account, 2 Tim. ii. 24–26: "And the servant of the Lord must not strive; but be gentle unto all men, apt to teach, patient, in meekness instructing those that oppose themselves; if God peradventure will give them repentance to the acknowledging of the truth; and that they may recover themselves out of the snare of the devil, who are taken captive by him at his will."

Hence it is, that those who have a strong inclination to oppress and destroy other men, which their interest prompts them unto, do endeavour to make every the least dissent from themselves, on one pretence or other, by sophistical arguments and strained consequences, to be a fundamental error, and such as makes them incapable of life eternal. But no men can give a greater evidence of their disinterest in Christian religion, of their unacquaintedness with the virtues and powers of it, wherein the glories of it do consist, and what is of real price with God, than those who are so minded. Blessed be God, that Christ will not leave his seat of judgment unto such persons, neither here nor hereafter!

But such differences as those mentioned will probably continue among Christians so long as they continue in this world; for although all those among whom these differences are do choose the same guide, yet they do not in all things equally hear and understand his voice. Perfection in light and knowledge are required unto a perfect agreement in all the conceptions of our minds about spiritual things; wherefore it is reserved for heaven, where every thing that is imperfect shall be done away. Here we have different measures. "We know but in part," and therefore "prophesy in part," 1 Cor. xiii. 9. It is love or charity alone that supplies this defect, and gives such a harmony unto the different parts of the mystical body of Christ, which is the church, as renders them all useful, and the whole beautiful, 1 Cor. xiii.; Col. iii. 14.

But these are not the differences which at present I intend. There are those which in their nature are of greater importance; such as are about the fundamentals of Christian faith, worship, and obedience; such as upon whose determination the eternal welfare and misery of the souls of men do depend. And not only so, but they are such also which, on that wretched management of religious concerns that late ages have embraced, have an influence into the peace or disturbance of human society, the tranquillity, the liberty, and lives of men. Yea, they are by some promoted and pursued by all ways of fraud and violence, with that height of impiety as is utterly destructive of all religion. Many we have who plead themselves to be *Christians;* which might be allowed them, if they pleased themselves, would they not do such things as Christian religion abhorreth. But this is the least part of their claim: they will also be the *only Christians;* all others who differ from them, however falsely so called, being only a drove of unbelievers, hasting unto hell. Now, although this be intolerable presumption, yet, because they hurt none by it but themselves, if they will not be awakened from this pleasing dream, they may be suffered to sleep on. But they rest not here. These Christians, who *only are so,* and so alone know truly what is in

Christian religion, will do such things under a pretence of it, will perpetrate such execrable crimes, avowing them to be the dictates and commands of that religion, that if men were not sure that their former pretences are presumptuously false, it would be a sufficient warranty for them whereon to question the whole truth of the gospel. And these things are done in the pursuit of these differences in religion which abound among us. Wherefore, if we would not contribute unto that intolerable scandal against the gospel, that the religion it teacheth is pernicious to the peace of mankind and all that is praiseworthy in the world, which must be accounted for; if we have any care about our own eternal salvation,—we ought to use our utmost diligence to arrive unto a safe conduct through all these difficulties.

This being our present case, there being such differences in, and divisions about religion among us, the management of them being grown incurably scandalous and perilous, our inquiry is, What guide or conduct a man that takes care of his own salvation, that would know the truth, and have the benefit of it, that would please God here, and come unto the eternal enjoyment of him hereafter, ought to betake himself, and firmly adhere unto, as that which will safely lead and direct him unto all these ends? for "if the blind lead the blind, both will fall into the ditch."

Two things are pleaded to be this *safe and infallible guide*, to have that conduct committed unto them, which every one who takes care of his salvation is obliged to betake himself unto.

The first is *the church of Rome*. She it is who at this time lays a most vehement claim to be the only authoritative, infallible guide of all Christians, as unto their faith, worship, and obedience. We inquire not after a ministerial guide, and the benefit which we may receive thereby. This they regard not, as that which leaves men the exercise of their own understandings, and use of all divine aids and assistances, as unto the information, direction, and determination of their minds in all that they are to believe and practise in religion. But such a guidance as whereunto, by virtue of its authority and infallibility, we are entirely and absolutely to resign our understandings and consciences, whatever it leads us unto, is that which this church claimeth, and without which she is nothing, nor can stand one moment. This is that which those who plead the cause of that church at present do wholly betake themselves unto the promotion of; declining, what lies in them, all other differences and controversies between them and us. Such a guide, they say, there must be of all Christians; and this guide is their church. And they do wisely consult their own interest therein; for if they can once gain this point, all other things which they aim at will follow of their own accord, and they may satisfy the desires of their hearts on the consciences of men.

Wherefore, this claim of theirs consists of these three parts, or may be reduced unto these three heads:—

1. That *they*, and *they alone*, are the church of Christ; all others who are called Christians in the world are heretics and schismatics, who belong not unto it, nor have any interest in it. Howbeit, if the description given us of the church of Christ in the Scripture be right and good, it is almost impossible there should be any society or combination of men, on a religious account, more unlike it than that which is called the Church of Rome. This, therefore, must be taken upon their own credit and vehement affirmation by them who have a mind so to do.

2. That this church, which they alone are, is intrusted with authority over the souls and consciences of all Christians, and all that would be so, to be their *only guide* in all that they are to know, believe, and do in religion; so that whoever gives not themselves up unto their conduct must perish eternally. It were no hard task to manifest that a supposition hereof is destructive unto the nature of evangelical faith and obedience, as also of all the directions and precepts given by Christ and his apostles for the discharge of our duty with respect unto them. But this they must obtain, or the whole present papal interest falls unto the ground. Yet neither will a supposition that there is such a church secure them, their own pretences to be this church being openly contradictory to the Scripture. Nor is the power claimed herein derived from the apostles, who professed themselves not to be lords of the faith of believers, 2 Cor. i. 24; 1 Pet. v. 3.

3. They plead that hereon no more is required of any man who takes care of his salvation, but that he *give up himself absolutely and entirely* unto the conduct of their church, believing what it proposeth, and that on this ground alone, that it is proposed by it, and obeying all its commands; whereby they seem to set this pretended guide "in the temple of God, showing him that he is God."

This is the claim of the church of Rome,—these are the principles whereinto it is resolved; which whether they have any thing in them of truth or modesty, will immediately be made to appear.

Secondly, *The holy Scripture*, with the divine aids and assistances for the understanding thereof which God hath promised unto all that diligently seek him, is pleaded to be the *only rule* and guide that men ought to betake themselves unto, in case of those important differences in religion which are under consideration. And the plea on the behalf thereof is reducible unto these five heads:—

1. That this Scripture is a *divine, supernatural revelation* of God, his mind and his will. This foundation is unquestionable, and will never fail them that build upon it. Those of the Roman religion will

propose ensnaring questions about it unto them on whom they design. They will be asking how they know the Scripture to be the word of God, labouring to disprove the evidences they produce to prove it so to be. But this bold artifice is of no use in this case, for themselves confess it so to be: only, they prefer the authority of their church testifying it so to be, as more safely to be rested in and trusted unto than that of God himself; which cannot be unto the advantage of their cause with any considerate persons.

2. That it is a divine revelation of *the whole will and mind of God*, as unto all things that are necessary unto his glory and our salvation. This it frequently testifieth of itself; and, on the former supposition of its being such a divine revelation, its testimony must be granted to be infallibly true. Both these assertions the apostle expressly conjoineth, 2 Tim. iii. 15–17. Somewhat they except here in respect of their unwritten traditions, but dare not positively deny that the Scripture is a sufficient revelation of all things absolutely necessary unto salvation; indeed, to do so will leave no assurance unto any man that he can ever know what is necessary unto salvation. But they have a reserve whereunto they betake themselves on a concession hereof,—namely, that whatever be contained in it, it cannot be understood but as the sense of it is declared by their church. But this is a bold, unproved presumption, contrary unto the design of God in giving us his word, and the experience of all who have been exercised in it.

3. The way, manner, and method of this revelation are such as are *suited unto divine wisdom and goodness*, whether they please men or no. It is with reference unto these things that they expatiate and enlarge themselves in charging the Scripture with obscurity, and unfitness thereon to be our only rule and guide; for the Bible, they say, is a book composed of histories, prophecies, songs, prayers, and epistles, and is therefore unmeet for any such use or end. But these things are of no consideration in our present case. It is thus given out immediately by God himself, and therefore every way answers divine wisdom and goodness; whether men are pleased with it or no, we are not at all concerned. He who designed it for the instruction of the church alone knows what was to be the method of its composure unto that end. And it hath been proved on another occasion, that, considering the state of the church in its several ages, the nature of that faith which is to be wrought and confirmed by this divine revelation, with the manner of teaching becoming the authority of God, the holy Scripture could not have been given out unto us in any other order or method than that wherein it is disposed.[1]

4. On these suppositions, there neither is nor can be more required of us, in order unto our eternal salvation, but that we *understand*

[1] See the "Reason of Faith," vol. iv.

aright, firmly believe, and yield obedience unto, the revelation of the mind and will of God that is made therein. The assurance hereof is so evidently included in the foregoing assertions that it needs no confirmation. Every thought unto the contrary is so injurious unto the wisdom, goodness, grace, and truth of God, so opposite unto all the notions of the minds of men, on a supposition of God's speaking unto them, that it ought to be rejected with detestation.

5. There are *efficacious aids promised* and assured means appointed by God himself, to help all that diligently seek him unto a certain infallible understanding of his mind in the Scripture, so far as the knowledge of it is necessary unto our salvation. This, also, I have lately confirmed in a peculiar discourse.[1] These are the heads whereunto the plea for the guidance of the Scripture in all differences and divisions about religion may be reduced.

The case being thus plainly stated, the inquiry hereon is, Whether of these guides a man that takes care of his own eternal salvation should betake himself, and firmly adhere unto to the end?

In answer unto this inquiry, I shall prove that no wise man who feareth God, and is careful of the eternal condition of his own soul, can choose the church of Rome for this guide, foregoing the other of the Scripture, with the divine aids promised and given for the understanding thereof.

The person of whom I speak I suppose to be a *wise man;* that is, one who prefers things eternal unto those that are temporal, so as not to be ensnared by earthly interests and advantages unto the forfeiture of his interest in things above, and will be careful not to be imposed on by men who design their own advantage in what they would persuade him unto. He who is otherwise minded is a fool. He is also one that feareth God, and therefore is real and in good earnest in religion, as desiring to please him in all things; for there are many who give the world no small disturbance about religious concerns who do on all occasions manifest that they have little or no regard unto God in what they say or do. But in the persons whom I address unto, I suppose that they really take care, above all other things, of the eternal salvation of their souls. And I shall not deal with them by abstruse arguments nor by testimonies of men, that may be bandied up and down on the one side and the other, but by such plain reasonings as are accommodated unto the common understanding of all sober, sedate, rational persons, who own the principles of Christian religion, which have their force from the general usage of mankind in things of an alike nature,—the common natural principles of men's minds, where they are not vitiated and depraved; with the experience of what they have found already in any duties

[1] See the "Causes, Ways, and Means of Understanding the Mind of God," vol. iv.

of religious worship. Indeed, if we could but prevail with men to be persuaded that every man must believe for himself, and obey for himself, and give an account for himself, this difference would be at an end; for the choice of the church of Rome to be the guide inquired after, is nothing but the putting of the care of saving our souls unto others, who will not be able to answer for us when our trial shall come.

And this subject in particular I have chosen at present to insist upon, for two reasons:—

1. Because, as was before observed, those who at present do plead *the interest of this church* among us do decline what they can all particular controversies, and, under various notions, betake themselves to this alone, about an authoritative guide and leader of all Christians, which they pretend their church to be. They do not, in their projection for proselytes, go to them and enter into disputes about transubstantiation, the sacrifice of the mass, adoration of images, or the like, no, nor yet about the pope's infallibility; but, supposing themselves to be greatly advantaged by the differences in religion that are among us, which usually they enlarge upon, without either truth or modesty, under a concealment of greater differences among themselves, they insist only on the necessity of such a guide, which they pretend their church alone to be. Hereby have they prevailed on many, who, on one account or other, do think themselves unmeet any longer to take care of their own salvation; and when once they have prevailed herein, there is nothing so horrid, nothing so wicked, that they cannot impose on the consciences of their proselytes. They will not now scruple or stick at all at those things which they would have dreaded to have thought of whilst they had the care of themselves in any measure upon them. Not one man of a thousand who supposeth that he hath himself and his own soul in charge, that he must give an account of and for himself, will venture on those ways and practices which they will with great satisfaction rush into under their conduct.

2. Because of the strange ways they have lately taken to put this pretence into use and practice, and to *take us all* under their conduct. Pretending unto the guidance of our souls in the things of God, they have attempted to take us into their power as unto our lives, liberties, laws, and all other our concernments in this world; which whosoever doth unlawfully forfeits all his own. And a sufficient indication it is of what guidance we were like to meet withal, when way was to be made unto it by fire, confusion, blood, massacres, and sedition.

Should there be a school erected, pretending unto an easy certain way of teaching all sciences, divine and human; should it pretend a grant that nothing of this nature should be taught or learned but in and by it; yet, if I saw the posts of the house hung like shambles with the limbs of slaughtered persons,—if the ground about it be strewed with the bones and ashes of men burned to death,—here lying one strangled, there another stabbed, a third poisoned, all for no other cause but either because they would not submit to the teaching thereof, or would not learn things foolish and wicked,—I should avoid such a school and its power so far as I were able. But yet, because there hath of late among us a great accession been made really unto this guidance by persons formerly professing the Protestant religion, I shall a little inquire into the causes of it, or the means whereby it hath been brought about; and I shall not fear to say, that, as unto the most of them who have relinquished the Protestant religion, they are these that follow:—

1. A *profound ignorance* of the internal powers of religion, with an utter want of all experience of them in themselves, makes them an easy prey to seducers. Persons who have never had any concernment in religion beyond the outside solemnity of it, with some notions and opinions about the doctrines of it, are easily "tossed to and fro" from one religion unto another, or unto none at all, through the "cunning sleights of men who lie in wait to deceive."

When men have only a "form of godliness" in the profession of the truth, but know nothing of the "power of it," it is an uncertain accident whether they persevere in that profession or no. There are internal powers of true religion which are efficacious on the minds of men to enlighten them, to purify them, and give them liberty from the adverse powers of darkness, vanity, and bondage unto sin. Where men have experience of them in their own hearts, there and there alone, if a vigorous impression unto the contrary do befall them, will they be constant in the profession of the truth. The success of our Roman emissaries is confined almost unto that sort of persons who, under the outward profession of the Protestant religion, have been totally ignorant of the virtue and power of the truth contained therein.

2. *Wickedness of life*, taking shelter in the promises of eternal security which that church, with presumptuous confidence, tenders unto all that will give up themselves unto her conduct, though in the last moments of their lives, gains them a multitude of proselytes. This engine they apply unto many when they are leaving the world, even unto such as, having lived in sin and ignorance, are ready to receive condign punishment for their villanies, deceiving them of those few minutes which might be improved in seeking after evangelical faith and repentance. But this is the least use they make of it. There are in the world, among those that are called Protestants, mighty men, nobles, men of dignity and revenue, who live in their

sins, and are resolved so to do; yet are they not able by any means to secure their consciences from troublesome fears of eternal miseries that will ensue on the course wherein they are. By all crafty ways of access and compliance, the factors of this church do insinuate themselves, or by others are introduced, into the acquaintance of this sort of persons; and the first thing they offer unto them is absolute security of eternal salvation, if they will but relinquish heresy, wherein it is impossible they should ever be saved, and betake themselves unto the conduct of the church of Rome. Of the change of their lives, the relinquishment of their sins, of repentance from dead works, of the life of God, and universal obedience therein, there are no words between them. Many of these persons, who are resolved beforehand rather to part with all the religion in the world than with one of their lusts and sins, do readily embrace the composition offered; for really that which is tendered unto them is a consistency between living in sin and assured going unto heaven, which before they knew not that they could be reconciled. For however they shall live for the future, suppose in the sins of adultery, fornication, profane swearing, luxury, drunkenness, or the like, the church will take care that, by confessions, masses, and purgatory, they shall be undoubtedly saved. At this door have entered great numbers of "unclean beasts," unto the increase of the herd, who often prove the most forward zealots for the Catholic cause.

3. *Secular interests* and advantages, accommodated unto all sorts of persons, are another means of their prevalency. There are no sorts of persons, from the highest to the lowest, that come within their walk and compass, or unto whom they can have access with the least probability of success, unto whom they have not in a readiness to propose some secular advantages suited unto their state, condition, inclinations, and abilities. *Great men* shall have favour and correspondences with potentates abroad, besides a principal interest in that alteration in national affairs which they doubt not but they shall introduce. *Scholars* shall be used and preferred; at least, when they have any eminency in abilities, they shall not want esteem and advancement. *Mechanics* shall be employed, and the poorest one way or other provided for. And for all sorts of discontented persons who may be of any use unto their interest, they have the refuge of their monasteries for their entertainment. And is it any wonder if, in this degenerate age, wherein the most of men do openly and visibly declare a predominancy in their minds and affections of things carnal and temporal, above those that are spiritual and eternal, many be ensnared by these promises, which either shall be made good unto them, or at least are sufficient to keep them in expectation until they are engaged beyond recovery?

4. Many, it is feared, fall under the dreadful account given of God's righteous dealings with those who obstinately live in sin, under the profession of the truth, 2 Thess. ii. 10–12: "Because they received not the love of the truth, that they might be saved, God shall send them strong delusion, that they should believe a lie; that they all might be damned who believed not the truth, but had pleasure in unrighteousness." This is that which we have more cause to fear, with respect unto this nation, than all the artifices of the Roman church.

Lastly, How powerful and prevalent the last voice of this church may prove I know not. The motto of some potentates on their great guns is, "Vox ultima regum,"—"The last voice of kings:" that of this church is, "Fire and fagot;" wherewith I pray and hope that they shall never more be heard to speak in England.

Allowing them these advantages, I shall now prove that no wise or sober man, who takes care of his own salvation, can give up himself to the conduct of the church of Rome in his choice of religion, then when there are the most abounding contests about the truth and the right way of its profession, which is supposed [to be] our present case.

In my first reason I shall proceed no farther but to render this pretended guide suspected with all wise and sober men; for it will be granted, I suppose, that we ought thoroughly to consider who or what that guide is whereunto we do absolutely resign the disposal of all our spiritual concernments, without power of revocation.

If any men were to make such an absolute trust of their lives, estates, and liberties into the hands of another man, or of other men, putting them all absolutely out of their own power, certainly they would think it their wisdom and interest to consider aright who and what they are unto whom they do so fully and absolutely resign themselves and all that they have. And if they have any just suspicion of their honesty or faithfulness, or that they seek themselves, or their own advantage, in taking this trust upon them, they will not easily be induced to resign up their all unto them; yea, the more earnest they are to persuade them, the more will they suspect that there is knavery in the cause. How much more careful ought we to be in the choosing a guide into whose power and disposal we must resign all the eternal concernments of our souls!—which all men do who absolutely give up the conduct of themselves unto the church of Rome in all matters of religion; for, notwithstanding all their pleas of a sure and safe bank for the consciences of men, there are great presumptions that they will break at last, and leave them who have intrusted them unto eternal beggary.

I shall give but one reason, which renders this pretended guide so justly suspected as that no wise man can commit himself thereunto in things of this importance. And this is, the *prodigious worldly secular advantages* which the church of Rome hath made unto itself by this pretence of being the only guide of all Christians in matters of religion; for this pretence is the sole foundation of the whole Papacy, which, when the sand of it is removed, must fall to the ground. And we may consider both what they have obtained by it, and how they use their acquisition. For,—

1. By virtue of this pretence alone they have erected their popedom, obtained principalities and sovereignties, possessed themselves of the principal revenues of most nations of Europe, have heaped up *huge treasures* of wealth, wherewith they maintain innumerable persons who have nothing to do but by all arts to promote their interest, especially that numerous society which is grown at this day the pest and terror of the world. These things are evident in other nations; they were so formerly in this. And in all the zeal which of late they have pretended for the conversion, as they call it, of this nation, it is legibly written in all the parts of their design and the whole management of it, that it was power, dominion, wealth, and revenue unto themselves, that they intended; this place, that dignity, and the other revenue, and the carnally-sweet dominion over the consciences of all sorts of persons, were in their eye.

2. We may consider what *use they make* of these secular advantages and revenues, which they have obtained merely by virtue of this pretence. And it may be said with modesty that these things were never forced to be wickedly serviceable unto the lusts of men among the heathens themselves more than they are and have been among all sorts of men in the church of Rome. Ambition, avarice, pride, luxury, sensuality, cruelty, are the deities that they sacrifice the spoils of the souls and consciences of men unto. There is no sort of wickedness, not the highest and most provoking, not the most vile and sordid, that human nature is capable of, but multiplied instances may be given of the perpetration of them, by the advantage which they make of this pretence.

This consideration, I say, is sufficient unto all wise men to render this pretended guide justly suspected, and to bring the vagabond unto the strictest and severest examination that the law and word of God doth direct unto in such cases.

(1.) It is so, on the account of *reason* and common usage, amongst men in cases of an alike nature. If it be notoriously known and evident that any sort of persons, whatever else they seem to be or act, do make great and unaccountable advantages unto themselves by any trusts that are committed unto them, pretending nothing in the meantime but the good of them who so intrust them, a wise man will not absolutely give up the disposal of himself and all his concerns unto such persons. Yea, when men are more than ordinarily urgent to have such trusts committed unto them, we do ordinarily inquire what is their interest in this matter of care and trouble that makes them so earnest. And if we find that they have made their own advantages on all such occasions, we shall not be too forward to give up unto them all that we have; especially if the resignation of ourselves and our concerns, desired by them, be such as we shall never more have the disposal of any thing in our own power, nor shall they be accountable for any thing they do thereon. It may be you will say, those who desire this great trust to be reposed in them are in all other things of virtue and piety most eminent above others. But what if, by various ways and means, they discover themselves to be for the most part of the very worst of men? It will assuredly be said that such a kind of trust as that mentioned would be ridiculous, and was never made by any wise man, fools and madmen being only meet to be confined unto it.

Yet such is the trust that the church of Rome requireth that we should commit unto her, and that in affairs of infinitely greater importance than all other earthly concerns; for she would have us *absolutely* resign up our souls and consciences, with all our eternal interests, unto her conduct and guidance, without any reservation for the use of our own light, reason, knowledge, or faith, and without power of revocation, on pain of damnation. In the meantime, it is evident and notorious that by virtue of this pretence she hath erected the popedom, obtained principalities and dominion, endowed herself with the principal revenues of the nations, and erected a supremacy over kings and kingdoms, to be disposed of at their pleasure. Is it not the duty of a wise man, when any of these persons are importunate with him to forsake the Scripture and his own understanding, with all the experience which ever he had of the power of religion, and to give up himself absolutely unto their conduct, to inquire what is the interest of these men in these things which makes them thus importunate?

And if this appear openly to be an increase or confirmation of their secular advantages, he will say that this is a trust fit only for them to make whom darkness, ignorance, the love of sin, and a vicious conversation, have rendered spiritual fools and bedlams, that can in nothing guide themselves. Especially he will do so, when he shall find that these high pretenders to be the *only guides* of the souls and consciences of other men, do for the most part walk in paths themselves that go down to the chambers of death; that they are so far from giving examples of Christian meekness, humility, self-denial, faith, love, or real holiness,—from giving a just representation of Christ in the image of God on themselves,—as that in many great, notable, prodigious instances they represent the devil, with all his malice, cruelty, and blood, unto the world.

(2.) There is that which doth hereon yet farther increase a just suspicion of this pretended guide; and this is *the way of our Lord Jesus Christ*, and of his apostles under him and after him,—unto whom that conduct of our souls which the pope and church of Rome do now lay claim unto was really committed by God, even the Father. It is known that our Lord Jesus Christ himself, though in his divine person he was the sovereign possessor of heaven and earth, yet in that ministry wherein he took the guidance of men's souls, he obtained nothing, possessed nothing beyond food and raiment, nor made the least outward advantage by any good that he did or by any miracles that he wrought. This state in general belonged unto his humiliation, and was a part of his sufferings: but withal it was chosen by himself for this end,—to convince and satisfy the souls of men that he designed nothing in all his instruction and guidance of them but the glory of God in their eternal welfare; gaining nothing unto himself but reproaches, persecution, and the cross. This he did as knowing that there was that glory, beauty, power, and usefulness in the truth wherein he instructed men, that nothing was outwardly needful to give it an effectual entrance into their minds but only to deliver them from prejudices, which all self-advantages made by him would have given unto them. The Pope and Mohammed, who have since pretended unto the same conduct of men's minds in religion which was intrusted originally with Him whom the Father sealed, knowing that what they had to teach of their own, and to lead men into, had no glory, beauty, evidence, nor use in itself, have wisely betaken themselves unto the ways of fraud and force, to impose their doctrine on the consciences of men, with this bait and allurement, that what profit and advantage they make unto themselves by the conduct which they have assumed, others, according to their proportion, shall be sharers therein.

The holy apostles succeeded unto the personal ministry of our Lord Jesus Christ, as unto this conduct of the souls of men. Such power was committed unto them by him who sent them, "even as the Father sent him." Such assurance was there in their conduct, through infallible inspiration, and the presence of the Holy Ghost with them in an extraordinary manner, as that all men were bound to give up themselves unto their conduct and guidance. Howbeit they judged that there was no duty more incumbent on them than to make it evident unto all the world that they neither sought nor would accept of any temporal advantages unto themselves by the trust reposed in them; but were contented that their portion in this world should lie in all the extremities and calamities of it. And this they willingly submitted unto, that all men might be encouraged to trust them in their everlasting affairs, when they saw what losers they were by it in this world, without desire, hope, or expectation of any better condition.

The church of Rome lays claim to the very same authority over and conduct of the consciences of men in religion as were committed unto Jesus Christ and his apostles. It is as safe, as they pretend, for a man to cast off the authority and institutions of Christ himself as to dissent from those of the pope. "But what," in the meantime, "meaneth this bleating of the sheep and lowing of the oxen?" whence is it that they have managed the pretence hereof to the gaining of power, dominion, wealth, and revenues unto themselves, beyond that of the greatest kings and princes in this world? Let others do as they shall think fit, I shall never commit the conduct of my soul unto them, who, for aught I know, would never look after me nor any other were it not for the advantage they make by it unto the service of their earthly desires.

It may be said, that *other churches* and persons do make advantages unto themselves by that conduct of the souls of men which they lay claim unto; and if this be sufficient to render such guides suspected, we shall scatter the churches, and leave none to guide them. I answer, It doth no way follow; for the rules, measures, and outward allowances, for and in the name of their labour and guidance, unto the ministers of the gospel, are in general so stated in the Scripture as that men cannot mistake therein unto their prejudice. But we are not at all concerned in what advantages men make unto themselves hereby, provided that the conduct they pretend unto be such as is accompanied with no *dominion* over our faith, but is proposed only as a *help* thereunto. Whilst men require not an absolute resignment of our souls and consciences unto them, but leave us unto the perfect liberty of our own minds, to judge upon and receive what they propose unto us, to examine and try all that they instruct us in,—which we may reject or refuse, according as it evidenceth itself to be good or evil unto us,—there is no great danger in our conduct.

This, I say, is sufficient to render this pretended guide, which with so much vehement importunity would impose itself upon us, to be so justly suspected unto all men not forsaken as well of common reason as of all due reverence unto the word of God, as that they will not readily embrace it.

Secondly, As what hath been spoken is sufficient to render this pretended guide *suspected* with all sober and considerate persons, so there are cogent reasons why it ought to be absolutely *rejected* by all who take care of their own eternal salvation. The cause peculiarly under consideration is stated on a double supposition:—

1. That there are such *differences* in and about religion among us as wherein the eternal salvation of the souls of men are immediately concerned; for some of them consist in opinions, principles, and practices, pernicious and destructive unto salvation, as each side doth acknowledge and contend. And it is meet the cause at present should be expressly stated on this supposition, because those of the Roman church design their great advantage from it.

2. That in this case we ought diligently to apply ourselves unto some *safe guide* which may lead and conduct us in the right way, wherein we may glorify God and obtain eternal blessedness unto our own souls. This also is not only allowed by them, but fiercely contended for, as a foundation of their whole cause. Wherefore, to determine our thoughts aright in our inquiry on these suppositions, we may consider the things that follow:—

(1.) The first supposition is plainly *stated in the Scripture.* It is plainly affirmed therein that such things were then beginning in the church, that they would fall out in after ages, and increase towards the end and consummation of all things. See to this purpose Acts xx. 29, 30; 1 Tim. iv. 1–3; 2 Tim. iv. 3, 4; 2 Pet. ii. 1–3; 1 John iv. 1–3,—all in compliance with the holy warnings and predictions of our blessed Saviour himself unto the same purpose, Matt. xxiv. 4, 5, 11, 23–26. In all these places, and many others, the cause, as stated in our supposition, is expressly foretold, with the pernicious effects of opinions and heresies, overthrowing the foundation of faith and destroying the souls of men. In this cause is a certain guide necessary in a peculiar manner.

(2.) In *no one place,* either in express words or by direct consequence, are believers or the disciples of Christ directed in this case to betake themselves unto such a guidance of the church of Rome. They are not so in any one place where these divisions are foretold, where properly such directions should be expected, or nowhere; nor yet in any other place whatever. Any one divine testimony unto this purpose, giving this direction on that supposition, shall for ever determine this controversy.

Shall we think that the Lord Jesus Christ, foreknowing, foretelling, and warning all his disciples of such a dangerous state and condition, as from which they cannot escape or be delivered without a guide that will safely lead and conduct them, if there were but *one* such guide prepared and appointed by him, should nowhere, in any divine revelation, direct them thereunto? Doth a supposition hereof truly represent unto us his love, care, and compassion towards the church? Can any thing more injurious unto his wisdom, faithfulness, and honour be once imagined? It is impossible, therefore, that any man, in the case supposed, should betake himself unto the sole conduct of the pope or church of Rome without casting contempt on him and his authority. But,—

(3.) Yet there is farther evidence of his mind herein, in that we are expressly in this case directed unto *another guide*, without any mention of the church of Rome, which is utterly exclusive of this pretence. For,—[1.] All believers are commanded themselves to examine and try all false teachers, prophets, and spirits that are not of God, doctrines subverting the faith, and endangering the souls of men; which is utterly inconsistent with that absolute, universal resignation of themselves unto the guidance of the church of Rome which is claimed by it. See 1 John iv. 1–3. [2.] They are directed unto the way, means, and rule whereby they must make this trial, and come unto the final determination in their own minds, Isa. viii. 20; 2 Pet. i. 19; 2 Tim. iii. 15–17. And this also is diametrically opposite unto that resignation of themselves unto the church of Rome which it requireth of them. [3.] They have a guide promised unto them, to give them an understanding of the rule in the discharge of this duty, and to enable them to make a right and safe determination thereon, John xvi. 13; 1 John ii. 26, 27. These things are consistent with a *ministerial guide*, such as is found in all true churches, wherein none pretend to be lords of our faith, but only helpers of our joy; but with a supreme authoritative guide, requiring an absolute resignation of our understandings and consciences unto itself, they are altogether inconsistent.

This is the substance of our case, and this is the determination of it given us by the Holy Ghost. Diversities and divisions in principles, opinions, and practices in religion, are supposed unto as great a height as they can be at, at this day in the world. Teachers "speaking perverse things; departures from the faith, giving heed to seducing spirits and doctrines of devils; teachers not enduring sound doctrine, turning away men's ears from the truth, and turning them unto fables; false teachers, bringing in damnable heresies, denying the Lord that bought them, many following their pernicious ways; spirits of false prophets going out in the world, the spirit of antichrist;"—these things, I say, are all supposed and foretold in the Scripture. In this case and state of things, that we be not seduced, that our souls be not ruined, we are commanded ourselves to try and examine all those who teach such things, whether they be of God or no; and by the Scripture we are to try them, if we intend not to be deceived and undone for ever. Unto the right understanding hereof a sure and faithful guide is promised unto us, to lead us into all truth; so that no concernment of religion is more plainly stated, and, as unto our duty, more expressly determined in the Scripture, than this is.

It is so in a peculiar manner in the First Epistle of John the apostle. Before the end of his days, divisions, errors, heresies, began to abound in Christian religion. This he fully testifieth, chap. iv. 1–3, and 2 Epist. 7. According unto his duty, he writes unto believers to warn them of their danger, with reference unto them that seduced them, or attempted so to do, 1 Epist. chap. ii. 26. And he writes unto this purpose unto "fathers, young men, and children," or professed believers of all sorts, degrees, and endowments, verses 12, 13; and this not "because they did not know the truth, but because they did know it," and had experience of its power, verse 21. But in all the directions he gives them for the discharge of their duty, so as that they might escape the dangers they were exposed unto, there is not any one word, any intimation that they should betake themselves unto the guidance of this, or that, or any church, much less that which is called the church of Rome. But the sum of his direction is, that they should rely on the unction they had received from the Holy One, or the aids and supplies of the Spirit of God, to understand the Scripture in the examination and trial they were to make of all these things, chap. ii. 20, 27.

But to preserve their interest, they tell us that these precepts and promises are given unto the church, and not unto individual believers; as though the church were any thing materially but individual believers, and formally but a disposition of them into a sacred order for their edification. "Man was not made for the Sabbath, but the Sabbath was made for man." Believers were not made for the church, but the church is made for believers, and is of no use but with respect unto their edification. And to deny all individual persons to be the first object of all gospel precepts and promises,—churches, in what sense soever you take them, being so only as they are directive of their faith and obedience,—is to exempt their consciences from the authority of Christ, to turn them into beasts, and to overthrow the gospel.

Let men now who take care of their own eternal salvation, place themselves in their thoughts in that condition which the present case and their own circumstances do place them in. The world, the place where they live, the people whereunto they do belong, are filled with different apprehensions, principles, opinions, and practices in and about religion. Some of these, as those between the Papists and the Protestants, have immediate influence into their eternal condition of blessedness or misery, as both parties contend. Dreadful disorders and confusions have followed, and are like to follow, these differences even in this world. They will, in this case, find that it highly concerns them to take care that they be not deceived, and thereby ruined eternally, as multitudes are; that they "be not high-minded, but fear." A guide is that which they are to look after, that may carry them safely through all these difficulties and dangers. Two immediately offer themselves unto them, tendering the utmost assurance in these things which the nature of man is capable of in this world. The one is the Pope or church of Rome, which requires no more of them but a blind submission unto its guidance,—a way, I confess, to extricate themselves, and to deliver them from all care about their own souls, easy and facile, if safe. The other is the holy Scripture, with the promised aids of the Spirit of God to lead us unto the understanding of it and the truth contained in it. But in this way it is required of men that they make use of their own reason, understanding, judgment, diligence, with fervent prayer for divine assistance.

The present question is, Whether of these two guides such persons ought to betake themselves unto? I am on the consideration of one directive reason only; others shall be afterward spoken unto. And this is, that the Scripture, which all acknowledge to be the word of God, to speak in his name, expressly supposing this case and all the circumstances of it before laid down, doth thereon frequently direct and command us to make use of this latter guide, if we desire to be saved; and doth nowhere, no, not once, on a supposition of this case, send us unto the guidance of the church or pope of Rome, or any other church whatever. Wherefore, for men to suffer themselves to be inveigled, their souls to be perverted, and their faith overthrown by a few captious, sophistical reasonings of men of perverse minds, pursuing their own secular interest; to turn aside from the commandments of our Lord Jesus Christ and his apostles, in so plain, evident, and indisputable a case and duty,—is such a folly in itself, such an impiety against God, such a contempt of the Lord Christ, his wisdom, authority, and care, as must be eternally accounted for.

Thirdly, The things, for the most part, which this pretended guide proposeth unto and imposeth on the consciences, faith, and practice of them who give up themselves unto its conduct, are so unreasonable, —so contrary unto the common sense of Christians and the very first notions of the minds of men any way enlightened with the doctrine of the gospel,—so directly opposite unto the design of God in the revelation of himself unto us, and his commands concerning our faith and obedience,—that it is a thing astonishable how they should attain an access unto them who have any sense of these things. But when once men have their eyes bored out,—as they do it for themselves in the resignation they make of their understandings and consciences unto the conduct of this church,—they must grind whatever is brought unto them. I shall briefly instance in some few things of this sort:—

1. *The keeping of the Scripture from their daily and continual use.* I speak not directly unto them who, being brought up from their infancy in that church, know nothing of the Scripture but that the Bible is an obscure, dangerous book unto all laymen, which heretics make use of unto their advantage,—such persons can be contented to want it, or be without it all their lives, especially seeing it is full of light and principles inconsistent with their carnal lusts and interest;—but I speak of such who, many of them, like Timothy, have known the Scriptures from children, and having been conversant in them, have had some experience of their power.

Unto such as these come persons in the name and on the behalf of this pretended guide; and a compass of plausible words they will use, fit to distract and amuse weak and unstable minds. But the plain sense of what they say in this case is, "Cast away this Bible, this book; it doth but perplex you and disturb your minds with things that are above you, which you cannot understand, and is therefore an occasion of almost all the pernicious errors that are in the world." Will not any such person be ready to say, "Hath God given this book, this alone, as the only revelation of his mind and will unto us, as the guide and rule whereby we may come unto the eternal enjoyment of him (which you dare not directly deny); hath he commanded me to read, study, meditate, and be conversant in it continually; have I found the benefit of the light, counsel, and consolation administered by it in my own soul; and shall I now forsake it, cast it away, to betake myself unto your guidance and direction? Shall I forsake God, and Christ, and the Holy Spirit, all the prophets and apostles, who daily speak unto me in and by this word, to comply with you?" The very horror of the proposal is enough to secure the minds of any who have the least spark of spiritual light or grace from a compliance with it. Wherefore, whether it be reasonable to leave the word of God, which is full of light, shining like the sun in the firmament, to follow the glimmerings of this wandering meteor, which arose out of a horrible pit, and there will end, is left unto their consideration who take care of the eternal salvation of their own souls.

2. The *solemn worship* of God, by the guides of the church, in a tongue and *language which the people do not understand*, is another of their proposals. This they are bound to attend unto, on pain of damnation. But how any thing can be more contrary unto the common sense of them who know what it is to pray in a due manner, no man can conceive. As unto them who do not, yet is it not hard to convince them, where they are not obstinate on other prejudices, how irrational this proposal is, how inconsistent with that reasonable service that God requireth of us. Others will say that they find hinder-

ances and difficulties enough from and in this duty, from the weakness of their faith and instability of their minds, the suggestions of Satan, with diversions from outward objects; if you add thereunto that they shall not understand a word of what is spoken in prayer, and they know well enough they shall never pray at all. And the truth is, did we not know whence they took occasion for this strange contrivance, so contrary to the nature of all religion, and what advantage they make of it unto themselves, it could never be sufficiently admired how such a senseless imagination should befall their minds. I do not design to show how contrary it is to Scripture precepts and examples, to the practice of all the saints under the Old Testament and the New, with that of the primitive churches, and, on all accounts, what an abominable sacrilege it is so to rob the church of its chiefest treasure; it hath been done by others sufficiently. I only give it as an instance how unmeet this pretended church is to be such a guide as whereunto we are to make an absolute resignation of our understandings and consciences in all concerns of religion; and there is nothing that can make them who have any regard unto their own souls to reject its guidance with more detestation. Shall they accept them for their guide in religion, who, under pain of damnation, confine them, in all the public worship of the church, unto the use of a language that they do not understand? [so] that, instead of praying with their understandings, they must be content with a dumb show, with postures and gestures, with altars and pictures, the antic actings of a priest, and a noise of words whose sense they know not at all? If a man would seek for an infallible guide to hell, it is hard to find one more likely and better qualified unto that purpose than is this church of Rome.

3. There is, at the same instant, proposed unto us by this guide, the doctrine of *transubstantiation*, with the sacrifice of the mass thereon depending. This, they say, we must believe, at least avow that we do believe, on pain of eternal and temporal destruction also. But herein they require of us, that, on the mere credit of their conduct, we must renounce the use of our senses, the exercise of our reason, and actings of faith on divine revelations, all things whereby we are either men or Christians, that we may become blind idolaters. But they who, pretending to be our guides in religion, do thereon impose this monstrous imagination on our credulity, with the idolatrous practice wherein it issues, had need give us better security of their divine infallibility than the angels in heaven can do; for if an angel from heaven should preach this doctrine unto us, we may safely esteem him accursed, Gal. i. 8.

4. The last thing I shall instance in of this kind is the *adoration or worship of images*. God says concerning it expressly, "Thou shalt

not make unto thyself any graven images; thou shalt not bow down to them, nor worship them." They say contrary, "Thou shalt make unto thyself graven images; thou shalt bow down to them, and adore them." And in their use they make them the stage-plays in religion, wherewith the minds of ignorant, unstable persons are allured and seduced into all manner of superstitious practices, and turned off from the simplicity of the gospel; for being once persuaded, on the credit of their guide, that the making, use, and adoration of them are lawful, there is enough in the carnal minds of men to make them "dote" and even be "mad" upon them. Wherefore, no less service is done unto the interest of sin and the kingdom of Satan hereby, than if they should have taken off all sense of the authority of God from the consciences of men in the prohibition of those things which their sensual lusts are most prone unto. Could they have dissolved the obligation of the commands of God against adultery or stealing, and left men unto the guidance of their own lusts and inclinations, it is evident what abominable excesses the generality of men would run into. Neither do the lusts of the mind engage persons with less fierceness into the pursuit of their objects than do those of the flesh; and thence the disannulling of this command of God hath been an inlet unto all abominable idolatry. But herein they will not allow those who give up themselves unto their conduct once to consider the direct contradiction that is between God's commands and theirs; but believe they must what their church believes, and practise accordingly,—which is the most intolerable tyranny over the souls of men that ever was attempted. Only they will tell us of "latria," and "dulia," and "hyperdulia," of religious worship that is direct or reductive, transient or terminated on this or that object; and, after a maze of the like insignificant terms, the conclusion is positive, "You shall worship graven images."

There are also sundry other things wherein they do or would impose on the credulity of men,—in open contradiction unto their sense, reason, and experience, as well as unto all evidence of truth from the light and guidance of the Scripture,—which are somewhat of another nature than those foregoing. I shall only mention some of them; as,—1. They would have us believe that "we cannot believe the Scripture to be the word of God but upon the testimony and authority of their church." All the evidence that a man is capable of in his own mind that he doth so believe it; all that can be given in ordering our lives according unto it as the word of God; the assurance and peace which multitudes of all sorts have in resolving all their interest in things eternal into the faith of it; the sufferings and martyrdoms which many have undergone in the confirmation of it; the uncontrollable pleas that are made of the sufficiency of the motives whereon we believe it so to be,—are nothing with them: but we must say, we cannot believe the Scripture to be the word of God but only on the testimony and authority of their church; and therein both give ourselves the lie as unto what we know and are assured of, and judge millions to hell who have lived and died in the faith of it, without any respect unto that testimony or authority. 2. They will have *us to believe what they do not indeed believe themselves;* as, for instance, justification by our own works: for practically many of them do for this end trust unto absolutions, masses, the sacraments, and sacramentals of the church, with a reserve for the complement of it in purgatory,—which are not our own works; and some of the wisest of them do betake themselves at last to the "only mercy and grace of God." So would they have us to venture our souls on that whereon they will not adventure their own. 3. *Papal personal infallibility* was once a principal article of their creed; and the generality of their proselytes do receive it from them with no less firm assent than they do unto that of Christ himself. But among themselves they have so multiplied their wrangling disputes about it, as makes it evident that they believe it only so far as holds proportion with their interest, and is subservient thereunto; indeed, not at all. Their disputes of a difference between the court of Rome and the church of Rome, of the pope in his chair and out of it, in the use of help and advice of others and without this, in a general council and without it, in a particular council and without it, in matter of right and of fact, and the like, make it evident that they know not in what sense to believe it; and so indeed believe it not at all. And whereas they do themselves confess that some of their popes have been of the worst of men, yea, monsters for luxury, uncleanness, and violence, that which they require of us is not only hard and unreasonable, but impossible for any sober man to grant,—namely, that we believe such persons to have been infallible in the declaration of all divine, heavenly mysteries, so as that we ought to acquiesce in their declaration of them. 4. They would have us believe that the same body of Christ which was once "in the fulness of time made of a woman," by the power of God, is every day made of a wafer by the power of a priest. And what indignities are hereby cast on his person hath been sufficiently demonstrated.

These are some of the proposals which this pretended guide makes unto all them who give up themselves unto its conduct, to be believed with a suitable practice, on the pain of eternal damnation. But yet evident it is that they are all of them contrary unto the common sense, reason, and experience of all Christians, all that believe the gospel, as well as directly contradictory unto the Scripture and example of the primitive church. It is therefore left unto the judgment of all sober persons, such as are not yet made drunk with the cup of their abominations, to determine whether any thing but either profound ignorance and spiritual darkness, or love of sin, with a desire to live securely therein, or secular interests, or a hardening judgment for the abuse of the truth, or a concurrence of all [of] them, can prevail with men to make an entire, absolute resignation of their souls, and all their eternal concernments, unto the conduct of this pretended guide.

Fourthly, The *way* for the attaining the knowledge of the truth proposed by this guide is opposite unto the way and means prescribed by God himself unto that end. It is so whether we respect the internal qualifications of our minds, or the duties that he prescribeth, or the aid that he promiseth thereunto. For, as unto the first, he requireth that those who would learn the truth ought to be meek, and lowly, and humble, for such alone he will teach, Ps. xxv. 8, 9, 14; John vi. 45,—and if we are not taught of God we learn nothing as we ought, or not unto any purpose; that they cast out all "wickedness and superfluity of naughtiness," that so they may receive the ingrafted word with meekness, James i. 21. Without these things they may be always learning, but shall never come unto the knowledge of the truth. And as unto means and duties, two things he enjoins and indispensably requires of us in order unto this end:—1. That we study the word continually; that we meditate upon it, and place our delight in it, Josh. i. 8; Deut. vi. 6, 7; Ps. i. 2; Isa. viii. 20; John v. 39; 2 Tim. iii. 15–17; Ps. cxix. 18; John xvi. 13; 1 John ii. 20. 2. Fervent and diligent prayer, that we may be led into and preserved in the truth, that we may be enabled to receive it, and hold it fast against temptations and oppositions. For our aid and assistance herein he commands us to wait for it, and expect the Spirit of wisdom and revelation to open our eyes, to bring us unto the full assurance of understanding, or to lead us into all truth. Of these things, of the necessity of them unto the due knowledge of the truth, we hear nothing from this pretended guide. She knows well enough that to put the minds of men into these ways and the use of these means, whereby they may be taught of God, and "learn the truth as it is in Jesus," is to loose them from herself for ever. Howbeit, they are the only ways and means prescribed and blessed of God unto this end, with those other especial duties which belong unto them.

They will say, it may be, that they do instruct their converts in these things, and press them withal unto higher acts of devotion and mortification than others do. But there are two things which deprive them of any advantage by this pretence. For,—1. We see and know of what sort, for the most part, their converts are. I shall not give that character of them in words which generally they give of themselves in their works: for I have nothing to do with the persons of men; and I should rejoice to see them give a better evidence of being instructed in these things than as yet they have done. But, 2, Whatever of this nature they propose and prescribe unto them, it is not unto this end, that they may learn and know the truth. They require no more of any hereunto but that, on their sophistical and frivolous pretences, he give up himself unto their guidance, or submit himself unto the authority of the pope: for hereby he formally becomes a member of the Catholic church, whose faith, whether he know it or no, immediately becomes his; and for particulars he must wait for the priest's information, as occasion shall require.

This is, I confess, their great advantage in this world:—The way they propose to attain the knowledge of the truth is easy, consistent with the lusts of men, exposed equally to the wise and foolish, to the sober and intemperate, puts men out of all doubts, giving them all the quiet assurance which deceit and falsehood can communicate.

The way of God unto the same end is difficult unto flesh and blood, destructive unto the lusts of the flesh and of the mind, requiring diligence, humility, and watchfulness, in the exercise of grace all our days; which things few are pleased withal. Yet is this way of God so suited unto the nature of religion; so becoming the importance of this duty; so effectual not only unto the attainment of the knowledge of truth, but unto all the ends of it in the life of God; is so necessary, on the account of the infinite greatness and holiness of God, with the nature of divine revelations,—as that no man, who is not blinded with prejudices and corrupt affections, can decline it to embrace the other.

There are other things yet, if it be possible, of a higher abomination, to deter all sober persons from touching with this guide, than those already insisted on. And such they are as the present contrivances and practices of our adversaries do unavoidably compel us to plead in this cause, and are in themselves sufficient for ever to divest that church of this great and gainful pretence of being the only guide of all men in religion. For,—

Fifthly, Consider what it is wherein they instruct many of them who betake themselves unto their conduct and guidance,—I mean of the agents for and in the name of the church of Rome. The first thing which they labour to fix on their minds and consciences is absolute obedience unto their immediate guides, with a blind belief of what they propose unto them; and this they prevail on them unto by assuming a twofold authority unto themselves. 1. And the first is, that of *forgiving them all their sins*, though against the light of nature and of their own consciences, which they confess unto them;

and this confession they are obliged unto under pain of damnation. Some things, indeed, they do require of them in order unto a participation of priestly absolution; but they are all in the power of the priest to prescribe, decline, or accept; which latter they will not be uneasy unto when it conduceth unto their advantage. The issue is, that in this pardon of their sins the souls of men may as safely acquiesce as if they were immediately pardoned by Christ himself. And if they have occasion, for the advantage of the Catholic cause, to put them on things that are openly sinful, as murder and sedition, either by virtue of the direction, guidance, and commands of the priests, they lose their nature and become no sins at all, or they are so assured of pardon as puts them, in their consciences, into as good a state and condition as if they had not sinned. And,—

2. They assume unto themselves an authority to grant especial privileges and rewards, in heaven and earth, to the doing of what they command or require, whatever it be. As unto the earth, so many prayers, so many masses, shall be assigned unto their advantage; and in some cases canonization, with all the glorious privileges of it. And as unto heaven, what they so do shall have such a proportion of merit as shall exalt them unto the second, third, or fourth place of precedency and honour therein among all the holy martyrs. It is incredible what power and dominion over the consciences of their proselytes they obtain by these means, with other artifices of the like nature. Hence many of them know of no other dependence on any, as unto present peace and eternal blessedness, than that on the priests alone.

Woful practices do follow on these principles: for the minds of men being thus prepared, they dispose of them unto such occasions or services, for the interest of the Catholic cause, as their own nature, inclinations, the fierceness or softness of their tempers, their outward greatness, power, and wealth, or their straits, wants, and necessities, render them meet unto; for now they are ready for such things, which, if they had not relinquished the care and charge of their own souls, if they had not absolutely resigned them unto others, they would never have entertained a thought of without detestation and abhorrency. Poor deluded creatures! who could sufficiently bewail their condition, but that, for the most part, through the love of sin and the wages of it, they choose these delusions? Some now shall fire cities; some shall murder innocent persons; some shall assassinate kings and potentates; some shall creep into houses and lead captive silly women, laden with sins, led about with divers lusts; and some shall prostitute themselves unto the carnal lusts and pleasures of others;—all, as they judge, conducing unto the Catholic cause, and their own interest therein! These are they who must answer, not only for the blood of them that are murdered, but of their murderers also. I heartily wish these things were not so, that they never had been so; but, being so, it is well that they are known so to be, and that they are written in such legible characters in most nations of Europe, especially in this wherein we live, as that he who runs may read them. I shall not descend unto particular instances; every one's mind and thoughts will suggest them unto them, or they may learn them in Westminster Hall.

It will be said, that on a supposition that these things are so, yet this is the crime of but a few, it may be of a few Jesuits, which others, especially the church, is not concerned in. They are but a *few* who teach and instruct their converts unto such purposes,—but a few that are possessed with those maxims and principles which lead unto these practices. Notwithstanding their miscarriages, the church itself may be a safe guide unto the souls of men.

I answer two things:—1. That those who have these principles, who teach these practices, are all of them appointed unto their office and work, imposed on the consciences of men as their only guides, by the *authority of the church* itself. No caution is given by it against them,—no rule prescribed whereby they may know them; but they come all armed with the authority of the church, and as such are received by their credulous followers. The whole, therefore, of what they do may justly be ascribed unto the church itself. 2. It may be made to appear that, for about a hundred and fifty years past, no plot, no design, hath been conceived or perpetrated, wherein kings, princes, private persons were to be murdered or destroyed, wherein nations were to be embroiled in blood and confusion, in order unto the promotion of the Catholic cause, but the *church itself* was either the contriver or approver of it. Who approved of the murder of the two kings in France, one after another? of the massacre there of a hundred thousand Protestants? Who designed and blessed all preparations for the murder of Queen Elizabeth, with the unjust invasion of the nation in '88?[1] Who blessed and protected, what in them lay, the horrible massacre of Ireland, with the slaughters that have been made in other places on the same principles? Was it a few Jesuits only? was it not the church itself, in its head the *pope*, and its horns the *cardinals* at Rome?

Wherefore, although it seem good unto this church to assume unto itself the sole conduct of the souls of all men, in the matters of religion, which hath thrived in its hands unto an incredible grandeur, in dominion, power, and wealth; yet other men of an ordinary wisdom and capacity, who are not yet taken alive by them at their pleasure, will be ready to judge (especially now the cave of Cacus is opened) that it is necessary for them to take more care of their own souls.

[1] The reference is to the Spanish Armada of 1588.—ED.

Some will say that all these things, principles, and practices, are separable from their religion, and that they will take sufficient heed unto themselves that they give admittance unto none of them, especially such as are against the light of nature and the known rules of common honesty. Both the goodness of their own natural temper, and the principles of morality, which they will never part withal, will give them and others security herein.

God forbid I should ever charge any persons with any thing that is criminal, whereof they are not or may not be easily convicted. Those who make these professions shall pass with me at the rate and upon the credit of their professions; as shall all men in this world, until they contradict and disprove themselves by their actions. But even such persons had need be very careful that they are not deceived herein. The resignation which they are to make of themselves and their consciences unto the conduct of this church doth quite change both their light and rule; for it includes a renunciation of all principles and persuasions, in things divine and moral, that do or may in the least interfere with that conduct. It is true that neither that church nor any else can change the nature of things moral in themselves: for although they may call good evil, and evil good,—light darkness, and darkness light,—yet they cannot make that which is good evil, nor that which is evil good; but they may make a false representation of the one and other unto the minds of men. Hence, what was evil unto them antecedently unto this resignation of themselves,—as the firing of cities, the murder of innocent persons, the overthrow of governments and nations for their own ends,—shall be imposed on them by this pretended infallible guide as things good and meritorious with reference unto their Catholic ends. These are the two most pernicious devices in all their superstition:—1. That the consciences of men are exempted and taken off from an immediate dependence on and subjection unto the authority of Christ, and put in immediate subjection unto the priest's; seeing he neither promiseth any thing unto them, nor commands any thing but by the church. 2. That their commands, because they are theirs, do regulate their consciences even as unto moral good or evil. Nor is it safe for these men to trust too much unto the goodness of their own natures, nor, it may be, unto others who are concerned in what they shall do. For as it is the glory of the doctrine and grace of the gospel to change the wolf, the lion, and the leopard, Isa. xi. 6–9, persons of the fiercest and most violent inclinations, into quiet associates of lambs and children; so it is to be feared, from many instances, that by virtue of their conduct they can change appearing sheep, at least as unto their natural tempers, into that which is violent, bloody, and poisonous.

Sixthly, Under pretence of being this guide, and to impose their pretensions thereunto on the minds and consciences of men, this church hath filled most nations of Europe with *blood and slaughter;* making horrible devastations of innumerable persons, both fearing God and living peaceably in the world. Ten times more blood of Christians hath been shed by them unto this end than was shed in all the primitive Pagan persecutions. All that dissent from them may say, "Quæ regio in terris nostri non plena cruoris?"—"Is there any nation in Europe that is not filled with our blood?" The last day alone can discover the blood that hath been shed secretly or with little noise by the Inquisition, in the Spanish and some of the Italian territories. England, France, Germany, Flanders, Holland, Ireland, can speak for themselves, in the cruelties which unto this end have been executed in them. The sole reason of all this inhuman violence hath been, that men would not submit their souls and consciences unto that absolute power over them and conduct of them which their church claimeth unto itself.

And it is most probable that their absolute conduct is of the same nature with the ways and means whereby they do attempt it or have obtained it. When men by force and fraud, blood and slaughters, do endeavour to impose their rule upon us, we are not to expect but that the rule will be answerable unto the means that are used for the attaining it. As in the first planting and propagation of Christian religion the way and means of them were spiritual light, and the evident exercise of all graces, especially meekness, humility, patience in sufferings, and contempt of the world, hereon men had just grounds to believe and expect that the conduct which they were invited and called unto, under the rule of Christ, would be of the same nature,—meek, holy, just, and good,—whereof by experience they found full assurance: so where the rule of our souls and consciences is attempted and carried on by violence, blood, cruelty, and desolation of nations, we have just ground to believe that if those who use them do prevail therein, their leading and rule will be of the same nature.

It is but reasonable, therefore, for any man, before he make choice of this guide, to ask of himself or others these few questions:—Is there any thing in the gospel which gives countenance unto this way of imposing a guide in religion on the minds and consciences of men? Was there any thing like it in the practices of our Lord Jesus Christ, his apostles, or the primitive churches? Doth this way make a just representation of the spirit, the meekness, the holiness, the love, the patience of our Lord Jesus Christ? Is it consistent with the genius of the doctrine of the gospel, the religion taught therein, as unto its nature and ends, concerning our deportment in this world, and our tendency unto another? Can any man think without horror that our Lord Jesus Christ should be the author of this way; that he hath appointed that all men should be starved, or hanged, or burned, or otherwise slaughtered, who would not submit unto the doctrine or rule of this or any church, as some of the worst of men shall please to state them? Is not this that which, among other things, gives us assurance that the doctrine and superstition of Mohammed were from hell, from the old murderer, in that it is a prime dictate of them that those who will not submit unto them are to be destroyed with fire and sword? By that time a man hath a little weighed these inquiries, with such other of the same nature that may be added unto them, if he be not forsaken of all sense of the glory of Christ, of the honour of the gospel, of the reputation of Christian religion, and all care of the salvation of his own soul, he will make a long stand before he give up himself absolutely unto the conduct of this church.

Seventhly, I cannot but mention, in the next place, that which, because it is commonly pleaded, I shall but mention. And this is, that many *important principles* and practices of the religion which this pretended guide would impose upon us are evidently suited unto the carnal interests and lusts of them who have the conduct of it. Such are purgatory, papal pardons, sacrifices for the dead, auricular confession, with priestly absolution thereon. Many have already declared how the notion and superstition of these things did both raise and do maintain their revenues, and are otherwise made use of to make provision for the flesh to fulfil the lusts thereof. And there lieth no encouragement herein to engage wise men to give up themselves unto its conduct. But,—

Eighthly, Considerate men will be afraid of that conduct under which Christian religion hath *lost all its native beauty*, simplicity, spiritual glory, and power. How are these things represented unto us in the gospel? How were they exemplified unto us in the lives of the apostles and of all the sincere primitive converts? The church was through them "a new heaven and a new earth, wherein dwelt righteousness." The whole of religion, as it was at first professed, was nothing but a representation of the wisdom, truth, holiness, love, and compassion of Christ; an evident and glorious means to recover mankind from its apostasy from God, and to re-introduce his image on the souls of men; a blessed way continually to exercise the power of love, goodness, charity, bounty, zeal, and delight in God; a testimony given unto the truth, reality, and substance of things spiritual, invisible, and eternal, with their preference above all earthly things. Under their conduct is this beauty, this glory of Christian religion, lost and defaced. We may say, with the prophet of old, "How is the faithful city become an harlot! righteousness lodged in it, but now murderers," Isa. i. 21. The church is the temple of God. Could we have looked into it of old, we might by faith have seen Christ sitting on his throne, the train of his light, holiness, love, and grace, filling the whole temple;—look into it under their conduct, and there is the dreadful appearance of the "lawless person," the Man of Sin, sitting in the temple of God, showing himself to be God, to our horror and amazement. Look into the primitive assemblies of Christians, 2 Cor. iii. 8–11, you shall see meekness, humility, and the glorious ministration of the Spirit in outward simplicity;—look into those of this guide, and you shall see them like the house of Micah, Judges xvii. 5, a house of gods, with molten images, graven images, ephods, and teraphims, multiplied instruments of superstition and idolatry. Look on their conversation of old in the world, and it was humble, peaceable, useful, profitable unto mankind, with a contempt of earthly things in comparison of those that are eternal;—but under the conduct of this guide, ambition, pride, sensuality, and profaneness have covered the nations of its communion; in all things have they lost and defaced the native beauty and glory of Christian religion. It will be of no advantage unto any voluntarily to come in into a participation in this woful apostasy.

Ninthly, The *insupportable yoke* that this guide puts on kings and sovereign princes, on pretence of its divine right of a universal guidance of them and all their subjects, deserves the consideration of them that are concerned, before they give up themselves unto it. It is true, that by and since the Reformation, as this power of these men who call themselves this guide hath been utterly cast off by many, so in those places where on other accounts they maintain their interest, it hath been greatly weakened and impaired,—hence those of the greatest power in the nations of Europe have had little regard unto their authority, unless it be used unto their interest and advantage;—but their principles are still the same as they were, their pretence of divine right the same that it was, and their desires after the exercise of it, unto their own ends, not at all abated. Could they once again enthrone themselves in the consciences of kings themselves and all their subjects,—could they destroy the balance of a contrary interest,—could they take away the reserves of reliefs against their encroachments, by engaging the assistance of subjects against their princes, of one prince against another, as in former days,—there is no reason to think but that they would return unto their former usurpations and insolency. And wise men, yea, princes themselves, may be deceived, if they take their measures of the nature of the Papacy, with respect unto civil government, from its present deportment and attempts, though bad enough. Take away the perplexities and difficulties they are cast into, through the rejection of their authority by so many nations, and by the divided interests of kings and potentates thereon,—heal their deadly wound, and restore them unto a catholic power over the consciences of all sorts of men, by the destruction of them by whom it is opposed,—and it will quickly appear with another aspect on the world, another manner of influence on the governors and governments of kingdoms and nations, than now it doth. But the consideration hereof belongs principally unto them who are not wont to be unconcerned in the preservation of their just authority. Yet, if occasion require it, a demonstration shall be given of the necessary and unavoidable consequences of the re-admission of the papal power in any of the nations of Europe who have cast it out, and that with respect unto the governors and governments of them.

Among many other considerations which offer themselves unto the same purpose, and which shall be produced if occasion is given, I shall add one more, and close this discourse. And this is, that the foundation of all the religious worship which this guide directs unto, whence all other parts of it do proceed, and whereon they do depend, consists of the overthrow of one of the principal articles of the Christian faith; and this is, that "our Lord Jesus hath by one offering for ever perfected them that are sanctified," as it is expressed by the apostle, Heb. x. 14. In direct opposition hereunto, the ground and reason of their mass, and the sacrifice therein,—which is the life, soul, centre, and foundation of all their religious worship,—lies in this, that there is a necessity that Christ be offered often, yea, every day, in places innumerable; without which, they say, the church can neither be sanctified nor perfected. Such a guide is this church, as that it lays the foundation of all its sacred worship in the overthrow of the principal foundation of the Christian faith.

God, in his appointed time, will put an end unto all these extravagancies, excesses, and distractions in his church, "when violence shall be no more heard in her land, wasting nor destruction within her borders; when she shall call her walls Salvation, and her gates Praise."

SOME CONSIDERATIONS

ABOUT

UNION AMONG PROTESTANTS,

AND THE

PRESERVATION OF THE INTEREST OF THE PROTESTANT RELIGION IN THIS NATION.

M.DC.LXXX.

PREFATORY NOTE.

This tract appears to have been published anonymously in 1680. The excitement prevailing throughout Britain at the time has been described in the prefatory note to the preceding treatise. The precise aim of our author in the tract which follows is not very easily ascertained; nor does it at first sight appear why, in order to strike a blow at Popery, and advance the interests of Protestantism, he should insist so strongly on the fact that the Anglican hierarchy, in its claims and pretensions, was the chief cause of the lamentable divisions among British Protestants, and, consequently, of the weakness of the Protestant interest at this juncture. It was, however, not an unusual plea with the adherents of the English Church, and more especially with the abettors of the high-handed measures adopted by the Court for discountenancing and suppressing dissent, that the Church of England was the bulwark of Protestantism, and that to strengthen it was the wisest course which the nation in the present crisis could pursue, in order to avert the threatened restoration of papal influence in Britain. Churchmen, accordingly, who were alarmed at the prospect of Popery regaining its ascendency in the land, might, under this consideration dexterously and plausibly urged, be not only confirmed in their attachment to the Established Church, but look with increased jealousy upon Nonconformists, as traitors to the cause of Protestantism; while the latter might be led to abate, in some degree, the strength of their conscientious opposition to the polity of the Established Church.

Our author, on the other hand, shows in this tract that in reality the Church of England—dreaded at the Court of Rome, and respected by Reformed Churches abroad, as the representative of British Protestantism—was not confined within the pale of the Established Church, but consisted of "the body of Christian people professing Protestantism, with a detestation of Popery." It is next his object to show that the hierarchy of England, or, more generally, "the authoritative national church-state," was a source of weakness rather than a tower of strength to the Protestant interest, on account of (1.) its encroachment on the civil rights and government of the nation; (2.) the oppression of Nonconformists in order that its claims and dignity might be upheld; and (3.) the spirit it fostered of subserviency to royal aggrandizement, in order to secure a share in the preferment which is under the patronage and at the disposal of the Crown. So long as the Anglican church was maintained in its claims, it was "vain to expect peace and union among Protestants." He proceeds farther, and affirms that Popery may seize possession of it, and make use of it for its own purposes, till the whole nation be insensibly "betrayed into Popery, as it were, they know not how."

In the absence of a National or Established Church, Protestantism would not be endangered, if the State gave civil and public securities for the maintenance of the Protestant religion. He specifies the securities requisite for this purpose:—a national renunciation of, and protest against, the errors of Popery; a confession of faith, to be subscribed by all enjoying a public ministry; and the exercise of magisterial authority to the encouragement of Protestantism, in providing for the support of the gospel, and in protecting the church in the enjoyment of its spiritual power. He contends that the church should be protected in the exercise of its spiritual power by spiritual means only.

His design, accordingly, in this tract, is not so much to enforce the duty of union among Protestants, as to indicate the danger which, in his judgment, threatened the Protestant cause from the "national church-state," or, to come nearer the modern phrase, the state-church; though, from the view he takes of the duty of the magistrate to support Christian ordinances, his objections to it have not much in common with the opposition now offered to the principle of a state-church. The subject of the tract is continued, and his views in regard to the course which apostasy to Rome might take, are more fully developed, in the succeeding treatise.—Ed.

SOME CONSIDERATIONS

ABOUT

UNION AMONG PROTESTANTS.

1. THE protestant religion, introduced into this nation by the apostolical way and means of the holiness and laborious preaching of its professors, confirmed with the martyrdom of multitudes of all sorts, being now thoroughly fixed in the minds of the body of the people, and confirmed unto them by laws and oaths, is become the principal interest of the nation, which cannot be shaken or overthrown without the ruin of the government and destruction of the people. Nothing, therefore, less being included in the attempts of the Papists, with all their interest in Europe, for the re-introducing of their religion amongst us, the nation hath been constantly filled for a hundred years with fears, jealousies, and apprehensions of dangers, to the great disturbance of the government and disquietment of the subjects; nor can it be otherwise whilst they know that there is a pregnant design for their total subversion, together with the ruin of the protestant religion in other places, which would have ensued thereon. But,—

2. This religion, so received and approved by the people as the only true way to salvation (accompanied with an abhorrency of the superstition, idolatry, and heresies of the church of Rome, partly on the general account of their own nature, and partly on particular reasons and provocations, from the attempts of those that belong unto that church for the ruin of them and their religion), and jointly professed in the same confession of faith, hath been preserved by the means of a faithful, laborious ministry, under the care, protection, and outward government of the supreme power, as the greatest bulwark of the protestant religion in Europe.

3. The only weakness in it, as the interest of the nation (before it was infested with novel opinions), was the differences that have been

amongst many of the professors of it, from the very first beginning of the Reformation, and which are continued unto this day.

4. These differences, though consisting now in many particulars of less moment, arose originally solely from the constitution of an authoritative national church-state. For some would have it to be of one sort, namely, episcopal; some of another, namely, presbyterian; some would have it of a divine original, others of a human, which must be the judgment of the king and parliament, who know it to be what they have made it, and nothing else; and some judge it a mere usurpation on the power of the civil government and the liberties of the people.

5. It is therefore acknowledged that the body of Christian people in this nation professing the protestant religion, with a detestation of Popery, having the gospel preached unto them, and the sacraments duly administered, under the rule of the king, are the church of England. But as unto an authoritative national church, consisting solely in the power and interest of the clergy,—wherein the people, either as Christians, Protestants, or subjects of the kingdom, are not concerned,—such as is at present established, farther inquiry may be made about it.

6. There is a threefold form of such a church at present contended for. The first is Papal, the second Episcopal, and the third Presbyterian.

7. The first form of an authoritative national church-state amongst us, as in other places, was papal; and the sole use of it here in England was, to embroil our kings in their government; to oppress the people in their souls, bodies, and estates; and to sell us all, as branded slaves, unto Rome. These things have been sufficiently manifested. But in other places, especially in Germany, whilst otherwise they were all of one religion, in doctrine and worship, all conform to the church of Rome, yet, in bloody contests, merely about this authoritative church-state, many emperors were ruined, and a hundred set battles fought in the field.

8. At the Reformation, this church-state was accommodated (as was supposed) unto the interest of the nation, to obviate the evils suffered from it under the other form, and render it of use unto the religion established. Yet experience manifests that, partly from its constitution, partly from the inclinations of them by whom it is managed, other evils have accompanied or followed it; which, until they are removed, the weakness of the protestant interest, through mutual divisions, will remain among us. And, among others, they are these:—

(1.) An encroachment on the civil rights and government of the nation, in the courts and jurisdictions pretended to belong or to be annexed unto this church-state, over the persons, goods, and liberties of the subjects (yea, in some cases, their lives). It is the undoubted right and liberty of the people of this nation, that no actual jurisdiction should be exercised over their persons, estates, or liberties, in a way collateral unto, and independent on, the public administration of justice unto all, derived from the sovereign power, and executed by known officers, rules, and orders, according unto the laws of the realm. If this be taken from them, all other pretences of securing the liberty and property of the subjects are of no advantage unto them: for whilst they have justice, in legal public courts, duly administered unto them, they may be oppressed and ruined (as many are so every day) by this pretended collateral irregular power and jurisdiction over their persons, goods, and liberties; from which it seems to be the duty of the parliament to deliver them. And it is the right of the kings of this nation that no external power over the subjects be exercised but in their name, by virtue of their commission, to be granted and executed according unto the laws of the land. This right of kings, and this liberty of subjects also, are so sacred as that they ought not to be intrenched on by any pretence of church or religion; for what is of God's own appointment will touch neither of them. But the administration of this jurisdiction, as it is exercised with a side-wind power, distinct, different from, and in some things contrary unto, the public justice of the nation (wherein all the subjects have an equal interest), and by the rules of a law foreign unto that of the kingdom, is a great cause of the continuation of divisions among Protestants, unto the weakening of the interest of religion itself.

(2.) It is accompanied with the prosecution and troubling of peaceable subjects in their liberties and estates, —not for any error in the Christian faith, not for any declension from the protestant religion or compliance with Popery, not for any immoralities, but merely and solely for their non-compliance with and submission unto those things which are supposed necessary for the preservation of their church-state, which is of itself altogether unnecessary; for the whole complex of the imposed conformity in canonical obedience, ceremonies, rites, and modes of worship, hath no other end but the sustentation and preservation thereof, being things otherwise that belong not to Christian religion. This began, this will perpetuate, our divisions; which will not be healed whilst it is continued. And whilst the two parties of Papists and Protestants are at this day contending, as it were, for life, soul, and being (the long-continued design of the former, under various pretences, and by great variety of attempts, being come unto its fatal trial, as unto its issue), it will not be thought meet by wise men, whose entire interest in religion and the liberties of the nation are concerned in this contest, to continue the body of Protestants in divisions, with mutual animosities and the distrust of multitudes, on such unnecessary occasions.

(3.) Whereas, by virtue of this state and constitution, sundry persons are interested in honours, dignities, power, and wealth, in all which they have an immediate (and not merely legal) dependence on the king since their separation from the pope, they have constantly made it their business to promote absolute monarchical power, without respect unto the true constitution of the government of this nation; which in sundry instances hath been disadvantageous to kings themselves, as well as an encumbrance to the people in parliament: for although their constitution doth really intrench upon the king's legal power in the administration of their jurisdiction, yet, to secure their own interests, and to make a seeming compensation for that encroachment, many of them have contended for that absolute power in the king which he never owned nor assumed unto himself.

9. The evils and inconveniences of this constitution of an authoritative national church-state have been greatly increased and propagated in this nation, as unto the heightening of divisions among Protestants, by the endeavours that have been [made] to confirm and continue this state in an extraordinary way. Such were the oath called "Et cetera,"[1] and the late oath at Oxford,[2] whereon many sober, peaceable protestant ministers have been troubled, and some utterly ruined; which hath much provoked the indignation of the people against those who occasioned that law, and for whose sake it was enacted, and increased the suspicion that those who manage these things would have men believe that their state and rule is as sacred as the crown or religion itself, unto the great disparagement of them both: which things are effectual engines to expel all peace and union among Protestants.

10. Those who are for the presbyterian form of an authoritative

[1] The convocation of the English church held under Laud in 1640, drew up seventeen articles, entitled "Constitutions and Canons Ecclesiastical," etc. They contain extreme views of the royal prerogative, and authorize the infliction of ecclesiastical and civil penalties upon Dissenters. The sixth canon embodies an oath to be taken by the clergy of the church; and in this oath these words occurred, "Nor will I ever give my consent to alter the government of the church by archbishops, bishops, deans, and archdeacons, etc." This "etc." was the subject of complaint, and gave rise to the nickname by which the oath is commonly known.—Ed.

[2] While the plague was ravaging London in 1665, the parliament met at Oxford, and imposed an oath on all Nonconformists, binding them never to take up arms against the king, or "endeavour any alteration of government, either in church or state." All who refused to take the oath were forbidden to approach within five miles of any city that returned a member to parliament, and any place where they had been ministers, or where they had preached after the act of oblivion. Strange requital for the faithfulness which many nonconformist ministers were at this time evincing in abiding by their posts in London, and supplying consolation to its inhabitants, diseased and dying in multitudes around them!—Ed.

national church-state do, indeed, cut off and cast away most of those things which are the matter of contest between the present dissenting parties, and so make a nearer approach towards a firm union among all Protestants than the other do; yet such an authoritative church-state, in that form, is neither proper for nor possible unto this nation, nor consistent with that pre-eminence of the crown, that liberty of the subjects, and freedom of the consciences of Christians, which are their due. But this being not much among us pretended unto, it need not farther be spoken of.

11. It is evident, therefore, that whilst the evils enumerated are not separated from the present authoritative national church constitution, but the powers of it are put in execution, and the ends of it pursued, it is altogether vain to expect peace and union among Protestants in England. It neither hath been so, nor ever will be so; fire and fagot will not be able to effect it. Who shall reconcile the endless differences that are and have been about the power, courts, and jurisdictions of this church-state, whether they be agreeable unto the laws of the land and liberty of the subjects? The fixed judgment of many, that they have no legal authority at present, nor any power given unto them by the law of the land, whereon they dare not submit unto them, is no less chargeable, dangerous, and pernicious unto them, than are their uncouth vexations and illegal proceedings unto them who are unwillingly forced to submit unto them. And, whatever may be expected, the people of this nation will never be contented that their persons, goods, or liberties shall be made subject unto any law but the public royal law of the kingdom, administered in legal courts of justice. Who shall undertake that all Christians or Protestants in this nation shall ever submit their consciences and practices to a multitude of impositions no way warranted in the Scriptures? or how any of the other evils that are the causes of all our divisions shall be removed, cannot easily be declared.

12. If it shall be said, that if this authoritative national church-state should be removed, and no other of another form set up in the room of it, or be divested of the powers claimed at present by it, it will be impossible to preserve the protestant religion amongst us, to keep uniformity in the profession of it, and agreement amongst its professors, it is answered,—(1.) Nothing ought to be removed but what is a real cause, or unnecessary occasion at least, of all the deformity and disorder that is amongst us, and is likely so to continue. (2.) That whilst we have a protestant king and a protestant parliament, protestant magistrates and protestant ministers, with the due care of the nation that they may so continue, and a protestant confession of faith duly adhered unto, I shall not, under the blessing of the holy Providence, fear the preservation of the protestant religion

and interest in England, without any recourse unto such a church-power as fills all with divisions. This, I say, is that church of England which is the principal bulwark of the protestant religion and interest in Europe,—namely, a protestant king, a protestant parliament, protestant magistrates, protestant ministers, a protestant confession of faith established by law, with the cordial agreement of the body of the people in all these things, esteeming the protestant religion and its profession their chief interest in this world. To suppose that a few men, having obtained honours, dignities, and revenues unto themselves, exercising a power and authority (highly questionable, whether legal or no) unto their own advantage, oppressive unto the people, and by all means perpetuating differences among Protestants, are that church of England which is justly esteemed the bulwark of the protestant religion, is a high and palpable mistake. The church of England, as unto its national interest in the preservation of the protestant religion, is not only separable from it, but weakened by it. Yea, if there be such a national constitution as, in its own nature, and by the secular advantages which it supplies men withal, inclines them to prefer their own interest above that of the protestant religion in general, it will always endanger that religion in any nation; for hereon they will judge, when they are pressed on any occasion or circumstance of affairs, that it is better to preserve their own interest, by virtue of some dispensations securing unto them their power and secular advantages, than to venture all by a rigid contest for the protestant religion.

Nor is it morally possible that ever Popery should return into this or any other nation, but under the conduct of such a church constitution; without this it hath no prevalent engine but mere force, war, and oppression.

But if the interest of Popery can possess this church-state, either by the inclinations of them, or the greater number of them, who have the management of it, or by their dependence, as unto their interest, on the supreme authority; if that happen in any age to give countenance thereunto, the whole nation will quickly be insensibly influenced and betrayed into Popery, as it were, they know not how. Hence have been such national conversions to and fro in England as have been in no other places or countries in the world; for the care of the public preservation of religion being, as it is supposed, intrusted in this church-state and the managers of it, if by any means it be possessed by Popery, or influenced by a popish prince, the religion of the whole nation will be lost immediately.

For as unto all other ministers who have the immediate guidance of the people, they will suppose that they can do nothing of themselves in this matter, but are only obliged unto the conduct of the church-state itself. And having their station therein alone, and depending thereon, they may easily be either seduced by their interest or excluded from their duty by the power of that church-state whereunto they are subject. By this means the whole interest of the protestant religion in this nation, as unto its preservation, depends on such a state as, being the concernment of a few, and those such as have an especial interest of their own, distinct from that of the protestant religion in general, may be easily possessed by Popery, and probably would be so, if they should have a popish prince to influence them.

But whereas the people are now possessed and fully persuaded of the truth of protestant religion, if there be no public machine or engines insensibly to turn about the whole body of them, but they must be dealt withal individually or parochially, it will, as was said, be morally impossible that ever Popery should become the religion of this nation any other way but by the destruction or killing of the present inhabitants.

Allow that the church-state supposed may, in those who have the trust and power of it, be seduced, corrupted, or any way induced or disposed unto the interest of Popery, as it may be; it is possible some individual persons may be found that, for the sake of truth, will expose their lives to the stake or otherwise,—so did many in the days of Queen Mary, though now esteemed, by not a few, foolish zealots for their pains,—but the body of the people, through their various legal relations unto this church-state, deserting the care of their own preservation, by their trust in the conduct thereof, whereunto they are unavoidably compelled, will quickly be inveigled so as not to be able to extricate themselves. But set them at liberty, so as that every parliament, every magistrate, every minister, every good Christian, may judge that the preservation of their religion is their own duty in all their capacities, and Popery with all its arts will know neither how to begin nor how to proceed with them.

If, then, there were no such church-state as, being in the management of a few, is seducible, and not difficult to be possessed by the interest of Popery, whereby the whole nation would be at once betrayed, the protestant religion is now so firmly seated in the minds of the people, so countenanced by law, so esteemed by all to be the principal interest of the nation, that the wit of all the Jesuits of the world knows not how to attack it, much less endanger it; which, if there be need, shall be farther demonstrated.

13. Nor is it a matter of art or difficulty to declare a way for the security of the protestant religion, with the rights of the government and liberties of the subjects, with the due freedom of conscience, without any such church-state; but it is what the principles of religion, common prudence, and the honest interest of the nation do

direct unto: as, to instance in the things that are most material unto that end,—

(1.) Let a solemn renunciation of Popery, suited unto the general principles of the protestant religion, be established by law, to be made publicly by every person that is to partake of the rights and privileges already confirmed unto that religion, or which afterward shall be so; to be renewed as occasion shall require.

(2.) Let there be one solemn stated confession of the Christian protestant faith, such as is the doctrine of the Articles of the church of England, especially as explained in the public authorized writings of the church in the days of Queen Elizabeth and King James, before the inroad of novel opinions among us, to be subscribed by all enjoying a public ministry.

(3.) Let the magistrate assume unto himself the exercise of his just power, in the preservation of the public peace in all instances; in the encouragement and protection of the professors of the protestant religion; in securing unto all men their legal rights, already granted unto them, in their several places and stations; in the punishment of all crimes cognizable by human judgment; in deposing of men from their enjoyments or privileges, which they hold on any condition,—as, suppose, their orthodox profession of the protestant religion,—if they fail in, or fall from, the performance of it; leaving only things purely spiritual and evangelical to the care and power of the churches, and all litigious causes, of what sort soever, with the infliction of all outward penalties, unto the determination of the laws of the land;—and a great progress will be made towards order and peace amongst us.

(4.) Yea, these few things, in general, are only needful thereunto:—[1.] Let the king and parliament secure the protestant religion, as it is the public interest of the nation, against all attempts of the Papacy for its destruction, with proper laws, and their due execution. [2.] Let the wisdom and power of the nation, in the supreme and subordinate magistrates, be exerted in the rule of all persons and causes, civil and criminal, by one and the same law of the land,—in a compliance wherewith the allegiance of the subject unto the king doth consist; without which, government will never be well fixed on its proper and immovable basis. [3.] That provision be made for the sedulous preaching of the gospel in all parts and places of the land, or all parochial churches; the care whereof is incumbent on the magistrates. [4.] Let the church be protected in the exercise of its spiritual power by spiritual means only,—as preaching of the word, administration of the sacraments, and the like. Whatever is farther pretended as necessary unto any of the ends of true religion or its preservation in the nation, is but a cover for the negligence, idleness, and insufficiency of some of the clergy, who would have an outward appearance of effecting that by external force which themselves, by diligent prayer, sedulous preaching of the word, and an exemplary conversation, ought to labour for in the hearts of men.

(5.) It is evident that hereon all causes of jealousies, animosities, and strifes among the Protestants, would be taken away; all complaints of oppression by courts and jurisdictions not owned by the people be prevented; all encroachments on the consciences of men (which are and will be an endless and irreconcilable cause of difference among us) be obviated; all ability to control or disturb the power and privilege of kings in their persons or rule, and all temptations to exalt their power in absoluteness above the law, will be removed; so as that, by the blessing of God, peace and love may be preserved among all true Protestants.

And if there do ensue hereon some variety in outward rites and observations, as there was in all the primitive churches, who pleaded that the unity of faith was commended and not at all impeached by such varieties; yet, whilst the same doctrine of truth is preached in all places, the same sacraments only administered,—wherein every protestant subject of the nation will be at liberty to join in protestant Christian worship, and to partake of all church ordinances in the outward way, and according unto the outward rites, of his own choosing, without the authoritative examination or prohibition of any pretended church power but what, in his own judgment, he doth embrace,—no inconvenience will follow hereon, unless it be judged such, that the protestant religion, the liberty of the subjects, and the due freedom of the consciences of men sober and peaceable, will be all preserved.

A BRIEF AND IMPARTIAL ACCOUNT

OF THE

NATURE OF THE PROTESTANT RELIGION;

ITS PRESENT STATE IN THE WORLD; ITS STRENGTH AND WEAKNESS; WITH THE WAYS AND INDICATIONS OF THE RUIN OR CONTINUANCE OF ITS PUBLIC NATIONAL PROFESSION.

BY A PROTESTANT.

M.DC.LXXXII.

PREFATORY NOTE.

Whether we regard the deep sagacity pervading this treatise; the calm and nervous dignity of its reasonings; the statesman-like view it gives of the condition and prospects of the Protestant cause; or the noble strain with which it concludes, of confidence in God and the ultimate triumph of his cause, amid all the fears and forebodings which the author had been led to entertain,—we are inclined to ascribe to it a pre-eminent value among the smaller productions of Dr Owen. It is very far from being of merely ephemeral interest. It was reprinted in 1822, when the claims of the Roman Catholics to be admitted into Parliament were under discussion. To this edition there was prefixed a letter, addressed to Mr Wilberforce, by Bishop Burgess; and from the following extract it will be seen in what estimation that accomplished prelate held this brief treatise: "The extensive knowledge, the powerful intellect, the ardent piety of Dr Owen, are too well known to you to require eulogium or recommendation. The little tract which I have reprinted, and which I am desirous of submitting to your perusal, is distinguished by all his talents, and is calculated to excite feelings superior to any considerations of partial and temporary policy."

I. The first part of the tract is occupied with an account of the Protestant religion,—*generally*, in its origin and principles; and then more *particularly*, as it is opposed to Popery. He specifies the four essential elements in Protestantism, from which the Reformation took its rise and character:—1. Some great apostasy had been foretold in Scripture; 2. The Church of Rome embodied this predicted apostasy; 3. All true Christians were bound to separate from this antichristian church; and, 4. It was their duty not merely to separate from it, but to maintain a public protest against its errors and abominations. II. Then follows an account of the way in which Protestantism had arisen; of the costly sacrifices made in order that it might be established, its martyrs exceeding in number those who had fallen under the Pagan persecutions; and, lastly, of the happy effects which had ensued from the Reformation, not merely to Protestant nations, but even in countries where though Popery still reigned, it was held in check by the contiguity of Protestant light and freedom, and the possibility that now existed of turning against it "the balance of power." III. The political weakness of Protestantism, from its manifold divisions, is exhibited, and the importance is urged of establishing a great Protestant interest throughout Europe. IV. Then follows a discussion of the probable way in which the Papacy may regain predominance;—either by *defection*, or *force*, or *reconciliation*. The author dwells chiefly on the danger to be apprehended from the last source, inasmuch as some learned men now conceded a *patriarchal primacy* to the Bishop of Rome; novel opinions had been widely spread, which, so far as they set aside the doctrines of grace, narrowed the difference between Popery and Protestantism; it was now denied that the Pope was Antichrist; atheism prevailed; vital religion was at a low ebb; the clergy, losing confidence in the spiritual power of truth, sought to retain their influence over the people by recourse to superstitious expedients and appliances, such as Romanism sanctions; and, lastly, forgetfulness of the persecuting spirit of Popery induced many to bethink themselves of an "ecclesiastical coalescency with the Church of Rome." V. The folly and wickedness of such a movement are exposed. The tract closes by stating the grounds of hope amid prevailing discouragements, and the true means for the preservation of Protestantism,—in prayer, union, and repentance.

The works of Owen are commonly more exhaustive than suggestive; but the following tract is an exception to the truth of the remark, and no analysis can do justice to the range of thought embraced in it. His views as to the danger of reconciliation being attempted with Rome may be thought extravagant, but accord with an apprehension entertained by many British Protestants at the time, and which there was much to justify in the notorious leanings of the Court. See "Neal's History," vol. iv. 458, 463. Louis Du Moulin, professor of History at Oxford, published in 1680 "A Short and True Account of the Several Advances the Church of England hath made towards Rome; or, a model of the grounds upon which the Papists for these hundred years have built their hopes and expectations that England would ere long return to Popery." While no authors have done more effective service in the controversy with Rome than Tillotson, Tenison, Stillingfleet, and other divines of the English Church, the necessity which they felt to engage in a vigorous exposure of the errors of Popery, as well as the spirit and scope of their treatises in many instances, indicate that they too wrote under feelings of alarm lest, through the Romanizing policy of the Court, the Anglican Establishment should revert to the Papacy.—Ed.

THE STATE AND FATE

OF

THE PROTESTANT RELIGION.

THE world is at this day filled with discourses about the protestant religion and the profession of it; and that not without cause. The public opposition that is made unto it, the designs that are managed with policy and power for its utter extirpation, and the confidence of many that they will take effect, must needs fill the minds of them whose principal interest and concerns lie in it with many thoughts about the event. Never was there a greater cause brought on the stage for a trial;—a cause wherein the glory of God is concerned above any thing at this day in the world; a cause wherein the most eminent prevailing powers of the earth are visibly engaged as unto its ruin, and whereunto all the diabolical arts of men are employed; a cause wherein those who embrace that religion do judge that not only their lives, but the eternal welfare of them and their posterity, is inevitably concerned. This cannot but fill the minds of all men with various conjectures about the issue of these things, according as their interest works in them by hopes and fears. Some of them, therefore, do endeavour, by their counsels and other ways, for the preservation and continuance of this protestant religion amongst ourselves, according as they have an accession unto public affairs; and some, whose lot is cast into a private capacity, do engage faith and prayer unto the same purpose. The enemies of it, in the meantime, are powerful, active, and restless; many amongst us being uncertain in their minds, as not resolved where to fix their interest; and a greater multitude, like Gallio, care for none of these things. This being a matter, therefore, wherein all men, who have any sense of religion, are so deeply concerned, it may not be unseasonable briefly to inquire, What is this protestant religion which is so contended about? what is its present state in the world? what its strength and weakness, as unto its public profession? and what is like to be the issue of the present contest? This is that which the ensuing leaves are designed unto; and it is hoped they may be of use unto some, to extricate their minds from involved, fruitless thoughts, to direct them in their duty, and to bring them unto an acquiescency in the will of God.

The protestant religion may be considered either as it is religion in general,—that is, Christian religion; or as it is distinct from and opposite unto another pretended profession of the same religion, whereon it is called Protestant.

In the first sense of it, it derives its original from Christ and his apostles. What they taught to be believed, what they commanded to be observed in the worship of God,—all of it, and nothing but that,—is the protestant religion. Nothing else belongs unto it; in nothing else is it concerned. These, therefore, are the principles of the religion of Protestants, whereinto their faith and obedience are resolved.

1. What was revealed unto the church by the Lord Christ and his apostles is the whole of that religion which God will and doth accept.

2. So far as is needful unto the faith, obedience, and eternal salvation of the church, what they taught, revealed, and commanded is contained in the Scriptures of the New Testament, witnessed unto and confirmed by those of the Old.

3. All that is required of us that we may please God, be accepted with him, and come to the eternal enjoyment of him, is, that we truly believe what is so revealed and taught, yielding sincere obedience unto what is commanded in the Scriptures.

Upon these principles Protestants confidently propose their religion unto the trial of all mankind. If in any thing it be found to deviate from them,—if it exceeds, in any instance, what is so revealed, taught, and commanded,—if it be defective in the faith or practice of any thing that is so revealed or commanded,—they are ready to renounce it. Here they live and die; from this foundation they will not depart: *this is their religion.*

And if these principles will not secure us, as unto our present acceptance with God in religion, and the eternal enjoyment of him, he hath left all mankind at an utter uncertainty, to make a blind venture for an invisible world; which is altogether inconsistent with his infinite wisdom, goodness, and benignity.

Being in possession of these principles of truth and security from Christ and his apostles, it belongs unto the protestant religion not to change or forego them, and to repose our confidence in the infallibility or authority of the pope of Rome, or of the church whereof he is the head. For these principles of assurance are such as every way become the wisdom and goodness of God; and such as that our nature is not capable in this life of those which are higher or of a more illustrious evidence. Let the contrary unto either of these be demonstrated, and we will renounce the protestant religion. To forego them for such as are irreconcilable unto divine wisdom and goodness, as also to the common reason of mankind, is an effect of the highest folly and of strong delusion.

For that all mankind should be obliged to place all their confidence and assurance of pleasing God, of living unto him, and coming unto the enjoyment of him for eternity, on the pope of Rome and his infallibility, however qualified and circumstantiated, considering what these popes are and have been, is eternally irreconcilable unto the greatness, wisdom, love, and kindness of God, as also unto the whole revelation made of himself by Jesus Christ. The principles of protestant religion before mentioned do every way become, are highly suited unto, the nature and goodness of God,—no man living shall ever be able to instance in one tittle of them that is not correspondent with divine goodness and wisdom;—but on the first naming of this other way, no man who knows any thing what the pope is, and what is his church, if he be not blinded with prejudice and interest, will be able to satisfy himself that it is consistent with infinite goodness and wisdom to commit the salvation of mankind, which he values above all things, unto such a security.

Neither hath this latter way any better consistency with human wisdom or the common reason of mankind,—namely, that those who are known, many of them, to be better and wiser men than those popes, should resolve their religion, and therein their whole assurance of pleasing God, with all their hopes of a blessed eternity, into the authority and infallibility of the pope and his church, seeing many of them, the most of them, especially for some ages, have been persons wicked, ignorant, proud, sensual, and brutish in their lives.

This, then, is the foundation of the protestant religion, in that it is built on those principles which are every way suited unto the divine nature and goodness, as also satisfactory unto human reason, with a refusal of them which are unworthy of infinite wisdom to give, and the ordinary reason of men to admit or receive.

Secondly, As the name Protestant is distinctive with respect unto some other pretended profession of Christian religion, so it derives this denomination from them who in all ages, after the apostasy of the church of Rome came to be expressly antichristian, departed from the communion of it, opposed it, reformed themselves, and set up the true worship of God according unto the degrees and measures of gospel light which they had received.

This was done successively in a long tract of time, through sundry ages, until, by an accession of multitudes, princes and people, unto the same profession, they openly testified and protested against the papal apostasy and tyranny; whence they became to be commonly callèd Protestants. And the principles whereon they all of them proceeded from first to last, which constitute their religion as protestant, were these that follow:—

1. That there are in the Scripture, prophecies, predictions, and warnings, especially in the book of the Revelation and the Second Epistle of Paul the apostle to the Thessalonians, that there should be a great apostasy or defection in the visible church from the faith, worship, and holiness of the gospel; and, in opposition unto what was appointed of Christ, the erection of a worldly, carnal, antichristian church-state, composed of tyranny, idolatry, and persecution, which should for a long time oppress the true worshippers of Christ with bloody cruelty, and at last be itself "consumed with the spirit of his mouth, and destroyed by the brightness of his coming."

This defection was so plainly foretold, as also the beginning of it, in a "mystery of iniquity," designed even in the days of the apostles, that believers in all ages did expect the accomplishment of it by the introduction of an antichristian state and power, though the manner of it was hidden from them, until it was really fulfilled. I say, from the days of the apostles, and the giving out of those prophecies and predictions of the coming of antichrist and an apostate church-state with him, all Christians in all ages did believe and expect that it should come, until its real coming, in a way and manner unexpected, confounded their apprehensions about it.

2. Their second principle as Protestants was, that this defection and antichristian church-state, so plainly foretold by the Holy Ghost in the Scriptures, was openly and visibly accomplished in the church of Rome, with the nations that had subjected themselves unto the yoke thereof. Therein they found and saw all that tyranny and oppression, all that pride and self-exaltation above every thing that hath the name of God upon it, all that idolatry and false worship, all that departure from the faith of the gospel, all that contempt of evangelical obedience, which were foretold to come in under and constitute the fatal apostasy.

3. Hereon their third principle was, that as they valued the glory of God, the honour of Christ and the gospel, their own salvation, and the good of the souls of others, they were obliged to forsake and renounce all communion with that apostate church, though they saw that their so doing would cost many of them their dearest blood or lives.

4. They were convinced, hereon, that it was their duty publicly to *protest* against all those abominations, to reform themselves, as unto faith, worship, and conversation, according unto the rules before laid down, as those that are fundamental unto Christian religion.

These were the principles whereon Christian religion, as it is protestant, was re-introduced into the world, after it had been not only obscured, but almost excluded out of it, as unto its public profession. And these principles are avowed by all true Protestants as those whereon they are ready at all times to put their cause and profession on the trial.

The way whereby the profession of this protestant religion was introduced on these principles, and made public in the world, under the antichristian apostasy, was the same whereby Christian religion entered the world under Paganism,—namely, by the prayers, preaching, writings, sufferings, and holiness of life of them who embraced it, and were called to promote it. And herein their sufferings, for the number of them that suffered, and variety of all cruel preparations of death, are inexpressible. It is capable of a full demonstration, that those who were slain by the sword and otherwise destroyed for their testimony unto Christ and the gospel, in opposition unto the papal apostasy and idolatry, did far exceed the number of them that suffered for the Christian religion in all the pagan persecutions of old. A plant so soaked and watered with the blood of the martyrs will not be so easily plucked up as some imagine. Nay, it is probable it will not go out without more blood (of sufferers, I mean) than it was introduced by; which yet no man knows how to conceive or express.

But it had no sooner fixed its profession in some nations, but it was loaden with all manner of reproaches, charged with all the evils that fell out in the world after its entrance, and, by all sorts of arts and pretences, rendered suspected and hateful unto princes and potentates. Whatever is evil in or unto mankind, especially unto the interest of great men, was with great noise and clamour charged on it; for so it was in the first entrance of the Christian religion under Paganism. There was neither plague, nor famine, nor earthquake, nor inundation of water, nor war, nor invasion by enemies, but all was charged on that new religion. And the reason hereof was, not only the hatred of the truth through the love of sin and unrighteousness, and an ingrafted power of superstition through blind devotion, but principally because, for a long tract of time, the whole of the profession of religion had been suited unto the secular interests of men, supplying them, under various pretences, with power, domination, territories, titles, revenues, wealth, ease, grandeur, and honour, with an insinuation into and power over the consciences of all sorts of persons;—a thing very desirable to men of corrupt minds, and easily turned into an engine unto very bad and pernicious ends. That the whole complex and all its parts, in their various motions and operations, of the Christian religion in the Papacy, is framed and fitted unto these ends, so as to give satisfaction unto all corrupt and ambitious desires in men, is palpable unto all that are not wilfully blind. But this protestant religion, so introduced, stated the interest of Christian religion in a way and design utterly inconsistent herewith, and destructive of it; and this was to give all glory and honour to God and Christ alone, and to teach the guides of the church to be humble, holy, zealous, ensamples of the flock, utterly renouncing all secular power and domination, with territories, titles, and great revenues on the account of their office and the discharge of it. And was it any wonder that those who were in possession of three parts of the power and a third part of the revenue of most nations in Europe, should look on this principle as the worst of devils, and so represent it as to frighten above half the monarchs of these nations from once looking steadily upon it, whereby they might have easily discovered the cheat that was put upon them? And thus was it with the first planters of Christian religion with respect unto the Pagans, Acts xix. 27.

But herein many labour to make a difference between the introduction of religion under Paganism, and the reformation of it under Antichristianism: for they say that the first professors of Christian religion for three hundred years endured their persecutions with all patience, never once stirring up either wars or commotions in the defence of their profession;—but since, upon and after the introduction of protestant religion, there have been many tumults and disorders, many popular commotions and wars, which have been caused thereby. For if all the professors of it had quietly suffered themselves to have been killed with the sword, or hanged, or burned, or tortured to death in the Inquisition, or starved in dungeons (and more was not required of them), there would have been no such wars about religion in the world; for their enemies intended nothing but to destroy them in peace and quietness, without the least disturbance unto the civil rule among men.

I say, this difference did not arise from any difference in the religion of the one and the other, nor of the principles of those by whom they were professed; but it hath proceeded from external causes and circumstances that were greatly different between the primitive Christians and the Protestants in some places and nations. For the primitive Christians, whose story we have, were all of them placed in and subject unto *one* empire. In that whole empire, and all the provinces of it, there was not one law, custom, or usage, giving the least countenance unto *right of protection of liberty*. There was not one prince, ruler, senate, governor, that had the least pretence of legal right to protect or defend them in their profession against the will and law of the emperor or empire. The outward rights of religion were no way *allied* in any thing unto the civil rights of men. However numerous, therefore, the Christians were in those days, they were all absolutely private persons, without pretence of law or right to defend themselves: in which state of things it is the undoubted principle of all Protestants, that where men are persecuted merely on the account of religion, without relation unto the civil rights and liberties of mankind, their duty is patiently to suffer without the least resistance. But it hath been otherwise upon the Reformation and since; for the protection and preservation of religion was taken up by sundry potentates, free princes, and cities, who had a legal right and power to protect themselves and their subjects in the profession of it. It hath been, and is at this day, incorporated into the laws, rights, and interests of sundry nations; which ought to be defended. And no instance can be given of any people defending themselves in the profession of the protestant religion by arms, but where, together with their religion, their enemies did design and endeavour to destroy those rights, liberties, and privileges, which not only the light of nature, but the laws and customs of their several countries, did secure unto them as a part of their birth-right inheritance. And in some places, though the name of religion hath been much used on the one side and the other, yet it hath been neither the cause nor occasion of the wars and troubles that have been in them; and this makes their case utterly different from that of the primitive Christians.

This religion being thus re-instated in many nations, it brought forth fruit in them; even as the gospel did at its first preaching in the places whereinto it came, Col. i. 6.

It brought forth fruit in them by whom it was received, such as is the proper fruit of religion,— namely, it did so in light, knowledge, truth, in holiness, in the real conversion of multitudes unto God, in good works, in the spiritual comfort of believers in life and death, with all other fruits of righteousness which are to the praise of God. Thereby, also, was the worship of God vindicated from idolatry and superstition, and restored in many places unto its primitive simplicity and purity.

It brought, also, no small advantage even unto those nations, both princes and their subjects, by whom the profession thereof was never received, as Christian religion also did of old unto the pagan world; for hereby it is that the kings and potentates of Christendom, even those of the Roman profession, have much eased themselves of that intolerable yoke of bondage that was on them unto the pope's pretended power and his impositions. For whilst all nations were in subjection to him, it was at their utmost hazard that any one king or state should contend with him about any of his demands or assumptions: for he could stir up what nation he pleased, and give them sufficient encouragement to avenge his quarrels on rebellious princes; which he also did in instances innumerable. But since so many nations fell off from all dependence on him and subjection to him, by the light and profession of the protestant religion, there is a balance of power against him, and an awe upon him in his presumptions, lest he should be dealt withal by others in the like manner. Had these western parts of the world continued under a superstitious sense of a fealty and obedience in all things due to the pope, as they were before the Reformation, the king of France himself should not so easily have rejected his personal infallibility and jurisdiction[1] as he seems to have done. But he hath now no way left to avenge himself but assassinations; which at this time may prove of very evil consequence unto himself. Wherefore, the princes of Europe, as well those by whom the protestant religion is not embraced, yea, is opposed and persecuted, as those by whom it is received, seem not so sensible of the benefit and advantage which doth accrue unto them all thereby; for from thence alone it is, with the interest and power which it hath obtained in the world, that they are freed in their minds and in their rule from as base a servitude and bondage as ever persons under their denomination were subject unto.

The common people, also, who yet continue in the communion of the papal church have received no small advantage by that effectual light which shines in the world from the principles of this religion, even where it is not received; for, from the fear of the discoveries to be made by it, hath a curb been put upon the flagitious lives of the priests and friars, wherewith all places were defiled; shame, also, with necessity, having stirred them up to deliver themselves in some measure from their old stupid ignorance. Many retrenchments have been made, also, in some of the most gross parts of

[1] Louis XIV. had several disputes with the papal court. The main ground of quarrel at this time was the determination of Innocent XI. to insist upon his rights in the matter of the Regale. This was a royal privilege, according to which, on the demise of a bishop in certain French sees, the king of France was entitled to collect and enjoy the revenues, and to act in some respects as bishop, till a new bishop was appointed. It was the aim of Louis to extend this right to all sees in his dominions, but Innocent would suffer no abatement on the ancient prerogative of the church. A fierce contest ensued, in which pontifical epistles were met with royal mandates. Louis proceeded to induct into office bishops whose nomination the pope had refused to sanction, and, when the thunders of the Vatican had been put in requisition to overawe him, summoned a convention of bishops in 1682, at which four propositions were adopted,—the first limiting the supremacy of the pope to spiritual matters; the second representing, according to the council of Constance, the authority of the pope to be subordinate to a general council; the third affirming the validity of the canons and usages of the Gallican church; and the last maintaining the assent of the church to be requisite, before the decision of the pope, even on matters of faith, could be received as valid. These propositions were registered in the Parliament of Paris, and ordained to be read from year to year in the schools, and to be subscribed by all professors in universities. New disputes arose in regard to certain immunities possessed by the French ambassador at Rome, and the pontificate of Innocent closed without any reconciliation being effected between the Roman see and the French court.—Ed.

idolatry, that were for many ages in general practice among them. And they are hereby, also, in some good measure, freed from the terror of evil spirits wherewith they were continually haunted; for before the Reformation, possessions, apparitions, sprites, ghosts, fiends, with silly miracles about them, filled all places, and were a great annoyance unto the common people. Somewhat there was, no doubt, of the juggling of priests in these things, and somewhat of the agency of the devil; each of them making use of the other to further their own designs. But upon the first preaching of the gospel there was an abatement made of these things in all places; which hath gone on until they are everywhere grown the matter of scorn and contempt.

This religion being thus planted, and producing these effects, the house of Austria, in both the branches of it, the imperial and the regal, espoused the antichristian interest and quarrel against it; and for eighty years or thereabouts endeavoured, by all ways of force and cruelty, its utter extirpation. What immense treasures of wealth they have spent and wasted, what an ocean of blood they have shed, both of their own subjects and others, in the pursuit of this design, cannot be well conceived. But what hath been the issue of all their undertakings to this end? They have so far broken themselves and their power in their obstinate pursuit of them, that those who not long since thought of nothing less than a universal monarchy, are forced to seek unto protestant states and nations to preserve them from immediate ruin. So vain, foolish, and fruitless, for the most part, are the deep counsels and projections of men, so destructive and ruinous unto themselves in the issue, when their desires and designs are enlarged beyond the bounds which right and equity have fixed unto them; especially will they be so when they are found fighting against God and his interest in the world. And if the same design be now pursued by another, it will in time come unto the same catastrophe.

I shall not speak any thing of the present state of this protestant religion as unto its political interests in the world. It is in general known to most, and hath been particularly inquired into by many. I shall only briefly consider something of its weakness, its danger, and what is like to be the issue of it, as unto its public profession, in the world; which are the subjects of many men's daily converse.

The political weakness of the protestant religion ariseth solely from the *divisions* that are among them by whom it is professed: and these are of two sorts;—first, Such as are of a civil nature, amongst princes and states; and, secondly, Such as are religious, among divines and churches. As unto the first of these, some good men, who value religion above all their earthly concerns, measuring other men, even princes, who profess religion, by themselves, have been almost astonished that there is not such a thing as a *protestant interest* so prevalent amongst them as to subordinate all particular contests and designings unto itself. But whereas there was formerly an appearance of some such thing, which had no small influence on public counsels, and produced some good, useful effects, at present it seems to be beyond hopes of a revival, and is of little consideration in the world. Could such a thing be expected, that the nations and the powers of them which publicly profess the protestant religion should avow the preservation and protection of it to be their principal interest, and regulate their counsels accordingly, giving this the pre-eminence in all things, their adversaries would be content tc dwell quietly at home, without offering much at their disturbance. But these things are not of my present consideration. Nor do I think that any sort of men shall have the glory of preserving the interest of Christ in the world; he will do it himself.

Again: the religious differences that are amongst them as churches do weaken the *political interest* of Protestants. They have done so from the very beginning of the Reformation. And when the first differences among them were in some measure digested and brought unto some tolerable composure, about sixty years ago, there was an inroad made on the doctrine that had been received among the reformed churches by novel opinions, which hath grown unto this day, to the great weakening of the whole interest; and, as far as I can see, it is in vain to dissuade men from contending about their small allotments in the house, or, it may be, but some supposed appurtenances of them, whilst others are visibly digging at the foundation, to oppress them all with the fall of the whole fabric. In these things lies the sole outward political weakness of the protestant interest in the world, whose direful effects God alone can prevent.

We may hereon inquire, what at present is like to be the issue and event of this protestant religion, as unto its public profession in the world; for the adversaries of it do every day discover, not only their desires and endeavours for its extirpation, but their expectations also of its speedy ruin. They suppose the time is come when that heresy, as they call it, which hath so long infested the northern nations, shall, by their arts, contrivances, and power, be utterly rooted out. And it is known that those discoveries of their minds and hopes herein, which have occasionally come unto light amongst us, are but indications of those counsels and combinations, in other places and among other persons, whereby their hopes are to be accomplished. And if it were unto our present purpose, much might be offered to manifest that those consultations and contrivances, which are constant in the managers of the papal interest, both at Rome and elsewhere, for the utter extirpation of the protestant religion, have been ordered, disposed, and cast into such methods, as not only to stir up all means of expedition, but also with respect unto a speedy, immediate execution.

We shall, therefore, briefly inquire by what way and means this may be effected, or what is like to give this design an accomplishment, giving every thing its due weight and consideration; for what the event will be, God only knows.

The ruin of the protestant religion, as unto its public profession, must be either by a general DEFECTION from it, or by a FORCE upon it, or by a RECONCILIATION and coalescency with the Roman church.

1. This DEFECTION must be either of the *princes*, or of the *clergy*, or of the *people*, or of them all in conjunction.

(1.) Of the first, or the defection of princes unto the Papacy, we have had some instances in the last age, but scarce of any who have been absolutely sovereign or supreme; unless it be of one who, together with her religion, wisely and honestly left her crown. But I suppose there lieth here no great danger or fear as to kings, or such as on whose authority the profession of religion in their dominions doth much depend; for they are too wise to be weary of their present station and liberty. Who can suppose that any of them would be willing to stand at the gates of the pope's palace barefoot, for a night and a day, and be disciplined to boot, as it was with one of the greatest kings of England? or to hold the pope's stirrup whilst he mounted his horse, and be rebuked for want of breeding in holding it on the wrong side? or would they lie on the ground, and have their necks trod upon by the pope, which a courageous emperor was forced to submit unto? or have their crowns kicked from their heads by the foot of a legate? or be assassinated for not promoting the papal interest in the way and mode of them concerned, as it was with two kings of France?

It will be said that these things are past and gone; the popes have now no such power as formerly; and the kings that are of the Roman church do live as free from impositions on them by the pretensions of papal power as any kings on the earth. But supposing such a change, and that the king of France, as great as he is, do find in the issue that there is such a change, yet if we do not know the reasons of it, they do. Is it because the maintainers of the Papacy have changed their principles and opinions in this matter? Is it that they have disclaimed the power and authority which they exercised in former ages? Is it from any abatement of the papal omnipotency in their judgment? Do they think that the popes had not right to do what they did in those days, or that they have not yet right to do the like again? It is none of these, nor any reason of this sort, that is the cause of the pretended change. The true and only reason of it is the balancing of their power by the protestant interest. So many kings, princes, potentates, states, and nations, being not only fallen off from that blind obedience and subjection wherein they were universally inthralled unto them in those days, but ready to oppose them in all their attempts to execute their pretended power, they are forced for a season to lower their sails, and to pluck in those horns wherewith formerly they pushed kings and princes unto their ruin. Should there be a restoration of their power and interest in the minds of men, which would ensue on the extirpation of the protestant religion, the greatest kings of Europe should quickly find themselves yoked and overmatched both in their own dominions, and by such as will be ready to execute their designs. And on this supposition, they will cross all experience of former ages if, having weathered their difficulties and conquered their opposers, they be not more haughty and secure in the execution of their power and pretended office than ever they were before.

Whatever delusion, therefore, may befall sovereign princes in their personal capacities, none of them can be so forsaken of common understanding as not to see that by a defection unto the Papacy, they bring a bondage on themselves and their subjects, from which God by his providence, through the light and truth of the protestant religion, had set them free. And it is certain enough that there is at this day so much rational light diffused in the world, that even those who, on various inducements, may comply with any of them in the re-introduction of Popery into any of their territories, will quickly find what condition of slavery and contempt they have brought themselves into; and thereon make the new posture of affairs very uneasy to themselves and their rulers. Yea, no sort of men will be given up unto more furious reflections, first on themselves, and then on others, than they will be, when they find themselves ensnared. Those who on such occasions have neither deceived themselves, nor suffered themselves to be deceived by others, may enjoy a sedate tranquillity of mind in all that shall befall them; but these, when they have digested the shame of being deluded, will be restless in their minds, and intent on new occasions. I suppose, therefore, there is no great danger to be feared on this hand, and if there should, that the event of counsels mixed with so much madness and ingratitude will be a sudden catastrophe.

(2.) And as unto the clergy, there can be no defection amongst them, unless it be from a weariness of their present station, upon the principles of the protestant religion; for they have most of them too much light to be corrupted any way but by interest. Now the principles intended are these two:—[1.] That the reverence which they claim, and the revenues which they possess, are not due unto them merely on the account of their offices and the titles which they bear, but on that of their faithful discharge of their office in diligent, laborious preaching of the gospel, and sedulous endeavours for the conversion and edification of the souls of men. This principle lay at the foundation of the Reformation, and was one of the greatest means of its promotion. [2.] That a distinction from the people by sacred office requires indispensably a distinction from them in gravity, usefulness, and holiness of conversation. If men should grow weary of their station in the clergy on these principles (and others the protestant religion will not afford them), it is to be feared that on provoking occasions they may verge unto that church-state wherein all things desirable unto them in this world will be secured on easier terms. And the danger will be increased, if they are capable of envy and vexation from those principles of light and liberty, which have been communicated unto the people by the protestant religion, rendering all expectations of reverence and honour but what ariseth from and is proportionate unto real worth and usefulness altogether vain. And if hereon they are exposed to impressions from the wealth, ease, and power proposed unto them in the papal church, it is to be feared that they may regulate themselves by opportunities. And on these grounds not a few ministers in France, being withal at the same time under the dread of trouble and persecution, have gone over unto the adverse party. In the meantime, there is some relief herein, that the generality of mankind is so far enlightened that no pleas or pretences of other reasons for such a change or defection will bear the least admittance, but it will be ascribed unto corrupt affection and carnal interest. However, if it be contained, as many judge it is, in the prophecies of the Revelation, that the churches of the nations who were once of the communion and in subjection unto the church of Rome shall be restored unto her power and possession again, at least for a short season, this sort of men must be signally instrumental therein. And if there be any nations where these two things concur:—that all church or ecclesiastical power and jurisdiction is, by the law of the land, vested in the king, being as unto its whole exercise derived from him alone, whereby that which he is, the church is, as to power and jurisdiction, and nothing else; and where the clergy do hold and derive their spiritual power, their power of order and office, by a flux and descent of it from the church of Rome and the authority thereof,—upon the accession of a Papist unto supreme rule, it will be very difficult, if not impossible, long to secure the public profession of the protestant religion in such nations. I say, in this case, although the protestant religion may be preserved in multitudes of individuals and their voluntary societies in the communion of it, yet in such a church-state its public profession cannot long be continued; for it will quickly be dissolved by its own intestine differences, which every wise man may easily foresee. But the force of law, interest, and inclination is hardly to be withstood.

(3.) The danger of defection from the profession of the protestant religion in the people must be measured from the preparations for it that are found amongst them, and the means of their furtherance. Now, these are nothing but the vicious habits of the minds of men, inclining their affections to take shelter in the papal superstition. Such are ignorance, lewdness of conversation, provocations from the power of religion in others, atheism, and interest, from hopes of advantage proposed unto some of them who have an influence on others. There can be no defection unto Popery in or among the people who have ever known any thing of the protestant religion but what proceeds from these causes, which wholly obliterate all sense of its power, all delight in its truth, and dispose men unto any thing wherein they hope they may find a better compliance with their inclinations, or at least free them from that whereof they are weary, and wherein they find no advantage. And the means whereby these things are promoted in them are, want of due instruction, examples of sin and impunity therein, public discountenance of the power of religion, personal and family necessities through pride or sensuality, with desire of revenge.

Where these things abound in any nation, amongst any people, there is no security of their stability in that profession of religion which yet they avow: for all these things will continually operate in their minds, and occasions will not be wanting, in the watchful diligence of the devil and his instruments, to excite and provoke their corrupt lusts unto a declension from their profession; which with many of them will be carried on gradually and insensibly, until they find themselves ensnared in the papal interest beyond what they can extricate themselves out of.

I shall make no conjectures concerning the ruin or total loss of the public profession of the protestant religion, from those ways and means of a general defection from it: for if there were more danger in them than there is, I know there is yet a way whereby they may be all defeated; and this being in the hand of God alone, with him it is to be left, and unto his care it is to be committed.

2. Force is the next way whereby the same effect may be produced; and this is that which those of the Roman interest do place their principal confidence in, and it is that which they judge they may lawfully make use of, whenever they are able so to do. Be the force esteemed necessary unto this end of what sort it will,—be it by private assassinations, legal persecutions, national oppressions, foreign invasions,—all is alike unto them; they are all of them to be made use of as their supposed opportunities do require. That which at present

doth most encourage their hopes and expectations, on this ground of them, is the power and inclinations of the French monarch, and the influence they have on the counsels and actings of other nations. But that whole business seems to me, on many accounts, to be but "res unius ætatis" at most; many countries may be ravaged and spoiled, and new work cut out for another age, but a stated interest for the papal advantage will scarcely be fixed thereby. They must be a people of another temper and complexion of mind than our neighbours are, of a more profound melancholy and superstition than they are subject unto, of less vehement desires of their own, and less subject to alter in their designs on provocations and disappointments, who are fit pertinaciously to pursue the advancement of the papal power and dominion, wherein themselves at length shall be no sharers. But where there is a concurrence of all these things,—namely, an inclination in many of all sorts unto a defection, preparations in the minds of more thereunto, the persecution of some so far as the laws will permit, and just fears of a greater outward force,—relief and safety is to be expected only from divine power and goodness.

3. The third way whereby the public profession of the protestant religion may be ruined in any nation, or universally, is by a RECONCILIATION unto the church of Rome. For although this be really of the same nature and kind with that of the defection before spoken of, yet seeing it is to be effected by a pretended mutual condescension, it will be averred to be different from a total defection. That which I intend is a coalescency in the same church-state, faith, worship, and rule with the church of Rome, on such concessions and reliefs from some present impositions as shall on both sides be agreed on. And this is the most plausible engine for attaining the fatal end designed that can be made use of, and possibly the most likely to take effect. The pretences of the peace of Christendom, and the union of Christians (though nothing less be intended than that peace and union which Christ hath appointed, nor will the peace pretended be ever attained by it), are suited to cover and overwhelm men with reproaches who shall but endeavour to discover their falsity and folly. But the present posture of counsels and affairs in the world calls for somewhat a more distinct consideration of these things, which yet shall be but preparatory unto what shall be farther discoursed unto the same purpose, if the process in the design do farther manifest itself.

From the very beginning of the Reformation there have been various attempts for a composition of the differences between the church of Rome and those who were departed from it. Councils of princes, conventions of divines, imperial edicts, sedate consultations of learned men, have all been made use of unto this end; and all in vain. And it was for a while the judgment of most wise men, that the council of Trent had rendered all reconciliations, so much as by a pretence of any condescension on the part of Rome, utterly impossible; for it hath bound itself and all the world that will own its authority, under solemn curses, not to make any change or alteration in the present state of the papal church, though the salvation of all men living should depend thereon.

Yet notwithstanding the fixing of this impassable gulf between the two churches or religions, some persons professing the protestant religion, either angry at their station and disappointments in the world, or ambitious above their station in the protestant church, though of the highest dignity attainable in it, or out of an itch or curiosity of venting their conciliatory notions, as they suppose them, and so to entitle themselves unto the name of peace-makers, have, in the foregoing and present age, revived the same fruitless design; but hitherto without success.

But it must be confessed that at present things are more prepared for the plying of this engine, and making it effectual unto the ruin of the protestant religion, than they were in former ages; whereof I shall give some instances.

Sundry learned men, who have made themselves of great name and reputation thereby, have, in their public writings, granted a patriarchal primacy in the west unto the bishop of Rome, which is meet to be restored; and therewithal they have relinquished the true grounds of the Reformation. For whereas the real causes and reasons of it were the idolatry, heresies, and tyranny of the church of Rome,—which every private Christian might understand, and was bound to separate from in his own person, were there no other of his mind in the world but himself alone, and had right so to do,—they have resolved it into the power of a national church in that patriarchate, with their supreme civil ruler, to reform itself from such things as they esteem abuses. Now, as this is a matter wherein the consciences of the people or private Christians are not concerned, so it is built on sundry arbitrary presumptions that have not the least countenance given unto them from the word of God. And as this endeavour tends directly to divert the minds of men from the true causes and reasons of the Reformation, whereon all the martyrs died, so it leads directly upon a relief against the pretended abuses to return unto the pope as a head of unity and peace unto all churches, at least in these western parts of the world; which is all that at present is pleaded for by many of the Papists themselves. "For the dispute," they say, "about the pope, his power and infallibility, you need not trouble yourselves. Let the bishop of Rome in his succession from St

Peter be acknowledged as a head of unity and peace unto all Christians, with a patriarchal power, and no more shall be required of you:" that is, at present; for the pope will be pope whilst he is so,—that is, until he is utterly cast out of the church. But by such concessions as these, the way is preparing for a composition as unto the outward order and rule of the church.

As unto the internal part of religion, in doctrines of faith, there is no small advance towards a reconciliation, in the introduction of novel opinions into the protestant profession; for although, on their first entrance among us, they were publicly protested against by the Commons of England in parliament, as introductory of Popery, yet their prevalency since hath been so great as that their abettors are ready to avow them as the doctrine of the present church. Yet are they all of them opposite unto the fundamental principles of the Reformation, which were to exalt the grace of God and debase the pride of men; from the contempt of which principles all the abominations of the Papacy did arise. And this progress towards a reconciliation is daily improved by the endeavours of some to lessen all the doctrinal differences between the Papists and Protestants, and to make them appear as things not worth the striving or contending about.

The same work is carried on by the labours and endeavours of many in their public writings to divert the making application of Scripture prophecies and predictions of an apostatical, antichristian church-state unto the church of Rome. The persuasion hereof (as it is a most undoubted truth, wherein the souls of men are concerned) is the principal means of preserving the body of the people in an aversation unto Popery. If you can once persuade them that the pope is not antichrist, that the church of Rome is not that idolatrous, tyrannical state foretold in the Scripture, many would be very indifferent how you treat with them, or what composition you shall make for yourselves. But it is hoped that the broad light which ariseth from the evidence the pope and his church for many ages have given of themselves so to be, by their idolatries, persecutions, murders, Luciferian pride, trampling on the power and persons of kings and all sorts of persons, in conjunction with the characteristical notes of times, places, rise, progress, nature, and actings of that church-state in the Scripture, will not easily be extinguished.

There is no small prevalency in the world of an atheistical principle lately advanced,—namely, of resolving all respect unto the public profession of religion into the wills and laws of men in supreme power. It is supposed herein that men may be in their own minds of what religion they please, and be as religious as they will; but, for the preservation of society, it is meet that the wills of lawgivers, in all nations, should be the sole rule of the outward profession of religion.

Now, although this atheistical opinion be destructive of Christian religion, condemning all the professors of it, from its first entrance into the world, of the highest folly imaginable, yet, being suited to accommodate all the lusts and interests of men profane and ungodly, it is incredible what a progress in a short time it hath made in the world; and those who have imbibed it are ready for all such compositions in religion as may be supposed any way commodious unto their inclinations and interests.

I shall only mention that which, of all other things, is of the worst abode,—namely, the loss of the power of religion in all sorts of persons. The protestant religion will not anywhere long maintain its station any otherwise than by an experience of its power and efficacy on the souls of men. Where this is lost through the power of prevalent vicious habits of the minds of men, the whole of that religion will be parted withal at an easy rate; for there is another continually proposed unto them, with those entertainments for men's fancies and carnal affections, with those accommodations for their lusts, living and dying, with outward secular advantages, that this religion is not capable of, nor accompanied withal.

This is that which, guided with an eye to outward advancement, hath in the last age lost great numbers of the nobility of France and Poland, and other places, from the profession of the gospel, whose ancestors were renowned champions for the truth of it: for to what end should men entertain a religion which they find no inward spiritual advantage by, and are for the profession of it exposed unto all sorts of outward disadvantages? And this sort of men will at any time greedily embrace such a reconciliation with the church of Rome as by the terms of it may a little shelter their reputation, and make a pretence of satisfying some traditional convictions of the truth which they had professed.

Moreover, unless it be diligently watched against, weariness is apt to grow on many of the clergy of that spiritual rule and conduct of the people which, according to the principles of the protestant religion, is committed unto them: for there hath, by virtue thereof, so much light and knowledge been diffused among the people, and such a valuation of their spiritual liberty thereon, which formerly they knew nothing of, that there is an excellent virtue and piety, with continual care and watchfulness, required unto the rule of them; and yet, when the best of men have done their utmost herein also, they will meet with that which shall exercise their wisdom and patience all their days. Neither hath Christ granted any rule or office in his church on any other terms; nor will the state of his subjects, who are all volunteers, permit it to be otherwise. No wonder, then, if some do like those engines of an easy rule, namely, ignorance and blind devotion in the people, and so are ready to return unto them again: for it is a monstrous wearisome thing for men of heroic, governing spirits to be obliged to give conviction from the Scripture, unto such persons as they judge impertinent, of what they do; much more to order their conversation with strictness, that no offence be taken at them. This posture of things men seem to be weary of, and therefore do daily relinquish them, so far as they can pretend any consistency between what they do and the religion which they profess. But the utter shaking off of those bonds and manacles, unworthy of men of generous spirits, must needs seem more eligible unto them; and if hereon such terms of reconciliation be offered, as shall not only secure unto them their present possessions and dignities, but give them also a prospect of farther advancement, it is to be feared that many of this sort will judge it better to embrace things so desirable than to die in a prison or at a stake.

Besides all these, there is at present a coincidence of two things that exceedingly incline the minds of many unto an ecclesiastical coalescency with the church of Rome. And these are,—first, an ignorance or forgetfulness of what the Papacy was, and will again be; and then a sense of some provocations given, or supposed to be given them by the protestant religion, or those that profess it. Alas! what harm hath the Papacy ever done to them? It may be they can give instances wherein they have had advantage by it, or by them that belong unto it. But every thing which they suppose evil, and find inconvenient unto their present inclinations, they suspect to proceed from the principles of the protestant religion, from whence they have already received many provocations.

These are some of the reasons which make it evident that there may be no small danger unto the public profession of the protestant religion (the thing inquired after), from the present design of not a few, to make a reconciliation of the two religions, and to bring all men into a coalescency in faith, worship, and rule with the church of Rome. Now, as there is little hope to prevail with them who are under the power of these things and considerations, or are influenced by them, by arguments religious and rational, seeing they have all of them their foundation in such corrupt affections, inclinations, and interests, as are more deaf than an adder unto such charms; yet, for the sake of others not as yet engaged by such prejudices, I shall manifest in a few instances the folly and wickedness of attempting or complying with any reconciliation with the church of Rome.

For, in the first place, be it on what terms it will, it is a renunciation of the fundamental principle of the Reformation,—namely, that the church of Rome is that idolatrous, antichristian state which is foretold in the Scriptures. For if it be so, the persons that belong unto it may be converted, but the state itself is to be destroyed. And to join ourselves unto, or coalesce in, that church-state, on any terms whatever, that the Lord Christ hath designed to destruction, is both foolish in itself, and will be ruinous in the issue unto our souls.

For it will hence also follow that we interest ourselves in the guilt of all that innocent blood which hath been shed by the power of that church-state for a dissent from it; for this guilt,—which is next unto that of the church of the Jews in murdering the Head of the church, and every way equal unto that of the pagan world in the blood shed in their persecutions, for which it was temporally and eternally destroyed,—lies charged on this church-state, and will reach unto all that shall choose an ecclesiastical conjunction therein. And let such persons flatter themselves whilst they please, and slight these things as those wherein they are not concerned, they will find them true to their cost, here or hereafter.

Neither will men of any light or ingenuity easily renounce the whole work of God's grace and power in the Reformation, and cast the guilt of all the divisions that have been in the world on the part of the Protestants. For, seeing they have all been on the account of the church-state of Rome, in opposition whereunto the martyrs laid down their lives, a coalescency on any terms in and with that church-state doth include a condemnation of all that hath been done or suffered in opposition thereunto. "The preaching of the gospel hath been but a fancy, the suffering of the martyrs was the highest folly, the glory given to God on these accounts little less than blasphemy," is the language of such a coalescency.

The vanity, also, of *the terms of reconciliation* which are or may be proposed, is obvious unto all that are not wilfully blind; for the church of Rome, preserving its essentially constitutive principles and its being as such, can make no such condescensions as shall not keep safe and secure the whole malignity of their faith and worship. When any thing that hath the show or appearance of a concession,—as, suppose, priests' marriage, the cup unto the laity, and the service of the church in a known tongue,—is proposed, it is natural for all men to commend and approve of what is so done, because it is a kind of relinquishment of things grievous and tyrannical. At the first proposal few will judge these things to be sufficient, but will encourage themselves in an expectation of farther condescensions, and will be ready to assure others that they will ensue; but yet, when they find themselves defeated herein, they will take up the management of the cause, and contend that this is enough at present for sober men, seeing no more can be attained. But, in reality, this reconciliation will prove a total defection from the protestant religion; for the church of Rome neither will nor can part with any thing that shall change its antichristian state and idolatrous worship. The whole of their pretension is but a decoy to get us into their power; where we shall be made to understand both where we are and where we have been also. And those which shall be most inclinable unto such a reconciliation as is designed, unless they also become flagitious persecutors of those whom they have left, as is the manner of most apostates, will find their former faults called over to the purpose, and such base acknowledgments required of them as ingenuous persons would rather choose to die than be brought unto. But although universal experience confirms this to be the certain and undoubted issue of a return unto their power, from which men are judged to have broken away unjustly, whatever salvos seem to be provided against it; yet those concerned cannot think it shall be so with them, but rather that they shall be dearly embraced and highly promoted, if not for their return, yet for their being early and sedulous therein. But if they find this entertainment with them, who have every thing which they think good, as conscience and religion, and every thing that is really evil, as pride, ambition, and revenge, to oblige them unto the contrary, I shall not be alone in being deceived. But this one consideration is sufficient to cast out all thoughts of any reconciliation with the church of Rome; for although they should never so earnestly desire it, as that which would bring dominion, profit, advantage, and reputation unto them, yet is it not in their power, continuing what they are, to make any such concessions as shall alter their state, or once touch the reasons of the Protestants' departure from them. And seeing what they suppose they may grant will not be upon a conviction of truth that such ought to be, as if before they had been in a mistake, but only to comply with a present exigence for their advantage, it will be recalled whenever they judge it meet to take it away again.

Upon the whole matter, the reconciliation, designed on the most plausible terms that have ever yet been proposed, is nothing but a hoodwinked defection to Rome, accumulated with a charge, on the consciences of them who shall comply therewith, of the guilt of all the miseries and blood of them by whom it will be refused.

But there are, on the other side, certain considerations that may be laid in the balance against these dangers, or the fears of them as unto the event; and I shall briefly mention them also. For,—

1. The honour of Christ himself seems to be engaged for the preservation of the light and truth of the gospel where it hath been professed. And so it is, undoubtedly, unless the sins and ingratitude of the generality of them by whom it is professed do require that they be dealt withal in his severity. In that case the glory and honour of Christ are more engaged to remove and take away the blessing of

it from any place or people, than to put forth his power for its preservation and continuance. Now, although it must be acknowledged that the sins of these and other protestant nations have been of a high provoking nature unto the eyes of his glory, yet it may be hoped that they have not exceeded the bounds of his patience and forbearance. And whether it be so or no, there will be a speedy discovery; for if, on the many intimations which he hath given them of his displeasure, his many calls to repentance mixed with threatenings, they will now at last return unto him from the evil of their ways, and make their repentance evident by the fruits of it, he will undoubtedly continue his presence among them and his care over them.

But if, notwithstanding all that they hear, and feel, and fear at present, notwithstanding all divine warnings and indications of his displeasure, they will go on frowardly in their own ways, unto the high dishonour of himself and his gospel, causing his name and ways to be blasphemed among the idolatrous nations, the event must be left, in the depths of infinite wisdom, with sovereign grace and mercy.

2. Notwithstanding all that profaneness and wickedness of life wherein multitudes are immersed who outwardly profess the protestant religion, there is a remnant in the nations where it is professed who manifest the power of it in their lives, and glorify Christ by their profession and obedience unto all his commands, walking worthy of the gospel in all holy conversation. Nor are this sort confined to any one party or peculiar way among them, but are found in the whole body or community of the protestant profession. What influence these have, on many accounts, into the preservation of the light of the gospel in the places, times, and nations wherein their lot and portion is cast by divine Providence, is not here to be declared; the Scripture will give a sufficient account of it.

3. There is evidently at present a spirit of courage and Christian magnanimity come upon many, whose other circumstances render them considerable in the world, to do and suffer whatever they shall lawfully be called unto for the defence of this protestant religion. This also is from God; and if his purpose were utterly to ruin that interest, it is more suited unto former dispensations of his providence in like cases to send weakness, faintness, cowardice, and despondency into the hearts of those concerned, than to give them a spirit of courage and resolution for their duty. And hereunto, also, belongs that revival of zeal for their religion and the concernments of it, which hath of late been stirred up even in the body of the people, taking occasion from the opposition made unto it, and the dangers whereunto it hath been reduced. If these things are from God, as they seem to be, they will not be so easily run down as some ima-

gine; for whatever means he will make use of, be they in themselves never so weak and contemptible, they shall be effectual unto the end whereunto they are designed. And therefore there is no small indication in them that it is in the counsel of the divine will as yet to preserve the profession of the protestant religion, though it may be sorely shaken.

4. The strange discoveries that have been made of the plots and designs of the enemies of this religion, with the disappointment of many of them, are also a pledge of the care of God over it. Wise and considering men knew well enough that they were at work, with all diligence, craft, and industry, for the accomplishment of what they had long designed, and which for some ages they had been engaged in various contrivances to bring about; but what they saw of the effects of their counsels they could not remove, and all the specialties of their design were hid from them. The generality of men, in the meantime, were in the highest security,—some enjoying themselves in the advantages which they hold by the profession of religion, and others altogether regardless of these things. But in this state of things, the providence of God, making use of the unparalleled confidence and precipitation of the enemies themselves, by strange and unexpected means, lays open their works of darkness, awakens the nation unto the consideration of its danger, variously disappoints their hellish plots, and puts the minds of multitudes, it may be millions, into a posture of taking care about those concernments of their religion which they had assuredly been surprised into the loss of, had they continued in the security from which their enemies awakened them. And it may be well supposed that nothing but sin and the highest ingratitude can divert or stop the progress of those streams of providence whose springs were undeserved mercy and bounty. For although the wisdom, justice, and honour of the nation, in the actings of the king as supreme, of both houses of parliament, in the judges and their legal administrations, with the piety of the church in the observation of a day of fasting and prayer with respect hereunto, be every day exposed to scorn and contempt in the papers and pamphlets of unknown persons, by decrying the plot and vilifying the discoveries [discoverers?] of it (a practice never allowed, never tolerated in any other well-ordered government, as that which would tend to its dissolution), yet all sober men have sufficient evidence of the hand of God in these things to make them an argument of his watchful care over the protestant religion.

And unto all these things we may add the fatal miscarriages and miserable ends of such apostates from the true religion as have not been contented to ruin their own souls alone, but have been active and instrumental, in their capacities, to draw or drive others into the same perdition. Examples in this kind might be multiplied sufficient to stop this sort of persons in their career, if an open discovery of the pit whereinto they will precipitate themselves may have any influence upon them.

Some few things may yet be added concerning the outward means of the preservation of the protestant religion as unto its public profession (for the thing itself will be preserved in despite of the world), which those concerned therein may do well to apply themselves unto; and I shall only name them at present.

And the first is, fervent prayers to Almighty God that the princes and potentates of the earth may have light to discern that their principal interest in this world lies in its preservation. And although some reasons that may induce them hereunto may not seem of force unto them, yet there is one that is uncontrollable; for where the protestant religion is received, publicly professed, and established by law, it cannot be changed without the extreme havoc and ruin of the greatest and best part of their subjects in all their temporal concerns. And this there is no doubt but that they are obliged, so far as in them lies, to prevent, as they will give an account unto God of the trust reposed in them: for as things are stated in the world, as the designs and interests of the parties at variance are formed, it is a madness to suppose that any alteration can be made herein without these direful effects; and if they should be covered for a season, they will break forth afterwards with more rage and fury. But I refer this unto the wisdom of them that are concerned.

It is also necessary hereunto that all those who sincerely own this religion, and make it the rule of their living unto God, in hopes of the eternal enjoyment of him in another world, do depose the consideration of the lesser differences amongst themselves, and unite in one common design and interest to oppose the entrances and growth of Popery among us. And it is a hard thing to persuade rational men that they are in earnest for its opposition and exclusion who are not willing so to do.

But that whereon amongst ourselves the event of this contest doth depend is the repentance and reformation of all them that profess this religion, upon the divine calls and warnings which they have received.

For a close of this discourse; if we may suppose, what we may justly fear, namely, that the holy God, to punish the horrible sins and ingratitude of the nations professing the protestant religion, should suffer the profession of it by any of these means, or any other that he shall think meet to use in his holy permission, to be extinguished for a season, and remove the light of the gospel from these nations, we may yet conclude two things:—

1. That it shall issue at last in the advantage of the church. Antichrist shall not be a final gainer in this contest; his success herein will be the forerunner of his utter destruction. The healing of his deadly wound will preserve his life but for a little while. Religion shall be again restored in a more refined profession. There shall ensue hereon no new revelations, no new doctrines, no new Scriptures, no new ordinances of worship; the substance of the protestant doctrine, religion, and worship shall be preserved, restored, beautified, in themselves and in their power, in them by whom they shall be professed; the demonstration whereof shall be given elsewhere.

2. In the meantime, to suffer for it, even unto death, is the most glorious cause wherein we can be engaged, and wherein we shall be undoubtedly victorious. It is no less glorious in the sight of God, no less acceptable with him, to suffer in giving testimony against the abominations of the apostate, antichristian church-state, than to suffer for the gospel itself in opposition to idolatrous Paganism.

END OF VOL. XIV.